SURVEY OF

American Industry
and Careers

SURVEY OF
American Industry and Careers

Volume 4

Logging Industry—Postal and Package Delivery Services

The Editors of Salem Press

SALEM PRESS
Pasadena, California   Hackensack, New Jersey

Editorial Director: Christina J. Moose
Project Editor: Rowena Wildin
Manuscript Editors: Stacy Cole, Andy Perry
Acquisitions Manager: Mark Rehn
Administrative Assistant: Paul Tifford, Jr.

Research Supervisor: Jeffry Jensen
Photo Editor: Cynthia Breslin Beres
Design and Layout: James Hutson
Additional Layout: William Zimmerman

Cover photo: ©moodboard/CORBIS

Library of Congress Cataloging-in-Publication Data

Survey of American industry and careers / The Editors of Salem Press.
    v.   cm.
    Includes bibliographical references and indexes.
    ISBN 978-1-58765-768-9 (set : alk. paper) — ISBN 978-1-58765-769-6 (vol. 1 : alk. paper) — ISBN 978-1-58765-770-2 (vol. 2 : alk. paper) — ISBN 978-1-58765-771-9 (vol. 3 : alk. paper) — ISBN 978-1-58765-772-6 (vol. 4 : alk. paper) — ISBN 978-1-58765-773-3 (vol. 5 : alk. paper) — ISBN 978-1-58765-774-0 (vol. 6 : alk. paper) 1. Business—Vocational guidance—United States. 2. Industries—United States. 3. Occupations—United States. 4. Vocational guidance—United States. I. Salem Press.
    HF5382.5.U5S87 2012
    331.7020973—dc23
                                                                    2011019601

First Printing

PRINTED IN THE UNITED STATES OF AMERICA

Contents

Complete List of Contents

VOLUME 4

VOLUME 5

VOLUME 6

List of Tables and Sidebars

SURVEY OF

American Industry and Careers

Logging Industry

©Dreamstime.com

INDUSTRY SNAPSHOT

General Industry: Natural Resources
Career Cluster: Agriculture, Food, and Natural Resources
Subcategory Industries: Cutting Timber; Piling Timber; Pulpwood Logging Camps; Rough Wood Rails Manufacturing; Stump Removal; Transporting Timber; Wood Chipping in the Field
Related Industries: Biofuels Industry; Building Construction Industry; Farming Industry; Natural Resources Management; Paper Manufacturing and Products Industry
Annual Domestic Revenues: $30 billion USD (First Research, 2008)
Annual Global Revenues: $270 billion USD (World Bank, 2008)
NAICS Number: 1133

INDUSTRY DEFINITION

Summary

The logging industry is an international business that utilizes an important natural resource for commercial purposes. The myriad wood products of logging and forestry have an equally wide range of uses, and logging serves a number of other important industries, such as papermaking, furniture manufacturing, and construction. The industry employs hundreds of thousands of workers throughout the world. It forms an important part of the economies of countries throughout the world, including industrialized nations.

History of the Industry

The logging industry owes its roots to some of the earliest human civilizations. Archaeologists have found evidence of the extensive use of wood in early architecture, furniture making, and other ancient crafts and industries—at sites in Jericho (in Israel) and in many sites in what is now Turkey—dating as far back as the Neolithic period, or New Stone Age (approximately 9500 B.C.E.). Neolithic civilizations originally used the trees closest to them for construction, but large settlements quickly exhausted that supply and obtained more wood by harvesting great numbers of trees from nearby mountain ranges. They used this wood in building foundations, walls, and rooftops, as well as in furniture and decorations. In ancient China, wood was also harvested during the late Neolithic period. The Chinese also began clearing forests in

The logging industry provides wood supplies that are crucial for construction and papermaking. (©Joseph Gough/Dreamstime.com)

order to establish farms along the Yellow River around 5500 B.C.E.

During the third millennium B.C.E., the first examples of the logging industry came into being. Ancient Egypt, lacking an adequate volume of local trees, looked to Byblos (modern-day Lebanon) to meet its growing demand for wood. The first pharaoh of Egypt's fourth dynasty, Snefru (or Sneferu), ordered forty ships filled with cedar from Byblos. Snefru and his successors saw a constant need to import wood, which they used to build and maintain the Egyptian fleet.

The availability of major wood resources in the Near East played a major role in the desire of ancient civilizations to build durable ships and buildings. In fact, wood was considered precious, accorded a value similar to that of gold and silver. In the twenty-third century B.C.E., Mesopotamian king Sargon of Akkad claimed that the god Dagan gave him a vast territory to rule that included a number of heavily forested areas, implying that those forests were part of his wealth. Some of Sargon's successors made similar claims.

The Roman Empire—like many other civilizations—used Middle Eastern lumber for shipbuilding, construction, and other important endeavors. Additionally, the Roman Empire expanded its resources to include ceramics, advanced weaponry, and other technologies. The vast empire's needs for wood and wood-based fire to fuel those technologies were great. In fact, the forests of the Lebanese mountains were not enough to satisfy the Romans' needs. Rather, many of the Romans' operations had to be moved to the heavily forested regions of what is now Germany.

By the advent of European colonialism in the fifteenth and sixteenth centuries, Europe had become extremely developed, and its forest resources were dwindling rapidly. When explorers came to the shores of the New World, they recognized its enormous potential for logging. The landscape was tremendous and untapped. Soon, ships traveling back to Europe contained large quantities of timber. The birth of the United States in the late eighteenth century continued this trend, as northern New England continued to be logged, both to build American houses and ships and to export timber to Europe.

The significance of the burgeoning logging industry was soon symbolized on the Massachusetts State House: A large golden pine cone was placed atop the building's dome as an homage to the importance of Maine (which was at the time part of the Massachusetts Bay Colony) and its successful logging industry. Maine (in particular, the city of Bangor) had become the largest logging center in the world, moving over 8 trillion feet of timber between 1832 and 1838. During the mid-nineteenth century, Maine and the rest of the northeastern United States saw the rise of another industry—papermaking—that added to the enormous demand for wood and logging.

The logging industry was long a linchpin of the American economy, and it became part of the new nation's cultural heritage. As Americans moved westward, much of their culture developed alongside logging. For example, the stories of Paul Bunyan, a giant lumberjack, and his pet ox Babe were part of the American mythology during its early years. As American movement westward continued, New England was joined by other major logging operations. In particular, the Pacific Northwest had become an important center for the industry by the early twentieth century, producing nearly 8 billion board feet in 1926. Washington State replaced Maine as the country's top lumber-producing state, sending exported wood as far away as China and Australia.

The Industry Today

The logging industry is a global, multibillion-dollar business. It provides wood supplies that are crucial for construction, papermaking, and other uses. Countless types of wood are collected in the myriad forested areas around the world. The list of leading wood- and timber-exporting nations varies in rank based on the type of product being exported, such as fiberboard, paper, plywood, and other materials. The United States is both a major exporter and a major importer of certain types of wood products. Among the other leaders are Southeast Asian countries such as Malaysia, Vietnam, and Myanmar, as well as Russia and Canada.

One of the benefits of wood as a natural resource is that it is found in nearly every part of the world. Although highly developed, the United States still contains large forests, much of which have been purchased for the purposes of logging. Canada, Russia, and many European countries also contain considerable forested areas dedicated to

A logging operation uses water to transport and cure logs. (©Dreamstime.com)

logging. A significant proportion of these industrialized nations' forest resources is at least somewhat sustainable. When trees are harvested, they are also replaced with tree farms and nurseries. Such practices ensure that this vital natural resource is not completely eradicated.

The same care is not taken in many developing countries. Often, these countries lack viable manufactured products, crops, or other natural resources to drive economic development, so they have turned to timber. Logging has been both beneficial and harmful to these countries. The industry provides jobs, creates products for domestic and foreign sale, and increases the acreage of arable land. However, the logging pursuits of many developing countries have not been planned or executed in a sustainable fashion. In places such as Haiti, Brazil, Africa, and Southeast Asia, forest resources have been heavily logged without replacement. In Haiti, this practice has left a once highly forested nation barren of trees, while the country remains extremely poor. In regions with large rain forests, the removal of trees for short-term economic gain has generated considerable controversy among environmentalists concerned with the depletion of the ozone layer.

The logging industry may be separated into three major components. The first of these segments harvests timber. Cutters, traditionally known as lumberjacks, travel deep into forests and begin their work—first removing branches and large limbs, and then sawing down the large trunks of trees. This part of the industry is one of the most dangerous, as lumberjacks need to climb high into trees and use heavy and light machinery that can cause serious injury. Furthermore, the location of the work performed is often far from the nearest hospital, adding to the physical risks when accidents occur.

The industry's second segment transports timber. Workers pick up felled trees and move them to locations for processing. The felled timber may be transported by flatbed trucks or floated down rivers on barges or as makeshift rafts assembled by bundling the logs themselves. The latter practice, one of the longest-used tactics in logging, is also one of the most efficient and inexpensive options.

The third component of the industry processes trees into usable commodities. Timber has myriad uses. Some is cut down into boards and blocks of varying shapes and dimensions, while other quantities of it are processed into pulp for paper or into concentrated packs for fireplace logs. Mills and processing plants have long constituted the economic lifeblood of many small communities located in rural, forested areas.

The logging industry remains strong in the early twenty-first century. While the increased use of computers and Internet technology has significantly reduced paper use, logging continues to thrive overall as a global business. Demand remains strong for wood and wood-based products on virtually every economic level.

INDUSTRY MARKET SEGMENTS

Logging companies vary significantly in size. Some small concerns specialize solely in felling or transporting timber on property owned by others. By contrast, large, vertically integrated companies

A crane lifts cut logs. (©Terrance Emerson/Dreamstime.com)

may purchase and maintain forests, fell trees within them, and process those trees into products that the company then markets. Forestry or forest management is an important part of the long-term business of such large businesses, while smaller companies may simply provide labor in the service of a forest-management plan produced by others.

Small Logging Companies

Small logging companies employ fewer than one hundred persons. They are generally local companies, felling timber in a particular forest or forested region. As a result, their fortunes may be tied to those of their region to a greater extent than is the case for larger companies.

Potential Annual Earnings Scale. The average earnings for employees of small logging companies vary based on the work performed and the volume of work available, as well as the number of employees at the company. Budgets tend to be very tight for these companies in the light of these factors. According to the U.S. Department of Labor, the average annual wage in the logging industry in 2007 was an estimated $34,387. Loggers comprise the bulk of a small company's payroll and typically earn between $31,000 and $37,000 per year according to Salary.com.

Clientele Interaction. The level of client interaction within the logging industry varies based on the position involved. At a small company, employees are more likely to interact with clients than they would be at a larger firm since jobs may be directly negotiated between the loggers and their customers. Payments for such jobs are made immediately following their completion.

Amenities, Atmosphere, and Physical Grounds. Logging and much processing takes place outdoors, in forests. Loggers must work in all types of weather and conditions, living at times in logging camps deep in the forest rather than commuting to work from home. As a result, there is often a general spirit of camaraderie among loggers, especially given the high level of physical risk that accompanies their occupation.

Typical Number of Employees. Some small logging companies employ as few as two people, while others may employ up to one hundred full-time workers. For large jobs, some small companies may hire temporary personnel to augment the full-time staff and enable them to complete the jobs.

Traditional Geographic Locations. Small logging companies operate in areas where large concentrations of harvestable lumber are found, typically small, rural communities adjacent to or within highly forested areas. Such locations facilitate not just logging but also transport to and from logging sites, both of which are conducted with minimal expense to the customer and the company alike.

Pros of Working for a Small Logging Company. Small logging companies offer their employees a degree of comfort and independence that may not be found at larger companies. Employees work closer to home than they would at larger firms, and they are less likely to be required to travel for work. Additionally, a company's customers themselves are often based nearby and are typically familiar with the company and its employees, developing a stronger relationship than exists between larger companies and their clients.

Cons of Working for a Small Logging Company. Small logging companies are capable of performing only relatively small jobs. As a result, they may not have consistent revenue streams and may therefore be forced to branch out into other types of work. Small firms' limited budgets also limit the amount of wages they can pay, which are generally below the industry average. They may not be able to afford training for their employees, which can increase the prevalence of on-the-job injuries. Furthermore, many companies are so small that their employees cannot afford full health insurance, so any injuries they incur may be costly. Finally, when economic conditions deteriorate, small companies do not have the ability to adapt and reorganize in the same manner that larger companies can; company closures occur frequently, as do job losses.

Costs

Payroll and Benefits: Pay and benefits for small logging companies depend largely on the jobs involved. Generally, pay for employees of small logging companies is below average, in large part because of the limited scope of work performed by a small number of workers. Workers are typically paid by the job as opposed to earning a salary or hourly wages. Benefits are typically limited by a company's small workforce and budget.

Supplies: Small logging companies require a number of important tools and pieces of hardware.

Among them are motorized saws, axes and similar cutting equipment, climbing equipment, and towing equipment. Additionally, they may require modified trucks, cranes, backhoes, and other heavy machinery in order to remove and transport felled trees and limbs. If they own their own equipment, they must also have smaller tools and oil on hand to maintain this equipment.

External Services: Many small logging companies do not own their own equipment. Instead, they rent equipment from vendors. Additionally, they may need accountants to manage their finances and taxes and Internet marketing consultants to develop and maintain Web sites. They may also need to contract mechanics to fix broken machinery and vehicles.

Utilities: Among the utilities used by small logging companies are gasoline and oil, used to power and maintain heavy and light equipment, as well as trucks and similar vehicles. If they have their own office space, such companies may pay for telephone lines and electricity as well.

Taxes: Small logging companies must collect and report employee income taxes, as well as pay their own corporate income taxes. If these companies have the minimum number of employees to meet the standards of state or regional government requirements, they may be liable for unemployment insurance. If they own their own business space, they must also pay property taxes.

Midsize Logging Companies

Midsize logging companies employ between 100 and 250 persons. While less tied to a specific location than are small companies, they are often still largely regional entities, cultivating and dependent upon local relationships and infrastructure.

Potential Annual Earnings Scale. According to the U.S. Department of Labor, the average annual wage in the logging industry in 2007 was an estimated $34,387. Loggers themselves earn between $31,000 and $37,000 per year according to Salary.com. Midsize companies are likely to pay wages in accord with the industry average.

Clientele Interaction. The level of clientele interaction experienced by a midsize logging company employee depends largely on the employee's position. A company's owners or business managers will speak and coordinate directly with clients, as will administrative personnel, who may answer phones, take orders, and maintain records. Cutters and haulers may have little, if any, interaction with clients.

Amenities, Atmosphere, and Physical Grounds. Midsize logging companies operate in two types of environments. The first is the main office environment, in which records are kept, vehicles are stored and maintained, and sales are conducted. This environment is professional, with personnel performing a range of pertinent tasks to support the work being done on site. The second environment is the field, the forests in which logging camps are located. Loggers in the field experience unpredictable working conditions, involving variable weather conditions and physical dangers. Employees in both environments must remain in close contact with one another in order to ensure that each job is managed professionally while the safety and well-being of loggers is maintained.

Typical Number of Employees. Midsize logging companies have from 100 to 250 full-time employees. This number may be quite variable at a given company, fluctuating with the demand for the company's services.

Traditional Geographic Locations. Midsize logging companies may be found in municipalities in or near heavily forested areas in order to facilitate cost-effective logging and hauling. However, some companies maintain headquarters in larger cities and communities from which they coordinate logging activities in the field. While on a job, loggers reside in forested areas, operating out of logging camps and similar venues.

Pros of Working for a Midsize Logging Company. Employees of midsize logging companies are able to work on a diverse number of projects, from commercial logging to clearing and landscaping. They often have more consistent work opportunities than do employees of smaller companies. Additionally, the larger volume of available work may entail more competitive pay and benefits. Midsize companies, by virtue of having larger budgets, may also be able to afford better equipment and training for employees, which can help reduce the risk of injury.

Cons of Working for a Midsize Logging Company. Although the pay and benefits for midsize

A lumberjack at work in the woods. (©Martin Fischer/Dreamstime.com)

logging company employees is competitive, the physical risk remains, especially given the fact that these companies may perform larger, more dangerous jobs than do smaller companies. Additionally, the logging industry as a whole is still subject to significant ebbs and flows, which can result in work stoppage and workforce reductions. Midsize companies may also have a competitive disadvantage in comparison to larger companies that can offer better machinery and more personnel.

Costs

Payroll and Benefits: Midsize companies have more diverse pay scales than smaller companies. In addition to loggers, truck drivers, and field workers, these companies employ senior managers, who command higher salaries, and lower-level administrative personnel.

Supplies: Midsize logging companies use office supplies such as stationery, business cards, accounting and filing materials, and telecommunication equipment. Logging operations require heavy equipment, such as cranes and backhoes; light equipment, such as chain saws and trimmers; parts and tools to maintain and repair the equipment; hand tools; and transport vehicles.

External Services: Midsize logging companies have more resources than do small companies, so they may address many of their needs internally. However, they may still rent equipment or vehicles and hire outside maintenance services. Additionally, many outsource accounting, Web site design, marketing, and advertising.

Utilities: Midsize logging companies use a large amount of gasoline and oil to fuel heavy and light logging equipment, as well as transportation vehicles. Additionally, they require electricity and telephone services for their headquarters, as well as cellular phones for on-site personnel.

Taxes: Like most companies, midsize logging companies must withhold income taxes from employees, as well as reporting their own corporate income taxes. If they own their own headquarters or storage space, they must pay commercial real estate taxes. In many areas, companies must pay taxes to fund health insurance programs and unemployment insurance pools.

Large Logging Companies

Large logging companies have more than 250 employees. Rather than being tied to a particular region, a large company is likely to have multiple operations in multiple regions, while being headquartered in an urban center removed from those operations. It may even be based in a different country from those in which its operations are carried out. Large companies are more likely to be involved in every aspect of logging, including the processing of timber into wood and paper products.

Potential Annual Earnings Scale. The employees of larger logging companies, by virtue of the generally larger volume of high-value jobs on hand, have a greater potential to earn competitive salaries. However, larger companies also have more diverse employee groupings. The highest end of a company's pay scale will be occupied by its salaried executives, while field workers and administrative employees are usually paid hourly and at lower wages.

Clientele Interaction. The level of interaction between a large logging company employee and the company's clients depends largely on the position held by the employee. Much client interaction is left to those employees who manage jobs from the corporate headquarters, including administrative personnel who oversee accounting and client relationships. Moreover, during the course of prospecting, business development managers have a high degree of interaction with potential new clients.

Amenities, Atmosphere, and Physical Grounds. Logging workers in the field must deal with certain risks and dangers, long hours, and physically demanding work. These workers tend to work closely with other cutters and lumber industry personnel. Personnel employed at a corporate headquarters or regional office must work together to ensure the safety and effective teamwork of those in the field. In both cases, personnel must act in a particularly tight group dynamic in order to complete their projects effectively.

Typical Number of Employees. Large logging companies have anywhere from 250 to thousands of full-time employees. For example, Canada's AbitibiBowater, one of the world's largest logging and paper companies, employed about 18,000 workers before it declared bankruptcy in 2009.

Traditional Geographic Locations. Large logging companies are often international corporations. They have headquarters in major cities, along with subsidiary offices and facilities in or near forested areas, with logging camps and mills established within each region of operation. In some cases, these businesses are multinational companies, conducting logging, processing, and transferring operations in and among various countries while maintaining their home bases elsewhere.

Pros of Working at a Large Logging Company. Employees of a large logging company are part of a sizable network that potentially offers a wide range of work options, leading to work diversity and opportunities for advancement. In addition, because such a company's contracts tend to be lucrative, worker pay and benefits are often better than at midsize and small logging companies. Large firms tend to have more buying power, enabling them to equip workers with the best trade tools. They can also afford to train employees in the use of their equipment. Furthermore, in the event of an economic downturn, large companies are often more resilient, able to downsize or reorganize rather than folding completely.

Cons of Working for a Large Logging Company. Because many large logging companies are multinational and not specific to a certain region, workers may be transferred to job sites and subsidiary locations away from home or even out of the country. Employees do not necessarily have a chance to cultivate familiarity with a given region or forest and to help steward its continued sustainability. Additionally, large companies' broad operational reach leaves them susceptible to broad economic issues. For example, when stocks fall or national economies falter, larger companies with stakes in foreign countries may suffer as well.

Costs

Payroll and Benefits: Pay and benefits for employees of large logging companies are among the most competitive in the industry. Executives earn the highest industry salaries, while administrative and hourly employees tend to earn lower base pay. Those working on at-risk job sites may also enjoy greater health, disability, and life insurance benefits than would employees working for small or midsize firms.

Supplies: Large logging companies require a great deal of equipment, both heavy and light, as well as the means and materials to maintain it. They also need large vehicles of all kinds to facilitate the transfer of harvested lumber. They also need factory equipment and materials to process lumber into commodities. Furthermore, they require a considerable quantity of office supplies, computer hardware, and software at corporate locations to maintain contact with worksites and subsidiaries, generate new business, and conduct internal operations.

External Services: Although much of the operations conducted by large logging companies are managed internally, these companies may still require the services of a number of external vendors. One of the largest external services is transportation—from trucking to rail to air and water shipping companies. Additionally, many large companies contract public relations companies and legal representation, as well as lobbyists to advance their agendas at state, regional, and national capitols.

Utilities: Large logging companies, particularly those with large corporate headquarters and regional offices, use a large quantity of utilities. Among these utilities are electricity and other energy resources. Large companies also require extensive telephone and Internet services in order to generate new business, as well as for internal communications among regional offices and with remote worksites.

Taxes: Large logging companies are required to withhold employee income taxes, as well as to report their own corporate income taxes on state, regional, and national levels. Many are also required to contribute to public unemployment insurance and health insurance pools. Because of these companies' multinational operations, many national and international leaders are seeking to increase the taxes levied for global logging operations in an effort to curtail those operations in order to combat global warming.

ORGANIZATIONAL STRUCTURE AND JOB ROLES

The organizational structure of the logging industry constitutes a diverse network centered on the felling, clearing, transportation, and processing of timber. Many logging companies perform different jobs: Some clear trees primarily to use as raw materials for commercial manufacturing, while others clear them to make room for land development or agriculture. There is thus significant variation in the composition and goals of different logging companies. The logging industry does, however, contain a number of general organizational consistencies.

The following umbrella categories apply to the organizational structure of businesses in the logging industry:

- Executive Management
- Business Development
- Manufacturing
- Transportation
- Maintenance and Engineering
- Lumberjacks
- Public Relations
- Legal Counsel
- Marketing
- Human Resources
- Accounting
- Administrative Support

Executive Management

At the top of a logging company is its executive team, which is charged with managing the overall operations and endeavors of the business. This group is responsible for ensuring that all activities of the company run smoothly, from business development to project completion to the distribution of the final product. Executive managers head a company's various departments, overseeing special projects and proposals as well as day-to-day operations.

Executive management is responsible for setting corporate goals and strategies; assessing, approving, or passing on requests for business; and developing and implementing budgets. Executive managers and personnel are generally highly experienced individuals with strong educational backgrounds. They may have secondary, under-

OCCUPATION PROFILE

Forestry Worker

Considerations	Qualifications
Description	Performs a variety of tasks to reforest and protect timber tracts and maintain forest facilities.
Career cluster	Agriculture, Food, and Natural Resources
Interests	Data; things
Working conditions	Work outside
Minimum education level	On-the-job training; high school diploma/technical training; junior/technical/community college
Physical exertion	Medium work
Physical abilities	Unexceptional/basic fitness
Opportunities for experience	Volunteer work; part-time work
Licensure and certification	Usually not required
Employment outlook	Average growth expected
Holland interest score	RES

Note: See volume 1, "Publisher's Note," for an explanation of the Holland interest score.

graduate, and graduate degrees in business administration, forestry, marketing, or other related fields. However, training and experience are the most important aspects of executives' qualifications, giving them strong familiarity with the work being conducted and the processes by which that work may be performed.

Executive management occupations may include the following:

- President/Chief Executive Officer (CEO)
- Chief Operating Officer (COO)
- Chief Financial Officer (CFO)
- Chief Information Officer (CIO)
- Vice President of Marketing

Business Development

The business development department is responsible for securing new jobs and business partners. The logging industry relies heavily on contracts from clients seeking logging services for both timber collection (to be used in wood-based products) and landscaping purposes. The business development department is responsible for seeking out clients and designing work plans and schedules that will meet the needs of those clients.

Business development personnel have considerable experience with and knowledge of their companies' operations. They must be well-organized and capable of developing strong proposals that meet the budget and operational needs defined by their customers. Business development personnel are usually college educated, although some are former field workers who, by virtue of their logging experience, can apply extensive and comprehensive knowledge to the proposal at hand.

Business development occupations may include the following:

- Vice President of Business Development
- Business Development Manager/ Coordinator

- Sales Manager
- Recruiter

Manufacturing

The logging industry is strongly linked to a number of other industries, including manufacturing. In many cases—and in particular, those cases in which the company is large or multinational in size—logging companies themselves contain manufacturing wings that process the materials they harvest into products that are sold on the market or delivered to middlemen for distribution.

The manufacturing side of the logging industry often involves arduous operations. Personnel are exposed to dangerous heavy machinery and toxic chemicals. Although manufacturing personnel may not have education beyond secondary schooling, in the light of these dangers, they are expected to have vocational training that may be obtained in school or on the job. They must be skilled with tools and heavy equipment and be able to adapt quickly to the often high-speed environment of a factory or processing mill.

Manufacturing occupations may include the following:

- Quality Assurance Manager
- Engineer
- Digester Operator
- Foreman
- Forklift Operator
- Inspector
- Line Worker

Transportation

The logging industry relies heavily on personnel who are skilled in operating the heavy trucks and equipment that are used to move and transport felled trees to processing plants and manufacturing facilities. These workers operate large vehicles such as bulldozers, tree clamps, and cranes to help fell trees and place them on the backs of trucks. Others drive the trucks themselves once the wood has been loaded. Logging vehicle drivers may not have formal education, but they must be experienced in operating large trucks that carry extremely heavy loads. They must be able to operate their vehicles in adverse weather and environmental conditions, as well as on the open road, as worksites are typically located off major roads.

Transportation occupations may include the following:

- Truck Driver
- Crane Operator
- Forklift Operator
- General Contractor

Maintenance and Engineering

The maintenance and engineering department is responsible for all equipment and systems utilized by a logging company. Personnel are usually based near the company's main equipment depots, although they may be called into worksites and subsidiary organizations to perform field repairs and upkeep. Maintenance and engineering personnel must be familiar with all the equipment with which they are assigned to work. They are well trained in the repair and maintenance of a broad range of logging-related equipment. Some of their training comes from general vocational and engineering training in the classroom (many will have equipment certification from accredited programs), although their understandings of specific equipment, both heavy and light, may predominantly come from on-the-job training.

Maintenance and engineering occupations may include the following:

- Truck Mechanic
- Engineer
- Equipment Repair Specialist
- Systems Engineer

Lumberjacks

At the heart of any logging company are the people responsible for felling trees. So-called lumberjacks, or timber cutters, are teams of individuals who, in careful fashion, remove trees from a forested area. Each individual has a role (or series of roles) to play in bringing down and removing timber, from climbing tall trees and trimming branches, to removing limbs, to felling trunks and removing stumps.

Lumberjacks may not receive much classroom training but rather obtain their experience in the field. Many come from logging families and learn the trade from peers and family members. Many loggers receive their training from the companies for which they work. Loggers must be proficient with the tools of logging and be able to use such equipment at significant heights, as well as in all types of weather. They must be physically strong and able to work closely together as a team.

Lumberjacking occupations may include the following:

- Cutter
- Logging Tractor Operator
- Dogger
- Barker
- Tree Trimmer
- Tree Faller
- Rigging Slinger
- Chaser
- Logging Operations Inspector
- Deckhand
- Log Grader/Scaler
- Choke Setter
- Bucker
- Cable Puller

Public Relations

Although many midsize and small logging companies use external public relations services (if any), many large logging companies have their own public relations departments. These departments manage all external communications, press statements, interviews, promotions, and other forms of public information dissemination. Public relations personnel are charged with promoting the interests and activities of their companies to the general population, as well as to targeted media outlets.

A logging company's public relations department is the primary vehicle by which the company establishes its official position or responds to emergency situations, political and environmental issues, and other time-sensitive matters. Public relations personnel must be effective communicators, as well as professionals able to react quickly to sensitive issues in an evenhanded, diplomatic manner. In many cases, a logging company's political endeavors, such as lobbying and government relations, are conducted through this department.

OCCUPATION SPECIALTIES

Lumber Production Workers

Specialty	Responsibilities
Buckers	Trim branches and tops off trees and then cut the logs into specified lengths.
Chainsaw operators	Trim limbs, tops, and roots from trees and saw logs to predetermined lengths using chain saws.
Cruisers	Hike through forests to assess logging conditions and estimate the volume of marketable timber.
Fallers	Cut down trees with chain saws or other mechanical felling equipment.
Log graders	Inspect logs for defects, determine their quality and volume, and estimate their market value.
Log markers	Determine the points at which logs will be sawed into sections.
Logging supervisors	Manage one or more crews, usually consisting of four or fewer workers.
Rivers	Split logs to form posts, pickets, stakes, and other objects.
Tree cutters	Fell trees of specified size and species, trim limbs from trees, and cut trees into lengths for firewood, fence posts, or pulpwood, using axes, measuring tools, and chain saws.

Public relations personnel are typically college educated, and many have advanced degrees in such fields as public relations, communications, public affairs, law, and public policy. They must be professionally experienced in the logging industry, demonstrating a strong understanding of the issues faced by the industry, as well as how each such issue relates to their companies' stated goals and activities.

Public relations occupations may include the following:

- Public Relations Director
- External Affairs Coordinator
- Government Relations Manager/Lobbyist
- Event Planner
- Marketing Manager
- Administrative Assistant

Legal Counsel

Logging companies (particularly midsize and large corporations) often employ (or retain) teams of full-time legal experts to advise them. One of the most important roles legal counsel plays is reviewing contracts to ensure that a company's best interests are served by them. Additionally, lawyers are frequently called upon to review local, state, regional, and national regulatory or statutory changes that may affect their companies. They may also facilitate or respond to employee complaints, negotiate employee contracts with collective bargaining representatives, and litigate external civil suits concerning their companies' work.

Legal counsel must be fully versed in the law. They must know federal and local laws pertaining to environmental regulation and forestry, and they must also carefully observe local ordinances. In the light of the complexities of legal statutes and regulations, legal counsel must pay an extraordinary amount of attention to detail.

Legal counsel team members must have advanced degrees in law. Most are experienced in the

A truck hauls spruce tree logs on a snowy road. (©Kelly Boreson/Dreamstime.com)

logging industry as well, giving them insight into relevant legal and regulatory issues. They must also have extensive understanding of how the laws in a given region affect the activity of their companies in that region.

Legal occupations may include the following:

- Chief Counsel
- Staff Attorney
- Associate Attorney
- Paralegal
- Administrative Assistant

Marketing

Logging companies must advertise themselves in order to generate business. For smaller and midsize companies, such efforts may enable them to compete with better-established and better-known companies. The responsibility for this area of operations falls to a company's marketing department.

Marketing personnel put together promotional brochures, create advertising campaigns and strategies, and even establish mutual partnership connections with other companies and trade associations in order to generate the maximum amount of visibility. Marketing personnel must therefore be very well educated not only in such endeavors but also in the industry itself, ensuring that any marketing materials distributed are delivered to the right media, groups, and individuals.

Marketing personnel at a logging company must have extensive experience in both the industry and in advertising. They also tend to have undergraduate and advanced degrees in such fields as marketing, advertising, communications, and business management.

Marketing occupations may include the following:

- Marketing Director
- Marketing Manager
- Marketing Coordinator
- Communications Specialist
- Administrative Assistant

Human Resources

Logging companies must seek out the most experienced and capable employees in order to ensure that the work performed will generate return business and spread the company's positive reputation. To this end, logging companies of all sizes have a human resources and recruitment department, or at least a person skilled in this capacity.

Human resources personnel are charged with recruiting, hiring, and terminating employees. They help organize employee benefits packages, insurance programs, and training programs for full-time employees. They may also be involved in conducting background checks to ensure that potential employees are not and have not been connected with any criminal activity. In the event that a logging company is competing with other companies for contracted business, human resources personnel play an active role on proposal teams, reviewing the best internal and external personnel for contract positions and, if the proposal is accepted, applying them to the stated positions. Furthermore, human resources managers are called upon to work with collective bargaining units when dealing with union employees.

Human resources professionals are highly conversant in issues pertaining to federal and state employment practices, as well as protocols for hiring and terminating employees. They are typically college educated, and many have advanced training or degrees in business management, human resources, and similar fields.

Human resources occupations may include the following:

- Human Resources Director
- Vice President of Human Resources
- Human Resources Coordinator
- Recruitment Manager
- Administrative Assistant

Accounting

The responsibility of overseeing financial operations, including accounts payable (money that is owed by the company) and accounts receivable (money that is owed to the company) falls to a logging company's accountant or accounting department. This area of the company must carefully review and record employee expenses within the context of a given project, as well as in terms of overall company operations.

Accounting departments are extremely vital elements of often budget constrained logging companies, especially in the light of the fact that clients are usually equally sensitive to budgets. Employees in a logging company's accounting department must be extremely organized and show strong attention to detail, taking into account a wide range of expenses, including maintenance, procurement, vehicle rentals, and payroll. Accountants also prepare annual and quarterly tax reports and filings.

Accountants are typically college educated, while some have advanced degrees in related fields. In the United States, most such personnel have licenses as certified public accountants (CPAs) as well.

Accounting occupations may include the following:

- Accounts Payable Manager
- Accounts Receivable Manager
- Accounting Director
- Office Manager

Administrative Support

Logging companies (particularly midsize and large companies) need personnel to perform administrative tasks in a variety of departments and as part of the company's overall operations. Administrative personnel answer a company's main telephone lines and redirect calls, organize accounting records, take meeting minutes, and coordinate visitor protocols.

Administrative support personnel in the logging industry must have strong organizational skills, as well as an ability to communicate effectively with internal and external personnel. They must also quickly become familiar with office computer, telephone, and filing systems. Many have high school diplomas, although some administrative support personnel are relatively new to the workforce, having recently graduated from undergraduate programs.

Administrative support occupations may include the following:

- Receptionist
- File Clerk
- Administrative Assistant

INDUSTRY OUTLOOK

Overview

In many societies, the logging industry has long had a degree of nobility attached to it. In lands with rich forests, including the United States and Canada, those who engaged in the felling of trees projected an image of strength and courage. Today, loggers retain that image, as their line of work continues to require great physical strength and fearlessness. The logging industry has undergone a steady evolution, however, during a period of change that coincided with the need to sell a viable natural resource. In developing countries, the wood trade has skyrocketed, spurring the creation of multinational corporations that remove large swaths of forest in regions with delicate ecosystems (as well as illegal deforestation and logging operations).

Southeast and southern Asia, for example, have long been rich with rain forests and tropical timber, and the market for their wood products on the international stage has been consistently strong. By the end of the twentieth century, it is estimated that more than 4.2 million people were employed as loggers in the Asia-Pacific region, part of over seventy-six hundred commercial enterprises in that area. The largest logging country at the time was Malaysia, employing about 206,000 workers.

The increasingly unsustainable clearing of tropical forests in particular has generated a political backlash, especially in the light of growing concerns about global warming and climate change. Forest conservation has seen considerable growth as an industry, while logging has remained stagnant. Conservation was long part of the overall logging industry since loggers were often called upon to clear overgrown forest areas.

Political concerns are not the only factor causing stagnation in the logging industry. Logging has benefited from the appearance of improved technologies. Modern technology has rendered the dual saw and the axe obsolete, replacing them with high-powered chain saws and other equipment that can fell trees with greater speed and efficiency and with fewer personnel. Furthermore, the increased use of the Internet and computer-based communications has caused a reduced demand for paper. Additionally, the increased number of large, multinational companies has reduced the number of midsize and smaller companies, as these larger companies have either absorbed the smaller ones or put them out of business.

Another element playing a major role in the logging industry's malaise is the global economy. Logging and forestry are industries that rely on demand. As housing and building construction declined at the start of the 2007-2009 recession, so too did the need for a wide range of hardwoods and other materials. The logging industry has thus suffered a major blow as a result of the economic downturn, and it does not appear that it will reverse that downward trend in the near future.

In addition to the politically generated and technological shifts that have created a reduction in logging jobs and production in many locations, another trend is having a significant impact on the industry as a whole. In European and North American forest regions, logging is heavily regulated and

PROJECTED EMPLOYMENT FOR SELECTED OCCUPATIONS

Logging Industry

Employment		
2008	Projected 2018	Occupation
1,600	1,800	Conservation scientists and foresters
500	400	Fallers
6,700	6,900	Forest, conservation, and logging workers
200	200	Forest fire inspectors and prevention specialists
1,700	1,500	Logging equipment operators
1,120	1,600	Sawing machine setters, operators, and tenders, wood

Source: U.S. Bureau of Labor Statistics, Industries at a Glance, Occupational Employment Statistics and Employment Projections Program.

carefully monitored. This regulation can increase the price of logging operations. The considerably lower cost of felling and manufacturing timber and related products in developing countries is causing many operations to move to those countries. A nine-year survey of hardwood production from 1999 to 2008 revealed a reduction of more than 2 billion board feet during that period. That survey suggests that this trend will likely continue in the short term, continuing another trend as well: the reduction in available jobs for forestry and hardwood workers.

Adding to the challenges facing the logging and timber industry is the fact that illegal logging has grown exponentially, particularly in the aforementioned developing countries. Illegal logging entails crews clearing undesignated areas or failing to report income to tax agencies. According to the World Wide Fund for Nature (WWF; formerly the World Wildlife Fund), the practice is extensive. In Bulgaria, for example, 45 percent of the entire timber harvest is illegally obtained. The World Bank estimates that illegal logging drains $10 billion each year from the global market as well as $5 billion in tax revenues. It drives prices down by as much as 16 percent. This growing trend, which shows no sign of abatement, will likely continue negatively to affect the legitimate logging industry's growth in the foreseeable future.

Employment Advantages

Employees in the logging industry, particularly those who are employed to cut and transfer timber, are potentially offered a great deal of excitement and adventure. They work predominantly in the outdoors in often picturesque environments. Those who seek to use their strength and familiarity with a wide range of tools find logging work to be extremely satisfying.

The logging industry has suffered a decline over the last several years as a result of economic and environmental concerns, as well as illegal logging activities and changes in technology. Despite declines in the number of loggers and companies operating successfully in the industry, the logging industry still remains global and profitable.

Although much debate continues over unsustainable and illegal logging's impact on the environment, the legitimate logging industry enables workers to respond to one of the world's most vital and longest-standing natural resource needs. Wood meets an abundance of demands—from energy to construction materials to paper—and those engaged in this global industry work to meet that demand.

Annual Earnings

Overall, the global logging and forest-products industry generates an estimated $270 billion per year. In the United States, which is both a major producer of timber and a major wood-products importer, that figure was about $30 billion in 2008, although revenues have been declining since 2006.

The greatest growth in the industry comes from East and Southeast Asian countries, where a wide range of high-demand woods and wood products is being exported by both legitimate, taxpaying businesses and illegal operations whose revenue figures are difficult to determine. Illegal logging has a significant impact on industry revenues. According to a 2008 study, if illegal operations ceased, countries with little illegal logging (such as the United States and Canada) would experience almost a doubling in their logging revenues, while worldwide inventories of harvestable forest would increase.

In an increasingly global economy, an important factor in discussing the performance of the logging industry is the quantity of wood and wood products exported by a given nation. Canada, for example, has long stood as the largest exporter of wood and wood products, with nearly $18 billion in exports in 2004. The European Union (EU) generated just over $10 billion during that same year, although that figure does not include trade between EU member countries. Indonesia's export market has increased significantly, while the U.S. export market hovered around the $6 billion mark in revenues between 2000 and 2004.

RELATED RESOURCES FOR FURTHER RESEARCH

AMERICAN FOREST AND PAPER ASSOCIATION
  1111 19th St. NW, Suite 800
  Washington, DC 20036
  Tel: (202) 463-2700
  http://www.afandpa.org

EUROPEAN BIOMASS INDUSTRY ASSOCIATION
  Renewable Energy House
  Rue d'Arlon 63-55
  B-1040 Brussels
  Belgium
  Tel: 32-2-400-10-20
  Fax: 32-2-400-10-21
  http://www.eubia.org

FOREST INDUSTRY NETWORK
  300-1585 Bowen Rd.
  Nanaimo, BC V9S IG4
  Canada

  Tel: (877) 755-2762
  Fax: (866) 758-8665
  http://www.forestindustry.com.

INTERNATIONAL TROPICAL INDUSTRY ASSOCIATION
  International Organizations Center, 5th Floor
  Pacifico-Yokohama 1-1-1, Minato-Mirai
  Nishi-ku, Yokohama 220-0012
  Japan
  Tel: 81-45-223-1110
  Fax: 81-45-223-1111
  http://www.itto.int

TRUCK LOGGERS ASSOCIATION
  725-815 W Hastings St.
  Vancouver, BC V6C 1B4
  Canada
  Tel: (604) 684-4291
  Fax: (604) 684-7134
  http://www.tla.ca

ABOUT THE AUTHOR

Michael P. Auerbach has over sixteen years of experience in government, international development, and public policy. He is a 1993 graduate of Wittenberg University and a 1999 graduate of the Boston College Graduate School of Arts and Sciences. He is the author of a comprehensive annotated bibliography on environmental awareness campaigns for USAID and has written papers about environmental policy and bureaucracy. He is a veteran of state and federal government, having worked for seven years in the Massachusetts legislature and for four years as a federal government contractor.

FURTHER READING

Adams, Darius M., and Richard W. Haynes, ed. *Resource and Market Projections for Forest Policy Development: Twenty-five Years of Experience with the U.S. RPA Timber Assessment.* New York: Springer, 2007.

American Forest and Paper Association. "Our Industry—Forestry." http://www.afandpa.org/forestry.aspx.

Baldwin, Richard F. *Maximizing Forest Product Resources for the Twenty-first Century: New Processes, Products, and Strategies for a Changing World.* San Francisco: Miller Freeman Books, 2000.

Huber, Tim. "Timber Trouble: Hard Times Are Hitting the Timber Industry." *Desert News* (Salt Lake City), April 9, 2008.

Iannone, Don. "Industry Profile: Timber Operations." *Economic Development Futures Journal,* January 23, 2006. http://www.libertyparkusafd.org/lp/Jefferson/timber%20companies%5CProfile%20Timber%20Operations.htm.

Kallen, Stuart A., ed. *Managing America's Forests.* Detroit: Greenhaven Press, 2005.

PayScale.com. "Logging Workers, All Other Job Descriptions." http://www.payscale.com/Job_Description/Logging_Workers,_All_Other.

Rae, Stephen. "North American Forestry Outlook." In *ForestBook*, 2006. http://www.forestindustry.com/static/ForestBook/09outlook.html.

Ruhong, Li, et al. "Long-Term Effects of Eliminating Illegal Logging on the World Forest Industries, Trade, and Inventory." *Forest Policy and Economics* 10 (October, 2008): 480-490.

Solomon, Barry D., and Valerie A. Luzadis, eds. *Renewable Energy from Forest Resources in the United States.* New York: Routledge, 2009.

Talwar, Himanshu. "Wood Industry." 2009. http://www.economywatch.com/world-industries/wood-industry-timber-industry.html.

U.S. Bureau of Labor Statistics. *Career Guide to Industries,* 2010-2011 ed. http://www.bls.gov/oco/cg.

_____. "Forest, Conservation, and Logging Workers." In *Occupational Outlook Handbook,* 2010-2011 ed. http://www.bls.gov/oco/ocos178.htm.

U.S. Census Bureau. North American Industry Classification System (NAICS), 2007. http://www.census.gov/cgi-bin/sssd/naics/naicsrch?chart=2007.

U.S. Department of Agriculture. *An Economic Overview of the United States Solid Wood Industry.* Washington, D.C.: Author, 2007. http://www.fas.usda.gov/ffpd/Economic-Overview/An_Economic_Overview_of_the_U.S_Solid_Wood_Industry.pdf.

U.S. Department of Commerce. International Trade Administration. Office of Trade and Industry Information. Industry Trade Data and Analysis. http://ita.doc.gov/td/industry/otea/OTII/OTII-index.html.

Mass Transportation Vehicles Industry

INDUSTRY SNAPSHOT

General Industry: Manufacturing

Career Clusters: Manufacturing; Science, Technology, Engineering, and Math; Transportation, Distribution, and Logistics

Subcategory Industries: Bus Body Manufacturing; Motor Vehicle Parts Manufacturing; Railroad Rolling Stock Manufacturing; Ship and Boat Building and Repairing

Related Industries: Freight Transport Industry; Passenger Transportation and Transit Industry; Shipbuilding, Submarines, and Naval Transport Industry; Travel and Tourism Industry

Annual Domestic Revenues: Shipbuilding (ferries and water taxis): $60.7 million USD; light rail, passenger train, and subway rolling stock: $3.9 billion USD; bus manufacturing: $1.5 billion USD (IBISWorld, 2010)

Annual International Revenues: Shipbuilding (ferries and water taxis): $737.4 million USD; light rail, passenger train, and subway rolling stock: $14.9 billion USD; bus manufacturing: $28.9 billion USD (IBISWorld, 2010)

Annual Global Revenues: Shipbuilding (ferries and water taxis): $798.1 million USD; light rail, passenger train, and subway rolling stock: $18.8 billion USD; bus manufacturing: $30.4 billion USD (IBISWorld, 2010)

NAICS Numbers: 3363, 336211, 3365-3366

INDUSTRY DEFINITION

Summary

The mass transportation vehicle industry manufactures intercity (IC), commuter rail, subway, and light rail cars, as well as trolleys, buses, ferries, and water taxis. It is an international industry that employs people in design, quality assurance, engineering, planning, testing, and managing positions. Mass transportation manufacturing serves the needs of commuters, point-to-point travelers, and tourists. In addition to manufacturing, maintaining, and refurbishing both land vehicles and water vessels, the industry partners with other industries that build and maintain tunnels; bridges; elevated train lines; railways; terminals; ferry docks; waterways and related infrastructure, such as dredging and buoys; and bus, train, and boat stations.

History of the Industry

As urban areas grew in the United States, mass transit began to develop. In the early 1820's in New York, Phila-

Most of Chicago's L (or El) train is elevated, although the Red Line does go underground. (©Victor Pelaez Torres/Dreamstime.com)

more than one hundred railcar manufacturers in the late nineteenth and early twentieth centuries.

Rapid transit cars were initially designed with vestibules and doors only at either end, making boarding and detraining large groups of passengers slow processes. The development of side doors greatly improved logistics. Steam locomotives were disguised in car bodies, called "dummy cars," to avoid scaring horses. The locomotives became larger, heavier, and faster. Passenger cars were heated with coal stoves. Oil, and later gas lamps, provided lighting.

With the advent of electricity, horsecars eventually gave way to trolleys, or streetcars. Richmond, Virginia, had the first electric trolley line in 1889. By 1902, 94 percent of city public rail and trolley transportation was electric. As streets became unbearably congested, New Yorkers began moving to New Jersey and Brooklyn, where ferries across the Hudson and East Rivers provided faster transportation. Intercity steam trains were used by wealthier patrons to connect "bedroom communities" to the nearby metropolises. While horse-drawn vehicles were smelly and noisy, so were the steam trains, whose noisy engines spewed ash along their routes.

The search for functional underground subways or elevated trains as alternatives to street transportation began in the 1850's. Throughout the late 1800's, many schemes were designed and proposed for both subterranean and elevated rail transport, including Alfred Ely Beach's underground pneumatic tube system (1849) and James H. Swett's elevated railway (1853). Various inventors tried monorail systems, cable and other steam-powered systems, and even suspended rail

delphia, Boston, and Baltimore, stagecoaches were modified to become horse-drawn omnibuses. Primitive and uncomfortable, they were only marginally faster than walking. By 1832, horsecars with wooden wheels that ran on street-mounted rails were in use in several cities. These modes of transportation were run by private companies.

The first railroad cars were of wooden construction, built by small independent companies. By the end of the nineteenth century, advances in iron and steel technology made the use of wood for passenger cars obsolete. Iron and steel cars were safer, being fireproof while wood was not. There were

cars. By 1873, cable-car propulsion, a cleaner mode of transportation, was invented by Andrew S. Hallidie. Cable cars use underground cables, driven by central, stationary steam engines. In 1876, New York City completed the first elevated "rapid transit" train line, carrying people between fixed-point stations. Cable was replaced with electric traction by 1890, with the notable exception of San Francisco, where cable cars still operate today. Montgomery, Alabama, had the first city-wide electrified transportation system by 1886. Electrified third rails or overhead power lines, called catenaries, were used to provide power to the cars. Mass-transit subway trains are generally self-propelled.

Locomotives pull or push rail cars while also supplying auxiliary power for lighting; heating, ventilation, and air-conditioning (HVAC); doors; and other systems. Steam was used to power locomotives until the 1940's, when more efficient diesel engines, sometimes combined with electrical power, were adopted. Rail was the most common mass transportation system until the 1940's. Despite a spike during World War II, passenger rail service was practically defunct by the 1960's, having lost ridership to automobiles and airlines. In the mid-1990's, manufacturers developed lighter, more efficient, less expensive railcars. Self-propelled diesel railcars were adopted in North America in the mid-1990's.

Contemporary ferries and water taxis use marine diesel engines and are built in shipyards. They are designed by naval architects and marine engineers. Although a small ferry was in operation in Connecticut as early as 1655, the first steam ferry between New York and New Jersey began operating in 1811. There were even horse-driven ferries on Lake Champlain in the nineteenth century. Diesel engines have now replaced steam engines. Regulated by the U.S. Coast Guard, some ferries operate as part of urban mass-transit systems, such as the Staten Island Ferry (carrying only passengers since 2001) in New York City. Washington State has an extensive ferry system that carries cars as well as passengers. Water taxis are smaller water vessels, usually employed in

Cable cars are still being used in San Francisco. (©Dreamstime.com)

urban areas. Most follow a set route and make multiple stops, operating similarly to buses. Such urban water taxis can carry up to 150 passengers. (Some small vessels are literally water taxis: They take individual fares door to door. Venice, Italy, for example, employs such private, door-to-door water taxis.)

Bus mass transit began in the late nineteenth century, when the Gillig Corporation began modifying horse-drawn buggies and carriages. Entrepreneurs adapted personal vehicles to carry several passengers at a time. Carl Eric Wickman began transporting workers to mines in a seven-seat Hupmobile in Hibbing, Minnesota, in 1914. His company became Greyhound Corporation in 1930. Automobile manufacturers began building vehicles capable of carrying large numbers of passengers. Truck manufacturers started building chassis specifically for buses in the 1920's. Better roads, paved with concrete, enabled manufacturers to build heavier and longer buses that could accommodate more passengers.

In 1921, the Hall-Scott Motor Car Company was the first to build a vehicle specifically designed to be a bus. Before that, wagon, automobile, and coach builders had just adapted their vehicles. That same year, Safety Coach of Muskegon, Michigan, manufactured the first Greyhound intercity bus, so named for its grey paint and sleek design. It had seven rows of four seats each. As the highway system grew, regional lines flourished. By the late 1920's, buses were manufactured with metal bodies. Many automobile companies, such as Studebaker, Packard, and Pierce-Arrow, began to manufacture buses.

Horse and electric power gave way to gasoline engines with advances in internal combustion engines. While rail flourished in the Northeast, buses were more prevalent in the Midwest and the South. The first buses were not enclosed, so both passengers and luggage were exposed to the elements. By 1925, design of buses had developed a center aisle with seats on both sides and a single-entry side door.

Other bus manufacturers included the Thomas Built Buses, founded by Perley A. Thomas in North Carolina in 1916. Thomas took over a failed streetcar company and became the main manufacturer of streetcars in the United States. With the advent of automobiles, however, streetcars were becoming obsolete. In 1936, he retooled the business to manufacture school buses.

Western Flyer began as Western Auto and Truck Body Works in 1930, and in 1941 it produced the first front-engine intercity bus. Most buses used gasoline-powered engines until Gillig introduced the first rear-engine diesel-powered bus in 1959, and the first bus powered by liquified natural gas (LNG) entered production in 1992. In the early 1970's, automatic transmissions began to replace manual transmissions. In the 1980's, Ontario Bus produced the first buses powered by compressed natural gas (CNG). Buses grew in length, from thirty-foot buses to sixty-foot, articulated buses in the mid-1980's. Low-floor models were introduced as well. Passenger capacity increased, and by the 1950's buses were able to accommodate over forty passengers each. In 2003, the first diesel-electric hybrid buses entered production.

The Industry Today

Today, mass-transit systems include subways, light-rail intercity and high-speed trains, water taxis, fast ferries, buses, and—in a few cases—trackless trolleys. Using clean fuels that create less pollution and relying less on fossil fuels in general are two of the most important challenges mass-transit vehicle designers and manufacturers face in the twenty-first century. However, these goals must be met if congestion and air and noise pollution are to be reduced.

The commuter and intercity rail manufacturing industry is overseen and regulated by the Federal Railroad Administration (FRA), part of the U.S. Department of Transportation (DoT), while transit authorities create their own specifications based on the Code of Federal Regulations (CFR). Water taxis and ferries are overseen by the Coast Guard, now part of the U.S. Department of Homeland Security (DHS). In 1996, the Surface Transportation Board (STB) succeeded the Interstate Commerce Commission (ICC) as the overseeing authority for regulating and resolving railroad fees and service. In 2000, the Federal Motor Carrier Safety Administration (FMCSA) was established to oversee safety in the bus industry. These federal agencies monitor everything from construction standards to safety regulations to requirements for training and licensing operators.

Ferries have evolved from using steam to using

This Metro Local bus in Los Angeles, California, is powered by natural gas. (©Publicimage/Dreamstime.com)

marine-diesel or gas-turbine power, with waterjet propulsion. They have increased in speed, are often built of aluminum, and often use a catamaran hull design. Fast ferries may be hydrofoils or hovercraft and use propellers, turbo fans, or waterjets for propulsion. They may carry cars as well as passengers and make trips that last only a few minutes or overnight. Some overnight ferries provide amenities such as guest rooms, casinos, and other entertainment on board. They may carry from two or three to over two hundred vehicles and up to twenty-five hundred passengers.

Shipyards build hull infrastructures and may then partner with boat builders to build superstructures such as pilot houses and passenger cabins, or they may partner with other shipyards to construct vessels' sides, called "curtain plates." For example, the large Todd Shipyards has contracted with Nichols Brothers Boat Builders and Everett Shipyard, both much smaller companies, to complete a project for the Washington State Ferry.

Ferry designers and builders are developing cleaner-burning engines to lower air and water emissions in an attempt to reduce harm to marine animals. High fuel prices could have a negative impact on the industry, as today's fast ferries were developed in the 1980's, when fuel prices were relatively low. These vessels are fuel inefficient by today's standards: They require expensive fuel and lack modern fuel-saving technologies. There are several types of fast boat hulls that need further research and development to ensure passenger comfort. Monohulls, catamarans, hovercraft, and hydrofoils lack stability in high seas. Perfecting these types of ships will be a goal for fast-ferry designers and builders.

Buses today often use clean-air technology. Many are hybrids that can use electric batteries and either diesel fuel or natural gas. Articulated buses are longer than traditional buses but bend in the middle in order to negotiate city streets. Low-floor models were introduced in the 1980's. Partner industries include manufacturers of tires, engines, seating, windows, and signage. Chassis manufacturers may partner with engine manufacturers such as Cummins, Ford, or Caterpillar.

Future buses may have doors on both sides for quicker boarding and unloading and may use CNG and other clean fuels. Fuel-cell-powered buses may be developed. Such cells would be superior to lead-acid batteries, resulting in cleaner energy use. Ethanol-diesel, hydrogen, other alcohols and biofuels, and synthetic fuels are all possible fuels for buses, which have proven to be useful prototype vehicles for such new technologies, since there are fewer of them in each production run, so fewer need be purchased to justify manufacturers' production costs. New lightweight construction and propulsion systems will change bus design and manufacture to work with the Global Positioning System (GPS) and bus rapid transit (BRT). With new propulsion systems and magnetic guidance, steering mechanisms will change. Speed can be automatically controlled. Many such systems are already in use.

Acela Express, built by a consortium of Alstom and Bombardier, is a high-speed intercity train service that was introduced into service by Amtrak in 2000, running between Boston and Washington, D.C. These trains use advanced tilting technology to allow high speed on curves. Using new propulsion equipment, energy normally lost in friction braking is recovered and transformed back into electricity to be used by other trains, a process known as regenerative braking. Diesel-electric locomotives are now more powerful and more efficient than they once were, and they, along with electric traction motor technology, have made the industry greener. Computer technology has been used to reduce noise pollution as well. All-electric zero-emissions locomotives may replace diesel-electric trains. Computerization of signal and communication systems began in the early twenty-first century. Diesel-electric light-rail vehicles running without overhead wires have also been developed. Subindustries include manufacturers and distributors of wheels, communication equipment, seating, windows, toilets, paints and coatings, and flooring.

Modern streetcars are different from light-rail cars in that their tracks are embedded in streets that are also traveled on by automobiles, rather than being installed on dedicated rights of way. They are similar to buses, but streetcars can accom-modate up to 170 passengers, more than even articulated buses, which have an 80-passenger capacity.

Magnetic levitation (maglev) is an emerging technology that is being tested and coming into use. In 2001, the FRA investigated using maglev for a Baltimore to Washington, D.C., train. In 2005, the FRA authorized publication of a study regarding implementation of a maglev project in Pennsylvania. Projects have also been proposed in Georgia and California, but the technology has thus far been too expensive to implement in the United States. Maglev is capable of reaching speeds above 300 miles per hour, and maglev trains are in operation in Shanghai and Germany. Adopting the technology in the United States would require making enormous changes, not only to the transportation infrastructure but also to railcar manufacturing facilities.

Today's mass-transit manufacturing industry is computer driven from conception to design to maintenance. The tools for technicians are as likely be laptop computers as they are to be wrenches or screwdrivers.

INDUSTRY MARKET SEGMENTS

The mass transportation vehicles industry is segmented among water, road, and rail transportation. Its customers are municipal transportation authorities and private companies. Ancillary industries manufacture parts and furnishings to outfit and maintain vessels and vehicles.

Water Transportation Vessels

Shipyards that build ferries and water taxis are a specialized subsector of the shipbuilding industry. Revenues from ferry construction represent only about 6 percent of all shipbuilding revenues in the United States. Some shipyards are small, family-owned businesses, while others are international companies. Many of the larger ferry builders began as family operations. The quantity of vessels built is very small compared to the number of railcars and buses built in the industry's other segments.

Potential Annual Earnings Scale. Wages at shipyards vary according to the job and skills level required for any position. According to 2008 figures of the U.S. Bureau of Labor Statistics (BLS)

Office of Employment Statistics (OES), average managers' salaries vary between technical and office positions. For example, benefits managers earned, on average, $38.69 per hour, or $80,480 annually, while human resources managers earned average wages of $44.44 per hour, or $92,430 annually. Engineering managers' average hourly wages were $52.21, or $108,000 per year. There is a wide range of salary scales among technicians, naval architects, drafters, and mechanical engineers. While mechanical engineering technicians earned an average of $20.31 per hour in 2008, mechanical engineers earned $38.10. Most other installation and repair jobs paid between $17 and $28 per hour.

A car boards a ferry. (©Paula Fisher/Dreamstime.com)

Clientele Interaction. Most shipyard employees have no interaction with clients (who are often transit authorities). Those who do are most often personnel whose primary functions involve client negotiation and satisfaction, such as sales staff and warranty support staff. Maintenance workers who travel to customers to service their vessels also belong in this category. In addition, some executives and design or engineering personnel are likely to discuss large contracts with clients, especially if those contracts involve customization of the vessels to be delivered. During construction, a customer's representatives are generally present for periodic tests conducted by the manufacturer on the vessel. Once the vessel has reached construction completion, it undergoes static testing of its operating systems, followed by dynamic testing, known as sea trials, at the manufacturer's facility. Once the vessel has successfully passed these tests, it is inspected and accepted for service. Training, maintenance, and parts contracts may be provided as deliverables, if specified in the contract.

Amenities, Atmosphere, and Physical Grounds. Shipyards are located on the water, usually in industrial zones. Smaller shipyards may be close to towns. Cranes, dry docks, and machine shops are the main components of shipyards. One example is Derecktor's shipyard, which occupies three acres on Long Island Sound and is accessible to airports, railways, and highways in the New York City metropolitan region.

Typical Number of Employees. The number of employees in ferry shipyards depends on the size of the company and the vessels. Kvichak Marine Industries and Nichols Brothers run small shipyards near Seattle, Washington. They hire laborers for each contract rather than maintaining a permanent corps of employees. Even though they are small, they are able to obtain contracts to build ferries for large agencies.

Derecktor is a private company with shipyards for commercial vessels in New York and Connecticut. It employs approximately 180 people between both yards and typically realizes sales revenues of about $33 million. The Gladding-Hearn Duclos Corporation builds steel and aluminum fast ferries, monohulls, and catamarans, as well as water taxis, for both public and private companies. Based in Massachusetts, it has customers in many different states. It has built over thirty-five ferries since 1985. Gladding-Hearn employs over one hundred people, including naval architects, marine engineers, shipfitters, welders, and office personnel. Both it and Derecktor offer health insurance and retirement benefits to their employees, and Gladding-Hearn offers profit sharing.

Todd Shipyards, a corporation that began as a family business in 1916, has about 550 employees and is traded on the New York Stock Exchange, realizing annual sales revenues of about $113.5 million. Crowley Marine integrates manufacturing and transit management through its vessel construction and architecture service, which maintains ownership of the vessels it constructs and charters vessels for use in lines that the company operates. Crowley is a privately owned international company employomg forty-three hundred people.

VT Halter Marine is an international, publicly held subsidiary of a larger corporation. With eight shipyards in the United States, it builds ferries for transit authorities and private companies both in the United States and abroad. From 1989 to 1999, it built over thirty ferries and earned revenues of over $1 billion. Individual shipyards may employ as few as fifty people.

Traditional Geographic Locations. Shipyards are always located on water. Shipyards may be located on rivers, lakes, or oceans, as long as the water is deep enough for the vessels under construction. For example, Gladding-Hearn Duclos is located in a deepwater port on the Taunton River, in southeastern Massachusetts. Direcktor is located on Long Island Sound in New York. There are shipyards on the Mississippi Gulf Coast, as well as the Puget Sound and rivers in the state of Washington.

Pros of Working for a Ferry Manufacturer. Shipyards are always on the water, most often in industrial areas. Such locations can be quite pleasant in nice weather. The maritime industry is unique in its products and procedures and represents a potentially interesting career choice. Anticipated technical advancements may add to the allure of a career building ferries.

Cons of Working for a Ferry Manufacturer. As in other segments of transportation manufacturing, shipyards may operate twenty-four hours per day, and second- and third-shift crews must adapt to these unusual hours. Most of the work at such facilities is performed outside, in all weather conditions. While coastal facilities may be pleasant in nice weather, they can be quite unpleasant during inclement weather. Spaces on the vessels under construction may be small or awkward to get into. Workers must also climb over uneven gangways and climb ladders to perform their jobs.

Costs

Payroll and Benefits: The salary structures of large companies are complicated, because they employ many different people in many different kinds of positions. International corporations may need offices in the United States to process payroll and comply with local, state, and national regulations and taxes. Technicians may be paid on an hourly basis, while administrators may be salaried. Benefits include vacation time and sick time, although it is becoming more common for companies to give personal time off in lieu of either sick or vacation time.

Some companies are unionized or have a mix of union and nonunion jobs, while others have no union positions at all. Some employees must be treated in accord with federal and state regulations governing wages, while others, generally those in management positions, are exempt from Fair Labor Standards Act (FLSA) rules.

Supplies: Ferry construction companies require materials, machinery, and parts, as well as supplies to service and maintain such equipment. Field offices require basic office equipment (computers, phones, cell phones, and paper), as well as basic supplies for employee use, such as coffeemakers and water. Companies may have microwaves and refrigerators for employee use as well.

External Services: Ferry construction companies may contract some core production tasks rather than employing permanent staff to perform these duties, and they may lease machinery rather than purchasing it. They may also contract uniform laundry services, custodial services, industrial trash and waste removal, security, information technology support, legal counsel, or accounting and payroll services.

Utilities: In the field, utilities must be set up through local companies on each site and may include water and sewage, electricity, gas or oil service, telephone, and Internet access.

Taxes: Payroll taxes must be withheld from all employees and paid to the federal, state, and local governments as required by each locality. Companies must also pay corporate income and property taxes, as well as international taxes and tariffs as appropriate.

Railroad Vehicles

The core of the mass transportation vehicle industry is the manufacture of railcar rolling stock for passengers, which includes long-distance intercity rail, commuter rail, light rail, and subway cars. There are no small manufacturers of railroad rolling stock, although suppliers of parts may be small or midsize companies. Most manufacturers are international, with plants around the globe.

The railcar manufacturing process is generally overseen by a company known as an integrator. This railcar manufacturer must integrate all systems to complete the vehicle, beginning with the car body. Bombardier Transportation, Kawasaki Rail, Siemens, and Alstom are the leading international manufacturers of passenger railcars that function as integrators. Research and development is concerned with new designs for car bodies and exterior structures, as well as noise reduction, aerodynamics, and bogies (or trucks). Computer-assisted design and computer-assisted manufacturing (CAD/CAM) are used to design new sys-

tems. Robotics may be used for some production operations.

After a railroad sends specifications to a qualified manufacturer, the integrator puts together a package with subcontractors while negotiating parts of the specs and contracts with the customer. It then presents a best and final offer (BAFO) to the railroad. Upon acceptance of the offer, the manufacturer usually builds a prototype, or pilot car, that undergoes qualification testing before final production begins.

First, a railcar's body is manufactured, beginning with a frame that may be made from either aluminum or steel. This frame is bolted or welded together. Windows, insulation, flooring, and the outer shell are installed. After the car bodies have been constructed, the integrator, working with subcontractors, arranges and supervises delivery and installation of the following systems in an assembly plant: trucks (wheel and axle sets upon which the cars sit, also known as bogies); brakes; propulsion; HVAC; toilets; interior and exterior

The New York City subway average weekday ridership was 5.1 million in 2009. (©Jordan Tan/Dreamstime.com)

communication systems; and automatic train control (ATC), which includes auto-signaling and train control (monitoring and limiting speed). Employees in the plant include assemblers, welders, pipefitters, electrical technicians, testing technicians, and quality assurance technicians.

United Streetcar, in Oregon and Washington State, is a subsidiary of Oregon Iron Works, which is where the streetcar production takes place. Modern streetcars have low floors like those of modern buses, allowing for wheelchair, carriage, and bicycle access. Streetcars generally operate only within a city, while light rail may have longer routes. Streetcars are also lighter than light rail vehicles.

Potential Annual Earnings Scale. According to the BLS, industrial production managers in railcar manufacturing facilities earned an average of $39.74 per hour, or $82,650 per year, in 2008. Operations managers earned an average of $55.73 per hour, or $115,920 per year. Engineers of various types earned averages between $33.36 and $39.03 per hour. Nonsupervisory production and installation workers earned averages between $14.00 and $23.88 per hour, depending on the level of skill required by their particular jobs.

Clientele Interaction. Warranty support is generally part of railcar contracts. Such support provisions require managers, supervisors, and technicians to maintain, repair, and support successful implementation and operation of the cars. Interaction is between the manufacturer's representatives and the customer, usually a public transit company. During construction, the customer's representatives are generally present for periodic tests conducted by the manufacturer on the ordered equipment.

These include static tests of operating systems, followed by dynamic tests on tracks at the manufacturer's facility. Once the car has successfully passed these tests, it is inspected and accepted for shipment to the customer's facility. Usually, there is additional testing (static and dynamic) in the environment where a rail system is to be operated. Once that final testing is complete, the car is conditionally accepted by the customer (pending open issues, modifications, and punch list completion) and placed into revenue service. The manufacturer may also provide other deliverables, such as training, maintenance, engineering support, and parts support.

Amenities, Atmosphere, and Physical Grounds. There are few amenities in a rail yard, or even in an assembly plant. There may be a cafeteria or lunchroom. Indoor facilities have bathrooms, but there may only be portable toilets on the grounds. In the field, the manufacturer may have offices in a trailer, with electricity and plumbing. Rail yards are busy and potentially dangerous with trains moving through. Workshops must comply with Occupational Safety and Health Administration (OSHA) standards for safety.

Typical Number of Employees. Small suppliers may have fewer than ten employees, while about three or four hundred or more may work in an assembly plant or rail yard.

Traditional Geographic Locations. Manufacturing sites are most often located in or near small towns, away from large metropolitan areas, while repair and maintenance facilities and yards are in or near urban areas where the trains run revenue service.

Pros of Working for a Railroad Manufacturing Company. Some 90 percent of all railcar manufacturing is concentrated in the fifty largest companies, which makes employment more likely in a large manufacturer.

Cons of Working for a Railroad Manufacturing Company. Railcar manufacturing is very cyclic. While peak production times offer very good employment opportunities, the low periods can be devastating. Rail yards are noisy and dangerous. Production requires work with grease and oil. There may be fumes from paints and chemicals, and work may be dirty.

Costs

Payroll and Benefits: Wages are usually hourly, with benefits such as vacation, health care, sick time, and often education as added costs.

Supplies: Manufacturers purchase raw materials, including steel products, which may represent 70 percent of the cost of producing a railcar. Equipment is a large expense, including maintenance and replacement, as are parts. Standard office supplies, as well as computers and furniture, are a basic cost.

External Services: Companies may contract out payroll services to specialized companies rather than processing payrolls in-house. Depending on the size and revenues, a company may contract out computer services, vending machines, or dining facilities. Other contracted services may include building and grounds maintenance, machine maintenance, security, or industrial trash and waste disposal and removal.

Utilities: Utilities may include water and sewage, electricity, gas or oil service, telephone, and Internet access.

Taxes: Payroll taxes are withheld from all employees, and paid to the federal, state, and local governments as required by each locality. Companies must also pay corporate income and property taxes, as well as international taxes and tariffs as appropriate.

Buses

A mass-transit bus is defined as a rubber-tired vehicle with its own engine that runs on a road, rather than on tracks. As in the rail industry, bus manufacturers integrate components and systems from subcontractors, including propulsion systems, suspension systems, drive trains, seating, wheels, and tires. The integrated chassis is assembled in a plant and then shipped to a production facility, where the engine, seats, axles, and electrical heat and air-conditioning systems are installed and vehicles are tested. There are small, midsize, and large subsegments of the bus manufacturing segment of the mass transportation vehicles industry.

Gillig Corporation, established in California in 1890, is privately owned and employs about seven hundred people. It offers retirement, education, and health benefits. As the second-largest bus manufacturer in North America, it produces between twelve hundred and thirteen hundred vehicles per year.

New Flyer is a midsize, publicly traded company, employing about twenty-four hundred people in two plants in Minnesota and one in Winnipeg, Canada. New Flyer produces over twenty-two hundred buses per year.

El Dorado National is a subsidiary of the publicly traded Thor Company. It builds buses in both California and Kansas. Champion Bus is another Thor subsidiary and builds over twelve hundred midsize buses in its plant in Michigan. Champion's 250 nonunion employees work in a 194,000-square-foot plant on a 73-acre site. Daimler Buses North America has over twelve hundred employees and sells over forty thousand buses worldwide. Its Oriskany, New York, plant for assembly and manufacturing occupies 206,000 square feet.

Potential Annual Earnings Scale. According to the BLS, machine operator supervisors in bus manufacturing facilities earned an average of $14.26 per hour in 2008, while industrial engineers earned an average of $29.55 per hour. At an average of $667 per week, these wages were high compared to all manufacturing jobs. Industrial production managers earned, on average, $40.17 per hour, or $83,550 annually, while engineering managers earned $44.78 per hour, or $93,140 per year.

Clientele Interaction. Employees in sales or customer support interact with clients, but most workers in the plants themselves do not.

Amenities, Atmosphere, and Physical Grounds. Bus manufacturing facilities are indoor spaces, unlike shipyards or rail yards, so weather does not affect working conditions.

Typical Number of Employees. Companies may employ from 250 to over 1,000 workers. The size of the company, the facility, and the stage of the production process all impact the size of the workforce.

Traditional Geographic Locations. Assembly plants and manufacturing facilities are usually located away from urban areas. Most bus manufacturing is located in the Midwest, but that is changing as plants open in California and the South.

Pros of Working for a Bus Manufacturing Company. Less than half of motor vehicle parts manufacturing jobs are found in small- and midsize companies.

Cons of Working for a Bus Manufacturing Company. Less than 16 percent of motor vehicle and parts manufacturing is involved in bus chassis manufacturing. Almost half of all bus manufacturers are large businesses with over five hundred employees. Although offices are typically clean and modern, workers on assembly lines have to tolerate noise, fumes, grease, and higher-than-average injury rates. Newer facilities mitigate these problems with modern, ergonomic assembly lines.

Costs

Payroll and Benefits: In times of high production, overtime wages for hours in excess of forty per week are 1.5 times the normal rate, or double for work performed on Sundays or holidays. Most bus manufacturers provide health, retirement, and education benefits and may provide life and accident insurance, especially if they are union shops.

Supplies: Standard office supplies as well as computers and furniture are a basic cost. Manufacturers purchase raw materials, including steel products, which may represent 70 percent of the cost of producing a bus. Equipment is a large expense, including maintenance and replacement.

External Services: Manufacturers may contract out accounting services or payroll services. Computer service companies may be used for maintaining and upgrading hardware and software. Larger companies may have in-house divisions for these needs. Grounds and machinery maintenance are costs, whether contracted out or not.

Utilities: Companies that own facilities must pay for electricity, water, sewage, telephone, and Internet access.

Taxes: Payroll taxes are withheld from all employees, and paid to the federal, state, and local governments as required by each locality. Companies must also pay corporate income and property taxes, as well as international taxes and tariffs as appropriate.

ORGANIZATIONAL STRUCTURE AND JOB ROLES

The mass transportation vehicles industry can be divided into three segments: bus, rail, and water. All are subject to federal and international environmental and safety regulations, which vary by segment. All employ technical and mechanically hands-on workforces, as well as experts in specific types of engineering. Employees in each segment who serve in managerial and supervisory roles usually have advanced degrees in design, engineering, or business administration. While smaller shipyards may have owner-operators, the industry is, for the most part, large, and corporate officers are not likely to participate in a hands-on manner. Both bus manufacturers and railroad rolling stock manufacturers are large, often international companies, although they may contract out specific parts of vehicles to smaller, more specialized companies.

The following umbrella categories apply to businesses in the mass transportation vehicles industry:

- Business Management
- Facilities and Security
- Technology, Research, Design, and Development
- Production and Operations
- Sales and Distribution
- Human Resources

Business Management

Corporate officers, or executive managers, oversee the highest-level operations of vehicle manufacturing companies, but they are often somewhat detached from day-to-day operations. On-site managers, including shipyard managers and rail yard managers, oversee and coordinate production and ensure that projects proceed on time and within budget. Managers must also ensure that safety regulations are followed and enforced.

Business management occupations may include the following:

- President/Chief Executive Officer (CEO)
- Chief Operating Officer (COO)
- Chief Financial Officer (CFO)
- Chief Technology Officer (CTO)
- Vice President
- Production Manager
- General or Operations Manager
- Project Manager
- Engineering Manager
- Project Engineer
- Project Coordinator

Facilities and Security

Shipyards can range in size from 130,000 to 225,000 square feet, and rail and bus manufacturing plants can reach the same size, although some may be smaller. Construction plants are often secure facilities, requiring identification badges for entry and monitored by guards and surveillance systems. Some companies contract security services to external vendors, but others prefer to hire their own security crews. Guards often have backgrounds in law enforcement or military service and must be proficient with weapons, as well as able to enforce security protocols governing both employees and visitors. Some security jobs may also require technical proficiency with computer or security systems.

In addition, facilities must be maintained and cleaned regularly. Cleaning and maintenance crews are employed both in administrative offices and in production plants, and they also maintain and repair extremely heavy machinery.

Facilities and security occupations may include the following:

- Security Guard
- Security Manager
- Custodian/Janitor
- Maintenance and Repair Worker
- Mechanic
- Network Security Specialist
- Custodial Services Manager
- Maintenance Supervisor

Technology, Research, Design, and Development

Engineers and other specialists design, test, and oversee construction of vehicles and vessels. They design not only entire vehicles and vessels, including necessary parts, but also production machinery required to construct their companies' products. As a result, they also help coordinate production workflow, especially as it relates to the systems they have designed.

Technology and development personnel may work with vendors to determine specifications and pricing of parts their companies have decided to purchase rather than construct. They often require degrees in very specialized fields, such as marine engineering, naval architecture, or railroad engineering, as appropriate. They must also understand the practical business side of the industry and the relationship between their designs and the full process required to bring those designs to fruition.

Commercial and industrial designers often work with computer design systems instead of models. Mechanical engineers design and improve on working parts, such as engines and transmissions. Electrical and electronics engineers design electrical and electronic systems and components and may work with robotic equipment for vehicle assembly. Industrial engineers may design the plan and oversee assembly-line production, including quality control. Engineering technicians usually need postsecondary education, such as associate's degrees. Engineers may earn close to $40 an hour, or between $45,000 and $55,000 a year if they have a postsecondary or associate's degree. Licensing as a professional engineer (PE) generally requires a bachelor's degree from an ABET-accredited engineering program, as well as formal testing and certification by a state entity.

Technology, research, design, and development occupations may include the following:

- Vice President of Research and Development
- Marine Chief Engineer
- Marine Engineer
- Naval Architect
- Railroad Engineer
- Vehicle Engineer
- Industrial Engineer
- Mechanical Engineer
- Electrical Engineer
- Environmental Engineer
- Engineering Technician
- Project Engineer
- Engineering Manager

Production and Operations

Production and operations personnel perform the work of actually creating and assembling parts, vehicles, and vessels. They may be skilled or unskilled, and most companies employ a mixture of both. Shipyard crews must have working knowledge of marine equipment, including diesels and hydraulics, and have a basic understanding of the theory and practice of internal combustion engines. They may need welding skills as well. Most require at least a high school or vocational school education. Some are required to have experience in the field or to have completed approved technical training, which might include electrical or electronics training. They must be able to use an extensive assortment of tools. Some shipyard positions require the ability to read and follow blueprints, as well as to use computers. Color vision may also be a requirement.

Some railcar production workers need to be able to use multimeters, which measure voltage, current, and resistance; advanced multimeters, which measure capacitance, inductance, and current gain of transistors for troubleshooting and diagnosis; and

OCCUPATION SPECIALTIES

Welders

Specialty	Responsibilities
Arc welders	Join metal parts using electric welding equipment.
Combination welders	Use arc, gas, or resistance welding equipment on the same project, depending on the materials and type of welding needed.
Gas welders	Use an intense gas flame to join metal parts.
Production line welders	Join metal parts on a production line using previously set up gas or arc welding equipment.

oscilloscopes, as well as traditional hand tools. Equipment installers generally work indoors in well-lit areas and are less prone to injury than are workers who must frequently lift heavy equipment. Electrical and electronics repairers and installers may earn anywhere from $13 to $39 hourly, depending on the level of experience required and the complexity of the task. Job growth in this subsector is expected to be slower than average, or about 4 percent a year. Suppliers to railcar manufacturers may be located in or near the assembly plants. This might include major systems propulsion, brakes, HVAC, doors, and communications. These suppliers support the integration of the systems during production.

OCCUPATION PROFILE

Metal/Plastic Working Machine Operator

Considerations	Qualifications
Description	Runs machines that produce thousands of parts that are used in automobiles and nearly every other manufactured product.
Career cluster	Manufacturing
Interests	Things
Working conditions	Work inside
Minimum education level	On-the-job training; high school diploma or GED; high school diploma/technical training; apprenticeship
Physical exertion	Medium work
Physical abilities	Unexceptional/basic fitness
Opportunities for experience	Internship; apprenticeship; part-time work
Licensure and certification	Recommended
Employment outlook	Decline expected
Holland interest score	RCE

Note: See volume 1, "Publisher's Note," for an explanation of the Holland interest score.

OCCUPATION PROFILE

Riveter

Considerations	Qualifications
Description	Operates different types of machines that fasten together pieces of metal for assembling such articles as aircraft, space vehicles, or fabricated parts.
Career cluster	Manufacturing
Interests	Things
Working conditions	Work inside
Minimum education level	On-the-job training; high school diploma or GED; high school diploma/technical training
Physical exertion	Medium work
Physical abilities	Unexceptional/basic fitness
Opportunities for experience	Part-time work
Licensure and certification	Usually not required
Employment outlook	Decline expected
Holland interest score	RSE

Note: See volume 1, "Publisher's Note," for an explanation of the Holland interest score.

About 25 percent of jobs in the heavy vehicles manufacturing industry are unionized, a somewhat higher figure than in other industries. At peak production times, workers may be paid 1.5 to 2 times their hourly wage if working on weekends or holidays. Hourly workers may earn between $15 and $30 per hour, depending on the skill and education level required in any position. Many aspects of assembly are now automated, but people are needed both to operate and guide the machines and to perform tasks too small or too complicated to be automated. Jobs in the electrical or electronics field usually require certification and associate's degrees.

Some companies provide training, maintenance, and parts to their clients, based on terms specified in contracts. Operations staff at such companies must travel to their clients' facilities to train their personnel and to perform maintenance and repairs on vessels, railcars, rail systems, or buses.

Production and operations occupations may include the following:

- Project Engineer
- Project Manager
- Production Manager
- Production Supervisor
- Electrical Engineer
- Fabrication Supervisor
- Marine Diesel Mechanic
- Marine Electrician
- Marine Estimator
- Marine Pipefitter
- Marine Welder
- Marine Mechanical/Piping Engineer
- Marine Painter
- Sandblaster
- Rigger
- Lofter
- Joiner

- Metalworker
- Assembly Worker/Team Member
- Fabricator/Fabrication Team Member
- Electrician
- Industrial Machinery Mechanic
- Machine Operator
- Machinist
- Material Mover/Handler
- Painter/Coater
- Welding, Soldering, and Brazing Worker
- Grinder/Polisher
- Tester, Sorter, Sampler, and Weigher
- Field Technician
- Millwright
- Tool and Die Maker

Sales and Distribution

Sales and distribution personnel secure contracts from customers, maintain relationships with those customers (keeping them apprised of developments in the design and production process), and ensure delivery of finished products. Ferry shipyards and rail yards sell vessels and vehicles directly to transit authorities and other customers. They do not sell through dealers or other intermediaries. Bus manufacturers may sell their products directly as well, or they may employ dealers to conduct sales.

Sales and distribution occupations may include the following:

- Vice President of Sales
- Sales Manager
- Sales/Customer Representative
- Distribution Manager
- Truck Driver
- Pilot
- Shipping and Receiving Clerk

Human Resources

Human resources personnel recruit, hire, orient, train, promote, and fire employees. They also administer payroll and benefits, coordinate safety training, and monitor company compliance with federal, state, and local work rules. They resolve workplace disputes and respond to employee grievances. Managers generally have degrees in human resources administration.

Human resources occupations may include the following:

- Human Resources Manager
- Human Resources Assistant
- Human Resources Generalist
- Benefits Specialist
- Administrative Assistant
- Payroll Clerk
- Training Manager

INDUSTRY OUTLOOK

The future of the mass transportation vehicle industry is best examined through a look at three areas: water vessels, rail vehicles, and buses.

Ferry and water taxi construction represent a small part of the large shipbuilding industry. While the U.S. industry grew by about 10 percent between 2006 and 2009, it is projected to decrease production slightly thereafter. Orders for new vessels from public transportation agencies are expected to fall as public expenditures decrease in the wake of the recession of 2007-2009. The BLS projects employment of marine engineers and architects at the manufacturing level to decrease by almost 10 percent between 2008 and 2018, while some other industry jobs are projected to decline by as much as 28 percent.

Until tracks and overhead catenaries are updated, the United States will continue to lag behind the rest of the world in true high-speed train service capable of competing with regional air service in both cost and speed. However, several impetuses exist for such development. After the September 11, 2001, terrorist attacks, train travel became more desirable, involving fewer security headaches for passengers than air travel (although train tracks are easier to sabotage than is the sky). Trains also have the advantage of being able to provide downtown-to-downtown service. As a result, railcar manufacturing has been growing steadily since 2005. The American Recovery and Reinvestment Act of 2009 should increase this growth as it allocates $8.4 billion in new funds for public transportation and $9.3 billion for intercity and high-speed rail. In 2009, United Streetcar received $50 million worth of new orders, and it anticipated growth as eighty cities were considering streetcar implementation in the future.

Bus transportation is the largest mode of public transportation. Buses continue to adopt cleaner

PROJECTED EMPLOYMENT FOR SELECTED OCCUPATIONS

Transportation Equipment Manufacturing

Employment		
2009	*Projected 2018*	*Occupation*
53,700	48,300	Machinists
29,610	30,000	Mechanical engineers
171,230	167,900	Team assemblers
46,120	45,700	Welders, cutters, solderers, and brazers

Source: U.S. Bureau of Labor Statistics, Industries at a Glance, Occupational Employment Statistics and Employment Projections Program.

energy technologies, such as parallel hybrid propulsion, electric propulsion, and fuel-cell power. Future developments may include intelligent vehicles, accident-avoidance technology, and wireless communication. Concerns in urban areas over massive traffic, gridlock, and air pollution, as well as greenhouse-gas emissions, are likely to improve the outlook for the bus industry. Demand for buses is projected to grow, as fuel prices for automobiles rise and urban congestion increases.

Employment Advantages

Water Vessels. In 2008, there were only eighty-five hundred marine engineer and naval architect jobs in the United States. Nevertheless, employment prospects in this field are good because a limited number of students are pursuing these occupations. The median income of these positions, moreover, is high at $74,000. Overall, the number of jobs in the industry is estimated to decline by 11 percent, with the greatest decline among upper management, human resources personnel, drafters, maintenance workers, and administrative support staff.

Rail Vehicles. According to the BLS, employment opportunities in rail manufacturing are expected to grow, but at only about 4 percent per year, slower than the average for all industries. Those job seekers with associate's degrees, technical certification, and experience will be most successful. However, automation and robotics are expected to eliminate some production jobs. Although welding jobs are expected to de-

PROJECTED EMPLOYMENT FOR SELECTED OCCUPATIONS

Rail Transportation

Employment		
2009	*Projected 2018*	*Occupation*
41,850	49,700	Locomotive engineers and operators
12,040	13,500	Rail car repairers
22,450	25,400	Railroad brake, signal, and switch operators
37,380	39,600	Railroad conductors and yardmasters
10,530	11,900	Rail-track laying and maintenance equipment operators

Source: U.S. Bureau of Labor Statistics, Industries at a Glance, Occupational Employment Statistics and Employment Projections Program.

cline, employment prospects remain positive for those with the latest training and certification. Declines will be most severe among unskilled positions. The BLS projects a decline of almost 40 percent in employment across the entire spectrum of jobs in manufacturing rolling stock between 2008 and 2018. With federal stimulus money and new streetcar projects on the horizon, however, some job prospects may improve.

Buses. Employment opportunities in bus manufacturing are expected to decline overall, according to the BLS, even as demand for buses increases. The decline will be most severe among unskilled workers. As factories automate, there will be jobs for those who service and repair robotic equipment. Management opportunities will decline, as there will be fewer employees to supervise. As in the rail industry, production may be cyclical. The BLS projects a decline in employment of about 8 percent between 2008 and 2018, with upper management, support services such as cleaning and maintenance, and drafting experiencing the highest rates of decline.

Annual Earnings

Water Vessels. Shipbuilding revenues for ferry and water taxi construction in 2009 were $60.7 million, a substantial increase from $50.8 million in 2006.

Rail Vehicles. Rail rolling stock revenue in the United States in 2009 was $3.896 billion. Both the rail rolling stock industry and the bus industry rely in some part on public policy and public funding. If a company receives direct funds from government agencies, it will be affected by the financial state of those agencies. For example, when states face fiscal crises, mass-transit budgets are cut, delaying or halting orders for new cars. After steadily increasing annual revenues between 2006 and 2009, revenues are projected to decline to about $3.712 billion in 2010.

Buses. Bus manufacturing revenues in the United States were $1.52 billion in 2009, a large decrease from 2006 earnings of $2.826 billion. Growth was predicted to rise slightly in 2010, to about $1.579 billion.

RELATED RESOURCES FOR FURTHER RESEARCH

AMERICAN BOAT BUILDERS AND REPAIRERS
    ASSOCIATION
50 Water St.
Warren, RI 02885
Tel: (401) 247-0318
Fax: (401) 247-0074
http://www.abbra.org

AMERICAN BUS ASSOCIATION
700 13th St. NW, Suite 575
Washington, DC 20005-5923
Tel: (202) 842-1645
Fax: (202) 842-0850
http://www.buses.org

AMERICAN PUBLIC TRANSPORTATION
    ASSOCIATION
1666 K St. NW, Suite 1100
Washington, DC 20006
Tel: (202) 496-4800
Fax: (202) 496-4324
http://www.apta.com

AMERICAN SOCIETY FOR ENGINEERING
    EDUCATION
1818 N St. NW, Suite 600
Washington, DC 20036
Tel: (202) 331-3500
Fax: (202) 265-8504
http://www.asee.org

AMERICAN SOCIETY OF MECHANICAL ENGINEERS
3 Park Ave.
New York, NY 10016
Tel: (800) 843-2763
Fax: (973) 882-1717
http://www.asme.org

FEDERAL TRANSIT ADMINISTRATION, U.S.
    DEPARTMENT OF TRANSPORTATION
East Building, 4th Floor
200 New Jersey Ave. SE
Washington, DC 20590
http://www.fta.dot.gov

INSTITUTE OF ELECTRICAL AND ELECTRONICS
ENGINEERS
3 Park Ave., 17th Floor
New York, NY 10016-5997
Tel: (212) 419-7900
Fax: (212) 752-4929
http://www.ieee.org

INSTITUTE OF INDUSTRIAL ENGINEERS
3577 Parkway Ln., Suite 200
Norcross, GA 30092
Tel: (800) 494-0460
Fax: (770) 441-3295
http://www.iie2net.org

NATIONAL BUS RAPID TRANSIT INSTITUTE,
CENTER FOR URBAN TRANSPORTATION
RESEARCH
4202 E Fowler Ave., CUT100
Tampa, FL 33620-5375
Tel: (813) 974-9833
Fax: (813) 974-5168
http://www.nbrti.org

NATIONAL COUNCIL OF EXAMINERS FOR
ENGINEERING AND SURVEYING
P.O. Box 1686
Clemson, SC 29633
Tel: (800) 250-3196
Fax: (864) 654-6033
http://www.ncees.org

NATIONAL SOCIETY OF PROFESSIONAL ENGINEERS
1420 King St.
Alexandria, VA 22314
Tel: (703) 684-2800
Fax: (703) 836-4875
http://www.nspe.org

RAILWAY SUPPLY INSTITUTE
50 F St. NW, Suite 7030
Washington, DC 20001
Tel: (202) 347-4664
Fax: (202) 347-0047
http://www.rsiweb.org

SAE INTERNATIONAL
400 Commonwealth Dr.
Warrendale, PA 15096
Tel: (724) 776-4841

Fax: (202) 463-7319
http://www.sae.org

SOCIETY OF NAVAL ARCHITECTS AND MARINE
ENGINEERS
601 Pavonia Ave.
Jersey City, NJ 07306
Tel: (800) 798-2188
Fax: (201) 798-4975
http://www.sname.org

TRANSPORTATION RESEARCH BOARD, THE
NATIONAL ACADEMIES
500 5th St. NW
Washington, DC 20001
Tel: (202) 334-2934
Fax: (202) 334-2519
http://www.trb.org

ABOUT THE AUTHOR

Jane Brodsky Fitzpatrick is a librarian at the
Graduate Center of the City University of New York
(CUNY). She worked at the State University of New
York (SUNY) Maritime College for ten years. She
earned a bachelor of arts degree from Lake Forest
College in 1969, a master's degree in library science
from Simmons College, in Boston, in 1994,
and a second master's degree in liberal studies
from the CUNY Graduate Center in 2006.

FURTHER READING

American Public Transportation Association.
2009 Public Transportation Fact Book.
Washington, D.C.: Author, 2009.
Brown, Betty J. *Transportation.* Vol. 2 in
Encyclopedia of Business and Finance, edited by
Burton S. Kaliski. 2d ed. Detroit: Macmillan
Reference, 2006.
Cheape, Charles W. *Moving the Masses: Urban
Public Transit in New York, Boston, and
Philadelphia, 1880-1912.* Harvard Studies in
Business History 31. Cambridge, Mass.:
Harvard University Press, 1980.
Cudahy, Brian J. *Cash, Tokens, and Transfers: A
History of Urban Mass Transit in North America.*
New York: Fordham University Press, 1990.

Karr, Ronald Dale. *Railroads.* Vol. 2 in *Encyclopedia of American Urban History.* New York: Sage Reference, 2007.

Levinson, Herbert S. "Bus Transit in the Twenty-first Century: Some Perspectives and Prospects." *Transportation Research Record: Journal of the Transportation Research Board* 1760, no. 1 (2001): 42-46. http://trb.metapress .com/content/q073w13683w14255.

McHoes, Ann McIver. *Computer Sciences: Railroad Applications,* edited by Roger R. Flynn. Vol. 3. New York: Macmillan Reference, 2002.

Meier, Albert E. *Over the Road: A History of Intercity Bus Transportation in the United States.* Upper Montclair, N.J.: Motor Bus Society, 1975.

Middleton, William D. *Metropolitan Railways: Rapid Transit in America.* Bloomington: Indiana University Press, 2003.

Miller, John A. *Fares, Please! A Popular History of Trolleys, Horse-Cars, Street-Cars, Buses, Elevateds, and Subways.* New York: Dover, 1960.

Parker, Jeffrey A. "Private Financing of Mass Transit." In *Private Innovations in Public Transit,* edited by John C. Weicher. Lanham, Md: University Press of America, 1988.

U.S. Bureau of Labor Statistics. *Career Guide to Industries,* 2010-2011 ed. http://www.bls.gov/ oco/cg.

U.S. Bureau of Transportation Statistics. *National Transportation Statistics,* 2009-2010 ed. http:// www.bts.gov/publications/national _transportation_statistics.

U.S. Census Bureau. North American Industry Classification System (NAICS), 2007. http:// www.census.gov/cgi-bin/sssd/naics/ naicsrch?chart=2007.

U.S. Department of Commerce. International Trade Administration. Office of Trade and Industry Information. Industry Trade Data and Analysis. http://ita.doc.gov/td/industry/ otea/OTII/OTII-index.html.

Wallace, Jonathan. *Railroads.* Vol. 3 in *Encyclopedia of Science, Technology, and Ethics,* edited by Carl Mitcham. Detroit: Macmillan Reference, 2005.

Walsh, Margaret. *Making Connections: The Long-Distance Bus Industry in the United States.* Burlington, Vt.: Ashgate, 2000.

Wang, J., and S. McOwan. "Fast Passenger Ferries and Their Future." *Maritime Policy and Management: The Flagship Journal of International Shipping and Port Research* 27, no. 3 (2000): 231.

Medicine and Health Care Industry

INDUSTRY SNAPSHOT

General Industry: Health Science

Career Cluster: Health Science

Subcategory Industries: Family Planning Centers; Freestanding Ambulatory Surgical and Emergency Centers; HMO Medical Centers; Home Health Care Services; Kidney Dialysis Centers; Medical and Diagnostic Laboratories; Nurses' Offices (Centers, Clinics); Offices of Physicians; Offices of Podiatrists; Outpatient Clinics and Care Centers

Related Industries: Complementary and Alternative Health Care Industry; Counseling Services; Dental and Orthodontics Industry; Health and Fitness Industry; Hospital Care and Services; Pharmaceuticals and Medications Industry; Public Health Services; Residential Medical Care Industry; Scientific, Medical, and Health Equipment and Supplies Industry

Annual Domestic Revenues: $1.75 trillion USD (U.S. Census Bureau, 2008)

Annual Global Revenues: $4.7 trillion USD (World Health Organization, 2006, estimate)

NAICS Numbers: 6211, 62132, 62149-6216, 62139-62141

INDUSTRY DEFINITION

Summary

The medicine and health care industry is dedicated to the prevention, diagnosis, treatment, and management of disease and the preservation of health through services provided by trained medical and allied health care professionals. These professionals usually have specific educational degrees, as well as certifications and licensure, qualifying them to provide care. Health care providers include medical doctors (M.D.s), dentists, nurses, dieticians, physical therapists, occupational therapists, speech therapists, recreational therapists, audiologists, chiropractors, optometrists, and mental health professionals. Many of these providers, however, may also be categorized in other industries. For example, dentists work in the dental and orthodontics industry, chiropractors work in the complementary and alternative medicine and health care industry, and mental health professionals work in the counseling services industry.

History of the Industry

The practice of caring for the sick in the United States predates the American Revolution. In 1751, Pennsylvania Hospital, chartered by Thomas Bond and Benjamin Franklin,

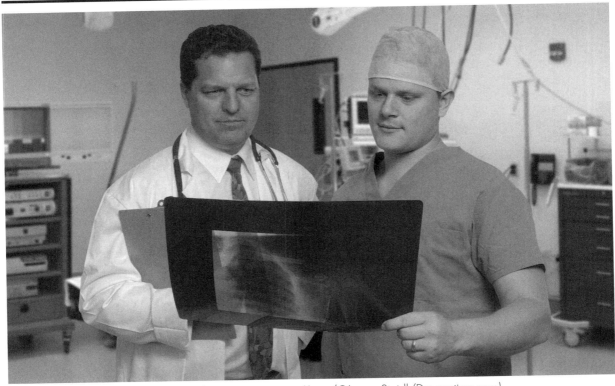

A physician and surgeon review an X ray. (©James Steidl/Dreamstime.com)

cared for the poor, sick, and insane from the streets of Philadelphia. To launch this institution, Franklin pursued political support and private donors. Public welfare through almshouses included basic health care. Americans supported dependent people through public taxes and lotteries.

The American colonies had few educated physicians and many health care needs. Poor sanitation practices, such as pouring waste into local streams, bred infectious diseases. Doctors had little formal training, often limited to knowledge of stabilizing broken bones and administering herbs and liquors. In 1765, the College of Pennsylvania founded the first medical school in the United States, modeled after the school at the University of Edinburgh. Courses included basic anatomy, and students received experience in bedside care at the Pennsylvania Hospital.

Historically, care of the sick was delegated to women with little training. Generations passed down various folk remedies. In the late 1800's, nurses, sponsored by charitable organizations and churches, delivered care in the homes of new mothers and people with infectious diseases. Following the standards of Great Britain's pioneering Florence Nightingale, American nurses established a professional training process through schools of nursing. By the early 1900's, nurses were licensed and credentialed by the states. In 1909, Jane Delano established the American Red Cross Nursing Service to complement the Army Nurse Corps. The need for nurses expanded during World Wars I and II, so the federal government funded nursing education and provided stipends.

For years, physicians held a place of respect and power in America. Central to both medical practice and its reputation is the belief that physicians have a moral obligation to act as healers. Traditionally, they valued the sanctity of life and embraced the unique nature of the patient-physician relationship. Physicians were viewed as selfless professionals putting the welfare of their patients before any other concerns. However, over time physicians became central figures in the business of health care in order to be paid for their services.

Physician practices and the business of medicine

are linked to the formation of health insurance companies to guarantee payment for services. In 1929, Dr. Michael Shadid formed a health care co-operative for farmers in Oklahoma, requiring a pre-determined fee to receive services. Baylor Hospital in Dallas, Texas, began a prepaid health care plan called Blue Cross to provide hospital services for teachers. Physicians joined this plan as Blue Shield to cover the cost of their services, forming Blue Cross Blue Shield. These examples represent the beginning of insurance and managed care to secure payment for medicine and health care services.

With advanced technology and disease man-agement, the life expectancy of Americans in-creased, resulting in more seniors needing health care. In 1965, the federal government enacted landmark legislation, establishing Medicare and Medicaid. Medicare was a federal government-funded program designed to pay for basic medi-cal care for Americans over sixty-five years old. Medicaid, funded with federal dollars but man-aged by the states, paid for basic health care ser-vices for indigent citizens and children.

For many years, Americans received health care under fee-for-service plans provided through em-ployer insurance. In these plans, physicians charge separate fees for each service performed. Usually, patients pay a portion of each bill while their insur-ance companies pay another portion.

The last three decades of the twentieth century witnessed the growth of managed care programs such as health maintenance organizations (HMOs) and preferred provider organizations (PPOs), de-signed to save health care dollars. Still, millions remained uninsured and health care costs skyrocketed. It remained a chal-lenge to provide access to medicine and health care services at reasonable cost for all citizens.

The Industry Today

In the twenty-first century, many new advances have been made in diagnosis, treatment of illness, and disease manage-ment. The health care industry contin-ues to offer a wide range of services and products to prevent, treat, and manage disease, as well as to promote wellness. Emphasis on healthy lifestyle choices has heightened, as U.S. health care costs have escalated alongside increased diagnosis and treatment of preventable diseases. Americans have been encouraged to take an active part in their health, and portions of the industry are transition-ing from thinking of themselves as providing sick-ness care to instead providing health and wellness. Living healthful lifestyles remains the most cost-effective solution to the many complications and adverse outcomes of sickness and disease, as far more than half of all U.S. health care dollars are spent to treat and manage illnesses that can be pre-vented or reduced through lifestyle change.

The U.S. Surgeon General's *Healthy People: The Surgeon General's Report on Health Promotion and Dis-ease Prevention* (1979) contained recommendations for Americans to follow. These recommendations were updated in 1990 as *Healthy People, 2000*; in 2000 as *Healthy People, 2010*; and in 2010 as *Healthy People, 2020*. States, communities, businesses, and professional groups have adopted these plans to improve the health of Americans and lower the cost of medical and health care.

Key goals of *Healthy People, 2010* were increased quality and length of life and elimination of health care disparities. This government initiative de-fined twenty-eight focus areas, including access to quality health care, injury and violence prevention, healthy communication, community-based educa-tion and supporting programs, safety of medical products, occupational safety, and environmen-tal safety and health. Target diseases for preven-tion and improved treatment included diabetes, cancer, chronic kidney disease, arthritis, chronic back conditions, osteoporosis, human immunode-

Ambulatory Health Care Services' Contribution to the U.S. Economy

Value Added	Amount
Gross domestic product	$485.9 billion
Gross domestic product	3.4%
Persons employed	5.697 million
Total employee compensation	$366.2 billion

Source: U.S. Bureau of Economic Analysis. Data are for 2008.

ficiency virus (HIV), heart disease, stroke, infectious disease, respiratory disease, sexually transmitted disease, nutrition, obesity, oral health, and mental health. Other focus areas were maternal, infant, and children's health, as well as disability, tobacco use, substance abuse, hearing, vision, immunizations, food safety, and the public health infrastructure. The top ten leading indicators of health in America were defined, in order, as physical activity, overweight and obesity, use of tobacco, substance abuse, responsible sex, mental health, violence and injury, quality of environment, immunization, and access to health care.

Another major project that has significant implications for medicine and health care practice is the Genome Project. This international project began in 1990 and was completed some thirteen years later in 2003. The purpose of this work was to discover and review the projected twenty thousand to twenty-five thousand human genes. The program studied the sequence of some three thousand units of deoxyribonucleic acid (DNA). Knowledge of DNA sequencing can enable scientists to crack the code of human genetics and treat and prevent devastating infectious and inherited diseases. These discoveries are especially important to understand the human immune system and to predict how each person will take in and utilize medications; this level of genetic analysis is expected to produce a future field of personalized medicine, in which care will be tailored meticulously to the genetically determined needs of each individual body. One day, these discoveries may also assist people to stay well by uncovering the secrets in the human genes that enhance health. Although ethical dilemmas surround this type of health science research, the benefits could prove useful to decrease disease and to manage human health, greatly affecting the medicine and health care industry.

Medical and health care services today are provided by a diverse group of providers in various settings. In the past, the majority of services were delivered within health care institutions such as hospitals. Today, many procedures and treatments once limited to inpatient settings have moved to outpatient settings and to patients' homes. Ambulatory health care services help patients remain in their residences within their communities, decreasing costs and improving patient satisfaction. Many medical procedures can be performed safely in physician or dentist offices. Physical, speech, and occupational therapists offer their services in outpatient centers, rehabilitation centers, and patients' homes. Innovative medical equipment allows patients to remain outside the walls of institutional care facilities such as hospitals.

Ambulatory outpatient settings include mental health and substance abuse centers, family planning centers, kidney dialysis centers, and surgical centers. Medical and diagnostic laboratories play an important role in patient care, as do diagnostic imaging centers. Although many hospitals offer these services through dedicated department staff and high-technology equipment, laboratories and diagnostic imaging establishments are becoming more available in the ambulatory health care setting. The improved technology of these services allows more options for diagnosis and treatment than ever before in health care history.

Traditional medicine still remains primary in patient care management; physicians and nurses provide the majority of care. However, many people have also adopted alternative practices to enhance wellness and treat illness. Specialists such as optometrists, chiropractors, podiatrists, homeopaths, acupuncturists, hypnotherapists, and naturopaths offer Americans additional choices for medical and health care services. Consultants in nutrition and fitness provide services to support lifestyle changes for disease prevention and wellness. Health care professionals work as educators as well as care providers to improve patients' quality of life.

Inputs Consumed by Ambulatory Health Care Services

Input	Value
Energy	$4.6 billion
Materials	$82.3 billion
Purchased services	$194.7 billion
Total	$281.6 billion

Source: U.S. Bureau of Economic Analysis. Data are for 2008.

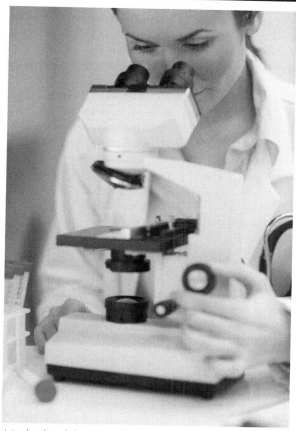

Medical and diagnostic laboratories play an important role in patient care, as do diagnostic imaging centers. (©Yuri Arcurs/Dreamstime.com)

Today, Americans enjoy many options for high-technology, sophisticated drug therapies and advanced medical and health care services. However, millions remain uninsured. Attempts to address this problem have resulted in incremental improvements, as the costs of medicine and health care services have continued to rise. Individuals and families pay higher prices each year for health care coverage and copayments, as insurers raise rates to cover their increasing costs. The promise of managed care as a cost-efficient way to decrease costs without lowering quality of care has not been fulfilled.

By 2010, the United States was spending 17.6 percent of its gross domestic product (GDP) on health care. While health costs were rising dramatically, real wages were falling. Some economists linked the two trends, asserting that the rising costs

to business of providing health insurance benefits contributed to the falling wages of American workers. In March, 2010, the federal government passed the Patient Protection and Affordable Care Act (PPACA), which was designed to expand greatly the availability of affordable medicine and health care services. The provisions of the act were to be phased in over the course of the 2010's, with most provisions beginning in 2014. The law is projected by the Congressional Budget Office to result in more than 30 million Americans gaining health insurance, but more than 20 million U.S. residents (including undocumented immigrants) will still lack insurance according to these projections.

INDUSTRY MARKET SEGMENTS

The U.S. medicine and health care industry includes more than 595,700 establishments, varying in size, services, and location. Ambulatory (outpatient) health care services are provided either directly or indirectly. These services constitute about 87.3 percent of all health care establishments. Ambulatory care includes outpatient care centers, home health care services, medical and diagnostic laboratories, radiology services, and offices of physicians and other health care professionals. The U.S. Bureau of Labor Statistics (BLS) notes that hospitals account for only 1 percent of these establishments, but they account for 35 percent of jobs in the industry. Similarly, outpatient health care providers may be divided into small, midsize, and large businesses based on the percentage of establishments and of jobs that they represent. This principle is used in the following section to discuss various segments of the industry.

Small Businesses

Small health care businesses include diagnostic laboratories, where ambulatory outpatients have their blood samples drawn and analyzed and secure other clinical tests. These laboratories represent 2.4 percent of all medical and health care establishments and employ about 1.6 percent of all health care workers.

Potential Annual Earnings Scale. Medical and diagnostic laboratory outpatient services offer both salaries and hourly wages. Laboratory operations managers earn an average of about $109,660 per year, whereas service administrators earn an average of $78,360. The hourly rates for clinical technologists and technicians vary based on education and training, as well as certifications. Clinical laboratory technologists earn an average of $53,360 annually, and clinical laboratory technicians earn an average of $32,630. The American Society for Clinical Pathology differentiates hourly wages further by specialty; specialized occupations include cytotechnologist, histotechnologist, medical technologist, histotechnician, medical technician, and phlebotomist.

Clientele Interaction. Delivery of medical and diagnostic laboratory services requires direct one-on-one interaction with patients. Patient contact begins prior to the laboratory visit, when patients make appointments for their blood to be drawn. When a patient arrives at a laboratory, a receptionist registers the patient and documents the laboratory tests to be performed, as well as the insurance plan that will pay for them. The patient is called back to the collection room, where a technician takes the blood samples. Afterward, a patient report is sent to the patient's health care provider, and a copy may be sent to the patient upon request.

Amenities, Atmosphere, and Physical Grounds. Medical and diagnostic laboratory centers may be located in business or medical office buildings, or they may occupy their own freestanding buildings. They have reception areas, where patients check in and document insurance and health information. They may provide patients with comfortable chairs and reading material in their waiting areas. The better medical and diagnostic laboratories are located in clean and safe neighborhoods and have attractive landscaping outside. Multistory buildings should have elevators, as medical laboratories may serve patients who have trouble climbing stairs. Patient treatment areas provide clean, sanitary conditions for blood collection, as well as sinks where gloved technicians can wash their hands between patients. Laboratories attempt to provide adequate parking with good lighting and area security.

Typical Number of Employees. The number of employees in a medical and diagnostic laboratory center varies based on size, geographic location, and number of specialties. Some centers have as few as five employees, while larger ones may have

sixty, including directors, medical technologists and technicians, pathologists, and microbiologists. Staffing needs may be calculated through the College of American Pathologists' (CAP) method of recording workload, a common practice in hospitals. A minimum staff includes a medical and diagnostic laboratory manager, a receptionist, and sufficient clinical technologists or technicians to cover the average number of patients and tests performed at the center. Medical records and billing services are also required, but these may be outsourced by small labs.

Traditional Geographic Locations. Medical and diagnostic laboratory centers can be in freestanding buildings or located in office space close to hospitals or to concentrations of health care practices for the convenience of patients and providers. They are usually established in more populated areas close to medical centers. A given medical and diagnostic laboratory business may operate multiple collection centers in various geographic locations.

Pros of Working for a Small Medical Business. Small medical businesses provide excellent employment opportunities in various settings and geographic locations. Employees participate as part of patient care teams. Their workload may be lighter than at larger businesses, with fewer patients spaced throughout the workday, and employees may experience less stress as a result. Medical and diagnostic laboratory employees usually work daytime hours only, and they can close for lunch.

Cons of Working for a Small Medical Business. Small medical businesses have fewer employees, so workers may need to cover for one another when one is ill or absent. Small businesses tend to offer fewer employee benefits. Medical businesses such as diagnostic laboratories may be certified or accredited. When the effort to compete those processes falls on fewer employees, it can increase their workload and stress levels. Despite wearing gloves and taking other precautions, employees who draw blood specimens and work with human fluids may experience accidental exposure to bacteria, viruses, or fungi and contract laboratory-acquired infections.

Costs

Payroll and Benefits: Medical and diagnostic laboratory employees are generally hired at hourly wages, while managers are salaried. Depending on the size of the agency, employees may receive benefits such as health insurance; vacation and sick time; education, tuition, and licensure reimbursement; dental, long-term disability, basic life, and accidental death insurance; retirement benefits; or a relocation package upon employment.

Supplies: Small medical businesses require specialized supplies, as well as general office supplies and equipment, including folders, papers, desk supplies, postage supplies, computers, copiers, and telephones. Diagnostic laboratories require such supplies as analyzers, reagents, stains, microscopes and slides, and tourniquets, as well as consumable and disposable supplies such as syringes, gloves, capillary tubes, lancets, swabs, and applicators.

External Services: Small medical businesses may contract billing and record-keeping services, as well as financial management, accounting, cleaning, maintenance, and technical support. They may also use couriers and other external delivery systems beyond the U.S. Postal Service.

Utilities: Typical utilities for a small business include water, sewage, electricity, telephone, and Internet access.

Taxes: Medical and diagnostic laboratory centers must pay local, state, and federal corporate and property taxes, as well as payroll taxes.

Midsize Businesses

Home health care agencies make up around 3.7 percent of all health care establishments and employ 7.2 percent of all health care workers. They provide cost-effective, skilled and unskilled health care services in patient residences, allowing patients to remain at home. Home care is especially useful for patients recently discharged from hospitals or after outpatient procedures. Some home care agencies also offer hospice care. Their annual revenues can vary from $500,000 to $10 million depending on size and geographic location. They may be challenging to operate, however, because they are primarily reimbursed by the federal government through Medicare payments that are subject to changing guidelines and reimbursement-rate cuts.

Potential Annual Earnings Scale. Home health care agencies employ a team approach to patient care. Each member has a different pay scale. The average earnings for a home care agency administrator range between $60,000 and $85,000, depending on the size of the agency, its geographic location, and the experience level of the manager. Professional home health nurses' national annual salaries average from $58,740 to around $66,000. Physical therapists average $39.36 per hour, or $81,870 annually. Medical social workers at home care agencies receive salaries in the range of $35,550 to $57,690, with an average salary of $46,930. While home health aides are employed by some home health agencies for about $7.75 per hour, the average wage ranges from $8.62 to $11.69 per hour, or about $16,000 to $24,000 annually, depending on agency size and location. General nonsupervisory office staff are paid in the same salary range as they are in other health care industries based on geographic market; the national average wage for this group is $16.17 per hour.

Clientele Interaction. Home health care agencies depend on patient referrals from hospitals, skilled nursing facilities, and physician offices. Most patients are recovering from illness or surgery, have chronic diseases with or without disabil-

Home health care nurses manage patient care after patients are discharged from hospitals. (©John Keith/Dreamstime.com)

ity, or have terminal illnesses. Care is primarily short term but can be ongoing when skilled medical services are needed. Patients are the focus of the service, along with their families or caregivers. Home care personnel interact with patients and families in their residences from once a week to daily, depending on the level of service needed. When a patient is receiving extensive therapy, such as intravenous treatment, a registered nurse (RN) may visit the home to provide treatment more than once a day. However, the average home care patient receives visits twice each week from one or more care providers. The same patient may be seen by a nurse, a therapist, and a home health aide. Care providers communicate by phone with patients and their families throughout the week, and home care agencies provide answering services and on-call personnel twenty-four hours per day, seven days per week. Establishing rapport and a positive patient-provider relationship are critical to care planning and successful treatment in the home.

Amenities, Atmosphere, and Physical Grounds. A home care agency's office houses its administrator and office staff, with cubicle space allocated for professional caregivers to plan their days. Offices generally include computers and telephones and have multipurpose rooms for team meetings and staff education. Medical storage areas house basic home care supplies, while other areas house patient files and other medical records. Many home care agencies are located on lower floors of their office buildings to facilitate the transport of equipment and supplies from their offices to staff members' cars for patient use. Some agencies are in freestanding buildings. Because care is delivered outside the office, most home care agency offices are relatively utilitarian and lack amenities.

Typical Number of Employees. The number of employees at a midsize medical business varies depending on size and the types of service provided. At a minimum, the agency requires an administrator, an RN, a physical therapist and other therapists, a medical social worker, and home health aides, as well as medical record, secretarial, financial management, and human resources personnel. Some services, such as billing, can be contracted or outsourced depending on the size of the agency and its geographic location.

Traditional Geographic Locations. Home care agencies may be located within or close to a hospi-

tal, or they may be freestanding within the community. Home health care is provided in all geographic locations, most often in densely populated cities. Rural care is usually available, but services may be more limited. Proximity to interstates and highways is a concern, as time management and driving distance are key factors to consider when managing home care visit costs.

Pros of Working for a Midsize Medical Business. Work at midsize businesses such as home care agencies is likely to remain plentiful, as the population ages and greater numbers of elderly persons enter the health care system needing health care services at home. Private insurance programs and Medicare provide reimbursement for services. Unlike the situation at hospitals, where one provider is typically assigned many patients to care for at the same time, home care professionals make one home care visit at a time, focusing on only one patient at a time. Providers have the freedom and responsibility to schedule each visit based on their time availability, as well as the needs of each patient. Providers who enjoy working outdoors may find home health care desirable, as much time during the day is spent in travel and in the community. Home health care practice may appeal to providers who enjoy autonomy, team work, and one-on-one patient interaction.

Cons of Working for a Midsize Medical Business. Home health care has some disadvantages, such as the need to have a working car and automobile insurance in order to make home visits reliably. Providers must carry supplies to patients, and they must sometimes work in less than optimal conditions within patients' homes. Patient visits must be made regardless of adverse weather conditions, and patients' homes may be in challenging locations, including high-crime areas that require security escorts. This environment is less controlled than are institutional settings. Home care typically requires completing many forms and other paperwork in order to receive payment and to maintain legally required documentation, especially when reimbursements are being made through Medicare. Providers must also recognize that patients may be more likely to exercise their rights not to comply with prescribed therapy when they are at home than they would be within institutional settings. Thus, to achieve the best care outcomes, patients may require education, and providers may have to invest more effort to establish positive patient-provider rapport.

Costs

Payroll and Benefits: Home care providers are generally hired at hourly wages, while administrators are salaried. Agencies often use contract providers to handle the flexible needs of the patient census. Depending on the size of the agency, employees will receive benefits such as health insurance; vacation and sick time; education, tuition, and licensure reimbursement; dental, long-term disability, basic life, and accidental death insurance; cell phone stipends; and 403(b) plans with employer contributions.

Supplies: Midsize medical businesses require specialized supplies, as well as general office supplies and equipment, including folders, papers, desk supplies, postage supplies, computers, copiers, and telephones. Home health care agencies require medical supplies for patient care, hand sanitizer to be used between patients, and cell phones or other mobile communication devices. Skilled service providers may use electronic medical records, requiring handheld documentation devices to record notes during care.

External Services: Midsize medical businesses may rent medical equipment and other durable supplies. They may contract answering services, staffing agencies, financial management, billing services, security services, storage facilities, cleaning, or maintenance, and they may also hire some health care providers on a contract basis.

Utilities: Typical utilities for a midsize business include water, sewage, electricity, gas or oil service, telephone and cell phone service, and Internet access.

Taxes: Taxes can vary depending on whether the business is nonprofit or for-profit. Nonprofit businesses are exempt from many taxes, but they must still pay payroll taxes. For-profit businesses must pay local, state, and federal corporate and property taxes. Medical businesses may also maintain accreditation from various review boards, adding to their business costs.

Large Businesses

About 36 percent of all health care establishments are physician offices, employing 17 percent of health care workers. Most physician offices include several physicians who practice as a group and hire diverse professionals and nonprofessional staff to support the practice. Most physicians see group practice as a way to share overhead expenses and to ensure that their patients will be covered when they take time off from work. Another benefit of group practice is quick access to peers for patient care consultations.

Potential Annual Earnings Scale. The earnings of employees of group medical practices vary depending on the medical specialties and number of physicians in the practice. The most common specialty of physicians in private practice is internal medicine; these specialists earn an average of $87.98 per hour, or $183,080 per year. By contrast, oncology physicians earn an average of $335,000 and neurosurgeons average more than $500,000 per year.

Among other physician office employees, office managers typically earn between $60,000 and $100,000 per year. Nurse practitioners earn an average of $82,590, while physician assistants earn an average of $80,440. RNs earn an average of $31 per hour, or $66,000 per year. Physical therapists in physician offices average $35.83 per hour, or $74,530 per year. General, nonsupervisory office staff are paid in the same general salary range as are other health care support staff. Administrative assistants, for example, average about $27,000 per year.

Clientele Interaction. Employees of private medical practices have extensive one-on-one contact with patients. Various employees speak to patients on the phone, make appointments, greet patients when they arrive at the office and help them fill out paperwork, conduct measurements of baseline vital signs such as blood pressure and pulse rate, and otherwise prepare patients to meet with their physicians. Physician-patient interaction forms the heart of most medical practices. Other support staff such as medical technicians and nurse practitioners interact with patients before and after they see their doctors, taking blood and administering radiological scans, for example. After they have completed their visits, patients may meet with billing staff to clarify their insurance information.

Amenities, Atmosphere, and Physical Grounds. Physician group practices may be in office buildings or in freestanding structures. Offices generally include reception areas where staff members check in patients and document their insurance and health information, as well as waiting areas with comfortable chairs, reading material, and sometimes a television. The better offices are located in clean and safe neighborhoods and have attractive landscaping outside. Multistory buildings have elevators. Treatment rooms are fitted with examining tables, basic vital signs equipment, and privacy gowns for patient use. Exam rooms have sinks where physicians can wash their hands between patients. Emergency equipment is standard within physician offices. Physician offices may be located in crowded areas such as medical centers, which can pose a challenge to patients who prefer adequate parking with good lighting.

Typical Number of Employees. The number of employees in a physician group practice office varies based on size, geographic location, and number of specialties. The positions needed may include an office manager, nurses, physician assistants, nurse practitioners, laboratory technicians, billing and business office workers, receptionists, housekeeping staff, and sometimes radiology technicians. Practices may outsource services such as transcription, cleaning, and other nonmedical office services.

Traditional Geographic Locations. Group practices can be in freestanding buildings, in medical or professional office buildings, or in office towers of hospitals. They are often located near at least one hospital for the ease of patients and the convenience of physicians who may need to make hospital rounds. Physician offices may have more than one location for the convenience of patients in different parts of a city. They are usually located in more populated areas for easier access to patients.

Pros of Working for a Large Medical Business. Physician practices may enjoy more up-to-date technology and more adequate personnel to share workloads than do diagnostic labs or home health care businesses. Offices are usually open only during business hours, which may be attractive to those seeking to avoid the more grueling schedule of a hospital or other emergency establishment. Physicians and other health care professionals in group practice can share on-call duties and have more coverage availability in case of illness, family emergency, or vacation or while securing continuing education.

Cons of Working for a Large Medical Business. Physician office practices may or may not of-

fer benefits to the workers, depending on the business's size and specialty. The workday can be extremely busy and may include overtime hours. Some employees, such as RNs, may be paid less than they would be in hospitals. Working with sick people can mean increased exposure to infectious and viral illnesses.

Costs

Payroll and Benefits: Physician offices generally hire staff members at hourly wages, while physicians and office administrators are salaried. Depending on the size of the practice, employees may receive benefits such as health insurance, vacation and sick time, and the costs of continuing education. Some offices may use contract services to decrease labor costs.

Supplies: Private practices require routine office supplies and equipment, such as folders, paper, desk supplies, computers, copiers, telephones, and cell phones. They also need durable and disposable medical supplies and equipment, pharmacological supplies, and basic laboratory testing equipment.

External Services: Medical practices may contract some or all laboratory tests beyond the most basic, or they may simply send patients to independent laboratories to have their tests done. They may also contract record storage, courier services, accounting and tax preparation, maintenance, and cleaning, including laundry.

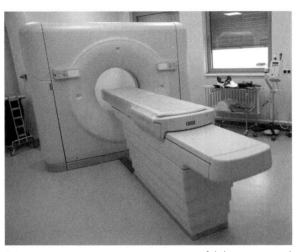

Magnetic resonance imaging is a powerful diagnostic tool. (©Tomas Hajek/Dreamstime.com)

Utilities: Typical utilities include water, sewage, electricity, gas or oil, telephone, and Internet access. Offices may incur additional expenses related to operating testing equipment such as magnetic resonance imaging (MRI) or computed tomography (CT) scans.

Taxes: Physician offices may pay taxes related to business operations, or the partners may pay business-related taxes on their personal returns, in which case they must also pay self-employment taxes. Offices must pay payroll taxes. Some offices need accreditation from various review agencies if they offer certain services, such as laboratory testing. Such accreditation can require additional expenses.

ORGANIZATIONAL STRUCTURE AND JOB ROLES

The organizational structure of the medicine and health care industry is usually based on the size and function of the establishment. Job roles within the organization will vary by title and function, demonstrating the diversity in this industry. In smaller to midsize health care businesses, some employees may perform more than one function depending on the needs of the organization. An example is a referral coordinator who also works as a marketing representative a few days a week. Another is the receptionist or administrative assistant who doubles as a customer service representative. Certain tasks may be outsourced, such as information technology, billing, facility management and security, housekeeping, and maintenance. However, large health care businesses may have entire departments that manage these functions.

The following general job categories can be found in some form in small, midsize, and large health care businesses:

- Business Management
- Customer Service
- Sales and Marketing
- Professional Staff
- Support and Allied Staff
- Human Resources
- Billing and Payments

Business Management

Managers oversee the general and specific operations of medicine and health care businesses. They help define and support the mission of their businesses and set strategic goals for operational success. A board of directors is legally responsible for the compliance of the establishment with accreditation and business regulations, which may vary between nonprofit and for-profit agencies. The management team is accountable to the board for hiring the best employee for each position, developing an environment where employees can excel in their jobs, creating energy that motivates middle managers and employees to do their best, and monitoring progress toward organizational objectives. They articulate and model the values of their organizations.

Many industry leaders have advanced degrees and demonstrated experience in their business areas. Some common educational backgrounds of health care leadership include health care administration, business administration, and clinical services administration. Executives are salaried employees and usually earn higher wages than staff employees. They are responsible and accountable for every aspect of their businesses, from human resource management to service delivery to financial management.

Business management occupations may include the following:

- Sole Practitioner/Owner
- Partner
- Chief Executive Officer (CEO)
- Chief Financial Officer (CFO)
- Administrator of Home Health Care Services
- Physician Office Administrator/ Manager
- Director of Clinical Services
- Director of Medical Records
- Director of Business Office
- Director of Sales and Marketing
- Director of Outpatient Services
- Director of Medical and Diagnostic Laboratories
- Director of Medical Equipment Services
- Director of Diagnostic Imaging
- Director of Physical Therapy Services

Customer Service

Customer service is critical to any business, including those in the medicine and health care industry. All employees play roles in promoting good customer service. In the health care industry, most department employees interface with patients and family members in some way, so excellent customer service is important. Employees should remember that patients may be ill or stressed when seeking or receiving health care services and need special patience and attention. For example, many older adults use the diverse departments of ambulatory health care services. They may be slower or walk with an assistive device or be hard of hearing and need to make certain adjustments to come to a physician's office or medical and diagnostic laboratory. Sensitivity to such patients can go a long way in customer satisfaction, which results in repeat business.

Health care industry employees who have direct effects on customer service are front-line secretaries, administrative assistants, and receptionists. These employees, usually paid lower wages than professional staff members, often represent the first contact that patients and their families have with their health care establishments. Because these employees answer the phone and take messages, they should have positive and pleasant voices and be able to take messages accurately and deliver them in a timely fashion. Speaking clearly and transferring calls without dropping callers are important. Training on how to listen to customer concerns and complaints without reacting in a negative or defensive manner is essential for conflict resolution. Knowing which manager to call when conflict arises may help defuse frustration on the part of the customer.

These front-line employees usually have a minimum of a high school diploma, and some hold college degrees. They often have special skills, such as word processing and database management, but acquire advanced skills, such as project management, through on-the-job training. Receptionists in physician offices earn an average of $12.20 per hour, or $25,400 annually, for full-time employment. Administrative assistants earn an average of $31,000. In larger health care businesses, full-time customer service representatives may be hired to respond to customer concerns and queries. These employees are usually trained on the job and average salaries of about $29,000 to $30,000 per year.

Customer service occupations may include the following:

- Customer Service Representative
- Receptionist
- Administrative Assistant
- Executive Secretary
- Department Secretary
- Medical Records Secretary
- Business Office Secretary

Sales and Marketing

The sales and marketing staff of any establishment can make or break the business. In the medicine and health care industry, not every business has a sales force, but each staff member is a salesperson through the quality of service provided. In smaller establishments, marketing may consist of making calls and mailing materials to possible referral sources. Some agencies or offices have a multipurpose role, such as referral coordinator, that includes making visits to current and potential referral sources to explain new or added services. A midsize firm may have only one part-time or full-time sales and marketing staffer, or it may have a team of positions dedicated to building its business. Large establishments often have sales and marketing departments that call on referral bases daily and may even be responsible for writing marketing materials and developing their companies' branding strategies.

Several health care businesses, such as general medical equipment and supply providers, pharmacy and biotech companies, and home equipment and infusion therapy providers, lend themselves to more aggressive marketing approaches. These are niche businesses that offer products and services that complement patient care and may be part of a health care business's diversification strategy. Sales and marketing excellence are critical to the success of these businesses.

Employees with detailed technical knowledge of the services their companies offer may be promoted to sales and marketing positions despite having little or no previous sales or marketing training. In health care, RNs and other health care professionals are recruited to sales and marketing. The average starting salary for new college graduates with marketing degrees is about $43,000. Sales and marketing managers generally need a baccalaureate or master's degree in business administration, with an emphasis in marketing, as well as experience in the business service area. These managers generally earn between $100,000 and $175,000 based on the type and size of the company, geographic location, education, and experience.

Sales and marketing staff spend most of their time outside the office in their communities, building the referral bases of their companies. They travel various distances, based on the geographic locations of the referral bases. They may work long hours, evenings, and weekends.

Sales and marketing occupations may include the following:

- Marketing Director
- Marketing Coordinator
- Sales Representative
- Referral Coordinator
- Business Development Manager/ Coordinator

Professional Staff

The medicine and health care industry is a service business that relies heavily on the professional staff who provide skilled patient care services. Many jobs are available for those seeking a career in this industry. Most professional staff roles require a college education with a minimum of a baccalaureate degree. Some, such as physicians and nurse practitioners, require graduate and postgraduate education and internships. Additional certifications are available for health care professionals desiring specialization or economic enhancement. Many professional roles require licensure by state boards. If providers move to a different state, they may need to apply for new licenses to continue practicing.

Just as education varies from job to job, wages and salaries vary as well. General practice physicians in rural areas may earn incomes of $100,000, while urban neurosurgeons may earn $500,000. Pay, practice parameters, and patient base depend on the selected area of practice, size of the business, and geographic location. Physicians are regulated by the states where they are licensed and work, and they may be required to complete continuing education to keep current on their chosen specialty areas.

RNs make up the largest segment of health care professionals, with around 6.2 million positions in the United States. Their basic educational path may be through two-year associate's degrees, three-year diploma degrees, or four-year baccalaureate degrees. Additional education to the master's or doctoral level offers more career opportunities. RNs can work in diverse settings, as almost all medicine and health care establishments utilize these health care professionals. They offer assessment, treatments, health teaching, resource referral, and support for patients and families.

Nurses are licensed under the regulations of the states where they live and work, and they may be required to complete continuing education to keep current on their chosen areas of practice. Their work environment depends on the setting where they work. Annual salaries for staff RNs range from around $57,000 to $68,000. Salaries may also vary based on the shifts nurses work, as evening and night shifts usually pay a differential. Advanced degree nurses, such as nurse practitioners, earn

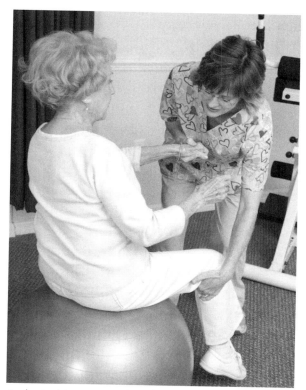

A physical therapist works with a patient. (©Lisa F. Young/ Dreamstime.com)

$80,000 to $85,000 or more depending on the place of employment.

Continued rehabilitation therapy is needed by many Americans in the course of their illness, or after injury or surgery, to restore function and return to the activities of daily living. Common health care professionals who provide these therapies are physical, occupational, and speech therapists. The work options for these professionals are diverse, with good opportunities for employment. Education necessary for these roles includes a minimum of a baccalaureate degree and a further degree from an accredited program in a specialty area. Annual salaries range from $72,800 to $78,000 for physical therapists, $60,00 to $75,000 for occupational therapists, and $58,000 to $79,000 for speech therapists, but they may be higher depending on the work setting and level of experience.

As health care delivery changes under new reimbursement guidelines and more Americans acquire insurance, new jobs may emerge, while traditional ones may evolve into new roles. Job seekers would be wise to research thoroughly roles of interest and contact someone in the field for further discussion before committing the time and financial investment necessary to achieve these occupations.

Professional occupations may include the following:

- Physician
- Nurse Practitioner
- Physician Assistant
- Registered Nurse
- Physical Therapist
- Speech-Language Therapist
- Occupational Therapist
- Audiologist
- Recreational Therapist
- Industrial Therapist
- Respiratory Therapist
- Radiation Therapist
- Optometrist
- Podiatrist

Support and Allied Staff

Allied health care providers are important to the delivery of services in the medicine and health care industry. Their specialized skills support patients in many settings. A growing group of health care providers with increasing job opportunities consists of health care technologists and technicians. Education requirements for these positions usually include baccalaureate degrees with one to two years of additional training and licensure or certification. Examples of jobs in these areas include clinical laboratory technologists and technicians, radiologic technicians, medical records and health record technicians, dental hygienists, and diagnostic medical sonographers. Salaries depend on the setting and specialty area of practice. Medical or health record technicians can expect to earn between $26,000 and $47,000, dental hygienists between $55,000 and $79,000, and radiologic technicians between $42,000 and $63,000.

Many health care industry support jobs require high school diplomas, associate's degrees, specialized vocational training, or on-the-job training. The BLS has stated that most health care jobs require less than a four-year college degree. For example, licensed practical or vocational nurses require one year of dedicated training and earn $35,000 to $45,000. Other allied health jobs include opticians ($20,000 to $43,000), medical assistants ($25,000 to $30,000), medical transcriptionists ($14.50 per hour to $17.00 per hour), and home health aides ($7.65 per hour to $13.93 per hour, or $15,620 to $28,980 annually).

Support and allied staff occupations may include the following:

- Licensed Practical Nurse
- Physical Therapist Assistant
- Clinical Technologist
- Clinical Technician
- Nuclear Medicine Technologist
- Surgical Technologist
- Diagnostic Medical Sonographer
- Radiologic Technician
- Home Health Aide
- Optician
- Medical Record and Health Information Technician
- Medical Transcriptionist
- Medical Assistant

Human Resources

The medicine and health care industry is primarily a service business that employs many and diverse workers. Critical to the success of any business is hiring the most qualified and motivated workers possible. The link between service delivery and employment is best managed by human resource managers. Although the title may vary based on the focus and size of the health care business, these employees play important roles in the medicine and health care industry.

Administrative duties of human resources managers include developing job descriptions; recruiting, interviewing, and hiring organizational workers; developing employee policies; monitoring federal and state employment regulations; maintaining consistent, fair, and equitable hiring practices; and conducting strategic planning with health care executives, department directors, and area managers. Human resources managers can help health care businesses promote employee productivity, minimize costly job turnover, increase retention, and provide employee education. In smaller health care businesses, a worker such as a staffing coordinator or manager may have divided duties that include some human resources functions.

Human resources managers are challenged to stay current on regulation and licensure requirements of professional and allied health care workers. They may be responsible for checking the licenses of their employees and keeping employment files up to date. This role is important to the accreditation process because review bodies such as the Joint Commission on Accreditation of Health Care Organizations (JCAHO) and the Centers for Medicare and Medicaid Services (CMS) require employee licenses to be current as a condition of accreditation. Human resources managers also develop policies that assist businesses in meeting federal standards enforced by such agencies as the Occupational Safety and Health Administration (OSHA) and the United States Equal Employment Opportunity Commission (EEOC).

Human resources professionals generally must have bachelor's degrees in business administration, social sciences, behavioral sciences, or human resources management. Advanced degrees may prove useful, especially degrees in labor and industrial relations. Pay scales vary among health care businesses, but human resources managers generally earn between $75,000 and $125,000; some may earn up to $163,000.

Human resources occupations may include the following:

- Human Resources Director
- Human Resources Coordinator
- Human Resources Manager
- Human Resources Generalist
- Benefits Specialist
- Administrative Assistant
- Payroll Clerk
- Staffing Coordinator
- Staffing Manager

Billing and Payments

Billing and payments personnel manage health care businesses' accounts receivable and payable. Smaller businesses may outsource business functions but may retain a billing clerk within the medical records area to secure payments based on the service codes used by the insurance industry and Medicare claims officers. These workers can expect to make between $12 and $18 per hour. In some larger businesses, an entire department may be responsible for these functions.

Billing and payment occupations may include the following:

- Billing Manager
- Billing Clerk
- Accounts Receivable Clerk
- Accounts Payable Clerk
- Collections Coordinator

INDUSTRY OUTLOOK

Overview

The outlook for this industry shows it to be on the rise. The medicine and health care industry has a long history of positive employment and economic growth. In 2008, a recession year, the BLS reported that the industry employed 14.3 million people. On the bureau's list of the twenty fastest-growing occupations, half were in the medicine and health care industry. The BLS has projected that 3.2 million new jobs will be created in the industry between 2008 and 2018, more than in any other industry.

Although the medicine and health care industry will continue to offer many job opportunities, several factors may influence these growth predictions and affect the wages and salaries of health care employees. The PPACA is projected to enable

PROJECTED EMPLOYMENT FOR SELECTED OCCUPATIONS

Health Care and Social Assistance Industry

Employment		
2009	Projected 2018	Occupation
899,980	1,296,600	Home health aides
623,210	764,100	Licensed practical and licensed vocational nurses
222,450	251,000	Medical and health services managers
1,317,360	1,559,200	Nursing aides, orderlies, and attendants
2,225,330	2,729,000	Registered nurses

Source: U.S. Bureau of Labor Statistics, Industries at a Glance, Occupational Employment Statistics and Employment Projections Program.

up to 32 million Americans currently lacking insurance to be added to the health insurance rolls. It is also designed to decrease the rate of inflation within the health care industry, bringing it closer to the overall U.S. inflation rate and making health care more affordable. To accomplish this, over the long term, providers will be paid less in real dollars per patient or per service than they would otherwise have been paid. At the same time, more patients will see providers, so the total spent on health care will increase.

With revenues per patient decreasing, medical businesses will need to rethink how they spend their limited resources. More people entering Medicare and Medicaid, coupled with less funding for providers, will challenge businesses to create less expensive ways to care for patients. This may result in capped payments for the work of highly educated, extensively trained professional health care providers. Opportunities will increase for workers who can gain skills through on-the-job training, including nursing aides, home health aides, medical assistants, dental assistants, and housekeeping and cleaning assistants. Regardless of changes, people will continue to need health care services, making this industry a good career choice.

Employment Advantages

The health care industry has a long history of employment growth offering good to excellent wages and benefits. Work environments are generally positive. Most health care employees receive access to health insurance and other benefits such as retirement plans. Some claim that this industry is recession-proof, as, even in economic decline, people need and seek health care services. Some sectors, such as nursing, are usually in a state of shortage to meet the country's needs. The choice of vocations available is diverse, with new roles evolving yearly to meet developing needs. Economic challenges encourage creative thinking and allow variations on traditional approaches to care. Workers can choose among various settings, from institutional to community-based businesses. Skills are sometimes transferable to other settings or industries and allow for advancement. For example, businesses may hire occupational health care nurses. Although professional health care providers usually require four-year college degrees or higher education and training, most roles in the health care field require either two-year associate's degrees, vocational training, or on-the-job training, minimizing the educational investment costs to support staff and other nonphysician workers.

Annual Earnings

The overall health care industry accounts for about one-sixth of the total U.S. economy, or more than $2.5 trillion. This figure includes pharmaceutical manufacturing, hospital services, and other related industries. According to the U.S. Census Bureau, in 2008 the medicine and health care industry alone experienced revenues of $1.75 trillion. The industry, moreover, is growing faster than the rate of inflation—one of the primary factors motivating passage of the PPACA—but one of the most important provisions of the new law designed to reduce health care inflation (an excise tax on very expensive health insurance plans) will not kick in until 2018. As a result, health care revenues not only will increase in absolute terms but also are very likely to increase as a percentage of GDP through 2020.

RELATED RESOURCES FOR FURTHER RESEARCH

AMERICAN MEDICAL ASSOCIATION
515 N State St.
Chicago, IL 60654
Tel: (800) 621-8335
http://www.ama-assn.org

AMERICAN NURSES ASSOCIATION
8515 Georgia Ave., Suite 400
Silver Spring, MD 20910
Tel: (301) 628-5000
Fax: (301) 628-5001
http://www.nursingworld.org

AMERICAN SOCIETY FOR CLINICAL LABORATORY SCIENCE
6701 Democracy Blvd., Suite 300
Bethesda, MD 20817
Tel: (301) 657-2768
Fax: (301) 657-2909
http://www.ascls.org

CENTER FOR HEALTH CARE STRATEGIES
200 American Metro Blvd., Suite 119
Hamilton, NJ 08619
Tel: (609) 528-8400
Fax: (609) 586-3679
http://www.chcs.org

CENTERS FOR MEDICARE AND MEDICAID SERVICES
75 Security Blvd.
Baltimore, MD 21244
Tel: (877) 267-2323
http://www.cms.hhs.gov

NATIONAL ASSOCIATION FOR HOME CARE AND HOSPICE
228 7th St. SE
Washington, DC 20003

Tel: (202) 547-7424
Fax: (202) 547-3540
http://www.nahc.org

ABOUT THE AUTHOR

Marylane Wade Koch is a registered nurse with a master of science in nursing degree and has been a health care professional for more than thirty-five years. She serves as adjunct faculty for Loewenberg School of Nursing, University of Memphis. She has written several health care books; has contributed to books published by Elsevier-Mosby, Harcourt Health Sciences, Delmar/Thompson-Cengage, F. A. Davis, Salem Press, and Jones and Bartlett; and has published many professional articles. She works as both an editor and a coach for private clients, including physicians and health care professionals. A member of the American Medical Writers Association, she also serves as faculty for an annual Memphis-area writing workshop run by the American Christian Writers.

FURTHER READING

Dill, Monda. "A Brief History of Health Care in America." *Associated Content*, August 13, 2007. http://www.associatedcontent.com/article/339640/a_brief_history_of_health_care_in_america.html.

Dillon, Tamara. "Health Care Jobs You Might Not Know About." *Occupational Outlook Quarterly*, Summer, 2008. Available at http://www.bls.gov/opub/ooq/2008/summer/art03.pdf.

Fried, Bruce, and James A. Johnson, eds. *Human Resources in Health Care: Managing for Success*. Washington, D.C.: AUPHA Press/Health Administration Press, 2002.

Jonas, Steven, Anthony R. Kovner, and James Knickman. *Jonas and Kovner's Health Care Delivery in the United States*. New York: Springer, 2008.

Koss, W., and T. Sodeman. "The Workload Recording Method: A Laboratory Management Tool." *Clinical Lab Management Review* 12, no. 2 (June, 1992): 337-50.

Kotlikoff, Laurence J. *The Health Care Fix: Universal Insurance for All Americans*.

Cambridge: Massachusetts Institute of Technology, 2007.

Merrit-Hawkins. *Physician Salary, Compensation, and Practice Surveys*. http://www.merritt hawkins.com/compensation-surveys.aspx.

Plunkett, Jack W. *Plunkett Health Care Industry Update*. Houston, Tex.: Plunkett Research, 2010.

Stevens, Rosemary, Charles E. Rosenberg, and Lawton R. Burns. *History and Health Policy in the United States: Putting the Past Back In*. New Brunswick, N.J.: Rutgers University Press, 2006.

Swanson, Barbara M. *Careers in Health Care*. 5th ed. New York: McGraw Hill, 2005.

U.S. Bureau of Labor Statistics. *Career Guide to Industries*, 2010-2011 ed. http://www.bls.gov/oco/cg.

U.S. Census Bureau. North American Industry Classification System (NAICS), 2007. http://www.census.gov/cgi-bin/sssd/naics/naicsrch?chart=2007.

U.S. Department of Health and Human Services. Office of Disease Prevention and Health Promotion. *Healthy People*. http://www.healthypeople.gov/.

World Health Organization. "Health Financing Policy." http://www.who.int/health_financing/functions/functions/en.

Metals Manufacturing Industry

INDUSTRY SNAPSHOT

General Industry: Manufacturing

Career Cluster: Manufacturing

Subcategory Industries: Alumina and Aluminum Production and Processing; Electrometallurgical Ferroalloy Product Manufacturing; Foundries; Iron and Steel Mills; Nonferrous Metal (Except Aluminum) Production and Processing; Steel Product Manufacturing from Purchased Steel

Related Industries: Building Construction Industry; Chemicals Industry; Mining Industry

Annual Domestic Revenues: $250 billion USD (First Research, Primary Metals Manufacturing, 2009); steel: $60.6 billion USD (American Iron and Steel Institute, 2008), $70 billion USD (IBISWorld, 2009)

Annual International Revenues: Steel: $488 billion USD (estimate based on data from Iron and Steel Institute and U.S. Geological Survey, 2009)

Annual Global Revenues: Steel: $558 billion USD (estimate based on data from Iron and Steel Institute and U.S. Geological Survey, 2009)

NAICS Number: 331

INDUSTRY DEFINITION

Summary

The metal processing and manufacturing industry converts raw or scrap materials into finished metals, ready for use as materials in other industries. Primary processing involves the smelting of metals from their ores to produce such things as liquid metal or metal ingots, whereas secondary processing consists of transforming liquid metal or ingots into sheets, bars, wires, and other forms. Workers create other metal products by pouring molten metal into casts or molds. The metals manufacturing industry includes companies engaged in smelting both ferrous metals and such nonferrous metals as aluminum and copper. The industry also creates many alloys, or amalgams of two or more metals. Because such mixed products have valuable properties, they have become an essential part of the industry; steel, which is an alloy of iron and carbon, is a prime example.

History of the Industry

Metals manufacturing has prehistoric roots. Evidence exists that copper was smelted in Europe in the Chalcolithic and early Bronze ages (2200 to 700 B.C.E.). Scholars often credit the Hittites, in eastern Anatolia, with being the first to successfully smelt iron from its ores between

Steel pipe at a steel mill in Indiana. (©Cheng Zhong/Dreamstime.com)

1900 and 1600 B.C.E. This development marked the end of the Near Eastern Bronze Age and the start of the Iron Age. The ancient Greeks, who, by trial and error, advanced smelting techniques, attributed great religious and astrological significance to the seven basic metals: gold, silver, iron, mercury, tin, copper, and lead. These metals were also known to other peoples because of their natural occurrence or the ease with which they could be isolated from ores. Alchemists of the ancient and medieval periods were profoundly interested in metals, especially those that might help them discover the so-called Philosopher's Stone that would enable them to transmute less valuable metals into gold. Their quest proved to be quixotic, but they were able to refine methods for producing metals and many other useful chemical compounds.

Despite their ignorance about the scientific principles underlying the smelting of metals and the manufacture of metallic products, artisans were able, because of the empirical knowledge built up in their craft traditions, to manufacture excellent daggers, swords, and other metallic objects. With the development of the phlogiston theory in the eighteenth century, Europeans had an explanatory system that could account for metals and their manufacture. According to this theory, metals were combinations of their ores (called "calces," or powdery minerals) and phlogiston (the principle of combustibility that also accounted for the shininess of metals). According to some historians,

modern chemistry began when Antoine Lavoisier replaced the phlogiston theory with his oxygen theory, according to which metals are elemental and calces are compounds of a metal plus oxygen. In this interpretation, when iron ore is smelted with charcoal, the heated mixture reacts, leading the carbon of the charcoal to bond with the oxygen in the ore. The compound escapes as the gas carbon dioxide, thus isolating the iron.

In the early nineteenth century, Humphry Davy used electricity to discover several new metals, including such alkali metals as sodium and potassium and such alkaline-earth metals as calcium, barium, strontium, and magnesium. Other chemists discovered still more metals, and Dmitri Mendeleyev proposed that these metals, as well as all other elements, could be organized into a useful table, where the properties of the elements, including the metals, were periodic functions of their atomic weights. He was even able to predict that new metals would be found, for instance, "eka-aluminum," which would account for an empty space in his table; the discovery of this metal, now known as gallium, as well as others, did much to cement the popularity of Mendeleyev's periodic table.

The Industrial Revolution transformed the ways in which metals were manufactured. The blacksmith's forge and bellows were replaced by ever-larger blast furnaces and rolling mills. When an extremely rich iron-ore deposit was discovered in the Mesabi Range of upper Minnesota, new techniques were developed so that this fine-dust ore would not clog the circulatory systems of blast furnaces. For example, pelletizing involved rolling the ore in a cylindrical drum to form small balls, later hardened by heat; sintering involved mixing the Mesabi ores with coke across a moving heated grate to form lumps suitable for charging the blast furnace. By 1900, the Mesabi ores supplied three-quarters of the needs of the American iron and steel industries.

In the Bessemer process, invented by Sir Henry Bessemer and perfected by the American Alexander Holley, a pear-shaped converter removed unwanted impurities in molten pig iron by blowing air through it. The process made it possible to manufacture high-quality steel inexpensively in England and the United States. The resulting availability of large quantities of cheap steel led to the expansion of railroads in the second half of the nineteenth century.

In the early decades of the twentieth century, American steel production grew at a rate of 7 percent (compared with 6 percent in Germany, a principal competitor). This significant growth was due to abundant sources of raw materials, innovative technologies, and such other factors as a highly efficient transportation system. During this period, the United States was the world's largest, most efficient, and cheapest producer of steel.

During the Great Depression years of the 1930's, U.S. steel production varied from a low of 13.9 million metric tons of raw steel in 1932 to a high of 51.4 million metric tons of raw steel in 1937. During World War II, annual production increased significantly, reaching a high of 81.3 million metric tons in 1944. During the late 1940's and through the 1950's, production soared to over 100 million metric tons, followed by declines in the early 1960's and a recovery in the late 1960's. By the 1970's, American steel producers discovered to their chagrin that they were losing market share domestically and internationally to a variety of companies. Sparrows Point was making steel with antiquated open-hearth furnaces, while the Europeans and Japanese were using the superior basic-oxygen process. Reluctance to embrace new technologies and other poor decisions by American steel executives led to bankruptcies and mergers.

Some scholars have described the 1980's as a period of near anarchy in the American steel industry. Some observers blamed greedy managers who placed short-term profits ahead of long-term advantages. Managers in turn blamed avaricious union leaders for negotiating ultimately unrealizable and overly generous benefits packages. Others blamed engineers and technicians for "technological timidity" in not keeping production facilities abreast of innovative technologies. Still others blamed government policies that allowed inexpensive steel from foreign countries to deluge the American market. Often, the steel from Japan, Europe, and Brazil was cheaper and of higher quality than American products.

The Industry Today

The modern metals manufacturing industry owes much to the discoveries of physicists and chemists and to the ingenuity of engineers. For example, the American physicist Josiah Willard Gibbs formulated an equation expressing the relationship between the number of component chemicals in a system, the phases of matter in that system, and the number of independent intensive properties in the system. One consequence of Gibbs's phase rule is that it reveals the conditions under which certain microstructural constituents, including certain alloys, can exist. In this way, the quality of steel, an alloy of iron and carbon, could be predicted based on scientific evidence rather than on such trial-and-error observations as the appearance of fractures in a sample. The next stage in the scientific understanding of metals and alloys involved the determination of the actual arrangements of atoms or ions within crystals of metals or alloys through the process of X-ray diffraction.

A man grinds steel in a metal fabrication factory. (©John Casey/Dreamstime.com)

The story of the modern metals manufacturing industry in the United States, especially that of iron and steel manufacturers, has often been told in terms of a rise-and-decline model. The American iron and steel industry was by far the world's most dominant in the first half of the twentieth century, and its extraordinary productivity during World War II contributed significantly to the Allies' victory. American inventors and engineers had developed a version of the open-hearth process that was extremely efficient in producing inexpensive, high-quality steel. In the American version of the process, the enclosed-system open-hearth furnace was increased in size, with improved design and better refractories (ceramic materials resistant to high temperatures), and producer gas was replaced by heavy fuel-oil residues. During the decade after the end of World War II, Americans were making steel faster, better, and in greater quantities than anyone else. The situation changed dramatically in the second half of the twentieth century, and the decline of American Big Steel can serve as a paradigm case.

By the end of the twentieth century, the United States was no longer the world's principal producer of steel, and many American steelmakers were closing or downsizing their plants, leading to the vanishing of hundreds of thousands of lucrative jobs. Several authors have tried to make sense of this dispiriting phenomenon. For example, Mark Reutter, in *Sparrows Point: Making Steel—The Rise and Ruin of American Industrial Might* (1988), used a case study of what was once the world's larg-

Inputs Consumed by the Primary Metals Manufacturing Industry

Input	Value
Energy	$21.5 billion
Materials	$138.1 billion
Purchased services	$31.0 billion
Total	$190.6 billion

Source: U.S. Bureau of Economic Analysis. Data are for 2008.

est steel mill, near Baltimore, Maryland, to argue that executives, devoted to a "bigger is better" policy, inflated steel prices in an increasingly competitive global economy and shortchanged innovative research. Consequently, within three decades Sparrows Point was producing half as much steel as it had at its peak, and the workforce had shrunk from more than twenty-eight thousand to less than eight thousand. Similar problems occurred in other American steel companies, and their executives, aware of the problem, explained their woes as being due to "overpaid" workers and "unfair" foreign competition, but others pointed out that neither federal limits on imports nor union wage concessions had slowed the decline.

Sparrows Point was but one example of what was also taking place in the steel manufacturing industry in Buffalo, New York; Gary, Indiana; and Pittsburgh, Pennsylvania. In *The Decline of American Steel* (1988), Paul A. Tiffany criticized the role of federal officials in this decline. For example, the policies of the Harry S. Truman administration encouraged plant expansion and wage increases for steelworkers. Officials in Dwight D. Eisenhower's administration urged international agencies to provide substantial financial aid to Japan's steelmakers. Other analysts blamed onerous federal environmental regulations for substantially adding to the cost of making steel in America. Still others blamed changing technologies and markets. For exam-

The Primary Metals Manufacturing Industry's Contribution to the U.S. Economy

Value Added	Amount
Gross domestic product	$58.5 billion
Gross domestic product	0.4%
Persons employed	445,000
Total employee compensation	$33.2 billion

Source: U.S. Bureau of Economic Analysis. Data are for 2008.

ple, the aluminum industry increasingly wrested control over the metal container business away from steel. Other industries were abandoning expensive steel for inexpensive plastics, and the steel content of American automobiles declined while their plastic content increased.

The most important technical development in steelmaking in the second half of the twentieth century was the oxygen furnace, which was, in Europe and Japan, largely replacing the open-hearth process. By the year 2000, the basic oxygen furnace accounted for more than half of the steel production in the world. This furnace converted iron ore and pig iron to steel by blowing oxygen through a molten mixture of these compounds, which were intensely heated by a water-cooled steel lance. These furnaces allowed Japanese and German steelmakers to produce 200 tons of steel every 45 minutes, whereas American open hearths required eight hours to produce that much.

In an electric arc furnace, carbon electrodes provide the heat to convert the charge (with a high percentage of steel scrap) into high-quality steel. Since these furnaces do not need pig iron or blast furnaces, the cost of making steel is considerably less than it is when utilizing traditional processes. This cost-effective device has led to an increase in the number of mini-mills, which produce steel on a small scale, diverging from the "bigger is better" dogma that so long dominated American steelmaking. These downsized operations generally consist of electric arc furnaces and continuous casting machines for producing plates, bars, rods, or wires.

In terms of world metal production, aluminum is second to steel in total tonnage. Because it is a very abundant metallic element in the Earth's crust, aluminum has become a significant competitor to steel in many products, from airplanes to beverage containers. The most important aluminum ore is bauxite, which is converted to aluminum by an electrolytic process. After bauxite is chemically converted to alumina, electrolytic cells perform the conversion of alumina into metallic aluminum. Similar electrolytic reduction processes exist for other nonferrous metals. In the second half of the twentieth century, researchers became adept at creating new alloys containing aluminum, which helped make the aluminum manufacturing industry a dominant force among metal producers.

Liquid iron from the smelting stove. (©Oleg Fedorenko/ Dreamstime.com)

Alloys have become significant parts of both the steel and the aluminum industry. An early example of an influential alloy is manganese steel. Because of the great strength of this and other alloys, they have been in high demand for armor plate for ships and tanks. A steel alloyed with tungsten and molybdenum proved to be an excellent product for high-speed cutting tools. Stainless or rust-resistant steels are generally alloyed with chromium, nickel, and manganese. Stainless steels have been used in tableware as well as in the pharmaceutical, chemical, and military industries.

Superalloys involve amalgams of such elements as iron, cobalt, and nickel, but several other elements can be present, such as molybdenum, tungsten, aluminum, titanium, and zirconium. The first superalloys to be developed were iron-based, but in the quest to create alloys that could operate without corrosion at high temperatures, cobalt-based superalloys were developed. Manufacturers have used these superalloys in jet engines and gas turbines.

INDUSTRY MARKET SEGMENTS

Throughout the history of metals, differences in the scale of manufacturing concerns have existed, from the bloomeries of blacksmiths to the blast furnaces of early industries, from "maxi-mills," such as open-hearth furnaces, to mini-mills with their electric arc furnaces. The following sections illustrate some of these small, midsize, and large businesses for a sample of various metals manufacturers within the metals manufacturing industry.

Small Businesses

With nearly seventy known metals, the metal processing industry varies considerably in business size, which is often related to the specific metal produced. For example, the total world production of tin and titanium is much less than 1 percent of that of iron and steel. Differences also exist in the cost of producing a given quantity of metal; in the case of tin and titanium, the respective costs are twenty and twenty-six times that of producing an equivalent amount of steel. The United States has not mined or smelted tin for some time, but several firms produce tin from secondary sources. In 2006 this amounted to 15,000 metric tons. Using the average price on the New York market, this constituted a value of $137,261,250. Evenly dividing this among 25 firms gives a very rough estimate of over $5 million per firm.

Potential Annual Earnings Scale. According to the U.S. Bureau of Labor Statistics (BLS), in 2009, the average annual income of production workers in the nonferrous, nonaluminum metals manufacturing industry, which includes tin and titanium, was $37,110. The most common production position, extruding and drawing machine operator, earned an average of $35,100, while production supervisors earned an average of $55,250. Sales representatives earned an average of $74,020, industrial engineers earned an average of $71,530, and materials engineers earned an average of $79,530. General and operations managers earned an average of $132,070. Salaries at small firms such as those making tin products are likely to be below these averages.

Clientele Interaction. Since China, Indonesia, Malaysia, and Bolivia are some of the chief producers of tin, U.S. firms deal with these and other pro-

ducers. Most major imports of tin enter the United States duty free. The United States also has the Defense National Stockpile Center, which operates a sales program offering tin to firms under long-term negotiated contracts. With increased emphasis on environmental quality, recycled tin has been entering American processing plants in increasing amounts. Many American companies using tin or tin alloys tend to deal with American rather than foreign suppliers.

Amenities, Atmosphere, and Physical Grounds. The conversion of ores into metals involves conditions different from the conversion of metals into finished products. In some businesses, especially those with an integrated manufacturing process, the sharp distinction between primary and secondary metals processing no longer holds. The transformation of molten metal into semifinished or fully finished parts largely influences the nature of the workplace. Firms generally have technologies for continuous casting. Sometimes, parts are forged starting with metal powders. Various mechanical machining methods are then used to produce finished products. For example, tin can be used by itself, but, most commonly, it is alloyed with other elements. Bronze, for instance, is an alloy of copper and tin. Although tin alone does not have physiological effects on humans, tin compounds do, and the possible negative health effects of these are of concern in the workplace.

In general, metals manufacturing plants are industrial facilities that employ heavy machinery and extreme heat. Production workers must wear basic protective equipment at all times and must follow established safety procedures. Other personnel usually work in standard office buildings that—in small firms—are usually located on the grounds of the production plants, and all employees must generally pass through the same guard stations or checkpoints when arriving at or leaving work.

Typical Number of Employees. The employees needed to construct a metal-processing facility differ from those needed to keep it running efficiently once it is established. It is a principal duty of chemical engineers to construct bridges between the scientific knowledge of metals and practical principles governing their economic and efficient production. Initially, a small number of these engineers design equipment and develop processes for small-scale manufacturing. Once a plant has been set up, workers are hired, generally fewer than one hundred. Engineers and chemical technicians monitor manufacturing methods for efficiency, economy, and safety, as well as for environmental protection. With the increasing cost of labor, engineers also experience pressure to automate and computerize production as much as possible, but trained workers are still necessary to maintain, repair, and run machinery.

Traditional Geographic Locations. Metal manufacturing plants are usually located near major highways and railroads, outside cities or in rural areas, where real estate is affordable and industrial manufacturing will not conflict with the needs of homeowners and other residential property owners. Historically, metal processing industries were located near their main sources of ore, but, with the development of improved transportation by land and water, facilities can now be located near transportation hubs. For example, in the United States, business officials deemed it uneconomic to transport tin ores from Alaska, where the deposits were viewed as insignificant. They decided instead to import either tin ore or refined tin from elsewhere in the world.

Pros of Working for a Small Metal Manufacturer. The advantages of working at a small metal manufacturer depend on the metal produced and the market conditions governing its use. Chemical engineers often experience satisfaction in making use of their scientific and technological knowledge to set up and monitor a metal-making facility. If the firm has a modest number of employees and they are treated as essential elements in the enterprise, they may enjoy a beneficial spirit of cooperation that causes all employees to feel they have a stake in the progress of the business.

Cons of Working for a Small Metal Manufacturer. Small companies tend not to be widely diversified, so they can suffer disproportionately when markets for their metals and alloys shrink or collapse. During such times of economic distress, irresistible pressure may be brought to bear on small firms to merge with large ones. The prices of metals are also subject to political changes in countries where they are produced. For example, prices tend to climb when political upheavals cause a decline in the production of ores or metals from a country that was previously a major supplier. If a metal or metal derivative turns out to have dangerous

health or environmental effects, this can then lead to a negative effect on a small business producing the metal or its derivatives. Large decreases in the use of a metal typically lead to plant closings and the laying off of workers.

Costs

Payroll and Benefits: Small metal producers generally pay hourly wages or salaries, depending on the position. They often do not provide health benefits unless they are unionized. Companies outside the United States often need not provide health benefits, as those are provided directly by the government in many nations.

Supplies: Small metal manufacturers require ores and raw metals, old and new scrap, and other processing materials such as chemicals. They need heavy machinery, production tools, and production computers, as well as the tools and supplies necessary to maintain their machinery. Manufacturers also require storage, packaging, and transportation equipment, as well as standard office supplies and equipment, including not only business computers but also computer workstations and software for engineers.

External Services: Small firms may contract accounting and payroll services, computer and machine maintenance, and food services.

Utilities: Modern metal manufacturers, even small ones, need access to abundant water supplies and electricity. Managers, administrative staff, engineers, and researchers also require access to telephones and the Internet.

Taxes: Historically, some small metal companies have been given tax breaks in order to keep them competitive with foreign firms, but generally they have to pay local, state, and federal corporate and property taxes and, in some cases, even foreign taxes and tariffs.

Midsize Businesses

In terms of global manufacture, the processing of such metals as copper and zinc occupies a middle position between the larger companies producing steel and aluminum and the small producers of such metals as tin and titanium. Detailed production data for many metals are not commonly available because certain manufacturers tend to keep such data secret. Nevertheless, it is possible to categorize certain subindustries as intermediate between the giant and small producers.

Potential Annual Earnings Scale. According to the BLS, in 2009, the average annual income of production workers in the nonferrous, nonaluminum metals manufacturing industry, which includes copper and zinc, was $37,110. The most common production position, extruding and drawing machine operator, earned an average of $35,100, while production supervisors earned an average of $55,250. Sales representatives earned an average of $74,020, industrial engineers earned an average of $71,530, and materials engineers earned an average of $79,530. General and operations managers earned an average of $132,070. Salaries at midsize firms such as those making copper and zince products are likely to be in line with these averages.

Clientele Interaction. Because midsize manufacturers of metals depend on the same clientele as small firms, they, too, require interactions with foreign, domestic, and governmental personnel. With larger staffs than those of small firms, midsize companies have more people to deal with customers, government officials, and personnel at other concerns with which they do business.

Amenities, Atmosphere, and Physical Grounds. Because the commercialized continuous casting of such metals as copper, lead, and zinc preceded the continuous casting of steel, successful techniques were developed early for casting strips of copper, zinc, and lead. Other casting techniques led to metal slabs or bars. Researchers also discovered that continuous casting was not economically feasible for most alloys because it was too difficult to control the solidification process. In 2003, the United States produced about 8 percent of the world's zinc (the chief producers were China, Australia, and Peru). The United States does not produce enough zinc from its own ores, and it therefore imports zinc from several countries, principally Canada, Mexico, Peru, and Australia. Zinc is mainly used for galvanizing, a process in which iron or steel is coated with rust-resistant zinc, and for making brass, an alloy of copper and zinc. In the first half of the twentieth century, Waterbury, Connecticut, became home to many midsize firms making brass products. These firms declined in the post-World War II period, though other American midsize companies manufacturing metals and metal derivatives prospered during the second half of the twentieth century. These firms are able to provide amenities such as free parking and access to food services.

Typical Number of Employees. The great variety of midsize metal manufacturers is matched by great variation in the size of their labor forces. In general, each company employs hundreds of workers. Market forces also influence the number of employees, as more workers are hired during periods when demand for their particular product is high, and layoffs generally follow market declines.

Traditional Geographic Locations. Historically, because of the chemical and noise pollution associated with the manufacture of metals, facilities were often located outside of cities and towns but near transportation hubs to make the influx of raw materials and the output of finished products more efficient. In some countries, midsize industries tend to be more integrated than small firms, so ore is smelted and then the raw metal is finished and made into various products at the same facility. Since countries such as China and Mexico have much more lenient environmental laws than the United States, zinc, copper, and lead can be produced more cheaply in these venues.

Pros of Working for a Midsize Metal Manufacturer. By their very nature, midsize metal manufacturers often produce metals and metal derivatives that neither small nor giant firms produce. Therefore, chemical engineers who are skilled in the manufacture of a particular metal may find that midsize firms are the only firms where they can employ their expertise. Some engineers favor the challenges of working in such an environment. Sometimes, they have the opportunity to participate in the design and construction of metal-making facilities; other times, they are hired to oversee production or to participate in research to find ways to improve the economic creation of metal products, both quantitatively and qualitatively.

Cons of Working for a Midsize Metal Manufacturer. Midsize companies tend to be more integrated and diversified than small companies, but they, too, tend to suffer when markets for their metals and alloys decline, although diversification usually prevents them from collapse. Because metals are nonrenewable resources, markets for them have been and will continue to be increasingly competitive, and the market for metals is also subject to great volatility in response to changing political conditions in certain producer countries. Unexpected events such as earthquakes and other natural disasters have also affected markets for metals. Personnel with advanced scientific and technical degrees generally have the best opportunities for weathering unpredictable declines in the marketplace.

Costs

Payroll and Benefits: Midsize metal manufacturing firms often hire personnel on contract, including engineers and technicians. These contracts usually include health and time-off benefits.

Supplies: Midsize metal manufacturers require ores and raw metals, old and new scrap, and other processing materials such as chemicals. They need heavy machinery, production tools, and production computers, as well as the tools and supplies necessary to maintain their machinery. Manufacturers also require storage, packaging, and transportation equipment, as well as standard office supplies and equipment, including not only business computers but also computer workstations and software for engineers.

External Services: Midsize metal manufacturers typically contract maintenance and repair of their production machinery and computer systems, as well as accounting and payroll services, on-site food services, and both on- and off-site medical services.

Utilities: Besides relying on local water and sewage, electrical power, and heating services, midsize companies sometimes locate near rivers because of their high demand for water, and they also make use of telephone and Internet services.

Taxes: Some midsize metal-making firms have been able to negotiate favorable tax arrangements with local and state officials, particularly when these officials want a company to establish itself or remain in a certain community. Regardless, they must pay some local, state, and federal corporate and property taxes. They may also pay foreign taxes and tariffs, when, as is often the case, they have dealings with companies in other countries.

Large Businesses

Worldwide, the two largest metal manufacturing industries make steel and aluminum. The approximate world production of iron and steel is forty-three times that of aluminum. Iron, steel, and aluminum production and use are often seen as basic measures of advanced industrialized societies.

Potential Annual Earnings Scale. According to the BLS, the average annual income of a production worker in the iron and steel mill industry in 2009 was $43,810, and the average annual income of a production worker in the aluminum industry was $36,070. In iron and steel mills, the average income of production supervisors was $62,860, the average income of industrial engineers was $78,120, the average income of industrial production managers was $107,270, and the average income of general and operations managers was $133,770. At aluminum manufacturers, the average income of production supervisors was $56,140, the average income of industrial engineers was $71,820, the average income of industrial production managers was $90,380, and the average income of general and operations managers was 116,750.

Clientele Interaction. Because of the larger numbers of managers and specialists dealing with clients, such as sales and customer service representatives, interactions with customers are more frequent and extended than is generally the case in small and midsize businesses. Greater investment in advertising, marketing, product promotion, and public relations also fosters greater interaction with clients.

Amenities, Atmosphere, and Physical Grounds. Sparrows Point in its heyday was the largest steel manufacturing plant in the world. It produced enough steel to make over 100 million automobiles, manufacture over 400,000 miles of railroad track, and construct over 1,000 skyscrapers the size of the Empire State Building. So large was the industrial landscape at Sparrows Point that the open-hearth department alone occupied about one hundred acres of flatland. During World War II, close to thirty thousand workers produced over 424 million tons of steel, 3.6 times the amount produced by Germany's Saar region in the same time period. This scene was repeated in Pittsburgh, where many blast furnaces and rolling mills churned out massive amounts of steel.

In the half century after the war, the workforce at Sparrows Point declined to fewer than eight thousand, and similar declines occurred elsewhere in the United States. This naturally led to fully and partially abandoned facilities in Pittsburgh; Gary; Youngstown, Ohio; and other steel towns. At Sparrows Point, some blast furnaces were dynamited and the scrap was sold, but some open-hearth structures and abandoned coke ovens still remained, as did the company town where families had purchased household goods.

In contrast to the decline in steel properties, companies such as Alcoa, Reynolds Metal, and Kaiser Aluminum expanded their physical plants to meet the demand for an expanding aluminum container business. Eventually, nearly all beer cans and about 90 percent of all soft-drink cans were made of aluminum. Increasing numbers of employees led to expanded plants for making aluminum and its alloys, along with such amenities as cafeterias and large parking lots.

Typical Number of Employees. Large metal manufacturers each employ thousands of workers.

Traditional Geographic Locations. America's first major steel city was Pittsburgh because iron ore and coal were both readily available there. Pittsburgh continued its growth because Mesabi Range iron ore could be efficiently transported to its blast furnaces. Other large iron and steel facilities were located in Gary, Youngstown, Buffalo, and Sparrows Point.

Pros of Working for a Large Metal Manufacturer. Large corporations have significant resources and are likely to weather temporary economic setbacks. They provide high salaries, significant opportunities for advancement, and research budgets that may enable their engineers to develop major new processes and products.

Cons of Working for a Large Metal Manufacturer. The decline of the U.S. steel industry demonstrates that even large manufacturers are not immortal. In addition, large companies have significant bureaucracies, and employees may feel anonymous and distant from the decision-making process.

A blast furnace at a plant. (©Oleksiy Mark/Dreamstime.com)

Costs

Payroll and Benefits: Large metal manufacturers may pay various employees hourly wages, annual salaries, or on a contract basis. They often provide benefits.

Supplies: Large iron and steel facilities require immense amounts of raw materials and lesser amounts of fine chemicals in order to manufacture metals, alloys, and various finished products. They also require heavy machinery, spare parts, and tools; engineering computer workstations; office supplies and equipment, including business computers; and laboratory equipment and chemicals.

External Services: Large companies often sign contracts with outside firms to handle payroll, computer maintenance, and food services on site. Some giant steel facilities, such as Sparrows Point, fostered the development of steel towns with housing and stores for their workers.

Utilities: Large metal manufacturing companies need massive amounts of electrical power and water. In the early days of the U.S. steel industry, little attention was paid to air and water pollution, but in the last third of the twentieth century governmental regulations have forced these companies to control their pollutants. Companies also need telephone, cable television, and Internet services.

Taxes: Some large metal-making firms have been able to negotiate favorable tax arrangements with local and state officials, particularly when these officials want a company to establish itself or remain in a certain community. Regardless, they must pay some local, state, and federal corporate and property taxes. They may also pay foreign taxes and tariffs, when, as is often the case, they have dealings with companies in other countries.

ORGANIZATIONAL STRUCTURE AND JOB ROLES

Metal manufacturing companies of different sizes and different ages vary significantly in their internal structures. However, all companies must fulfill the same basic job roles in order to function. Even at small companies in this industry, each role is likely to be performed by a different employee, although some employees will take on multiple roles as necessary.

The following umbrella categories apply to the organizational structure of businesses in the metals manufacturing industry:

- Executive Management
- Marketing and Sales
- Customer Service
- Office and Administrative Support
- Research and Development
- Maintenance and Repair
- Production
- Information Technology
- Distribution

Executive Management

Executive managers oversee all aspects of their companies' operations. Historically, as exemplified by steel magnate Andrew Carnegie, top executives did not possess technical knowledge and skills in the metals being manufactured; instead, they possessed general business savvy. Modern executives, however, are frequently persons with substantial scientific knowledge and technical expertise and experience. New technologies and changing business patterns have influenced the structure of executive management. Frederick Winslow Taylor, the father of scientific management, studied how to make more efficient not only the output of skilled and unskilled laborers in the steel industry but also the productivity of managers.

Executive management occupations may include the following:

- President/Chief Executive Officer (CEO)
- General or Operations Manager
- Chief Financial Officer (CFO)
- Vice President of Sales and Marketing
- Engineering Manager
- Public Relations Manager

Marketing and Sales

Marketing and sales personnel find, attract, cultivate, and maintain clients. In the metals manufacturing industry, clients are usually other manufacturing companies who require metals as raw materials. Sales staff must understand both their own corporations' production processes and those of their clients, and they must be able to negotiate profitable contracts for their firms. Marketing and sales personnel often have at least two-year technical degrees or, more commonly, four-year college degrees. Because many metals manufacturing concerns have foreign customers, particular language skills are necessary for those marketing metal products to a specific country.

Marketing and sales occupations may include the following:

- Marketing Manager
- Marketing Analyst
- Sales Manager
- Sales Representative
- Business Operations Specialist
- International Sales Director

Customer Service

Because of the great diversity of metals and alloys sold by manufacturing companies, both to individuals and to other firms, customer relations representatives have many tasks to perform. For example, they typically deal with misunderstandings by customers about products, customer complaints, replacements of defective products, and so on. Since they often have to handle detailed questions about various metal products, they need to have the requisite scientific and technical background to deal knowledgeably with customers.

Customer service occupations may include the following:

- Customer Relations Manager
- Customer Relations Representative

Office and Administrative Support

Large metals manufacturers need relatively large staffs to handle the many clerical and business tasks that keep them running smoothly. Keeping track of raw material inputs and finished product outputs, along with records of sales, requires many office workers. Because much of this information is now computerized, office workers need professional expertise in information management systems.

Office and administrative support occupations may include the following:

- Bookkeeper
- Accountant
- Auditor
- Administrative Assistant
- Secretary
- Computer Support Specialist
- Payroll Clerk
- Human Resources Generalist

Research and Development

Most large metals manufacturing companies have research and development personnel to improve traditional products and create new ones. These scientists, engineers, and technicians work with customer relations representatives to handle customer complaints. Many workers in this division have advanced college degrees. Chemists and materials scientists, for example, analyze products to make sure that they live up to industry and governmental standards. They also modify existing metals, develop new alloys, and create new finished products. Chemical engineers, who are often heavily involved in setting up metal-making plants, design equipment and develop various processes for manufacturing metals and alloys on a large scale. Chemical technicians conduct tests for quality control.

OCCUPATION SPECIALTIES

Metallurgical/Materials Engineers

Specialty	Responsibilities
Extractive metallurgists	Extract metals from ores through processes such as smelting or refining, develop uses for scrap metal and low-grade ores, control temperature, and charge mixture furnaces.
Foundry metallurgists	Conduct research to develop and improve sand-molding, melting, alloying, and metal-pouring methods.
Materials engineers	Evaluate technical and economic factors to recommend engineering and manufacturing strategies to attain the design objectives of products and processes by applying their knowledge of material science and related technologies.
Metallographers	Conduct tests to develop new and improved metals and alloys and improve production methods.
Physical metallurgists	Study the structure of metals in order to develop new alloys, new uses for metals through alloying, and ways to produce alloys commercially.
Welding engineers	Specialize in the development and application of welding equipment and welding techniques for hard-to-weld metal alloys and assemblies.

Certain chemists specialize in developing knowledge about the many metals in the periodic table, and other chemists specialize in particular alloys. This knowledge can be beneficial to metals manufacturers concerned with those metals and alloys. Chemical research engineers conduct experiments to discover how most efficiently to transform raw materials into commercial metals and alloys. They perform these experiments not only to improve traditional techniques but also to discover potential new products and processes. Materials engineers concerned with metals and alloys may try to develop production techniques for these materials that meet the commercial requirements of their employers. They make use of their knowledge of the microstructure of these materials to devise alloys with the desired hardness, electrical properties, resistance to fracture or cracking, malleability, ductility, and other properties.

An open-hearth furnace at a plant. (©Oleksiy Mark/Dreamstime.com)

Research and development occupations may include the following:

- Chemist
- Chemical Engineer
- Chemical Technician
- Chemical Engineering Technician
- Metallurgist
- Materials Scientist
- Materials Engineer
- Materials Engineering Technician
- Industrial Engineer
- Industrial Engineering Technician
- Mechanical Engineer
- Mechanical Engineering Technician

Maintenance and Repair

The devices used to manufacture metals require periodic maintenance and repair. For example, open-hearth furnaces are still being used, and, because of extensive dust and high temperatures, furnace parts often need to be cleaned, and occasionally complete replacement of the furnace roof is necessary. Laborers must replace front and end walls after about one to two hundred cycles. Proper maintenance and repairs allow open-hearth furnaces to last about ten years. In advanced steelmaking technologies, basic oxygen furnaces, electric furnaces, primary and secondary rolling devices, rheocasting, and spray-casting devices need to be maintained. Repairs are often essential to extending the life and efficiency of these new metal-processing machines.

Maintenance and repair occupations may include the following:

- Maintenance and Repair Worker
- Metal-Manipulation Machinery Mechanic
- Custodian/Janitor
- Machinist

Production

Contemporary production personnel may be skilled or unskilled workers who operate one or more machines in production plants. Some work as part of teams and trade responsibilities among teammates; others specialize in a single, sometimes extremely repetitive task. Production workers may require only high school educations, or they may require bachelor's degrees in a relevant technical or scientific field.

Production occupations may include the following:

- Industrial Production Manager
- Production Supervisor
- Rolling Machine Setter and Operator

- Metal-Refining Furnace Operator
- Metal Pourer/Caster
- Inspector, Tester, Sorter, Sampler, and Weigher

Information Technology

Although computer specialists have a role to play in such divisions as administration, sales, and office support, they have also become important to production and floor operations. With the growth of mini-mills in the steel industry came an increase in computer-controlled rolling and casting processes. Automatic control of rolling operations has been necessitated by higher rolling speeds, developed to make greater quantities of high-quality product speedily and efficiently. Uniformity of product is especially valued. As knowledge of various metal-making processes has increased over time, so has the capacity for precise computer control of those processes, with attendant improvements in quality and yield of various metals and alloys. Such computerized control require specialized software, either proprietary software developed in-house or commercial or open-source software that must often be customized in-house. In either case, computer programmers and software engineers must ensure that their companies' code matches their needs and priorities.

Information technology occupations may include the following:

- Computer Scientist
- Computer Programmer
- Computer Technician
- Software Engineer

Distribution

Distribution personnel transport raw materials to manufacturing plants, store both materials and finished metals, and transport finished metals to purchasers. Truck drivers in this industry generally require commercial driver's licenses, while warehouse workers may require certification on vehicles such as forklifts. College degrees are not usually required for entry-level distribution positions.

Distribution occupations may include the following:

- Heavy Truck Driver
- Light Truck Driver

- Material and Freight Mover
- Packer and Packager
- Warehouse Supervisor
- Dispatcher
- Shipping and Receiving Clerk

INDUSTRY OUTLOOK

Overview

The metals manufacturing industry is complex, comprising as it does the making of nearly seventy metals and many more alloys. Even a single giant subindustry, such as steelmaking, has several subfields of its own, such as ironmaking and iron products, steelmaking and steel products, and the manufacture of many steel alloys. However, generally speaking, the outlook for the metals manufacturing industry shows it to be in decline. The BLS projects that the steel industry, for example, will shed 13 percent of its jobs between 2008 and 2018. However, the same report indicates that job prospects in the industry are "very good" for engineers and other skilled workers despite this overall decline. In the bureau's parlance, "very good" means that there will be more open positions than applicants.

The steel industry in particular has been in decline for some time. Employment in the U.S. steel industry decreased from over 500,000 workers in 1975 to fewer than 200,000 workers in 1987. In 2008, the steel industry provided about 159,000 salaried jobs. Close to 100,000 workers were employed in iron and steel mills and ferroalloy production, and about 60,000 worked fabricating steel products from purchased steel.

The American primary metals industry encompasses approximately four thousand companies, including those producing steel, aluminum, and copper. The fifty largest companies are responsible for more than half of industry revenues. Analysis of manufacturers' shipments of durable goods suggests that the industry's decline is due in part to a decline in demand for its products. For example, the demand for primary metals in the first eleven months of 2009 was 17 percent lower than demand during the same period in 2008. Steel demand in December, 2009, was 11 percent less than demand in December, 2008. The demand for aluminum can sheet, a key product in the metals manufacturing industry, declined by 3.7 percent by the start of 2010.

The 2009 decline in the U.S. steel industry was its greatest since 1982. Explanations offered for this decline include a decrease in the nation's gross domestic product, the recession of 2007-2009, and weaknesses in many markets that have traditionally used steel and other metals. Whatever the reason, 2009 witnessed a dramatic fall in the American consumption of steel and steel products.

By the late twentieth and early twenty-first century, American steel production was rebounding from its dramatic decline of the 1970's and 1980's. Some companies had built new facilities using such new technologies as basic oxygen and electric furnaces, as well as automated rolling mills. This development led to the increased production of high-quality steel. In 1997, the United States produced 107.5 million metric tons of raw steel, a more than 20 percent increase over 1991, the decade's low point. In the decade from 1998 to 2008, the total production of crude steel in the U.S. varied from a high of 101.8 million metric tons in 2000 to a low of 90.1 in 2001. The average total production for the decade was 95.7 million metric tons. Some optimists believe that shortsighted managers and union conflicts are things of the past, and that American steelmakers, after having passed through the gauntlet of very hard times, now understand that attention must be paid to the complex interactions among social, economic, technological, and political forces in order for the industry to enter a period of prosperity.

Employment Advantages

BLS projections indicate that some occupations within the metals manufacturing industry will be in demand, and those positions are likely to be among the higher-paying positions in the industry. However, employment overall in the industry is in serious decline, which may breed a certain amount of resentment toward in-demand workers within companies. Although jobs in old, giant facilities will decline, employment in mini-mills and automated rolling mills will increase. The very technologies, such as automation and computerization, that have fostered a small but more efficient workforce have also increased the need for highly trained computer programmers and maintenance workers. Some analysts even believe that this modernization may lead to a growth in American steelmaking, with a consequent need for more workers at some point in the future. A hopeful sign is the increased demand for special metal products used in the aerospace industry and by chemical equipment manufacturers. If the American nuclear industry revives, steel products will play a role in new plant construction.

Employment in the steel industry is sensitive to market conditions, technological developments, and domestic as well as international competition. Those companies that intelligently and imaginatively adapt to changes in markets, technology, and competition will prosper and have room for

PROJECTED EMPLOYMENT FOR SELECTED OCCUPATIONS

Fabricated Metal Product Manufacturing

Employment		
2009	Projected 2018	Occupation
62,800	58,300	Cutting, punching, and press machine setters, operators, and tenders, metal and plastic
61,000	61,400	First-line supervisors/ managers of production and operating workers
120,920	115,900	Machinists
75,270	81,400	Team assemblers
90,620	94,700	Welders, cutters, solderers, and brazers

Source: U.S. Bureau of Labor Statistics, Industries at a Glance, Occupational Employment Statistics and Employment Projections Program.

like-minded employees. For example, markets are opening in several developing countries, and companies willing to meet the needs of these emerging markets will be helped. Environmental concerns may also foster domestic demand for steel, for example, in the wind turbine industry. Consequently, even with overall declines, opportunities still exist for several occupations, including chemical and materials engineers, metallurgists, and experts familiar with automation and computerization.

Annual Earnings

Annual earnings of the entire metals manufacturing industry are difficult to determine precisely, both because of the large number and variety of companies and because many companies tend to keep this knowledge secret or charge large amounts for its publication and use. First Research estimates that the domestic primary metals industry earned $250 billion in revenues in 2009. More accurate information exists about certain metals industries, such as steel. Domestic steel revenues are variously estimated at steel: $60.6 billion in 2008 by the American Iron and Steel Institute and $70 billion in 2009 by IBISWorld.

Good data exist for the world production of raw steel (it went from 770 million metric tons in 1998 to over 1.25 billion metric tons in 2008). On the other hand, average wholesale prices for raw steel have varied considerably from country to country and from company to company. Within segments of the steel industry, earnings and wages vary by the kind of production and occupation of the worker.

According to the BLS, earnings and wages in the steel industry for 2008 were higher than the average earnings in private industry as a whole. The average weekly salary of production workers in 2008 was $1,117 in iron and steel mills and $736 in companies making steel products from purchased steel. The median hourly wages of managers over all segments of steel manufacturing were $24.25 in

PROJECTED EMPLOYMENT FOR SELECTED OCCUPATIONS

Primary Metal Manufacturing

Employment		
2009	Projected 2018	Occupation
12,690	12,400	Cutting, punching, and press machine setters, operators, and tenders, metal and plastic
18,400	18,700	First-line supervisors/managers of production and operating workers
14,460	14,100	Inspectors, testers, sorters, samplers, and weighers
14,370	14,800	Metal-refining furnace operators and tenders
13,140	13,600	Molding, coremaking, and casting machine setters, operators, and tenders, metal and plastic
13,980	12,000	Rolling machine setters, operators, and tenders, metal and plastic

Source: U.S. Bureau of Labor Statistics, Industries at a Glance, Occupational Employment Statistics and Employment Projections Program.

May, 2008. For rolling machine operators, the hourly wage was $16.40. For furnace operators, the wage was $17.47, and for laborers in stock and freight, the hourly wage was $10.89.

During its years as a world leader, the U.S. steel industry was highly unionized, and its members enjoyed excellent benefits, including health insurance, paid vacations, compensated sick leaves, and generous pension plans. During the last decades of the twentieth century and the first decade of the twenty-first, union membership declined, though it remained higher than the average across American industries. In 2008, approximately one-quarter of steel manufacturing workers were union members (compared to 14 percent in all manufacturing). As with production workers, the number of highly trained personnel, such as chemical engineers, has also declined over the past two decades, though earnings of such people in the steel industry tend to be higher than average.

RELATED RESOURCES FOR FURTHER RESEARCH

AMERICAN CHEMICAL SOCIETY
1155 16th St. NW
Washington, DC 20036
Tel: (800) 227-5558
Fax: (202) 872-6257
http://www.acs.org

AMERICAN INSTITUTE FOR INTERNATIONAL STEEL
3400 Westpark Dr., 2d Floor
McLean, VA 22102
Tel: (703) 245-8075
Fax: (703) 610-0215
http://www.aiis.org

AMERICAN INSTITUTE OF CHEMICAL ENGINEERS
3 Park Ave.
New York, NY 10016-5991
Tel: (800) 242-4363
Fax: (203) 775-5777
http://www.aice.org

MINERALS, METALS, AND MATERIALS SOCIETY
184 Thorn Hill Rd.
Warrendale, PA 15086-7514
Tel: (800) 759-4867
Fax: (724) 776-3770
http://www.tms.org

ABOUT THE AUTHOR

Robert J. Paradowski is a historian of science and technology who specializes in the history of chemistry with a particular emphasis on the life and work of Linus Pauling. He graduated summa cum laude from Spring Hill College, earned a master's degree in chemistry from Brandeis University, and received a Ph.D. in the history of science from the University of Wisconsin in 1972. He has taught at Brooklyn College, Eisenhower College, and the Rochester Institute of Technology, where he is a professor in the Department of Science, Technology, and Society/Public Policy.

FURTHER READING

Beddoes, J., and M. J. Bibby. *Principles of Metal Manufacturing Processes.* New York: John Wiley & Sons, 1999.

Creese, Robert C., et al. *Estimating and Costing for the Metal Manufacturing Industry.* Boca Raton, Fla.: CRC Press, 1992.

_____. *Introduction to Manufacturing Processes and Materials.* New York: Marcel Dekker, 1999.

Hoerr, John P. *And the Wolf Finally Came: The Decline of the American Steel Industry.* Pittsburgh: University of Pittsburgh Press, 1988.

Khare, Mukesh, et al. *Aluminium Smelting: Health, Environment and Engineering Perspectives.* Miami: Ian Randle, 2008.

Lankford, William T., Jr., et al. *The Making, Shaping, and Treating of Steel.* 11th ed. Pittsburgh: AISE Steel Foundation, 1998.

McDavid, Richard A., and Susan Echaore-McDavid. *Career Opportunities in Engineering.* New York: Ferguson, 2007.

Madar, Daniel. *Big Steel: Technology, Trade, and Survival in a Global Market.* Vancouver: University of British Columbia Press, 2009.

Peck, Merton J. *The World Aluminum Industry in a Changing Energy Era.* Baltimore: The Johns Hopkins University Press, 1988.

Preston, Richard. *American Steel: Hot Metal Men and the Resurrection of the Rust Belt.* New York: Prentice Hall, 1991.

Reutter, Mark. *Sparrows Point: Making Steel—The Rise and Ruin of American Industrial Might.* New York: Summit Books, 1988.

Rogers, Robert P. *An Economic History of the American Steel Industry.* New York: Routledge, 2009.

Tiffany, Paul A. *The Decline of American Steel: How Management, Labor, and Government Went Wrong.* New York: Oxford University Press, 1988.

U.S. Bureau of Labor Statistics. *Career Guide to Industries,* 2010-2011 ed. http://www.bls.gov/oco/cg.

U.S. Census Bureau. North American Industry Classification System (NAICS), 2007. http://www.census.gov/cgi-bin/sssd/naics/naicsrch?chart=2007.

U.S. Department of Commerce. International Trade Administration. Office of Trade and Industry Information. Industry Trade Data and Analysis. http://ita.doc.gov/td/industry/otea/OTII/OTII-index.html.

World Steel Association. *Steel Statistical Yearbook, 2009.* Brussels, Belgium: Committee on Economic Studies, 2010.

Mining Industry

©Brad Sauter/Dreamstime.com

INDUSTRY SNAPSHOT

General Industry: Natural Resources

Career Cluster: Agriculture, Food, and Natural Resources

Subcategory Industries: Metal Ore Mining; Nonmetallic Mineral Mining and Quarrying; Support Activities for Metal Mining; Support Activities for Nonmetallic Mineral Mining

Related Industries: Batteries and Fuel Cells Industry; Coal Mining Industry; Metals Manufacturing Industry; Nuclear Power Industry; Watches and Jewelry Industry

Annual Domestic Revenues: $69.6 billion USD (United States Geological Survey, 2007)

Annual International Revenues: $1.592 trillion USD (Research and Markets, 2008)

Annual Global Revenues: $1.661 trillion USD (Research and Markets, 2008)

NAICS Numbers: 2122-2123, 213114-213115

INDUSTRY DEFINITION

Summary

The mining industry extracts useful substances from the earth. These substances include metals, such as copper, silver, and gold, as well as nonmetals, such as gypsum, clay, and gemstones. Exploration determines whether the desired substances are present in commercial quantities. Miners then either use surface methods, such as dredging, stripping, quarrying, and open pits, for extraction or create underground shafts, tunnels, and large openings known as stopes to reach and remove ore. Miner safety is a major concern, as is the health of the environment. After a mine is closed, the area must be reclaimed for other purposes.

History of the Industry

Humans have been extracting valuable substances from the earth since the earliest times. Some of the first substances to be extracted were the harder nonmetallic ones, such as flint, chert, and quartz, which were used in making arrowheads and spear points. Softer nonmetallic substances, such as soapstone and limestone, were used for carving and making utensils. Clay was probably the basis for the first large-scale mineral industry. It could easily be shaped into bricks or tiles that were used for construction or writing. Quarrying of blocks of stone was another major industry involving nonmetallic

The ghost town of Bodi, California, (site of the Bodie gold mine) is a popular tourist destination.

substances. The Egyptian pyramids contain millions of blocks of dressed stone that average 2.5 tons apiece.

Decorative stones early attracted the attention of ancient peoples, and several nonmetallic minerals were used to ornament their clothes or burial garments. Color was the characteristic most valued, so that lapis lazuli (azure), carnelian (red), malachite (green), and turquoise (blue) were especially prized, although these are semiprecious stones and not of great value today. The first recorded underground mines were dug in search of gemstones: turquoise mines in the Sinai and emerald mines along the shore of the Red Sea, where the shafts were said to be 820 feet deep.

The first metals ancient people used were the so-called native metals. These are found in the pure or uncombined state. Gold attracted attention right away because it had a bright luster. Flakes or nuggets could easily be spotted in streams. Soon, gold was valued because it was malleable and could be shaped into jewelry and coins. Silver and copper were valued too, and some of the first underground metal mines were gold and silver mines in Cassandra, Greece, where miners drove tunnels into the rock along fractures known as faults. Bronze, made by melting tin with copper, was the preferred metal for weapons and implements in early times as it was rigid and did not corrode. Iron did not replace it until around 1000 B.C.E. because

of the difficulty of separating it from its ore, which requires smelting: The crushed ore must be melted with a flux, such as limestone or charcoal, to form a slag that accumulates at the top of the container, permitting the molten iron to be drained off.

During the Middle Ages, the variety of minerals that was mined increased, as did the sophistication of the ways of extracting the ore. As late as the 1500's, however, when the Conquistadores were searching for gold in Arizona, mining methods were still primitive. The mines were lit by candles that were set in wrought iron holders stuck in the tunnel walls. If the rock was soft, the miners used picks and shovels or pointed sticks to loosen it. If the rock was hard, black powder was used when available, or else fires were built against the tunnel walls, which were then doused with cold water to shatter the rock. Carts carried the ore out to rock-lined pits called arrastras, where donkeys dragged boulders around in circles, crushing the ore for processing. Today, thanks to the invention of the electric motor and modern steel-making methods, the mining industry has leaped forward with a host of new methods.

The Industry Today

The mining industry still performs the same functions it always has, namely extracting desirable substances from the surface of the earth or below it, but today's methods are more technologically sophisticated than they were in the past. No longer do lonely prospectors trudge into the wilderness with bedrolls strapped to their pack animals to explore for minerals. Today exploration is conducted by trained geologists, probably paired with mining engineers, who travel by four-wheeled vehicles or helicopters. A variety of exploration tools are available, including geologic maps, aerial photographs, and geophysical studies that show the bedrock's magnetic and electrical variations in the area to be explored. Once a likely mineral prospect has been located, the geologist and mining engineer evaluate the character, shape, size, grade, and prospective tonnage of the ore and estimate its value.

The mining methods that are used have changed as well. When the mineral is low-grade, it is generally mined by surface methods. Large pits called quarries are commonly used for mining stone. Flat, sedimentary deposits such as clay and phosphate are strip-mined, provided that the overburden that must be removed is not too thick. Extremely large,

near-surface accumulations, such as porphyry copper, are worked using huge open pits. The one at Bingham Canyon, Utah, is 4 kilometers (2.5 miles) wide. Here, the ore is excavated using power shovels that can scoop up 98 tons at a time. These move about on benches of rock that circle the pit and spiral downward to the pit's bottom. Placer mining is another type of surface operation. Giant dredges screen hundreds of cubic yards of gravel per hour as they plow up river beds in search of gold or diamonds.

Underground mining methods are used when a mineral of value is too deep to be worked by a surface pit. Entry into the ground is made by means of horizontal tunnels or vertical shafts. From these, workings are driven off laterally in various directions, following the traces of the ore. The workings may extend long distances outward from the entry point, and in the case of one South African gold mine, the total length of these workings is 800 kilometers (500 miles). After the rock is freed by blasting or drilling, it is drawn off through chutes lead-

The Bingham Kennecott copper mine near Salt Lake City. (©Gary Whitton/Dreamstime.com)

ing down to a train of small ore cars. These carry the ore to a hoisting shaft, where it is lifted to the mill above.

Just as mining methods have become more varied and sophisticated, the ways of separating minerals from their ores have become more sophisticated too. Gravity concentration is probably the oldest method, used since earliest times. Miners ran their crushed gold ore through sluice boxes lined with shrubs to collect the heavy particles and then freed the gold from the shrubs by shaking. A more sophisticated method was amalgamation, in which the particles of gold were allowed to combine with mercury, which was then burned off. Today, the milling of gold and silver uses a process known as cyanidation, similar to amalgamation, except that the medium used is potassium cyanide.

Minerals are also recovered from their ores by leaching with ammonia or acid, and water is used

The Mining Industry's Contribution to the U.S. Economy

Value Added	Amount
Gross domestic product	$48.8 billion
Gross domestic product	0.3%
Persons employed	224,000
Total employee compensation	$17.3 billion

Note: Includes all mining except petroleum and natural gas.
Source: U.S. Bureau of Economic Analysis. Data are for 2008.

to extract salt from underground deposits through drilled holes. Early methods of purifying iron ore by heating were revolutionized in 1856 by the invention of the Bessemer converter, which made possible the production of high-quality steel. Cop-

A train hauls coal. (©Brad Sauter/Dreamstime.com)

per is purified by electrolytic refining. Plates of crudely refined "blister" copper are placed in tanks of acid electrolyte and an electric current is passed through the solution, causing the blister copper to be dissolved off one plate (the anode) and be deposited as pure copper on the other (the cathode). Impurities drop off as sludge.

Reclamation of exhausted mines is now mandatory in the United States. Formerly, when a mine was exhausted, the owners simply walked away. Today, that is no longer possible. Stringent federal, state, and local environmental laws govern the closing of mining properties. Contamination of the groundwater and of the soil must be remedied, often at considerable expense. Shafts and tunnel openings must be closed up, and the tailings ponds must be revegetated after contaminants are removed. Even the open pits must be turned into lakes or reshaped with waste rock, on which fresh soil is placed with seed mixtures to start new plant growth.

INDUSTRY MARKET SEGMENTS

Mining companies may be small, family businesses or massive multinational ventures. They may concentrate on a single substance (or a single mine), or they may mine any substance of value on the open market.

Small Businesses

The smallest mines are usually one-family operations, where the owners do the mining themselves, with the help of a few employees. Frequently, the mine is open to tourists as an additional source of revenue. Good examples of these mines are the gemstone mines of North Carolina and the old-time gold mines in Colorado.

Potential Annual Earnings Scale. According to the U.S. Bureau of Labor Statistics (BLS), in 2009 the average overall salary of all workers in the metal ore mining industry was $53,010 and the average overall salary of all workers in the nonmetallic mineral mining industry was $40,730. In the metal ore mining industry, on average, mining and geological engineers earned $78,780, construction and extraction workers earned $49,080, construction and extraction supervisors earned $70,900,

and general and operations managers earned $145,800. In the nonmetallic mineral mining industry, on average, mining and geological engineers earned $72,040, construction and extraction workers earned $39,660, construction and extraction supervisors earned $58,900, and general and operations managers earned $99,940.

Clientele Interaction. If the mine is tourist-oriented, personal attention to visitors is essential, especially if visits to the gift shop, museum, cafeteria, and other attractions are anticipated. The guides who lead the visitors through the mine must be friendly and able to answer a variety of questions about the mining operation. They will also have to be watchful of small children, as both surface and underground mines have numerous safety hazards. If the mine offers visitors the opportunity to dig for minerals on their own, which is common in the gemstone mines of North Carolina, employees need to be available to answer questions, offer instructions, and help visitors identify their mineral finds.

Amenities, Atmosphere, and Physical Grounds. Small mines are generally located in remote areas, often with an attractive mountain setting. Part of the charm of the tourist-oriented ones is that they are so unlike the urban environment from which their visitors come. The approach to the mine will be a narrow dirt road that winds up into wooded hills. At the mine itself, the look is always rustic: signs are hand-painted, the parking lot is unpaved, and the buildings have a weath-

Inputs Consumed by the Mining Industry

Input	Value
Energy	$8.5 billion
Materials	$22.9 billion
Purchased services	$15.3 billion
Total	$46.7 billion

Note: Includes all mining except petroleum and natural gas.
Source: U.S. Bureau of Economic Analysis. Data are for 2008.

ered appearance. All the employees wear old clothes or jeans.

The tourist-oriented gold mines in Colorado are generally entered through a dark opening in a rock face. After a tour of the underground workings, visitors may be given the opportunity to pan for gold in a nearby stream, or to visit the gift shop, where small rock samples and various books are for sale. The gemstone mines in North Carolina offer more amenities for tourists. After a tour of the mine, which may be underground or just a water-filled pit from which gravel is extracted, visitors can purchase a bucket and scratch for gems on a hill-side covered with loose rock. There is generally a gift shop and sometimes a museum as well, with a display of minerals, old mining equipment, and antique tools.

Gemstone mines may also have a lapidary shop, where a visitor's finds can be turned into attractive cut stones and jewelry. Wire-wrap courses may even be offered. And if the mine has fluorescent minerals, there will be a black-light exhibit and perhaps even a black-light tour of the mine. Several of the North Carolina gemstone mines have evolved into sophisticated commercial operations. They have Web pages, flyers displayed at tourist centers around the state, and offer picnic areas and campgrounds with bathrooms and hot showers. A number of the gemstone mines even have online stores.

Typical Number of Employees. The number of employees working in a small mine will depend on whether the mine is tourist-oriented or not. Some of the gold mines in Colorado are operated by their owners without assistants, and visitors must ring a bell or honk the car horn to attract attention if the owner is underground giving other visitors a tour. These gold mines are seasonal because of heavy winter snows, so if owners need tour guides, they will hire high school students. The tourist-oriented gemstone mines in states such as North Carolina have more employees and may operate on a year-round basis. Full-time personnel, such as the gift shop manager, will probably be family members. High school or college students will be hired in the summer when the number of tourists is large, along with a few local adults who can help visitors identify their finds and perform routine maintenance work.

Traditional Geographic Locations. Mines are located where minerals exist to be mined. Most small mines are located in remote areas, often with attractive mountain scenery. Few people may live in the vicinity of the mine.

Pros of Working for a Small Mining Company. The owners and workers in a small mine in many ways resemble an extended family, with persons often being related to each other. This means that the work environment is a collegial one where occasional absences and minor mistakes can be overlooked, and if there is an accident or other misfortune, people can be expected to rally round supportively. Because the owner has total control of the operation, the owner will probably be on the premises daily, which provides an opportunity to ensure that instructions are carried out. Some business and financial skills are needed, of course, as well as knowledge about property maintenance and the legal requirements that come with having an income-producing property with paid employees. If the owner lacks these skills, people will have to be paid to assist with the operation of the mine.

Cons of Working for a Small Mining Company. The owner of a small mine must be prepared to mediate conflicts among the employees, as well as to deal with issues that arise in connection with visitors to the mine. If an employee does not show up one day, the mine owner may have to do that employee's job, whether it is acting as a tour guide, serving as gift shop cashier, or filling in as an amateur plumber. In larger mining operations, managers are available on several levels to handle the various operations related to the business, but in small mines, owners are responsible for all aspects of the business themselves.

One of the major problems that the owner of a tourist-oriented mine has in trying to operate the mine profitably is the matter of seasonality. The people who visit the mine come as a vacation activity, and most people take their vacations in the summer. Owners of tourist-oriented mines in Colorado must conduct all their business during an interval of three to four months, and once the snow starts to fly they will have to board up and find some other activity to occupy their time until spring. Although some of the gemstone mines in North Carolina announce that they are open "year round," the number of visitors that they get in the winter is bound to be small. Owners will have to decide if it is cost-effective to keep the mine open for so little business.

Costs

Payroll and Benefits: To keep costs low, the tourist-oriented small mines hire all their workers on a part-time basis and at local hourly wages. Since most workers are generally hired only for the summer months, benefits such as sick leave and vacation time will not be expected.

Supplies: Office supplies will be required, including a cash register, telephone, and computer. Cleaning supplies and maintenance items are needed too. If there is a gift shop, it will have to be restocked periodically, and sodas and snacks should be available for purchase by visitors.

External Services: Tourist-oriented small mines may contract computer maintenance, credit card processing, vending machine maintenance and stocking, and portable toilet services.

Utilities: Electricity will be required if there is an office and a gift shop, and to provide lights in the mine if there are underground tours, but if the mine is small and far from town, an on-site generator may serve this need. Telephone and Internet access are also needed if the mine is tourist-oriented. Water can come from the mine's own well, and either portable toilets or a bathroom with its own septic tank can deal with waste.

Taxes: In addition to property taxes, small mines need to pay any applicable local, state, and federal taxes. Sales taxes on items sold in the gift shop must be collected as well.

Midsize Businesses

Midsize mining companies will generally have a market capitalization of somewhere between $50 million and $500 million. The company may operate several mines, but these will usually all be located in the same geographic area. The headquarters office for these companies is invariably in Vancouver, Canada, and the company's stock is always listed on the Toronto Stock Exchange.

Potential Annual Earnings Scale. According to the BLS, in 2009 the average overall salary of all workers in the metal ore mining industry was $53,010 and the average overall salary of all workers in the nonmetallic mineral mining industry was $40,730. In the metal ore mining industry, on average, mining and geological engineers earned $78,780, construction and extraction workers earned $49,080, construction and extraction supervisors earned $70,900, and general and operations managers earned $145,800. In the nonmetallic mineral mining industry, on average, mining and geological engineers earned $72,040, construction and extraction workers earned $39,660, construction and extraction supervisors earned $58,900, and general and operations managers earned $99,940.

Clientele Interaction. Midsize mining companies pay a great deal of attention to their current and prospective stockholders because they depend on their interest to keep the price of the company's stock high. They also hope to generate funds from them through stock offerings to pay the costs of developing new mining prospects. Toward this end, company officials such as the chief executive officer (CEO) and the chief financial officer (CFO) tour the country giving presentations known as "road shows." These are company-paid luncheons or dinners at exclusive restaurants in cities where current or prospective investors might be found. Boston, New York, Palm Beach, Miami, Houston, and San Francisco are favored. Investment brokers are invited to the luncheons and often bring their wealthy clients with them. No expense is spared. While the guests dine on filet mignon or salmon, company officials present illustrated updates on their companies in hopes that the brokers will encourage their clients to invest.

Amenities, Atmosphere, and Physical Grounds. Most midsize mining companies maintain corporate offices in Vancouver, Canada, so this will be the place where the company's officers live. Because most of these companies' investors do not live in Vancouver and have no plans to visit it, their corporate offices do not need to be luxurious. Rather, these offices are workplaces where officers can catch up on their mail, direct operations, and interact with one another as they plan future strategies. As the officers are on the road much of the time, support staff manage the business while they are gone.

One or more additional offices will also be maintained in the field, close to the mining operations. A company's investors are never going to see these offices either, so they are unpretentious places where geologists and mining engineers come and go in hard hats and muddy boots as they supervise the company's day-to-day operations. These operations tend to be in far-off locations, and company personnel may need helicopters to reach these places until the company puts roads in.

Typical Number of Employees. The corporate staff of midsize mining companies is generally small: a CEO, a CFO, perhaps a chief operating officer (COO), maybe one or two vice presidents, and a company secretary. There will also be a handful of directors, paid in stock options, whose role is to provide advice. A support staff will be required for the Vancouver office, and at the field offices there will be geologists, mining engineers, and supervisory personnel. The rest of the company's employees will be hard-hat workers. In total, the company may have just a few hundred employees.

Traditional Geographic Locations. For years, Vancouver has been the place where the corporate offices of midsize mining companies are located. This is probably because it is the largest city in western Canada and most of the country's mines are in the western part of the country. The field offices of midsize mining companies will be wherever the minerals that the company is looking for are found.

Pros of Working for a Midsize Mining Company. For the officials of midsize mining operations, a major attraction of the job is the possibility of a large financial payoff when the company is finally sold. Each official owns company stock, often purchased for just a few pennies a share. Stock options, granted in lieu of salary increases, increase their holdings each year. The typical midsize mining company is bought out by a major mining company after a few years, and each company official then pockets a windfall. After that, they may go on to join other midsize companies and repeat the process. The pattern of waiting to be taken over has become so common that many midsize mining companies simply stake out proved reserves and then wait to be taken over without ever mining a single load of ore.

Cons of Working for a Midsize Mining Company. Mineral prospects have to be located and then evaluated by mining companies. If these prospects are located in foreign countries, contacts with their governments must be made and matters such as royalties agreed upon. Environmental concerns must be addressed too, no matter where the prospect is located, and good relations must be established with the local people who will be affected by the mining operation. Once the operation be-

gins, facilities must be built, equipment purchased, and specialists and hard-hat workers employed. There are also matters to be addressed back at company headquarters: salaries, loans, financing, shareholder relations, and government relations. The Sarbanes-Oxley Act of 2002 established new standards of accountability for companies in the United States that have greatly increased expenses.

Costs

Payroll and Benefits: Midsize mining companies pay their officers minimal salaries, augmented by generous stock options, in order to keep costs down. Full-time workers generally receive standard benefits.

Supplies: In addition to the usual supplies for the home and field offices, midsize mining companies have significant expenses for vehicles, especially of the all-terrain type. Drilling rigs may be required for exploration, and underground mining brings new costs. A helicopter may also be required.

External Services: Midsize companies may contract computer maintenance auditors, legal counsel, a transfer agent and registrar to deal with stockholder issues, and public relations firms to assist with new stock issues and setting up road shows.

Utilities: The needs of midsize mining companies for utilities are the same as those for other companies their size, except that electronic communications are especially important because of the widespread nature of the company's activities. On-site power supplies for mining operations may be needed too.

Taxes: In addition to paying local, state, and federal income and property taxes in the country where the home office is located, companies may have to pay taxes in the country or countries where the field offices and the mining operations are conducted. They may also have to pay excise taxes on minerals removed, land leases on land occupied, and other industry-specific taxes and fees.

Large Businesses

Large mining companies are global behemoths, with market capitalizations that often exceed $100 billion. They run far-flung mining operations spread across several continents and produce a number of different mineral products. Company headquarters may be located anywhere on the globe, and their stocks are traded on leading stock exchanges. The number of employees is usually in the tens of thousands.

Potential Annual Earnings Scale. According to the BLS, in 2009 the average overall salary of all workers in the metal ore mining industry was $53,010 and the average overall salary of all workers in the nonmetallic mineral mining industry was $40,730. In the metal ore mining industry, on average, mining and geological engineers earned $78,780, construction and extraction workers earned $49,080, construction and extraction supervisors earned $70,900, and general and operations managers earned $145,800. In the nonmetallic mineral mining industry, on average, mining and geological engineers earned $72,040, construction and extraction workers earned $39,660, construction and extraction supervisors earned $58,900, and general and operations managers earned $99,940.

Clientele Interaction. Because the big mining companies are so large, they will interact with many different types of people, such as purchasers of their mineral products, individuals who live around their mining operations, and governmental representatives from the states or countries where they are located. Relations with stockholders are fairly routine; the annual meeting is attended by only a tiny fraction of the stockholders and management usually gets its way when critical items are up for a vote.

Amenities, Atmosphere, and Physical Grounds. A large mining company's operations are spread around the globe, and there may be more than one corporate office. This office will be a handsome place in a prestige building, always located in a major city. Senior officers will spend most of their time here, providing overall direction for the company's far-flung enterprises. The entertainment of prospective business partners or purchasers of the company's products will be a major activity for the top company officials, and for this purpose they will need fine restaurants, a beautiful home in which to entertain, and access to a country club that offers golf as one of its amenities.

Field operations will be centered around the company's mines. These may be surface operations, with enormous open pits, or underground mines with miles of tunnels. If the mine is a metal mine, nearby there will probably be a concentrating plant to enrich the ore, a smelter to remove the waste material from it, and a refinery to purify the metal for sale.

The mine itself may be in a remote and rugged place. Freeport-McMoRan's Grasberg Mine, the largest gold mine in the world, is located at a height of over 4,000 meters (14,000 feet) atop a mountain in Papua, Indonesia. Working conditions in such faraway places can be harsh. Grasberg is cold—a glacier is nearby—and many people experience altitude sickness at that elevation. There are other disadvantages as well. Two workers died in landslides in 2000 and two in a 2003 slide; five were also injured in the second slide, and six were reported missing. Separatist rebels are also a problem. Three teachers employed by Freeport, including two Americans, were killed in an ambush on the company road in 2003. Three more died in two separate incidents on the same road in 2009, and six were wounded in an ambush on January 24, 2010.

Typical Number of Employees. The number of employees in large mining companies can be huge. Freeport-McMoRan has thirty thousand, and Rio Tinto has thirty-five thousand. Most of these are hard-hat workers. Executive management staffs remain fairly small.

Traditional Geographic Locations. The corporate headquarters for large mining companies can be anywhere in the world, perhaps near the company's first mines, or in a major financial center where the company can obtain financing. Field offices are always located near the company's mines.

Pros of Working for a Large Mining Company. For corporate officers, large mining businesses offer highly paid careers with excellent fringe and retirement benefits. Officers and their families enjoy affluent lifestyles in major metropolitan settings with fine health care and excellent schools. Similar advantages apply for the rest of the corporate office personnel, but on a smaller scale. Managers of field operations may be able to create a comfortable lifestyle for themselves, but for average workers in the company's far-flung operations, the biggest advantage is a fairly reliable job with an adequate salary and some benefits. If the company provides housing, a store, and other amenities, that will be even better.

Cons of Working for a Large Mining Company. For a corporate officer, the stress of the job can be considerable. Huge sums of money are at risk every day, and mishaps due to poor judgment or unanticipated economic events may cost officers their jobs. Directors represent stockholders and can terminate CEOs' tenures at any time. Employees at lower levels may encounter job stresses too. A large mining company is not a supportive, family-type operation. Supervisors can be ruthless because their overall concern is for the "bottom line." Added to a lack of job security at all levels are the dangers that personnel may face. Corporate officers and managers often travel to remote locations by company jets and mishaps are not unheard of. Hard-hat workers perish in industrial accidents.

Costs

Payroll and Benefits: Pay scales in large mining businesses are lush for the corporate elite, providing generous bonuses and incentives awards in addition to a salary that may be in the millions. Pay scales for middle-level employees and mine workers will be standard for the industry, with the usual fringe benefits, such as vacation time and sick leave. The skyrocketing cost of health insurance has been a growing concern for all companies and this may result in gradual cutbacks in these benefits in the years ahead.

Supplies: Large mining companies require a variety of supplies for the offices and the mines. Each phase of the operation has its special needs. Exploration geologists need helicopters to reach remote destinations and rigs to drill for underground samples. Surface mines need huge power shovels and giant trucks. Underground mines need mechanized drilling equipment and plenty of explosives. Processing of metal ores requires concentrators, smelters, and refineries, each one a large and complex operation in itself. There has to be a company jet so the corporate elite can travel in style.

Utilities: The power needs of large mining companies are huge, especially in the underground and ore-processing operations. Telephone, cable, and Internet needs are complex too, in order for the officials at corporate headquarters to keep in touch with distant operations.

Taxes: Large companies must pay local, state, federal, and international income and property taxes, as well as any applicable excise taxes, land leases, and so on.

The organizational structure of the mining industry depends greatly on the size of the operation. In the smallest mines, the owner may handle all the tasks associated with the operation or may be assisted by family members and a few part-time workers. As mining companies increase in size, however, more and more people will be required to do a greater variety of tasks.

The following umbrella categories apply to the organizational structure of businesses in the mining industry:

- Executive Management
- Administrative Support
- Information Technology
- Exploration
- Surface Mines
- Underground Mines
- Mineral Processing
- Ancillary Job Roles

Executive Management

A relatively small core of experienced executives will direct and coordinate the daily operations of the company. Their role is to oversee the various subdivisions, many of which may be conducted in other countries, ensure that the company is doing well financially, set goals for the company's future development, and see that these goals are carried out. Most of the executives will have degrees in business administration, marketing, accounting, or related fields. Their compensation will be generous, with high salaries, stock option grants, and incentive awards for reaching certain targets. They will also have a variety of perks, such as country-club memberships, travel allowances, company cars, and use of the company jet. A board of directors, which is elected by the stockholders, is the ultimate source of authority for the company. The board meets regularly, picks the company's CEO, and deals with such matters as the CEO's compensation and the award of stock options to officers. A large mining company's executives will have salaries from hundreds of thousands of dollars a year to over a million dollars a year for those in the highest positions.

Executive management occupations may include the following:

- Chief Executive Officer (CEO)
- Chief Financial Officer (CFO)
- Chief Operating Officer (COO)
- President
- Vice President of Exploration
- Vice President of Investor Relations
- Secretary-Treasurer

Administrative Support

Because senior officials are out of the office much of the time, either dealing with local issues or visiting the company's mining operations, a large and highly trained administrative staff is needed to manage the headquarters and regional offices while they are gone. There will be executive secretaries and administrative assistants for company officials, and an office supervisor to direct the large number of clerks, interns, and other personnel doing data entry and other routine chores. Bookkeepers, accountants, and auditors will be on the payroll, and the company will either employ a high-priced legal team or have lawyers on staff. Someone will have to deal with stockholder relations and send the necessary information to a transfer agent. In addition, the company has to communicate its story to the public, so there will be a public relations or media office to send out press releases about company doings and prepare the company's annual report and other publications. Administrative support staff will be employed full time, with generous fringe benefits. Salaries will range from $40,000 a year to $110,000 a year depending on the position.

Administrative support occupations may include the following:

- Office Supervisor/Manager
- Executive Secretary
- Administrative Assistant
- Bookkeeper
- Accountant
- Auditor
- Public Relations Officer
- Sales Manager
- Purchasing Manager
- Clerk

Information Technology

Computer specialists are needed to build the company's information technology (IT) networks and maintain the company's Web site. High-speed and protected networks are required throughout the company, especially if there are numerous overseas operations. Senior officials and managers need to be able to communicate with one another on a moment's notice regarding developments requiring urgent attention. CEOs may have to reach directors regarding possible takeover threats, and geologists want to inform their supervisors of discoveries before other companies get there first. In the field and overseas, handheld devices are useful, allowing personnel to read their e-mail while away from their desks; information can also be recorded on these devices for later retrieval. In the mines and at ore-processing operations, such devices can enable personnel to digitally record data as procedures take place or send pictures of what is happening to superiors at the office. All these systems need constant attention, so IT personnel are employed full time. Salaries range between $50,000 and $80,000 per year, with excellent benefits.

IT occupations may include the following:

- Information Systems Manager
- Network Administrator
- Software Engineer
- Computer Programmer
- Computer Support Specialist

Exploration

The exploration for new mineral deposits is an essential operation for a mining company because natural resources are not renewable. Once they are removed from the ground, they are gone forever and must be replaced by new reserves elsewhere if the company is to remain viable. This means that the exploration for new mineral prospects is an ongoing activity for mineral companies, and a staff of geologists and other trained personnel is required to perform this activity. Geologists need to study maps and published reports about the area to which they are going before going into the field, and they must collect the necessary equipment and supplies. If the location is in a foreign country, they

OCCUPATION SPECIALTIES

Mining and Geological Engineers

Specialty	Responsibilities
Design engineers	Design mining and oil-field machinery.
Mine safety engineers	Inspect underground or open-pit mining areas and train mine personnel to ensure compliance with state and federal laws and accepted mining practices designed to prevent mine accidents.
Mining and oil well equipment research engineers	Conduct research to develop improved mining and oil-well equipment.
Mining and oil-field equipment test engineers	Conduct tests on mining and oil-field machinery and equipment.

need to learn about the culture and obtain permission from the foreign government before departing. Frequently, the location they are heading for will be so remote that the only way to reach it is by helicopter. When they arrive, they may camp at the site or return each night to the nearest settlement. Drilling equipment may be called for if the prospect is underground and surveyors may be needed to map the prospect's dimensions. When the potential value of the prospect has been determined, they will send their findings to corporate executives who will decide whether to proceed with mining. Salaries for exploration personnel will range from $40,000 to $110,000 per year, depending on the job description.

Exploration occupations may include the following:

- Exploration Manager
- Geologist
- Geological Assistant
- Mining Engineer
- Earth Driller
- Surveyor
- Drafter
- Helicopter Pilot

Surface Mines

Open-pit mines can be huge. The Bingham Canyon copper mine in Utah is 4 kilometers (2.5 miles) across and 1.2 kilometers (0.75 mile) deep.

It is said to be the largest human-made excavation on Earth, and astronauts say they are able to see it as they pass overhead in the space station. The mine is roughly circular, with a series of benches that spiral downward to the pit bottom. Ore is loosened from the bench walls by drilling holes and blasting the ore out with explosives. Several blasts take place each day. Following each blast, giant electric power shovels that can scoop up to 98 tons at a time move into the area and load the broken rock on huge haul trucks that cost $3 million apiece. These trucks wind down to the ore crusher where the pieces of rock are reduced to the approximate size of grapefruits. These are then loaded on a conveyor that slopes down to a refinery at the mouth of the canyon. The conveyor belt at Bingham Canyon has a total length of 8 kilometers (5 miles). Salaries for workers in surface mines range from $40,000 to $110,000 per year depending on the position.

Surface mine occupations may include the following:

- Surface Mine Supervisor
- Blast Hole Driller
- Explosives Worker
- Electric Power Shovel Operator
- Haul Truck Driver
- Mobile Heavy Equipment Mechanic
- In-Pit Crushing Machine Operator
- Conveyor Operator

Underground Mines

The layout of an underground mine is complex. Entrance is provided by means of a horizontal tunnel if the operation is at ground level or by a vertical shaft if the ore is deeper down. From the shaft, horizontal passageways called workings are driven laterally at 160-meter (100-foot) intervals so that miners can follow the veins of ore. In the TauTona Mine in South Africa, there are 800 kilometers (500 miles) of these workings.

Mining methods in underground mines depend on the type of mineral being mined. If the mineral is soft, it may be sliced off the tunnel walls or roof by scaling machines. When the bedrock is hard, holes must be drilled and the ore blasted out. By working the vein upward, it may be possible to have the loosened ore slide down through a chute into the car of an ore train known as a "tram." The tram then carries the ore to a hoist where it is lifted to the surface in "skips" for processing. Timbers may be used to hold up the mine roof as the ore is removed. The deepest underground mines in the world are the South African gold mines. The TauTona Mine is the deepest of all, with a depth of 3.9 kilometers (12,792 feet). Earth temperatures in this mine are extreme. On the rock face in the lowest workings, the temperature is 60 degrees Celsius (140 degrees Fahrenheit), and air-conditioning is required to bring mine temperatures down to a level of 28 degrees Celsius (82.4 degrees Fahrenheit). Underground mining is a dangerous business, and four men died at this mine in 2008. Salaries in underground mines will vary from $40,000 to $110,000 per year, depending on the position.

Underground mine occupations may include the following:

- Underground Mine Supervisor
- Mining Machine Operator
- Mobile Drill Operator
- Explosives Worker
- Excavating Machine Operator
- Loading Machine Operator

An excavator works at a mine. (©Sergey Milovidov/Dreamstime.com)

- Heating, Ventilation, and Air-
    Conditioning (HVAC) Specialist
- Tram Operator
- Hoist Operator

Mineral Processing

Processing methods in the mining industry vary according to the mineral being mined. In some mines, such as those where clay is dug, the mineral is ready to be sent to the consumer, with appropriate packaging, as soon as it comes out of the ground. In metal mines, processing is more complex. When the crushed ore leaves the mine, further reduction in size by grinding may be required. The powdered ore goes to concentrators to remove waste rock, which is known as "gangue." Concentration methods for the various minerals vary from hand sorting for gemstones and other fragile minerals, to gravity separation for heavy minerals, various flotation methods, or the dissolving of the ore in fluids like potassium cyanide, mercury, and acid. Magnetic and electrostatic concentration methods are used. For metals that are tightly bonded to other elements, additional processing known as smelting may be required. Here the ore is melted in a blast or reverberatory furnace with a flux, which combines with the unwanted elements to form a floating slag. The metal is then drained off at the base of the furnace. Even after smelting, copper must be purified by electrolytic refining in order to produce a product suitable for industrial use. Salaries for personnel in mineral processing will vary from $40,000 to $110,000 per year, depending on the position.

Mineral processing occupations may include the following:

- Concentration Mill Supervisor
- Smelter Supervisor
- Refinery Supervisor
- Separating Machine Operator
- Metal-Refining Furnace Operator
- Power Plant Operator
- Industrial Machinery Mechanic
- Inspector

Ancillary Job Roles

Mining companies require a number of departments that are ancillary to the administrative staff. One is a department of human resources, which is responsible for personnel matters such as hiring and dismissal of employees, their overall supervision, and financial matters affecting employees such as payroll, preparation of W-2 forms, health insurance, benefits, and retirement. Complaints by employees about unfair treatment or sexual harassment are handled by the department of human resources as well. The company will also employ a labor relations specialist to deal with union matters and a compliance officer to be sure that company operations are in accordance with federal, state, and local laws.

A security office will be needed to watch over the company's various operations. Much confidential information is kept in company files, especially at the headquarters office, and must be protected; overseas operations may face threats from local agitators who may oppose the company for political reasons. Freeport-McMoRan's employees have been fired on several times at its Grasberg mine in Indonesia. Buildings and grounds is another important ancillary department. The company's image is important, and facilities must look well, especially the headquarters office. Salaries for these personnel will vary from $30,000 to $110,000 per year, depending on the position.

Ancillary occupations may include the following:

- Human Resources Director
- Labor Relations Specialist
- Compliance Officer
- Security Director
- Security Officer
- Director of Buildings and Grounds
- Maintenance and Repair Worker

INDUSTRY OUTLOOK

Overview

The outlook for this industry shows it to be in decline. This is especially true for the mining of metals, which is the predominant segment of the industry. The BLS predicts that employment in the metal mining industry will fall by 10 percent between 2008 and 2018. On the other hand, employment in the mining of nonmetals, which is the smaller segment of the industry, is expected to be stable.

The predicted employment drop in metal mining can be attributed to several factors. One is the rapid increase in metal prices during the years prior to 2008. The higher prices encouraged metal producers to expand their exploration efforts and to ramp up production. In many locations, older mines, which had been closed previously because they were uneconomical, were put back into production. A good example of this was the announcement on January 22, 2008, by the American Bonanza Gold Corporation of Vancouver, British Columbia, that it was going to reopen Arizona's Copperstone Mine. This mine had been closed in 1993 because it was deemed uneconomical based on the price of gold at that time. The company stated that the reason for reopening the mine in 2008 was that the price of gold had reached $900 per ounce. As prices for gold and other leading metals level off in the years ahead, it is believed that companies will slow down their hiring or start cutting back. This, in turn, will reduce the demand for new employees in the years leading up to 2018.

Another factor that will keep employment low in metal mining is that mining companies can no longer ignore environmental concerns. The days when a large company could dig a hole 1.6 kilometers (1 mile) across and 0.8 kilometers (0.5 mile) deep without permits are over. Not only did those companies create massive eyesores, but also the waste rock was simply dumped in the area surrounding the mine, and chemical effluents from the processing plant flowed into the nearest river. Today, numerous regulations define the steps needed before any kind of mining operation can begin in the United States; similar regulations are beginning to affect foreign operations as well.

An article in *The New York Times* for December 27, 2005, describes the environmental impact that Freeport-McMoRan's Grasberg Mine in Indonesia has had on one of the world's last untouched landscapes. About 1 percent of what is dug out of the mine each day is copper and gold. The remaining 99 percent is waste rock that has to be disposed of.

PROJECTED EMPLOYMENT FOR SELECTED OCCUPATIONS

Mining and Quarrying

Employment		
2009	Projected 2018	Occupation
10,850	10,400	Continuous mining machine operators
11,420	13,700	Excavating and loading machine and dragline operators
215,500	179,400	Extraction workers
8,450	23,900	First-line supervisors/ managers of construction trades and extraction workers
23,090	31,400	Operating engineers and other construction equipment operators
13,820	24,200	Truck drivers, heavy and tractor-trailer

Source: U.S. Bureau of Labor Statistics, Industries at a Glance, Occupational Employment Statistics and Employment Projections Program. Data are for 2008.

The mine generates nearly 700,000 tons of this waste rock daily, and the only place to put it is around the mine itself. In 2005, the last year for which accurate figures are available, this waste rock had accumulated to a depth of 275 meters (900 feet) in some places and covered 8 square kilometers (3 square miles) of formerly pristine mountain valleys.

The crushed ore from the mine is in the form of a slurry composed of ore mixed with water, and it goes down a river valley to the concentrators for processing before it is shipped to the smelters. Chemically charged waste from the concentrators, with the color and consistency of wet cement, is then spread as "tailings" over 230 square kilometers (90 square miles) of former wetlands around the river mouth. The levees surrounding the tailings ponds are 21 meters (70 feet) high and will soon be overtopped.

Residents say that the river no longer has any fish in it and that drinking water from their wells has a greenish color. The company states that it is following the country's environmental regulations to the letter, but the country is a 9.3 percent stockholder in the mine and the country's soldiers are the armed guards that keep unwanted visitors away.

Another factor that will contribute to the predicted drop in employment opportunities for workers in metal mining is that many existing mines are now approaching exhaustion. New mineral prospects are needed to replace them, and these are becoming more difficult to find. In addition, the metal mining industry has always provided poor returns for stockholders because metals prices are so cyclical. Freeport-McMoRan earned $2.9 billion in 2006, earned $6.5 billion in 2007 when metal prices peaked, had a loss of $12.7 billion in 2008 when they collapsed, and then earned $6.5 billion in 2009 when prices rose again. Such volatility makes it difficult for mining companies to raise money for new undertakings.

The BLS predicts that employment opportunities in nonmetallic mining will remain stable between 2008 and 2018. The nonmetallic minerals that are now being mined on a large scale are sand, gravel, and crushed stone for road building and construction. Large deposits of these substances are available, and provided that the economy remains stable through 2018, these deposits are more than adequate for anticipated needs. Nonmetallic minerals are bulky and heavy, so that their transportation costs are high. This means they are used locally and not shipped overseas. As a result, their prices are not subject to the wide swings of international markets. This makes for stability of prices until 2018 and anticipated stable job opportunities in the industry.

Employment Advantages

Even though employment in metal mining is predicted to decline between 2008 and 2018, segments of this industry still offer interesting opportunities. The prospect of "striking it rich" is always present when working for a midsize mining company. These companies are constantly prospecting for new mineral deposits, and company stock, which has often been bought for pennies a share or received as an option grant, may suddenly be worth a large sum if a significant metal find is made.

Larger mining companies offer interesting job opportunities too. Persons employed in exploration work, such as geologists and mining engineers, will visit remote and scenic areas in search of new mineral finds, so these jobs are attractive for the adventure-minded with a love of nature. Opportunities for supervisory jobs are also a possibility. Because of retirements, supervisory personnel will be needed at all levels in the mining industry during the years ahead. This will give capable individuals at the lower levels an opportunity to move ahead to more challenging and financially remunerative positions.

Job opportunities in the mining of nonmetallic substances such as sand, gravel, and crushed stone are generally part time as these substances are mined from surface operations that may close down when demand is slack, or during the winter months if the climate is severe. Part-time work is also characteristic of the tourist-oriented gem mines, so both fields are well suited to the financial needs of high school and college students.

Annual Earnings

According to the United States Geological Survey's Minerals Yearbook, the total nonfuel mineral industry earnings for the United States in 2007 were $69.6 billion, up 6 percent from the $65.5 billion earned by the industry in 2006. These figures are deceptive, however, for 2007 was a boom year for commodity prices. Subsequently, in 2008 and 2009, commodity prices collapsed during a global economic recession. Freeport-McMoRan's 2009 earnings were down 15.5 percent from its earnings in 2008, for example.

During 2010, world economies began to show signs of a recovery. Hopefully, this will be reflected in improved commodity prices and in higher earnings for both the nonmetal and metal mining companies. Such improvement should, in turn, result in more favorable prospects for job opportunities in these industries.

RELATED RESOURCES FOR FURTHER RESEARCH

American Institute of Mining,
  Metallurgical, and Petroleum Engineers
8307 Shaffer Parkway

Littleton, CO 80127-0013
Tel: (303) 948-4255
Fax: (303) 948-4260
http://www.aimehq.org

NATIONAL MINING ASSOCIATION
101 Constitution Ave. NW, Suite 500 East
Washington, DC 20001-2133
Tel: (202) 463-2600
Fax: (202) 463-2666
http://www.nma.org

NATIONAL STONE, SAND, AND GRAVEL
ASSOCIATION
1605 King St.
Alexandria, VA 22314
Tel: (703) 525-8788
Fax: (703) 525-8788
http://www.nssga.org

ABOUT THE AUTHOR

Donald W. Lovejoy holds an A.B. degree cum laude in geology from Harvard College and A.M. and Ph.D. degrees in the same subject from Columbia University. He is associate professor and coordinator of the Department of Earth Science/Oceanography at Palm Beach Atlantic University in West Palm Beach, Florida. Among his many publications are reports on the Rip Van Winkle Gold Mine near Elko, Nevada, the Carrefour Raymond marble near Jacmel, Haiti, and the coquina and shell rock deposits found along the east coast of Florida.

FURTHER READING

Ali, Saleem H. *Treasures of the Earth: Need, Greed, and a Sustainable Future.* New Haven, Conn.: Yale University Press, 2009.

Bateman, Alan M. *Economic Mineral Deposits.* 2d ed. New York: John Wiley & Sons, 1950.

Bishop, A. C., A. R. Woolley, and W. R. Hamilton. *Guide to Minerals, Rocks, and Fossils.* Buffalo, N.Y.: Firefly Books, 2005.

Bouquet, Tim, and Byron Ousey. *Cold Steel: The Multi-Billion-Dollar Battle for a Global Empire.* Toronto: Key Porter Books, 2008.

Burke, D. Barlow, and Robert E. Beck. *The Law and Regulation of Mining: Minerals to Energy.* Durham, N.C.: Carolina Academic Press, 2010.

Dietrich, R. V., and Brian J. Skinner. *Gems, Granites, and Gravels: Knowing and Using Rocks and Minerals.* New York: Cambridge University Press, 1990.

Erlichman, Howard J. *Conquest, Tribute, and Trade: The Quest for Precious Metals and the Birth of Globalization.* Amherst, N.Y.: Prometheus Books, 2010.

Hill, Mary. *Gold: The California Story.* Berkeley: University of California Press, 1999.

Horberry, Tim, Robin Burgess-Limerick, and Lisa J. Steiner. *Human Factors for the Design, Operation, and Maintenance of Mining Equipment.* Boca Raton, Fla.: CRC Press, 2011.

Perlez, Jane, Raymond Bonner, and Evelyn Rusli. "Below a Mountain of Wealth, a River of Waste." *New York Times* late ed. (East Coast), December 27, 2005.

Thompson, Tamara. *Uranium Mining.* Detroit: Greenhaven Press, 2010.

Tilton, John E., ed. *World Metal Demand: Trends and Prospects.* Washington, D.C.: Resources for the Future, 1990.

United Nations Statistical Division. *Statistical Yearbook.* 51st ed. New York: United Nations, 2007.

U.S. Bureau of Labor Statistics. *Career Guide to Industries,* 2010-2011 ed. http://www.bls.gov/oco/cg.

U.S. Census Bureau. North American Industry Classification System (NAICS), 2007. http://www.census.gov/cgi-bin/sssd/naics/naicsrch?chart=2007.

U.S. Department of Commerce. International Trade Administration. Office of Trade and Industry Information. Industry Trade Data and Analysis. http://ita.doc.gov/td/industry/otea/OTII/OTII-index.html.

U.S. Geological Survey. *Mineral Commodity Summaries, 2006.* Washington, D.C.: U.S. Government Printing Office, 2006. Available at http://minerals.usgs.gov/minerals/pubs/mcs/2006/msc2006.pdf.

_____. *Minerals Yearbook, 2007.* Washington, D.C.: U.S. Government Printing Office, 2007. http://minerals.usgs.gov/minerals/pubs/myb.html.

Motion Picture and Television Industry

INDUSTRY SNAPSHOT

General Industry: Arts and Entertainment

Career Cluster: Arts, A/V Technology, and Communication

Subcategory Industries: Cable Broadcasting; Motion Picture and Video Distribution; Motion Picture and Video Exhibition; Motion Picture and Video Production; Postproduction Services; Satellite Television Broadcasting; Television Broadcasting Networks; Television Broadcasting Stations

Related Industries: Advertising and Marketing Industry; Apparel and Fashion Industry; Broadcast Industry; Internet and Cyber Communications Industry; Music Industry; Publishing and Information Industry; Theater and Performing Arts Industry; Themed Entertainment Industry; Video, Computer, and Virtual Reality Games Industry

Annual Domestic Revenues: Film industry: $9.8 billion USD (Motion Picture Association of America, 2008); television industry: $17 billion USD (MediaBuyerPlanner, 2009)

Annual International Revenues: Film industry: $18.3 billion USD (Motion Picture Association of America, 2008)

Annual Global Revenues: Film industry: $28.1 billion USD (Motion Picture Association of America, 2008); television industry: $280 billion USD (£194 billion GBP; OFCOM, 2008)

NAICS Numbers: 5121, 515120, 515210

INDUSTRY DEFINITION

Summary

The motion picture and television industry creates and disseminates audiovisual entertainment, news, sports coverage, documentary material, and other film and video content to viewers worldwide. The industry comprises two major components: The film industry provides small-, medium-, and large-scale productions spanning a wide range of genres. The television industry provides similar entertainment products for broadcast directly to viewers' homes. Each of these components has seen dramatic growth over the last several decades, and both have enjoyed relative stability.

Motion picture and television production constitute a multibillion-dollar industry with visibility in virtually every country in the world. Employing millions of workers across a broad spectrum of professional pursuits, the industry is perhaps best known for its high profile in Hollywood, New York, Canada, Great Britain, and India. However, it has seen consistent growth into other regions, maintaining a presence in every developed country and in most developing nations as well.

History of the Industry

The motion picture industry owes its roots to the eighteenth century, when moving projected images were first introduced by the magic lantern. This device, the first slide projector, projected images that had been drawn on glass slides. Some of these slide projectors incorporated levers and other devices to bring simple movements to the screen; for example, in a comic slide, a man's pants might fall down when the lever was pushed.

Magic lanterns remained popular through the mid-1800's. Even those that did not move helped form the foundation of the later cinema by creating a language for telling stories on a screen. Such cinematic conventions as the establishing shot and shot-reverse shot were invented by magic lantern devisers who used them to order the still images from which they formed their narratives.

The photographic camera was invented in 1826 and became popular beginning in 1839. In 1879, Eadweard Muybridge developed the zoopraxiscope, a device that created the illusion of motion by projecting a series of still images based on photographs he had taken of people and animals in motion. (Because of the way the device worked, it was necessary to project elongated drawings based on photographs to compensate for the zoopraxiscope's tendency to shorten images.) The zoopraxiscope was itself based on an earlier device, the phenakistoscope, which similarly created simple moving images that were viewed by individual spectators looking through a series of slits in the side of a spinning disc.

In 1888, Muybridge and American inventor Thomas Alva Edison met at Edison's West Orange, New Jersey, laboratory. The two collaborated on the development of the zoopraxiscope and Edi-

Movie theaters are just one source of revenue for the motion picture industry. (©Alexander Podshivalov/Dreamstime.com)

son's groundbreaking phonograph. Edison, however, balked at the notion of full collaboration, looking instead to develop a motion picture system that could both capture and recreate motion directly. Edison introduced the kinetoscope, a peep-show device that was capable of recording and reproducing objects in motion, for which he received a patent in October, 1888.

When Edison's product was unveiled a year later, the search began for a medium by which the new technology might record its images. After exploring several avenues, Edison and his colleagues settled on celluloid film purchased from Eastman. From that point forward, the technology attracted considerable attention. In 1891, kinetoscopes began to appear in the form of coin-operated machines in public parlors in New York and Europe. Edison resisted creating motion picture projectors based on the kinetoscope, however, for simple economic reasons. A coin parlor would purchase six or eight kinetoscopes, so it could serve six or eight

customers at a time. A machine that projected an image onto a screen would serve many more customers, so Edison feared he would sell far fewer of them.

In 1895, the development of film technology took a great leap forward when the French brothers Auguste and Louis Lumière introduced their cinematograph, a single portable device that was a camera, film developer, and projector all in one. The Lumières began producing short films for public viewing. One of their most well-known films was *L'Arrivée d'un train à La Ciotat* (1896; *Arrival of a Train at La Ciotat*; better known as *Train Arriving at a Station*). Viewers unaccustomed to moving images reportedly thought the train was coming toward them and reacted with shock at the realism of the image. Over the course of the decade after the Lumière films gained prominence, film production became more standardized and marketed to audiences around the world.

With the increased popularity of films in the

There are more than a dozen film studios, as well as nearly a dozen television studios, in greater Los Angeles and Hollywood alone. (©Dreamstime.com)

Lumière vein, known as "actualities," filmmakers concurrently sought new ways to develop their technology. In one of the first examples of special effects, for example, French magician Georges Méliès discovered that by stopping the camera mid-scene, rearranging the scene, and starting the camera again, he could cause characters and objects to appear and disappear in a variety of manners. The novelty and creativity that films fostered at the end of the nineteenth century helped lay the groundwork for the industry's explosive growth during the twentieth century. Films were produced by the hundreds in Europe and the United States, with new techniques being employed to develop characters and scenes. Over the decade from roughly 1907 to 1917, the language of classical cinema was developed and standardized. By the end of the 1910's, film was both an industry and a medium of standardized communication.

During the 1920's, the industry began to move and jell in Hollywood. Large studios were built that could produce countless films to meet audience demands. Grandiose productions such as those of producer Cecil B. DeMille, comedies featuring the Keystone Kops and the legendary Charlie Chaplin, and many artistic pieces appealed to a growing audience. Hollywood was not the only place in the world to produce films, however. From Germany came such classics as *Nosferatu* (1922) and *Metropolis* (1927). In France, artistic and avant-garde films emphasized characters and scenery. The Soviet Union used well-crafted and emotional filmmaking as part of its communist propaganda.

In 1927, Warner Bros. released *The Jazz Singer*, which used a new synchronized sound technology. (Sound experiments date back to the 1890's, but the technology used in *The Jazz Singer* proved more effective and popular than had earlier attempts.) *The Jazz Singer* was followed by *Steamboat Willie* (1928), the debut of Walt Disney's cartoon character Mickey Mouse. The introduction of sound opened the floodgates for cinema, powering a

Would-be actors flock to film capitals such as Hollywood and New York. (©George Mayer/Dreamstime.com)

highly lucrative and diverse industry that would continue to grow and revolutionize over the course of the next several decades.

The so-called studio system in Hollywood lasted roughly from 1917 to 1960. During that time, it was common for creative talent—including actors, writers, directors, costumers, and so on—to work "on contract" at a given studio. These professionals received weekly salaries year-round, and they worked on whatever project their studio assigned them. After the end of the studio system, reliable salaries independent of a given production became a thing of the past. Instead, creative professionals were paid by each production on which they worked and had no source of income between jobs. Studios continued to employ executives, including some producers, but they no longer permanently employed actors, writers, directors, and other creators.

When World War II came to an end in 1945, another medium began to grow in popularity. Televi-

A television show host gestures to get his point across. (©Haider Yousuf/Dreamstime.com)

sion had been introduced several years earlier at the 1939 World's Fair, but with the economic boom of the postwar period, television became both extremely popular and affordable for consumers. The number of television stations increased dramatically, as sales of television sets grew by 500 percent. Over the course of the next few decades, picture quality improved. The diversity of programs also grew, as comedies, game shows, mysteries, dramas, and other shows were broadcast, in addition to news programs and other scheduled items. Advances in television technology also made it easier to produce shows anywhere, increasing viewers' access, as well as the volume of entertainment options available. By the late twentieth century, television and film had become the most popular forms of entertainment, not just in the United States but also around the world.

The Industry Today

The motion picture and television industry remains healthy, despite the negative global economic conditions of the early twenty-first century. In fact, many economy-weary consumers around the world consider television viewing and motion picture attendance to be cost-effective "therapies." Motion picture and television production are lucrative, revenue-generating businesses. Their impact on local economies has led them to be sought after by economies seeking a strong boost, and local governments compete to bring productions to their areas by offering tax breaks and other incentives. In the United States, the industry accounts for 2.5 million jobs, paying over $41 billion in wages to its employees, as well as over $38 billion for external vendors and businesses. In 2008, it generated $13 billion in federal and state income and sales taxes.

The industry provides a wide range of entertainment opportunities for viewers and audiences around the world. There are more than a dozen film studios, as well as nearly a dozen television studios, in greater Los Angeles and Hollywood alone. Each of these studios generates a large volume of films and programs to suit a broad variety of audience tastes. Hollywood does not hold a monopoly on the industry, however. Greater New York boasts over two dozen television studios, and a growing number of major studios are appearing in such areas as western Canada. One of the fastest-growing venues for film studios is located in Mumbai (formerly Bombay), India, where the Bollywood style of filmmaking has gained increasing worldwide popularity. The world's largest broadcasting company is the British Broadcasting Company (BBC), with one of the planet's biggest studio campuses located just outside London.

The expanse of the motion picture and television industry is demonstrative of its profitability. For example, Bollywood (so-named by merging the location, Bombay, with the more well-known icon of the industry, Hollywood) grew in profits by 12.5 percent over five years to achieve a total worth of about $21 billion. Global box office receipts totaled just over $28 billion in 2008, with the North American box office accounting for about 35 percent of that total, or $9.8 billion. Interestingly, the Motion Picture Association of America (MPAA), which normally issues an annual assessment of global box office receipts for the film industry, issued a statement in 2009 indicating that it would no longer report such figures with respect to film production costs, which can provide a more effective profile of the true nature of the industry's revenues. The reason, it said, was that the unreliable nature of contemporary data on costs made it too difficult to assess global profits accurately.

Inputs Consumed by the Motion Picture and Sound Recording Industries

Input	Value
Energy	$0.6 billion
Materials	$5.0 billion
Purchased services	$35.4 billion
Total	$41.0 billion

Source: U.S. Bureau of Economic Analysis. Data are for 2008.

The Motion Picture and Sound Recording Industries' Contribution to the U.S. Economy

Value Added	Amount
Gross domestic product	$61.1 billion
Gross domestic product	0.4%
Persons employed	385,000
Total employee compensation	$27.2 billion

Source: U.S. Bureau of Economic Analysis. Data are for 2008.

The world's film and television studios have increased not only in number but also in diversity. In addition to large-scale studios such as Universal, the BBC, and Walt Disney, many small and midsize studios are in operation. These smaller studios have surged in popularity, as filmgoers have flocked to theaters to see such independent films as Sony Pictures Classics' Academy Award winner *Crouching Tiger, Hidden Dragon* (2000) and Blumhouse Productions' *Paranormal Activity* (pr. 2007, rl. 2009). Each year, these smaller studios and arthouse films are featured at a number of major film festivals, including the Sundance Film Festival and the Tribeca Film Festival.

Still, motion pictures and television programs are expensive undertakings and often rely heavily on major studio support. Peter Jackson's sweeping *The Lord of the Rings* trilogy (2001-2003) was designed by his small studio, Wingnut Films, but was funded heavily by the much larger New Line Studios. Many major studios have branched out into the arthouse market, giving them the ability to capitalize on the small, independent market while retaining their significant funding and resources. Twentieth Century Fox Film Corporation, Disney, and Miramax Films have all created smaller subsidiary studios with this trend in mind.

The television industry has not seen as much explosive growth in the early twenty-first century as it did in the second half of the twentieth century. Television does continue to enjoy growth, however, despite the economic downturn of 2007-2009 and the rise of the Internet as a significant new competitor. Total global revenues for the television industry dropped in 2009 but were predicted to rebound consistently in the following years.

The motion picture and television industry is an extremely complex business, comprising a wide range of networks and professions. The studio (which may be defined as both a facility in which productions and programs are filmed and a centralized business housing every component of film and television production) is a microcosm of the larger industry. Studio executives, writers, directors, actors, technical crews, and other business professionals all collaborate to create feature films, broadcast programming, and other films and television shows. It is an exciting field, offering its employees opportunities to help build films and programs that will be viewed by millions of people at a time. Much of the industry is also extremely competitive, with would-be actors and screenwriters flocking to film capitols such as Hollywood, New York, and Mumbai to join the industry.

The creation of a major motion picture or television show is not limited to the studios. In fact, the industry frequently relies on many outside companies to assist in special effects, graphics, set design, and other aspects of film production. Films and programs are often filmed on location (meaning anywhere outside of a controlled sound stage or other studio set). Many film and television locations, however, do not correspond to their settings. For example, Los Angeles may be represented on screen by Los Angeles, Vancouver, Cincinnati, a sound stage in London, or any combination thereof. Indeed, many film and television locations are pieced together by filming in a number of cities or areas that present the most aesthetic and cost-effective sites.

The film and television industry has experienced significant challenges during the early twenty-first century. Motion picture studios have consistently been challenged by illegal copies of their films being made available in many locations (most prominently East Asia and Eastern Europe). Such practices, referred to as piracy, cost the global industry an estimated $18.2 billion in 2005, according to the MPAA. The rise of the Internet has also cut into

profits for the industry, particularly in television, which has had to adapt quickly and repeatedly to the World Wide Web's rapid growth as an entertainment medium. The motion picture and television industry continues to evolve, updating both its production technologies and its marketing tools. It is a worldwide business that has largely proven very durable in the face of tumultuous economies and other conditions.

INDUSTRY MARKET SEGMENTS

Both films and television programs are created and distributed by production companies of various sizes. Often in contemporary practice, content is distributed by a different company than the one that creates it. It is standard practice for a studio to attempt to line up distribution for a given film in advance, because such contracts often entail investment by the distribution company to help finance completion of the film. The result of this arrangement is that both small and large studios may be involved in the same project to varying degrees. This is particularly true in the television industry, in which a major network may provide financial backing to and assert creative veto power over a show otherwise produced by a small, stand-alone company.

Small Studios and Production Companies

Small film and television businesses include small studios, as well as the minor production companies assembled to create individual properties. In television, such companies include Bad Robot, Mutant Enemy Productions, MTM Enterprises, and a host of other companies whose logos are flashed briefly at the end of television shows. Most small production companies establish relationships with major studios, and some are even housed entirely on the lots of those studios. Small studios, meanwhile, create or acquire independent films. Some produce films that are distributed by major studios. Others act primarily as arthouse distributors, finding and sometimes funding promising small-scale films and paying for their distribution to movie theaters in return for a percentage of their profits.

Potential Annual Earnings Scale. The average annual salary of a motion picture studio executive, according to the U.S. Bureau of Labor Statistics (BLS), was $224,820 in 2009. The average salary for an entertainment lawyer was $166,420, while film producers and directors earned an average of $108,420, writers earned an average of $86,820, film and video editors earned an average of $70,100, and camera operators earned an average of $52,420 per year. Actors earned a median hourly wage of $27.14, or a mean hourly wage of $47.65 (the discrepancy is indicative of the gap between the average salary and the highest salaries). For almost all of these occupations, salaries of employees of small studios are generally equal to or below these averages.

Clientele Interaction. Client interaction in the motion picture and television industry varies based on the position held. The primary clients of a motion picture company are members of the film-going audience, while the primary clients of a television company are the advertisers who purchase television air time. Two-way interaction with individual fans is extremely limited, so film clientele interaction mostly takes the form of public relations ventures that are directed to fans and meant to make them feel addressed or that facilitate the formation of fan clubs and similar groups. Some film marketing professionals may also conduct focus groups to help plan future projects or shape the direction of current ones. By contrast, television companies carefully cultivate their relationships with advertisers, and account executives may interact quite closely with their most important show sponsors.

Amenities, Atmosphere, and Physical Grounds. Motion picture and television studios, even small ones, are often relatively secure facilities, with guarded gates to keep random members of the public off their lots. Many small studios are located on the lots of major studios and share in their atmosphere and amenities, from studio cafeterias to sound stages. Studios are often charged with excitement tinged with tension, as the glamor of the business is constantly mixed with the reality of extremely long hours, frayed nerves, and tight budgets. In addition, film and television productions often operate on location, taking over entire neighborhoods with large trailers and police-provided security and converting city streets into ad hoc film sets.

Typical Number of Employees. The number of employees at a small motion picture or televi-sion studio depends largely on the size and volume of films being produced. Some studios employ only a few people full time, drawing actors and performers on a contract basis as necessary. Others may have as many as one hundred full-time employees.

Traditional Geographic Locations. Small studios are capable of operating in a wide range of venues. Their independence of Hollywood (both real and perceived) enables them to develop films in many settings. Many small studios, however, realizing the need to have access to actors and other film industry segments (such as sound stages and directors), operate in or near major film-industry centers such as Southern California, greater New York, London, and Mumbai.

Pros of Working for a Small Studio or Production Company. Some small studios have less-corporate, top-down atmospheres and structures than do large studios, so creative employees may experience or perceive less artistic intrusion by executives at smaller companies. These employees may be able to take on projects that they find more artistically satisfying, as well as to enjoy more artistic control over their projects. Many small studio features are created by one person, who may write, produce, direct, and star in the film. While small productions are not always financially rewarding, many workers appreciate the process of creating original and unique work.

Cons of Working for a Small Studio or Production Company. Small studios may afford creative employees no more artistic control than do large studios, and they may lack the financial resources of larger companies. Although many small films flourish despite low budgets, the norm is that films require financial backing. If small companies seek such backing from large distribution companies, for example, they give up some of their creative independence as a result. Pay for employees (including actors) on a given film is generally lower at small studios than it is at larger studios. Limited budgets may also preclude small studios from filming in a particular locale or acquiring a marketable star or stars to act in a film. If a small studio seeks to distribute a film itself, the scope of its distribution may be seriously curtailed, limiting its ability to reach audiences and maximize its revenue potential and cultural impact.

Costs

Payroll and Benefits: Small studios pay executives, administrative support staff, and other permanent employees annual salaries. Those working on a particular film are generally paid either a monthly salary or an hourly wage for the duration of the project, although it is common for some positions (such as actor, writer, and director) to receive a flat fee for the entire project.

Supplies: Small film and television studios require production equipment, artistic supplies, costumes, film editing hardware and software, lighting, microphones, and other light and heavy filmmaking equipment. They also require office supplies such as paper, files, computers, copiers, telephones, and so on.

External Services: Because of their size and their limited resources, small studios often contract a number of external vendors. They may hire such vendors to provide such services as marketing and distribution, accounting, and casting. On production sets, they may also contract out equipment rentals, transportation services, and makeup and wardrobe services. They may also contract postproduction services, including special effects and sound mixing. Furthermore, smaller studios may rely on the funding of larger studios to support filming and distribution to theaters.

Utilities: Small motion picture and television studios use a significant amount of electricity, as well as heating, water, and sewage services. They must also pay for telephone and Internet service.

Taxes: Motion picture and television studios must pay income and property taxes, as well as any permitting fees levied for location shoots on public property. However, small studios are often given tax breaks by local and state governments in order to encourage their activities in communities that benefit from the film crews' business.

Midsize Studios

Midsize studios are generally significant corporations that are nonetheless smaller than the major studios. They may include the largest production companies, as well as the creative divisions of some television networks and the largest independent film studios.

Potential Annual Earnings Scale. The average annual salary of a motion picture studio executive, according to the BLS, was $224,820 in 2009. The average salary for an entertainment lawyer was $166,420, while film producers and directors earned an average of $108,420, writers earned an average of $86,820, film and video editors earned an average of $70,100, and camera operators earned an average of $52,420 per year. Actors earned a median hourly wage of $27.14, or a mean hourly wage of $47.65 (the discrepancy is indicative of the gap between the average salary and the highest salaries). Generally speaking, employees of midsize companies tend to earn salaries in line with these national averages.

Clientele Interaction. Client interaction in the motion picture and television industry varies based on the position held. The primary clients of a motion picture company are members of the filmgoing audience, while the primary clients of a television company are the advertisers who purchase television air time. Two-way interaction with individual fans is extremely limited, so film clientele interaction mostly takes the form of public relations ventures that are directed to fans and meant to make them feel addressed or that facilitate the formation of fan clubs and similar groups. Some film marketing professionals may also conduct focus groups to help plan future projects or shape the direction of current ones. By contrast, television companies carefully cultivate their relationships with advertisers, and account executives may interact quite closely with their most important show sponsors.

Amenities, Atmosphere, and Physical Grounds. The work environment at a midsize television or motion picture studio is usually a dynamic and exciting one. The hours are sometimes long (although sometimes hours are shorter than the average work week), but the work is rarely dull. Each of the studio's employee teams is expected to show professionalism and an ability to work with other areas of the operation.

Typical Number of Employees. The number of people working at a midsize film or television studio depends on the size and volume of the productions underway at that institution. Often, such projects may have as many as a few hundred full-time employees, as well as external vendors working in direct support of the production. As many midsize studios are part of larger studio complexes, the number of employees varies greatly.

Traditional Geographic Locations. Midsize film and television studios are typically located in major metropolitan areas or regions in which the motion picture and television industry are well established. Hollywood, Toronto, Mumbai, and London are home to some of the most extensive film and television studio systems, and many midsize studios are located within those larger company campuses.

Pros of Working for a Midsize Studio. Midsize studios offer those who work for them the opportunity to work not only on independent films but also on major productions. Because they are often part of, or closely connected to, much larger production companies, midsize studios tend to have more diverse productions, some of which target the arthouse crowd and some of which are more commercial, major productions. In light of this diversity, midsize studios may achieve greater influxes of producer money, enabling them to provide above-average salaries.

Cons of Working for a Midsize Studio. Many midsize film and television studios are subject to absorption into larger production companies. Thus, those who work for them may find their job stability somewhat unpredictable. Additionally, the increased potential for major productions may increase competition for jobs on those productions, making work more difficult to come by.

Costs

Payroll and Benefits: Studios pay executives, administrative support staff, and other permanent employees annual salaries. Those working on a particular film are generally paid either a monthly salary or an hourly wage for the duration of the project, although it is common for some positions (such as actor, writer, and director) to receive a flat fee for the entire project. Midsize studios may employ a significant number of full-time workers, including cafeteria staff, security guards, maintenance workers, and a host of other auxiliary personnel.

Supplies: Midsize film and television studios require production equipment, artistic supplies, costumes, film editing and effects hardware and software, lighting, microphones, and other light and heavy filmmaking equipment. They also re-

quire office supplies such as paper, files, computers, copiers, and telephones.

External Services: Although many midsize motion picture and television studios are capable of performing a number of production effects and programs, many use external contractors. They may contract such services as special effects, casting, set construction, accounting, postproduction, and distribution.

Utilities: Midsize studios use a large amount of energy, particularly electricity. They also, by virtue of their size, expend a significant quantity toward heating, water, and sewage service. Furthermore, midsize studios require extensive telephone and Internet capabilities to facilitate both intra- and intercompany communications.

Taxes: Midsize motion picture and television studios must withhold income taxes from their full-time employees for state and national tax agencies. They must also pay real estate and corporate taxes, as well as permitting fees for location shoots on public property. They may receive tax breaks from states and municipalities seeking to draw film and television productions to their locations in order to benefit their local economies.

Major Studios

The major motion picture and television studios are the icons of the industry, located on studios whose back lots have hosted some of the most famous productions in history. Almost all major studios in the twenty-first century either are owned by or are portions of even larger multinational corporations with multiple entertainment and nonentertainment properties. For example, Disney owns the Walt Disney Studios, the Walt Disney Theme Parks, the American Broadcasting Corporation (ABC), ESPN, and several other television stations. NBC Universal, which owns both the National Broadcasting Company (NBC) and Universal Entertainment (the parent company of Universal Studios), is itself owned jointly by General Electric and Vivendi Universal. In addition to the divisions that give the company its name, it also owns the USA Network, Syfy (formerly the Sci Fi Channel), and many other television and Internet properties. Through Vivendi, the company is also tied to Universal Music Group (formerly MCA), among many other entertainment properties. As these examples demonstrate, it is often very difficult to draw the line between a single major studio and the portfolio of properties of which it is a part and which it owns. As a result, though amorphous, the major studios are massive, multinational, multibillion-dollar corporations with many thousands of employees.

Potential Annual Earnings Scale. The average annual salary of a motion picture studio executive, according to the BLS, was $224,820 in 2009. The average salary for an entertainment lawyer was $166,420, while film producers and directors earned an average of $108,420, writers earned an average of $86,820, film and video editors earned an average of $70,100, and camera operators earned an average of $52,420 per year. Actors earned a median hourly wage of $27.14, or a mean hourly wage of $47.65 (the discrepancy is indicative of the gap between the average salary and the highest salaries). Generally speaking, employees of the major studios earn salaries at least equal to and sometimes significantly greater than the average for their positions.

Clientele Interaction. Client interaction in the motion picture and television industry varies based on the position held. The primary clients of a motion picture company are members of the film-going audience, while the primary clients of a television company are the advertisers who purchase television air time. Two-way interaction with individual fans is extremely limited, so film clientele interaction mostly takes the form of public relations ventures that are directed to fans and meant to make them feel addressed or that facilitate the formation of fan clubs and similar groups. Some film marketing professionals may also conduct focus groups to help plan future projects or shape the direction of current ones. By contrast, television companies carefully cultivate their relationships with advertisers, and account executives may interact quite closely with their most important show sponsors.

Amenities, Atmosphere and Physical Grounds. Major studios are dynamic settings, with many working parts for each production, as well as multiple simultaneous productions occurring all on the same grounds. Major studios are typically large campuses with multiple sets and soundstages of varying sizes and configurations, and they may even have outdoor areas designated for filming as well. Hours for employees vary, with some working fewer than thirty hours per week and others working more than fifty hours per week. Work is hardly routine, particularly when shooting on location, where work is concentrated and often intense in order to stay on budget and time.

Typical Number of Employees. The number of employees on hand at a major film or television studio varies based on the number of productions underway, as well as the size of those productions. One of the world's largest film and television studios, the BBC, has nearly twenty-three thousand employees. Twentieth Century Fox, based in Los Angeles, has twenty-five hundred employees.

Traditional Geographic Locations. Major film and television studios are located around the world. Although the heaviest concentrations have long been in Southern California, London, New York, Toronto, and Mumbai, an increasing number of major studios are appearing in other metropolitan areas as a result of tax credits and incentives offered by those locales. Film studios are under consideration in greater Boston and in Michigan, as well as in Cape Town, South Africa (which has seen a surge of interest since the popular 2009 science-fiction film *District 9* was shot on location there).

Pros of Working for a Major Studio. The notion of working at a major studio is attractive for many who would like to work with the biggest names on the biggest films. Indeed, a major studio is filled with many different projects, offering a high degree of diversity and energy that is rarely found in any other industry. Salaries at major studios tend to be higher on average than those offered at midsize or small studios, largely because the productions and programs have higher budgets.

Cons of Working for a Major Studio. One of the most challenging aspects of working at a major studio is the high level of competition for each position. Countless people actively pursue employment at major studios and, as a result, those who hold positions there are under heightened pressure to retain their jobs. In addition, actors and other members of the industry working for major studios on large-scale projects have high expectations. In light of these two factors, employees at major studios have very little margin for error during the course of their work.

Costs

Payroll and Benefits: Studios pay executives, administrative support staff, and other permanent employees annual salaries. Those working on a particular film are generally paid either a monthly salary or an hourly wage for the duration of the project, although it is common for some positions (such as actor, writer, and director) to receive a flat fee for the entire project. The major studios often have massive payrolls at any one time, and almost all of their employees are represented by collective bargaining units. In addition to their creative staffs and contractors, the major studios employ many full-time support staff, including cafeteria and craft-services workers, security guards, maintenance crews, and a host of other auxiliary personnel.

Supplies: Major studios use a sizable number of supplies during the course of their operations. During shooting, they require cameras, lighting, sound systems, and other equipment, as well as the tools and parts to maintain them. Off-camera, they need basic office supplies, including computers, telephones, presentation materials, and similar resources. Their technology requirements may be quite significant, including editing workstations, special effects workstations, and other postproduction computing resources, as well as networking systems and the general office support systems required by major corporations.

External Services: Although many studios are self-reliant in many ways, they still use a great many external vendors for their operations. On the set, for example, they may contract caterers and transportation services. On location, they may use local labor for set and equipment management. It is common for even the largest productions to outsource their most sophisticated special visual effects and sound needs to companies that specialize in those services, though those companies may sometimes be subsidiaries of the major studios. Studios may also hire external security companies to provide security both within the studios and on location. Furthermore, they may utilize casting agencies to locate the most appropriate actors for the roles they need to fill.

Utilities: Major film and television studios expect major utility expenses. Their operations, both while filming and in the course of their business activities, require a great deal of electricity and, in the case of colder geographical locations, heat (which may use oil or natural gas). Additionally, they must pay for water use, sewage, trash removal, and telephone and Internet services to handle inter- and intra-studio communications.

Taxes: Major motion picture and television studios must withhold income taxes from their full-time employees for state and national tax agencies. They must also pay real estate and corporate taxes, as well as permitting fees for location shoots on public property. They may receive tax breaks from states and municipalities seeking to draw film and television productions to their locations in order to benefit their local economies.

ORGANIZATIONAL STRUCTURE AND JOB ROLES

The organizational structure of the motion picture and television industry comprises myriad jobs and responsibilities. Often, many of the facets of a film or television production's development span a plethora of professional trades and industries, in addition to occupations within the film and television industry. Each of these components works as part of an overall organization centered on the production or program being developed.

The following umbrella categories apply to the organizational structure of businesses within the motion picture and television industry:

- Executive Management
- Directing
- Casting
- Acting
- Set Design
- Hair/Makeup/Costume
- Writing
- Special Effects
- Technical Crew
- Postproduction
- Marketing and Advertising
- Representation

Executive Management

The responsibility of managing the overall operations and productions of a given studio falls to studio executives. Studio executives are similar to a corporation's executive management team. They review all incoming scripts, approve (or "green light") productions, hire relevant personnel, fund productions, and ensure that projects are completed and distributed within a certain period of time. The task of managing multiple productions, approving future programs and films, and handling the overall operations of what is usually an extensive business enterprise requires a great deal of attention to detail, a strong ability to multitask, and a true love of the entertainment industry.

Most studio executives ascend to their professional positions through extensive training and experience within the film and entertainment industry. However, as their responsibilities entail oversight and management of a large company, they must also have relevant business management training. Moreover, as so many entertainment companies are now part of larger enterprises, some executives may become successful managers of other divisions and then move laterally into the motion picture or television business. Many receive their training by earning advanced degrees in business management or related fields. However, many others arrive at their positions by way of long careers of working for studios from the ground up.

Studio executives read and review countless potential films and programs and, as a result, must be able to quickly assess and approve or decline a large volume of scripts. They are supported in this regard by significant support staff, who read entire scripts and provide "coverage," or brief summaries of each script's plot, aesthetic quality, general marketability, and suitability for a studio's specific portfolio of properties. Executives must be careful business managers, capable of developing budgets and analyzing the potential returns of future films and programs.

Executive management occupations may include the following:

- President/Chief Executive Officer (CEO)
- Vice President
- Chief Operating Officer (COO)
- Chief Financial Officer (CFO)
- Executive Producer
- Producer

Directing

Each film or television episode is overseen by a director, who is responsible for every aspect of that production. The director is the creative force behind the development and filming of a film, and has significant control over a given television episode as well. Working in concert with producers, directors select their cast and crew, select locations and sets, and establish shooting schedules. They must be familiar with all technical aspects of producing films, including the use of various camera angles and any alterations to scripts required to meet the limitations of the film.

In addition to technical management, directors must manage films themselves, making adjustments to story lines, characters, or settings as necessary and guiding actors through their scenes. After shooting takes place, directors review footage to determine whether corrections are necessary. They select or approve final edits made by film editors, and they plan their shoots largely in order to provide editors with the material they need to do their jobs.

In addition to directors themselves, films' directorial staffs include first- and second unit directors (who oversee subsidiary shots on films, such as long shots of open desert and other establishing or atmospheric shots). They also include the professionals directly responsible for the look of the film. These professionals, who tailor their work to directors' specifications, include directors of photography and cinematographers.

Directors come from a variety of backgrounds within the film and television industry. They are not necessarily expected to receive advanced training in film direction. Indeed, it has become common for television actors to direct select episodes of their series. Directors must have extensive experience in the film or television industry, a strong understanding of each aspect of production (both technical and artistic), and a clear vision of the final product. Some are actors themselves, while others receive academic educations in film direction from formalized vocational programs. They must have strong organizational skills, keen artistic perspectives, and strong focus on narrative flow.

Directing occupations may include the following:

OCCUPATION PROFILE

Cinematographer

Considerations	Qualifications
Description	Composes the shots that constitute a film or television program, working with the director and providing instructions to camera operators.
Career cluster	Arts, A/V Technology, and Communication
Interests	Data; things
Working conditions	Work both inside and outside
Minimum education level	Bachelor's degree
Physical exertion	Light work
Physical abilities	Unexceptional/basic fitness
Opportunities for experience	Internship; apprenticeship; military service
Licensure and certification	Usually not required
Employment outlook	Average growth expected
Holland interest score	ASE

Note: See volume 1, "Publisher's Note," for an explanation of the Holland interest score.

- Director
- Director of Photography
- Cinematographer
- First Unit Director
- Second Unit Director
- Assistant Director

Casting

Casting personnel solicit and screen actors auditioning for parts in films and television programs. Working closely with directors and producers, casting personnel arrange script readings and auditions to find actors who are well suited to play the parts for which they are cast. They also help write and negotiate contracts between producers and actors and, when necessary, work with actors and their agents to resolve contract issues.

Casting personnel must have a thorough knowledge of both films and actors and an awareness of talent, as well as an understanding of those film genres where a particular actor or actress will excel.

Successful casting personnel have extensive client lists and strong networking ties within the industry. They must also have an ability to identify acting excellence and take strong direction from senior filmmakers.

Casting personnel do not necessarily have to have advanced degrees. Rather, what is most important is a strong understanding of the film and television industry, outstanding experience, and a keen eye for what studio executives require.

Casting occupations may include the following:

- Casting Director
- Casting Agent
- Administrative Assistant

Acting

Film and television performers come from a variety of backgrounds. Some are classically trained, while others begin their careers in other performance genres, such as comedy or music. They must understand not only the principles of drama or comedy performance but also the peculiar requirements of filmed performances, most particularly the craft of working with the camera.

Acting jobs are some of the most sought-after positions in the motion picture and television industry. Countless people move to areas such as Southern California and New York to join film and television companies, only to find that competition for roles is fierce. Actors may be paid small contracts or stipends at first, earning more per part as their experience grows.

The median hourly wage for an actor in 2009, according to the BLS, was $27.14, down a bit from the previous year's median, 28.72. Members of the Screen Actors Guild are guaranteed a minimum daily rate of $782 for any speaking part, with additional compensation for reruns (known as "residuals"). According to the Screen Actors Guild, only about 50 of their 100,000 members earn the salaries associated with Hollywood's biggest celebrities. Other actors and actresses generally work sporadically, as film and television work tends to be inconsistent.

Acting occupations may include the following:

- Leading Actor
- Series Regular
- Supporting Actor
- Series Recurring Role Actor
- Guest Star
- Character Actor
- Speaking Role Actor
- Extra
- Body Double
- Stunt Performer

Set Design

Set designers plan and construct the sets of motion pictures and television shows, as well as "dressing" filming locations. They help bring directors' artistic visions to fruition. Set designers employ both careful attention to detail and strong organizational skills with artistic, creative design ideas. They must develop detailed drawings and other plans, which are approved by directors before construction begins. Taking their cues from production designers or art directors, they draw up blueprints for construction and oversee the construction process. Set designers must have exten-

sive experience in both construction and the film industry, enabling them to understand the possibilities and limitations of set construction within the context of a motion picture or television production. They may have advanced degrees in art, graphic design, architecture, or related fields. According to the BLS, the mean annual salary of a set designer in 2009 was $65,050.

Set design occupations may include the following:

- Art Director
- Set Designer
- Construction Coordinator
- Production Designer

Hair/Makeup/Costume

The physical appearance of actors in motion pictures and television programs falls to hair and makeup artists and costume design teams. Costume designers design or rent clothing that best suits the characters within the setting of a given film or television production. Hair, makeup, and costume professionals are responsible for the look of the actors' characters, who may appear within a contemporary drama, a period piece, or a work of science fiction. Additionally, these professionals ensure that actors appear in a manner commensurate with the expectations of directors and producers. Hair, makeup, and costume personnel must be well schooled in cosmetology, as well as in the motion picture and television industry. They must understand how people appear on film and how to modify their appearances to achieve desired effects, including a natural look, which requires as much artifice as any other.

Hair, makeup, and costume occupations may include the following:

- Costume Designer
- Key Costumer
- Costume Assistant
- Key Makeup Artist
- Makeup Assistant
- Key Hair Stylist
- Hair Styling Assistant

Writing

While directors are the ones who ensure that a film develops according to plan, it is the writers who develop the plot, dialogue, and other critical areas of a film or television program's production. Moreover, on many television shows, the show's creators and creative overseers are writers rather than directors. Television directors and writers generally work on some but not all episodes, whereas a show's creators and executive producers provide the overall vision for a series. These leaders are commonly the heads of a show's writing staff.

Writers are often called in on a contract basis when a given script is approved. They then help flesh out any aspects of the screenplay that previously appeared thin or shallow, as well as making any necessary modifications to the story line. Such changes in a film screenplay are generally requested and approved by directors or studio executives.

Writers create scripts that are designed to be filmed. Often, initial ideas for a film or television program lack a great deal of detail, so writers use the limited information available to create characters, dialogue, dramatic situations, and other aspects of the film.

Writers generally receive some form of training in the liberal arts that enables them to focus on creative writing. Some, however, combine theater with writing-centric undergraduate degrees (such as English) in order to focus professionally on script development. Screenwriting is an extremely competitive endeavor, as film and television studios receive countless scripts from writers but choose only a few for production.

Writing occupations may include the following:

- Teleplay Writer
- Senior Writer
- Screenplay Writer
- Script Supervisor
- Executive Story Editor
- Story Editor
- Staff Writer

Special Effects

Most films and television productions rely on some form of special effects. Beyond the classic science-fiction type of special effect, these effects may be as mundane as using computer graphics to block out an unwanted advertisement in a location shoot or providing the sound of a person walking.

Special effects teams and subgroups are divided into two main areas: visual effects and sound effects. Within these arenas, there are computer-generated effects, makeup effects, synthesized sounds, foley effects (recorded sounds of footsteps, glass breaking, and other situations), and photographic images. Special effects professionals are well trained in the devices and fields on which they focus and, like other artists, enjoy a great deal of creativity in generating sights or sounds for productions.

Special effects professionals' educations vary based on the arenas in which they work. Some attend undergraduate or vocational schools to learn about computer systems and software, while others are trained in cosmetic fields. They also tend to start at the ground level within the industry, learning from mentors before succeeding on their own.

Special effects occupations may include the following:

- Sound Mixer
- Foley Artist
- Special Effects Director
- Makeup Effects Coordinator

Technical Crew

Each shooting location and set contains a number of important pieces of equipment. From cameras, to boom microphones, to lighting equipment, this equipment is employed by technical crews. These crews ensure that lighting systems, sound recording systems, and cameras, among other vital tools, are functioning properly and performing in the manner required. They must also ensure that the equipment is maintained and, where necessary, either repaired or replaced. Most important, they use the equipment to record the sounds and images from which films and television programs are composed.

Technical crewmembers often receive vocational training to become familiar with heavy machinery and technology, although they must receive on-the-job training on such equipment as well. Much of the work involved entails strenuous physical activity, so technical crewmembers must be able to handle such on-the-job physical stress. According to Simply Hired, the average annual salary for a technical film crewmember in 2010 was $37,000.

Technical crew occupations may include the following:

OCCUPATION PROFILE

Camera Operator

Considerations	Qualifications
Description	Covers news events as part of a reporting team, sets up and runs cameras on film sets, and otherwise operates equipment that captures or produces moving pictures for film or television.
Career cluster	Arts, A/V Technology, and Communication
Interests	Data; things
Working conditions	Work both inside and outside
Minimum education level	On-the-job training; junior/technical/community college; apprenticeship
Physical exertion	Medium work
Physical abilities	Unexceptional/basic fitness
Opportunities for experience	Internship; apprenticeship
Licensure and certification	Usually not required
Employment outlook	Average growth expected
Holland interest score	RCS

Note: See volume 1, "Publisher's Note," for an explanation of the Holland interest score.

- Dolly Grip
- Key Grip
- Camera Operator
- Technical Director
- Sound Engineer
- Clapper/Loader
- Focus Puller
- First Assistant Cameraman

Postproduction

Once the initial shooting of a film or television program is completed, the postproduction team reviews the resulting footage, pieces it together, and packages it. Postproduction staff are responsible for finalizing films and television programs and preparing them for distribution or broadcast.

Postproduction personnel must be very detail oriented, with a keen eye for ensuring that films are as perfectly shot and assembled as possible. Film editing, sound mixing, and other technical pro-

cesses are managed by postproduction teams, who ensure that films are well constructed. Many postproduction professionals are college-educated in liberal arts programs.

Postproduction occupations may include the following:

- Story Post Producer
- Assistant Editor
- Editor
- Digital Media Technician
- Sound Mixer

Marketing and Advertising

The commercial success of a film or television program depends heavily on the efforts of marketing, advertising, and other public relations professionals. Marketing and advertising personnel spread the word about a film's impending release in order to generate interest among potential viewers. Marketing campaigns may involve trailers (short advertising programs promoting films), viral marketing (clips and advertisements distributed on the Internet in such a fashion as to encourage people to spread the material to their friends via e-mail and social networking resources), and actor appearances in the media. Some marketing departments may also oversee distribution. In the case of the motion picture industry, that entails ensuring that films are shown in theaters with strong potential returns.

Marketing and advertising personnel tend to have undergraduate or advanced degrees in business and marketing. They must also have a strong understanding of the film industry and media outlets and how they operate. In addition to their work on behalf of individual productions, marketing personnel create campaigns to promote entire studios.

Marketing and advertising occupations may include the following:

- Marketing Director
- Marketing Manager
- Promotions Director
- Advertising Manager
- Distributor
- Intern

Representation

Talent agents represent actors and other performing artists who seek to join film and television productions. They work directly with studio executives, producers, and other agents to secure auditions for their clients and otherwise promote them. Once their clients are hired, they negotiate pay and contract stipulations and continue to represent their clients' interests to their employers throughout shooting and postproduction. In addition, agents are often the spokespeople for their clients, speaking out about issues facing them during the course of a film's development or off the set.

In light of the delicate yet intense environment in which they work, agents must be diplomatic, social, and direct on behalf of their clients. They must enter into negotiations with studios over money, seeking the maximum amount available, yet avoiding creating a negative image for their clients.

Agents are usually educated, with undergraduate or advanced degrees in business, marketing, or

similar fields. They usually begin their careers by working at large talent agencies. Once they have advanced to a high level, many agents strike out on their own and use their extensive contacts to start their own businesses. According to the BLS, the average annual salary for talent agents in 2009 was $81,310.

Representation occupations may include the following:

- Partner
- Senior Agent
- Junior Agent
- Manager
- Intern
- Administrative Assistant

INDUSTRY OUTLOOK

Overview

The motion picture and television industry has undergone a dramatic evolution since its roots were laid near the end of the nineteenth century. The rate of change over the course of the twentieth century was driven by the strong desire of viewers and audiences for new experiences to entertain them. The Lumières' footage of an oncoming train thrilled audiences, as did the "magic" of special effects a few years later. In 1933, audiences were mesmerized at the giant gorilla brought to life and interacting with real-life characters in *King Kong*, and in 1956 special effects icon Ray Harryhausen created an army of skeletal warriors to battle humans in *Jason and the Argonauts* in a scene that took special effects to an entirely new level.

Special effects are not the only aspects of motion picture and television entertainment that have evolved over the course of the industry's history. Revolutionary storylines, plots, and characters have contributed to both areas' respective and rapid growth. Hollywood and other industry centers continue to see high volumes of incoming candidates offering screenplays and acting talent; still others arrive looking for any sort of work on a film or television production. The industry continues to produce a great deal of content, spanning all genres and budget parameters. It is expected that this ongoing operational growth will continue as video distribution channels and technologies multiply.

There are two issues, however, that will likely create a change within the industry. The first is the international development of the industry—no longer are places such as Hollywood the epicenter of the film and television world. Instead, studios are being constructed around the United States, a thriving Canadian studio industry continues to grow, and European and Asian industries are also seeing growth. This trend will most likely draw business away from traditional production centers such as Southern California and redistribute it (and its revenues) around the world. This trend will also probably increase inter-studio competition, as newer studios outside Hollywood are constructed in response to large tax incentives, enabling them to produce films with significantly lower budgets. The rapid growth of so-called independent films provides evidence of this trend, changing the landscape of the industry.

The second issue that continues to arise is piracy. Illegally obtained films and television programs are receiving increasing circulation (largely in less developed countries in Asia and the former Soviet Union). The revenues generated from the sale of these pirated recordings have a significant impact on the industry, costing jobs and future revenues. With efforts to curtail the practice falling short in the early twenty-first century, it is expected that this issue will continue to influence the industry.

Although these trends have significantly altered the dynamics of the field, declines in growth of the motion picture and television industry are expected to be modest. The aspect of the industry that has been hardest hit overall is the television industry, affected by the recession of 2007-2009, as well as direct competition from the Internet. Nevertheless, the television market will continue to present job opportunities in many areas. Computer graphic artists, digital filming, editing, and other behind-the-scenes technical positions will likely continue to offer jobs. Acting, writing, and producing, long extremely competitive fields, will likely continue to be subject to intense competition, as large numbers of candidates seek a limited number of jobs.

Employment Advantages

The allure of working in the motion picture and television industry continues to attract countless candidates from all over the world. Indeed, the dynamic and exciting world of filmmaking and entertainment production serves as a major benefit for those who are fortunate enough to obtain a job in this arena. Employees are able to interact with celebrities and high-profile industry personalities during the course of their everyday tasks, a benefit that few other industries can present to their employees.

Additionally, motion picture and television professionals have the opportunity to use cutting-edge technologies to bring to life new visual realities. They create unusual and amazing new sights, such as alien worlds, dinosaurs, and natural phenomena. Similarly, nontechnical professionals can take pride in working in an industry that creates memo-

PROJECTED EMPLOYMENT FOR SELECTED OCCUPATIONS

Motion Picture, Video, and Sound Recording Industries

Employment		Occupation
2008	Projected 2018	
11,100	12,800	Actors
1,900	2,100	Art directors
800	800	Musicians, singers, and related workers
24,400	28,300	Producers and directors
19,300	22,500	Television, video, and motion picture camera operators and editors

Source: U.S. Bureau of Labor Statistics, Industries at a Glance, Occupational Employment Statistics and Employment Projections Program.

rable characters and tells the stories that define contemporary culture.

Finally, the industry presents its employees with stability. Although the industry is subject to great changes, and although they are employed by the project and subject to the vicissitudes of their projects, industry employees are able to work in a field that will continue to grow and produce. Although studios may fold or build, their personnel are part of a major, interconnected industry that will give them (once they have been accepted therein) a relatively strong sense of job security.

Annual Earnings

Although there are many connections between the motion picture and television sectors, the industry's earnings are best calculated when the two sectors are separated. Such a methodology reveals differences in revenue growth rates. Motion picture earnings have increased with relative consistency, with the exception of a drop of approximately 7 percent in 2005. In 2008, the motion picture industry earned $28.1 billion, up 5 percent from 2007. With the exception of 2005, the film industry's earnings have grown at modest but consistent rates.

Television earnings have seen a downward trend. In 2009, U.S. industry experts predicted total revenues at $17 billion, a drop of about 15 percent in revenues from 2008. In fact, the industry has seen an earnings decline since 2006, with the most precipitous drop, over 21 percent, occurring between 2007 and 2009. Analysts predict, however, that the recovering economy will fuel slight increases in revenues. On the global scale, revenues dropped from 2008 to 2009 by $3.5 billion. However, analysts predict a turnaround on that front as well.

RELATED RESOURCES FOR FURTHER RESEARCH

ACADEMY OF MOTION PICTURE ARTS AND SCIENCES
8949 Wilshire Blvd.
Beverly Hills, CA 90211
Tel: (310) 247-3000
Fax: (310) 859-9619
http://www.oscars.org

ACADEMY OF TELEVISION ARTS AND SCIENCES
5220 Lankershim Blvd.
North Hollywood, CA 91601
Tel: (818) 754-2800
http://www.emmys.org

BRITISH FILM INSTITUTE
Belvedere Rd.
South Bank, Waterloo, London SE1 8XT
United Kingdom
Tel: 44-20-7928-3232
Fax: 44-20-7928-3535
http://www.bfi.org.uk

CANADIAN FILM AND TELEVISION PRODUCTION ASSOCIATION
151 Slater St., Suite 902
Ottawa, ON K1P 5H3
Canada
Tel: (613) 233-1444
Fax: (613) 233-0073
http://www.cftpa.ca

CENTRE INTERNATIONAL DE LIAISON DES ECOLES DE CINEMA ET DE TELEVISION
Rue Theresienne 8
B-1000 Brussels
Belgium
Tel: 49-160-99-189-654
Fax: 49-160-99-52-584
http://www.cilect.org

MOTION PICTURE ASSOCIATION OF AMERICA
1600 Eye St. NW
Washington, DC 20006
Tel: (202) 293-1966
Fax: (202) 296-7410
http://www.mpaa.org

SCREEN ACTORS GUILD
5757 Wilshire Blvd., 7th Floor
Los Angeles, CA 90036-3600
Tel: (323) 954-1600
http://www.sag.org

ABOUT THE AUTHOR

Michael P. Auerbach has over sixteen years of professional experience in public policy and administration, economic development, and the tourism industry. He has worked closely with economic development advocates seeking to construct a major film studio in Massachusetts, a state that has passed tax incentives for film productions. He is a 1993 graduate of Wittenberg University and a 1999 graduate of the Boston College Graduate School of Arts and Sciences. He is a veteran of state and federal government, having worked for seven years in the Massachusetts legislature and four years as a federal government contractor.

FURTHER READING

Appleton, Dina, and Daniel Yankelevits. *Hollywood Dealmaking: Negotiating Talent Agreements for Film, TV, and New Media.* New York: Allworth Press, 2010.

Balio, Tino. *The American Film Industry.* Madison: University of Wisconsin Press, 1976.

_____. *Grand Design: Hollywood as a Modern Business Enterprise, 1930-1939.* New York: Maxwell Macmillan International, 1993.

Bielby, Denise D., and C. Lee Harrington. *Global TV: Exporting Television and Culture in the World Market.* New York: New York University Press, 2008.

Finney, Angus. *The International Film Business: A Market Guide Beyond Hollywood.* New York: Routledge, 2010.

Hoovers. "British Broadcasting Corporation." http://www.hoovers.com/company/British _Broadcasting_Corporation/hrfyri-1.html.

International Television Expert Group. "TV Market Data/Global TV Funding, 2008-2013." http://www.international-television.org/ tv_market_data/pay-tv-and-tv-funding- worldwide_2008-2013.html.

Koszarski, Richard. *Hollywood on the Hudson: Film and Television in New York from Griffith to Sarnoff.* New Brunswick, N.J.: Rutgers University Press, 2008.

Langford, Barry. *Post-Classical Hollywood: Film Industry, Style, and Ideology Since 1945.* Edinburgh: Edinburgh University Press, 2010.

Mehta, Rini Bhattacharya, and Rajeshwari Pandharipande. *Bollywood and Globalization: Indian Popular Cinema, Nation, and Diaspora.* New York: Anthem Press, 2010.

Motion Picture Association of America. *The Economic Impact of the Motion Picture and Television Industry on the United States.* Washington, D.C.: Author, 2009.

Musser, Charles. *The Emergence of Cinema: The American Screen to 1907.* New York: Maxwell Macmillan International, 1990.

Udelson, Joseph H. *The Great Television Race: A History of the American Television Industry, 1925-1941.* University: University of Alabama Press, 1982.

U.S. Bureau of Labor Statistics. *Career Guide to Industries,* 2010-2011 ed. http://www.bls.gov/ oco/cg.

U.S. Census Bureau. North American Industry Classification System (NAICS), 2007. http:// www.census.gov/cgi-bin/sssd/naics/ naicsrch?chart=2007.

U.S. Department of Commerce. International Trade Administration. Office of Trade and Industry Information. Industry Trade Data and Analysis. http://ita.doc.gov/td/industry/ otea/OTII/OTII-index.html.

U.S. Library of Congress. "History of Edison Motion Pictures." http://memory.loc.gov/ ammem/edhtml/edmvhist.html.

Museums and Cultural Institutions Industry

INDUSTRY SNAPSHOT

General Industry: Arts and Entertainment

Career Cluster: Arts, A/V Technology, and Communication

Subcategory Industries: Aquariums; Art Museums; Botanical Gardens; Halls of Fame; Historical Museums; Historical Ships; Historical Sites; Military Museums; Natural History Museums; Nature Parks; Nature Preserves; Nonretail Art Galleries; Observatories; Science and Technology Museums; Sculpture Gardens; Zoos

Related Industries: Libraries and Archives Industry; Outdoor Recreation Industry; Philanthropic, Charitable, Religious, Civic, and Grant-Making Industry; Themed Entertainment Industry; Travel and Tourism Industry

Annual Domestic Revenues: $9 billion USD (Hoovers, 2009)

NAICS Number: 712

INDUSTRY DEFINITION

Summary

The International Council of Museums (ICOM) defines a museum as

> a non-profitmaking, permanent institution in the service of society and of its development, and open to the public, which acquires, conserves, researches, communicates and exhibits, for purposes of study, education and enjoyment, material evidence of people and their environment.

The American Association of Museums (AAM) defines a museum as

> an organized and permanent non-profit institution, essentially educational or aesthetic in purpose, with professional staff, which owns and utilizes tangible objects, cares for them, and exhibits them to the public on some regular schedule.

These definitions are also applicable to similar institutions, such as nonprofit art galleries, historical societies, zoos, and aquariums.

History of the Industry

The institution of the museum as a place of cultural significance finds its roots in the classical world. Ancient Greece and Rome constructed and

People watching fish at an aquarium. (©David Miller/Dreamstime.com)

valued various "musaeums" or "mouseions" (places of music or poetry)—the Museum at Alexandria being perhaps the most famous. Though these early cultural institutions were largely centers of philosophical thought rather than repositories of valuable objects, the ancient world still had public collections of objects that resembled the modern concept of a museum. Greek temples and Roman forums, for example, often displayed gold and silver offerings, sculptures, and paintings.

During the Middle Ages, churches and other religious institutions throughout Europe acted as cultural repositories, collecting vast numbers of religious artworks and manuscripts. During the fifteenth century, the more modern concept of museums came into fashion in Europe. Over the following few centuries, museums such as the Ashmolean Museum of Art and Archaeology, in Oxford, England; the Vatican museums; the British Museum in London; and the Louvre in Paris, France—considered the first art gallery—were founded. The first modern museums began as pri-

vate collections of wealthy individuals who amassed extensive collections and then exhibited them to the public. These first museums were, however, rarely accessible to all members of the public, catering instead to the upper classes. In addition, though the ancient world is well known for its fantastic gardens, genuine botanical gardens began to appear at universities during the sixteenth and seventeenth centuries in the interest of scientific study.

Until the eighteenth century, museums were chiefly concerned with collecting the beautiful and the curious, and their collections were often motivated by personal interests. During the nineteenth and twentieth centuries, however, museums, cultural institutions, and public art galleries grew rapidly throughout Europe and the United States. It was during this intense period of proliferation that the concept of the museum as something more than just a storehouse for invaluable treasures was developed. Museums began to dedicate themselves to conservation, preservation, and, most important, research. Natural history, science, and art museums became scholarly centers of academic research and thought. Once museums and other cultural institutions became public, exhibition became a much more central concern. Prior museum goals, such as collection, conservation, and preservation, suddenly became the means to procure interesting and desirable exhibitions.

Museums developed slowly in the United States. American painter and naturalist Charles Wilson Peale founded a natural history museum in the late eighteenth century in Philadelphia. He is considered the first great American museum director. In 1846, James Smithson, a British scientist, made a bequest to the United States "for the increase and diffusion of knowledge" that led to the development of the Smithsonian Institution. In its formative years, however, the Smithsonian remained devoted to research; it was not until 1873 that it widened its scope to include all areas of the arts and humanities. The United States finally made its mark on the development of the modern museum

in 1870, with the founding of the American Museum of Natural History (AMNH) and the Metropolitan Museum of Art in New York, as well as the Museum of Fine Arts in Boston.

The influence and spread of the automobile also led to museums, historical sites, and cultural institutions being located outside major cities. Historic homes, battlefields, and other such sites became more popular, and sites that were maintained and opened for the public became more widespread. Throughout the twentieth century, museums and other cultural institutions began to focus on education. American museums, especially, became devoted to public education. Many such organizations also transformed themselves into cultural centers with performing arts, music, and film presentations.

The Industry Today

A 2007 AAM survey identified four critical challenges that museums will face over the coming years: obtaining increased public funding rather

Behind-the-scenes preparation for a museum exhibit. (©Dreamstime.com)

than relying on private funds and benefactors; adapting to changes in technology, including new educational technologies, while still maintaining current museum practices and standards; developing new leaders, particularly among recent graduates and young professionals; and maintaining their relevance in the face of rapid social and cultural change. Though the industry is predicted to rise, it still faces considerable challenges in the face of the changing cultural landscape. Whereas museums were once regarded as warehouses of knowledge and shrines to specific aspects of history or culture, they have recently come under fire as outdated, stale buildings devoted to antiquated ways of thinking. In response, many cultural institutions have dedicated themselves to updating their exhibitions, expanding their collections and gift shops, and refining and publicizing their research. They have attempted to become more accessible through alternative approaches, such as mobile and online exhibits, as well as adopting educational programs for adults and children alike, including guided tours, demonstrations, lectures, and study groups.

Germain Bazin (1901-1990), former chief curator of the Louvre, once commented,

> Perhaps the most significant contribution America has made to the concept of the museum is in the field of education. It is common practice for a museum to offer lectures and concerts, show films,

circulate exhibitions, publish important works of art. The museum has metamorphosed into a university for the general public—an institution of learning and enjoyment for all men. The concept has come full circle. The museum of the future will more and more resemble the academy of learning the "mouseion" connoted for the Greeks.

There are more than eleven thousand museums in the United States, more than half of which are free to the public. Rather than dusty storehouses of artifacts, these organizations have evolved into vital cultural institutions that strive to reach a wider population. They extend to classrooms, theaters, cinemas, performance halls, and the Internet. As they continue to evolve and adapt to the changing interests and habits of their visitors, museums have never been more exciting.

INDUSTRY MARKET SEGMENTS

Museums range in size from small storefronts to major institutions that occupy entire city blocks and form the cornerstones of some cities' cultural identities. Historical sites may be otherwise-unremarkable patches of ground marked by small plaques or large parks featuring elaborate historical diplays. Because they are not-for-profit institutions, the size of these organizations is measured by their operating budgets rather than their revenues.

Small Institutions

Museums may be classified as small if they have annual operating budgets of less than $250,000. Small institutions are commonly staffed by volunteers and generally have only two or three full-time paid employees. Many small organizations target specific communities or neighborhoods, serve local interests, and represent local and regional cultures and communities. With the rise of the Internet and digital access to col-

A man at an astronomical museum in California looks up. (©Dreamstime.com)

The Griffith Observatory is a great place to see the stars while visiting Los Angeles. (©Dreamstime.com)

lections and exhibitions, very small museums have been able to grow and reach a larger clientele that lives outside their immediate physical area.

An example of a small institution might be a historic home. The significance of such homes is intensely local; for example, one may have belonged to the founder of a small community, or it may have been the home or office of a local official who later went on to greater prominence. Staff might include only one or two full-time employees responsible for administration, maintenance, exhibitions, and visitor interaction. Curators or managers of small museums are generally experts in the relevant focus of the museum. They are in daily contact with visitors, becoming their institutions' primary educators. Volunteers may be involved in tours, interactive experiences, reenactments, and collections management.

Potential Annual Earnings Scale. The average annual salary for a museum curator according to the U.S. Bureau of Labor Statistics (BLS) was about $51,540 in 2008. A curator at a small museum can expect to receive a below-average salary.

Clientele Interaction. Small museums offer opportunities for close interaction between museum professionals (such as curators, historians, and art historians) and visitors, since most museum staff members often take on multiple roles. This interaction allows them insight into visitors' interests and enables them to hear feedback firsthand.

Amenities, Atmosphere, and Physical Grounds. Small museums and cultural institutions generally occupy small spaces of only a few thousand square feet or less. Some are housed in dedicated buildings, while others are located within larger buildings. Local history museums are usually located in spaces of historical relevance, while art galleries typically rent space in larger offices or retail complexes. Botanical and zoological gardens can be located anywhere, so long as the grounds have been sufficiently landscaped. Visitor amenities are typically few. Small museums may have gift shops, but they will usually lack additional amenities such as restaurants, classrooms, or libraries. Employees are expected to be pleasant, helpful, and informed about their museums' exhibits and collections. Since small museums are heavily dependent on visitor contributions and donations, interactions between staff and visitors are of paramount importance.

Typical Number of Employees. Small institutions are widely staffed by volunteers and generally have only two or three full-time paid employees. The total number of volunteers varies according to the location of the institution and the nature of its collections. For example, the number of volunteers at an aquarium in Chicago would likely be much higher than that at a historic home in Frederick, Maryland.

Traditional Geographic Locations. Small museums, zoos, gardens, and other fine arts or cultural institutions can be found in cities and towns of every size. Since many small organizations target specific communities or neighborhoods, they are found in major cities such as New York and San Francisco, as well as in smaller suburban and rural locations. A large percentage of small organizations, however, tend to be located outside major metropolitan areas in order to avoid competition from midsize and large institutions that have larger budgets, more publicity, and wider popularity among the general population.

Pros of Working for a Small Museum. Small institutions explore themes and topics of local relevance that are typically overlooked at larger institutions. This local relevance combined with a high level of staff-visitor interaction provides curators with the freedom to be more responsive to their communities' needs and interests. Collections and exhibitions at small institutions are usually immediately accessible, so visitors need not experience long waits. Such museums, then, can provide intimate visitor experiences unmatched at larger institutions. Volunteers at small museums tend to be committed and supportive, and both volunteers and staff enjoy relative freedom from bureaucracy.

Cons of Working for a Small Museum. The staff of a small museum or cultural institution often has a plethora of responsibilities, including collec-

tions management, conservation, exhibit design, administration, grounds maintenance, and facilities oversight. Budgets are usually small and tight, with no funds allocated for professional development or training. This means that staff members rarely have the opportunity to attend professional conferences or training sessions. Little time and few resources are spent on experimentation and collaboration. Small institutions tend to be undervalued in the wider industry, and board members tend to be unaware of protocols and procedures.

Costs

Payroll and Benefits: Small museums and fine arts institutions generally pay an hourly wage or yearly salary. Benefits can range from full to no benefits and may include health insurance, 401(k) plans, and paid vacation and sick time.

Supplies: Museums require the materials used to create and assemble exhibits and displays, including glass or plastic cases, audiovisual equipment, picture frames, pedestals, and so forth, as well as the tools to maintain them. They also require standard office supplies and equipment, such as paper, telephones, and computers.

External Services: Some small museums contract third-party landscaping services. They may also seek professional accounting or legal services, especially when taxes are due. Cleaning of exhibition and office space is typically performed by staff.

Utilities: Museums must pay typical utilities, including electricity, heating, water, telephone, and Internet access.

Taxes: Nonprofit organizations are often exempt from taxes, including income taxes and property taxes. There are exceptions in some jurisdictions, and all nonprofits must still pay employer payroll taxes on employees' wages and salaries.

Midsize Institutions

Museums may be classified as midsize if they have annual operating budgets of between $250,000 and $1 million. Midsize institutions have many more people on staff than do small institutions, but they still rely heavily on volunteer support for various job responsibilities. Like small institutions, many midsize organizations target specific communities or neighborhoods, serve local interests, and represent local and regional cultures and communities. However, midsize museums and cultural institutions also serve wider audiences with broader interest bases. Many such organizations are able to compete with larger institutions for visitors, publicity, and funding.

An example of a midsize institution might be a state natural history museum. While such a museum's exhibitions and research focus on subjects of general interest and significance, they usually have a local or regional flavor. For example, the museum might mount an exhibit of North American mammals (general interest) found in the North Carolina Piedmont (regional interest). Staff would include a full roster of museum professionals, including administrators, maintenance crew, exhibition designers, and visitor-services staff. Many midsize institutions have reciprocal membership agreements with partner museums, so paying members of one museum enjoy membership privileges at the museum's partners as well. Such a partnering group may include institutions of similar size or focus located in different regions, or it may include a set of nearby cultural institutions within the same region.

Potential Annual Earnings Scale. Employees at midsize institutions generally earn average salaries for their professions. According to the BLS, the average annual salary for a curator in 2008 was $51,540; the average salary for an archivist was $48,200; and the average salary for a museum technician or conservator was $40,750.

Clientele Interaction. Midsize museums offer opportunities for close interaction between museum professionals (such as curators, historians, and art historians) and visitors, since some museum staff members take on multiple roles. Positions at midsize institutions are significantly more specialized than are those at small organizations, so some staff members tend to have responsibilities that separate them from day-to-day public operations. Nevertheless, a large proportion of midsize museums' staffs experience a relatively high degree of direct contact with visitors.

Amenities, Atmosphere, and Physical Grounds. Midsize museums and cultural institutions generally occupy dedicated buildings of several thousand square feet, with separate exhibition, storage, and office spaces. History museums of this size are located in a space of historical relevance with regional or national significance. Botanical and zoological gardens can conceivably be located anywhere, so long as their grounds are sufficiently landscaped. Visitor amenities may include a wide range of options, including a permanent exhibition, temporary exhibitions, education programs, arts programs, a museum shop, a cafeteria or restaurant, and carefully landscaped or manicured grounds.

Visitor-services staff and docents have the most direct interaction with visitors. They are expected to be pleasant, helpful, and informed about their museums' exhibitions. Many midsize organizations depend heavily on visitor contributions, entrance fees, and membership, so this interaction is of paramount importance.

Typical Number of Employees. The total number of staff members at a midsize institution can range from as few as five to several dozen. This includes a full roster of museum professionals, with individuals trained and responsible for administration, maintenance, exhibitions, and visitor interaction. Most midsize museums employ design staff for graphic and environmental design projects, including exhibitions. In addition to traditional two-dimensional and three-dimensional designers and architects, design departments may include audiovisual specialists, software engineers, audience research and evaluation specialists, writers and editors, and art handlers. Many staff members possess advanced degrees in their particular areas of specialization.

Traditional Geographic Locations. Midsize museums and cultural institutions can be found in cities and towns of every size. A large percentage of midsize organizations, however, tend to be located in and around midsize and large metropolitan areas, where they have access to a wider potential audience and the resources necessary for operation. Because of their location, midsize institutions face competition from large institutions with larger budgets, more publicity, and wider popularity among the general population. However, they generally focus on more specialized subjects with specific regional interests.

Pros of Working for a Midsize Museum. Midsize institutions explore themes and topics of regional and national relevance that are typically glossed over at larger institutions. Staff members have the opportunity for more specialized positions, with the ability to focus on specific topics. The collections and exhibitions are also more accessible than at larger organizations. With larger budgets, larger membership, and wider publicity than small museums or cultural institutions, staff can afford more experimentation and collaboration in their work. There is also a greater possibility of career advancement; because of their larger budgets and wider renown, midsize institutions often have more qualified candidates for vacancies, and they are able to benefit from the skills, training, experience, and vision that such individuals bring to their work.

Cons of Working for a Midsize Museum. Some staff members at midsize institutions have a wide range of responsibilities, including collections management, registration, and conservation. Although budgets are significantly higher than at small institutions, they still remain tight in certain respects. While funds may be reserved for professional development, these are rarely sufficient to provide opportunities for all staff members. Many times, only those in supervisory roles receive training or attend conferences. Salaries and benefit packages also tend to be lower than they are at large institutions. While education and arts programs are offered, they tend to be individual events. Budgets are rarely large enough for the wide spectrum of rich programming found at large organizations.

Costs

Payroll and Benefits: Midsize museums and cultural institutions typically pay annual salaries. Benefits can range from full to no benefits and may include health insurance, 401(k) plans, and paid vacation and sick time.

Supplies: Museums require the materials used to create and assemble exhibits and displays, including glass or plastic cases, audiovisual equipment, picture frames, pedestals, and so forth, as well as the tools to maintain them. They also require standard office supplies and equipment, such as paper, telephones, and computers.

External Services: Landscaping and cleaning services are usually contracted out by midsize institutions. However, these cleaning services are usually limited to public areas and office space. Care and cleaning of objects on display are typically performed by staff.

Utilities: Museums must pay typical utilities, including electricity, heating, water, telephone, and Internet access.

Taxes: Nonprofit organizations are often exempt from taxes, including income taxes and property taxes. There are exceptions in some jurisdictions, and all nonprofits must still pay employer payroll taxes on employees' wages and salaries.

Large Institutions

Museums may be classified as large if they have annual operating budgets of more than $1 million. Large institutions have many people on staff, and they typically offer volunteer positions for students interested in learning more about museum studies or about the particular focus of the institution. Large museums and cultural institutions serve extensive audiences with broad interest bases. They typically are founded on wide-reaching topics, such as natural history, American art, or African American culture. Many such organizations command significant visitorship, membership, publicity, and funding.

An example of a large institution might be an established zoo, such as the San Diego or Philadelphia zoos. Exhibitions and research at a municipal zoo target subjects of general interest and usually of national or international significance, such as wildlife conservation and the protection of natural habitats. The staff of any large institution includes a full roster of professionals, including such employees as administrators, maintenance crew, exhibition designers, conservation specialists, veterinarians, and visitor services staff. Visitors enjoy a wide range of opportunities, including permanent exhibitions, temporary exhibitions, education programs, arts programs, family events, travel opportunities, special holiday events, several museum shops, and several cafeterias or restaurants. Visitors may participate in robust membership programs that include many incentives.

Potential Annual Earnings Scale. Large institutions often pay above-average salaries. According to the BLS, the average annual salary for a curator in 2008 was $51,540; the average salary for an archivist was $48,200; and the average salary for a museum technician or conservator was $40,750. The average salary for a zoologist was $58,820, and the average salary for a conservation scientist was $60,170.

Clientele Interaction. Large museums offer few opportunities for close interaction between museum professionals (such as curators, historians, and art historians) and visitors. Nearly all staff members are engaged in specialized work that keeps them separate from the public day-to-day operations of the museum. It is the responsibility of visitor services staff members to interact with the public, and they become the conduits through whom the professional work of the museum filters down to visitors and through whom the concerns and feedback of the visitors reach the rest of the staff.

Amenities, Atmosphere, and Physical Grounds. Large museums and cultural institutions occupy dedicated buildings that may be several hundred thousand square feet or more, with separate exhibition, storage, and office spaces. Many continually undergo renovation and expansion, and large institutions are generally state of the art in all respects. Often, the architecture and design of buildings and grounds are as much a draw for tourists as are the exhibitions housed inside. Visitor amenities include permanent and temporary (traveling) exhibitions, libraries or archives, education programs, arts programs, family events, travel opportunities, special holiday or seasonal events, several museum shops, several cafeterias or restaurants, and carefully landscaped or manicured grounds.

Visitor services staff have the most direct interaction with visitors, and they are expected to be pleasant, helpful, and informed about their museums' exhibits. Many large organizations depend on entrance fees and membership, so a positive visitor experience is of paramount importance.

Typical Number of Employees. The total number of staff members can range from a few dozen to several hundred. This staff typically includes a full roster of museum professionals, with individuals specially trained in and responsible for administration, maintenance, exhibitions, and visitor interaction. Large museums typically employ design staff for graphic and environmental design projects, including exhibitions. In addition to traditional two-dimensional and three-dimensional designers and architects, these staff departments may include audiovisual specialists, software engineers, audience research and evaluation specialists, writers and editors, educators, and art han-

dlers. Most staff members possess advanced degrees in their particular areas of specialization.

Traditional Geographic Locations. Large museums, zoos, gardens, and similar fine arts or cultural institutions are typically found in large cities, where they have access to wide audiences and the resources necessary for operation. Large institutions tend to face little competition from similar, smaller organizations. However, because of their locations and high entrance fees, they do face competition from other, unrelated tourist attractions. For example, the Metropolitan Museum of Art in New York City faces little competition from smaller art museums, but it competes for visitors' time and money with other attractions such as the Statue of Liberty and the Empire State Building.

Pros of Working for a Large Museum. Large institutions explore themes and topics of national and international relevance that simply cannot be covered in depth at smaller institutions. Staff members have the opportunity to occupy more specialized positions and focus on specific topics. Younger staff members also benefit from their proximity to senior professionals with significant knowledge and experience. With large budgets and membership, as well as wide publicity, staff can afford significant experimentation and collaboration in their work. Large institutional budgets also enhance program planning, exhibition design, and education programs.

Generally, large museums' budgets almost always have funds set aside for professional development and training. As a result of this funding, as well as of their larger and more hierarchically organized staffs, these institutions provide significant opportunities for career advancement. Because of their large budgets and wide renown, large institutions often receive applications from the most qualified candidates for vacancies, and they are able to benefit from the skills, training, experience, and vision that such individuals bring to their work. Salaries and benefit packages also tend to be among the most competitive available.

Cons of Working for a Large Museum. Because of their size and popularity, large institutions cannot offer the intimate, personal visitor experience that smaller institutions can. Exhibitions are typically conceived, planned, and implemented based on staff research interests, current events, or prevailing trends in the industry, rather than visitor feedback or the unique and specific interests of the local community. Many large institutions have such large collections that only a fraction can be displayed at any one time, thereby keeping a majority of the collection unknown to the general public. Staff members tend to become isolated within their departments, and interaction with other divisions (for example, between the collections and education departments) can be rare or limited.

Costs

Payroll and Benefits: Large museums typically pay annual salaries, including full benefits such as health insurance, 401(k) plans, and paid vacation and sick time.

Supplies: Museums require the materials used to create and assemble exhibits and displays, including glass or plastic cases, audiovisual equipment, picture frames, pedestals, and so forth, as well as the tools to maintain them. They also require standard office supplies and equipment, such as paper, telephones, and computers.

External Services: Landscaping and cleaning services are usually contracted out by large institutions. However, these cleaning services are usually limited to public areas and office space. Care and cleaning of objects on display is typically performed by staff. Many large institutions also contract external security services.

Utilities: Museums must pay for typical utilities, including electricity, heating, water, telephone, and Internet access.

Taxes: Nonprofit organizations are often exempt from taxes, including income taxes and property taxes. There are exceptions in some jurisdictions, and all nonprofits must still pay employer payroll taxes on employees' wages and salaries.

ORGANIZATIONAL STRUCTURE AND JOB ROLES

Any size museum or cultural institution needs to account for activities in the following areas. In smaller institutions, one person generally holds several roles within several groups. In larger organizations, specialists fulfill unique requirements in specific groups. Regardless of size and scope, the functions must be fulfilled.

The following umbrella categories apply to the organizational structure of museums and cultural institutions:

- Business Management
- Education and Programming
- Collections and Registration
- Visitor Services
- Exhibitions
- Sales and Marketing
- Development
- Human Resources
- Libraries and Archives
- Facilities and Security

Business Management

Business managers are responsible for the day-to-day operations of their institutions. Responsibilities include establishing the vision or direction of the organization, directing a group of employees who can implement that vision, and managing finances. The typical employee in this area will have an advanced degree, usually with a focus on business. Typically, salaries for employees in this area are the highest in the institution. In addition to overseeing strategy and finance, business managers coordinate an institution's relationships with its partners, suppliers, and distributors.

Business management occupations may include the following:

- Chief Executive Officer (CEO)
- Chief Financial Officer (CFO)
- Chief Operating Officer (COO)
- Museum/Zoo Director
- Legal Counsel
- Business Manager
- Accountant

Education and Programming

Education and programming staff are responsible for the educational initiatives of an institution. They develop and teach classes for children and adults, organize outreach programs to local schools and community centers, program special events, and schedule and promote performing arts presentations, film screenings, and lectures. They are also responsible for recruiting and managing volunteers and docents.

Education and programming staff usually have advanced degrees in education or communications. They typically receive salaries that are on par with those of other nonadministrative staff at their institutions. In addition to programmatic responsibilities, individuals in education and programming roles coordinate relationships with local schools, community centers, parent groups, and special events vendors.

Education and programming occupations may include the following:

- Public Programming Director
- Special Events Director
- Education Curator
- Education Specialist
- Volunteer Coordinator

Collections and Registration

Collections and registration staff manage and preserve their institutions' collections and govern access to them. They ensure the proper care and handling of the objects in collections, including three-dimensional, multimedia, and document collections. These staff members store objects, register them in an institution's collections database, manage and track their documentation and provenance, package and ship them, and arrange access to them for researchers and scholars.

Collections staff usually have advanced degrees in art history or museum studies. They typically receive salaries that are on par with those of other nonadministrative staff at their institutions. Conservators have additional responsibilities to care for and conserve delicate or damaged objects. Many professional conservators tend to specialize—for example, in paper, textile, wood, art, or film conservation.

Collections and registration occupations may include the following:

- Collections Curator
- Collections Manager
- Registrar

OCCUPATION PROFILE

Archivist and Curator

Considerations	Qualifications
Description	Evaluates, classifies, and protects historical items and documents and maintains records regarding their acquisition and status.
Career clusters	Arts, A/V Technology, and Communication; Hospitality and Tourism
Interests	Data; people
Working conditions	Work inside
Minimum education level	Apprenticeship; master's degree; doctoral degree
Physical exertion	Light work
Physical abilities	Unexceptional/basic fitness
Opportunities for experience	Internship; apprenticeship; volunteer work; part-time work
Licensure and certification	Usually not required
Employment outlook	Faster-than-average growth expected
Holland interest score	AES; IRS

Note: See volume 1, "Publisher's Note," for an explanation of the Holland interest score.

- Conservator
- Museum Technician

Visitor Services

Visitor services staff are responsible for day-to-day public interaction with visitors. They conduct guided tours, staff information booths and customer-service counters, respond to visitor needs and questions, and ensure that the flow of visitors throughout buildings and grounds remains uninterrupted. They may or may not have advanced degrees, and their salaries are typically slightly lower than those of other nonadministrative employees of their institutions. Their duties may entail physical or manual activities, such as moving supplies, setting up or taking down chairs and tables for daily events, or participating in interactive tours and activities. They must also coordinate their activities with their institutions' sales, marketing, development, and security departments.

Visitor services occupations may include the following:

- Guest Services Coordinator
- Docent
- Coat Check Attendant

Exhibitions

Exhibitions staff design and construct exhibits. They plan and design new exhibits, then construct and produce exhibit spaces, displays, and supporting materials. They must plan electric wiring and lighting for exhibits, as well as designing or commissioning the security devices and procedures necessary to protect fragile or valuable objects from damage or theft. They are also responsible for security and maintenance of existing and permanent exhibits.

Exhibitions staff members may or may not have advanced degrees, but they typically have either degrees or experience in design, architecture, or carpentry. They typically receive salaries on par with, or slightly lower than, those of other nonadministrative employees of their institutions. They often work with their hands, using power tools and construction equipment to engineer, design, and build unique exhibits. They must coordinate their activities with their collections and facilities departments, as well as with relevant external vendors.

Exhibitions occupations may include the following:

- Exhibitions Curator
- Exhibit Designer
- Electrician
- Lighting Technician

Sales and Marketing

Sales and marketing staff manage publicity for their institutions. They publicize and market temporary and permanent exhibits, special events, and institutions' broader social and cultural objectives. Their responsibilities include managing museum stores, conducting promotional campaigns to build membership and attendance, and publicizing their institutions' social, educational, and humanitarian efforts in order to build their brands and reputations. They must build relationships with news agencies, advertising agencies, and retail-store suppliers in the service of their organizations.

Sales and marketing staff members usually have advanced degrees in journalism, communications, or marketing. They typically earn salaries that are on par with those of other nonadministrative employees of their institutions.

Sales and marketing occupations may include the following:

- Retail Store Manager
- Retail Sales Associate
- Public Relations Director
- Marketing Manager
- Graphic Designer

Development

Development staff raise money for their institutions by cultivating and retaining members and by mounting fund-raising campaigns. They coordinate and implement initiatives to attract new members, organize membership benefit programs, identify potential donors, and organize and implement fund-raising efforts. They must coordinate relationships with charitable organizations and relevant foundations, as well as individual members. They may or may not have advanced degrees and typically earn salaries that are on par with those of other nonadministrative employees of their institutions.

OCCUPATION SPECIALTIES

Archivists and Curators

Specialty	Responsibilities
Art conservators	Coordinate the examination, repair, and conservation of art objects.
Historic-site administrators	Manage the overall operations of a historic structure or site.
Museum registrars	Maintain records of the condition and location of objects in museum collections and oversee the movement of objects to other locations.
Museum technicians	Prepare specimens for museum collections and exhibits. They preserve and restore specimens by reassembling fragmented pieces and creating substitute pieces.

Development occupations may include the following:

- Membership Coordinator
- Fund-Raising Coordinator
- Director of Planned Giving

Human Resources

Human resources staff are responsible for recruiting, hiring, training, and firing personnel, as well as managing payroll and administering benefits. They coordinate relationships with relevant benefits providers, such as 401(k) plan administrators and health insurance providers, as well as recruitment agencies and payroll management companies. They may or may not have advanced degrees and typically earn salaries that are on par with those of other nonadministrative employees of their institutions.

Human resources occupations may include the following:

- Human Resources Manager
- Human Resources Generalist
- Benefits Specialist

Libraries and Archives

Librarians and archivists organize and manage their institutions' public libraries and internal archives. They acquire new materials, update and maintain internal databases, lend materials to re-

searchers and general patrons, and organize and maintain internal records related to their archives. They coordinate relationships with libraries and archives at similar institutions, as well as with publishers and other staff members. They typically have advanced degrees in library science and earn salaries that are on par with those of other nonadministrative employees of their institutions.

Library and archive occupations may include the following:

- Librarian
- Archivist

Facilities and Security

Facilities and security staff are responsible for the maintenance and security of their institutions' physical grounds and buildings. They landscape grounds, clean buildings and grounds, guard exhibits, and otherwise provide security for their institutions (including maintaining emergency alert and video surveillance systems). They also maintain and repair wiring; lighting; heating, ventilation, and air-conditioning (HVAC) systems; and electric systems such as elevators and escalators.

Facilities and security personnel are typically experienced in relevant skills and do not have advanced degrees. They are usually paid less than other nonadministrative employees. Much of their work is physical or manual. Individuals often work with their hands, using power tools and other specialized equipment to maintain, upgrade, and repair buildings and grounds. They must also coordinate relationships with external security agencies and facilities and maintenance vendors.

Facilities and security occupations may include the following:

- Facility Manager
- Building Maintenance and Repair Worker
- Employee Workplace Safety Manager
- Heating, Ventilation, and Air-Conditioning (HVAC) Technician
- Building Security Manager
- Security Guard
- Collections Warehouse Supervisor
- Computer Security Specialist

INDUSTRY OUTLOOK

Overview

As a result of the economic downturn of 2007-2009, museums and cultural institutions have experienced a decrease in revenue and donations (as well as a loss in the value of investments held in trusts), even though for many admissions have remained somewhat steady. For example, the American Folk Art Museum, located in midtown Manhattan, saw its revenue drop by half—from $6.4 million to $3.2 million—from fiscal 2008 to fiscal 2009. In addition, New York City's Metropolitan Opera reported in 2009 that its $300 million endowment had decreased in value by one-third. More glaring, the Nevada Department of Cultural Affairs cut its budget in 2009, resulting in state museums being closed four days per week. Other museums and institutions, facing similar fiscal cutbacks, have postponed exhibitions or suspended daily operations.

Nonetheless, according to the BLS, faster-than-average growth is expected in the museum industry, with employment expected to increase by approximately 18 percent by 2016. In addition, the National Employment Matrix projects employment for curators, archivists, and museum technicians to increase from twenty-seven thousand positions nationwide in 2006 to thirty-three thousand positions in 2016. Occupational employment statistics indicate that the median hourly wages and annual salaries for these positions are also on the rise. A growing interest in establishing and maintaining museum collections, in preserving the growing volume of records and information, and in exhibiting various collections publicly are all contributing factors to this growth.

However, competition for museum positions is, and will continue to be, high. As more people choose to pursue museum studies as a career option, the number of qualified candidates will continue to outnumber vacancies. Students who establish themselves in a more competitive position tend to hold advanced degrees and have a keen ability to work in a digital environment. This is particularly true as cultural institutions are increasingly making their collections available online and offering education opportunities and exhibits on the Internet and in other digital forms.

PROJECTED EMPLOYMENT FOR SELECTED OCCUPATIONS

Museums, Historical Sites, and Similar Institutions

Employment		
2009	Projected 2018	Occupation
5,790	8,100	Curators
3,940	5,600	Museum technicians and conservators
4,790	5,800	Nonfarm animal caretakers
1,980	2,700	Public relations specialists
11,670	13,600	Tour guides and escorts

Source: U.S. Bureau of Labor Statistics, Industries at a Glance, Occupational Employment Statistics and Employment Projections Program.

(Digital media and skills are equally relevant and in demand in the for-profit art industry.)

Many museums and cultural institutions are highly dependent on outside funding to continue their operations. Budgets are largely based on fund-raising efforts, grant acquisition, and membership support, and museums generally generate revenue based on earned income, membership, and philanthropy. As a result, job security and institutional budgets can fluctuate with periods of strong and weak national economic growth. The number of visitors is also influenced by trends in the wider travel and tourism industries. When tourism is on the rise, museum visitorship and membership also increase. When tourism is on the decline, museums and other cultural institutions have fewer visitors, fewer members, and smaller funds from external sources.

Employment Advantages

Most people who work in museums, zoos, galleries, and other cultural institutions find that their work combines learning and entertainment. Such organizations are natural fits for individuals with an interest in history, art, or the natural world. While academic environments are potentially static, museum work can be engaging and stimulating. Employees can work with subject material they enjoy in an environment that fosters appreciation of and interaction with that material on a variety of levels. Such work can also afford many opportunities for interaction with the general public. The number of small and midsize institutions is surprisingly large and growing. Job opportunities, though influenced by economic cycles, are usually available for a variety of roles in a variety of organizations.

Annual Earnings

According to Hoovers, museums and cultural institutions in the United States took in revenues of $9 billion in 2009. Although museums and cultural institutions are widespread and successful throughout the United States and many European countries, the industry is in relative infancy elsewhere. Many developing nations are currently home to only a few state-funded national museums, but there has recently been tremendous growth in the number of new museums that target local history, arts, and issues. These institutions tend to be private, for-profit organizations, but, ow-

ing to the current state of the industry, revenue and earnings statistics are unreliable.

RELATED RESOURCES FOR FURTHER RESEARCH

AMERICAN ASSOCIATION FOR STATE AND LOCAL
  HISTORY
1717 Church St.
Nashville, TN 37203-2991
Tel: (615) 320-3203
Fax: (615) 327-9013
http://www.aaslh.org

AMERICAN ASSOCIATION OF MUSEUMS
1575 Eye St. NW, Suite 400
Washington, DC 20005
Tel: (202) 289-1818
Fax: (202) 289-6578
http://www.aam-us.org

ASSOCIATION FOR LIVING HISTORY, FARMS, AND
  AGRICULTURAL MUSEUMS
8774 Rte. 45 NW
North Bloomfield, OH 44450
Tel: (440) 685-4410
http://www.alhfam.org

ASSOCIATION OF CHILDREN'S MUSEUMS
1300 L St. NW, Suite 975
Washington, DC 20005
Tel: (202) 898-1080
Fax: (202) 898-1086
http://www.childrensmuseums.org

ASSOCIATION OF COLLEGE AND UNIVERSITY
  MUSEUMS AND GALLERIES
40 Arts Circle Dr.
Evanston, IL 60208-2410
Tel: (847) 491-5893
Fax: (847) 467-4609
http://www.acumg.org

ASSOCIATION OF ZOOS AND AQUARIUMS
8403 Colesville Rd., Suite 710
Silver Spring, MD 20910-3314
Tel: (301) 562-0777
Fax: (301) 562-0888
http://www.aza.org

INTERNATIONAL COUNCIL OF MUSEUMS
1 rue Miollis
75732 Paris CEDEX 15
France
Tel: 33-1-4734-0500
Fax: 33-1-4306-7862
http://icom.museum/

MUSEUM STUDIES AND REFERENCE LIBRARY
National Museum of Natural History
Smithsonian Institution
10th and Constitution Ave. NW
Washington, DC 20560
Tel: (202) 633-1700
http://www.sil.si.edu

SOCIETY OF AMERICAN ARCHIVISTS
17 N State St., Suite 1425
Chicago, IL 60602-3315
Tel: (312) 606-0722
Fax: (312) 606-0728
http://www.archivists.org

ABOUT THE AUTHOR

Jamie Greene attended the University of Virginia, where he studied cultural anthropology and archaeology. He has held various curatorial and collections-management positions at the Academy of Natural Sciences in Philadelphia, the University of Virginia Art Museum in Charlottesville, and the U.S. Holocaust Memorial Museum in Washington, D.C. He also has considerable experience in the publishing and education industries.

FURTHER READING

Alexander, Edward P. *Museums in Motion: An Introduction to the History and Functions of Museums*. Walnut Creek, Calif.: AltaMira Press, 1996.

Burdick, Jan E. *Creative Careers in Museums*. New York: Allworth Press, 2008.

Center for the Future of Museums. *Museums and Society, 2034: Trends and Potential Futures*. Washington, D.C.: American Association of Museums, 2008. Available at http://aam-us.org/upload/museumssociety2034.pdf.

Chew, Ron. "In Praise of the Small Museum." *Museum News*, March/April, 2002. http://www.aam-us.org/pubs/mn/MN_MA02_SmallMuseums.cfm.

Institute for Career Research. *Careers in Museums: Director, Curator, Conservator, Exhibit Designer, Archivist*. Chicago: Author, 2007.

Rentzhog, Sten. *Open Air Museums: The History and Future of a Visionary Idea*. Stockholm: Carlsson, 2007.

Schlatter, N. Elizabeth. *Museum Careers: A Practical Guide for Novices and Students*. Walnut Creek, Calif.: Left Coast Press, 2008.

Society of American Archivists. "So You Want to Be an Archivist: An Overview of the Archival Profession." http://www2.archivists.org/profession.

U.S. Bureau of Labor Statistics. "Archivists, Curators, and Museum Technicians." In *Occupational Outlook Handbook*, 2010-2011 ed. http://www.bls.gov/oco/ocos065.htm.

———. *Career Guide to Industries*, 2010-2011 ed. http://www.bls.gov/oco/cg.

U.S. Census Bureau. North American Industry Classification System (NAICS), 2007. http://www.census.gov/cgi-bin/sssd/naics/naicsrch?chart=2007.

U.S. Department of Commerce. International Trade Administration. Office of Trade and Industry Information. Industry Trade Data and Analysis. http://ita.doc.gov/td/industry/otea/OTII/OTII-index.html.

Music Industry

©Dreamstime.com

INDUSTRY SNAPSHOT

General Industry: Arts and Entertainment

Career Cluster: Arts, A/V Technology, and Communication

Subcategory Industries: Instrument Manufacturing and Repair Industry; Integrated Record Production/Distribution; Music Arrangers; Music Directors; Music Publishers; Musical Groups and Artists; Musical Performance Organizers and Promoters; Sound Recording Industries

Related Industries: Broadcast Industry; Internet and Cyber Communications Industry; Motion Picture and Television Industry; Publishing and Information Industry; Retail Trade and Service Industry; Theater and Performing Arts Industry

Annual Domestic Revenues: $9.2 billion USD (*Pollstar*/International Federation of the Phonographic Industry, 2008; includes live performance industry)

Annual International Revenues: $12.6 billion/year (International Federation of the Phonographic Industry, 2008; not including live performance industry)

Annual Global Revenues: $18.4 billion USD (International Federation of the Phonographic Industry, 2008; not including live performance industry)

NAICS Numbers: 5122, 7113, 339992, 711130, 711510, 811490

INDUSTRY DEFINITION

Summary

The music industry encompasses multiple and diverse for-profit and nonprofit businesses that provide live and recorded music to listeners. Although the sound recording segment makes up a large share of the industry, concerts, music publishing and licensing, artist management, and fine arts outlets such as symphony orchestras all play important roles in the field. Industry products include both tangible goods, such as compact discs (CDs) and digital video discs (DVDs), and intangible products, such as electronic music files and concert performances. Musicians also rely on products and services supplied by the musical instrument manufacturing and repair industries, while listeners obtain physical or electronic recordings through the music retail industry.

History of the Industry

Although people have written and performed music for entertainment

By the 1990's, the CD had become the dominant music format, replacing the vinyl album on retail shelves. (©Sandra Van Der Steen/Dreamstime.com)

and cultural reasons for millennia, today's commercial music industry dates back only to the sheet music and concert industries of the 1700's. For over a century, music listeners consumed popular music exclusively through live performances. Musicians and singers performed at public venues or were hired to appear in private homes, and amateurs relied on printed sheet music to learn and play popular songs.

By the early twentieth century, the invention of the phonograph had changed the music industry dramatically. Standardized discs called records could hold about four-and-a-half minutes of recorded sound, and the sound recording industry had already begun to emerge. The first record companies, known as record labels, issued recordings of classical and popular music. New labels thrived during World War I, but the popularization of radio, which brought music and other programming to a wider audience, had a negative impact on the early record business during the 1920's. In 1931, two early record companies combined to form EMI (the only privately owned major music corporation as of 2007), beginning a long history of mergers and acquisitions within the industry.

During the 1940's, technological innovations brought the first tape recording, and the perfection of polyvinyl chloride (PVC) led to the development of the familiar vinyl album. Magnetic tape cartridges—first commercially available as eight-track tapes—proved to be a major addition to the industry, allowing many new recording studios to appear throughout the world. For the first time, serious efforts to record lesser-known music began, widely expanding the available catalog of recorded music.

Although the 1950's had begun with only five major record labels, the success of rock-and-roll music during that decade encouraged a spate of new, independent imprints dedicated to the emerging genre. Shifting consumer tastes were influenced by the increasing popularity of rock, particularly after the British Invasion of 1964. Demand for the singer-songwriter-driven sounds of previous decades declined. Instead, music became a force for social protest and change. Cassette tape recording techniques improved, and the format grew in popularity and availability throughout the 1970's. Airwaves offered new sounds such as rock and funk and, later, disco and punk to avid music listeners.

During the 1980's, the dual emergence of Sony's Walkman, a portable personal tape player, and the cable television network MTV contributed to a musical revolution. Music videos became a vital promotional tool for artists—to the extent that the premieres of videos by artists such as Michael Jackson, marketed as "world premiere video" events, became cultural touchstones. Music became mobile for the first time with the Walkman, and the cassette tape enjoyed a brief heyday as the dominant musical format stretching from the late 1970's into the next decade.

The CD emerged as the dominant music format by the beginning of the 1990's, eventually replacing the increasingly outdated vinyl album on retail shelves. (Vinyl sales, however, have increased since 2006, propelled by both nostalgia and their accurate sound, though their place on the commercial scale remains minuscule.) This same decade saw an end to the pop-driven sounds that had dominated the 1970's and 1980's, with grunge rock and hip-hop becoming the defining styles of the era. By the end of the century, the rise of the Internet had provided listeners with a new source of recorded music: digital music. Soon, digital music formats such as MPEG-1 audio layer 3, or MP3, grew in importance and popularity, and the first online peer-to-peer (P2P) sharing service, Napster, electrified an industry concerned about music piracy.

The Industry Today

The twenty-first century music industry is experiencing significant change. Modern technologies, particularly the Internet and its associated technologies, have greatly altered the ways that people discover, acquire, and listen to music. As of 2009, just four companies—Sony BMG Music Entertainment, Warner Music Group, Universal Music Group, and EMI—dominated the sound recording industry.

In the 2000's, the popularity of digital music format began to alter the music industry. (©Yuri Arcurs/Dreamstime.com)

However, technology shifts and the rise of online music downloading have contributed to steep declines in record label revenue. According to a 2007 study conducted by the think tank Institute for Policy Innovation, illegal music downloads and physical sales of pirated recordings cost the United States economy $12.5 billion annually.

Record companies and trade organizations have acted vigorously to halt the flow of illegally downloaded music since the early 2000's, and within a few years, legitimately purchased downloads began to steadily increase. By 2008, digital music sales had grown to encompass about one-fifth of all global music purchases, according to statistics gathered by the International Federation of the Phonographic Industry (IFPI). This trend was even more pronounced in the United States, where digital sources represented about one-third of total sales. Rock music remains the most popular genre by far, according to sales figures from the Recording Industry Association of America (RIAA); it is trailed closely by country and western, hip-hop, and rhythm and blues (R&B), respectively.

Rising online music sales and competition from big-box retailers such as Walmart and Best Buy have also hit brick-and-mortar specialty music retailers hard, contributing to widespread store and chain closures. According to figures published by the RIAA, the percentage of music purchases made at traditional record stores declined from just over 44 percent in 1999 to only 30 percent in 2008. Consequently, according to a January, 2008, report from marketing research company NPD Group, the top five music retailers of 2007, in order, were digital-only retailer Apple, Walmart, Best Buy, Amazon, and Target. (A large percentage of sales at each retailer were attributed to gift cards.) In addition, according to Research and Markets in 2007, the top fifty music retailers earned 80 percent of music-store revenue. In the spring of 2009, the largest music store in the United States by volume—the Virgin Megastore in New York City's Times Square—closed its doors.

At the same time that traditional retailing industries have declined, the live performance industry has grown significantly. Year-over-year, revenue increases have been the norm since the early 2000's, bolstered greatly by the high ticket prices commanded by the world's top acts and, to a lesser extent, a general upward trend in live performance attendance. According to concert trade publication *Pollstar*, live performance revenues for North American tours reached $4.2 billion in 2008, which represents a strong 7 percent increase over the previous year. That same year, country artist Kenny Chesney sold more than one million tickets to performances in North America alone, a testament to the immense selling potential of top artists.

In addition, live events promoter and venue owner Live Nation has begun actively courting major recording artists for its so-called 360 deals. These agreements give the concert promoter a stake in all of the signed artists' musical output, including albums, music merchandise, Web sites, concert films, and DVD sales, as well as exclusive rights to promote the artists' associated tours. As of 2009, four big-name acts—pop singer Madonna, rock bands U2 and Nickelback, and hip-hop performer Jay-Z—had signed on. (In 2009, Live Nation also merged with Ticketmaster, the nation's largest ticket broker, in a $2.5 billion deal that was scrutinized for antitrust implications.)

Licensing and product integration remain vital to the music industry. Much as filming a successful music video could make or break an artist during the height of the MTV era, placing a song in a commercial, television program, or video game offers performers, songwriters, and record labels needed exposure and significant revenue streams.

INDUSTRY MARKET SEGMENTS

The music industry is highly segmented into a plethora of enterprises. Advancements in sound recording technology have made high-quality recording affordable for almost anyone. Professional quality recordings that once required a full studio and significant resources can now be made in private homes with a personal computer and minimal recording equipment. At the same time, a handful of key corporations dominates the music distribution subsector. As a result, the music industry is one

Live performances are popular and generate substantial revenue. (©Dreamstime.com)

of the most variable industries in existence in terms of business size. It is one of the few economic sectors in which individuals and multinational corporations alike exert significant influence and constitute significant brands.

Small Businesses

Small businesses make up an important segment of the music industry. Nearly any type of business that can exist in the industry is represented in the small business segment. These businesses may be as small as one person—such as a solo musician, talent manager, agent, or music retailer. Other small businesses may be considerably larger, with twenty or twenty-five employees. Small businesses often gain success by focusing on a certain niche, such as retailers selling specialty products—used equipment or CDs, for example—or agents or venues that book acts only in a specific genre of music. Some music retailers have closed their brick-and-mortar operations and conduct their business solely online.

Because of the wide revenue spread between those working part time in the industry and those who have become widely successful, such as top-earning acts and agents, a small music business may earn practically no money or millions of dollars each year.

Potential Annual Earnings Scale. Because many individuals pursue music as a hobby, some part-time musicians, promoters, and record label owners may net practically nothing from their businesses. According to the U.S. Bureau of Labor Statistics (BLS), the median earnings of professional musicians who perform with a symphony orchestra or religious organization were $19.73 per hour in 2006. Highly successful recording artists may make millions of dollars each year.

Clientele Interaction. Small businesses can allow for a great deal of interaction between workers and clients. A small venue owner, for example, may take on multiple roles, such as talent booking, accounting, supply ordering, and human resources, while generally managing the nuts and bolts of the business. The venue might have fifteen or twenty employees who sell and take tickets for musical performances, staff the venue's bar, assist the touring musicians who play at the venue, and provide general security during events. All of these workers interact with attendees at performances and may deal directly with the artists and their road crew. Also, independent bands and musicians are often responsible for selling their own wares, such as T-shirts and CDs, after or before shows.

At traditional small or independent music stores, a sense of community was often important to the success of the operation. For example, in the heyday of music stores, store employees often served as "tastemakers," suggesting new music for their customers. While this has largely changed, as online sales and big-box retailers are pushing mom-and-pop stores aside, personal interaction is still an important part of fostering success.

Amenities, Atmosphere, and Physical Grounds. Some music businesses may be operated in the most basic setups, such as an extra room of an apartment or home. Others may rent limited office or retail space. The atmosphere is often casual, in accord with the nature of the work, but it may also be quite stressful. For example, a small-business operator engaged in booking acts for a summer festival may spend a great deal of time listening to new groups or reading music magazines, all the while juggling phone calls, scrambling to arrange a successful lineup, and negotiating contract details.

Many bands spend long hours traveling from venue to venue in a van packed with the group's members, road crew, and equipment. More successful artists may travel in relative comfort aboard large buses, with separate vehicles carrying their gear and road staff. Bands typically have access to a private area to relax, and these areas can range greatly in terms of comfort and cleanliness.

Typical Number of Employees. Most small businesses in the music industry have relatively few employees, ranging from just one to twenty or twenty-five. For example, Chris Lombardi started independent record label Matador in 1989. At first, he ran the label by himself out of his apartment. Twenty years later, the business had expanded to include an artist roster of about twenty and a staff of twenty-three. Perhaps the most common small music business, the musical artist or group, typically has one to five members.

Traditional Geographic Locations. A small music business may be located practically anywhere. Although many bands relocate to New York and Los Angeles in the hopes of increased exposure, many other cities, such as Nashville, Tennessee; Austin, Texas; and Atlanta, Georgia, have been hubs for varying styles of music. Smaller cities may be home to independent record labels and promoters that release music and put on shows by local or regional artists.

Pros of Working for a Small Business. Many people establish small music businesses for the personal satisfaction of being part of the industry. Small-business owners perform a range of job duties and generally have the freedom to make creative decisions, such as what music to perform, what bands to book, or what albums to release. Music industry business owners and staff often attend live performances for free and may work with famous musicians. Artists have the remote chance of achieving great financial success.

Cons of Working for a Small Business. Small-business owners are often sole proprietors, meaning that all the financial risks of their organizations lie with them. Thus, an event such as a lawsuit for copyright infringement could bankrupt not only a record label, but also its owner. Musicians, whether self-employed or on the staff of a small arts organization, often experience extended periods of unemployment between tours or performing arts seasons. Because musicians typically earn the bulk of their income from performances, this can leave them short of cash or forced to seek alternate employment.

In addition, small retailers and independent record stores are often subject to cost-cutting efforts from large labels. For example, in June of 2009, EMI informed its smaller accounts, mostly small and independent stores, that it was no longer selling its products directly to them, instead directing them to third-party distributors, who sell at higher prices.

Costs

Payroll and Benefits: Small businesses may pay workers on an hourly or salaried basis, and benefits can range from extensive packages with health insurance and retirement plans to nothing at all. Even small record labels typically pay advances to signed artists. Self-employed musicians often earn money sporadically through quarterly royalty payments, as well as through licensing and performance fees.

Supplies: Musicians typically own their own instruments and sound equipment, while business managers and record labels need office supplies and computers.

External Services: Necessary external services depend on the type of business operated. Artists employ many outside services, often having business managers and booking agents, as well as employing road crews such as touring managers, soundboard operators, and instrument technicians. Record labels pay for studio time and production services for signed artists and may employ outside accountants or lawyers. Small retailers such as music stores or online ventures may also contract outside services for printing catalogs, accounting or ordering systems, and other related services.

Utilities: An office-based business, such as a record label or a small music retailer, requires physical utilities such as heat, water, electricity, telephone, and Internet access. A touring band would need to pay for travel, lodging, and vehicle costs.

Taxes: Small private businesses and self-employed workers must pay applicable local, state, and federal taxes on all revenues. Nonprofit organizations, such as symphony orchestras, must file tax forms but do not pay taxes. Any small business that has employees must pay a portion of those employees' Social Security and Medicare taxes, while self-employed workers instead pay a special self-employment tax to cover their share of Social Security and Medicare taxes.

Midsize Businesses

Midsize companies and businesses generally employ a few hundred employees and have much higher revenues than do small businesses, with some topping half a billion dollars. Examples of companies at this level include record labels, music venues, and large symphony orchestras, as well as regional, independent music-store chains. During the late twentieth and early twenty-first centuries, mergers and buyouts led to many small and midsize companies becoming subsidiaries of larger corporations. Some of these companies continue to operate largely as independent businesses, while others have been more or less completely subsumed by their parent companies.

Potential Annual Earnings Scale. A typical midsize music business takes in revenues between $1 million and hundreds of millions of dollars. Diversification into fields such as merchandising or publishing can significantly increase a company's earnings potential. For example, record label Bad Boy Entertainment (now Bad Boy Records) earned about $600 million in 2008 from its music, television, fashion, and other business activities. Similarly, regional midlevel music retailer Newbury Comics, which has twenty-eight locations in the New England area as of 2009, sells pop-culture-related goods and comics in addition to music CDs and DVDs. Company-wide revenue for the store was projected to be $77 million in 2008.

Clientele Interaction. The increased size of midsize businesses often brings a greater structural hierarchy. Staff members at performance venues or who work for a fine arts organization may interact with the general public, but many music businesses of this size function on a business-to-business model. For example, midsize record labels may employ regional representatives, who call on retail business owners and managers to promote their labels' albums. In midlevel music stores, clientele interaction may not be as personal as that in small, independently minded stores, but employees may still be instrumental in influencing consumer tastes.

Amenities, Atmosphere, and Physical Grounds. Although some employees may spend time traveling with performing artists, seeking out new acts at clubs, or conducting other business, staff members are likely to have permanent work spaces in cubicles or offices. Symphony orchestras may have office space in a performing arts complex. For example, the New York Philharmonic both performs and has administrative offices at New York City's Lincoln Center. Large performance venues may be extensive outdoor complexes with seating areas, food and beverage outlets, and extensive landscaping.

The atmosphere of midsize companies varies but is likely to be more relaxed than a traditional corporate environment. Many music companies promote a laid-back, jeans-and-T-shirt corporate culture. Many midsize businesses have grown from small business roots, and these may retain a similar atmosphere.

Typical Number of Employees. Midsize music businesses may employ from one hundred to one thousand people, either at a central location or spread throughout multiple locations. These employees are more likely than their small business

counterparts to have defined job duties. For example, for a record label, defined job duties would be in such areas as artist development, marketing and public relations, legal affairs, talent management, and business administration. For midlevel music retailers, beyond storefront personnel, other areas would be warehouse and distribution.

Traditional Geographic Locations. Unlike small businesses, midsize companies are likely to cluster around traditional entertainment meccas such as New York, Los Angeles, and London. Some may operate offices or outlets in more than one of those cities. For example, the New York-based Knitting Factory operates concert venues in Brooklyn and Los Angeles, as well as Spokane, Washington, and Boise, Idaho. Substantial symphony orchestras employing significant numbers of musicians and administrative workers can be found in New York City, Boston, Chicago, Los Angeles, and other major metropolitan areas throughout the world. Because certain types of music are associated with particular cities—for example, country music with Nashville—businesses that cater to specific segments of the industry are likely to maintain offices in those cities.

Pros of Working for a Midsize Business. The greater scope of a midsize business means that jobs are generally more specialized. This specialization may appeal to those business owners who prefer to handle top-level decision making or management rather than deal with the variety of day-to-day concerns that can occupy much of the time of small-business owners. Midsize businesses typically have higher revenues than small businesses and may offer the opportunity for greater profit. With mergers and acquisitions common in the industry, the owner of a midsize business may receive a substantial sum of money for the sale of that business to a larger company. For example, in 2002, BMG Entertainment paid nearly $2.75 billion for the Zomba Label Group, the home of successful pop and R&B issuers Jive Records and LaFace Records.

Cons of Working for a Midsize Business. For a business owner who enjoys working closely with music listeners or having a direct hand in the differing aspects of the organization, the increased structural hierarchy inherent in a midsize business can be a distinct disadvantage. With larger numbers of employees come higher levels of personnel management, a task that not everyone enjoys. Record labels and music retailers of this size face stiff competition from larger companies, which may have greater financial resources, lower overhead costs, and increased product integration.

Costs

Payroll and Benefits: Midsize businesses often have both hourly and salaried employees and may also employ unpaid interns. Such companies typically offer additional benefits such as health insurance, paid time off, and retirement plans to full-time staff. Record labels pay artists an advance when signing them and pay additional royalties once sales take off. It is hoped that an artist's recording earnings will be enough to repay the advance costs of recording and promotion.

Supplies: Offices typically require a wide range of supplies, including computers and recording equipment for studios. Companies that manufacture physical products require specialized equipment. Performance venues may operate food and beverage services, requiring cooking equipment, raw ingredients, and disposable eating utensils.

External Services: Because businesses typically maintain office space, they are likely to employ cleaning services. Those with freestanding buildings may contract landscaping services. Performance venues typically contract security guards. Sound recording companies that do not have on-staff lawyers typically hire independent attorneys, as well as hiring time at studios and necessary production staff for artists to record albums.

Utilities: Offices and venues alike must pay for basic utilities, including electricity, gas, heat, water, telephone and Internet access.

Taxes: Because most midsize businesses are corporations rather than sole proprietorships, they pay corporate taxes at the federal and state levels. Some may also pay local taxes. Nonprofit organizations must file tax forms but are exempted from taxes. Additionally, midsize businesses contribute to their employees' Social Security and Medicare taxes.

Large Businesses

The large businesses of the music industry are few but powerful. In the sound recording segment of the industry, eight companies garner about 80 percent of the segment's total revenue. Live Nation dominates the performance segment of the industry, with 2008 sales exceeding $4 billion. These revenues are representative of the massive earning potential at the upper tiers of the industry. As of 2009, Universal Music Group was the largest music business in the world, with branches dedicated to album production and distribution, artist management, music catalogs and publishing, merchandizing, and digital ventures. Such diversified operations contribute to the immense influence exerted on the global music industry by the industry's large businesses. The largest businesses in the music retail industry are typically big-box retailers such as Walmart, Best Buy, and Target, though digital-only retailer Apple has garnered the top spot in recent years through the success of its iTunes Store, which offers music and videos available for download.

Potential Annual Earnings Scale. Large music businesses earn revenues ranging from hundreds of millions to billions of dollars. They employ workers of all types, from unpaid interns and minimum wage office clerks to entertainment executives who may earn more than $1 million per year, plus perks.

Clientele Interaction. Employees at a large corporation typically have highly defined job duties and may have little interaction with those outside of their immediate fields. For example, a public relations representative might deal with music journalists, magazine editors, and event coordinators to ensure coverage of an artist, album release, or other newsworthy event. The average listener has little, if any, contact with the staff of sound recording companies. Equally, although some employees of performance operations companies may deal directly with concert attendees, such as ticket sellers and venue workers, the bulk of the administrative staff is removed from the end user of its products.

Amenities, Atmosphere, and Physical Grounds. Large music businesses typically maintain substantial office presences in major cities around the world. Because of music's integration with mainstream culture, the physical buildings associated with its major businesses hold their own iconic appeal. For example, Los Angeles's Capitol Records building is one of the city's best-known landmarks.

These businesses may have relatively formal corporate cultures that are influenced by the practices of their international owners. For example, some have argued that Sony BMG's corporate culture reflects its Japanese parent company with a distinct hierarchical decision-making structure. As record labels have struggled with declining revenues, some have tried to reinvigorate their organizations by hiring creative individuals to manage business operations. Notable music producer Rick Rubin became the head of Columbia Records in 2007, and other artists, producers, and songwriters, including Jay-Z (Def Jam Recordings) and Amanda Ghost (Epic Records), have served in executive roles. Such individuals may lead to shifts in existing cultures, as when Rubin moved the staff of Columbia Records into nicer offices in a building designed by famed architect I. M. Pei.

Typical Number of Employees. Large music businesses generally have at least a few thousand and as many as ten thousand employees. For example, the 2010 merger between performance giant Ticketmaster and Live Nation created a company with about ten thousand employees. However, the challenges facing the sound recording industry have forced significant reductions in staff—between 2003 and 2007, the number of employees at Sony BMG declined by about 40 percent, from 4,880 to 2,851. Employees of large companies work in many capacities, ranging from business administration to creative services to sales and marketing.

Traditional Geographic Locations. In the United States, large music companies cluster in the entertainment capitals of New York City, Los Angeles, and Nashville. Internationally, these businesses can be found in such major capitals as London, England, and Tokyo, Japan. Vivendi, the parent company of industry giant Universal Music, is headquartered in Paris, France.

Pros of Working for a Large Business. Large businesses in the music industry may offer high salaries and the prospect of working with some of the music world's biggest names. The industry's renowned glamour revolves around the artists and executives attached to major labels, and the prestige level of working at these organizations can be high.

Cons of Working for a Large Business. The overall challenges facing the industry have hit large

sound recording companies especially hard. Major record labels often invest hundreds of thousands of dollars in developing freshly signed artists through recording sessions, promotion, and tour support; if an artist fails to achieve widespread success, these outlays may never be repaid. Because of their size, large companies may face government scrutiny before being able to complete proposed mergers. The media typically pay greater attention to the problems experienced at these well-known companies than to those of smaller, less prominent music businesses.

Costs

Payroll and Benefits: Large companies employ hourly and salaried employees, as well as interns, and offer full benefits packages to full-time employees. These may include stock options, bonuses, and other incentives, in addition to standard health insurance, paid time off, and retirement investment plans. Artists signed to major record labels often receive hefty contract advances and tour support.

Supplies: Integrated music production and distribution companies must support multiple offices and their accompanying business supplies, as well as operate merchandising and physical music-production facilities. Live performance companies may operate food and beverage businesses at their venues.

External Services: Large offices may contract their cleaning and maintenance services, while performance venues may employ external security companies. Record labels may rent recording studios for artists to cut albums. However, the size of these companies makes it possible that any of these functions may be filled by regular internal staff rather than contract workers, and artists may choose to record albums in studios owned by major record labels.

Utilities: Large business offices and performance venues alike pay for utilities, such as electricity, heat, water, telephone, and Internet access.

Taxes: Large businesses pay necessary federal and state corporate taxes, and may additionally pay local taxes. These businesses must also contribute to their employees' Social Security and Medicare taxes. Multinational corporations may be subject to taxes in other countries in addition to those paid in the United States.

ORGANIZATIONAL STRUCTURE AND JOB ROLES

Although the types of businesses in the music industry vary depending on their particular industry segment, size, and purpose, most of these companies must address organizational needs in each of the following activities. A few specialized firms, such as music publishing businesses, may not maintain operations in each field. Typically, in small businesses, one person juggles responsibilities in more than one of these areas, while in midsize and large businesses, the increased size allows employees to have a greater degree of specialization in their work.

Variations in the specifics of each broad job category exist primarily among music businesses that fill different industry roles rather than among businesses of different sizes. That is, a small record label has an organizational structure more similar to a large record label than to an equally small performance venue. These differences are explained more thoroughly in the descriptions of the relevant individual categories that follow.

The following umbrella categories apply to the organizational structure of businesses in the music industry:

- Creative Services
- Business Management
- Sales and Marketing
- Design, Technology, and Manufacturing
- Facilities and Security
- Production and Operations
- Distribution
- Human Resources/Artist Recruitment

Creative Services

Artists who provide creative services lie at the heart of the music industry. Creative artists may be responsible for any combination of writing, recording, performing, arranging, or conducting music. Musicians and singers typically have some degree of formal training. Some may have only rudimentary instruction acquired through regular schooling, while others may have years of personal instruction and advanced degrees under their belts. Composers, conductors, and arrangers typically pursue highly specialized studies in addition to

Musicians are at the heart of the music industry. (©Dreamstime.com)

normal musical training. All creative services workers rely on extensive practice and on-the-job training to maintain and improve their technical skills. Many have skills on more than one instrument or can perform various styles of music.

According to the BLS, about half of all creative artists in the music industry are self-employed. Of those who work regularly part or full time, nearly all work for religious or performing arts organizations. Some musicians and other creative artists belong to labor unions, such as the American Federation of Musicians (AFM) or the American Guild of Musical Artists (AGMA).

Although artists are the most important players in the music industry, they typically operate outside of the business structure that exists to support and profit from their work. For example, a rock musician under contract to a specific record label would have little to no involvement with any of that label's business operations. Music directors, however, may be exceptions to this rule. These individuals are typically the head conductors at performing arts organizations and may work closely with an organization's executive director to select musical programming that fulfills both artistic and business goals.

Creative services occupations may include the following:

- Musician
- Singer
- Songwriter
- Composer
- Arranger
- Music Director
- Conductor
- Music Video Director

Business Management

Top music executives hail from various walks of life. Some, such as symphony orchestra executive directors and certain corporate officers, may hold advanced degrees in arts or business administration. These executives may draw on professional backgrounds in the music industry or related fields, such as film and media, or may come from a corporate background outside of the entertainment field. Other music executives assume business leadership roles on the basis of their successful creative careers. For example, hip-hop performer Sean "Puffy" Combs founded and oversees the running of Bad Boy Entertainment. Small-business owners generally serve as their own chief executives, and this role may grow significantly if their business becomes successful.

Business administrators are responsible for the overall management and financial success of an organization. They create and implement long-term business development plans and strive to achieve maximum business profitability. Such employees typically work at a corporate headquarters, although many travel frequently to ensure smooth business operations and develop business partnerships or other relationships. Business administrators typically earn higher salaries than do employees in other parts of the music industry.

Attorneys may work on behalf of artists, music publishers, or record labels to negotiate contracts, mediate disputes, and defend against censorship. Music business specialists may have extensive experience working with entertainment clients or on in-

OCCUPATION SPECIALTIES

Musicians and Composers

Specialty	Responsibilities
Arrangers	Transcribe musical compositions or melodic lines to adapt them to or create a particular style.
Choral directors	Conduct vocal music groups, such as choirs and glee clubs.
Instrumental musicians	Play musical instruments as soloists or as members of a musical group, such as an orchestra or band, to entertain audiences.
Musical directors	Plan and direct the activities of personnel in studio music departments and conduct studio orchestras.
Orchestra conductors	Lead instrumental music groups, such as orchestras and dance bands.
Orchestrators	Write musical scores for orchestras, bands, choral groups, or individuals.
Singers	Singers entertain by singing songs on stage, radio, and television or in nightclubs.

tellectual property matters, or they may have more generalized experience in corporate and tax law. All music businesses are likely to retain the services of an attorney at some point.

Some specialized professions also exist in this category. Royalties administrators work for record labels and publishing-rights organizations to oversee the collection and distribution of royalty payments for the physical sale, usage, or public performance of a recorded work. (This has become more pertinent as a result of the rise of the Internet and associated technologies, such as smart phones, Web broadcasting, and Internet and satellite radio.) Artist managers work directly with musicians and singers to handle the business end of their careers.

Managers help their clients find work, set goals, take care of finances, and fulfill contractual obligations. Typically, managers also act as intermediaries between artists and business organizations such as record labels and publishing-rights houses. They may also work closely with artists' talent agents. Talent agents deal with promoters and others who book artists for live appearances to negotiate contracts, pay rates, and other details relating to concert performances. Agents also act as customer-service point persons should artists or bookers fail to live up to their contractual obligations.

Business management occupations may include the following:

- Chief Executive Officer (CEO)
- Executive Director
- Business Manager
- Legal Counsel
- Artist Manager
- Talent/Booking Agent
- Acquisitions and Mergers Director
- Royalties Administrator
- Accountant

Sales and Marketing

Sales and marketing are vital to the success of all segments of the music industry. Small and large

OCCUPATION PROFILE

Musician and Composer

Considerations	Qualifications
Description	Creates and performs music.
Career cluster	Arts, A/V Technology, and Communication
Interests	Data; people
Working conditions	Work inside
Minimum education level	High school diploma or GED; junior/technical/community college; apprenticeship
Physical exertion	Light work
Physical abilities	Unexceptional/basic fitness
Opportunities for experience	Apprenticeship; military service; volunteer work; part-time work
Licensure and certification	Usually not required
Employment outlook	Average growth expected
Holland interest score	ASE; ASI

Note: See volume 1, "Publisher's Note," for an explanation of the Holland interest score.

record labels must have employees or entire departments dedicated to public relations, marketing, promotions, and sales. Music publishers work to place their artists' songs in films, television programs, video games, and commercials. Performing arts organizations and concert promoters market their events to attract listeners and sell tickets.

Public relations workers are responsible for getting their artists, recordings, and events mentioned in publications. They conduct such activities as writing press releases, contacting journalists, setting up photo shoots, and working with media outlets to secure maximum coverage for a given topic. Closely related to

Studio musicians may experience less travel than band members. (©Dreamstime.com)

public relations are promotional staff, who work to secure radio or television time for artists, songs, or events. Public relations and promotions employees may work in offices or attend events, and they typically have bachelor's degrees in English, journalism, public relations, or mass communications. Similarly, members of the marketing staff help coordinate these efforts, as well as conduct and analyze market research to help create overall marketing plans.

Artists, record labels, and concert promoters may all build street teams, which are groups of individuals who market artists or events by such activities as hanging flyers, collecting marketing lists on college campuses, or handing out promotional materials. Street team members are often college students or other young people trying to break into the music industry.

Sales and marketing occupations may include the following:

- Public Relations Manager
- Marketing Manager
- Public Relations Representative
- Publicist
- Market Research Analyst
- Sales Representative
- Street Team Member

Design, Technology, and Manufacturing

Graphic designers and photographers provide images to help promote artists, recordings, and events. Graphic designers are responsible for the visual conceptualization and creation of digital artwork, including packaging materials such as liner notes, promotional posters and flyers, advertisements, and other printed pieces. They typically work in an office setting. Photographers capture still images used in these types of products. They may work in a studio or on location. On-location photo shoots may produce staged photos or may rely on events such as concerts to provide opportunities for candid shots. After photographers have completed their shoots, either they or trained photo editors correct their images to prepare them for use. This work may be as simple as cropping or enlarging an image or as complex as balancing color, adding or removing details, or merging several images together.

Music industry companies often have staffers responsible for maintaining up-to-the-minute Web sites to promote artists or services. Some may operate online sales outlets or encode digital music files for sale through marketers such as the iTunes Store. Technology workers typically hold associate's or bachelor's degrees in a computer-technology field. They generally work in offices, although some may travel from site to site as needed.

OCCUPATION SPECIALTIES

Musical Instrument Repairers

Specialty	Responsibilities
Piano technicians	Repair and refinish pianos in addition to tuning them.
Piano tuners	Adjust piano strings so that they will be in proper pitch. They may tune pianos in both public and private establishments, and they make initial adjustments in the factory.
Pipe-organ tuners and repairers	Tune and repair organs that make music by forcing air through flue pipes or reed pipes.
Violin repairers	Adjust and repair bowed instruments such as violins, violas, and cellos, using hand tools.
Wind instrument repairers	Clean, adjust, and repair brass, wind, and woodwind instruments.

Large sound recording companies typically employ workers who manufacture physical music products, such as CDs or DVDs. Specialized manufacturing companies that make musical instruments and accessories also exist. Artisans use factory or handcrafting techniques to build various types of instruments to company specifications, or they may create custom instruments ordered by artists. Instrument-repair technicians may work for such companies or operate independently to service damaged instruments.

Design, technology, and manufacturing occupations may include the following:

- Graphic Designer
- Photographer
- Photo Editor
- Web Designer
- Systems Engineer
- Information Technology Technician
- Artisan
- Instrument Repairer

Facilities and Security

In the music industry, facilities and security staff are responsible for the maintenance and oversight of physical locations such as offices and performance venues. Businesses that lease space in large office complexes may rely on facilities services provided with their leases, while freestanding companies may employ or contract their own maintenance, landscaping, and cleaning crews.

Performing arts venues typically employ house managers. These individuals oversee operations in the public spaces of the venue, including auditorium seating areas, lobbies, ticketing areas, and bars or restaurants. Because many performing arts organizations may share the use of a venue, such individuals typically work for the venue itself rather than for a particular organization. However, ushers (staffers who show patrons to their seats) may be provided by either the venue or the organization. Often, these people are volunteers rather than paid employees.

All performance venues have on-site security guards to prevent members of the public from entering private areas. These employees also help ensure the safety of all attendees in the event of an emergency. Highly prominent creative artists may employ one or more personal bodyguards. These staffers ensure the safety of the artists when they appear in public by protecting them from paparazzi and overly intrusive fans.

Facilities and security occupations may include the following:

- House Manager
- Usher

- Security Guard
- Bodyguard
- Safety Manager
- Maintenance and Repair Worker

Production and Operations

Production and operations employees have diverse roles in the music industry. Perhaps the best-known job in this field is that of the music producer. Producers manage music recording in studios and have some degree of creative input into final products. Recording engineers also work in studios, where they operate equipment to accurately capture the sounds made by singers and musicians. Production and operations staff members also play vital roles in the live performance segment of the music industry. Touring acts, performance venues, and performing arts organizations rely on the skills of production and operations personnel to ensure that musical performances run smoothly.

Many performances begin with the work of concert promoters, who hire artists to appear at concerts and music festivals. Promoters may work alone, or they may represent small or large associations and businesses, ranging from college student groups to massive corporations such as Live Nation. Concert promoters' responsibilities include hiring and paying artists, overseeing event promotion, and coordinating supplies and staffing needs at venues. Performing arts organizations essentially act as their own concert promoters. Occasionally, private companies or individuals may contract with artists directly or through a talent broker.

For a live performance to be successful, certain roles need to be fulfilled. Artists and their equipment must travel to the performance site, and instruments and other equipment must then be unloaded and set up at the venue. Maintenance must then be performed to ensure that the items are in working order. A large touring act may employ extensive stage sets or complex light shows, and trained technicians must build those sets and set up necessary lights. During the show, sound quality must be managed to ensure that both performers and audience can adequately hear the music.

On-site individuals must also manage the overall workflow to make sure everything happens on time and on schedule. Artists often bring many of these workers with them, and even small touring acts are likely to travel with at least one person who may double as a tour manager and sound technician. Alternatively, performance venues or promoters may provide some staff. At a performing arts organization, one or more people typically make up the operations department. This department conducts productions and operations backstage and may also oversee activities in the theater or the front of the house.

Production and operations occupations may include the following:

- Producer
- Recording/Sound Engineer
- Promoter
- Production Manager
- Tour/Road Manager
- Stage Manager
- Stagehand
- Sound Technician
- Instrument Technician
- Bus/Truck Driver

Distribution

Once a record label has released an album, that recording must find its way to listeners. The distribution sector of the music industry handles this process, taking physical or electronic music products from the point of creation to the point of sale. While large record labels handle their own distribution, smaller labels often strike deals with larger companies to distribute their products. Physical items, such as CDs and vinyl albums, travel from a manufacturing facility to a distribution center. From there, employees ship goods to individual retail facilities.

Retail record stores may be independently owned or part of a chain. They are often located in urban and suburban shopping districts or malls. If a store is part of a chain, it may be overseen by a district or regional manager who is responsible for the performance of a number of retail outlets. This job involves a great deal of travel, and a typical district manager has a college degree and retail-store experience. At the store level, retail sales staff are responsible for stocking, sales, and customer service. A typical store includes a manager, at least one assistant manager, and a number of part-time and full-time store associates. These employees may have high school or college educations, or they may still attend school.

During the early twenty-first century, online distribution has become increasingly common. Through online distribution, smaller record labels can sell their products without relying on a partnership with a larger distributor. Some retail stores have also expanded into online sales. When an online order is received, an employee must pull, pack, and ship the item to the purchaser.

Distribution and sales staff may also work in a live performance venue. These employees sell merchandise including recordings, T-shirts, posters, and other goods to attendees of live performances. Often, these crew members are employed by and travel with particular artists rather than being on the staff of a performance venue.

Distribution occupations may include the following:

- Distribution Manager
- Shipping and Receiving Clerk
- Truck Driver
- Regional Manager
- Store Manager
- Store Associate
- Merchandiser

Human Resources/Artist Recruitment

Human resources staff oversee employee recruitment, hiring, and termination processes. They are also typically responsible for mediating disputes between employees and employers, administering payroll and benefits, and contributing to employee and organizational policies. Small companies may have only one person to perform these functions, or they may be assumed by the financial manager or business owner. Large companies may have entire divisions dedicated to human resources, with an executive-level director managing the work of several departments. A typical human resources staffer has at least an associate's degree in the field.

Record labels must have one or more individuals responsible for artists and repertoire, commonly called A&R. A&R managers scout new musical talent and recruit artists for their record labels. After artists have been signed to a particular label, that label's A&R manager may help develop the artists' careers, make suggestions about recording decisions, and help choose singles for radio airplay. Typically, A&R managers become intermediaries between creative artists and their managers on the one hand and the record label on the other. At small labels, the label owner may fulfill these functions.

At performing arts organizations, music directors and other trained listeners from each orchestral section determine which musicians to hire based on live auditions. Typically, these auditions are "blind," meaning that those performing cannot be seen by the people for whom they are auditioning. This practice helps ensure unbiased decisions. In fact, researchers determined in 2001 that use of blind auditions led to a 50 percent jump in the likelihood of a female musician advancing beyond the first round of auditions.

Human resources and artist recruitment occupations may include the following:

- Vice President of Human Resources
- Vice President of Artists and Repertoire
- Human Resources Manager
- Human Resources Generalist
- Human Resources Assistant
- Benefits Specialist
- Payroll Administrator
- A&R Manager

INDUSTRY OUTLOOK

Overview

The outlook for this industry shows it to be in decline. However, while the sound recording industry is expected to continue an overall trend of decline, not all segments of the music industry face the same challenges. Some subindustries face somewhat stronger outlooks.

The BLS projects rapid growth in the overall field of arts, entertainment, and recreation as both the incomes and the leisure time of American workers increase. However, performing arts fields such as music are expected to remain unchanged. This discrepancy is due to significant growth expected in the other portions of the larger industry. For example, people are increasingly expected to choose to spend money on health-club memberships rather than on recorded music. Because of this shift in consumer tastes, the BLS does not anticipate occupational growth for musicians or singers to outpace the average for all jobs. Moreover, music jobs are anticipated to remain highly competitive because many people desire them.

Some segments of the music industry are struggling with other difficulties stemming from consumer taste and lifestyle changes. For several years, the sound recording industry has experienced declining sales, both in terms of revenue and in terms of units sold. Industry analysts have attributed at least part of this decline to the rise of online music piracy. Although record companies have found ways to capture revenue streams by offering content through popular paid download services such as the iTunes Store, this rise in paid electronically delivered music has not compensated for the consistent drops in physically delivered music formats such as CDs. In 2009, financial analysts at accounting and consulting firm Deloitte predicted that overall revenues for the sound recording industry were likely to continue their downward trend for quite some time.

These shifts have had a negative impact on traditional retail music outlets. Entertainment retailer Trans World Entertainment has steadily purchased failing record-store chains over the past several years, yet it has experienced disappointing revenues that have forced individual store closures. Throughout the industry, even those outlets that survive face such severe continued challenges that the BLS anticipates that the number of workers at book, periodical, and music stores will decline by nearly 20 percent by 2016.

On the other hand, the concert industry has generally enjoyed strong growth over the past several years. Although analysts predict that the worldwide economic downturn of 2007-2009 is likely to bring diminished returns for the concert industry as consumer discretionary spending declines— and industry reports of live-performance returns for the first half of 2009 indicate a decrease of more than 10 percent—bright spots have emerged. For example, concert producer and venue operator Live Nation enjoyed revenue growth during the period of general decline. A 2010 merger between Live Nation and ticket powerhouse Ticketmaster has created a music company of unparalleled scope, to the extent that the two corporations had to agree to several U.S. Department of Justice demands before the merger was approved. In the wake of the deal, Live Nation's product expansion through its "360 deals" seems all the more likely to continue.

Employment Advantages

Despite the challenges facing the music industry as consumer consumption habits shift, the industry offers exciting opportunities for those who love music. The few performers who achieve worldwide success can earn huge sums of money in a short period of time, and the possibility—no matter how remote—of achieving fame and fortune attracts many musicians to the field. However, most musicians work part time for low pay, simply for the satisfaction of playing an instrument or singing before an appreciative audience. Full-time musicians and their support crews often spend much of their time on the road, making the lifestyle attractive to individuals who enjoy visiting new places.

The range of jobs available in the music industry is quite diverse, and many positions exist for nonperformers. Students who love music but prefer not to take on the risks or the extensive training that come with being a performer may enjoy working for a record company, publishing company, or performance venue. Such workplaces may also offer opportunities for staff members to meet well-known stars or attend publicized events.

Annual Earnings

Revenue outlooks for the overall music industry vary greatly depending on the particular market segment. Analysts widely expect the revenues of traditional sound recording companies to continue to decline for the foreseeable future, both domestically and internationally. These declines will presumably bring further staff reductions at large record labels and eventually usher in transformed business models. Dropping sales also seem to be heralding the end of the traditional specialty music store. By 2007, Trans World Entertainment, the largest operator of music retail outlets in the United States, had begun working to diversify into other entertainment products, such as video games.

In 2008, the sound recording industry posted annual revenues of nearly $5 billion in the United States, a decline of 18.6 percent from the preceding year. International revenues were more than $12.6 billion, with the music industry bringing in $18.4 billion worldwide. These figures include sales of physical and digital music media, as well as performance rights.

Live performance companies have a much rosier outlook. Steadily increasing concert revenues, paired with innovative artist agreements, seem likely to guarantee strong revenue streams in upcoming years, despite temporary challenges brought on by overall economic woes. In 2008, the U.S. concert industry brought in about $4.2 billion, an increase of 7 percent over 2007.

RELATED RESOURCES FOR FURTHER RESEARCH

AMERICAN SOCIETY OF COMPOSERS, AUTHORS, AND PUBLISHERS
1 Lincoln Plaza
New York, NY 10023
Tel: (212) 621-6000
http://www.ascap.com

AMERICAN SYMPHONY ORCHESTRA LEAGUE
33 W 60th St.
New York, NY 10023
Tel: (212) 262-5161
http://www.symphony.org

BILLBOARD
BPI Communications
1515 Broadway
New York, NY 10036
Tel: (800) 745-8922
http://www.billboard-online.com

INTERNATIONAL FEDERATION OF THE PHONOGRAPHIC INDUSTRY
IFPI Secretariat
54 Regent St.
London W1B 5RE
United Kingdom
Tel: 44-20-7878-7900
http://www.ifpi.org

MUSIC WEEK
Ludgate House
245 Blackfriars Rd.
London SE1 91S
United Kingdom
http://www.musicweek.com

POLLSTAR
4697 W Jacquelyn Ave.
Fresno, CA 93722

Tel: (559) 271-7900
http://www.pollstar.com

RECORDING INDUSTRY ASSOCIATION OF AMERICA
1025 F St. NW, 10th Floor
Washington, DC 20004
Tel: (202) 775-0101
http://www.riaa.com

ABOUT THE AUTHOR

Vanessa E. Vaughn is a freelance writer who has experience in both the commercial and the non-profit sides of the music industry. While completing her bachelor's degree in mass communications at Boston University, she interned at a small music management and booking company in London, England. Later, she spent two years on the staff of the Dayton Philharmonic Orchestra in Dayton, Ohio, before earning a master's degree from Wright State University. From 2004 to 2007, her husband played drums for a successful rock band, giving her a behind-the-scenes look at such music institutions as Radio City Music Hall and Chicago's Lollapalooza festival.

FURTHER READING

Allen, Katie. "Downloads Fail to Stem Fall in Global Music Sales." *The Guardian*, July 3, 2007.

Borg, Bobby. *The Musician's Handbook: A Practical Guide to Understanding the Music Business.* New York: Billboard Books, 2008.

Cosper, Alex. "History of Record Labels and the Music Industry." Playlist Research, 2009. http://www.playlistresearch.com/recordindustry.htm.

Deloitte. "2009 Industry Outlook: Media and Entertainment." January 28, 2009. http://www.deloitte.com/view/en_US/us/Industries/Media-Entertainment/article/a5391ec6f6001210VgnVCM100000ba42f00aRCRD.htm.

The Economist. "Digital Music Sales." May 28, 2009.

Espejo, Roman, ed. *What Is the Future of the Music Industry?* Detroit: Greenhaven Press, 2009.

Gordon, Steve. *The Future of the Music Business.* 2d ed. Milwaukee: Hal Leonard Books, 2008.

Hefflinger, Mark. "Sony BMG Revenue Down 27.8%; Digital Up 40%." Digital Media Wire, March 20, 2008. http://www.dmwmedia.com/news/2008/03/20/sony-bmg-revenue-down-27.8%25%3B-digital-40%25.

Krasilovsky, M. William, and Sydney Shemel. *This Business of Music: The Definitive Guide to the Music Industry*. 10th ed. New York: Billboard Books, 2007.

Miller, Warren. "Live Nation, Ticketmaster Announce Plan to Merge." Morningstar, February 12, 2009. http://quicktake.morningstar.com/Stocknet/san.aspx?id=279588.

Negus, Keith. *Music Genres and Corporate Cultures*. New York: Routledge, 1999.

Rapaport, Diane. *A Music Business Primer*. Upper Saddle River, N.J.: Prentice Hall, 2003.

Thall, Peter W. *What They'll Never Tell You About the Music Business: The Myths, the Secrets, the Lies (and a Few Truths)*. New York: Billboard Books, 2006.

U.S. Bureau of Labor Statistics. *Career Guide to Industries*, 2010-2011 ed. http://www.bls.gov/oco/cg.

———. "Musicians, Singers, and Related Workers." In *Occupational Outlook Handbook*, 2010-2011 ed. http://www.bls.gov/oco/ocos095.htm.

U.S. Census Bureau. North American Industry Classification System (NAICS), 2007. http://www.census.gov/cgi-bin/sssd/naics/naicsrch?chart=2007.

U.S. Department of Commerce. International Trade Administration. Office of Trade and Industry Information. Industry Trade Data and Analysis. http://ita.doc.gov/td/industry/otea/OTII/OTII-index.html.

National and International Security Industry

INDUSTRY SNAPSHOT

General Industry: Government and Public Administration

Career Clusters: Government and Public Administration Occupations; Law, Public Safety, and Security

Subcategory Industries: Intelligence Agencies; Intelligence and National Security Consultants; International Development; International Security Organizations; Technology Manufacturers; Think Tanks

Related Industries: Civil Services: Public Safety; Defense Industry; Federal Public Administration; Legal Services and Law Firms; Public Health Services

Annual Domestic Revenues: $302 billion USD (U.S. Department of State, 2001)

Annual International Revenues: $534 billion USD (U.S. Department of State, 2001)

Annual Global Revenues: $839 billion USD (Stockholm International Peace Research Institute, 2002)

NAICS Numbers: 928, 336992

INDUSTRY DEFINITION

Summary

The national and international security industry is an overarching network of private and public corporations and agencies dedicated to locating, assessing, and defending against threats to a nation's interests. The industry is often interconnected with various branches of the military, but it focuses on systems and analysis as opposed to policy making.

The national and international security industry has been in a constant state of evolution throughout history, adapting to meet an ever-changing threat environment. Generally, this industry comprises two manifested areas. The first area involves systems, such as computer networks, early-warning systems, and satellite technology. The second of these areas is more academic and focuses on events, organizations, and key individuals that may strengthen or destabilize the interests of a given country.

History of the Industry

In the mid-seventeenth century, the governments of Europe coalesced to address common economic issues. Europe had long been in crisis from war and economic stagnation, and the leaders of each major government sought to move away from past conflicts to create a framework whereby the many nations of the continent could work together. This common desire resulted in the signing of two peace treaties, commonly known as the Peace of Westphalia, that fostered the creation of a new type of political entity—the sovereign nation-state, with defined interests and goals.

After the establishment of the Peace of Westphalia in 1648, countless regional and imperial governments began to form nation-states with borders, individual governments, and discernable cultures and social groups. They also demonstrated their own interests and goals, in some cases coincidental with the pursuits of other nation-states. Nonetheless, these nation-states remained independent of one another. The military remained the primary tool of national defense throughout preindustrial history. Designed to defend or attack with blunt force, armies and navies were organized and dispatched to challenge threats to a given nation-state's way of life.

After World War I, many new nation-states rose from the ashes of defeated European and Asian empires. Each of these emerging countries developed its own government, military, and other institutions. With time, the interests and goals of these new states coincided with the interests and goals of

neighboring countries. Often, two or more neighbors identified a potential mutual threat in some other nearby country or countries. As a result, it became necessary for nations to set forth policies that would protect each country's interests and people in the event of a foreign attack. As more countries emerged on the global stage, an increasing volume of national and international security plans were effected.

Although espionage, one of the oldest aspects of security, dates as far back as ancient Egypt, the boom of modern nation-states that followed World War I caused a surge in intelligence institutions and organizations. In the interests of protecting their lifestyles and assets, new nation-states created systems designed to analyze the actions of other nation-states to assess any potential threats. In the years leading up to World War II, some of the most elaborate and far-reaching security networks were operated by Nazi Germany and Japan. In the United States, the Office of Strategic Services (OSS) was developed as a wartime intelligence agency in 1942, although the key intelligence-gathering entity used by the Allies in the war was that of the British government.

Following World War II, the Cold War between

A U.S. Air Force MQ-1 Predator unmanned aerial vehicle flies over a U.S. Marine Corps AV-8B Harrier at Creech Air Force Base in Nevada. (U.S. Department of Defense)

the Soviet Union and the United States brought about a renaissance in national and international security pursuits. The Soviet Committee for State Security (Komitet Gosudarstvennoy Bezopasnosti, or KGB) and the U.S. Central Intelligence Agency (CIA)—of which the OSS was the predecessor—engaged in a decades-long cat-and-mouse game.

The Industry Today

Modern national and international security endeavors did not subside with the 1991 dissolution of the Soviet Union and the end of the Cold War. Rather, the industry changed significantly along with the rest of the international environment. In fact, the end of the Cold War helped foster an increase in two new potential security threats: international terrorism and rogue states. These two threats, long in the background during the Cold War era, were brought to the forefront after the terrorist attacks on the United States of September 11, 2001, and the increasing penchant for aggressive

The nano-hummingbird is a tiny remote-controlled aircraft designed by the AeroVironment facility in Simi Valley, California. (AP/Wide World Photos)

countries to combat their adversaries by funding terrorists.

The national and international security industry has become one of the most pivotal global industries in the early twenty-first century. Generally, government agencies and organizations are the primary drivers of this industry, as they set and implement security policy. In most cases, these agencies have become clients of private security and defense companies, which have entered into development and manufacturing contracts to meet a country's security needs. Thus, government intelligence and security agencies such as the CIA, the National Security Agency (NSA), and the Department of Homeland Security (DHS) are not the only components of the national and international security industry, as private corporations work closely with government agencies to develop surveillance and weapons technologies.

The vast collection of public and private organizations constituting the national and international security industry spans a wide range of fields. For example, the aerospace industry, long dedicated to creating military aircraft, increasingly emphasizes surveillance aircraft used to track the movements of hostile elements in such areas as Iraq and the Afghanistan-Pakistan border. Similarly, the naval defense industry is changing its focus from defenses against naval attack toward long-distance detection systems such as radar. The naval defense industry is also shifting from larger ships to smaller patrol craft. This evolution toward a focus on security rather than combat is not accidental: With the demise of the Cold War, the primary threat to national interests comes from smaller, more agile, and stealthy nonmilitary enemies. As a result, military contractors across the spectrum are now meeting the demand for national security-oriented technologies and hardware.

In addition to public and private institutions concerned with the security of individual nations, entities exist to coordinate international security. These entities administer international security partnerships, which are usually forged between two or more countries with common interests and which are seeing greater participation than in previous decades. Two of the most prominent of these organizations are the North Atlantic Treaty Organization (NATO), which was created among Western nations to counter the perceived Soviet threat during the Cold War era, and the European Union (EU), which was established to concentrate and strengthen the economic and political interests of the tightly knit countries of Western Europe.

These organizations are hardly alone in terms of their focus on integrated regional and international security. In 2003, the twenty-one-member Asia Pacific Economic Cooperation (APEC) established the APEC Counter-Terrorism Task Force, and in Central and South America, the Organization of American States (OAS) created the Inter-American Committee Against Terrorism (Comité Interamericano Contra el Terrorismo, or CICTE). Additionally, the United Nations maintains a number of security and counter-terrorism committees and organizations under its umbrella.

Beyond government agencies and partnerships and the private manufacturing and contract support corporations they utilize, there exists another element of this industry that is critical to analyzing issues and implementing proper reactive policies: think tanks. National security think tanks are research companies and academic nonprofit organizations that assess potential security threats and submit reports to governments and their security agencies. Often, these think tanks, also known as policy institutes, operate as the primary policy actors or counsels within an organization or government.

The FBI recruits prospective candidates at Cleveland State University in March, 2011. (AP/Wide World Photos)

INDUSTRY MARKET SEGMENTS

The national and international security industry today is a diverse network, offering potential employees a wide range of fields and career paths. Whether one comes from a law enforcement background, academic environment, or engineering field, this growing field continues to offer a host of options for professional development.

Government Security Agencies

U.S. government agencies include intelligence and espionage services, such as the CIA and NSA, as well as investigative and enforcement agencies, such as the Federal Bureau of Investigation (FBI). The DHS integrates both functions, as well as assuming primary responsibility for monitoring and securing the United States' national borders against illegal entry.

Potential Annual Earnings Scale. The average hourly salary for many positions in the Department of Homeland Security, for example, is between $18 and $33, while the average pay at the Central Intelligence Agency is $70,000 per year.

Clientele Interaction. Federal national security employees have varying degrees of public interaction. Those who work in such agencies as the CIA or NSA rarely interact with private citizens outside of their workplace. Homeland Security personnel, including airport screeners employed by the Transportation Security Administration (TSA), and protective service personnel, including law enforcement officers and some members of the U.S. Secret Service, have constant contact with private civilians as part of their job descriptions.

Amenities, Atmosphere, and Physical Grounds. Federal security agents may work in offices, at airports, at border stations, or in military installations. These work settings are typically team oriented, with peers working closely alongside one another, often in compartmentalized divisions of labor.

Typical Number of Employees. The number of people employed by government security agencies is rarely disclosed. However, it is believed that

A Border Patrol agent watches trains passing through Montana, looking for any illegal activities. (Gerald L. Nino/U.S. Department of Homeland Security)

the CIA employs about 22,000 (excluding private contractors), while the NSA is believed to have considerably more employees. The Department of Homeland Security is estimated to have about 196,000 employees around the country, many of whom are civilians.

Traditional Geographic Locations. Although most federal agencies are headquartered in the greater Washington, D.C., area, positions with such agencies as the CIA and DHS may be based in virtually every state and in offices around the world. In some cases, national and international security jobs are located on both domestic and foreign military bases.

Pros of Working for a Federal Security Agency. Despite the 2007-2009 global economic crisis, the federal government continues to hire personnel for national and international security agencies. The government offers competitive salaries and benefits and, in the light of the ongoing nature of security concerns, relative stability.

Cons of Working for a Federal Security Agency. Federal salaries, while typically competitive, are also regimented according to experience and limited by budgets, so increases in such salaries are not as frequent or dramatic as they are in the private sector. Additionally, jobs are beholden to the federal budget, which may cause layoffs or work furloughs when legislative budget impasses occur. Furthermore, security agencies in particular are managed strictly with protocols and oversight, which may frustrate those who prefer organizational flexibility in the workplace.

Costs

Payroll and Benefits: Pay for employees of federal security agencies varies based on the job performed and the experience of the individual. Such agencies pay both hourly and salaried rates for their employees. For full-time employees, benefits such as health insurance are provided.

Supplies: Federal agencies must procure a wide range of office and personnel supplies. In addition to up-to-date computer and communications systems (along with office supplies and furniture), many agencies must pay for vehicles, weapons, and uniforms.

External Services: Like most federal agencies, national security agencies use contractors as administrative, logistical, and consultative support resources. Such "stringers" often work in offices alongside agency personnel and receive their salaries and benefits from the private company by which they are employed. Because of the sensitive nature of the data handled (and the security clearance required to work in such an environment), other external services would be limited to activities that do not provide access to key internal areas.

Utilities: Because of their sheer size, federal agencies pay a considerable percentage of their budgets to utilities, including heat, electricity, and telecommunications providers. Utility providers and government procurement offices usually negotiate a lower rate for such utilities than is paid in residential areas.

Taxes: Public national security agencies rarely pay property or corporate taxes. However, in many cases, such federal departments offer a payment in lieu of taxes to the communities or states in which they are located. National security employees are also often exempt from certain kinds of sales taxes as long as they are traveling on official government business.

Private National and International Security Corporations

Private corporations form a crucial portion of the national security sector, although as is the case with government-agency employment figures, the precise proportion and distribution of security roles filled by private contractors are not public knowledge. Private contractors have been increasingly integrated into military and intelligence operations, and many have job descriptions—such as interrogation of suspected terrorists or providing personal security for government officials in war zones—that were once the sole purview of public employees. Many contractors previously worked for the government, whether in the armed forces or in the intelligence community, and they capital-ize on the skills, experience, and security clearances they obtained as public employees.

Potential Annual Earnings Scale. The salaries of private contractors depend on the size and scope of their contracts. According to a 2007 U.S. Senate report, the average national security private contractor earns about $250,000 per year, while the average federal agency employee earns about half of that figure.

Clientele Interaction. Private contractors provide hands-on support to national security agencies. Typical contractors spend a large percentage of their work time in communication with (if not at the offices of) their clients, presenting frequent reports, assisting in financial reviews, and conducting program audits to ensure quality service.

Amenities, Atmosphere, and Physical Grounds. While many private contractors work alongside federal agencies, often in the same offices, others are located in their own office spaces, although usually near the client. In many situations, private contractors work in the field, alongside their clients. Arlington, Virginia, which is located just outside Washington, D.C., and is home to the Pentagon, contains a large number of office buildings filled with national and international security companies.

Pros of Working for a Private National Security Corporation. Private contractors are able to perform many of the same tasks as public employees for greater pay and benefits. Many contractors also receive per diem payments to cover travel expenses. In addition, private contractors are not necessarily beholden to the stringent internal policies found in military branches and other government agencies, so private companies are able to attract a more diverse base of employees.

Cons of Working for a Private National Security Corporation. Private corporations risk losing their government contracts, which could result in them laying off the staff funded by those contracts. Additionally, contractors must compete for contracts by offering cost-effective budgets to potential government clients, so they must keep salaries in check. In some cases, this competition can keep pay levels lower than some federal employee salaries (as the federal government has no competition). Additionally, national security firms must work within parameters set by the government, fostering little creativity for those who work under such contracts.

Costs

Payroll and Benefits: Salaries for employees of private national and international security agencies vary based on the job performed and the experience of the individual. Such agencies pay both hourly and salaried rates for their employees. Benefits such as health insurance are provided for full-time employees.

Supplies: Private corporations must procure a wide range of office and personnel supplies to support their efforts. They must have up-to-date computer and communications systems (along with office supplies and furniture), as well as audiovisual capabilities in order to assist in client reports.

External Services: Private national and international security agencies may employ subcontractors to help manage administrative, logistical, and systemic support services. Such workers remain beholden to the same parameters and guidelines established by the main contract and the private company, although they receive pay and benefits from the company through which they are employed.

Utilities: Private national and international security companies must pay for such operational utilities as heat, electricity, and telecommunications. Although some are large enough to own their offices, others must pay rent to building owners or leasing companies. Such costs may or may not be attached to the contracts they hold with the federal government.

Taxes: Unlike public national and international security agencies, private companies must pay property and corporate taxes. Under some circumstances, they may be exempt from sales tax, hotel occupancy tax, and other such taxes. In many instances, however, they are not.

Technology Manufacturers

National security technology includes everything from spy satellites and military hardware to proprietary software used to intercept and evaluate telecommunications. Manufacturers of this technology often receive government contracts to create it, and they may receive support in their quest for such contracts from the members of Congress representing their districts.

Potential Annual Earnings Scale. Average salaries for engineers, scientists, and other personnel working for aerospace and security technology manufacturers range from just over $60,000 per year for mechanical engineers to as much as $110,000 per year for project managers at aviation plants and other producers of military and security hardware.

Clientele Interaction. The level of client interaction for technology manufacturers varies based on job responsibilities. For example, sales managers and senior officials are responsible for designing proposals for technology delivery that can fit the needs of clients, and they therefore have a great deal of interaction with clients. Project managers and engineers, on the other hand, may spend more time in their plants conducting research, operations, or assembly endeavors; they often have very little interaction with clients.

Amenities, Atmosphere, and Physical Grounds. The work environment of a security technology manufacturer varies based on the type of work performed. Many such manufacturers operate in large complexes of interconnected plants and warehouses, rather than in office buildings. Because of their size, many of these campuses offer employees walking areas outside of the buildings, cafeterias, and other amenities. Project managers and more senior personnel may have individual offices, while other workers are grouped together in teams, whether in shared office space or in cubicle settings. Typically, these manufacturing complexes are carefully monitored and protected by security personnel, gates, and systems.

Typical Number of Employees. Security technology manufacturers often employ a great many people. For example, the Raytheon Company, which is an industry leader in producing homeland-security-oriented intelligence-gathering and information technology, employs seventy-three thousand workers worldwide. Saab, the Sweden-based producer of aerospace, aviation, and coastal security systems, has about thirteen thousand employees at its various international locations and has plans to grow significantly in the future. Such large employee pools are usually broken up and departmentalized, with small teams working on individual projects under the oversight of project managers. Major projects such as coastal defense systems and integrated satellite technologies, however, require much larger groups of interconnected teams.

Traditional Geographic Locations. Because producers of security and military technology must have access to transportation systems, reliable telecommunications systems, and employee bases from which to draw, plants are often located near urban centers. For example, Hughes Missile Systems, which produces the Patriot interceptor missile, is located just outside Tucson, Arizona. Northrop Grumman, one of the world's largest global security manufacturers, has plants just outside Los Angeles and Washington, D.C. Many manufacturers require an enormous amount of real estate in order to produce their systems and maintain sufficient building security. As a result, they tend to remain near but outside cities, where sufficient land is available and affordable.

Pros of Working at a Technology Manufacturer. Security technologies are among the most advanced, best funded, most cutting edge technologies in the world. As a result, employees take a great deal of pride in their work, as well as enjoying opportunities for invention and innovation that exceed those afforded by most other technology subsectors. Additionally, because security manufacturers seek the best engineers and teams available, they usually pay higher than average salaries and benefits.

Cons of Working for a Technology Manufacturer. Security technology manufacturers enforce strict rules governing the workplace. These include a wide range of security protocols, some of which are company-imposed and some of which are imposed on companies by clients, such as the military. Many of these requirements involve frequent administrative reporting, strict project oversight, concrete deadlines and timelines, and tightly controlled access. This level of control, combined with the size of manufacturing facilities, can make leaving those facilities for lunch or brief breaks challenging. Additionally, the workplaces themselves are not always accommodating and may include makeshift offices and workstations and occasionally inefficient air and heating systems.

Costs

Payroll and Benefits: Security technology manufacturers generally pay annual salaries. Benefits are usually competitive and tailored to those who work in a hands-on environment: Most major manufacturers offer accidental death and dismemberment insurance, as well as short- and long-term disability plans.

Supplies: Manufacturers require a great deal of office, machine, hardware, computer, and other supplies in their day-to-day operations. In addition, they need wiring, computer modeling software, heavy machinery equipment, power generators and other tools, as well as hard-hats and uniforms for personnel working in environments in which clothing may be damaged on the job. Manufacturers that produce aircraft, ground vehicles, or naval systems need gasoline, jet fuel, or other energy sources. Finally, they may need audiovisual equipment to present their technologies to prospective buyers.

External Services: Because of the classified nature of the systems and equipment they produce, security technology manufacturers often perform in-house many operations that other manufacturers would normally contract to external vendors. Nonetheless, they may still contract groundskeeping services (including winter snow removal), shuttle-bus services (to transport staff from building to building on large campuses), and even gate security. Snack machine maintenance services and cafeteria operations may also be staffed by external vendors who are kept away from secured areas. Even with limited access, these external vendors must often pass background checks as a condition of employment on-site.

Utilities: Security technology manufacturers use a relatively large amount of energy and utility services during the course of their daily operations, including electricity to run computers, heavy machinery, lights, and other key systems. Because of the size of their facilities and the large number of on-site personnel employed at a given time, trash, water, and sewage utilities are also heavy components of a manufacturer's monthly expenses. In order to mitigate the cost of utilities, manufacturers may implement green technologies such as solar power, low-pressure faucets, and recycling programs.

Taxes: Technology manufacturers are often among the largest property tax contributors in a given area. Unlike federal agencies, they are not exempt from state and local taxes (although, in many cases, they are able to negotiate their corporate and property tax rates with local governments, which benefit from their presence as high-paying employers of large workforces).

International Security Partnerships

International security organizations often exist by virtue of treaties among their member states. Their immediate mission may be to administer and execute the terms of those treaties, while their larger mission is to protect the mutual interests of their members. These interests may include maintaining the relative stability of strategically important global regions, so international security partnerships often engage in peacekeeping missions in third-party nations.

Potential Annual Earnings Scale. The earnings of employees at a given international security organization are usually dependent on the civil service standards of the participating countries. These standards usually include pay scales for various positions, such as senior leadership, managers, support staff, and administrative personnel.

Clientele Interaction. Employees of an international security partnership act as representatives of their respective countries while in service to the overarching organization. They work closely with representatives of other states, as well as project administrators from higher levels. They remain, however, beholden to the countries they represent, taking orders from their home countries' international relations leadership (such as the U.S. Department of State or the British Foreign and Commonwealth Office).

Client interaction varies at these organizations based on the position involved, as does the definition of a client. In some contexts, a client may be a project team, while for others it will be an ambassador. In any case, partnership staff must have strong communication and interpersonal skills, and they must be able to relate to and interact effectively with people of vastly different cultural backgrounds.

Amenities, Atmosphere, and Physical Grounds. The work performed at an international security organization is professional and diplomatic in nature. Many such organizations' operations are conducted in or near government or military installations. In the interest of cost-effectiveness, many such organizations lack the personalized décor of an Internet start-up or the grandiose architecture of a skyscraper. In fact, many staff must share office space or work in cubi-

cle settings. Those who work in the field are often sent to unstable zones, where they are charged with combating the elements that create threats to regional security.

Typical Number of Employees. The number of employees at a given international security organization varies based on the size of that organization. For example, NATO employs thousands of nonmilitary personnel in its efforts to maintain international security, while similar organizations dedicate smaller task forces to their regional efforts.

Traditional Geographic Locations. International security partnerships have headquarters and other facilities throughout the world. Because of the large volume of high-level diplomats and leaders that frequent them, they are usually headquartered in major cities. Smaller offices are found in locations throughout their regions of influence or in strategically important centers. Additionally, these organizations may have offices located on military bases, at transportation centers, or in other key facilities.

Pros of Working for an International Security Partnership. Working for an international security partnership offers employees unique opportunities. International security professionals assess and address regional, national, and international security threats in diverse and cosmopolitan settings. They are able to work with people from other countries, analyzing information from sources to which they may not have access on a national level. While working in international settings, they are able to receive the benefits and salaries typically provided by their home countries. Workers from wealthy nations such as the United States and those in Western Europe thus receive competitive pay, even when they are located in regions with much lower annual salaries than those of their home countries.

Cons of Working for an International Security Partnership. In most cases, work at international security partnerships is not conducted over the long term; assignments may last only a year or two, which may hinder professional growth. Additionally, although the directives of an individual working for an international security partnership are clear (as they originate in the individual's home country), the diversity of the environment entails being surrounded by colleagues from other countries with conflicting directives and interests. Such divisive conditions may hinder the work being performed or slow its progress considerably. Furthermore, employees' duties may require them to travel to unstable or dangerous areas for prolonged periods of time.

Costs

Payroll and Benefits: International security organizations pay salaries and benefits based on the pay scales of member countries' civil services. These salaries, like most of the organizations' operating budgets, are supplied by the member nations themselves.

Supplies: Like any large government agency, international security partnership organizations must procure large amounts of office supplies, such as computers, telecommunications hardware, and audiovisual equipment (such as overhead projectors and screens). Because of the large quantity of supplies purchased, the managing organization and its individual members may negotiate lower procurement costs with suppliers.

External Services: While most international security partnership organizations are staffed primarily by public employees, some contract external services for less integral positions. Because of the sensitivity of the data they handle and the level of security clearance necessary to view such data, externally contracted positions may be limited to janitorial services, building security, or systems maintenance (such as groundskeeping and building engineering).

Utilities: International security partnerships must pay for standard utilities such as electricity, heat, water usage, and waste management.

Taxes: The tax status of an international security partnership organization can be vague, particularly when it operates in a third-party country. In the case of the former Yugoslavia, for example, NATO's establishment of operations depended on the Croatian, Serbian, and Bosnian governments' willingness to exempt NATO employees from any national income, property, or sales taxes, as long as their presence was part of official NATO business. When they do not secure such exemptions, the organization and its employees must pay the relevant taxes of the countries in which they are operating.

Think Tanks

National and international security think tanks conduct research and engage in advocacy in order to shape the foreign and defense policies of national governments. Some think tanks are avowedly partisan, embracing a progressive or a conservative point of view. Others strive to be nonpartisan and seek a balance of diverse opinions from their staffs. Some—particularly in the national and international security realm—are funded by the government itself. These government-funded institutes evaluate current and prospective policies and provide reports and recommendations directly to the government. They bring together governmental, industrial, and academic resources in a way that a fully governmental entity cannot.

In addition, some think tanks are funded by particular business interests, such as defense contractors. Their job is to shape policy for the specific benefit of their funders—usually for their financial benefit. Even those nonpartisan entities funded by public donor contributions may have a vested interest in producing analyses that confirm the opinions of their particular donor bases. If so, they tend to shy away from expressing opinions that those bases will find controversial.

Think tanks may employ researchers and analysts with varying levels of academic credentials versus practical experience in government and national security. Indeed, one of the benefits of the think tank as an entity is its ability to bring together academics and those with real-world experience to work cooperatively on the same project.

Potential Annual Earnings Scale. The earnings of a national and international think tank vary based on the contracts under which the organization is operating, as well as the security clearance required for a given position. In 2006, the average uncleared staff member earned about $50,000 per year, while the average staff member with a higher security clearance earned about $66,000 per year. At the largest security think tank, the Rand Corporation, the average annual salary is about $56,000, although high-level economists and policy analysts may earn more than $100,000.

Clientele Interaction. Government-funded think tanks report directly to government agencies, while other institutions tend to issue press releases and reports and hold public events to disseminate their findings. In either case, at small think tanks it is likely that most if not all employees will present findings and publicize positions in forums outside their institutions. By contrast, large institutions generally employ specific staff members tasked with client relations, public relations, or government relations. Other employees are unlikely to interact much with clients or the general public.

Amenities, Atmosphere, and Physical Grounds. The environment of a national and international security think tank is typically an office setting with individual offices, cubicles, or a combination thereof assigned according to seniority. The environment is professional, and most of the work is performed with computers and telecommunications technologies.

Typical Number of Employees. Think tanks vary in size, from small, nonprofit organizations staffed by only a few individuals and administrative personnel to large corporations with hundreds of staff members working on a large number of contracts. Small institutions may supplement their small staffs with unpaid interns or part-time workers. Large corporate think tanks often divide employees into teams that are each assigned specific projects.

Traditional Geographic Locations. National and international security think tanks are typically located either in major urban areas or in major university environments. Urban areas facilitate transportation and access to a large amount of information, whereas academics and staff may dedicate a larger percentage of time analyzing data and utilizing a wide range of information resources within an academic setting.

Pros of Working for a Think Tank. Working at a think tank involves a great deal of academic research and policy analysis (if not recommendations). It is intellectually stimulating work that allows specialists in such fields as political science, defense, economics, and national security to capitalize on their training and expertise. Additionally, although think tanks study threats to a nation's security, their employees are not typically placed in harm's way (though they may have previ-

A U.S. Navy SH-60B Seahawk helicopter flies over an Arleigh Burke-class guided missile destroyer in the Pacific Ocean. (U.S. Department of Defense)

ous experience in high-risk environments, including battlefields and front-line counter-terrorism assignments).

Cons of Working for a Think Tank. The work conducted at a think tank is done in something of a vacuum, in that it is shielded from the reality of the political process or the dangers of physically repelling a security threat. The think tank is an academic setting, dependent on models and theoretical concepts as well as actual data. Those seeking a real-world career environment may become frustrated with the approach of a think tank.

Additionally, while the larger, corporate think tanks have sufficient financial resources to offer high salaries to their employees, the same cannot be said for a significant number of think tanks, which are often nonprofit entities. As a result, salaries, while at times competitive for higher-level managers and executives, are typically set at the level of the nonprofit sector rather than at the level of the corporate sector. A corporate employee doing comparable work is likely to be better paid.

Costs

Payroll and Benefits: Think tanks generally offer annual salaries and benefits to employees, although small institutions that receive contractual funding for specific projects may pay the staff working on those projects on a contract (per-project) basis.

Supplies: Think tanks require office hardware and equipment, such as phones, computers, photocopiers, and fax machines, as well as stationery, writing implements, staples, and similar supplies. They also require computer software that is capable of collating and modeling large amounts of data.

External Services: Think tanks may use external accounting services, employment agencies, custodial services, and private security agencies. Small institutions that are only occasionally in the public spotlight may also hire external public relations professionals or legal counsel.

Utilities: Think tanks pay for standard utilities, which may include electricity, water, sewage, and trash removal, as well as telephone and Internet access.

Taxes: Nonprofit think tanks are exempt from most taxes, though they must still pay payroll taxes on employees' salaries. For-profit institu-

tions must pay corporate and real estate taxes to state and federal governments.

ORGANIZATIONAL STRUCTURE AND JOB ROLES

The organizational structure of a national or international security agency or company is dependent on its size and duties. Many such institutions have multiple purposes and, as a result, are compartmentalized into mission- or project-specific groups.

Many components of the industry are considerably different in terms of the types of employees who fill particular job roles. For example, an aerospace company that is responsible for developing intelligence satellite technology will likely have a high volume of engineers and technical experts in senior leadership. By contrast, a public policy organization that gauges political instability in certain regimes is more likely to have leaders with academic or diplomatic backgrounds.

Because of the sensitivity of the industry and its endeavors, most employees of a national or international security organization must undergo extensive background checks. Upon passing, they are given security clearances appropriate to their job functions.

The following umbrella categories apply to the organizational structure of agencies and institutions within the national and international security industry:

- Senior Leadership
- Project Management
- Analysts
- Field Personnel
- Administrative Personnel

Senior Leadership

At the top of a national or international security agency or corporation is a seasoned leadership team. It is responsible for overseeing the activities and operations of the entire organization. Many members of such teams are retired military officers or former legislators, both of whom are fully experienced in not just the issues involved in national security but also the operations directed toward addressing those issues. They must also be capable budgeters and often serve as the official representatives of their organizations, reporting to legislators, officials, and even members of the media.

The education of senior leadership in this industry varies, but they must be fully experienced in the issues at hand. Some are academics with extensive university experience and degrees in relevant fields. They must also be effective bureaucrats and leaders who can command employees and implement plans effectively.

Senior leadership occupations may include the following:

- President/Chief Executive Officer (CEO)
- Vice President
- Chief Operating Officer (COO)
- Director
- Deputy Director
- Supreme Commander
- Chief Financial Officer (CFO)

Project Management

Project managers oversee projects from conception to completion, and they manage the teams dedicated to carrying out those projects. They are responsible for overseeing team members, developing and maintaining project budgets and schedules, and assigning duties and tasks to team members. They report to senior leadership and, in the case of private contractors, to clients on a frequent basis.

Project managers in the national and international security industry are typically former military personnel or college-educated civilians who have spent a number of years ascending through the industry. They are expected to have leadership skills and be effective administrators.

Project management occupations may include the following:

- Program Manager
- Project Coordinator
- Contract Writer

Analysts

Most international and national security teams include trained analysts. These individuals assess data, conduct audits, study trends, and assess threats. Analysts must be effective communicators who are adept at writing and speaking, as they are called upon to present coherent explanations of often-complex situations and systems. The recipients of these briefings may include senior officials who may not be familiar with the intricacies of the relevant concepts, as well as underlings who must understand the information they are given well enough to relay it up the chain of command. Analysts typically have advanced degrees, including at least a bachelor's degree in the field most directly relevant to their projects. In many cases, they must be proficient (if not fluent) in a foreign language, which makes them far more effective at assessing data.

Analyst occupations may include the following:

- Senior Analyst
- Analyst
- Senior Researcher
- Researcher

Field Personnel

Field personnel operate on the front lines against those who threaten national or international security. They are often the most visible of the agents in this industry, positioned at airports and other ports of call, assisting in maintaining security in combat zones, and even conducting investigations and interrogations. Field personnel vary in experience and educational background according to the type of work they are charged with performing. Some have law enforcement or military training, while others are trained after they have been hired, following strict procedures set forth by their agency or company.

Field occupations may include the following:

- Security Officer
- Intelligence Officer
- Site Manager
- Special Agent
- Section Chief
- Peacekeeping Officer

Administrative Personnel

Like any effective corporation or agency, in order to be efficient, a national or international security organization must have a highly capable group of administrative personnel to oversee the day-to-day operations. Administrative personnel manage paperwork, answer phones, organize files and computer networks, and handle other tasks of vital importance. They may or may not have postsecondary educations, but they are expected to have exceptional organizational skills so that their offices will function both efficiently and effectively.

Administrative occupations may include the following:

- Receptionist
- Administrative Assistant

INDUSTRY OUTLOOK

Overview

Since the earliest development of the modern nation-state, the security of a country and of the regions in which it has interests has been a high governmental priority. However, the environment in which the national and international security industry operates has changed considerably over the last several decades, and it will no doubt continue to evolve. What has emerged as a sizable, diverse, and global industry has been modified in response to changes in the nature of the threats against which it guards. While the need still exists for nations to have military and police presences to deter and defeat would-be attackers, the industry increasingly employs technological solutions to combat terrorism, monitor national instability and the behavior of rogue states, and protect against other threats.

Concerns over security have major implications for other important national and international sectors and, as a result, may affect their operations. For example, it has been estimated that the heightened state of vigilance stemming from the terrorist attacks of September 11, 2001, helped spur American defense spending by as much as 60 percent over a six-year period. The growing national security industry continues to have strong ties to the arenas of aerospace, maritime, and conventional weapons (such as missiles, armor, and small arms), with which it has long been connected. Additionally, computer and communications surveillance, fields overseen in part by the NSA, continue to be a mainstay for the national and international security industry.

The changing landscape of potential threats to a nation's security has required adaptation and expansion into other areas. Although the NSA has been pursuing suspected combatants by monitoring telephone and electronic communications since the turn of the twenty-first century, the agency and its contractors have also had to defend against attempts to breach the country's economic, governmental, and other vital systems via the Internet (so-called cyberterrorism). In doing so, the industry has needed to train personnel to create online defenses, as well as tracking and destroying viruses and other programs that pose a danger to a nation's infrastructure.

Additionally, biological and chemical weapons, while not necessarily new to the world, are seeing a renaissance of sorts. With the collapse of the Soviet Union, most countries eschewed the development of such weapons. However, many former Soviet chemical weapons scientists and their products disappeared after the Soviet collapse. Their disappearance gave rise to anxiety that they would resurface among terrorists and rogue nations. Fears persist that terrorist groups such as al-Qaeda will obtain such weapons and deploy them in heavily populated urban centers. As a result, the national and international security industry has paid a considerable amount of attention to the myriad biological and chemical agents that might be used in terrorist weapons. The industry is also helping local law enforcement establish protocols in the event that such weapons are used.

National and international security industry representatives in both the government and the private sector have demonstrated an increasing interest in undoing the elements that foster terrorism. Working alongside military, diplomatic, and even nonprofit organizations, many such groups are helping train local law enforcement, develop democratic institutions, and help build business and social service networks. To this end, international development organizations and international security organizations increasingly work hand-in-hand to defeat terrorism at its roots.

Employment Advantages

The national and international security industry is constantly growing and adapting in response to a changing environment. The industry offers an extremely wide range of career areas and, with them, a large number of opportunities for advancement along different career paths. Additionally, individuals who are part of this industry are also buoyed by the fact that they are part of a network that works to protect their country and its allies. The tragic events of September 11, 2001, fanned passions about not just defeating al-Qaeda but also preemptively neutralizing other terrorist organizations around the world. This industry and those who work within it are dedicated to preventing another tragedy.

Annual Earnings

The ongoing global effort against terrorism, coupled with continued conflicts in the Middle East, South Asia, and the former Soviet Union, perpetuates a perceived need among policy makers for continued investment in national and international security efforts. Although the stagnant global economy resulting from the 2007-2009 financial crisis is affecting most industries, national and global spending on security continues to rise, and it is estimated that this trend will continue.

The only fiscal years for which the budget of the U.S. intelligence community is unclassified are 1997 and 1998. In those years, the total governmental expenditures on intelligence were $26.6 billion and $26.7 billion, respectively. Overall revenues in the American national security industry in 2001 were $302 billion. One study estimates that by 2018, U.S. spending on national and international security programs will increase by nearly 30 percent. The study also suggests that nineteen other major countries will see increases as well. The growing focus on combating terrorism through international development has also caused an increase in the industry's revenues, as U.S. spending on such efforts increased by nearly 4 percent from 2009 to 2010.

RELATED RESOURCES FOR FURTHER RESEARCH

ASIS INTERNATIONAL
1625 Prince St.
Alexandria, VA 22314
Tel: (703) 519-6200
Fax: (703) 519-6298
http://www.asisonline.org

LAWRENCE LIVERMORE NATIONAL LABORATORY
7000 East Ave.
Livermore, CA 94550
Tel: (925) 422-1100
Fax: (925) 422-1370
http://www.llnl.gov

NORTH ATLANTIC TREATY ORGANIZATION
Blvd. Leopold III
1110 Brussels
Belgium
http://www.nato.int

U.S. DEPARTMENT OF HOMELAND SECURITY
245 Murray Ln. SW
Washington, DC 20528
Tel: (202) 282-8000
http://www.dhs.gov

ABOUT THE AUTHOR

Michael P. Auerbach has over sixteen years of professional experience in public policy and administration, international relations, and defense. He is a 1993 graduate of Wittenberg University and a 1999 graduate of the Boston College Graduate School of Arts and Sciences. He previously worked as a project manager for a number of U.S. Navy international informational exchange programs in Washington, D.C., and has published a number of articles about defense and international security, including a comprehensive study of NATO and the Partnership for Peace.

FURTHER READING

Bullock, Jane A., et al. *Introduction to Homeland Security: Principles of All-Hazards Response.* 3d ed. Boston: Butterworth Heinemann, 2009.

CareerBuilder.com. Salary Calculator and Wage Finder. http://www.cbsalary.com/salary-calculator.

Defence.Professionals. "Saab Half-Yearly Result Shows Increased Sales." July 24, 2009. http://www.defpro.com/news/details/8775.

Federation of American Scientists. "Fast Facts." 2009. http://www.fas.org/asmp/fast_facts.htm.

Homeland Security Research Corporation. *Global Homeland Security, Homeland Defense, and Intelligence Markets Outlook, 2009-2018.* Washington, D.C.: Author, 2009.

Howard, Russell D., and Reid L. Sawyer, eds. *Terrorism and Counterterrorism: Understanding the New Security Environment.* New York: McGraw-Hill, 2009.

Jones, Elka. "Careers in Homeland Security." *Occupational Outlook Quarterly,* Summer, 2006. Available at http://www.bls.gov/opub/ooq/2006/summer/art01.pdf.

Method, Jason. "Fed Pay: Rank-and-File Tops Private Average, Managers Fall Below." *USA Today,* June 24, 2007.

Nemeth, Charles P. *Homeland Security: An Introduction to Principles and Practice.* Boca Raton, Fla.: Auerback, 2010.

PayScale.com. "Salary Survey for Industry: Aerospace and Defense." http://www.payscale.com/research/US/Industry=Aerospace_and_Defense/Salary.

Renshon, Stanley Allen. *National Security in the Obama Administration: Reassessing the Bush Doctrine.* New York: Routledge, 2010.

Rosenbach, Eric, and Aki J. Peritz. *Confrontation or Collaboration? Congress and the Intelligence Community.* Cambridge, Mass.: John F. Kennedy School of Government, Belfer Center for Science and International Affairs, 2009.

Simply Hired. "Average Central Intelligence Agency Salaries." http://www.simplyhired.com/a/salary/search/q-Central+Intelligence+Agency+cia.

Thomas, Douglas, and Brian D. Loader, eds. *Cybercrime: Law Enforcement, Security, and Surveillance in the Information Age.* New York: Routledge, 2000.

U.S. Bureau of Labor Statistics. *Career Guide to Industries,* 2010-2011 ed. http://www.bls.gov/oco/cg.

U.S. Census Bureau. North American Industry Classification System (NAICS), 2007. http://www.census.gov/cgi-bin/sssd/naics/naicsrch?chart=2007.

U.S. Department of Commerce. International Trade Administration. Office of Trade and Industry Information. Industry Trade Data and Analysis. http://ita.doc.gov/td/industry/otea/OTII/OTII-index.html.

White, Jonathan R. *Terrorism and Homeland Security.* 6th ed. Belmont, Calif.: Wadsworth Cengage Learning, 2009.

Natural Resources Management

INDUSTRY SNAPSHOT

General Industry: Natural Resources

Career Cluster: Agriculture, Food, and Natural Resources

Subcategory Industries: Administration of Conservation Programs; Environment, Conservation, and Wildlife Organizations; Forestry

Related Industries: Civil Services: Planning; Coal Mining Industry; Environmental Engineering and Consultation Services; Logging Industry; Mining Industry; Petroleum and Natural Gas Industry; Waste Management Industry; Water Supply Industry

Annual Domestic Revenues: $1.2 billion USD (Hoovers, 2010, natural resource management segment for private environmental consulting firms only)

Annual International Revenues: $1.65 billion USD (Hoovers, 2010, natural resource management segment for private environmental consulting firms only)

Annual Global Revenues: $2.85 billion USD (Hoovers, 2010, natural resource management segment for private environmental consulting firms only)

NAICS Numbers: 113, 92412, 813312

INDUSTRY DEFINITION

Summary

Natural resources management professionals provide direction in implementing and maintaining a balance between immediate human needs to exploit land and water resources and long-term needs to protect ecosystems so resources can recover, restock, grow, and renew. Natural resource managers function as planners, analysts, restoration specialists, preservationists, conservationists, fisheries and wildlife managers, forestry professionals, rangers, wetland monitors, social advocates, environmental consultants, and land-use managers. Natural resource managers work in private sector companies and consulting firms; public sector agencies within federal, state, and local governments; and nonprofit organizations and trusts. Many natural resource professionals build careers in academia doing basic and advanced research, providing the information necessary to promote sound resource management plans and policies.

History of the Industry

The modern era of environmental awareness began in the 1890's and lasted until the early 1970's; it was characterized by an emphasis on efforts to conserve and preserve wilderness areas or to identify areas of scenic interest and provide access and amenities, so urban dwellers could vacation in these natural environments. At the beginning of the 1970's, scientific studies indicated a growing danger to both the natural world and humans from increased levels of human-induced pollution. For the next thirty years, environmental sciences concentrated on methods to prevent, control, or remediate the effects of pollution of the environment. During the 1990's, a series of laws was enacted acknowledging that industrial pollution and human behaviors were affecting the natural world and, as a by-product, the quality of human life. This legislation assumed that to ensure current and future generations a livable world, environmental degradation resulting from pollution had to be monitored, controlled, or eliminated, and those in violation had to be penalized. Much of the legislation passed also set standards for recycling, treating, and disposing of human and industrial wastes. At the beginning of the twenty-first century, an emphasis was placed on remedia-

tion and reclamation of sites previously contaminated with pollutants.

As environmental awareness grew over the course of the twentieth century, it became clear the rate of human resource exploitation and consumption could not be maintained within the obvious finite limits of the resources themselves. Land, groundwater, timber, minerals, wildlife, grazing lands, farmlands, wetlands, and waterways needed to be observed, monitored, cataloged, managed, and maintained in a manner ensuring their continued biodiversity, prosperity, and renewal. It became clear to science professionals that maintaining sustainable ecosystems equated to maintaining a sustainable quality of life for humans: To do otherwise would court disaster. From this understanding, the modern role of the natural resource manager arose: Such managers were skilled professionals versed in the science needed to oversee and direct the use and preservation of natural resources.

Government agencies were the first to employ professional resource managers in an attempt to

Wetlands at Tomales Bay State Park in California. (©Christopher Russell/Dreamstime.com)

identify the resources available for exploitation on government lands. Knowledge of available resources allowed the government to promote specific territorial regions to business, industry, and settlers for development. Early resource specialists were most often interested in mineral reserves, groundwater availability, timberlands, wildlife numbers, and grazing lands. As the period of westward expansion in North America during the 1800's waned and the idea of preservation and conservation began, the primary role of the government-backed resource manager changed from being a promoter of the exploitation of public lands to being a vigilant protector of those lands. Often, the mission of government resource managers was, and still is, double-sided: While they were charged with protecting and safeguarding resources, they were also charged with cultivating a climate in which business and exploitation are encouraged within the relevant legal restrictions.

A sign in a conservation area alerts hikers that birds are roosting, so they must walk around them. (©Dreamstime.com)

At the same time the role of government resource managers was developing, other resource managers attached to industry approached the environment differently. They placed their major emphasis on coordinating and managing industrial and other activities in order to extract the maximum amount of resources in the most efficient manner possible. These early industrial and agricultural managers paid little to no attention to remediation, reclamation, sustainability, or any other considerations that did not contribute to their employers' profits.

The Industry Today

The profession of natural resources manager is growing rapidly, both in positions available and in importance. As human understanding of environmental interactions and sustainability collide with the ever-growing need for renewable and nonrenewable resources generated by the growth of the human population, resource professionals trained in implementing sound policy and decision making are in demand. Trained resources managers are necessary to ensure that both the needs and the rights of farmlands, wetlands, wilderness, watersheds, forests, and wildlife are considered in balance with the needs of growing human demands for resources. This is especially significant as urban boundaries expand and infringe on previously undeveloped areas. The same balance must also be taken into consideration as developing countries attempt to exploit their resource bases in order to modernize.

Much of the emphasis on natural resource management is based on strategies and policies initiated through legislation and regulation. As governments acknowledge the need to maintain sustainable ecosystems and resource bases and to preserve healthy environments for the long-term good of their citizens, they understand that the balance between resource exploitation and preservation or restoration requires the guidance of highly trained scientific professionals. Government agencies currently employ over 74 percent of land, water, mineral, wildlife, and forest resource managers. There are a limited number of large private-sector environmental consulting firms, and many rely heavily on contracts to government agencies. The reason the government relies on private consulting firms is that there are so many resource-

A California condor spreads its wings. (U.S. Fish and Wildlife Service)

related issues to address, so many stakeholders affected, and a constant shift in priorities within national and local agendas that those resource specialists in public service cannot handle the ever-increasing number of cases and projects put before them in a timely manner.

The awareness of global climate change has added a new aspect to the field of natural resource management. Earth is an integrated ecosystem of cycles and feedback loops fluctuating through time in varying states of equilibrium. Scientific evidence suggests human behaviors have upset certain chemical, hydrogeologic, and atmospheric cycles of the planet, altering the climatic regime at a scale in which extremes in climatic conditions are being generated as the planet attempts to reach a new equilibrium. The new equilibrium may turn out to be less hospitable to many of the planet's existing ecosystems. The science of global climate change offers new opportunities to natural resources managers. As global climatic conditions shift, there will be a determined need for natural

resource professionals skilled in energy matters, renewable resources, population dynamics, international policies, remediation, reclamation, pollution prevention, alternative resources, hydrogeology, desalinization, soil conservation, irrigation, air quality, and land-use management.

Because skill sets are generally focused to each specific branch of resource management, positions within the field require a minimum of a bachelor's degree in a specialized area of environmental, biological, botanical, or physical science. The majority of employers in both the public and private sectors search for candidates with graduate educations, especially those with cross-specialty training. Most research-based resource management positions within government agencies, and similar careers in academia, require doctoral degrees. Resource managers holding advanced degrees are more likely to see increased chances for advancement in their fields. Depending on education level and job responsibilities, average annual compensation for resource management jobs ranges from

Wild horses in Utah. (BLM/Utah)

$65,000 to $130,000. Resource managers with graduate educations can be expected to earn about $20,000 to $25,000 more annually than those with only bachelor's degrees. Salaries may be lower for resource managers working for underfunded government agencies, or considerably higher for upper managers, business owners, and technical specialists in the private sector. There are a small number of resource management jobs within private industries exploiting natural resources, such as mining, energy exploration, agriculture, construction, commercial fishing, irrigation, desalinization, and waste management. A very limited number of resource managers are also employed as advocates or lobbyists for nonprofit organizations or large industrial and business interests. A limited number of natural resource specialists are also employed in academia.

The field of resource management is predicted to grow as the need for more sustainable sources of natural materials increases. Increasing world population demands new or renewable sources of water, energy, minerals, and food products. The expansion of urban boundaries into previously wild or agricultural lands, the need for cleaner forms of energy, the loss of species habitat, ecosystem alteration from climate change, overharvesting of species, growing demands for timber prod-

ucts and minerals, and the need to protect resource areas from pollutants and waste products of modern societies all require the skill sets of modern natural resource managers. As long as human societies demand resources from their environment at a rate the planet cannot naturally renew, there will be a need for people willing to take on the responsibilities of natural resource management.

Many positions in the resource management field involve regulatory or compliance functions. As governments enact laws to protect natural resources and ensure a healthy environment for citizens, it is up to natural resource managers to make sure applicable laws are enforced. Natural resource managers are often embroiled in debates among economic demands, cultural values, environmental realities, political necessities, scientific fact, and social traditions. Some natural resource managers are also experts in public policy or environmental law, making them especially valuable in facilitating compromises that seek balances between resource needs, sustainability, conservation, and preservation. Those individuals willing to become natural resource managers, at whatever level of responsibility, must understand that they can never satisfy all stakeholders in the realm of resource exploitation versus resource preservation. One stakeholder's vision of sustainability and conservation is often the point of conflict with another person's source of income or traditional value system. The most successful natural resource managers will always be those who are able to provide positive direction in implementing and maintaining a balance between human needs and promoting resource bases and ecosystems that function in a meaningful and naturally healthy manner. Those natural resource managers with the ability to communicate complex problems in plain language, are skilled in facilitating conflict resolution and negotiations that stay well away from litigation, and are able to establish working relationships with stake holders of varying agendas will be the most successful.

Natural resource management jobs may occur in small, privately owned consulting firms or isolated field offices of government agencies; in large multinational environmental businesses and industries; or in large, statutory federal, state, or local government bureaus. The following sections give a generalized overview of what might be confronted while working for either a private or governmental natural resource management concern.

Small Businesses and Agencies

Natural resource management careers on the smallest levels include individual, contracted consulting firms that may have from one to a dozen employees. Of these, possibly only one to five are actual resource specialists in decision-making positions; the remaining are support staff. This is similar in the case of small government field offices, in which a limited number of environmental specialists may work alone or with shared support staff. Smaller municipalities or county agencies may be staffed with a limited number of permanent or part-time environmental specialists. In many instances, agency environmental specialists are hired on a seasonal basis for specific assessment or oversight responsibilities and are assigned to small permanent or mobile field stations.

Potential Annual Earnings Scale. The average earnings for natural resource managers is $65,000 to $130,000, but salaries will vary based on location and level of responsibility and decision making. According to the U.S. Bureau of Labor Statistics (BLS), government-employed conservation scientists earned an average of $62,360 in 2009, soil and plant scientists earned an average of $69,030, environmental scientists earned an average of $63,260, environmental engineers earned an average of $76,550, and natural sciences managers earned an average of $100,720.

Clientele Interaction. At the small business and agency level, the majority of client and stakeholder interaction occurs on the individual or small group level. Large groups may be encountered in public hearings, hearings of cause, park interpretations, educational lectures, or court testimony. When not collecting or analyzing environmental data, natural resource managers spend the majority of their time in conflict resolution. Being able to negotiate and build consensus and compromise are valuable skills, especially if the manager is working alone or in a limited group. Much of the interaction with stakeholders and the public requires the resource manager to be able to conduct one-on-one conversations in a rational and deliberate manner with emotionally stressed stakeholders. The ability to build a professional rapport with even the most distraught client or stakeholder, and to do so without backup or support, is a positive. In some state and federal agency positions, resource managers are armed, similarly to conservation law enforcement officers. Many stakeholders involved in controversial environmental problems have displayed powerful dislikes for government agencies they believe are standing in the way of their ability to exploit resources, and in the past such people have proven disruptive and even violent to lone environmental professionals in the field.

Amenities, Atmosphere, and Physical Grounds. The working conditions for natural resource managers at the small business and agency level vary by location and profitability. A successful private consulting firm may choose to upgrade the amenities, technology, and surroundings of its working conditions. On the other hand, a small consulting firm may work out of a natural resource manager's home office. The working conditions for small office agency postings may vary from quite upscale office space in a major metropolitan setting to a floorless tent in a wilderness logging camp. The most important aspect determining the amenities, working atmosphere, and physical grounds for working as a natural resource manager is what one is willing to live with while working the job. Many people want to live and pursue their profession in the most wild and isolated wilderness under the most physically demanding conditions; others prefer the comfort of a more urban environment. Wilderness jobs frequently have odd hours of work, not suited to people who prefer regular work schedules. Jobs in the wilderness may bring the natural resource manager in contact with a wide range of wildlife; some resource managers would as soon not have to deal with bears on a daily basis.

Typical Number of Employees. Number of employees for small natural resource consulting firms fluctuates with the needs of the marketplace: Marketplace needs are often determined by regulatory mandate, changes to existing laws, or environmental dilemmas or disasters. Government agencies staff their field offices and research stations based on need, funding, urgency, or political expediency. Many projects in both the private and public sectors are seasonally dependent, so numbers of employees vary widely.

Traditional Geographic Locations. Smaller consulting firms tend to remain regional in their project selection, choosing to specialize in the environmental problems of their local areas. Such regional specialization allows for the establishment of personal relationships with stakeholders and promotes the businesses as part of the local economy and culture. The building of a positive professional record in solving complex environmental problems that balance the needs of local stakeholders helps the smaller environmental consulting firms stay solvent. Agency natural resource management jobs of small-to-moderate size can be found in planning and environmental divisions of small towns and county governments. Federal and state environmental agencies have lone resource managers assigned anywhere from busy urban parks to isolated wilderness field stations to obscure mining and fishing operations spanning the width and breadth of most states and the entire nation. Job locations also revolve around resource specialties: Foresters will find jobs near timber regions, fishery specialists near fisheries, land-use planners in urban areas, and mineral managers near mining operations.

Pros of Working for a Small Business or Agency. Natural resource professionals who enjoy working independently and free from bureaucratic constraints often imposed in larger agencies or businesses will enjoy working at the smaller level. Also, many natural resource managers enter the profession because of strong stands on environmental ethics: A smaller consulting firm allows managers to pick and choose projects expressing their environmental commitments. Working in a small agency for a local government allows for the building of connections and relationships within a community: Many natural resource managers feel that their jobs are more satisfying and meaningful

when they are also stakeholders in solving problems. Resource managers who enjoy the solitude of the wilderness may find that living and working in a remote field station is perfect for the professional experience they seek.

Cons of Working for a Small Business or Agency. Negative aspects of working for a small consulting firm include the inability to compete with the resources of large consulting firms for certain jobs, even at the local level. Small firms often lack the access to advanced technology and additional staffing needed to complete tasks in a timely manner. The small consulting firm must rely on a constant stream of jobs to remain solvent, so downturns in business have a large effect on profitability. The negative aspects of working for a smaller agency office or field station are similar to the positives: isolation, lack of professional interaction, rugged living conditions, and minimal support staff.

Costs

Payroll and Benefits: Small consulting firms are free to establish whatever pay standards and benefits they determine, as long as they meet minimum wage requirements and the market is willing to accept their rates. Agency natural resource manager positions' pay grades and benefits are mandated by the governments they work for and are usually the result of negotiations between the government and bargaining units representing civil service employees. Benefits, pensions, annual leave, sick time, and pay grades vary from city to city and state to state—and often from agency to agency. Federal pay and benefits are set nationwide. Cost of living increases for agency positions are often linked to budget restrictions of the local, state, or federal government. Agency seasonal employees may receive overtime pay when jobs require extended hours.

Supplies: Most small agency offices and small businesses require telephones; mobile telephones; walkie-talkies; first-aid kits; personal and portable computers; printers; geographic information services (GIS)-capable computing devices; typical office supplies such as paper, pens, and office furniture; field equipment; safety equipment; business and staff vehicles—usually four-wheel-drive capable; Global Positioning System

(GPS) units; reference libraries; and occasionally firearms.

External Services: External services may include landscaping, janitorial services, bottled-water delivery, security services, document removal and shredding, temporary and seasonal hires, laboratory services, and outside auditors. Ready access to travel agencies is important. Established positive working relationships with regional colleges and universities are favorable services.

Utilities: Small environmental businesses and small agency offices require water, electricity, sanitation services, telephone, and Internet access. Additionally, local rubbish or recycling removal should be available.

Taxes: All employees and managers are subject to payroll taxes applicable where the business or agency is located. Businesses are also subject to business and property taxes. Many states also require environmental professionals to be registered or licensed, and these fees may be considered taxes.

Midsize Businesses and Agencies

Most midsize environmental consulting firms servicing natural resource management clients tend to be niche-market oriented: In regions with large timber or mineral operations, midsize consulting firms focus their energies on these resources and hire accordingly. Midsize environmental firms in urban areas may concentrate on land-use planning issues and environmental impact statements; firms in agriculture-dominated areas may specialize in hydrology or soil resources. Midsize governmental agency offices with natural resources managers are typically located in capital cities of smaller states, or are regional field offices of major agencies and may be responsible for overseeing territories of significant sizes. Both these midsize operations tend to have twenty-five to one hundred employees, with about 10 percent of their employees being natural resource managers.

Potential Annual Earnings Scale. The average earnings for natural resource managers is $65,000 to $130,000 USD, and salaries vary based on location and level of responsibility and decision making. According to the BLS, government-employed conservation scientists earned an average of $62,360 in 2009, soil and plant scientists earned an average of $69,030, environmental scientists earned an average of $63,260, environmental engineers earned an average of $76,550, and natural sciences managers earned an average of $100,720.

Typically, salaries for resource managers working for midsize consulting firms are higher than those of employees working for smaller operations. These higher salaries reflect rates the companies charge and the need for higher salaries to allow employees to live in the urban areas where most of the firms are based. Employees of midsize consulting firms are usually paid according to their corporate status, responsibilities, and levels of decision making. Government employees are paid based on civil service rankings and pay scales established through bargaining units. Some midsize field office operations are often central bases for seasonal employees; most of these seasonal employees work at hourly rates of pay and often have the option to earn overtime pay.

Clientele Interaction. Client interaction within midsize consulting firms and government agencies is dictated by the status of the resource manager within the corporate or agency hierarchy. Resource managers doing active oversight, assessment, research, and interviewing will have the most client interactions. Upper-level resource managers rely on the input and results of their subordinates to keep them informed of project progress. It is traditionally the midsize agency field office personnel who have the most frequent and extensive interactions with clients and stakeholders. Because of regional field offices' specialization with the local ecosystems and intimate understanding of problems and events within their region, they employ the natural resource managers on whom central agency supervisors rely to do specific resource managing tasks. As a result, regional resource managers often have nearly daily contacts with resource extraction operations, concerned stakeholders, law enforcement officials, wilderness visitors, lawyers, academics, and polluters.

Amenities, Atmosphere, and Physical Grounds. Most midsize consulting firms and agencies are housed in modern facilities with active technology networks, laboratories, and clerical staffs. Both types of operations are typically located in midsize communities with easy access to transportation and ancillary environmental support. While midsize environmental operations often are still highly career competitive, they also afford a greater opportunity for the development of collegial fellowship and long-term professional relationships.

Typical Number of Employees. The number of employees for midsize natural resource consulting firms fluctuates with the needs of the marketplace, which are often determined by regulatory mandate, changes to existing laws, or regional environmental dilemmas or disasters. Government agencies are staffed based on need, funding, urgency, or current project needs. Many environmental projects in both the private and the public sectors are seasonally dependent, so numbers of employees vary widely. It is not unusual for midsize consulting firms and regional governmental offices to have twenty-five to one hundred full-time employees.

Traditional Geographic Locations. Typical locations of midsize consulting firms and government agency regional field offices are midsize municipalities. Midsize consulting firms tend to specialize their resource management operations in those resources being exploited in their vicinities. Regional government agency offices are usually located in cities with necessary auxiliary operations that aid in their management operations: academic institutions, law enforcement, judiciary, testing laboratories, and other ancillary government agencies.

Pros of Working for a Midsize Business or Agency. One of the greatest benefits of working in a midsize private or public environmental operation is the chance for resource managers to use their scientific specialties on a day-to-day basis in geographic areas with which they have daily interactions. It also allows resource managers to focus their understanding of ecosystems and specific resources on those specific geographic locations. Such specialization helps stakeholders, clients, and the public feel that the resource managers addressing their concerns are well-versed in the economic, cultural, and environmental issues particular to their locations. Since the resource managers live within the regions and communities they work within, they can be considered stakeholders as well. This sense of environmental and community ownership by some natural resource managers is considered a positive.

Cons of Working for a Midsize Business or Agency. While being a visible part of the community one works within is a positive for some natural resource managers, it can be a serious negative at the same time. Because many of the midsize consulting firms and regional government agency field offices are in midsize communities, natural resource managers can gain notoriety for the exploitation operations they represent, or the results of their studies, environmental impact statements, assessments, oversight operations, and law enforcement. Trying to strike a balance between sustainable ecosystems and resource exploitation entails confronting a set of stakeholders who have opposing viewpoints, values, and preferred outcomes. If the results of a public hearing, court case, or resource management plan leave one of the stakeholders feeling unsatisfied, the resource manager can become the target of criticism. Whether deserved or not, the resulting notoriety can greatly affect future business and career opportunities.

Costs

Payroll and Benefits: Midsize consulting firms are free to establish whatever pay standards and benefits they determine, as long as they meet minimum wage requirements and the employment market will accept their rates. Bonus packages at successful midsize consulting firms are often incentive-based and linked to project outcomes or competitive client acquisition, with bonuses based on annual business profitability or established as incentives in client contracts. Statutory agency natural resource manager positions' pay grades and benefits are mandated by the local, state, or federal government they work for and are usually the result of negotiations between the government and bargaining units representing civil service employees. Benefits, pensions, annual leave, sick time, and pay grades vary from city to city and state to state—and often from agency to agency. Federal pay and benefits are set nationwide. Cost of living increases for agency positions are often linked to budget restrictions of the local, state, or federal government. Agency seasonal employees may receive overtime pay when jobs require extended hours. Typically, compensation time is given in lieu of overtime pay for civil service employees in nonclerical and nonmaintenance positions.

Supplies: Most midsize agencies' and environmental businesses' offices require telephones;

mobile telephones; walkie-talkies; personal and portable computers; printers; plotters; GIS-capable computing devices; typical office supplies such as paper, pens, and office furniture; fleet vehicles, some four-wheel-drive capable; GPS units; limited laboratory testing equipment; and reference libraries. Most midsize offices also have their own mainframe computers and servers. Since many midsize offices rely on their field offices for on-site actions, the midsize offices do not require the same field-oriented equipment.

External Services: External services may include landscaping, janitorial services, bottled-water delivery, security services, document removal and shredding, temporary and seasonal hires, information technology support, outside laboratory contracts; and outside auditors. Ready access to travel agencies is important. Established positive working relationships with regional colleges and universities are favorable services. Some regional hub agency and business offices may also have their own pilots and aircraft available for travel needs.

Utilities: Midsize environmental businesses and agency offices require water, electricity, sanitation services, telephone, and Internet access. Additionally, local rubbish or recycling removal is necessary.

Taxes: All employees and managers are subject to payroll taxes applicable where the business or agency is located. Businesses are also subject to specific business and property taxes. Many states also require environmental professionals to be registered or licensed, and these fees may be considered taxes.

Large Businesses and Agencies

There are estimated to be about nine thousand environmental consulting companies in the United States, but the fifty largest companies account for less than 30 percent of annual revenues. Corporate contracts are defined by the needs of clients seeking to comply with laws and regulations or to pick up the overload for government agencies unable to provide necessary assessment and analysis of environmental issues in a timely manner. The biggest advantage of both large government environmental agencies and big consulting firms is their ability to draw from an extensive pool of environmental

experts in their employ in developing problem-solving teams.

Potential Annual Earnings Scale. The average earnings for natural resource managers is $65,000 to $130,000, and salaries vary based on location and level of responsibility and decision making. According to the BLS, government-employed conservation scientists earned an average of $62,360 in 2009, soil and plant scientists earned an average of $69,030, environmental scientists earned an average of $63,260, environmental engineers earned an average of $76,550, and natural sciences managers earned an average of $100,720.

Typically, salaries for resource managers working for large consulting firms are higher than those of managers working for small or midsize operations; these higher salaries are a direct result of the reputation of the consulting firm and the rates it charges for services. Also, many of the major environmental consulting firms are located in large metropolitan areas with escalated costs of living, requiring employees to be paid at a level necessary to support local residency. Individuals within large consulting firms are also paid according to their corporate status, responsibilities, and levels of decision making. Government employees are paid based on civil service rankings and pay scales established through bargaining units. Those government employees in resource management positions that are appointed or on personal service contracts are often paid at a higher rate than career civil servants, but their job stability is often more tenuous and they are subject to termination with little to no advanced notice.

Clientele Interaction. Client interaction within large consulting firms and large government agencies is dictated by the status of the resource manager within the corporate or agency hierarchy. Resource managers doing the footwork, research, data assessment, and interviewing will have the most client face time. Upper-level resource managers rely on the input and results of their subordinates. As businesses and agencies grow in size and power, bureaucracy often grows as well. Upper-level decision makers will delegate differing levels of responsibility to stratified subordinates. The amount and degree of client interaction depends on the degree of hierarchy insulation provided in the bureaucracy: Lower-status resource managers will likely have the most client interactions; upper-status managers will interact with clients at final decision-making meetings, public hearings, court hearings, congressional investigations, or media events. While lower-status natural resource managers are the legs-on-the-ground of these large organizations, the upper-status managers are the public face and ultimate decision makers.

Amenities, Atmosphere, and Physical Grounds. The amenities, working atmosphere, and physical aspects of working for a large agency or corporate environmental business reflect the confidence, status, or power of the operation. The largest environmental consulting firms are headquartered on modern corporate campuses with modern structures and state-of-the-art technologies. Many of these campuses are also equipped with athletic facilities and extensively landscaped grounds and parks. The hivelike activity in large corporate operations is not for everyone but for resource managers who like the feeling of being part of a large-scale team effort and have little ego invested in being a worker bee, the day-to-day work on a corporate campus can be rewarding. Most large-scale government agencies are housed in older structures reflecting classical government architecture. However, as the interest in environmental problem solving has increased over the last forty years, many new agency structures reflect an open and more modern sensibility. As with corporate life, resource managers working in large government operations headquarters will find themselves a small cog in a big machine. However, for environmental professionals who excel in team efforts and enjoy the collegial aspects of working toward a common goal, large corporate or government operations may offer a rewarding career.

Typical Number of Employees. The number of employees for large natural resource consulting firms fluctuates with the needs of the marketplace, which are often determined by regulatory mandate, changes to existing laws, or environmental dilemmas or disasters. Government agencies are staffed based on need, funding, urgency, or political expediency. Many projects in both the private and public sectors are seasonally dependent, so numbers of employees vary widely. Estimates of environmental specialists currently working for corporate consulting firms place the number around 125,000. Environmental resource specialists working for local, state, and federal governments are estimated at 1.3 million. Within these employment numbers for environmental specialists, only about 11 percent are designated as natural resource managers.

Traditional Geographic Locations. The largest environmental consulting firms can be found in California, the Pacific Northwest, and the Eastern Seaboard states. Large regional consulting firms, and branch offices of the largest companies, can be found in most major metropolitan areas. Large government agencies responsible for resource management issues are located in Washington, D.C., in every state capital, and at regional agency field offices across the United States.

Pros of Working for a Large Business or Agency. One of the biggest positives of working in both large corporate and large agency settings is the opportunity for career advancement at a rate faster than that enjoyed by individuals working in annex or field settings. The chance for quicker advancement equates to the ability to earn more income. Some people find that the locations of larger consulting firms and central agencies allow them the opportunity to take advantage of cultural and social activities not afforded to employees in isolated regional or field locales.

Cons of Working for a Large Business or Agency. The downsides of working for a large environmental corporation include a highly competitive work atmosphere; strict deadlines involving long hours and labor-intensive projects; large amounts of long-stay travel; and quotas of billable hours and revenue streams. In both large corporate and large government environmental operations, employees are often subject to transfers to new work locations if they wish to keep their jobs; this can be upsetting to employees with families or well-established family roots. One of the major downsides of working for large government agencies is that the enthusiasm and dedication that drive many civil service environmental specialists can be easily lost or turned into cynicism as a result of political agendas. Many career environmental civil servants work entire careers to help mitigate, enforce, or create balances between ecosystems and human resource needs only to see their long efforts dashed by a change in political will.

Costs

Payroll and Benefits: Large consulting firms are free to establish whatever pay standards and benefits they determine, as long as they meet minimum wage requirements and the employment market will accept their rates. Bonus packages at large consulting firms are often incentive-based and linked to project outcomes or competitive client acquisition. Many corporate bonuses are portioned as golden parachute options established in contract negotiations, by annual business profitability, share prices, or stockholder votes. Agency natural resource manager positions' pay grades and benefits are mandated by the government body they work for and are usually the result of negotiations between the government and collective bargaining units representing civil service employees. Benefits, pensions, annual leave, sick time, and pay grades vary from city to city and state to state—and often from agency to agency. Federal pay and benefits are set nationwide. Cost of living increases for agency positions are often linked to budget restrictions of the local, state, or federal government. Agency seasonal employees may receive overtime pay when jobs require extended hours. Typically, compensation time is given in lieu of overtime pay for civil service employees in nonclerical and nonmaintenance positions.

Supplies: Large agency offices and large environmental business headquarters require telephones; mobile telephones; walkie-talkies; personal and portable computers; printers; plotters; GIS-capable computing devices; typical office supplies such as paper, pens, and office furniture; fleet vehicles, some four-wheel-drive capable; GPS units; reference libraries; microscopes; testing equipment; capable laboratory facilities; real-time distance conference capabilities; mainframe computers; and servers.

External Services: External services may include landscaping, janitorial services, bottled-water delivery, security services, document removal and shredding, temporary and seasonal hires, information technology support, outside auditors, professional lobbying, public relations, advertising, fitness, legal counsel, and contracted expert witnesses. Established positive working relationships with regional colleges and universities are a favorable service. Ready access to travel agencies is important, but most large agencies and businesses have their own corporate pilots and aircraft available for travel needs.

Utilities: Main headquarters of environmental businesses and agency offices require water, electricity, sanitation services, telephone, and Internet access. Additionally, local rubbish or recycling removal is necessary.

Taxes: All employees and managers are subject to payroll taxes applicable where the business or agency is located. Businesses are also subject to specific business and property taxes. Many states also require environmental professionals to be registered or licensed, and these fees may be considered taxes.

ORGANIZATIONAL STRUCTURE AND JOB ROLES

Unlike many other work environments, natural resource management is not an overarching umbrella industry or agency. People making a living as natural resource managers do so as individual specialists working within the framework of an agency or corporation. More than 74 percent of all natural resource management jobs are with government agencies at the federal, state, and local levels. Less than 30 percent of resource management positions are with private consulting firms or corporations. Because of the specialized nature of each resource management field, and because these jobs are spread throughout multiple agencies or corporate entities, there is no specific organizational structure defining the profession as a whole. The majority of individuals working as natural resource managers with private concerns actually started out within, or have spent some portion of their careers having worked within, the public sector.

The following categories encompass areas in which resource managers participate. The organizational structure of each of these sectors has no set practices and varies based on resource specialties, agency requirements, budgets, politics, business environment, individual contracts, legal dictates, legislative mandates, and working conditions: civil service, academia, private industry, and nonprofit organizations and lobbies.

Civil Service. The increased concern for environmental policy by governments at all levels has resulted in an expansion of natural resource management civil service jobs within statutory bodies.

Overall growth in natural resource management positions within the civil service grows or slows often because of political realities: As administrations often shift with elections, so to do policy directions for environmental exploitation, management, oversight, and problem solving. Differing political philosophies often have differing environmental values, priorities, interests, and agendas toward the natural world. As these priorities change, so do the organizational structures of each agency, as well as numbers and roles of resource managers required to staff statutory agencies.

Despite the political variations, government agencies—local, state, and federal—remain the dominant employers of natural resource managers and related environmental professionals. In the United States, government agencies are the largest employer of environmental specialists. The United States federal government employs nearly a quarter of a million resource and environmental specialists, from geologists to park rangers, foresters to soil scientists, biologists to oceanographers, and hydrologists to waste managers. They work for federal environmental, regulatory, conservation, preservation, or monitoring agencies. These environmental professionals may work in large administrative complexes in Washington, D.C., national parks, wildlife refuges, or solitary field stations in isolated wilderness areas.

In some cases, federal resource management jobs with international agencies such as the United States Agency for International Development (USAID) may place the employee in foreign countries. While the federal government is a large employer of environmental and resource specialists, state governments employ twice as many people to deal with environmental and resource-related issues. It is estimated that 10 to 15 percent of all jobs in state civil service professions involve some type of environmental work. Resource management jobs with state agencies usually involve roles in environmental protection, fisheries and wildlife, agriculture, land use planning, water resources, minerals management, parks and recreation, utilities, coastal management, community and economic development, and waste management. As with federal agencies, resource managers may find themselves working in large capital complexes, regional field offices, parks and reserves, or isolated wilderness research stations. It is estimated that five hun-

OCCUPATION SPECIALTIES

Foresters and Conservation Scientists

Specialty	Responsibilities
Forest ecologists	Conduct research upon the various environmental factors affecting forests.
Range managers	Study, manage, improve, and protect rangelands to maximize their use without damaging the environment; also called range conservationists, range ecologists, or range scientists.
Silviculturists	Manage tree nurseries and thin forests. They also conduct research in forest propagation, life span of seeds, and the effects of fire and animal grazing.
Soil conservationists	Assist farmers, ranchers, and others to conserve soil, water, and related natural resources.
Wood technologists	Conduct research on the methods of drying, preserving, and using wood and its by-products. They test wood for such properties as strength, moisture content, elasticity, and hardness and determine the best type of wood for specific uses.

OCCUPATION PROFILE

Marine Biologist

Considerations	Qualifications
Description	Studies saltwater plants and animals for medical, environmental, industrial, and entrepreneurial reasons.
Career cluster	Science, Technology, Engineering, and Math
Interests	Data; people; things
Working conditions	Work inside; work outside
Minimum education level	Bachelor's degree
Physical exertion	Light work
Physical abilities	Unexceptional/basic fitness
Opportunities for experience	Internship; volunteer work
Licensure and certification	Usually not required
Employment outlook	Faster-than-average growth expected
Holland interest score	IRS

Note: See volume 1, "Publisher's Note," for an explanation of the Holland interest score.

dred thousand people work as environmental or resource specialists for local county or city governments in the United States. The majority of these resource jobs revolve around solving problems linked to land-use planning, waste management, water quality and supply, pollution remediation, reclamation, and parks and recreation.

Academia. A very limited number of natural resource positions exist within academia. While students majoring in environmental studies have increased dramatically since 1985, there has not been a similar increase in the demand for qualified instructors, professors, and researchers. Numbers of academics teaching natural resource topics have risen in the last decades, but these numbers are small in comparison to the large increase in students interested in natural resources and environment-related fields. Despite the increased environmental awareness and concern of the public over natural resource topics, research funding has only increased in certain environmental fields such as alternative energy and climate change: Basic envi-

ronmental research grant funding tends to be erratic and reflects trends in political preferences and pressures. The organizational structure of each university or research institute varies greatly by departments within the institution. Often, the structure is linked to specialty, seniority, tenure, publication record, or research funding.

Private Industry. Conservation, preservation, and sustainability have become premiere concerns in governmental policy in most nations, and while the majority of natural resource management is directed by government agencies, there are still many efforts dependent on the efforts of private industries and voluntary nongovernmental organizations. Many private environmental consulting firms, as well as resource managers with industrial concerns, do not consider themselves as actively promoting the ethics of resource conservation, preservation, or sustainability, but at the same time are often unfairly labeled and criticized for any apparent lack of environmental conscience. These private and commercial natural resource profes-

OCCUPATION PROFILE

Range Manager

Considerations	Qualifications
Description	Studies, manages, improves, and protects rangelands to maximize their use without damaging the environment.
Career clusters	Agriculture, Food, and Natural Resources; Manufacturing; Science, Technology, Engineering, and Math
Interests	Data; things
Working conditions	Work both inside and outside
Minimum education level	Bachelor's degree; master's degree
Physical exertion	Light work
Physical abilities	Unexceptional/basic fitness
Opportunities for experience	Part-time work
Licensure and certification	Recommended
Employment outlook	Average growth expected
Holland interest score	IRS

Note: See volume 1, "Publisher's Note," for an explanation of the Holland interest score.

sionals, despite often being motivated for purely economic reasons, have a very large influence over how natural resources are managed, exploited, or protected.

It is professional planners, commercial foresters, energy specialists, agronomists, and land-use managers who establish many of the long-range plans directing the use and development of water, soil, mineral, wildlife, and land resources. It is the responsibility of many private natural resource managers to implement government policies directing the activities of industries exploiting the environment. These managers must make decisions affecting not only the environment but also the profitability of their businesses. They need to understand the structure and limitations of natural resources, as well as the seemingly endless circles of bureaucratic directives and governmental regulations to be successful. As technology has made it easier and more profitable for people to exploit the natural environment, the resulting often un-

planned and unrestrained rates of development have resulted in dangerous environmental side effects.

Since 1970, a strengthening of environmental legislation has resulted in the setting of environmental standards and safeguards to establish some sort of balance between a sustainable environment and the needs of people for natural resources. As a result, industries have been made to take their environmental and social obligations seriously or face financial penalties. Though the positions are limited, opportunities do exist for jobs as natural resource managers within industries such as forestry, mining, land development, agribusiness, water management, and commercial fisheries. Many of these industries require skilled and qualified specialists as monitors, evaluators, and planners to oversee their operations and fulfill policy obligations and limitations established by local, regional, or federal agencies.

The most difficult aspect of a natural resource

career in industry is the up-and-down nature of job assignments. Private industry most often must react and adapt to changes in government policies and mandates. Since 1990, legislation and statutes have shifted from pollution and resource control to remediation to sustainability. Natural resource managers that are overspecialized may find it difficult to adjust to this changing arena of work assignments. The fluid nature of change within the private and commercial natural resource management field, usually driven by profit margins, means defined organizational structures are always in flux, usually as new teams are developed to work on each new project based on budgets and client needs. Levels of management, researchers, project leaders, assistants, laboratory technicians, and specialists change with assignments and financial bottom lines. A major increase in employment for private natural resource managers exists in the de-

veloping world. While growth in new natural resource career opportunities outside government service is small, demand outside the United States is on the rise. Resource management jobs are expected to rise at a growth rate of 15 percent annually in Asia, especially China; 12 percent annually in Latin and South America; and 10 percent annually in Africa. Instilled cultural values and business practices define the organizational structure in both governmental and corporate resource management scenarios in foreign nations.

Nonprofit Organizations and Lobbies. The very idea of natural resource management owes a great debt to nonprofit organizations and lobbyists. Natural resource conservation, preservation, and sustainability originally began as a social reform movement over concern for degradation of the environment reflected in quality of life issues. Many of these environmental nonprofits are regis-

---

OCCUPATION PROFILE

Soil Scientist

Considerations	Qualifications
Description	Studies the chemical, physical, biological, and mineralogical composition of soils as they relate to plant or crop growth, as well as soil's response to fertilizers, tillage practices, and crop rotation.
Career clusters	Agriculture, Food, and Natural Resources; Manufacturing; Science, Technology, Engineering, and Math
Interests	Data; things
Working conditions	Work outside; work both inside and outside
Minimum education level	Bachelor's degree
Physical exertion	Light work
Physical abilities	Unexceptional/basic fitness
Opportunities for experience	Internship
Licensure and certification	Recommended
Employment outlook	Faster-than-average growth expected
Holland interest score	IRS

Note: See volume 1, "Publisher's Note," for an explanation of the Holland interest score.

tered as charities or special interest groups; many others are registered as pro-exploitation lobbies. These organizations may be purely fund-raising groups aimed at purchasing land, promoting research, paying for conservation and preservation projects, or funding education programs. Many such organizations establish trusts to finance or manage land or wildlife reserves, zoos, or animal rescue facilities or to foster basic research.

A number of nonprofit organizations maintain active lobbies running campaigns to pressure decision makers for new legislation or to raise concerns and support for environmental causes. Similarly, there are for-profit resource lobbyists whose sole purpose is to push back against regulation, campaigning for changes to legislation favoring exploitation of natural resources and limiting governmental oversight of commercial developments. Most nonprofit and for-profit organizations and lobbying concerns are organized in a similar manner; usually, there is a strong administrative staff directing personnel, financial, and legal matters, often hired more for their operational skills than for their commitment to the organizations' causes. Within these organizations, there are usually several units responsible for private and corporate fund raising, membership coordination, information and public relations, press management, and education. There is little actual hands-on natural resource management taking place in these organizations; their business is more influencing how active natural resource managers will eventually be directed to conduct their operations. There is no exact census as to how many environmental nonprofits or lobbying groups there are in the United States, but estimates range from a low of five thousand to as high as eleven thousand or more.

Job roles within natural resource management can be placed into four broad categories:

- Planning
- Policy Making
- Resource Assessment
- Sustainability

Planning

When building a career in resource management, whether in the public, private, or academic sectors, most positions will fall within certain broad environmental specialties: resource planning, for-estry, land-use management, water resources, minerals, coastal management, conservation, wildlife, fisheries, policy setting, remediation, reclamation, environmental protection and enforcement, practices and implementation, parks, and oversight. Land-use, resource, and environmental planning has been done throughout human history, but until the last hundred years it was seen not only as a means to exploit resources but also as a way to sustain and protect valued resources. Many resource manager jobs evolve into planning positions. Planning is an integral aspect of resource management because often a manager's job is not focused on a single aspect of the environment, but requires arriving at solutions spanning a variety of environmental factors over differing time scales, across ecosystem boundaries, multiple resource bases, and differing cultural, economic, and political agendas. Resource managers who solve problems via planning must conduct research and formulate data to define the questions they need to ask. Resource planners must be versed in the legal parameters that exist and how they either help or limit the manager's ability to plan a solution.

Policy Making

Resource managers may also be tasked with establishing boundaries for new regulations and laws that act to stimulate a balance between environmental sustainability and human needs. In this capacity many natural resource managers may find themselves in the role of policy setting. Many resource managers become involved in preparing environmental impact statements, an essential, and mandated, tool in land use planning. Often, the result of an extensive environmental impact statement is the finding of facts that lead to the enacting of new legislation, or the setting of a new standard by which policies are then established, ranging from the protection of an endangered species to banning of construction along threatened coastlines.

Resource Assessment

Natural resource managers who work in specialties involving land or water issues will most often find themselves dealing with issues surrounding resource assessment, habitat protection and restoration, preservation, or protection. Resource assessment involves the inventorying and evaluation of a

Trees vanish in the fog at Olympic National Park in Washington. Conflict often arises over the best use of forests. (©Lindsay Douglas/Dreamstime.com)

ing soil reclamation, pollution remediation, reconstituting a wetland, or reconstruction of damaged shorelines. Preservation resource managers work to make sure valuable land, water, and sensitive ecosystems are excluded from development or recreational usage and are maintained in their natural state. After the preservation of these lands and water resources the manager's job may shift to one of creating the necessary functions or legislation to conserve the ecosystem or resource for future generations. In addition, land and water resource managers may also be tasked with establishing priorities in protecting historic locations, archaeological sites, or other places of significant social, spiritual, or cultural value. Some resource managers will work in parks were they will monitor and maintain the integrity of the land or water resources, as well as wildlife.

Sustainability

Natural resource managers active in areas involving forestry, fish and wildlife, and minerals are charged with maintaining adequate resources for sustainable exploitation, while at the same time often being required to establish the limits at which point extraction of these resources is stopped. Natural resource managers dealing with fish and wildlife problems are almost exclusively trained in biology; mineral managers are geoscientists; and timber managers are forest scientists. These management specialists may be required to assess and protect habitats, monitor and assess toxins, enforce pollution and reclamation standards, identify nonnative species and develop eradication programs, monitor migrating species for hunting and health purposes, maintain public access to public lands, assess both natural and human-induced hazards in both wilderness and exploited environments, and enforce extraction limits and proration standards. As modern societies grow at an unprecedented rate the need for ex-

resource to rate its ecological wellbeing or economic value. Protection and restoration involve identifying and limiting hazards to the environment as a whole or to individual species or ecosystems. Protection of a resource may also involve mitigating and then restoring an ecosystem damaged by pollution, overuse of a resource, intrusion activities, or poorly planned development or exploitation. Restoration activities could involve reintroduction of lost species, reforestation, reclaiming and recontouring a damaged landscape, institut-

ploiting timber, minerals, and fisheries is expanding to levels at which sustainability of these resources is threatened. The role of the natural resource manager is growing in importance in regard to these social and economic essentials. While there is a clear need for these resources, there also exists a concerned aspect of society that demands preservation of the lands and waters in which these resources exist. It is resource managers, directed by legislation, who are responsible for establishing the balance between resource sustainability and managed extraction.

INDUSTRY OUTLOOK

Overview

The outlook for careers in natural resource management is positive. As concerns over resource sustainability, pollution, climate change, alternative energy, water, useable lands, and wildlife receive increasing attention, the need for qualified professional resource managers increases. The greatest demand will be for resource managers with expertise in earth sciences, chemistry, engineering, computer modeling, ecology, geographic information systems (GIS), resource sustainability, public policy, environmental law, and energy issues. Technical savvy with the latest advances in equipment, modeling programs, and computer technology will be a must skill set for anyone entering the natural resource management field. These points all suggest the necessity for an interdisciplinary education for college students considering resource management as a career path.

In the future, the majority of resource managerial jobs will still be with government agencies. Large federal and state agencies tasked with enforcing environmental laws and policies will remain the largest employers of resource managers. At the federal level, the Department of the Interior, Fish and Wildlife Service, Department of Energy, Bureau of Land Management, Department of Agriculture, Environmental Protection Agency, U.S. Geological Survey, Forest Service, National Parks Service, Department of Defense, National Marine Fisheries Service, Bureau of Indian Affairs, Bureau of Reclamation, the National Aeronautics and Space Administration, and individual branches of the military will require trained resource management professionals.

At the state level, departments of natural resources and departments of environmental quality and their subdivisions of parks, fish and wildlife, water quality, land management, geological surveys, waste management, soils conservation, and wetlands protection will all need new resource managers to assume new or vacated positions. Local governments will require more resource managers to help develop land-use plans, as urban boundaries and utility needs increase with growing populations. Fewer new jobs will be available in advocacy and lobbying, but the demand in these areas may shift with changes in political administrations or societal values. Industrial jobs in resource management will always be limited by the extent to which businesses are forced to be conscious of the need to manage the resources they profit from.

As pressure on government budgets increases, consulting firms will likely become larger players in the field of natural resource management. Businesses and government agencies unable to afford full-time resource professionals will rely more on hiring consultants on a need-to-need basis. Jobs in academia are projected to remain steady, but if governments begin to emphasize concerns over global climate change, an increased number of professionals engaged in basic and applied research will be needed. An increased social sensitivity to the issues of climate change will result in an influx of students interested in resource management, thus requiring more academic specialists to train and educate these students.

One of the biggest limiting factors in the future hiring of more natural resource managers, in any of the areas listed, is the increased reliance on technology. As field equipment and computer technology advances, a single resource manager becomes capable of completing numerous tasks that in the past might have required several resource professionals to complete. While this is a financial savings to agencies and companies, it limits career openings for natural resource managers, especially those not versed in advances in technology. The biggest fields of growth for upcoming resource managers will be in the areas of water management, land-use planning, fisheries management, energy resources, and timber management. In all these areas the concern will be over sustainability—resource sustainability in combination with economic sustainability. Natural resource managers with interdisciplinary skill sets and cross-fields of experience and training will be those in highest demand.

Employment Advantages

A job in natural resource management is a career often well suited for an individual with an environmental conscience and an aptitude for science or politics. The career path allows many people to put their science training to practical application in the pursuit of what they see as a higher goal for good. Some resource managers end up living in wilderness areas or may travel to different natural environments in connection with projects they are working on. To many people the ability to work in the outdoors is a sought after job benefit. Other resource managers find the problem solving aspect of the job to be most rewarding: the majority of issues surrounding resource management are those involving direct interactions with stake holders in the resource in question. The ability to communicate and use critical thinking skills to reach a balance between competing positions is a must for resource managers. People who enjoy outcome-based work will find resource management either rewarding or eternally frustrating depending on their abilities to work with people with competing values, goals, and traditions. People who enter the field of natural resource management with high environmental ideals are often disappointed when they come to realize their jobs will require them to set aside their personal feelings or beliefs to reach a compromise in the balance between environmental sustainability and societal needs and economic realities. On the positive side, completing a project balancing the needs of a sustainable environment with those of an ever-changing society can be deeply rewarding, and the outcome in many instances, is one that can be seen and appreciated for generations to come.

Annual Earnings

In a healthy economy, salaries for resource managers would be expected to rise about 5 percent per year over the first twenty years of the twenty-first century. This salary increase is dependent on the source of employment: government positions are less likely to see significant salary increases in comparison to profitable private businesses; non-profit advocates are less likely to see annual salary increases in comparison to professional lobbyists. Annual earnings are also dependent on location of employment; a state resource manager with an assignment in an isolated wilderness area is likely to see less financial gain than a resource manager working with a large petroleum corporation in a major metropolitan area. Annual earnings for resource managers are also linked with experience and education: managers with graduate educations and histories of increasing responsibilities and positive project outcomes will see greater chances for advancement and greater financial rewards. Resource managers employed as advocates or lobbyists may often be given bonuses based on positive outcomes of their efforts. Financial bonuses given to resource managers employed with businesses or consulting firms are sometimes linked to outcomes, but are more often based on annual corporate profits and the employee's place within the corporate hierarchy.

RELATED RESOURCES FOR FURTHER RESEARCH

EARTH WORK MAGAZINE
689 River Rd.
Charlestown, NH 03603
Tel: (603) 543-1700
Fax: (603) 543-1828

ENVIRONMENTAL CAREER OPPORTUNITIES NEWSLETTER
700 Graves St.
Charlottesville, VA 22902
Tel: (800) 315-9777
Fax: (434) 984-2331
http://www.ecojobs.com

ENVIRONMENTAL CAREERS CENTER
2 Eaton St., Suite 711
Hampton, VA 23669-4095
Tel: (757) 727-7895
Fax: (757) 727-7904
http://environmentalcareer.com

ENVIRONMENTAL CAREERS ORGANIZATION
68 Harrison Ave.
Boston, MA 02111

Tel: (617) 426-4783
http://www.eco.org

NATIONAL ASSOCIATION OF ENVIRONMENTAL
    PROFESSIONALS
P.O. Box 460
Collingswood, NJ 08108
Tel: (856) 238-7816
Fax: (856) 210-1619
http://www.naep.org

ABOUT THE AUTHOR

Randall L. Milstein has nearly thirty years of professional experience in the areas of natural resource and environmental enforcement, education, and research. He holds a bachelor's degree in earth sciences from Western Michigan University, a master's degree in earth sciences from the University of Northern Colorado, and a doctorate in geology from Oregon State University. He began his career in 1981 with the Michigan Department of Natural Resources' Geological Survey Division's Petroleum Geology Unit. After a decade, he left government service for academia and now teaches within nine different scientific disciplines at Oregon State University.

FURTHER READING

Cassio, Jim, and Alice Rush. *Green Careers: Choosing Work for a Sustainable Future.* Gabriola Island, B.C.: New Society, 2009.

DeGalan, Julie. *Great Jobs for Environmental Studies Majors.* New York: McGraw-Hill, 2008.

Education-Portal.com. Natural Resource Manager Career Summary. http://education-portal.com/articles/Natural_Resource_Manager_Career_Summary.html

Fasulo, Michael, and Paul Walker. *Careers in the Environment.* 3d ed. New York: McGraw-Hill, 2007.

Fraidenburg, Michael E. *Intelligent Courage: Natural Resource Careers That Make a Difference.* Malabar: Krieger, 2007.

Greenland, Paul R., and Annamarie L. Sheldon. *Career Opportunities in Conservation and the Environment.* New York: Checkmark Books, 2007.

Hoovers. "Environmental Consulting." http://www.hoovers.com/environmental-consulting/—ID__385—/free-ind-fr-profile-basic.xhtml

Hunter, M. J., D. B. Lindenmayer, and A. J. K. Calhoun. *Saving the Earth as a Career: Advice on Becoming a Conservation Professional.* Oxford, England: Blackwell, 2007.

Kroger, Richard. *Choosing a Conservation Vocation or a Bureaucratic Career: Your Personal Choices and the Environmental Consequences.* Victoria, B.C.: Trafford, 2006.

Llewellyn, A. B. *Green Jobs: A Guide to Eco-Friendly Employment.* Cincinnati: Adams Media, 2008.

Sharp, Bill. *The New Complete Guide to Environmental Careers.* Washington, D.C.: Island Press, 2001.

U.S. Bureau of Labor Statistics. *Career Guide to Industries,* 2010-2011 ed. http://www.bls.gov/oco/cg.

_____. "Conservation Scientists and Foresters." In *Occupational Outlook Handbook,* 2010-2011 ed. http://www.bls.gov/oco/ocos048.htm

U.S. Census Bureau. North American Industry Classification System (NAICS), 2007. http://www.census.gov/cgi-bin/sssd/naics/naicsrch?chart=2007.

U.S. Department of Commerce. International Trade Administration. Office of Trade and Industry Information. Industry Trade Data and Analysis. http://ita.doc.gov/td/industry/otea/OTII/OTII-index.html.

Nuclear Power Industry

INDUSTRY SNAPSHOT

General Industry: Energy
Career Cluster: Science, Technology, Engineering, and Math
Subcategory Industries: Nuclear Fuels Security; Nuclear Power Plant Construction; Nuclear Power Plant Operation; Radiation Safety
Related Industries: Alternative Power Industry; Biofuels Industry; Coal Mining Industry; Electrical Power Industry; Petroleum and Natural Gas Industry
Annual Domestic Revenues: $29 billion USD (U.S. Census Bureau, 2007)
NAICS Numbers: 541, 221113

INDUSTRY DEFINITION

Summary

The nuclear power industry generates electrical power using nuclear reactors and distributes it. Nuclear power production begins with uranium mining, followed by fashioning of fuel elements, operation of the actual reactors, distribution of electrical energy through the nationwide grid, and eventually the safe disposal or storage of nuclear waste. The industry is highly regulated and extremely security conscious. Care must be taken to prevent nuclear fuel from falling into the hands of domestic or international terrorists or other criminals. In the United States, the industry suffered setbacks following the nuclear power plant accidents at Three Mile Island in Pennsylvania in 1979 and at Chernobyl in the Ukraine in 1986, but it has revived somewhat as the environmental and political costs of heavy dependence on fossil fuels have become more salient.

History of the Industry

The nuclear power industry stems from the discovery of induced uranium fission after neutron bombardment by German scientists Otto Hahn and Fritz Strassman in 1939 and is in some sense a by-product of the development of the atomic bomb by the scientists and engineers working on the Manhattan Project during World War II. A nuclear reactor is an arrangement of radioactive materials and control elements enclosed in sufficient shielding material to block the release of radiation into the environment. The fission of uranium or plutonium fuel releases additional neutrons, which can stimulate further fissions. The rate at which the resulting chain reaction occurs is controlled by the presence of other elements in control rods. The

An aerial view of steam rising from a cooling tower at a nuclear power plant. (©Ken Cole/Dreamstime.com)

first successful reactor was built by physicist Enrico Fermi and tested in December, 1942. The vast majority of nuclear reactors function as heat generators, and the heat produced is used to run a turbine and electric generator. Some reactors are dedicated to isotope production for medical applications. Because nuclear reactors do not require an air intake or exhaust pipes, they were quickly adapted for submarine propulsion. Many of the reactor operators and other technical staff employed in the nuclear power industry received their training on submarines.

The fate of the atomic energy enterprise after the end of World War II was vigorously debated among scientists and political leaders. Military leaders wanted to maintain control in the interests of national security. Eventually, however, the advocates of civilian control prevailed, and the Atomic Energy Act of 1946 established the civilian Atomic Energy Commission to control both civilian and military uses of atomic energy. In 1954, the U.S. Congress approved private ownership of nuclear

reactors by power companies. In 1955 and 1956, the Atomic Energy Commission declassified most of the technology employed in nuclear reactors. An autonomous International Atomic Energy Agency was established in 1957 to encourage peaceful uses of atomic energy and ensure the safe handling of nuclear materials. In 1974, the Atomic Energy Commission was replaced by two agencies: the Nuclear Regulatory Commission and the Energy Research and Development Administration. In 1977, the Energy Research and Development Administration was combined with the Federal Energy Administration to form the U.S. Department of Energy.

The first practical production of electrical energy by a nuclear reactor occurred at the experimental breeder reactor (EBR1) in Arco, Idaho, in December, 1951. The electrical energy initially produced was enough to light four 200-watt lightbulbs. In 1954, the Obninsk Nuclear Power Plant in the Soviet Union (now in Russia) was able to contribute 5 megawatts to an electrical grid. The first commercial nuclear power plant, Calder Hall, in

Sellafield, England, was commissioned in 1956 with a capacity of 50 megawatts, and the first nuclear power plant in the United States, the Shippingport Atomic Power Station, began operation in Pennsylvania in 1957. The Shippingport reactor was similar to the type that Westinghouse Corporation was building for the U.S. Navy Submarine Service. Over the next two decades, 104 commercial nuclear reactors became operational in the United States and more than 400 went into service worldwide.

In 1979, an accident occurred at the Three Mile Island Nuclear Generating Station in Dauphin County, Pennsylvania. This accident, involving a partial core meltdown because of operator error, resulted in the evacuation of more than 144,000 people and raised significant questions about nuclear safety. In response to the Three Mile Island incident, the Nuclear Regulatory Commission tightened educational requirements for nuclear reactor operators, and the construction of new nuclear power plants ceased in the United States. In 1986, a far worse reactor breach occurred at the Chernobyl Nuclear Power Plant in the Ukraine (then part of the Soviet Union), resulting in a substantial discharge of radioactivity, a large-scale evacuation, and lingering medical and environmental problems.

The Industry Today

The nuclear power industry in the United States is experiencing something of a revival as people are becoming more aware of the political and environmental costs of coal mining, offshore drilling, and American dependence on imported oil and fossil fuels. Permits have been issued for the construction of at least twenty nuclear plants in the United States.

Of the 104 commercial nuclear reactors in operation in the United States, the majority, 69, use a pressurized water reactor, and the remainder, 35, use a boiling water reactor. In the pressurized water reactor, demineralized water serves as the moderator and is maintained in the liquid state at high pressure. The pressurized water is pumped through a heat exchanger, where it provides the

The nuclear power plant in Chernobyl in 2008. (©Dreamstime.com)

heat energy to an open supply of boiling water, which produces high-pressure steam to turn the blades of a turbine, which powers an electrical generator. In the boiling water reactor, the heat exchange step is skipped, and steam under pressure is produced in the core itself. Commercial nuclear power plants generally purchase prefabricated fuel elements consisting of uranium pellets sealed in aluminum cylinders. In principle, the spent fuel elements could be reprocessed to make additional fuel, but this technology is not considered cost-effective; therefore, reactor waste is stored, often at the site at which it was generated. Other types of nuclear reactors are possible, including the breeder reactor, which creates plutonium while producing power. Such reactors have not yet proven commercially viable in the United States.

Nuclear power plants are generally built by large utility companies and some government agencies, who sell the power produced to other utilities on a nationwide grid. Individual consumers thus have no control over the source of their electric power, which generally comes from a combination of hydroelectric, oil-fired, coal-fired, and nuclear sources. As of the start of the twenty-first century, nuclear power accounted for 17 percent of the electric power used in the United States. Nuclear power accounts for a far larger fraction of the power consumed in countries such as France and India, which have far fewer energy-producing natural resources.

Nuclear power plants are generally built in geologically stable areas, far from population centers. Building a power plant in an earthquake-prone area could lead to the rupture of the reactor core and the release of significant radiation into the environment during a seismic event. Plants are built away from cities to keep real estate costs low and to minimize public opposition. Every new nuclear facility must be licensed by the Nuclear Regulatory Commission following public hearings at which opponents and proponents can voice their opinions and concerns.

The concerns of the present-day nuclear power industry include safety, security, waste disposal, public relations, and the possibility of economic competition from new forms of energy production. The safety of power plant operations seems to be generally well established, provided power

The control panel at a nuclear power station. (©Aleksandar Andjic/Dreamstime.com)

plant executives resist the temptation to cut corners. Nuclear power plants are one of the major employers of health physicists, who specialize in making sure that personnel are not exposed to unacceptable levels of radiation.

Security is a particular concern of the nuclear power industry. Workers must generally obtain a security clearance, which requires proof of citizenship, evidence of personal reliability and mental stability, and the absence of any criminal history. The uranium used in reactor cores (the U-235 isotope) must be enriched, although not to the level required for nuclear explosives. Nonetheless, the location and amount of all reactor fuel in a plant must be carefully tracked and recorded because the diversion of some of the material to a rogue state or terrorist group could have dire consequences. Similarly, nuclear power plants must be protected from sabotage, which could result in the release of a harmful amount of radioactivity into the environment.

Yucca Mountain in Nevada was suggested as a storage facility for nuclear waste. (U.S. Geological Survey)

Nuclear power plants purchase nuclear fuel rods as aluminum tubes containing purified uranium extracted from uranium ore. Once the products of radioactive decay have built up in the rods to the point where they interfere with energy generation, the rods are replaced in the reactor. Although the technology exists to remove the fuel pellets and reprocess the uranium, it is not yet economically viable. Instead, spent fuel rods are generally stored under pools of water at the site where they were used, awaiting shipment to a long-term storage facility.

Nuclear waste is generally categorized as low, intermediate, and high level, depending on the length of time over which the waste presents a radiation hazard. Low- and intermediate-level wastes are those for which the radiation level can be expected to return to near ambient levels in one hundred years or less. Low- and intermediate-level wastes can be buried in sites about 100 meters below ground and will become harmless in the forseeable future. The storage of high-level waste, which could remain hazardous for thousands of years, is another matter. Much high-level waste is stored under water at the sites where it is generated. Plans to create a national high-level waste facility in the Yucca Mountains of Nevada have been developed, but concerns about the facility's safety and the hazards of transporting high-level waste have delayed implementation of these plans. As the generation of nuclear waste continues, the storage and removal of waste will become increasingly important. However, the disposition of nuclear waste presents scientific, environmental, and ethical issues that remain unsolved.

Public perception is a matter of great concern to the nuclear power industry. Many people have misconceptions of what nuclear power involves and mistakenly regard anything nuclear as dangerous. For example, physician concern about patients being reluctant to undergo nuclear magnetic resonance imaging (MRI)—a highly benign procedure not involving ionizing radiation—resulted in the dropping of "nuclear" from the procedure's name to gain patient acceptance.

Any industry faces the danger that its production methodology might be rendered obsolete by a new technology. Once controlled nuclear fusion becomes economically viable, the reactor technology used in the present-day nuclear power industry might be abandoned, and many of the physical plants of the industry could be decommissioned. Similar changes would most likely follow a breakthrough in solar energy conversion. The occurrence of an accident similar to the one at Three Mile Island in 1979 might again raise questions about the safety of nuclear plants, but at the same time, news of an ecological disaster, such as the Gulf oil spill of 2010, or development of efficient electric vehicles could greatly increase public acceptance of the nuclear industry.

Worldwide, some countries are far more dependent on nuclear energy than the United States. France, for instance, receives a far greater share of its energy from nuclear reactors than does the United States. Governments are always involved in the production of nuclear power for reasons of security, and some governments subsidize their nuclear industries. Producing nuclear power is cause for national pride in some countries. In some cases, nuclear facilities may be used to mask the production of weapons-grade nuclear material. For these reasons, it is difficult to gauge the economics of the worldwide nuclear industry.

Nuclear power production begins with the mining of uranium. (©Dreamstime.com)

INDUSTRY MARKET SEGMENTS

Because of the economics of nuclear energy production and the associated security and radiation safety concerns, there are no small or midsize nuclear energy generating plants. As of 2011, there were 104 licensed nuclear energy power plants in the United States and fewer than 500 worldwide. The exact nature of some of the overseas plants is uncertain. American nuclear power plants are generally owned by large utilities that also produce electrical energy by other means.

Small Businesses

Although there are no small nuclear power plants, there are numerous small and midsize businesses that affect the overall function of the nuclear industry, from the mining of uranium to the long-term storage of hazardous nuclear waste. For example, independent consultants provide access to expertise and services that are not provided by staff at a nuclear plant site. Safety regulations require that some instruments be calibrated by independent experts and that plans and operations be reviewed by individuals who do not have a financial stake in the plant. Independent consultants range from college professors of nuclear engineering who augment their income on a part-time basis to veterans of the nuclear power industry who make their expertise available to multiple clients. Consulting firms can be as small as a one-man office or can be staffed by dozens of professionals with offices in several large cities. Some consulting firms specialize in the calibration of radiation-measuring instruments. Of special interest are the firms that prepare and interpret the badges that personnel who work with radiation must wear to monitor their exposure.

Potential Annual Earnings Scale. Earnings in consulting firms that deal with nuclear energy range from $20,000 for a single-person, part-time consultancy to several million dollars per year for a high-level position.

Clientele Interaction. Consultants may be required to submit bids for certain projects. If they were previously employed by the nuclear industry or have a history of working with the industry, they may be known by reputation, and their interactions with clients are likely to be less formal.

Amenities, Atmosphere and Physical Grounds. Consulting firms dealing with nuclear energy generally maintain one or more small offices. The work of a consultant is generally pleasant, but it may involve substantial travel to nuclear plant sites. Nuclear plant sites are generally clean and well maintained but tend to be located in remote areas.

Typical Number of Employees. The number of employees can range from one to a dozen or more at a single-office consulting firm to hundreds at a multiple-office consulting firm.

Traditional Geographic Locations. Consulting firms generally tend to be located in big cities or college towns. Many have Washington, D.C., offices.

Pros of Working for a Small Nuclear Consulting Firm. In small firms involved in the nuclear energy industry, the consultants may actually be business partners and can share in the profits. Often, consultants may set their own business hours.

Cons of Working for a Small Nuclear Consulting Firm. Small firms are more vulnerable to economic downturns than bigger firms are. Workers will generally have fewer benefits. Firms with full-time employees may be at an economic disadvantage with respect to firms in which the consultants are working part time and rely on their full-time academic positions for employee benefits.

Costs

Payroll and Benefits: Except for the smallest operations, consulting firms require a full-time receptionist and a full- or part-time accountant. Salaries for experienced professional engineers and scientists can be in excess of $100,000 per year. Salaries of support employees range from $20,000 to $40,000 per year. Health insurance for full-time employees, if offered, is also a considerable expense. Firms that serve a number of clients can have appreciable travel expenses.

Supplies: In addition to the usual office supplies, consulting firms involved in nuclear energy will require a number of powerful computers, costing from $1,500 to $4,000 each. Software packages for engineering applications can cost from $900 to $20,000 or more. Some consulting firms maintain an inventory of radiological instrumentation. This must be kept up to date and frequently calibrated.

External Services: Consulting firms generally rent office space, and cleaning and groundskeepings services are incorporated into their rent.

Utilities: Consulting firms may obtain utilities as a part of the rent they pay or may pay for them separately.

Taxes: Consulting firms pay business taxes to federal, state, and local governments and must carefully track expenses to isolate profit from gross revenue.

Midsize Businesses

Midsize businesses include some of the extractors of uranium and fabricators of fuel elements for nuclear reactors. In the future, these midsize businesses are likely to include companies devoted to processing nuclear waste and safely shipping it to long-term repositories.

Potential Annual Earnings Scale. The pay earned by employees at midsize nuclear-related businesses ranges from low, hourly wages to six-figure salaries, depending on the position and the person's experience.

Clientele Interaction. The clients of midsize nuclear-related companies (such as extractors and fabricators) are the nuclear power plants. Therefore, the salespeople in these companies must be technically educated to effectively deal with their clients. Other employees of these companies, except for receptionists, are less likely to have much contact with clients.

Amenities, Atmosphere, and Physical Grounds. Nuclear fuel extractors and packagers will generally be located near nuclear power plants and away from population centers. The workplace, both the offices and the building surroundings, will generally be clean and secure although constructed with function rather than beauty in mind.

Typical Number of Employees. The number of employees at a midsize nuclear fuel extractor or fabricator can range from twenty to several hundred.

Traditional Geographic Locations. Midsize nuclear-related facilities are located close to nuclear power plants or disposal facilities.

Pros of Working for a Midsize Nuclear-Related Business. Midsize extractors and fabricators can generally provide better fringe benefits than smaller firms, including better health insurance plans and possibly subsidized education.

Cons of Working for a Midsize Nuclear-Related Business. The disadvantages of working in midsize nuclear-related firms include some uncertainty as to continued employment and the possibility of accidental exposure to radiation.

Costs

Payroll and Benefits: Midsize nuclear-related businesses will have professional staff consisting of professional engineers; a technical staff who may have bachelor's or associate's degrees or have received specialized training while working in the military; and a certain number of unskilled workers who receive on-the-job training. Salaries will range from $20,000 to more than $100,000 per year, depending on education and experience.

Supplies: Midsize nuclear-related industries generally must make a substantial investment in the equipment needed to handle radioactive materials. Computers are needed for record keeping. These industries also need the typical office supplies used by any business.

External Services: Midsize nuclear-related companies may hire contractors for janitorial services and groundskeeping.

Utilities: Midsize nuclear-related companies generally pay for their utilities, which include electricity, gas, telephone, Internet service, and water.

Taxes: Midsize firms pay business taxes to federal, state, and local governments and must carefully track expenses to isolate profit from gross revenues.

Large Businesses

Because of the high entry cost as well as the burdens imposed by security concerns and regulations, the nuclear power industry consists mainly of large businesses who sell electrical power to the national power grid. Nuclear reactors are operational more than 90 percent of the time but may need to be offline to allow time for refueling. Generally, the consumer is not affected by such shutdowns. Because the individual utility companies purchase power dependent on demand and cost, the actual mix of hydroelectric, oil, gas, coal, and nuclear power used by an individual energy consumer will vary from hour to hour and season to season.

Potential Annual Earnings Scale. The U.S. Census Bureau reports annual revenues of about $29 billion in 2007 for the nuclear power industry. In 2002, this quantity was only $12 billion. Revenues can be expected to grow over the long term as the supply of fossil fuels becomes scarcer or more expensive. There are, however, a number of significant uncertainties in this prediction.

Clientele Interaction. Because nuclear power plants sell the power they produce to the nationwide grid, there is little need for sales personnel, although some attention must be paid to keeping costs competitive with power produced from coal, oil, and other sources. However, nuclear plants do require public relations personnel to ensure the local community that their operations are safe and that the economic benefits balance the environmental costs.

Amenities, Atmosphere, and Physical Grounds. Nuclear power plants are generally remote from population centers; however, the plant workers and their families may form a tightly knit community. Because concern for safety is paramount, work spaces are generally clean, and some level of on-site medical care may be provided. The physical environment may involve a limited amount of landscaping. Plants will generally include reactor buildings and cooling towers, as well as high-tension wires to carry away the power produced.

Typical Number of Employees. Large nuclear power plants typically employ more than two thousand workers.

Traditional Geographic Locations. Nuclear power plants are located on the East and West Coasts, as well as in the South and the Midwest. Very few are in Western states.

Pros of Working for a Nuclear Power Plant. Large nuclear power plants offer job stability with some opportunity for advancement. They offer fringe benefits typical of other large business, including quality health insurance and pension plans. Employers often provide subsidies for education.

Cons of Working for a Nuclear Power Plant. The disadvantages of working in nuclear power plants include the remoteness of the work site and the anonymity typical of a large business, which may lead to slow advancement.

Costs

Payroll and Benefits: Nuclear power plants have professional staff consisting of professional engineers, a technical staff that may have bachelor's or associate's degrees or have received specialized training while working in the military, and a certain number of unskilled workers who receive on-the-job training. Salaries range from $20,000 to more than $100,000 per year, depending on education and experience, with executives often earning more than $100,000.

Supplies: In addition to normal office supplies, nuclear power plants must have radiological monitoring equipment, specialized protective clothing, leak monitors, and equipment to monitor the performance of the steam turbines.

External Services: Large nuclear-related companies may hire contractors for instrument calibration and short-term construction jobs or may rely on in-house staff.

Utilities: Nuclear power plants generally pay for their utilities, which include gas, oil, water, electricity, telephone, and Internet access.

Taxes: Nuclear energy producers pay business taxes to federal, state, and local governments and must carefully track expenses to isolate profit from gross revenues.

ORGANIZATIONAL STRUCTURE AND JOB ROLES

Nuclear power plants are high-tech production facilities requiring a technically skilled workforce that meets high standards of reliability and trustworthiness. Nuclear power plants offer employment for engineers in several disciplines, including nuclear, electrical, civil, and environmental; for scientists at degree levels from bachelor's through doctoral; and for technicians who may be graduates of community colleges or technical institutes or have received advanced technical training in the armed forces. In addition, nuclear power plants, like other large organizations, have a need for managers, human resources specialists, janitorial and maintenance staff, and security personnel. Generally, nuclear plant employees must pass a rigorous security screening, which includes interviews of neighbors and relatives.

Most nuclear plants are operated by energy-producing companies and are managed by a general manager who reports to the energy company. General managers and the shift managers that report to them are generally veterans of many years in the nuclear industry. Nuclear plants make a careful distinction between the reactor operators, who must be licensed and who actually control the reactor, and other technical personnel who are generally not allowed in the control room. Essentially all employees must obtain some level of security clearance.

The following umbrella categories apply to the organizational structure of nuclear power plants:

- Executive Management
- Engineering
- Analysis and Monitoring
- Operations
- Security

Executive Management

Like all large organizations, nuclear power plants are under the control of senior managers, generally individuals with considerable experience in the industry who may have added management training to a technical background. Such individuals may hold a bachelor's degree in science or engineering as well as a master of business administration. Executive management handles the general operations of the plant. These individuals help oversee the reactor operation, fueling and waste disposal, technical upgrades to the facility's major operations, goal setting, and the implementation of plans for the property. They also manage individual teams and departments, or, as in the case of the general manager, oversee departments. Many executive managers have advanced degrees. As with many industries, experience can sometimes serve as a substitute for advanced education.

Executive managers generally earn higher salaries than anyone else in the plant. Their job is to manage the overall functions of the property, address systemic issues, and ensure that all departments are functioning in a fluid fashion.

Occupations in the area of executive management include the following:

- Plant Manager
- Chief Financial Officer (CFO)
- Controller
- Chief of Engineering
- Security Manager
- Groundskeeping Manager
- Human Resources Manager

Engineering

Nuclear plants offer employment opportunities for engineers in numerous specialties. Generally engineers working at a nuclear plant will hold a bachelor's or master's degree in their engineering field and will have passed the professional engineer's examination for their field and state.

Engineers' salaries range from about $40,000 to more than $100,000. Successful engineers can move into executive management or become private consultants commanding somewhat higher incomes. Civil engineers are involved in the design of new nuclear power plants and in supervising upgrades to existing structures. Materials engineers are needed to ensure the integrity of reactor shielding and of the turbine's blades. Mechanical engineers monitor the function of the heat exchanger and the turbine blades. Electrical engineers are needed to ensure that all the electronic control systems of the reactor are functioning correctly. They are also needed to monitor the output of the generator powered by the turbine and the system of conductors leading electrical energy out of the plant.

Nuclear engineers are responsible for the reactor design and for making sure that it is operating within safe limits. They design and oversee the construction of new reactors and the modification of existing power plants. They develop procedures for the handling of radioactive materials.

Computer engineers are needed by the nuclear industry to maintain or develop computer systems for monitoring reactor operation as well as for fulfilling normal business purposes, ranging from accounting to inventory control. An important specialty is simulator engineering. Like airline and military pilots, reactor operators must constantly prepare for emergencies that they hope to never actually experience. To be prepared for any eventuality, power plant technical staff members must undergo extensive training using computer simulations. Writing the control software for nuclear reactor simulators requires knowledge of reactor operations as well as programming skill and familiarity with the field of human factors psychology.

Among the engineering specialties needed in the nuclear industry are the following:

OCCUPATION PROFILE

Nuclear Engineer

Considerations	Qualifications
Description	Designs and develops equipment and processes involving nuclear power.
Career clusters	Manufacturing; Science, Technology, Engineering, and Math
Interests	Data; things
Working conditions	Work inside
Minimum education level	Bachelor's degree; master's degree; doctoral degree
Physical exertion	Light work
Physical abilities	Unexceptional/basic fitness
Opportunities for experience	Apprenticeship; military service
Licensure and certification	Required
Employment outlook	Average growth expected
Holland interest score	IRE

Note: See volume 1, "Publisher's Note," for an explanation of the Holland interest score.

Nuclear Engineers

Specialty	Responsibilities
Nuclear equipment design engineers	Design nuclear machinery and equipment.
Nuclear equipment research engineers	Conduct research on nuclear machinery and equipment.
Nuclear equipment test engineers	Conduct tests on nuclear machinery and equipment.

- Civil Engineer
- Materials Engineer
- Mechanical Engineer
- Electrical Engineer
- Nuclear Engineer
- Computer Engineer

Analysis and Monitoring

Nuclear power plants generally have an in-house staff of scientists to monitor reactor function and environmental impact.

Analytical chemists are needed to verify the condition of the fuel elements and to confirm the absence of heavy elements in the water that flows through the turbine. Chemists working at a nuclear site generally will have bachelor's degrees in chemistry with graduate level training in analytical chemistry or radiochemistry. Biologists are needed to address the environmental impact of the plant. In addition to looking for signs that the plant might be releasing low levels of radiation or toxic chemicals into the environment, they may monitor the biological impact of heat generated by the reactor. Geophysicists have an important role to play in the storage of radioactive waste and in ensuring that the reactor can withstand any seismic activity likely to occur at its location.

Health physicists are responsible for protecting plant personnel from the dangers associated with the radioactive fuel and its products. In addition to having a minimum of a bachelor's degree in physics or a closely allied field, they must go through a specialized training program in health physics and a certification examination. They are experts in dosimetry (measuring radiation dose) and the environmental transport of radiation. Health physicists generally have the final word on the selection of radiation protection and detection equipment and are assigned to monitor it for proper function. They also have general responsibility for training all plant personnel in the safe conduct of their jobs. Health physicists may supervise as many as seventy technicians and chemists and may be responsible for monitoring exposure data for up to two thousand plant employees.

Materials scientists and metallurgists are responsible for ensuring that the physical properties of shielding and structural materials remain within safe limits. Because the mechanical properties of materials exposed to gamma rays and free neutrons will change as atoms are pushed out of their normal sites by radiation, degradation of material performance must be carefully monitored

Among the scientific specialties employed in the nuclear power industry are the following:

- Analytical Chemist
- Biologist
- Geophysicist
- Health Physicist
- Materials Scientist

Operations

The operation of a nuclear power plant requires many technicians. These technicians generally have less than a bachelor's degree but all have advanced technical training. Many have an associate's degree or have received extensive training at a trade school or during military service.

Nuclear reactor operators are charged with proper operation of the reactor and have responsibility of shutting down the reactor through the in-

OCCUPATION PROFILE

Nuclear Quality Control Inspector

Considerations	Qualifications
Description	Inspects machinery, equipment, working conditions, and materials produced at manufacturing companies, during power plant construction, and during nuclear facility operations.
Career clusters	Government and Public Administration; Manufacturing; Transportation, Distribution, and Logistics
Interests	Data; things
Working conditions	Work both inside and outside
Minimum education level	Junior/technical/community college
Physical exertion	Medium work
Physical abilities	Unexceptional/basic fitness
Opportunities for experience	Military service; part-time work
Licensure and certification	Required
Employment outlook	Faster-than-average growth expected
Holland interest score	ERS

Note: See volume 1, "Publisher's Note," for an explanation of the Holland interest score.

sertion of control rods if the reactor gets outside of acceptable operating limits. Nuclear reactor operators must obtain both an operator's license and a security clearance from the Nuclear Regulatory Commission. To obtain a license, individuals must both pass a test of knowledge and meet certain physical standards needed for the safe operation of a reactor. Generally, the nuclear reactor control room is staffed by several licensed reactor operators under a senior nuclear reactor operator who acts as shift supervisor. According to the Bureau of Labor Statistics, the median annual wage for a nuclear reactor operator was $70,410 in 2007.

Nuclear plants may also employ a number of auxiliary nuclear reactor operators, nonlicensed individuals who operate equipment outside the control room. These individuals may be gaining on-the-job experience while preparing for the nuclear reactor operator exam.

Instrument technicians, also called by several other titles, are responsible for maintaining and repairing the instruments used in a nuclear power generating plant. A nuclear power plant will generally have its own machine shop and electronics shop so that malfunctioning equipment may be quickly repaired.

Nuclear waste removal workers include decontamination technicians, radiation protection technicians, and decommissioning and decontamination (D&D) workers. Decontamination technicians are called in to clean up spills of radioactive materials, using for the most part standard janitorial equipment. This job may be done by robots if radiation levels are too high. Radiation protection technicians have more experience and training and may use may use high-pressure cleaning equipment. They may also be responsible for packaging radioactive materials. D&D workers break down contaminated laboratory equipment and build storage containers for nuclear waste. When a nuclear site is decommissioned, they are responsible for the removal and safe storage of nuclear material. All hazardous waste removal workers wear protective clothing with the level of protection depending on the job.

The essence of nuclear power plant operation is the use of heat produced in a nuclear reactor to boil water producing steam to turn an electric generator. The construction and maintenance of the large boilers required are the responsibilities of the boilermakers. Generally boilers are constructed on site, and considerable engineering know-how goes into their successful construction. Pipefitters are individuals who specialize in joining pipes for use under a variety of pressure and temperature conditions. Although some nuclear plants maintain an in-house staff of pipefitters, others contract for their services as needed. Boilermakers and pipefitters must be capable of reading blueprints and using computer-assisted design programs.

Occupations in the operations area of nuclear power plants may include the following:

- Nuclear Reactor Operator
- Instrument Technician
- Nuclear Waste Removal Worker
- Boilermaker
- Pipefitter

Security

Nuclear plants must be constantly on guard against theft of nuclear material, sabotage, and terrorist activity. A substantial security force must be hired, trained, and equipped. Although a high school education is usually sufficient to become a security guard, potential employees must undergo extensive background checks and some states require licensure. Guards at nuclear facilities undergo several months of on-the-job training. According to the Bureau of Labor Statistics, the median annual wage for a security guard was $23,460 in 2008.

Security occupations at a nuclear power plant may include the following:

- Security Manager
- Security Guard

INDUSTRY OUTLOOK

Overview

The outlook for the nuclear power industry is positive. The industry is in growth mode, but political and economic issues make for an uncertain future. According to the Bureau of Labor Statistics, the number of nuclear reactor operators is likely to increase by 19 percent between 2008 and 2018, although the percentage of new employees is expected to grow much faster as the result of older workers retiring. New power plants are scheduled for construction and the growth in demand for energy continues, but the problem of long-term storage of high-level nuclear waste persists, as does the problem of carbon emissions from conventional power plants. With the introduction of purely electric and hybrid electric-gasoline vehicles for private individuals and corporate use, the demand for electric power is likely to increase. The nuclear power industry is well positioned to respond to this demand, particularly during off-peak hours.

The nuclear power industry is particularly sensitive to the electoral process. For example, during the 2008 presidential election, those advocating expanded drilling for oil and removal of restrictions on coal mining were pitted against those advocating tougher restrictions on carbon emissions. Although nuclear advocates point to the lower environmental impact of properly run nuclear plants, the fear of possible nuclear accidents will be difficult to eliminate. On the other hand, the increasingly aggressive methods needed to maintain the flow of fossil fuels to the consumer and the increasingly stringent environmental regulations driven by a concern for global warming caused by excess carbon dioxide emissions make nuclear power generation increasingly attractive.

The nuclear power industry requires a technologically educated workforce. Educational standards for reactor operators were significantly increased in the wake of the Three Mile Island incident, and a nuclear industry concerned with safety and security will continuously update its infrastructure and monitor new technological developments.

Several types of reactors not yet in commercial operation may become practicable as the demand for electric power grows. These include breeder reactors, which actually produce additional radioactive fuel as they generate electricity, and liquid metal reactors, in which a liquid metal such as sodium replaces water as the heat exchange medium. The fuel produced in a breeder reactor is plutonium, an element that must be separated from uranium by reprocessing the spent fuel rods. Experimental fusion reactors, which generate energy by fusing hydrogen nuclei to form helium, are approaching a breakeven point, at which the energy released by fusion exceeds the energy input required to maintain the conditions of high-temperature plasma confinement needed for sustained fusion. Although some scientific and engineering breakthroughs may be needed for commercial fusion power to become a commercial reality, the basic skill sets needed to safely run a fusion power plant are likely to substantially overlap those required by the existing nuclear power industry.

Employment Advantages

The nuclear industry is in expansion mode, which is likely to continue barring a major nuclear accident. New nuclear plants will be constructed and older reactors refurbished, and the demand for electrical energy is likely to continue to grow. Significant new employment opportunities will occur as the baby-boomer generation begins to retire. Highly skilled workers will find their skills transferable to new technologies, if for instance, fusion power supplants nuclear fission as an energy source. Further, the demand for health physicists is likely to continue as medical applications for isotopes are identified. Particle accelerators for electrons and protons are routinely used for cancer therapy, and accelerators for ions of the heavier elements are used in the doping of semiconductors.

Scientific and technical staff in the nuclear power industry will therefore have many jobs open to them, even outside the traditional area of energy production. Students who prepare for engineering or science degrees or receive advanced technical training at a community college or in the military should be able to select from a number of attractive positions, particularly if they are willing to relocate for employment. Workers in nuclear power and its allied industries can expect to participate in continuing education throughout their lifetimes.

Annual Earnings

Electric power companies generally function as regulated monopolies and their profitability is unlikely to increase or decrease dramatically. It is probably safe to assume that power industry revenues will grow over time and that the fraction of electrical energy produced by nuclear power plants will increase, following the example of European countries. A marked increase in demand is possible as fully electric and hybrid vehicles capture more of the automotive market. The cost of hazardous reactor waste disposal or reprocessing is another economic variable. As spent nuclear fuel accumulates on site, there will be a push both for disposal at geologically safe sites as well as for the reprocessing of spent nuclear fuel. Transportation and security costs associated with transport of high-level waste by rail or truck will also enter into the equation.

In addition to their domestic operations, American companies are involved in exporting nuclear power technology to other countries, particularly those in Asia and the Middle East. In December, 2010, Westinghouse Electric Company announced the end of preparatory work on fuel for four of its AP1000 reactors, with the first scheduled for operation in Zhejiang, China. The AP1000 is a pressurized water reactor designed for robust performance. Meanwhile, the United Arab Emirates has announced that American construction giant Bechtel has been selected to build the first nuclear plant in the oil-rich Mideast.

RELATED RESOURCES FOR FURTHER RESEARCH

AMERICAN NUCLEAR SOCIETY
555 N Kensington Ave.
La Grange Park, IL 60526
Tel: (800) 323-3044
Fax: (706) 352-0499
http://www.ans.org

HEALTH PHYSICS SOCIETY
1313 Dolly Madison Blvd., Suite 402
McLean, VA 22101
Tel: (703) 790-1745
Fax: (703) 790-2672
http://www.hps.org

NUCLEAR ENERGY INSTITUTE
1776 I St. NW, Box 400
Washington, DC 20006-3708
Tel: (202) 739-8000
Fax: (202) 785-4019
http://www.nei.org

U.S. NUCLEAR REGULATORY COMMISSION
11555 Rockville Pike
Rockville, MD 20852-2738
Tel: (800) 368-5642
http://www.nrc.gov

ABOUT THE AUTHOR

Don Franceschetti has been a member of the physics faculty at the University of Memphis for more than thirty years. He received his bachelor of science degree from Brooklyn College in 1969 and his doctoral degree in physical chemistry from Princeton University in 1974. He came to the University of Memphis following research appointments in physics and materials science at the Universities of Illinois, North Carolina, and Utrecht (the Netherlands). He is Dunavant University Professor. He has taught a wide range of physics courses and courses for physics teachers and has written extensively about the physical sciences and their history.

FURTHER READING

CareerBuilder.com. Salary Calculator and Wage Finder. http://www.cbsalary.com/salary-calculator.

Careers.org. Occupation Profiles: Descriptions, Earnings, Outlook. http://occupations.careers.org.

Elliott, David. *Nuclear or Not? Does Nuclear Power Have a Place in a Sustainable Energy Future?* New York: Palgrave Macmillan, 2007.

Franceschetti, Donald R., David Rulloch, and Lee A. Paradise. "Can Radiation Waste from Fission Reactors Be Safely Stored?" In Vol. 2 of *Science in Dispute*, edited by Neil Schlager. Farmington Hills, Mich.: Gale, 2002.

Heppenheimer, T. A. "Nuclear Power: What Went Wrong?" *American Heritage of Invention and Technology* 18, no. 2 (2002): 46-56.

Herbst, Alan M., and George W. Hopley. *Nuclear Energy Now: Why the Time Has Come for the World's Most Misunderstood Energy Source.* Hoboken, N.J.: John Wiley & Sons, 2007.

Lejzerovič, Aleksander. *Wet-Steam Turbines for Nuclear Power Plants.* Tulsa, Okla.: PennWell, 2005.

Levy, Salomon. *Fifty Years in Nuclear Power: A Retrospective.* La Grange Park, Ill.: American Nuclear Society, 2007.

Newton, David E. *Nuclear Power.* New York: Infobase, 2005.

Taylor, Allan, and James Robert Parish. *Career Opportunities in the Energy Industry.* New York: Ferguson, 2008.

U.S. Bureau of Labor Statistics. *Career Guide to Industries,* 2010-2011 ed. http://www.bls.gov/oco/cg.

U.S. Census Bureau. North American Industry Classification System (NAICS), 2007. http://www.census.gov/cgi-bin/sssd/naics/naicsrch?chart=2007.

U.S. Department of Commerce. International Trade Administration. Office of Trade and Industry Information. Industry Trade Data and Analysis. http://ita.doc.gov/td/industry/otea/OTII/OTII-index.html.

Wood, J. *Nuclear Power.* London: Institution of Engineering and Technology, 2007.

Outdoor Recreation Industry

©Dreamstime.com

INDUSTRY SNAPSHOT

General Industry: Hospitality and Tourism
Career Cluster: Hospitality and Tourism
Subcategory Industries: Bicycle-Based Recreation; Camp-Based Recreation; Fishing Equipment; Fishing Guides; Hunting Equipment; Hunting Guides; Paddle-Based Recreation; Skiing Facilities; Skiing Instruction, Camps, and Schools; Trail-Based Recreation; Wildlife Viewing
Related Industries: Hotels and Motels Industry; Museums and Cultural Institutions Industry; Sports Equipment Industry; Themed Entertainment Industry; Travel and Tourism Industry
Annual Domestic Revenues: $289 billion (Outdoor Industry Foundation, 2006)
NAICS Numbers: 7192, 7199, 423910, 451110, 532292, 611620, 713920, 713990

INDUSTRY DEFINITION

Summary

The outdoor recreation industry provides equipment, training, and guidance for persons interested in such recreational activities as skiing, mountain climbing, hunting, and fishing, as well as hiking and bird-watching. Companies that offer tours of outdoor areas and training in outdoor activities form a major component of the industry. Retail stores that specialize in selling equipment for outdoor activities are also usually included in economic analyses of the industry.

History of the Industry

Many activities grouped under the umbrella term "outdoor recreation" have their origins in antiquity. After all, the hunting and gathering techniques and exploratory wanderings of prehistoric humans constituted the earliest forms of what would later become such recreational activities as hiking, hunting, and fishing. Exploring nature, by foot and later by horseback, allowed humans to find food and other resources and facilitated the colonization of new areas.

The transition of outdoor activities from necessity to leisure largely accompanied technological innovations, which led first to agriculture and animal husbandry, and later to industrial food production. As humankind relied more on innovations such as these, they inevitably experienced a reduced "need" for outdoor activities. Nonetheless, many humans still felt a desire to explore nature and engage in outdoor sports. The first out-door recreation industry was centered on hunting and fishing, and mainly developed around the sale of hunting and fishing equipment. It also included the breeding and sale of hunting dogs, horses, falcons, and other animals used for outdoor sporting activities.

Land ownership soon became the most significant factor in the creation of the outdoor recreation industry. With ownership, it was possible to charge a fee for the right to hunt, fish, ride horses, ski, or mountain climb. Those with experience in the outdoors began to market their services, leading amateur sporting enthusiasts on nature hikes, hunting expeditions, and other types of outdoor leisure activities.

In eighteenth and nineteenth century Europe, "sporting" activities became popular among the social and economic elite. A movement toward more realistic art depicting scenes of nature also helped foster a romantic urge to hike and explore. European settlers brought this renewed interest in nature activities to the United States, where sporting and nature exploration also became popular among various social and economic classes.

As mass fervor for the "great outdoors" began to peak in the United States, early American naturalists such as John Muir helped spread awareness of the value of natural areas. The United States was the first country to create wilderness reserves, largely through the work of Muir and other naturalists who promoted the value of preserving and protecting natural areas. Between 1830 and 1890, the U.S. government set aside several natural areas for public use and recreation. In 1916, the National Park Service was created to oversee the development and protection of the country's preserves.

As the twentieth century unfolded, there were still vast areas in both the United States and Western Europe where individuals could engage freely in nature exploration and outdoor sports. However, population growth and the industrial revolution gradually consumed most of the land during the first half of the twentieth century. The transformation of outdoor areas into residential, agricultural, or urban landscapes helped spur the evolving outdoor recreation industry. With encroaching suburban and urban sprawl, more individuals began seeking out nature in an effort to escape from their urban and suburban environments. In addition, new ways to explore nature's offerings developed, including pursuits such as spelunking, or exploring caves, and the revival of culturally oriented sports such as surfing.

The next major development in the outdoor recreation industry was the advent and subsequent popularization of the automobile, followed by the first national highways in the 1950's. Urbanites and their suburban counterparts could now travel to national parks and other natural areas and engage in hiking, bird-watching, and a number of other nature activities that their city environments did not offer, building an entirely new consumer base for the outdoor recreation industry. The completion of interstate highways led to a significant spike in the number of Americans engaging in hiking, camping, and other wilderness activities.

The next major milestone in the outdoor recreation industry was the development of ecological consciousness, strengthening the conservation movement first spearheaded by naturalists such as Muir. While naturalists and scientists had long warned of the damage being wrought on the environment, it was not until the 1960's that ecologi-

Hunting and fishing are a big part of the outdoor recreation industry. (©Dreamstime.com)

cal awareness became widespread in the United States. The movement had its roots in the writings of naturalists such as Rachel Carson, who brought the environmental crisis to a national audience with the publication of *Silent Spring* (1962).

The early 1970's witnessed the back-to-the-land movement, in which hundreds of urban dwellers began moving to the country to be closer with nature and engage in what they saw as a simpler, more natural existence. This movement coincided with the first international efforts to combat environmental destruction and to protect natural resources and ecosystems. The environmental movement of the 1960's and 1970's also popularized the idea of "ecotourism," or traveling to a location for the express purpose of enjoying the natural environment. By the late 1990's, ecotourism was one of the largest segments of the international tourism industry, and many countries began to focus on preserving portions of their natural environment to attract tourists.

In the early twenty-first century, the outdoor recreation industry established itself as one of the fastest-growing segments of the international tourism and leisure industries. In urban areas, a variety of retail stores emerged specializing in selling equipment and educational materials for persons interested in outdoor activities. Companies offering outdoor recreational activities vary in size, from simple one-person guided hiking tours to massive resorts where visitors can engage in a variety of activities such as skiing, hiking, boating, rapelling, and mountain climbing.

The Industry Today

The outdoor recreation industry services a diverse array of customers from different cultural and socioeconomic backgrounds. Outdoor recreation appeals to those hoping to find a relaxing environment away from the hectic pace of modern life, as well as to those who crave the adventure and excitement that only the outdoors can offer. Given the wide-ranging appeal of the industry and the large base of potential customers, outdoor recreation has developed into a multitrillion-dollar industry that accounts for almost $300 billion in sales and services in the United States every year.

The twenty-first century outdoor recreation industry can be divided into a number of subindustries, including hunting and fishing, snow-based recreation, trail-based recreation, camp-based recreation, water-based recreation, and wildlife-themed activities. Within each category, there are thousands of outdoor recreation businesses in the United States and abroad, ranging from small, privately owned operations to national and international corporations.

Recreational hunting and fishing are among the largest segments of the industry—and the most controversial. Each year, hunting and fishing enthusiasts spend millions of dollars on training, equipment, licenses, and permits for such sports as game hunting, fly fishing, angling, deep-sea fishing, and big game or trophy hunting. In the wake of the environmental movement of the 1970's, awareness of species extinction and loss of diversity increased. This increased awareness led to the development of vigorous antihunting and antifishing movements. In an effort to prevent the extinction of threatened species and curb overall gradual species loss, governments began creating more stringent laws regarding hunting and fishing licensing. Gov-

Camping is a popular outdoor activity. (©Stephen Spraggon/Dreamstime.com)

ernments also began more strictly to regulate and govern the numbers and types of animals that can be killed by sport hunters and fishers. Hunting and fishing remain widely popular around the world, and government agencies are currently attempting to adjust their laws and regulations to protect vulnerable species without damaging the lucrative sport hunting industry.

Camping is another major facet of the outdoor recreation industry. There are hundreds of national parks across the United States that sell permits allowing individuals to camp within their grounds. There are also thousands of private campgrounds, often located near protected areas or national parks, where visitors can camp or park their recreational vehicles (RVs) for a fee. Camping is often connected with trail-based activities, which include any recreation or sport that uses a planned route through a natural area. These activities include basic hiking and biking paths, as well as mountaineering and mountain biking. Most national parks contain hiking trails for public use, and a number of businesses take customers to exotic locations for biking, horseback, or hiking tours.

Other outdoor recreation companies specialize in wildlife-themed entertainment. Wildlife-themed businesses include zoological parks and wildlife parks, as well as guided tours designed to allow visitors to view wildlife in its natural habitat. Scuba diving, snorkeling, and other marine activities are a popular part of the modern ecotourism industry, as are bird- and whale-watching tours. Many companies offering wildlife tours donate portions of their profits to help support conservation and other environmental efforts. Horseback riding is also popular around the world and has developed into a multimillion-dollar industry.

Snow-based recreation includes downhill and cross-country skiing, sledding, snowboarding, and snowmobiling. The snow-based recreation industry is robust in the United States and Europe be-

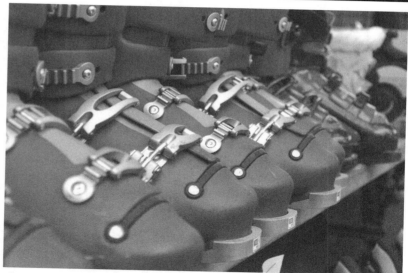

The snow-based recreation industry is robust in the United States because of the popularity of skiing and other snow-based activities at mountain resorts. (©Brian Balster/Dreamstime.com)

cause of the popularity of skiing and other snow-based activities at mountain resorts. (In recent years, the mountainous and newly economically empowered countries of Central Asia have also increased their respective profiles in the snow-based recreation and travel industry.) Snow recreation companies earn money by offering access to private skiing and snowboarding slopes, as well as by renting and selling equipment and clothing.

Water-based recreation involves boating, scuba diving, snorkeling, water skiing, parasailing, jet skiing, kayaking, canoeing, and a variety of other marine-based activities. Boating is among the most popular water-based recreation activities, as it includes activities such as recreational and competitive sailing, as well as boat tours, in both marine and freshwater areas. Much of the industry is focused on the renting or seasonal housing of boats and other watercraft. Water-based recreation also includes other wildlife-themed activities, such as whale watching, an industry that was estimated in 2009 to be worth $2.1 billion globally by the International Fund for Animal Welfare.

The various categories of outdoor activities overlap in practice. Ski resorts, for instance, might also offer bird-watching tours and horseback riding in the off-season, while businesses offering wildlife-viewing tours might also own trails for mountain biking. Similarly, a single business might try to cater to different types of clientele by offering some activities that are relaxing or family-oriented, as well as others that are more challenging and appeal to sporting or experienced consumers.

The most important forces driving the development of the outdoor recreation industry are the availability of natural areas for consumers and their evolving ecological awareness. Companies that once specialized in deep-sea fishing, for example, may find that their consumer base is shrinking as concerns over declining fish populations become more widespread. Companies marketing services that are environmentally friendly and ecologically responsible are beginning to have a major advantage in the market.

While the outdoor recreation industry includes numerous large and profitable companies, the industry is only partly driven by profit. Many companies and outdoor recreation organizations donate profits and volunteer services to the ongoing effort to preserve and protect wildlife and natural habitats. Those who work in the industry, especially in smaller businesses with ties to local communities, tend themselves to be avid participants in outdoor activities and to enjoy earning a living while sharing their passion with others.

INDUSTRY MARKET SEGMENTS

Outdoor recreation companies range in size from small operations with one or a few employees to massive companies with hundreds or thousands of employees. There are small, midsize, and large corporations for each category of outdoor activity, whether it is water-based, snow-based, or trail-based. The following descriptions list qualities common to recreation businesses, grouped according to size and number of employees.

Jet boats are a popular form of recreation on lakes and rivers. (©Dreamstime.com)

Small Businesses

Most outdoor recreation businesses would fall into the small business category, with between one and ten employees and established ties to their immediate communities. In addition to small companies, this category includes self-employed entrepreneurs who work alone, offering training or tours in some type of outdoor or recreational activity.

Potential Annual Earnings Scale. According to the U.S. Bureau of Labor Statistics (BLS), the average annual salary range for employees of outdoor recreation businesses in 2009 was between $14,000 and $37,000. Owners and managers of small recreation companies can earn salaries significantly higher than the average salary of all employees, which was $20,470. The potential earnings of outdoor recreation businesses' owners vary widely depending on their location and type of business. For example, the owner of a small fishing tour business along a midwestern river might earn a salary of less than $15,000 per year, while the owner of a private deep-sea fishing tour business, located near a busy tourist area, might earn well over $80,000 per year.

Clientele Interaction. Owners and managers of small recreation businesses generally work with small groups of clients and can therefore offer personalized service to their clientele. While some recreation businesses maintain a significant number of repeat customers, most businesses must maximize the number of new customers they bring in each season because a large portion of their customers engage in outdoor recreation only occasionally. In order to maintain revenues, smaller businesses must market themselves on the basis of their unique qualities, which often include offering personalized service.

Owners, managers, and employees of smaller outdoor recreation businesses are expected to have intimate knowledge of the activity in question. Owners of a surfing supply business, for instance, are generally expected to be surfers or at least to have firsthand knowledge of the local surfing scene. This intimate connection to the activity in question makes customers feel as if they are receiving expert service, and it is one of the primary reasons that customers choose smaller, independent businesses over larger companies.

Smaller companies are also able to offer more flexible services, as they accommodate smaller groups of customers. A common niche for smaller recreational businesses is to offer various types of training, tours, or services depending on the client's needs. A small hunting business might therefore offer private father-and-son hunting tours, while a hiking tour company might offer couples night hiking.

Amenities, Atmosphere, and Physical Grounds. Smaller businesses tend to present a less formal and more personalized atmosphere. Depending on the type of business, the layout may range from a single-room office to a small building. The décor of a small outdoor recreation business's office will often feature posters, photographs, and other souvenirs representing features of the local area. A small fishing shop might hang a stuffed fish caught by a local fisher, while a small mountain-bike-rental office might hang maps of local biking trails or pictures of wildlife commonly found on their trails. Because most small recreation businesses are independent, the choice of décor and the overall atmosphere of the establishment generally reflect the personality of the owner and employees. One common theme is to employ a rustic or outdoors decoration scheme that builds on the theme of sports and nature appreciation.

Smaller outdoor recreation businesses typically operate on low or limited incomes and may therefore keep amenities to a minimum. Depending on the type of business in question, the owners may make basic amenities such as restrooms and automated teller machines (ATMs) available on site. Few small businesses can afford to offer free souvenirs and other complimentary gifts, which is a popular strategy of larger recreation companies.

Typical Number of Employees. Small outdoor recreation businesses typically have fewer than ten employees, but they may have only one or two, depending on the type of business. A small canoe-renting facility might have between ten and twenty employees to handle customer service, make equipment and tour sales, shuttle visitors to and from the launch location, and maintain the office and grounds. A small bait shop or private deep-sea fishing operation, on the other hand, might have only one or two employees and might therefore operate only seasonally and during peak fishing hours.

Outdoor recreation businesses with significant equipment expenditures, such as bike rental companies, surfboard rental companies, and retail stores specializing in outdoor equipment, typically have larger numbers of employees to fulfill the demands of maintaining and handling inventory. Smaller businesses offering tours or training may only require a few employees, each of whom is responsible for small groups of customers during a typical business day.

Traditional Geographic Locations. Small outdoor recreation businesses are typically geographically specialized and situated as close as possible to the area in which their activities take place. Small fishing shops attempt to locate themselves near local lakes or rivers, surfing shops locate themselves coastally, and small skiing shops locate themselves near popular ski slopes. Most small businesses are operated by individuals who live near the area in question and have close ties to the community; for example, small surfing equipment stores are found in surfing towns. In general, those in the outdoor recreation industry are members of their local communities and build their livelihoods around the features that attract customers to the area.

Some outdoor recreation companies set up remote locations in urban areas in an effort to capitalize on the larger number of potential customers who live there. A small mountain bike store might therefore open in a city, offering equipment and arranging for biking classes with urban residents who then travel to the appropriate location to participate in the classes. Satellite locations of this kind are more common among midsize and larger companies, but some small businesses also try to attract customers from nearby, more populous urban areas.

Pros of Working for a Small Outdoor Recreation Business. Most owners and operators of small outdoor recreation businesses are not motivated primarily by potential earnings. Many entrepreneurs in the outdoor recreation industry have a genuine passion for their fields and open their businesses in an effort to earn a living while doing what that they love to do.

In addition to working in an industry with personal appeal, small-business owners benefit from having close ties to their communities. They may also enjoy interacting personally with their customers. Small-business owner-operators also typically have the freedom to tailor every aspect of their businesses according to their personal tastes. By the same token, they can adjust their business strategies according to changes in the market or in their personal lives. This type of flexibility may not be possible at larger establishments that have greater overhead and more employees to consider.

Cons of Working for a Small Outdoor Recreation Business. Small outdoor recreation industries, like many small and independently operated businesses, are especially vulnerable to both environmental and economic changes. While a large recreational venue or company might earn enough income to weather periods of economic downturn and reduced business, a smaller business might have more difficulty in meeting its payroll requirements, maintaining its inventory, and paying its expenses.

In addition, owners and operators of small businesses are typically responsible for a variety of activities in the daily operation of the business. For example, a manager at a small mountain-climbing equipment store might be responsible for, among other things, human resources management, cashier and customer service duties, inventory management, and accounting, while managers at midsize and large businesses often have more defined and less demanding roles.

Costs

Payroll and Benefits: Small businesses generally pay hourly wages, and few offer medical or other typical benefits.

Supplies: Small retail stores must make significant investments in inventory, while service-based businesses, such as those providing tours or training, may have smaller expenses in terms of inventory and supplies. They will still need to maintain a full stock of the tools of their trade, such as fishing equipment or stable supplies and horse-transportation vehicles.

External Services: Some small businesses pay for credit card processing services and other customer service amenities for their offices, such as vending machines. They may also hire accountants at tax season or small advertising firms or consultants to find and appeal to customers.

Utilities: Depending on the business, small recreation business owners may need to pay for electricity, gas or oil, telephone and Internet services, and sewage and water utilities.

Taxes: Small businesses pay local, state, and federal income taxes, as well as property taxes. In addition, many small businesses must maintain sporting licenses, and some also arrange to sell licenses to their customers. As many outdoor recreation activities are associated with significant physical risk, some businesses may carry highly specific insurance policies to protect themselves in cases of customer injury.

Midsize Businesses

Midsize outdoor recreation businesses are not as abundant as are small businesses, and they generally serve areas with high customer volume. Popular resort or vacation areas can support midsize businesses, where the number of customers necessitates larger size and more employees. Some midsize outdoor recreation businesses are part of larger chains, including a number of sporting-goods and other specialty retail shops. Midsize businesses may maintain between twenty and fifty employees, depending on the type of business and its location.

Unlike smaller businesses, midsize businesses commonly offer more than one recreational activity or service. For instance, a midsize boating business may sell boating equipment, as well as offer lessons in sailing and operating motor boats, guided boat tours, and other services. By contrast, smaller businesses are often limited to providing a single service or limited service in a few basic categories.

Potential Annual Earnings Scale. The wages for managers, owners, and operators of midsize recreation businesses vary widely depending on the type of business and location. According to the BLS, salaries for all employees of recreation businesses generally fall within a range of $14,000 to $37,000 per year, with owners and managers earning incomes at the upper half of the range. Managers of recreation businesses in busy areas with high customer volumes may earn as much as $80,000 or more annually.

Clientele Interaction. Midsize recreation businesses are more formal than their smaller counterparts, and generally have high customer volume, which translates into less personalized interaction between customers and staff. Because of high volume, midsize businesses are also sometimes less responsive and adaptable to the needs of individual customers.

While midsize businesses may not be as personable as some smaller businesses, they are often able to offer more reliable service and have longer hours than their smaller competitors. In addition, midsize businesses are sometimes able to hire staff specifically assigned to customer relations and satisfaction, allowing them to handle greater volume without sacrificing personal customer interaction. Because midsize businesses often bring in higher revenues than do small businesses, they are sometimes able to offer services and customer sales that would be impossible for smaller businesses with less profit.

Amenities, Atmosphere, and Physical Grounds. The appearance and layout of midsize outdoor recreation businesses varies widely according to the type of business and physical location. Most midsize businesses require larger spaces than do small businesses and typically provide at least basic amenities, such as restrooms and heating or air-conditioning in customer areas. A midsize nature park might, for instance, have two sets of restrooms for customers, as well as a cafeteria or refreshment stand. In addition, some midsize businesses are able to couple with other businesses to offer grouped services. For example, a midsize ski-rental business might be located next to a bed and breakfast or hotel to capitalize on business from tourists.

Like small businesses, the décor and atmosphere of midsize businesses often feature decora-tions, art, and colors reminiscent of their professional activity. A business specializing in surfing equipment and lessons will feature a décor derived from surf culture, while businesses specializing in saltwater fishing might be decorated with pictures of the ocean and may hang decorations such as mounted fish, sea creatures, and other items associated with the marine environment. Midsize businesses that are part of larger chains may be required to decorate in accordance with the policies of the national chain management. In contrast to the common rustic decoration scheme of many smaller recreation businesses, midsize companies often attempt to project a more businesslike and formal atmosphere.

Midsize recreation businesses are more likely than are smaller businesses to concentrate on branding their business. While a small business might rely on word of mouth and basic advertising as its only marketing efforts, a midsize business might create a logo and apply it to products and promotional items in an attempt to generate interest. In such a case, the business's logo might play a major role in its decoration scheme and in choices made regarding its atmosphere and physical design.

Typical Number of Employees. Midsize businesses may hire anywhere from ten to more than fifty employees, depending on the nature of the business and its physical location. A retail location, for instance, might need to have a full staff of ten or more employees divided over two or three shifts per day and operating from five to seven days per week, while a midsize nature park might need no more than ten or fifteen employees, because a minimal staff is required for the daily operation of the business.

Traditional Geographic Locations. As midsize businesses typically specialize in handling larger groups or high customer volume, they generally appear near resort locations or other areas that draw large numbers of tourists. Midsize retail establishments are an exception to this trend, as they tend to appear in locations with large populations, such as urban areas, where their customer volume will be higher even though the equipment and other goods they sell are typically used at some distance from their retail locations.

Many midsize outdoor recreation companies situate themselves close to other businesses that attract tourists to the area, such as hotels, restaurants, museums, or other popular recreational venues. Many midsize outdoor recreation companies are coupled with hotels and motels, often creating a resort environment and encouraging guests to enjoy outdoor recreation activities during their stay.

Pros of Working for a Midsize Outdoor Recreation Business. Midsize outdoor recreation companies offer employees higher average salaries and access to benefits such as health insurance that smaller businesses are typically unable to offer. As is the case in small businesses, employees of midsize businesses may enjoy the ability to use the company's equipment and services for their personal recreation, either without cost or at a substantially reduced rate.

Some employees may enjoy working at midsize establishments because the larger staff provides more flexibility and potential for advancement than is the case at smaller businesses that are constrained in terms of profit and resources. Midsize businesses are more likely than are small businesses to offer pay raises and other advancement opportunities. Working at a midsize business is therefore more likely to represent a long-term career choice than is working at a small business.

Some employees might also enjoy the more defined structure of a midsize business because it allows them to concentrate on their specific roles, rather than having to serve in a variety of functions. For owners and managers, the larger staff at a midsize business makes it more likely that, if one or more employees are unable to work, the manager will be able to fill the available hours among the remaining employees rather than having to do the work him- or herself.

Cons of Working for a Midsize Outdoor Recreation Business. In contrast to the informal, family-like atmosphere of many smaller establishments, midsize businesses must often adopt a more formal atmosphere. This may be a detriment to some employees who desire more personal relationships with other staff members and with customers. Midsize businesses are also dependent on maintaining significant customer volume in order to meet their costs of operation.

Additionally, while midsize businesses are more likely to build financial insulation to guard against slow business periods or prolonged periods of reduced business, they still commonly remain vulnerable to economic collapse, often leaving owners in poor financial shape because of the significant cost of maintaining a business. Another drawback to the midsize business is the large amount of capital needed to start it, including inventory (if applicable), staffing, building maintenance, and other costs. Compared to smaller businesses, which are able to more quickly adjust their business models to changing market conditions, midsize businesses are not as flexible, and any major change in their business will require another significant investment in capital.

Costs

Payroll and Benefits: Most midsize businesses pay support and sales staff hourly wages, while managers and executive personnel may be paid salaries. Midsize businesses are more likely than small businesses to offer benefits to employees, especially those that work for local or national chains.

Supplies: Depending on the type of business, midsize outdoor recreation businesses may require a significant number of basic supplies for operation, including equipment, cleaning supplies, inventory for retail sales, and a variety of other items. Retail stores have the highest cost in terms of supplies, while tour companies, wildlife parks, and other similar businesses have relatively low supply costs.

External Services: Because midsize businesses may require employees to wear uniforms, they are more likely to hire uniform or linen supply companies and laundry services. Some businesses may also hire payroll and accounting services, as well as tax services, from outside vendors. Retail equipment vendors also typically need to have accounts with shipping companies and electronic payment processing companies. They may also hire companies to provide and maintain vending machines and other supplies at their locations.

Utilities: Midsize outdoor recreation businesses are typically required to pay for water and sewage, oil or gas, and electricity and telecommunication services. Many midsize businesses also offer Internet and other interactive services specifically for customers.

Taxes: Many outdoor recreation activities require special licensing and fees, both for the business itself and for customers who want access to activities that require licensing, such as hunting and fishing. Depending on the location, customers may need to purchase a one-day license for certain activities. As many outdoor recreation activities are associated with significant physical risk, some businesses may carry highly specific insurance policies to protect their business in cases of customer injury. In addition, midsize businesses are responsible for playing federal and state income, property, and other business-related taxes.

Large Businesses

Large outdoor recreation companies include resorts and regional or national outdoor-equipment supply companies. Large companies typically offer more than one type of recreational activity or a host of related services, which may include services classified under different industries. A ski lodge, for instance, might offer skiing, snowboarding, snowmobile rental, hiking, food and beverages, lodging, and travel-arrangement services. Large outdoor businesses are not as common as small and midsize businesses and typically appear only in areas with large numbers of potential customers and tourists.

Potential Annual Earnings Scale. While the general earnings range for employees of the outdoor recreation industry falls between $14,000 and just over $37,000 per year, owners and managers of large outdoor recreation companies have the highest earning potential in the industry. Depending on the type of business and customer volume, some managers may earn more than $80,000 or $90,000 annually. Earnings for general employees at large outdoor recreation companies are usually commensurate with those of similar employees at smaller companies.

Clientele Interaction. Because of their larger size and more significant customer volume, workers at large outdoor recreation companies have fewer opportunities for direct interaction with their customers. Many large outdoor recreation businesses handle hundreds of customers in a typical business period and may therefore need to adopt an efficient system for customer service, creating a different atmosphere from the informal interactions characteristic of small businesses.

While the interactions in a larger outdoor recreation company may be formal by comparison to a small recreation company, larger companies sometimes hire personnel whose sole task is to handle customer relations and service. In this way, larger companies can maintain a more personal level of service, even with higher volume. At resorts, for instance, customer service is generally considered one of the keys to successful operation and most resorts will place significant investment in hiring and training staff to address customer needs.

Larger businesses must often create standard strategies and routines for many aspects of their business and are therefore not as responsive to customer needs. Smaller companies, on the other hand, may have the freedom to address customers on an individual basis.

Amenities, Atmosphere, and Physical Grounds. Because they serve larger numbers of customers, large outdoor recreation companies must provide a range of amenities for their customers, including restrooms with changing facilities, refreshments, and atmospheric controls. Resorts typically have entertainment amenities as well, including games, television, and Internet services.

Large outdoor recreation companies, such as ski resorts and water parks, often blend elements of a rustic decorative scheme with luxurious appointments. For example, a large ski lodge may use live evergreen trees as decoration and hang a stuffed moose head in a customer area, but it will juxtapose these bucolic reminders with luxurious leather furniture and central heating. The general idea is to capture the flavor of the outdoor or rural lifestyle without sacrificing luxury.

The physical layout of a large outdoor recreation business will differ depending on the type of business and its location. Some larger resorts may occupy huge complexes with several associated businesses, including restaurants, nightclubs or bars, lodging quarters, training facilities or venues, and a retail outlet. Other large outdoor recreation venues may occupy a single large building or warehouse space, as is true of some types of outdoor-equipment vendors.

Typical Number of Employees. Large outdoor recreation companies may have anywhere from fifty to several thousand employees. For example, Diamond Peak, a ski resort in Tahoe, Nevada, maintains a staff of three hundred full-time employees and as many as one hundred seasonal or part-time employees. REI Corporation, a vendor specializing in sports and outdoor activities equipment, employed more than nine thousand full-time employees in 2008. Similarly, outdoor recreation retailer L. L. Bean employed more than fifty-four hundred workers year-round in 2008, with an additional twelve thousand temporary employees during that year's holiday season. (The retailer also features a flagship store in Maine that is open twenty-four hours.)

Traditional Geographic Locations. Large recreational businesses tend to be located in areas with heavy foot or automobile traffic or large numbers of arriving tourists. The businesses are ideally located close to some natural feature that attracts visitors, such as a mountain, beach, or stretch of woodland appropriate for hiking. Large retail recreation stores are often located on the immediate outskirts of urban areas, where they can still capitalize on significant foot traffic. Large recreation venues are not frequently found within major urban areas because the cost of urban property is prohibitive for businesses.

Pros of Working for a Large Outdoor Recreation Business. Large outdoor recreation businesses are typically able to offer benefits for full-time employees. For managers and owners, larger businesses may also offer significantly higher salaries and advancement opportunities than do small and midsize businesses. Employees of large recreation facilities may also have access to better equipment and other amenities. In addition, employees of large companies with established reputations may have an advantage in terms of finding employment with other companies in the same industry, and they may be able to relocate to other locations while remaining employed by the company.

Cons of Working for a Large Outdoor Recreation Business. For some interested in a career in outdoor recreation, the formal atmosphere associated with the large business model might be unappealing. A majority of those seeking employment in the industry are outdoor activity enthusiasts, and many of these individuals might not relish the idea of working in a corporate environment. For managers, the sheer size and complexity of running a large business can be difficult and challenging. As large businesses are focused on attracting and handling large customer volume, daily operations can be hectic in comparison to those of smaller businesses that accommodate a more select clientele.

In addition, serving such a large volume of customers virtually guarantees that a variety of operational, customer-service, and human-relations problems will arise, creating additional difficulties for management and other staff.

Large businesses have significant overhead in terms of supplies, staffing, maintenance, and basic operating costs. With such significant overhead, large businesses are dependent on maintaining significant customer volume throughout the year, or at least throughout the busiest season. Environmental and economic changes can be a major obstacle for a large outdoor recreation business, though it is more likely to have the resources to endure reduced business for short periods.

Costs

Payroll and Benefits: Because large businesses typically have more complex corporate and labor structures, they generally have both hourly and salaried employees. Most large companies provide some benefits, including basic health coverage. In addition, many outdoor recreation companies provide discounts on equipment or other services for their employees' personal recreation.

Supplies: The types of supplies needed by large outdoor recreation businesses vary widely among companies. While resorts need supplies that fit into a variety of categories, including housekeeping, recreational equipment, and food service equipment, smaller companies may only require basic supplies to meet the requirements of their daily operations.

External Services: Large resorts often utilize laundry and linen services from an outside vendor. In addition, some companies may contract certain facets of their accounting and advertising, as well as other business services. Many companies hire outside vendors to process payments and handle credit transactions.

Utilities: Large businesses usually pay for gas or oil heating, air-conditioning, electricity, sewage and water service, and telephone and Internet services.

Taxes: Any large outdoor recreation business must pay local, state, and federal income taxes, as well as property taxes. Some businesses, such as hunting lodges and ski resorts, must also pay licensing and insurance costs on an annual basis. Many businesses pass on a portion of their insurance costs to customers through various service fees.

ORGANIZATIONAL STRUCTURE AND JOB ROLES

The organizational structure of an outdoor recreation business depends largely on the type of business. The sheer diversity of the industry, which includes businesses from a variety of categories, defies simple examinations of organizational structure; however, some basic roles need to be filled at every business, regardless of the company's specific niche.

The following umbrella categories apply to the organizational structure of businesses in the outdoor recreation industry:

- Executive Management
- Sales and Marketing
- Booking and Reservations
- Customer Relations
- Maintenance and Janitorial Services
- First Aid and Medical Care
- Food and Beverage Services
- Groundskeeping and Facilities Maintenance
- Naturalists and Tour Guides
- Education
- Information Technology

Executive Management

Executive managers oversee the operation of their businesses, and they may handle tasks in a variety of categories. A small-business owner may serve as the sole manager of a business, while some large companies have a variety of managers serving in different capacities. At a large retail operation, for instance, a manager may be hired solely to handle inventory.

Managers often have the most demanding roles in their businesses, but they also earn higher salaries than do other employees. Many managers earn annual salaries, while most other employees in the outdoor recreation industry work for hourly wages. In small companies, managers are often required to handle personnel management, such as hiring decisions, in addition to a variety of other tasks, including maintaining supply inventory and participating in sales and other daily operations.

Executive management occupations may include the following:

- Chief Financial Officer (CFO)
- General Manager/Managing Director
- Resort Manager
- Inventory/Sales Manager
- Facility Manager
- Customer Service Manager
- Food Service Manager
- Entertainment Director

Sales and Marketing

Some outdoor recreation companies have sales and marketing departments, while others rely primarily on word of mouth, walk-in customers, and basic advertising in local media. Companies that are part of regional and national chains are more likely to maintain separate departments or to assign specific employees to handle their marketing and advertising campaigns. Large chains may employ a variety of advertising methods, including sponsorship campaigns, as well as print, radio, television, Internet, and other types of advertising campaigns. With more complex advertising strategies, larger companies may hire individuals or advertising firms just to maintain their overall marketing and advertising efforts.

Sponsorship is a popular form of advertising and marketing for companies in the outdoor sport industry. For example, a mountain bike company may sponsor riders in return for their agreement to wear and use equipment featuring the company's logo. Other companies may attempt to hire well-known athletes to endorse their products. One important facet of advertising and marketing is branding. Logos and other methods of branding a company create public recognition and drive business to the company. Some larger companies and outdoor-equipment manufacturers may have employees specifically designated for branding and marketing management.

Sales and marketing occupations may include the following:

- Advertising Director
- Sponsorship Director
- Advertising Sales Associate
- Corporate Relations Specialist

- Marketing Representative
- Design and Branding Associate
- Marketing/Design Manager

Booking and Reservations

For recreation companies that offer guided tours, vacation packages, and other types of prearranged activities, booking and reservations employees handle customer service and scheduling. In large resorts and tour companies, the booking and reservation department might be divided into several distinct categories, including managers, reservations agents, and customer-fulfillment agents. Small companies may place booking and reservations in the hands of general customer-service personnel, who work under the supervision of one of the company's managers.

Booking and reservation occupations may include the following:

- Booking/Reservation Manager
- Customer Service Representative
- Receptionist
- Administrative Assistant

Customer Relations

Employees in the customer relations department focus on answering customer questions, resolving complaints, and assuring customer satisfaction. While some larger companies may have separate personnel for customer relations tasks, in many companies, customer relations duties fall on staff members from a variety of departments. Booking and reservations agents, for instance, often handle customer relations in resort hotels, while managers fill customer relations roles in many retail stores.

Customer relations occupations may include the following:

OCCUPATION PROFILE

Recreation Program Director

Considerations	Qualifications
Description	Plans, organizes, and directs activities for the public at parks, community centers, recreation areas, health clubs, places of worship, and camps.
Career clusters	Education and Training; Hospitality and Tourism; Human Services
Interests	Data; people
Working conditions	Work inside
Minimum education level	Bachelor's degree
Physical exertion	Light work
Physical abilities	Unexceptional/basic fitness
Opportunities for experience	Military service; part-time work
Licensure and certification	Recommended
Employment outlook	Faster-than-average growth expected
Holland interest score	ESA

Note: See volume 1, "Publisher's Note," for an explanation of the Holland interest score.

OCCUPATION PROFILE

Recreation Worker

Considerations	Qualifications
Description	Directs, plans, and organizes recreational activities.
Career cluster	Education and Training; Hospitality and Tourism; Human Services
Interests	Data; people
Working conditions	Work both inside and outside
Minimum education level	On-the-job training; high school diploma or GED; high school diploma/technical training; junior/technical/community college; bachelor's degree
Physical exertion	Light work; medium work
Physical abilities	Unexceptional/basic fitness
Opportunities for experience	Military service; volunteer work; part-time work
Licensure and certification	Recommended
Employment outlook	Faster-than-average growth expected
Holland interest score	SCR; SEI

Note: See volume 1, "Publisher's Note," for an explanation of the Holland interest score.

- Customer Relations Manager
- Customer Relations Representative

Maintenance and Janitorial Services

The maintenance and janitorial departments are responsible for maintaining the appearance of a business, from basic cleaning to decoration, and fixing any mechanical objects used in the operation of the business. Smaller companies rarely have separate employees to handle janitorial duties, but they may still need at least one employee with the knowledge and skills to fix and maintain equipment. For skiing companies, maintenance workers might need to repair and maintain a resort's ski lifts; fix damaged rental skis, boots, and poles; and perform upkeep on landscaping equipment.

In resort companies, janitorial services often overlap with housekeeping services, as housekeeping employees must handle laundry and basic cleaning for the resort's guests. Janitorial employ-ees are also responsible for removing garbage and, if applicable, organizing the company's recycling.

Maintenance and janitorial occupations may include the following:

- Custodial Services Manager
- Custodian/Janitor
- Maintenance and Repair Worker
- Equipment Technician
- Mechanic

First Aid and Medical Care

Companies offering outdoor activities and sports sometimes maintain on-site first-aid and medical specialists to help customers who are injured during their recreational activities. Ski slopes, rafting companies, and many other establishments offering vigorous outdoor activities must have some personnel trained in basic first aid. In addition, many companies offering water-based sporting activities

OCCUPATION SPECIALTIES

Recreation Workers

Specialty	Responsibilities
Camp counselors	Direct and plan children's camp activities, such as hikes, cookouts, and campfires, to provide a wide variety of camping experiences.
Recreation center directors	Plan, organize, and direct public and voluntary recreation programs at recreation buildings, indoor centers, playgrounds, playfields, or day camps.
Recreation leaders	Conduct recreational activities with assigned groups in public departments or voluntary agencies.

hire personnel with knowledge of cardiopulmonary resuscitation (CPR) and water-rescue techniques. Similarly, those operating mountain climbing areas must have staff who can tend to broken bones, various types of abrasions, and other injuries. In addition to providing first aid after an accident, medical personnel may be responsible for organizing a company's medical and first-aid supplies, including bandages, splints, pain relievers, and other basic medical supplies.

First-aid and medical occupations may include the following:

- Physician
- Lifeguard
- Emergency Worker

Food and Beverage Services

Some outdoor recreation companies offer food and beverages to their customers. This is especially common at resorts, which often have on-site restaurants. Other companies provide basic refreshments, such as drinks and wrapped foods, but do not have a full-service restaurant on premises. In large resorts, the restaurant department may function as an independent business with its own managerial and accounting departments. These businesses function under several industry classifications, including outdoor recreation, food service, and lodging.

Food and beverage service occupations may include the following:

- Cook
- Chef
- Restaurant/Kitchen Manager
- Server
- Server's Assistant
- Expediter
- Kitchen Maintenance Worker
- Kitchen Worker
- Cafeteria Worker

Groundskeeping and Facilities Maintenance

For ski resorts, nature parks, zoos, and similar businesses, groundskeepers and maintenance workers maintain the appearance and safety of the grounds. They may be responsible for, among other tasks, grass cutting, tree trimming, and landscaping, as well as maintaining plantings and other decorative elements such as statues, benches, and picnic areas. Groundskeepers fill an essential function at nature parks, where maintaining vegetation is very important for the safety of guests and visitors. In national parks, for instance, felled trees can pose a safety hazard for hikers and bikers, and they must therefore be cleared from roads frequently to prevent injury.

Groundskeeping and facilities maintenance occupations may include the following:

- Landscaper
- Gardener
- Horticulturist
- Groundskeeper

- Facility Manager
- Yard Worker

Naturalists and Tour Guides

Outdoor recreation companies that handle wilderness areas such as wildlife parks, zoological parks, and nature parks often hire naturalists to manage their animal and plant populations. A nature park that offers hiking and other trail-based activities may hire only a single naturalist, while a zoological park may hire different keepers for different types of animals. Naturalists help facilitate any research conducted in the park and are also charged with handling any wildlife problems, so they may have quite a wide variety of tasks. Naturalists may also function as educators, helping create informative materials to teach guests about the animals found in the park.

Many outdoor recreation areas offer guided tours, often conducted by trained tour guides who are experts in answering questions about the facility and about the plants and animals found in the area. In some facilities, naturalists function as tour guides, while other facilities have separate personnel for each department and may use naturalists to manage the tour team.

Naturalist and tour guide occupations may include the following:

- Park Naturalist
- Animal Keeper
- Tour Guide
- Docent
- Conservation Specialist
- Wildlife Manager

Education

Some outdoor recreation companies have education specialists who prepare and present educational materials to guests or customers. In wildlife parks and zoological parks, the education department prepares educational materials about plants, animals, and conservation and often gives lectures to guests.

Facilities specializing in outdoor sports may hire specialists to teach classes in outdoor activities. Many mountain-climbing facilities, for example, offer classes in various mountain-climbing techniques taught by experienced climbers. Similarly, rafting and canoeing companies hire individuals to

teach classes in swimming, rafting safety, and other topics.

Many outdoor recreation companies provide educational materials addressing conservation and wildlife preservation, issues that are important to any industry that depends on utilizing the world's preserved wilderness areas. Education department employees may also assist and facilitate scholarly research conducted on premises.

Education occupations may include the following:

- Teacher
- Educational Coordinator
- Education Presenter
- Training Supervisor
- Trainer

Information Technology

Many outdoor recreation companies hire employees to handle their information technology (IT) needs, including building and maintaining the company's Web site, handling Web marketing, and maintaining the company's internal e-mail system. While small companies may assign these duties to a general manager or to the basic advertising department, companies with specially designed information systems may require separate employees who concentrate only on the company's technological needs.

IT occupations may include the following:

- Information Technology Supervisor
- Web Marketing Supervisor
- Webmaster
- Information Technology Assistant
- Secretary

INDUSTRY OUTLOOK

Overview

In the first decade of the twenty-first century, the outdoor recreation industry experienced significant flux. On one hand, the industry became more robust thanks to increased global interest in ecotourism, environmental protection, and fitness. On the other hand, the industry suffered from the global economic crisis of 2007-2009, and many industries are also coping with the ongoing threat of environmental damage from pollution, overdevelopment, and global warming.

According to the BLS, the U.S. outdoor recreation industry will benefit from three related trends in the period from 2006 to 2016: an overall increase in disposable income, increased leisure time for American adults, and an increasing interest in health and physical activity. Because of these trends, the BLS estimated in 2006 that the recreation industry as a whole would grow by more than 31 percent in the following ten-year period, compared to 11 percent average growth for all U.S. industries.

The Outdoor Foundation estimates that the outdoor recreation industry contributes more than $730 billion to the U.S. economy each year. This figure includes not only earnings by outdoor recreation companies but also those of intermediary companies that provide services to the industry. The outdoor recreation industry itself generates more than $289 billion in direct annual revenues. Estimates also indicate that the industry generates at least $88 billion in taxes. (Information on the state of the industry worldwide is problematic because many countries that generate significant income from tourism and outdoor recreation have not calculated earnings for that portion of their economies; conservative estimates would indicate that the worldwide industry generates close to $1 trillion of the $5.4 trillion estimated for the global tourism and recreation industry as a whole.)

Growth in the industry is largely fueled by an increase in both fitness and environmental consciousness in the United States. The popular media's dissemination of information about environmental decay, global warming, and emerging trends in health and wellness has affected every industry in the United States and many countries around the globe. Today, more Americans take ecological consciousness and health into consideration when deciding where and how to spend their leisure time and evaluating the desirability of businesses and products. Outdoor recreation appeals to both the health and the environmental market, and the companies that dominate the industry are designing their marketing to cater to both facets of their consumer base.

According to the Outdoor Foundation, wildlife viewing is the most popular outdoor activity, accounting for 66 million participants in 2007-2008. Bicycling was the second most popular activity, accounting for 60 million participants, while trail-based activities and camping accounted for 56 million and 45 million participants, respectively.

A bicycle tourist on a desert road in India. (©Dreamstime.com)

While the outdoor recreation industry is currently experiencing robust growth, the industry has significant difficulties that may affect job outlook and earning potential in the next decade and beyond. First, the Outdoor Foundation and other organizations have noted a recent significant decrease in youth involvement in outdoor recreation. The Outdoor Foundation's 2008 participation survey found that the number of children aged six to seventeen who had participated in outdoor activities in the previous year fell by more than 11 percent. The decrease was most significant for young girls, whose participation decreased from 77 to 61 percent.

In another Outdoor Foundation study, responses indicated

that approximately 90 percent of U.S. adults who regularly participated in outdoor recreation were introduced to outdoor activities between five and eight years of age. Decreasing youth participation could therefore indicate a dangerous trend with the potential to affect the industry over the next ten years.

Surveys further indicate that media and advertising have little direct effect on stimulating youth involvement in outdoor activities. Companies must therefore concentrate on advertising toward parents of young children, while designing innovative programs that appeal to both children and parents. While fitness and environmentalism are appropriate marketing positions for companies seeking to attract adult customers, children are more responsive to activities that offer fun, adventure, or exploration. The success of the outdoor recreation industry in overcoming this marketing challenge will perhaps determine the growth of the industry as a whole for the next several years.

Climate change and other forms of environmental degradation also threaten the stability of the outdoor recreation industry. According to the U.S. Climate Change Science Program's 2003 investigation of the Rocky Mountain/Great Basin Region, climate change poses a significant threat to both the snow-based and the water-based recreation industries. Among the first businesses to be affected by global warming are ski slopes and resorts, where business depends on adequate snow levels during the peak skiing seasons. Even businesses that use artificial snow depend on weather conditions to maintain snow quality and to attract customers to the slopes. Warmer temperatures will also mean shorter skiing seasons and poor snow coverage in many areas.

Warmer temperatures will also be difficult for the water-based recreation industry. In some places, climate change will contribute to low water levels, which will prevent kayaking and canoeing in many areas. In other parts of the country, warming may lead to higher water levels and faster currents, making the waters too dangerous for casual enthusiasts. Other forms of environmental damage, including overdevelopment, also threaten the outdoor recreation industry. As the population increases and communities are left with little space for expansion, some individuals will support development in protected areas in an effort to provide more hous-

ing and commercial property. Many of these protected areas will be those currently used by companies offering outdoor recreation activities.

To combat the threat of development, outdoor recreation companies may utilize their resources and mobilize their consumer base to fight against development and support the preservation of public and private wilderness and outdoor recreation areas. Outdoor recreation companies may also support or become involved in efforts to prevent pollution and environmental decay, as part of an effort to preserve the substrate that supports their livelihoods.

From 2008 to 2009, the global economic crisis posed another challenge to the domestic recreation industry. Recreational spending fell across the board, as practically all recreation companies experienced reduced revenues. These lower revenues harmed employment. For example, outdoor retailer L. L. Bean, voted one of the best companies to work for nationwide in 2008 by organizations such as the AARP, announced layoffs estimated at between 200 and 240 employees in April, 2009.

While there have been no comprehensive estimates of how the recession has affected the overall outdoor recreation industry specifically, reports from some companies indicate that many vendors experienced reduced business during the two years of the crisis. Some companies have begun marketing specifically to consumers experiencing the economic turmoil of the recession. This marketing strategy may be successful, as some forms of outdoor recreation, such as camping on public lands and taking hiking trips, are more affordable than are resort or hotel vacations.

In summary, while the industry is currently enjoying growth and a positive outlook for the immediate future, the impact of the 2007-2009 recession and of emergent environmental and economic trends has not been well explored. It has been reported that some national parks have been forced to cut hours and employees and to raise fees and taxes in an effort to counterbalance reduced funds from government sources. To minimize loss of business and maximize profits, outdoor recreation companies need to stay abreast of current trends in consumer spending and emerging changes in consumer attitudes. The companies able to survive economic shifts will be those best able to adjust to changing market conditions without losing the aesthetic appeal that draws consumers to the great outdoors.

Employment Advantages

While the BLS estimates that the outdoor recreation industry will continue to display steady growth during the next decade, average wages within the industry are consistently low compared with other jobs requiring similar levels of experience and education.

The recreation and entertainment industries rely on young and temporary workers to compose approximately 24 percent of their entire employee base, as compared to an average of 14 percent for all national industries. Outdoor recreation companies provide an excellent source of temporary and seasonal work, ideal for students seeking part-time employment during the winter or summer seasons. As a whole, the U.S. outdoor recreation industry accounts for more than 6 million jobs nationwide.

In addition, the outdoor recreation industry stimulates economic development and creates jobs in rural communities. The industry thereby provides jobs for many young and semiskilled workers living in communities with otherwise limited opportunities for employment. By creating a competitive, sustainable industry to compete with the industrial, manufacturing, and engineering industries that typically buoy rural economies, the outdoor recreation industry helps create economic development that is also sustainable within small, rural communities.

While the outdoor recreation industry might not offer as many career-oriented employment opportunities as some industries, it does offer a number of alternative benefits to employees, including the opportunity to learn more about and take part in outdoor recreation activities. A vast majority of those involved in the industry are active participants in outdoor activities, and they seek employment in the industry partly out of a desire to earn a living while participating in outdoor recreation.

Annual Earnings

The outdoor recreation industry experienced annual revenues of $289 billion in 2006. According to the BLS, the average weekly income of an industry employee in that year was approximately $332, which was relatively low compared to the $568 per week average for all private industries. Employees of retail stores are more likely to be offered benefits in addition to their basic wages, while tour guides, park attendants, and other nonretail employees often work for hourly wages without benefits. As in other recreation industries, many employees in outdoor recreation are forced to hold multiple jobs in order to meet their cost of living. Despite low earnings, the outdoor recreation industry continues to attract employees because of the intangible benefit of being closer to nature and simply enjoying being outdoors.

RELATED RESOURCES FOR FURTHER RESEARCH

AMERICAN ALLIANCE FOR HEALTH, PHYSICAL
   EDUCATION, RECREATION, AND DANCE
   1900 Association Dr.
   Reston, VA 20191-1598
   Tel: (703) 476-3400
   http://www.aahperd.org

AMERICAN CAMP ASSOCIATION
   5000 State Rd. 67 North
   Martinsville, IN 46151-7902
   Tel: (765) 342-8456
   Fax: (765) 342-2065
   http://www.ACAcamps.org

AMERICAN RECREATION COALITION
   1225 New York Ave. NW, Suite 450
   Washington, DC 20005-6405
   Tel: (202) 682-9530
   Fax: (202) 682-9529
   http://www.funoutdoors.com

NATIONAL PARK SERVICE
   1849 C St. NW
   Org. Code 2220
   Washington, DC 20240-0001
   Tel: (202) 208-6843
   http://www.nps.gov

NATIONAL PARKS AND CONSERVATION
   ASSOCIATION
   1300 19th St. NW, Suite 300
   Washington, DC 20036
   Tel: (800) 628-7275
   http://www.npca.org

NATIONAL RECREATION AND PARK ASSOCIATION
22377 Belmont Ridge Rd.
Ashburn, VA 20148-4501
Tel: (800) 626-6772
http://www.nrpa.org

OUTDOOR AMUSEMENT BUSINESS ASSOCIATION
1035 S Semoran Blvd., Suite 1045A
Winter Park, FL 32792
Tel: (407) 681-9444
Fax: (407) 681-9445
http://www.oaba.org

OUTDOOR FOUNDATION
4909 Pearl East Circle, Suite 200
Boulder, CO 80301
Tel: (303) 444-3353
Fax: (303) 444-3284
http://www.outdoorfoundation.org

ABOUT THE AUTHOR

Micah L. Issitt is a freelance writer specializing in history, ethnography, and ecology. He has been involved in the wildlife park industry since 1993, working at wilderness sanctuaries, national parks, and other recreational facilities. He has been writing about nature and outdoor activities since 1996, and his writing has appeared in numerous magazines, newspapers, and reference publications.

FURTHER READING

Beech, John G., and Simon Chadwick. *The Business of Tourism Management.* Upper Saddle River, N.J.: Prentice Hall, 2006.

Bell, Simon. *Design for Outdoor Recreation.* New York: Taylor and Francis, 1997.

Broadhurst, Rich. *Managing Environments for Leisure and Recreation.* New York: Routledge, 2001.

Fennell, David A. *Ecotourism: An Introduction.* New York: Routledge, 2003.

Forbes, M. S., F. S. Liljegren, J. T. Liljegren, and V. E. Lovejoy. *Outdoor Recreation Business Plan Guidebook.* Denver: U.S. Department of the Interior, Bureau of Reclamation, Policy and Program Services, Denver Federal Center, 2008. Available at http://www.usbr.gov/recreation/publications/BusPlanGuide.pdf

Gartner, W. C., and D. W. Lime. *Trends in Outdoor Recreation, Leisure, and Tourism.* Oxfordshire, England: CABI Press, 2000.

Jenkins, John. *Outdoor Recreation Management.* New York: Routledge, 1999.

Jensen, Clayne R., and Steven Guthrie. *Outdoor Recreation in America.* Champaign, Ill.: Human Kinetics, 2006.

Pigram, J. J. J., and John Michael Jenkins. *Outdoor Recreation Management.* Abingdon: Routledge, 2006.

U.S. Bureau of Labor Statistics. *Career Guide to Industries,* 2010-2011 ed. http://www.bls.gov/oco/cg.

———. *Occupational Outlook Handbook,* 2010-2011 ed. http://www.bls.gov/oco.

U.S. Census Bureau. North American Industry Classification System (NAICS), 2007. http://www.census.gov/cgi-bin/sssd/naics/naicsrch?chart=2007.

U.S. Department of Commerce. International Trade Administration. Office of Trade and Industry Information. Industry Trade Data and Analysis. http://ita.doc.gov/td/industry/otea/OTII/OTII-index.html.

U.S. Global Change Research Program. "Regional Paper: Rocky Mountain/Great Basin Region." 2003. http://www.usgcrp.gov/usgcrp/nacc/education/rockies-greatbasin/default.htm

Zueflie, Matt. "Leisure and Tourism Changing through the Great Recession." *The Athens News* (Ohio), July 30, 2009.

Paper Manufacturing and Products Industry

INDUSTRY SNAPSHOT

General Industry: Manufacturing

Career Cluster: Manufacturing

Subcategory Industries: Other Converted Paper Product Manufacturing; Paper Bag and Coated and Treated Paper Manufacturing; Paperboard Container Manufacturing; Pulp, Paper, and Paperboard Mills; Sanitary Paper Product Manufacturing; Stationery Product Manufacturing

Related Industries: Household and Personal Products Industry; Logging Industry; Printing Industry

Annual Domestic Revenues: $167.3 billion USD (IBISWorld Industry Market Research, 2009)

Annual International Revenues: $241 billion USD (Datamonitor, 2009)

Annual Global Revenues: $408.3 billion USD (IBISWorld Industry Market Research, 2009)

NAICS Number: 322

INDUSTRY DEFINITION

Summary

The paper manufacturing and products industry makes pulp, paper, and paper products that have been converted into end products from boxes to writing paper. The industry is subdivided into two industry groups. Pulp mills, paper mills, and paperboard mills (NAICS sector 3221) constitute the first industry group. Establishments that make products from purchased paper and other materials make up the second industry group, "Converted Paper Product Manufacturing" (NAICS sector 3222). These products are grouped together because their manufacture comprises a series of vertically connected processes consisting of three essential activities. First, the manufacturing of pulp involves separating the cellulose fibers from other impurities in wood or used paper. Second, paper is manufactured from pulp by forming the fibers into a sheet. Third, paper and pulp are converted into a wide variety of products by various cutting and shaping techniques.

History of the Industry

Humans have always strived to record their experiences and observations in some way. Before the invention of paper, various media were employed to carry information, including cave walls, stone, clay, plants, bones, and animal skins. The word "paper" derives from the Greek term for the ancient writing material called papyrus, which was formed from beaten strips of the aquatic papyrus plant, common in Egypt. Actually, papyrus is not considered to be true paper, because of the process used to create it. True papermaking was first documented in China about 105 C.E. What was revolutionary about this writing surface was that it was created through the process of macerating materials into separate fibers, suspending these fibers in a watery pulp, and drying them into sheets of paper.

The art of papermaking spread from China to Japan and Korea and then to Samarqand and Baghdad. Uses for paper were expanding, as evidenced by reports from Arab travelers, around 875 C.E., of seeing toilet paper in use in China. By the eleventh century, paper had spread to the Byzantine world and medieval Europe, especially Spain and Italy, where mills were established. Around 1450, the printing of Johann Gutenberg's Bible marked the beginning of book printing in Europe and the commencement of the use of paper on a comparatively large scale. By 1487, every country in Europe had adopted printing, and large quantities of paper were consumed in the printing of books.

For hundreds of years, cotton and linen rags were the papermaker's raw materials. In 1666, a serious rag shortage in Europe resulted in the issue of a decree prohibiting the use of cotton or linen for burial, in order to save linen and cotton for papermakers. For colonists in America, paper had to be imported and was highly prized and treasured. Many goods imported from Europe were wrapped in paper, and scraps of these packaging papers were hoarded and used for writing. In 1690, William Rittenhouse, who had acquired papermaking skills in the Netherlands, established the first paper mill in America, near Germantown, Philadelphia, Pennsylvania.

By 1776, the need for paper in America was so great that legislation obtained exemption from military service for all skilled papermakers. Linen and cotton rags for papermaking had become so scarce that committees of safety were appointed to encourage the saving of rags. During the American Revolution, paper was so hard to find that soldiers ripped pages from books to use them as wadding for their rifles. Around 1800, a machine was invented that allowed paper to be manufactured continuously rather than one sheet at a time.

Following the Civil War (1861-1865), paper pro-

Piles of spruce logs waiting to be processed. (©Dreamstime.com)

duction underwent a major transformation. New technologies permitted papermakers to process wood, which was relatively abundant, instead of rags, and to generate far greater quantities of energy from waterways. These developments precipitated a dramatic rise in the productive capacity of paper mills and caused a steep decline in paper prices. The modern paper industry is, in fact, defined by its use of wood.

Paper manufacturing and consumption grew exponentially and the United States became both the top producer and the top consumer of paper products in the world. Even while the Great Depression of the 1930's severely hurt other industries, it did not affect the pulp and paper industry as much, since paper was being used in new ways throughout the economy. World production of paper and board increased by more than 650 percent in the fifty years between 1950 and 2000.

By the 1980's, demand had begun to slow and currency exchange rates and global competition had begun to put price pressure on U.S. papermakers at the same time that large outlays of corporate resources were required to comply with environmental regulations. In 1990, the global market began growing steadily, but revenues and profits for U.S. companies shifted dramatically, because of rapidly increasing commodity prices and weaker demand. Global competition continued to increase as production capacity grew in Asia and Latin America. Papermakers in these emerging markets have enjoyed lower costs for fiber, labor, and energy and are not required to fund environmental compliance. As demand retreated and competition grew, manufacturers in developed countries were faced with continual needs to reduce production costs.

Plagued by fragmentation, overcapacity, and low profitability, North American paper manufacturers were forced to take drastic measures in an effort to remain competitive and profitable. The industry was consolidated in a series of mergers and

Cellulose, obtained from wood pulp and cotton, is used primarily to produce cardboard and paper. (©Moreno Soppelsa/ Dreamstime.com)

The Paper Products Industry's Contribution to the U.S. Economy

Value Added	Amount
Gross domestic product	$59.7 billion
Gross domestic product	0.4%
Persons employed	442,000
Total employee compensation	$31.5 billion

Source: U.S. Bureau of Economic Analysis. Data are for 2008.

acquisitions involving more than $60 billion in assets. In 1980, the 150 largest companies accounted for only 45 percent of production, but by 2000 they accounted for 70 percent of production. Capital spending declined severely and planned projects were canceled. Capacity reduction was achieved by closing down many older and less efficient mills, plants, and machines and taking extensive market-related downtime. Employment in the industry went from 650,000 in 1990 to 400,000 in 2009.

The Industry Today

Today paper and packaging are essential components of modern life. There are thousands of applications with high practical value, ranging from specialized commercial applications to printing paper and cardboard boxes. Personal and household paper products, such as bathroom tissue and paper towels, are used by virtually everyone.

The modern industry consists of two industry groups: pulp, paper and paperboard mills, and converted paper products manufacturing. In the first group, pulp mills create the pulp, a concentrated mixture of fibers suspended in liquid, by separating the cellulose fibers from the impurities in wood or other materials, such as recycled paper. Paper and paperboard mills manufacture various grades and types of paper and paperboard from pulp. Paper mills and manufacturers are organized by the types and grades of paper they produce.

The second industry group converts pulp, paper, and paperboard into a vast array of other products. The largest segment in this group consists of establishments that use corrugating, cutting, and shaping machinery to form paperboard into containers, boxes, corrugated sheets, pads, pallets, paper dishes, and fiber drums and reels. Other establishments cut, coat, treat, and laminate paper to make paper bags, labels, wrapping paper, food and beverage packaging, packaging for the pharmaceutical and cosmetics industries, and an endless array of other products. These manufacturers alone generate almost $75 billion in sales every year. Sales in this segment are highly sensitive to economic conditions and tend to mirror trends in retail and food services.

The second largest segment consists of firms that convert pulp and paper into sanitary paper products for household and personal use. Toilet paper is used by nearly 100 percent of the population in the United States, and paper towels and facial tissue are found in the vast majority of households. Personal care products such as sanitary napkins and tampons are necessities to a large segment of the population. Disposable diapers and wipes are used by fewer households, but a higher percentage of personal income is spent on these products. As the population ages, there has been a steady growth in the demand for incontinent-care products. Household and personal care products are sold mainly to grocery wholesalers and retailers. Since most of these products are considered necessities, sales of products in this segment are less sensitive to economic downturns than other types of products tend to be.

About 70 percent of all paper is produced at mills

Inputs Consumed by the Paper Products Industry

Input	Value
Energy	$13.6 billion
Materials	$74.6 billion
Purchased services	$19.2 billion
Total	$107.4 billion

Source: U.S. Bureau of Economic Analysis. Data are for 2008.

This machine is used to make paper and cardboard from recycled paper. (©Moreno Soppelsa/Dreamstime.com)

that are "integrated" with a pulp mill and paper mill at the same site. Large manufacturers are even further integrated with converting facilities, all of which are typically owned by the same company.

Taken as a whole, the U.S. pulp, paper, and converted paper products industry is among the largest U.S. manufacturing industries in dollar sales. It is also the most capital-intensive industry in the world, requiring large investments in fixed assets. High levels of competitive rivalry, slowing demand, low product differentiation, and high entry and exit costs give the advantage to large, vertically integrated companies. High levels of production efficiencies and careful capacity management are required to achieve an acceptable return on investment.

Today's technologies and advanced machinery have made papermaking faster and more efficient. While there may be fewer facilities than in the past, the remaining ones are more efficient. Labor productivity has increased. Capacity has come closer to demand and producer prices are increasing. New technology also has led to increasingly technical training for workers throughout the industry.

Computers and computer-controlled equipment aid in many functions, and there is increased use of robotics to move material within the plant.

Pulp and papermaking are energy-intensive industries, so companies are highly sensitive to changes in the price of energy as well as consumer and legislative concerns about environmental issues. The environmental performance of the industry has dramatically improved with investments in cleaner technologies. Pollution from water and air emissions has been significantly reduced, and dioxide-producing bleach is no longer used in most facilities. Today's industry is much more energy-efficient than in the past. It uses 85 percent less water than it did thirty years ago and generates 50 percent of its own energy.

These improvements come with a price. Regulation has a negative financial effect on the industry, as it restricts operators from certain activities, increases production costs, and reduces global competitiveness. In one of its 10-k reports, Kimberly-Clark estimated 2011 expenditures of $170 million for environmental compliance, including pollution-control-equipment operation and maintenance costs, governmental payments, and research and engineering costs.

Increased consumer focus on sustainability is also reflected in the industry's work to promote recycling. Today recovered paper has become the main resource for paper manufacturers, followed by wood pulp. Recycled paper uses less water and energy, but efforts to clean, deink, and prepare it for use sometimes result in products made from recycled materials being more expensive. The amount of recycled paper used in paper manufacturing continues to grow, however. In 2009, 63.4 percent of the paper consumed in the United States was recovered for recycling.

North American paper and paper products manufacturers continue to face increasing international competition. Until recently, the United States produced more paper and paperboard than any country in the world, but it has recently been eclipsed by China. Despite these difficult operating conditions, however, the industry remains one of the largest in the world and employs hundreds of thousands of people.

INDUSTRY MARKET SEGMENTS

The paper manufacturing and products industry is dominated by large global firms because of the capital-intensive nature of the business and the commodity nature of most products. The purchase and operation of massive and very expensive paper machines and the development and implementation of sophisticated technologies require that large amounts of resources be invested in fixed assets and research and development. The result is that most employees in the industry work for large global corporations. The number of employees a large company retains depends on the size of the operation. An integrated manufacturer needs em-

Recycled paper uses less water and energy, but efforts to clean, deink, and prepare it for use sometimes result in products made from recycled materials being more expensive. (©Moreno Soppelsa/Dreamstime.com)

ployees for pulping, papermaking, converting, and distributing its products. International Paper, a global paper and packaging company, operates 23 pulp, paper, and packaging mills; 157 converting and packaging plants; 19 recycling plants; and 3 bag facilities in the United States. Internationally, the company employs about sixty thousand people in production facilities that are spread across Europe, Asia, Latin America, and South America. Kimberly-Clark, a company offering personal care and consumer tissue products, has 112 manufacturing facilities in thirty-eight countries with fifty-six thousand employees.

Midsize firms tend to manufacture specialty papers or specialized converted products. They are more heavily represented in packaging and containers and might make products such as egg cartons.

Small firms in the United States tend to be highly specialized and to excel in areas requiring more hand work and less machinery.

In developing countries, small firms that make art paper and handmade paper containing fibers from exotic plants are more common than in the United States.

The following sections provide a comprehensive breakdown of each of these different segments.

Small Businesses

In 2007, small businesses made up about 30 percent of establishments in the industry but accounted for only about 2.5 percent of employment in the industry and less than 1.5 percent of industry revenue. Papermaking by hand can use a wide range of natural materials and produce unique textures and qualities. These products tend to be more artistic than scientific in nature. Low-volume handcrafted paper and niche-converting operations that do not require large investments in fixed assets make up most of these businesses. Products may be sold to an intermediary, such as a wholesale or retail establishment, or directly to the final customer though the establishment's own retail outlet or the Internet. Small businesses in the paper industry are more common in underdeveloped countries than in the United States.

Potential Annual Earnings Scale. The average earnings for a small business vary substantially depending on the size of the operation. A sole proprietorship with a single owner working part time may earn just a few thousand dollars a year, whereas a small manufacturer or a converting operation might pay much more.

Clientele Interaction. Small establishments rely on orders that are often tailored to a specific customer or an occasion, resulting in extensive and highly personalized interaction with the client. These establishments may work with a wedding planner, for example, to design and manufacture handmade invitations or with a small-business owner seeking unique packaging for a product line or personalized wrapping paper and boxes for a retail operation. Because small businesses rely on referrals and recommendations from their clients, they tend to maintain close and personal relationships.

Amenities, Atmosphere, and Physical Grounds. Because of cost constraints, smaller operations are not able to offer many amenities to their employees. The physical grounds for a small papermaker may range from a private home to a small manufacturing or retail operation. Most consist of home, office, and manufacturing work environments. Those firms that operate from private homes will reflect that environment, while others might provide coffee machines and refrigerators to store food and drinks.

Typical Number of Employees. Small organizations in this industry generally have fewer than twenty employees. Employees may range from one entrepreneur crafting handmade paper and paper products from a home to a small manufacturing or converting operation employing a dozen or so employees.

Traditional Geographic Locations. Small establishments in the paper industry can be found all over the world. In developing countries, they are often located close to fiber and water sources as well as markets for the products. Makers of handmade papers tend to be spread out fairly evenly across the United States, while small pulp, paper, and converting operations are more concentrated. Box, bag, and packaging manufacturers and to a lesser extent paper manufacturers are concentrated in California, New York, Florida, and Illinois. Small pulp operators are concentrated in the Great Lakes and Southeast regions.

Pros of Working for a Small Paper Manufacturing Organization. Owners and employees in small establishments tend to wear more than one hat. Performing myriad functions can lead to a better view of the entire operation and help develop flexibility and versatile skills in multiple areas. From a psychological standpoint, an employee of a small business may feel that his or her contribution is important to the success of the business as a whole. This feeling can contribute to a high level of job satisfaction. Staff members tend to work together closely and can develop long-lasting personal relationships at work. The opportunity to work part time or flexible hours is more prevalent in smaller business establishments than it is in larger concerns.

Owners and managers of smaller establishments do not necessarily need to attend college or have sophisticated technical skills. If there are machines involved, they are smaller and simpler to operate and maintain. While compliance with some environmental regulations may be required, it is on a much smaller scale than that facing larger firms.

Cons of Working for a Small Paper Manufacturing Establishment. In addition to offering fewer jobs in general, small establishments may be able to offer only limited salaries and benefits. There may not be as much opportunity for formal training and development. Along the same lines, the opportunity to learn the best practices on getting things done may be better in a larger company. Because there are fewer employees, the ability to delegate work can be limited.

Costs

Payroll and Benefits: Small establishments are more likely to hire part-time employees and might pay by the hour, by the job, or based on output. Benefits such as vacation and sick time are rare for part-time employees but may be offered to full-time employees at the discretion of the business owner. A smaller firm may be more willing to offer more flexible working hours and conditions.

Supplies: Small companies typically do not have the resources to invest a lot of capital in equipment and supplies. Basic office supplies (one or more computers, a printer, a copier, telephones, paper, and other items typically consumed in an office environment) as well as the raw materials and equipment for paper manufacture will be found, usually in limited numbers.

External Services: In many smaller mills, large engineering projects are contracted out. Small paper manufacturers may use bookkeeping or accounting services to help manage the financial aspects of the business. Transportation and delivery services to receive raw materials and deliver finished products are often required. The selling of the products can require credit-card processing systems or e-commerce services that allow payments and money transfers to be made through the Internet.

Utilities: Papermaking operations of all sizes require access to lots of water. For small manufacturing entities, where processes are mechanized, access to a large amount of energy is also required. A handmade paper business operating a retail outlet or selling on the Internet also requires telephone, cable, and Internet access.

Taxes: Tax requirements for a small business vary, depending on how the business is organized and whether a separate property is purchased or leased for making and/or selling products. Someone making handmade paper products and selling them on the Internet would pay personal income taxes. A partnership or corporation with a dedicated physical plant might pay corporate taxes and applicable property taxes.

Midsize Businesses

Midsize paper companies typically operate in a niche market where long, continuous production runs and economies of scale are not as important as they are for smaller businesses. Midsize paper companies account for 67 percent of establishments in the industry, 32 percent of the employees, and about 20 percent of the revenue.

Many independent operators that convert pulp and paper into other products fall into this category. Boxes used by department stores and other retailers and for textiles, wearing apparel, and hosiery are often made by midsize firms. Other companies in this category produce labels, envelopes, gift wrap, pressed and molded products such as egg cartons, and filter paper.

Potential Annual Earnings Scale. Wages for managers at midsize firms depend largely on the size of the operation and the position itself. There are more technicians and fewer engineers, and technical salaries tend toward $40,000 annually.

The average salary of a production worker is between $30,000 and $35,000.

Clientele Interaction. While in midsize paper manufacturing establishments the owners and sales force will have extensive contact with customers, the production workers will have substantially less. These companies often hire manufacturers' representatives or independent salespeople to represent their products. In that case, the clients interact with the representative more than with the company.

Amenities, Atmosphere, and Physical Grounds. Most midsize companies consist of office and manufacturing work environments. They typically offer their employees break rooms with coffee and vending machines and refrigerators to store food and drinks. Midsize operations may offer their employees gym memberships and flexible working conditions.

Typical Number of Employees. Midsize manufacturers generally have between twenty and five hundred employees. There are fewer part-time employees, and temporary employees are often hired to handle tasks during periods of peak demand.

Traditional Geographic Locations. Like larger manufacturers, midsize establishments are often located in proximity to raw materials, power sources, and consumer markets. Midsize manufacturers of pulp and paper tend to be concentrated in the Great Lakes area, especially Wisconsin, followed by the Southeast and Middle Atlantic regions. Midsize paper-converting operations are more widely distributed across the country and tend to be close to major markets.

Pros of Working for a Midsize Paper Manufacturing Establishment. A midsize organization can offer the best of both worlds. Employees at midsize firms often derive the benefit and satisfaction of feeling that their contribution is important to the success of the business. Midsize organizations are more likely than smaller organizations to offer competitive wages and benefits such as insurance, vacation time, and sick time. There are often some resources allocated to training and development, while opportunities for advancement are more plentiful because of the midsize firm's wider variety and number of positions. Because plants may run multiple shifts, there may be opportunities to work overtime and weekends and earn additional pay.

Cons of Working for a Midsize Paper Manufacturing Establishment. Midsize paper manufacturers often have older equipment, which can result in periods of frustrating downtime and lost productivity. Noise levels in the manufacturing area can be bothersome and midsize companies often do not have the resources to invest in sophisticated noise-reduction materials and technologies. Salaries and benefits are likely to be somewhat less than those larger establishments may offer for similar positions. Training and development opportunities might be limited. Along the same lines, the opportunity to learn the best practices for task performance may be better in a larger company. Finally, because there are fewer employees, the ability to delegate work may be limited.

Costs

Payroll and Benefits: A midsize paper manufacturer may have a larger number of more specialized positions than a smaller organization but not as much variety as a large operation. Most nonproduction employees are paid an annual salary and accrue benefits such as health insurance, vacation, and sick leave. They are generally not eligible for overtime pay, although this varies by employer. Production and maintenance workers are paid by the hour and often earn a higher hourly rate for working overtime, weekends, and holidays. Most hourly workers earn benefits in both union and nonunion environments. Incentive bonuses may be offered for some employees. Flexible benefits are often available to pay for health care and child care with pretax dollars.

Supplies: Midsize paper manufacturers need office supplies such as computers, printers, copiers, telephones, paper, and other items typically consumed in an office environment. They also require supplies used in the manufacturing process, such as machine parts and supplies to maintain equipment, computerized process equipment, and the work space. Some midsize firms also use vending and food-service supplies as well as cleaning supplies.

External Services: Many midsize paper manufacturers depend on external services functions that are not related to manufacturing. They may have their own sales force but are more likely to utilize independent sales or manufacturers representatives. They may also use independent accounting services, audit and security firms, and cleaning and housekeeping services.

Utilities: Midsize pulp and paper manufacturing operations are heavy users of water and energy. Some manufacturers produce a percentage of their own energy and have processes in place to reuse large quantities of water. They must often pay for wastewater discharge.

Taxes: Tax requirements for a midsize business vary, depending on how the business is organized and whether a separate property is purchased or leased for making and/or selling products. A partnership or corporation with a dedicated physical property might pay corporate taxes and applicable property taxes.

Large Businesses

Paper manufacturers are heavily skewed to this segment, given the economies of scale that exist in the industry. In 2007, less than 6 percent of firms in the industry accounted for more than 80 percent of the revenue and accounted for almost 70 percent of the employment.

Potential Annual Earnings Scale. The earnings of employees who work for large paper manufacturers vary considerably, depending on the position. A housekeeper or grounds manager generally makes just over $20,000 per year, while a chief executive officer may earn several hundred thousand. Profit sharing and incentive bonuses for executives and managers are more prevalent in larger companies. Some companies offer incentive pay to all employees to encourage productivity.

Clientele Interaction. Most large paper manufacturers have an internal sales force. These sales representatives will have contact with the wholesalers and retailers that buy their products. Customer service representatives interact with consumers by phone and Internet and help answer questions and resolve problems.

Amenities, Atmosphere, and Physical Grounds. A wide variety of working environments are found in large establishments. Employees may work in an office, a laboratory, a manufacturing plant, or a warehouse. Large paper manufacturers are often located in industrial parks or areas where there might not be much access to places for employees to buy meals, especially for night-shift workers. They generally provide cafeterias or vending machines and often utilize traveling food-service providers.

Parking lots are usually provided by the company. Some companies provide on-site exercise classes and gyms, and some provide child-care facilities as well.

Typical Number of Employees. Large paper and paper products manufacturers have five hundred or more employees. Large, integrated firms, such as International Paper and Kimberly-Clark, can have more than fifty thousand employees.

Traditional Geographic Locations. Traditionally, requirements for the production of paper included suitable raw materials, an abundant water source, and proximity to the consumer market. Therefore, large paper manufacturers tend to be concentrated in the Great Lakes area, especially Wisconsin, followed by the Southeast and Middle Atlantic regions. These regions are home to 65 percent of paper mills in the United States.

Pros of Working for a Large Paper Manufacturing Organization. A large organization is more likely to offer benefits such as insurance, vacation time, and sick time. Some offer on-site workout facilities, child-care facilities, and perhaps even access to doctors and occupational health nurses. More resources are allocated to training and development in a large company, and opportunities for advancement are more plentiful as a result of a wider variety and number of positions. Because their plants tend to operate around the clock, large companies can offer substantial opportunities to work overtime and weekends, providing employees the chance to earn additional pay.

Cons of Working for a Large Paper Manufacturing Organization. Overtime, however, can also be viewed as a "con." Overtime is common in large, around-the-clock plants, and while earning more money is a benefit, working long hours or night-shift hours can cause stress and can prove detrimental in other ways. In large factories that run twenty-four hours a day, many operators work on rotating schedules, which can cause sleep disorders and stress from constant changes in work hours. Managerial and administrative support personnel typically work five-day, forty-hour weeks in office settings, although some of these employees (generally those who occupy salaried, exempt positions, rather than hourly, nonexempt workers) may also work long hours without the option of overtime pay. Travel is an important part of the job for many managers and specialists.

Costs

Payroll and Benefits: A large manufacturer typically has a very complex payroll and benefit structure, given the scope and variety of jobs. Most nonproduction employees are paid an annual salary and accrue benefits such as health insurance, vacation time, and sick leave. They are generally not eligible for overtime pay. Production and maintenance workers are paid by the hour and often earn good wages at an hourly rate and have opportunities to work overtime, weekends, and holidays. Most hourly workers earn benefits in both union and nonunion environments. Incentive bonuses and profit sharing are usually offered to executives and sales people, but some companies have some kind of incentive structure for all employees. Flexible benefits are common, and it is often possible to pay for health care and child care with pretax dollars.

Supplies: Large manufacturers require two basic categories of supplies. The first consists of supplies for offices, such as computers, printers, copiers, telephones, paper, and other items typically consumed in an office environment. Second are supplies used in the manufacturing process. These are parts and supplies that are needed to maintain large, expensive pieces of equipment, computerized process equipment, and the work space. Most large firms also use vending, food-service, and cleaning supplies.

External Services: Depending on its integration strategy, a large manufacturer will either outsource most service functions or retain in-house service functions. Firms that focus on the core manufacturing area may utilize a large variety of external services, such as an outside sales force, independent accounting services, off-site customer service call centers, audit and security firms, uniform supply and cleaning services, and housekeeping services. Firms that are more vertically integrated may keep some or all of these functions in house.

Utilities: Large paper manufacturers are heavy users of water and energy. Some manufacturers are producing a percentage of their own energy and have processes in place to reuse large quantities of water. They must often pay for wastewater discharge.

Taxes: Large manufacturers are required to pay federal, state, and local corporate income taxes and property taxes. Sometimes large corporations can take advantage of tax credits offered by the state or federal government, such as credits for generating and using biomass and biofuels.

ORGANIZATIONAL STRUCTURE AND JOB ROLES

The paper manufacturing industry offers a wide variety of employment opportunities, but production occupations and occupations related to transportation and material moving make up the majority of the workforce. The type of work is generally determined by the product being manufactured and the manufacturing process. Since papermaking is a series of vertically connected processes, job roles contribute to one of the three essential activities: the manufacturing of pulp, the manufacturing of paper, or the conversion of paper into other products.

The following umbrella categories apply to the organizational structure of small, medium, and large manufacturers of paper and paper products:

- Business Management
- Business and Financial Operations
- Science and Engineering
- Office and Administrative Support
- Craft, Maintenance, and Repair
- Production Occupations
- Transportation and Material Moving

Business Management

Chief executives and other executive managers establish goals and objectives for the organization and develop strategies and policies designed to meet those goals and objectives. Other executives and managers direct the activities of various departments, business units, and functional units within the organization. Most management positions share the goal of maximizing sales, profit, and customer satisfaction. Duties and responsibilities include formulating and implementing plans and policies, managing daily operations, and guiding the use of materials and human resources. Marketing and sales managers direct efforts to promote and sell a company's products. They are often responsible for identifying and developing new products and markets, determining sales potential, and estimating demand. Computer and information systems managers direct the administration of technology such as network security and Web services. Engineering, science, and research and development managers are generally in charge of developing systems, developing new products, improving processes, and solving technical problems. They are often responsible for quality control. Production managers and plant managers direct activities and resources necessary for manufacturing products within parameters for quality, quantity, and cost. In smaller organizations an owner, partner, or general manager can be responsible for multiple areas, including purchasing, hiring, training, quality control, and day-to-day supervisory duties.

Many executive managers have advanced degrees in business or engineering, while mid- and lower-level managers often achieve management status though experience and job performance. Managers generally earn higher salaries than others in the organization. Excluding chief executives, the average salary for a manager in the paper industry is about $100,000 per year. Actual compensation varies by position, level of responsibility, and years of experience.

Occupations in the area of management include the following:

- Administrative Support Manager
- Advertising and Marketing Manager
- Sales Manager
- Computer and Information Systems Manager
- Engineering Manager
- Research and Development Manager
- Financial Manager
- Human Resources Manager
- Industrial Production Manager
- Purchasing Manager
- Transportation, Storage, and Distribution Manager
- Top Executive

Business and Financial Operations

These personnel make up the functional areas of running an organization that are not directly in-

volved in the manufacturing of the product. Business operations specialists in finance, accounting, and auditing conduct quantitative analyses. They examine, analyze, interpret, and estimate costs and other financial and budgetary data and records for the purpose of giving advice, assuring compliance, or preparing statements.

Network and computer systems and support specialists support an organization's information networks and systems. They analyze user requirements, procedures, and problems to automate or improve existing systems and review computer system capabilities, workflow, and scheduling limitations, and they perform necessary maintenance to support network availability and security. They may also design software or customize software with the aim of optimizing operational efficiency.

Marketing and marketing research specialists analyze markets, trends, competitors, prices, sales, and consumers to determine the potential for products. They develop advertising, promotion, pricing, and public relations strategies and inform product development. Sales specialists sell the organization's products to members of the distribution channel or directly to end users.

Purchasing specialists buy raw or semifinished materials for manufacturing as well as the machinery, equipment, or services necessary for manufacturing. Many also examine, evaluate, and administrate contract compliance. Production planning and logistics specialists analyze and coordinate production with demand, internal allocation of resources, distribution, storage, and delivery of raw materials and finished products.

Human resources specialists analyze job descriptions and position classifications; determine compensation and benefits; and recruit, train, and develop employees. They may also conduct organizational studies and evaluations, design systems and procedures, conduct work simplification and measurement studies, and prepare operations and procedures manuals to assist management in operating more efficiently and effectively.

Most specialists in the business and financial operations area require at least a bachelor's degree, while many employees have advanced degrees. The average pay for a business and financial operations specialist is around $65,000 per year.

Job areas in business and financial operations include the following:

- Accountant/Auditor
- Market Research Analyst
- Salesperson
- Network Specialist
- Purchasing Agent
- Production Planning and Logistics Specialist
- Human Resources Specialist

Science and Engineering

The running of a paper mill relies heavily on engineers. Some of the components in paper machines are large and move at very high speeds. The main functions of engineering departments are repair, maintenance, monitoring, calibration, and keeping abreast of the latest environmental and safety regulations. Because of the increasing number of devices on paper machines, proactive and predictive maintenance is important to reduce breakdowns, since the cost of a machine being shut down is very high. Industrial engineers and technicians design, develop, test, and evaluate integrated systems for managing industrial production processes. They may study and record time, motion, method, and speed involved in performance of production and other operations to establish standard production rates or improve efficiency and develop economical solutions to technical problems.

Mechanical engineers and technicians deal with the machines and equipment. They plan and design tools, engines, machines, and other mechanically functioning equipment to keep the paper machine running continuously in order to optimize production time available. They are involved in installation, operation, maintenance, and repair.

Electrical and electronics engineers and technicians are involved with power use and power management in the mill. They design, develop, test, or supervise the manufacturing and installation of electrical or electronic equipment, components, or systems. Environmental engineers, scientists, and technicians are involved in research, prevention, control, and remediation of environmental health hazards. Work may include waste treatment, site remediation, or pollution control technology.

Health and safety engineers and industrial product engineers promote work-site or product safety by applying knowledge of industrial processes, mechanics, chemistry, psychology, and industrial health and safety laws. They work with occupational health and safety specialists to review, evaluate, and analyze work environments and design programs and procedures to control, eliminate, and prevent disease or injury caused by chemical, physical, and biological agents or ergonomic factors.

Materials engineers and scientists study various natural and human-made materials to determine ways to improve or develop new materials, processes, applications, and machinery with specific properties for use in new and improved products and applications.

The paper industry involves the use of many chemicals and compounds. Chemical engineers, chemists, and chemical technicians work with dye, sizing, and various other chemicals to improve efficiency and make the process more cost-effective and environmentally friendly.

Average annual salaries for engineers are slightly greater than $80,000; scientists earn around $70,000 and technicians somewhat less than $50,000.

The science and engineering occupations in the industry include the following:

- Industrial Engineer
- Mechanical Engineer
- Mechanical Drafter
- Electrical and Electronics Engineer
- Chemical Engineer
- Environmental Engineer
- Health and Safety Engineer
- Materials Engineer
- Technician

Office and Administrative Support

This category is made up of various secretaries, administrative assistants, representatives, clerks, operators, and their front-line supervisors. They interact with customers, perform routine clerical and administrative duties, verify and keep records, handle shipping and receiving, and coordinate and expedite the flow of work and materials within or between departments.

The average pay for this category is about $35,000 per year, with front-line supervisors earning close to $55,000. Advanced degrees are not typically required, but office and administrative support personnel are expected to have excellent organizational and computer skills.

Occupations within this department include the following:

- Bookkeeping, Accounting, and Auditing Clerk
- Customer Service Representative
- Office Clerk
- Production, Planning, and Expediting Clerk
- Shipping and Receiving Clerk
- Stock Clerk
- Administrative Assistant
- Receptionist

Craft, Maintenance, and Repair

These are primarily craft and maintenance positions that are involved in the installation, maintenance, and repair of all of the production and processing machinery and systems, wiring, equipment, fixtures, pipelines, heating, cooling, control systems, and facilities.

A period of apprenticeship is generally required to qualify for craft occupations, such as electricians, plumbers, pipefitters, steamfitters, and millwrights. Machinery maintenance workers generally learn on the job, while industrial machinery mechanics usually need some technical education after completing high school. There are union and nonunion manufacturers; for union workers, salaries and benefits may be determined largely through collective bargaining. The average annual salary for a nonsupervisory position in this category is about $50,000.

Occupations within this category include the following:

- Electrician
- Industrial Machinery Mechanic
- Maintenance and Repair Worker
- Millwright
- Plumber, Pipefitter, and Steamfitter
- Welding, Soldering, and Brazing Worker

Production Occupations

This category represents the majority of the employment in the industry. There are hundreds of distinct job titles for workers in pulp and paper manufacturing and converting, but most set up, operate, or tend paper-goods machines that perform a variety of tasks, such as cutting, folding, drying, rolling, slitting, calendaring, winding, converting, corrugating, forming, coating, and gluing. Others perform duties requiring fewer specialized skills, such as supplying or holding materials and cleaning up the work space. There are also paper graders, sorters, stackers, counters, and testers.

A high school diploma or general equivalency diploma (GED) is sufficient for most entry-level production occupations, although familiarity with computers and some postsecondary training are needed for technical jobs and to operate sophisticated machinery. Most production workers are trained on the job to understand complex automated machinery and to recognize and solve problems. The average annual pay for nonsupervisory positions is about $37,000.

Occupations within this category include the following:

- Production Manager
- Production Worker
- First-Line Supervisor
- Paper Goods Machine Setter and Operator
- Cutting and Slicing Machine Setter and Operator
- Printing Machine Operator
- Team Assembler
- Packaging and Filling Machine Operator
- Inspector, Tester, Sorter, Sampler, and Weigher
- Coating, Painting, and Spraying Machine Setter and Operator
- Cementing and Gluing Machine Operator
- Extruding, Forming, Pressing, and Compacting Machine Setter and Operator
- Mixing and Blending Machine Operator
- Machinist
- Tool and Die Maker

Transportation and Material Moving

These workers operate industrial trucks or tractors equipped to move materials around a warehouse, storage yard, factory, construction site, or similar location. They manually move freight, stock, or other materials or perform other unskilled, general labor. These workers feed materials into or remove materials from machines or equipment that is automatic or tended by other workers. They pack or package by hand a wide variety of products and materials.

Like production workers, transportation workers require only a high school diploma or GED for most entry-level tasks. Most workers are trained on the job. Nonsupervisory workers earn about $34,000 annually.

Occupations within this area include the following:

- Industrial Truck and Tractor Operator
- Laborer and Freight, Stock, and Material Mover
- Machine Feeder and Offbearer
- Packer and Packager
- Truck Driver
- Conveyor Operator
- First-Line Supervisor

INDUSTRY OUTLOOK

Overview

The outlook for the paper manufacturing and products industry shows it to be stable, despite the struggle of North American and European companies to remain profitable during the 2000-2010 period. Global demand is estimated to increase an average of 2.3 percent annually to 2030 as emerging and developing countries increase their consumption of paper products.

Developed economies will continue to lose market share as emerging economies, especially in China, Latin America, and India, continue to add capacity and profit from their lower cost structure, but most of their output will feed the increasing demand in local markets. The high cost of transporting goods encourages manufacturers to produce products close to the markets where they will be consumed.

Because of limited access to raw materials, developing economies will still rely on imported pulp to feed their paper manufacturing operations, providing U.S. pulp manufacturers with an alternative avenue for revenue. While U.S. demand is falling, export growth has been on the rise since 2005. Even with increased revenue, profitability suffers, since domestic markets typically provide pulp millers with higher prices than export markets.

The 2007-2009 global economic crisis severely affected the industry, but the economy began to show signs of recovery in the second quarter of 2009, when gross domestic product (GDP), a frequently used economic indicator, began a steady climb. The industry was expected to recover and grow, though more slowly than in the past.

A pulp and paper mill. (©Dreamstime.com)

PROJECTED EMPLOYMENT FOR SELECTED OCCUPATIONS

Paper Manufacturing

Employment		Occupation
2009	Projected 2018	
15,510	13,300	Cutting and slicing machine setters, operators, and tenders
16,800	13,400	First-line supervisors/managers of production and operating workers
4,870	3,800	Industrial production managers
17,740	14,700	Industrial truck and tractor operators
77,340	64,600	Paper goods machine setters, operators, and tenders
13,670	11,600	Printing machine operators

Source: U.S. Bureau of Labor Statistics, Industries at a Glance, Occupational Employment Statistics and Employment Projections Program.

In North America, substantial restructuring, elimination of excess production capacity, and increased operating and production efficiencies will continue to improve profitability, return on equity, and return on capital employed. Lower pulp and energy prices will improve cost structures, and profitability will begin to improve over the 2010-2015 period.

Research and development will continue to focus on the economic and environmental aspects of paper manufacturing, resulting in decreased consumption of raw materials, energy, water, and noise. Other anticipated improvements include increases in the runability and lifetime of equipment and machines, increases in product quality, and process improvements. Focused efforts will be made to improve the quality of recovered paper and improve the recyclability of paper products. The number of facilities available to gather recycled paper and process it into usable raw materials will continue to increase. It is also expected that substantial levels of innovation will lead to new products and materials.

Pulp mills will focus on higher energy recovery. The industry already produces 50 percent of its own energy using biomass by-products from the production process to create biofuels. Some companies produce all their own energy and generate excess power, selling it back to local utilities.

Alternative fuel tax credits enjoyed by producers in the past few years have ended, but many see making and selling biofuels as a potential future revenue stream. The paper manufacturing and products industry could become a clean-energy supplier, producing 100 percent of its own needs and selling the excess. The future company in the industry might employ an integrated process that includes pulp and papermaking together with energy generation and the production of chemicals and biofuels. A long value chain of wood and fiber products is resource-, energy-, and carbon-efficient.

Total employment is projected to fall because of growth in productivity resulting from automation and equipment upgrades, but there are still many opportunities in the industry.

Employment Advantages

In spite of the decrease in total industry employment, as of 2010 the paper manufacturing and products industry remained an extremely large employer and there were still a multitude of opportunities across a highly diverse range of occupations. Higher levels of competition in this industry indicate that students who excel academically will be more likely to obtain positions. Demand for graduates in core engineering disciplines and people with strong management skills will remain high, as well as for graduates in all computer-systems disciplines. Individuals interested in careers in the environmental and sustainability fields will find opportunities and satisfaction in the ongoing accomplishments in the industry.

Because most large paper mills and manufacturers are located near lakes, rivers, and oceans, employees can enjoy the recreational opportunities that exist in those areas. Many people in this industry have weekend cottages and enjoy fishing, boating, and other water sports. Hunters take advantage of well-forested areas. Individuals who have a love of nature and enjoy being outdoors may wish to consider an occupation in this industry.

Annual Earnings

As the global economic recovery has progressed since 2009, prospects for the paper manufacturing and products industry have improved. Income statements for corporations in the sector showed revenues increasing slowly but steadily in each quarter of 2009 and in the first quarter of 2010. The first quarter of 2009 saw losses, but by the last quarter profits before taxes had climbed out of the red. Balance sheets began to look better as cash positions improved and both short- and long-term debt declined.

As manufacturers in North America and Europe continue to eliminate excess capacity, utilization rates will improve. Gains in production speeds will increase return on investments, and capital spending will focus on efficiency improvements. Increased productivity and lower cost structures will improve both the competitive positions of domestic corporations and profit levels.

The performance of the global paper products market is forecast to accelerate, with an anticipated compound annual growth rate (CAGR) of 8.4 percent for the five-year period 2009-2014, which is expected to drive the market to a value of $427.1 billion by the end of 2014. The performance of the domestic market is forecast to accelerate more slowly than the global market, with an anticipated CAGR of 2.2 percent for North America and 2.1 percent for the United States for the five-year period 2009-2014.

RELATED RESOURCES FOR FURTHER RESEARCH

AMERICAN FOREST AND PAPER ASSOCIATION
1111 19th St. NW, Suite 800
Washington, DC 20036
Tel: (800) 878-8878
Fax: (202) 463-2700
http://www.afandpa.org

CENTER FOR PAPER BUSINESS AND INDUSTRY
STUDIES
500 10th St. NW, 3d Floor
Atlanta, GA 30332-0620
Tel: (404) 894-1488
Fax: (404) 385-2414
http://www.cpbis.gatech.edu

PAPER INDUSTRY TECHNICAL ASSOCIATION
5 Frecheville Ct.
Bury, Lancashire B19 0UF
United Kingdom
Tel: 0161-764-5858
Fax: 0161-764-5353
http://pita.co.uk

TAPPI (TECHNICAL ASSOCIATION OF THE PULP
AND PAPER INDUSTRY)
15 Technology Parkway South
Norcross, GA 30092
Tel: (770) 446-1400
Fax: (770) 446-6947
http://www.tappi.org

ABOUT THE AUTHOR

Leslie Farison is a business librarian and assistant professor at Appalachian State University, Boone, North Carolina. She received her master's degree in library science from the University of Kentucky and her master's degree in business administration from Indiana University. Prior to becoming a librarian, she spent many years as a marketing professional, including several years at Kimberly-Clark Corporation. She has published in the *Journal of Education for Library and Information Science* and has written a book chapter titled "Data-Driven Cancellation Decisions" for the American Library Association publication *The Frugal Librarian: Thriving in Tough Economic Times.* She has presented at the Charleston Conference and the University of Louisville. Her research interests include economics in collection development, business information literacy, and international librarianship.

FURTHER READING

Bjorkman, A., D. Paun, and C. Jacobs-Young. "Financial Performance, Capital Expenditures, and International Activities of the North American Pulp and Paper Industry at Mid-Decade." *TAPPI Journal* 80, no. 10 (October, 1997): 71-84.

Carson, Thomas, and Mary Bonk. *Gale Encyclopedia of U.S. Economic History*. Detroit: Gale Group, 1999.

Converter. "New Technology Active in Sector." 46, no. 6 (October 28, 2008). Retrieved from Business Source Complete database.

Datamonitor. *Global Paper Products: Industry Profile*. March 8, 2010. Retrieved from MarketLine database.

_____. *Paper and Paperboard in the United States*. March 15, 2010. Retrieved from MarketLine database.

Encyclopedia of American Industries. Millerton, N.Y.: Grey House, 2008.

Holik, Herbert. *Handbook of Paper and Board*. Weinheim, Germany: Wiley-VCH, 2006.

Hunter, Dard. *Papermaking: The History and Technique of an Ancient Craft*. New York: Knopf, 1947.

IBISWorld. *Cardboard Box and Container Manufacturing in the U.S.: Industry Report 32221*. February, 2010. Retrieved from IBISWorld Industry Market Research database.

_____. *Cardboard Mills in the U.S.: Industry Report 32213*. June, 2009. Retrieved from IBISWorld Industry Market Research database.

_____. *Coated and Laminated Paper Manufacturing in the U.S.: Industry Report 32222*. February, 2010. Retrieved from IBISWorld Industry Market Research database.

_____. *Labels, Egg Cartons, and Other Paper Product Manufacturing in the U.S.: Industry Report 32229b*. January, 2010. Retrieved from IBISWorld Industry Market Research database.

_____. *Office Stationery Manufacturing in the U.S.: Industry Report 32223*. May, 2010. Retrieved from IBISWorld Industry Market Research database.

_____. *Paper Mills in the U.S.: Industry Report 32212*. February, 2009. Retrieved from IBISWorld Industry Market Research database.

_____. *Sanitary Paper Product Manufacturing in the U.S.: Industry Report 32229a*. February, 2010. Retrieved from IBISWorld Industry Market Research database.

_____. *Wood Pulp Mills in the U.S.: Industry Report 32211*. November, 2009. Retrieved from IBISWorld Industry Market Research database.

Nurmi, Ville. "Future Trends of HRD in the Finnish Pulp and Paper Industry." *Human Resource Development International* 10, no. 1 (2007): 107-113.

O'Hara, Frederick M., Jr., and F. M. O'Hara III. *Handbook of United States Economic and Financial Indicators*. Westport, Conn.: Greenwood Press, 2000.

Organization for Economic Cooperation and Development. *OECD Environmental Outlook to 2030*. Paris: Author, 2008.

Packaged Facts. *The U.S. Market for Household Paper Products*. December, 2005. Retrieved from MarketResearch.com Academic database.

Parker, Philip M. *The 2006-2011 World Outlook for Paper Mills*. San Diego, Calif.: ICON Group, 2005.

Parsons, Charles K. *Workplace Transformation and Human Resource Management Practices in the Pulp and Paper Industry*. Atlanta: Center for Paper Business and Industry Studies, Georgia Institute of Technology, 2004.

Patrick, Ken, and Glenn Ostle. "Outlook: North America 2010." *Paper 360* 5, no. 1 (January/February, 2010): 8-11.

PricewaterhouseCoopers. *CEO Perspectives: Viewpoints of CEOs in the Forest, Paper, and Packaging Industry Worldwide*. Available at http://www.Pwc.Com/en_gx/gx/forest-paper-packaging/ceo2009/index.Jhtml.

_____. *Global Forest, Paper, and Packaging Industry Survey*. Available at http://www.Pwc.Com/en_gx/gx/forest-paper-packaging/2009-fpp-survey/index.Jhtml.

Smith, Maureen. *The U.S. Paper Industry and Sustainable Production: An Argument for Restructuring*. Cambridge, Mass.: MIT Press, 1997.

Standard and Poor's Industry Surveys. *Paper and Forest Products*. Available at http://www.netadvantage.standardandpoors.com.

Thompson, Claudia G., and the American Institute of Graphic Arts, Boston Chapter. *Recycled Papers: The Essential Guide.* Cambridge, Mass.: MIT Press, 1992.

U.S. Bureau of Labor Statistics. *Career Guide to Industries*, 2010-2011 ed. http://www.bls.gov/oco/cg.

_____. *Occupational Outlook Handbook*, 2010-2011 ed. http://www.bls.gov/oco.

U.S. Census Bureau. North American Industry Classification System (NAICS), 2007. http://www.census.gov/cgi-bin/sssd/naics/naicsrch?chart=2007.

Wilkinson, Norman B. *Papermaking in America.* Greenville, Del.: Hagley Museum, 1975.

Young, Rod. "Rollercoaster Ride in Recovered Paper Continues." *PPI: Pulp and Paper International* 52, no. 5 (2010): 48.

Passenger Transportation and Transit Industry

INDUSTRY SNAPSHOT

General Industry: Transportation, Distribution, and Logistics

Career Cluster: Transportation, Distribution, and Logistics

Subcategory Industries: Ambulance Service; Charter Bus Industry; Commuter Rail Transportation; Employee Bus Transportation; Handicapped Passenger Transportation; Interurban and Rural Bus Transportation; Rail Transportation; Scenic and Sightseeing Transportation; School Bus Transportation; Taxi and Limousine Services; Urban Transit Systems; Van Pool Services; Water/Ferry Transportation

Related Industries: Airline Industry; Automobiles and Personal Vehicles Industry; Freight Transport Industry; Mass Transportation Vehicles Industry; Shipbuilding, Submarines, and Naval Transport Industry

Annual Domestic Revenues: $40 billion USD (U.S. Economic Census, 2007)

Annual International Revenues: $134 billion USD (Organization for Economic Cooperation and Development, 2009)

Annual Global Revenues: $174 billion USD (Organization for Economic Cooperation and Development, 2009)

NAICS Numbers: 482-483, 485

INDUSTRY DEFINITION

Summary

The passenger transportation and transit industry comprises a diverse range of transport methods, all with the common goal of moving people to their desired locations. Modes of transportation are available to cover long or short distances, over land or water. The routes may be structured and scheduled, moving hundreds of people at a time, such as urban transit, rail, or ferry services, or under the direction of a single person or small group, as in taxi, limousine, or ambulance services. Companies in this industry can range from a single, independent owner-operator of a car service to a multibillion-dollar corporation covering great distances with thousands of vehicles and employees. Municipal transportation systems are transforming into highly efficient and economical options for travelers. Improvements in traffic patterns and planning in this industry are the focus of dedicated research departments within academic institutions and government agencies around the world.

History of the Industry

Since ancient times, people have needed to travel from place to place. Most early travel was done on foot or with the help of animals. People covered long distances on land, but ferries were created to assist with water crossings and were noted in early Greek mythology. In addition to providing safe water crossing, it was believed that ferries transported the souls of the deceased to their final resting place; the dead often were buried with a ferry coin under the tongue or covering each eyelid.

Early passenger transport involved the use of a cart pulled by an animal or person. The first taxi meter was used in ancient Roman cities. A reservoir of small balls was attached to the axle of a passenger cart. As the cart moved, the balls were released one by one, and the passenger paid a fare based on the number of balls that had fallen. The first structured transit line was organized in Paris in 1662 by physicist and mathematician Blaise Pascal, better known for his contributions to barometric pressure. This multiseat carriage service operated for fifteen years until influence from Parisian nobility raised the fares beyond the means of the general public. Similar stagecoach operations within cities did not reappear until the early 1800's. In England, Walter Hancock revolutionized public transportation with the creation of the first steam-powered bus. These buses were more cost-efficient and alleviated many troubles of horse-drawn carriages, but strict legislation and high tolls discouraged the new buses from running. Abraham Brower, an American entrepreneur, pioneered bus use in New York City in 1829. News of its efficiency quickly spread, leading to bus services being instituted in Philadelphia, Baltimore, and Boston by 1844.

The Metro Light Rail connects Phoenix, Tempe, and Mesa. (©Anton Foltin/Dreamstime.com)

Inputs Consumed by the Transit and Ground Passenger Transportation Industry

Input	Value
Energy	$5.4 billion
Materials	$2.8 billion
Purchased services	$2.5 billion
Total	$10.7 billion

Source: U.S. Bureau of Economic Analysis. Data are for 2008.

In Europe, Julius Griffiths first patented a passenger road locomotive in 1821, but it was not until 1825 that regularly scheduled passenger trains were developed by the Stockton & Darlington Railroad Company. The company's locomotives were designed by George Stephenson, an English inventor, and pulled six coal cars and 450 passengers in twenty-one cars, nine miles per hour. In 1830, the first steam-powered passenger train in the United States, called the Best Friend of Charleston, carried 141 passengers six miles on its first trip. Within the decade 2,218 more miles of rail track had been laid, linking even more communities. Passenger rail travel continued to expand and flourish, carrying more than 1.2 billion passengers annually by 1920. The advances in diesel engines in the 1930's made rail travel even faster, although passenger numbers did drop significantly during the Depression era.

Cable cars became a very popular mode of transport in the United States. They first were used in San Francisco in 1873, and within ten years, similar cars were operating in Chicago, New York, and Philadelphia. New York's Brooklyn Bridge cable car carried more than 9 million passengers during its very first year. In 1882, Ernst Werner von Siemens began experimenting with the Elektromote, the first electric trolley car, in Berlin. Richmond, Virginia, began testing North America's first electric street railway in 1888. At the Paris Exhibition in 1900, an experimental trolley line was used to move visitors. This innovation led to implementation of Europe's first urban trolley car service in Bielathal, Germany, in 1901.

As a solution to the congestion of New York City streets, *Scientific American* editor Alfred Ely Beach suggested taking transportation underground. His "Pneumatic Transit" opened in 1870 and used a 100-horsepower fan to propel a passenger car through a 312-foot (one city block) underground wind tunnel. This odd invention paved the way for modern subterranean subway systems. The first subway system in the United States was the Interborough Rapid Transit system in New York, which was completed in 1904 and carried more than 150,000 passengers on its first day.

The Industry Today

The passenger transportation industry has evolved from the simple movement of people across distances to a highly competitive, increasingly efficient means of transportation incorporating a wide range of service options to passengers. In the United States in 2008, there were more than 7,700 operational public transit systems taking people on some 10.5 billion trips, bringing public transit ridership to its highest level in five decades. Many large metropolitan public transportation corporations have diversified to include all modes of travel within their jurisdiction, including buses, commuter rail, ferry boats, light and heavy rail, paratransit, trolley buses, and vanpools.

The Transit and Ground Passenger Transportation Industry's Contribution to the U.S. Economy

Value Added	Amount
Gross domestic product	$23.2 billion
Gross domestic product	0.2%
Persons employed	438,000
Total employee compensation	$15.0 billion

Source: U.S. Bureau of Economic Analysis. Data are for 2008.

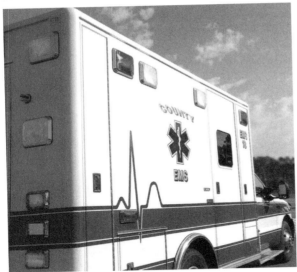

Ambulance services are included in the passenger transportation industry. (©Cheryl Casey/Dreamstime.com)

As metropolitan areas experience increased development and sprawl, demand grows for public transportation options. Although North Americans enjoy the convenience of driving their own vehicles, mounting fuel, parking, and insurance costs are leading many to look into alternate transportation options. Public transit systems are inexpensive alternatives, but predetermined routes and strict schedules do not work for everyone. Alternatives such as taxis, limousines, sedans, and shuttles offer more flexibility and convenience, but at higher costs.

Costs and concerns surrounding air travel have risen in the past decade, leading more people to explore bus and rail travel for both business and recreation. Distances may take longer to cover, but the scenic route options, scheduled stops, vast network of destinations, and low fares make land travel an attractive alternative.

Ambulance services are included in the passenger transportation industry. In many countries, ambulance service is operated as part of the health care system; in the United States, ambulance service generates billions of dollars in revenue. American Medical Response is one of the largest services, operating more than four thousand vehicles, and carrying some 3.5 million patients each year.

Many companies in the passenger transportation industry are investigating multimodal transportation options, partnerships, and expansion of core services. Metropolitan transit services may include several modes of transportation in order to cover a great geographic area and meet the needs of their ridership by linking them to additional services. New York City offers the public a linked system of rail, bus, subway, and ferry options. Several cities provide bike racks on buses and trolleys to accommodate people who wish to travel a portion of their commute on bicycle and link to public transit for another portion. Passenger transportation companies are expanding their services to provide scenic tour options and destination bus trips for holidays or sightseeing; rail companies such as Amtrak are partnering with hotels and attractions to provide package and themed vacations. Passenger transportation companies want to use all of their potential space and energy output to generate revenue, so many have combined passenger transport with freight transport. An example is Greyhound Lines, the bus company that carries passengers as well as packages.

All passenger transportation relies heavily on the infrastructure of the served area. Roads, rails, and ports must be maintained to ensure passenger safety, and a great deal of the responsibility and cost lies with municipal or other governments.

These buses are equipped with bike racks on front to accommodate those who wish to bike and bus to work. (©Bill Gillam/Dreamstime.com)

Passenger transportation modes are the focus of a great deal of research. Research highlights include improved efficiency, lower costs, and cleaner fuels to reduce environmental impact. Many metropolitan transit systems have made the switch to buses that run on natural gas. In 1999, commercial bus service in Christchurch, New Zealand, began using hybrid electric vehicles, and Seattle became the first city to put General Motors hybrid transit buses into service in 2004.

INDUSTRY MARKET SEGMENTS

Small Businesses

Small passenger transportation companies can be a one-person, owner-operator business or a service of up to fifty employees taking on a range of roles. The most common type of small business in this industry is a taxi, limousine, or car service. These companies can be completely independent, made up only of a driver who manages dispatch, transport, and all other aspects of the business. In other cases, a small-business owner might manage a fleet of up to twenty vehicles. The owner hires dispatchers and drivers to operate the vehicles, rotating their schedules so at least one vehicle is in operation around the clock. Another popular arrangement is to have drivers lease vehicles from the owner for a shift or other specified period of time. Most of these small businesses stay confined to a specific geographic area or route, such as airport transfers. They may be contacted through telephone or online dispatch, flagged down on the street, or contracted by organizations or corporations to transport people on an on-call basis. Common modes of transportation for most small businesses are rickshaw cart (foot, bicycle, or motorized), boat, motorcycle, taxi, limousine, van, or sedan car.

Potential Annual Earnings Scale. Small transportation operators earn approximately $18,000 to $27,000 per year, but earnings can vary widely by region and consistency of work available. Dispatchers and administrative positions in these small businesses usually are paid an hourly wage or salary, while drivers typically are not. If a driver is not the owner of the vehicle, he or she must make an arrangement to lease the vehicle from its owner and must pay the operating expenses. This can be a challenging arrangement because of fluctuations in traffic patterns, weather, and demand for services. Average fare revenue for a taxi driver in the United States is $150 per shift; however, fuel and lease costs can reduce this total by more than half. Tipping is customary for passengers and can increase revenue by 15 to 20 percent for good service.

Clientele Interaction. The drivers for small transportation businesses most often pick up clients and take them to their destinations, with minimal to no interaction with a remote dispatcher. For some car services, the dispatcher and driver are the same person. Repeat business and recommendations from happy customers are keys to success, so all clientele interaction must be positive. Employees often are encouraged to meet standards for personal appearance and vehicle cleanliness.

Hailing a taxi in New York. (©Zygomaticus/Dreamstime.com)

Amenities, Atmosphere, and Physical Grounds. Small passenger transportation companies may have a small hub or office space, but frequently their transport vehicles are considered their offices. The dispatch center may be located in a home office or in a vehicle, with calls managed by cellular telephone.

Typical Number of Employees. As in most small-business situations, the goal is to keep expenses low and revenues high. As fuel and insurance costs rise, a business might hire or lease its vehicles to operate twenty-four hours per day, rotating among operators. A small company usually is managed by a single individual, depending on the workload and geographic area the company serves. The typical number of employees for a small passenger transportation company can range from one to fifty.

Traditional Geographic Locations. Most small businesses serve specific geographic areas, such as a single city or districts or routes within a city. Many limit service only to downtown areas, resort districts, or to and from major airports. Most taxi or car services will take passengers to any desired destination, although fares to some distant locations may be declined because of the prohibitive cost of the return trip for the driver. Shuttle companies operate on structured schedules between predetermined locations. Smaller and nonmotorized transportation options typically remain within a very small, specific service district.

Pros of Working at a Small Passenger Transportation Company. Independent operators and driver have a great deal of flexibility and can usually decide how much and when they want to work. Small companies or individuals who hold contracts for service with other companies can have regular routes, allowing a familiarity with an area and frequent passengers. There usually is very limited direct supervision for employees of small businesses, and they most often work alone.

Cons of Working for a Small Passenger Transportation Company. Within smaller passenger transportation companies there is limited opportunity for advancement. A job with a small company also might require employees to take on roles and responsibilities outside their expected job description. Often, without set service contracts or scheduled routes, demand fluctuations, traffic patterns, and weather conditions can make income unpredictable. Passenger transportation operators often work long hours and can encounter challenging, dangerous, and possibly criminal situations.

Costs

Payroll and Benefits: Typically, small passenger transportation operators earn and record their own fares or can be paid hourly wages based on completed trips. Administrative or dispatch employees usually receive hourly wages or salaries and the same benefits as other workers, at the discretion of the owner or manager; however, most independent operators are not entitled to benefits.

Supplies: The mode of transportation determines the supplies required. Employees must have a clean, properly maintained vehicle with adequate fuel as well as any safety equipment required by local law. Some businesses require communication systems to connect dispatchers to operators; these systems must be maintained.

External Services: Maintenance of vehicles is the key to sustaining a small passenger transportation business. Fuel, repair, and insurance costs can be considerable. Also, a communication system such as cellular telephones, wireless devices, or two-way radios must be maintained.

Utilities: Many small businesses do not have central offices or service centers, so utility costs are minimal.

Taxes: Small businesses are required to pay local, state, and federal income taxes, as well as any required regional business and service taxes. Tips for service are common in this industry and also subject to federal income tax. In many cities, taxi drivers must possess a medallion issued by a regulatory agency. In New York City, a limited number of medallions are issued; they are transferable but can be very costly.

Midsize Businesses

Midsize passenger transportation companies usually operate within a larger geographic area and may have more services and employees than a small business. Midsize companies typically have a fleet of vehicles, focused on a single mode of transportation. They may confine transport within a specific area or offer service between several states or cities. Midsize businesses usually have centralized dispatch hubs and may offer online reservation services, schedules, and vehicle-tracking capabilities.

Potential Annual Earnings Scale. Midsize transportation businesses have more employees and more positions within the company, possibly including vehicle operators or drivers, dispatchers, ticket clerks, customer service agents, managers, supervisors, and technical support staff. Wages for these positions vary by region and job responsibilities. Entry-level or nonsupervisory workers can expect to earn $17,000 to $32,000 annually. Supervisory and management positions will have higher earnings, depending on qualifications and responsibilities.

Clientele Interaction. This industry is service- and customer-based, so clientele interaction is very common; however, as the size of the business increases, more positions become available that involve less direct interaction with customers. Telephone customer service and requests are still very common, although many midsize businesses have started implementing online service options. The vehicle operator or driver still has the greatest amount of interaction, and personnel such as guides for scenic tours are hired to provide additional service to riders As with any company in the service industry, repeat business and recommendations from happy customers are key to success, so all clientele interaction must be positive. Employees often are required to maintain appearance standards and wear uniforms.

Amenities, Atmosphere, and Physical Grounds. Midsize transportation service businesses often maintain service kiosks or station stops and waiting areas as well as dispatch offices, retail spaces, and lots for the storage and maintenance of fleet vehicles.

Typical Number of Employees. The typical number of employees for a midsize passenger transportation business depends on the service provided, mode of transportation, and geographic area served. It can range from fifty to one thousand employees, covering a wide range of positions.

Traditional Geographic Locations. Midsize transportation businesses usually serve larger geographic areas than do smaller companies. They also can simply have more vehicles in their service fleets. These businesses typically operate a single mode of transportation, such a shuttle buses, taxis, or water taxis, within a specific area.

Pros of Working for a Midsize Passenger Transportation Company. Midsize companies tend to pay employees an hourly wage or annual salary rather than giving them independent contractor status, although some drivers do operate independently under the umbrella of the larger company. Employees normally experience more income stability. Midsize companies often provide benefits and uniforms to their employees. Many have their own fleets of vehicles; therefore, employees are not required to provide and maintain their own.

Cons of Working for a Midsize Passenger Transportation Company. Midsize businesses usually operate on a more structured schedule than small companies, and employees receive more direct supervision and less flexibility.

Costs

Payroll and Benefits: Midsize passenger transportation companies typically pay their personnel an hourly wage, although drivers often are paid a portion of their completed trip fares. Full-time employees usually receive the same vacation and benefits as other workers.

Supplies: Midsize companies usually have fleets of transportation vehicles that require supplies for cleaning and maintenance. Supplies also may be necessary for ticketing and communication systems. Different modes of transportation require specific safety equipment, such as life preservers for water transportation.

External Services: Midsize businesses need to maintain the vehicles they use. Fuel, repair, and insurance costs for a fleet can be considerable. Often, vehicle maintenance and repair are contracted out as needed. Communication systems linking dispatchers to service personnel must be maintained, such as cellular telephones, wireless devices, Global Positioning Systems (GPSs), or two-way radios. Transportation businesses may rely on partnerships with other businesses, such a tourism operators, to provide referrals to potential customers.

Utilities: Utilities depend on the physical space or property type maintained by a business. Large office spaces will require electricity, heating, water, and sewer service. Internet and telephone services are the key to communication with customers and operators within the business and need to be maintained.

Taxes: Midsize businesses are required to pay local, state, and federal income taxes, as well as any required regional business and service taxes. Tips for service are common in this industry and also subject to federal income tax. In many cities, taxis must possess a medallion from a regulatory agency.

Large Businesses

Large passenger transportation companies are the most well known in this highly competitive industry. They may employ thousands of people and serve vast geographic areas or supply public transportation to a single metropolitan area. The Metropolitan Transportation Authority of New York City has an annual operating budget of more than $11 billion and employs more than 65,000 people in order to meet the travel needs of some 8 million people each day. Amtrak employs more than 26,000 people to maintain the daily service of more than 300 trains. ComfortDelGro is a transportation holding company based in Singapore that controls bus and rail operators and transit and taxi companies in Singapore but also has significant bus and taxi operations in several markets in the United Kingdom, Ireland, China, and Australia. Large companies might offer a variety of transit modes or provide a single service, covering a large geographic area. Large companies tend to diversify their services by providing passenger transport in combination with freight or courier service, or in partnership with other service providers to create package services. Some large companies are owned and operated by municipal governments and receive subsidy and stimulus funds in addition to fare revenue to provide service; others are contracted, privately owned, or publicly traded corporations.

Potential Annual Earnings Scale. The annual earnings for large passenger transportation businesses vary widely depending on position and job responsibilities. Hourly wages for transit drivers and operators across the United States range from $10.62 to $16.8, while fleet mechanics earn an hourly wage of $15.59 to $20.80. Managers, supervisors, and directors earn annual salaries over $60,000.

Clientele Interaction. Customer service is most often provided online or by telephone, but ticket agents and drivers have almost constant clientele interaction. Transit systems are becoming increasingly automated, limiting interaction in order to increase efficiency and improve safety of employees. By limiting the vehicle operators' customer interaction, there also is less opportunity for driver distraction, which is a significant safety risk. Personnel, as representatives of the company, are required to wear uniforms or identification, adhere to appearance standards, have good communications skills, and be knowledgeable about the services, safety, and policies of their specific company.

Amenities, Atmosphere, and Physical Grounds. Large passenger transportation compa-

nies can provide services throughout large metropolitan cities, states, or countries. Large companies have centralized corporate offices where administrative operations are managed and facilities for storing and servicing fleet vehicles. Some large companies maintain depots and waiting areas for their customers; these may simply be shelters from weather or large complexes with food, shopping, and business services. The atmosphere can be stressful as the movements of millions of people each day need to be efficient and safe.

Typical Number of Employees. Large passenger transportation companies typically have thousands of employees. Most are full-time employees, although casual and part-time staff can be brought in during high-volume periods, events, or commuter rush hours. Deutsche Bahn, a Germany-based international mobility and logistics company whose core business is rail activities, employs a workforce of more than 251,000 worldwide to transport more than 5 million passengers and 1 million tons of goods every day.

Traditional Geographic Locations. Large companies serve many diverse areas but often have their headquarters in major metropolitan cities.

Pros of Working for a Large Passenger Transportation Company. Transportation and transit workers in many regions are municipal employees with the ability to unionize and collectively bargain for better wages and benefits. Benefits provided to almost all workers include cost of living adjustments, paid sick days, overtime pay, health insurance, and pensions. Wages and benefits for large businesses are comparable to or better than the national average. Employees at larger companies normally are responsible for a specific job, rather than covering multiple roles as often is required by smaller companies.

Cons of Working for a Large Passenger Transportation Company. These companies are a very popular career choice for many people and entry-level positions require minimal education; therefore, the hiring process can be very competitive. Some metropolitan transit systems require potential employees to take qualification examinations. Many large companies provide around-the-clock service, and in order to accommodate this, many positions require a lot of shift work. The environment, time commitments, and strict schedules can be stressful for some people.

Costs

Payroll and Benefits: Large companies employ thousands of people with varying skills and job descriptions. Large teams of people are hired solely to manage payroll and benefits for employees.

Supplies: Transportation costs, including vehicles, fuel, and other maintenance and cleaning supplies, are significant for large companies. New York's Metropolitan Transit Authority budgets more than $160 million for fuel costs. Materials and supplies in a large business's operating budget consist primarily of items for maintenance and improvement of property and equipment as well as general supplies to run the business operations. In 2008, Amtrak reportedly spent more than $201 million for these materials. Many large companies are able to negotiate fuel-hedging programs in an attempt to stabilize fuel costs; most also are upgrading and retrofitting their fleets to use electric, hybrid, and hydrogen fuel-cell technology.

External Services: Large passenger transportation and transit companies tend to have internal staff to cover all requirements for operations. Maintenance of facilities and equipment often is managed on site by employees of the company. Communication services are provided by national carriers and need to be of the highest quality and reliability.

Utilities: Large companies operate thousands of offices, stations, ports, and hubs. Utilities include water, gas, sewer, electricity, heat and air-conditioning, and communication services.

Taxes: Large businesses are required to pay local, state, and federal income taxes, as well as regionally required business and service taxes. Tolls and services fees or international charges may be incurred. In many cities, taxis must be in possession of a medallion issued by a regulatory agency. Some companies receive federal grants that also may be subject to taxation.

ORGANIZATIONAL STRUCTURE AND JOB ROLES

The organizational structure of a passenger transportation company usually is based on the mode of transportation, size of the company, and purpose of the service being provided. In very general terms, passengers who need to travel from one place to another will solicit the service that best suits their needs and budgets. Transportation companies employ thousands of people in numerous positions to ensure safety and efficiency of travel. Because of the responsibility of ensuring passenger safety, employees in this industry are subject to random drug and alcohol testing and pre-employment investigation. The Metropolitan Transportation Authority, North America's largest transit system, which operates public transit in New York and its surrounding area, employed more than 68,000 people in 2008. Some larger companies operate internationally, such as ComfortDelGro, the world's second largest transport company, which is headquartered in Singapore but also operates in China, the United Kingdom, Ireland, Australia, Vietnam, and Malaysia.

The following umbrella categories apply to the organizational structure of businesses in the passenger transportation and transit industry:

- Business Management
- Customer Services
- Sales and Marketing
- Facilities and Security
- Technology, Research, Design, and Development
- Production and Operations
- Distribution
- Human Resources

Business Management

Management and executive positions are the highest ranking positions within passenger transport and transit companies. These positions normally comprise a small group of individuals, supported by a larger team of administrative and other professionals. The goal of this team is to make decisions that ensure that the company continues to generate maximum revenue, reduce costs, and improve safety and service.

The annual salaries for top positions in the transit industry are quite considerable. The chief executive officer (CEO) of New York's Metropolitan Transportation Authority reportedly negotiated a compensation package in 2008 that included an annual salary of $350,000 in addition to housing and retirement benefits. The average annual compensation package for the heads of city transit systems in North America is $305,000. Many public transit systems receive government financial assistance.

Executive positions in large, privately owned or publicly traded companies typically earn higher compensation. Greyhound Lines is the largest intercity bus company in North America; its executives receive annual compensation over $500,000.

Occupations in the area of executive and business management include the following:

- Chief Executive Officer (CEO)
- Chief Operating Officer (COO)
- Chief Financial Officer (CFO)
- Chief Information Officer (CIO)
- President
- Vice President

Customer Services

Customer service is critical to a company's success. Personnel in this field must provide accurate information and assistance to customers, respond to inquires, resolve problems, and sell services. In many transportation businesses, the operator of the vehicle may be the only company employee with whom the customer has direct contact; therefore, there is an overlap of responsibilities.

Customer service employees provide answers and resolutions to customer inquiries. This may include helping customers determine which mode of transportation best suits their needs, explaining route options, or providing fare quotes. Customer service representatives also handle customer complaints.

Positions in customer service do not often require previous training or specialized education. Employees need to demonstrate excellent communication skills, professionalism, patience, telephone etiquette, and good problem-solving and multitasking skills.

Occupations within the customer service department include the following:

- Customer Service Representative
- Ticketing Agent
- Customer Relations Executive
- Service Agent

Sales and Marketing

Passenger transportation is a highly competitive industry. Customers have many choices depending on their transportation needs, so brand recognition and a reputation for superior service are critical. Sales and marketing departments ensure that advertising dollars are well spent, the company's brand remains at the forefront of customer choice, and exceptional relationships with the customer are maintained.

Some smaller businesses in this sector, such as independent owner-operators, may not advertise. Instead, they locate their vehicles and services in places of opportunity, such as airport taxi queues or tourist districts. However, most businesses, regardless of size, have dedicated advertising budgets. Depending on the target customer demographic and area of service, advertising strategies may focus on small areas in a single city or the entire world, and the marketing team may be a single individual or a team of thousands.

Marketing and communications personnel need to project their message to potential customers and may handle a lot of public relations activities. Effective media relations and media monitoring is critical in the handling of a crisis and issues which may arise, and often marketing and communications staff need to protect the company's reputation by identifying and managing these emerging issues. A key measurement of corporate success is revenue; therefore, sales of products and services are imperative. In this industry, advertising and exposure are marketing keys. Many of the customers accessing transportation services remain anonymous and therefore direct sales rarely take place. Sales personnel may contact companies or event managers to make arrangements for people attending conventions, tours, or other events to be offered exclusive transportation services.

Marketing and sales analysts determine whether allocated advertising budgets have been effectively used. They report if the proposed sales goals and targets have been achieved and develop analysis and recommendations for future sales opportunities. Sales positions often are compensated by a base salary and commission structure. Key skills include communication, influence, negotiation, problem solving, and organization. Sales positions often require travel.

Marketing and communications positions usually require a degree or training. Salaries can start near $25,000 annually for entry-level positions and exceed $90,000 for marketing managers and directors. Key skills include communication and organization; knowledge of branding, promotions, trade shows, and event planning; database marketing; telemarketing; promotions; advertising; and research.

Occupations within the sales and marketing department include the following:

- Marketing Director
- Sales Account Manager
- Sales Analyst
- Sales Clerk
- Corporate Communications Specialist
- Media Relations Representative
- Business Solutions Specialist
- Business Liaison
- Market Research Manager

Facilities and Security

The goal of passenger transportation companies is to achieve the highest practical level of safety and security for all modes of transportation in order to protect passengers, employees, revenues, and property. The maintenance of facilities, routes, and transportation equipment is critical to the operation of any passenger transportation or transit company, and government and regulating bodies encourage all companies in this industry to develop and implement a safety and security plan.

In most countries, governments have strict regulations and requirements for modes of passenger transportation in order to ensure safety. The United States Department of Transportation is the umbrella governing agency and is divided into several more specific offices, such as the Federal Transit Administration, Federal Motor Carrier Administration, Federal Railroad Administration, and others. The vehicle used to transport passengers must be safe for passengers and mechanically maintained. Small companies may require that the operators or drivers perform required cleaning and maintenance or take the vehicle for regular maintenance. Specialized maintenance of equipment and vehicles often is contracted out to other companies, although larger companies may keep individuals on staff to perform repair and maintenance of fleet vehicles.

Urban transit systems may include a wide range of travel modes, including rail, trolley car, bus, and water taxi, and all of this specialized equipment has very precise maintenance needs. Occupations in this area often require specialized training and certification. Employees need to perform scheduled maintenance and install new equipment, troubleshoot, and make repairs as needed. Routes and other equipment also must be maintained, including places such as passenger stops, waiting areas, depots, rail lines, docking facilities, and ticketing kiosks, as well as signals and overhead wire systems. Maintenance and facilities positions cover a very wide range of employment options, anything that ensures the smooth running and maintenance of the larger operations. Managers, supervisors, and engineers in maintenance-related positions can expect to earn $50,000 to $75,000 annually. Fleet maintenance technicians can expect annual salaries between $32,000 and $45,000.

Passenger transportation security has been enhanced by installation of video cameras and protective barriers between customers and vehicle operators. This has been in response to increasing criminal activities and violence on public transit and taxi services to better protect passengers and operators. Personnel are needed to install, maintain, and monitor security equipment. There have been incidents around the world that have involved radical or terror attacks and threats to transit operations, leading to increased security measures and vigilance. Transportation companies and transit authorities work with local and federal law enforcement to perform security duties. Specialized security personnel normally require training and experience in law enforcement and transportation security and familiarity with applicable technical devices. Security personnel can expect annual salaries of $32,000 to $48,000 depending on required skills, experience, and level of responsibility.

Occupations within the facilities and security department include the following:

- Security Specialist
- Security Guard
- Security Analyst
- Maintenance Technician
- Car and Vehicle Maintenance Technicians

- Maintenance Supervisor
- Mechanic
- Electrical Engineer
- Cleaner (Vehicle and/or Facilities)
- Track Maintainer

Technology, Research, Design, and Development

Technology is becoming increasingly important to the passenger transportation industry. Programmers, analysts, and technical support personnel are experiencing the greatest job growth in the industry. Customers want to be able to plan travel and purchase fares and ticket vouchers online, all securely and in real time. The operation of transportation systems requires specialized equipment for security, scheduling, and tracking, such as video links and global positioning systems. There also is increasing demand for technical services onboard public transportation. Many buses, rail transport, and ferry systems now provide customers with convenience options like entertainment or wireless Internet service.

In order to remain competitive in the industry, advances in technology design also are crucial. Technology is constantly changing because the systems need to be efficient and effective but easy for customers and employees to use. Positions in the technology, research, design, and development require specialized training such as degrees in computer science and information systems. Programmer analysts' and systems programmers' salaries begin at about $32,000 and can go up to more than $84,000 annually.

Private companies and public transit authorities employ research and development teams to look for more cost-effective transportation options, including cleaner-burning fuel. Customers increasingly seek out transportation options that provide service while doing less damage to the environment.

Occupations within the technology, research, design, and development department include the following:

- Data Analyst
- Programmer Analyst
- Systems Analyst
- Technical Analyst
- Application Manager
- Application Analyst
- Technical Specialist
- Technology Consultant
- Technology and Application Support
- Application Project Manager
- Technological Adviser
- Environmental Impact Analyst

Production and Operations

Operations is the key to the passenger and transportation industry. A great deal of planning and scheduling goes on behind the scenes to ensure that customers are able to arrive at their intended destinations on time. When a taxi cannot be flagged down on the street, dispatchers are the liaison between the customer and driver of a taxi, limousine, or shuttle. A dispatcher collects location and service request information from customers or online requests and assigns them to appropriate drivers. Dispatchers can be asked to communicate to the customer in case of delays or complications. Dispatcher positions normally do not require any specialized training, but candidates need to be organized, patient, and good multitaskers. The annual median salary for dispatchers is about $30,000, although some earn as much as $50,000.

Operations workers keep various transportation modes on strict schedules and assure the operation of the system in the most cost-effective and efficient manner. This may include implementing recommendations for commencement, improvement, modification, or elimination of a particular transportation service. Operations services clerks perform duties that overlap between operations and customer service. They dispatch and assign work to drivers and allocate vehicles for routes. Clerks also respond to trouble calls and relay information to supervisors or emergency services. Operations staff also are responsible for receiving and transferring lost property to customer service and emptying and replacing fare boxes. Annual salaries for operations clerks range from $22,000 to $34,000.

Rail service requires employees to manage operations on the trains, the tracks, and in the rail yard. Rail yard and track workers spend most of their time outdoors in varying weather. Conductors must be at least twenty-one years of age and can be trained by their employers or required to complete training programs. In 2008, the U.S. Department of Labor estimated that the average annual salary for railroad conductors and yardmasters was $54,120, although many conductor positions are paid based on the number of miles traveled.

Passenger transportation across water does have different challenges and therefore requires a uniquely trained staff. Ferry, water taxi, shuttle, and commuter boat companies regularly look to hire mates, seamen, deckhands, and operations engineers in order to keep their service operations running smoothly. Entry, training, and educational requirements for the majority of water transportation positions are regulated by the Coast Guard, and officers and operators of commercial vessels must be licensed. No special training or experience is needed to become a seaman or deckhand on vessels operating in harbors or other waterways. Mates often are referred to as captain assistants, and seamen and deckhands assist with docking operations and other shipboard duties.

The annual wage range for ferry operations staff is $25,000 to $49,000.

Occupations within the production and operations department include the following:

- Operations Supervisor
- Operations Engineer
- Dispatcher
- Operations Service Clerk
- Deckhand
- Seaman
- Mate
- Rail Yard Worker
- Train Conductor

Distribution
Careers in distribution in the passenger transportation industry involve almost all modes of transportation, including drivers, chauffeurs, cyclists, motorcyclists, ferry captains, transit operators, and

The Washington State Ferry at Bainbridge Island, near Seattle. (©Natalia Bratslavsky/Dreamstime.com)

train engineers. Many of these careers also overlap with customer service, as these individuals have a lot of direct interaction with customers. Most of these positions require clean driving records and proper certification. Federal regulations require that drivers who operate commercial vehicles hold state-issued commercial driver licenses. The average annual salary for taxi drivers in the United States and Europe is $26,000. Income may vary because of arrangements with a parent company regarding vehicle maintenance and operating expenses.

Transit operators and drivers, such as bus drivers and subway operators, normally must work a range of shifts or split shifts to accommodate peak commuter travel times. North American wages for these positions range from $11.75 to $28.90 per hour, and most of these positions are unionized.

Ferry captains are expected to possess managerial and leadership skills in addition to proficiency in navigation, seamanship, docking, and passenger embarking and debarking procedures. All water transportation captain and officer positions are regulated and must be licensed by the Coast Guard. The average annual salary for a ferry captain is $80,000.

Train locomotive engineers must be at least twenty-one years of age, and these positions are customarily filled by workers who have had previous experience in other railroad-operating occupations.

Occupations within the distribution department include the following:

- Taxi Driver
- Bus/Trolley Driver
- Ferry Captain
- Light Rail Operator
- Train Engineer
- Chauffeur
- Ambulance Driver

OCCUPATION PROFILE

Bus Driver

Considerations	Qualifications
Description	Drives a passenger-carrying bus; may be responsible for some maintenance.
Career clusters	Hospitality and Tourism; Transportation, Distribution, and Logistics
Interests	Data; people; things
Working conditions	Work inside
Minimum education level	No high school diploma; on-the-job training
Physical exertion	Medium work
Physical abilities	Unexceptional/basic fitness
Opportunities for experience	Military service; part-time work
Licensure and certification	Required
Employment outlook	Average growth expected
Holland interest score	RES

Note: See volume 1, "Publisher's Note," for an explanation of the Holland interest score.

OCCUPATION PROFILE

Locomotive Engineer

Considerations	Qualifications
Description	Drives electric, diesel-electric, and gas-turbine-electric locomotives; monitors the operation of the engine; oversees the function of the entire train; and maintains prescheduled timetables.
Career cluster	Transportation, Distribution, and Logistics
Interests	Data; things
Working conditions	Work both inside and outside
Minimum education level	No high school diploma; on-the-job training; high school diploma or GED; high school diploma/technical training; apprenticeship
Physical exertion	Light work
Physical abilities	Unexceptional/basic fitness
Opportunities for experience	Apprenticeship; military service; part-time work
Licensure and certification	Required
Employment outlook	Average growth expected
Holland interest score	IRS

Note: See volume 1, "Publisher's Note," for an explanation of the Holland interest score.

Human Resources

The human resources department is responsible for the employees. They ensure that each employee has the tools and training that they need in order to be effective and productive in their position. They manage a variety of tasks, beginning with the hiring of personnel, their training and development, compensation and benefits, retirement and dismissal. Human resources also ensures that all employee relations and practices comply with legal requirements and corporate policies.

Most positions within human resources require a degree or equivalent experience. Managers in this field earn approximately $80,000 annually. This is often a challenging area, and employee relations require patience, collaboration, negotiation, and conflict resolution skills.

In many smaller companies, managers and supervisors take on the roles of human resources as part of their job responsibilities.

Occupations within the human resources department include the following:

- Human Resources Director
- Human Resources Manager
- Human Resources Coordinator
- Human Resources Analyst
- Administrative Assistant
- Human Resources Generalist

INDUSTRY OUTLOOK

Overview

The outlook for the passenger transportation and transit industry appears to be on the rise. The

PROJECTED EMPLOYMENT FOR SELECTED OCCUPATIONS

Transit and Ground Passenger Transportation

Employment		
2009	Projected 2018	Occupation
12,060	12,400	Bus and truck mechanics and diesel engine specialists
160,130	170,200	Bus drivers, school
71,530	77,000	Bus drivers, transit and intercity
14,700	14,400	Dispatchers, except police, fire, and ambulance
76,220	89,900	Taxi drivers and chauffeurs

Source: U.S. Bureau of Labor Statistics, Industries at a Glance, Occupational Employment Statistics and Employment Projections Program.

United States Bureau of Labor Statistics expects to see an increase in ground passenger transportation of 2.1 percent and water transportation of 4.2 percent by 2018. The gains expected in this industry can be attributed to a number of factors, including fuel costs, vehicle maintenance costs, urban sprawl, and convenience. Safety and convenience are important to passengers, and many transportation businesses and municipal transit services are making improvements to service and implementing increased safety measures.

People are finding it increasingly expensive to operate, insure, and park their vehicles and are looking to transportation options to reduce their costs but maintain convenience. According to the American Automobile Association, the estimated annual cost of driving a single-occupant vehicle ranges from $4,826 to $9,685, depending on vehicle type and mileage; the annual average cost for public transportation ranges from $200 to $2,000. A commuter who travels 120 miles daily round trip could save more than 1,888 gallons of gasoline every year by switching from using a car to using public transportation.

Many transportation and transit companies have expanded hours and routes and upgraded fleet vehicles in order to increase ridership. Environmental concerns also provide incentive to riders to use mass transit. Without mass transit, there would be more than 2.6 million more cars on New York City streets. For each mile traveled, fewer pollutants are emitted by transit vehicles than by single-passenger automobiles. Emissions and fuel efficiency will continue to improve as passenger transportation vehicles transition to cleaner-burning fuels.

As improvements in service and convenience continue to be made in the passenger transportation industry, more customers will consider it a viable option. Governments around the world are providing cash and incentives to transit systems to make these improvements in order to reduce traffic congestion and environmental impact. Teams of researchers are working on ways to improve fuel efficiency, alternative fuel options, and transportation planning.

Globally, private-sector influence over the transportation industry is growing. In many cases, inability of governments to efficiently administer public transportation has led to privatization. These collaborations have improved the performance of transportation modes and infrastructure. Examples of successful privatization include railroads in several European countries and privatized subways in Tokyo and Hong Kong.

Employment Advantages

The transportation industry was identified by the High Growth Job Training Initiative, which recognizes the need to prepare workers for new and increasing job opportunities in high-growth/high-demand and economically vital industries. Many of the positions in this industry do not require advanced education, and some companies will provide training, licensing assistance, and certification. Careers in transportation often are a popular choice for new immigrants. Some larger companies may provide above-average wages and benefits, while employees of smaller and independent transportation companies usually are able to determine their own benefits and working conditions. Many of the large transportation companies and urban transit systems have labor unions and provide opportunities for advancement, career development, and job security. Transportation employees are needed to work a range of shifts to accommodate around-the-clock service.

Annual Earnings

The passenger transportation and transit industry is strongly influenced by fuel costs and convenience. Despite the love that North Americans have for their vehicles, between 1996 and 2001 public transportation travel increased by 23 percent and continues to rise annually. In 2007, the United States Economic Census reported that annual revenues for this industry were more than $40 billion. Global annual revenues in this industry in 2009 were more than $174 billion, and the average growth rate is projected to be between 2 and 4 percent annually to 2014.

Occupations in the transit, rail, and ground passenger transportation sector that are expected to have the greatest projected employment by 2014 are bus drivers, taxi drivers/chauffeurs, conductors, engineers, and dispatchers. Occupations in the industry projected to have the greatest job gains are bus drivers, taxi drivers/chauffeurs, engineers, heavy mechanics, and service technicians.

RELATED RESOURCES FOR FURTHER RESEARCH

AMERICAN PUBLIC TRANSPORTATION
   ASSOCIATION
   1666 K St. NW, Suite 1100
   Washington, DC 20006
   Tel: (202) 496-4800
   Fax: (202) 496-4324
   http://www.apta.com

FEDERAL TRANSIT ADMINISTRATION, U.S.
   DEPARTMENT OF TRANSPORTATION
   East Building, 1200 New Jersey Ave. SE
   Washington, DC 20590
   Tel: (202) 366-4043
   Fax: (202) 366-9854
   http://www.fta.dot.gov

PROJECTED EMPLOYMENT FOR SELECTED OCCUPATIONS

Support Activities for Transportation

Employment		
2009	Projected 2018	Occupation
27,490	31,800	Aircraft mechanics and service technicians
44,920	58,600	Cargo and freight agents
14,800	14,600	Dispatchers, except police, fire, and ambulance
53,370	56,700	Laborers and freight, stock, and material movers, hand
45,860	67,800	Truck drivers, heavy and tractor-trailer

Source: U.S. Bureau of Labor Statistics, Industries at a Glance, Occupational Employment Statistics and Employment Projections Program.

INSTITUTE OF TRANSPORTATION STUDIES,
    UNIVERSITY OF CALIFORNIA, BERKELEY
109 McLaughlin Hall
UC Berkeley, Mail Code 1720
Berkeley, CA 94720-1720
Tel: (510) 642-3585
Fax: (510) 643-3955
http://its.berkeley.edu

INTERNATIONAL ASSOCIATION OF PUBLIC
    TRANSPORT
Rue Sainte-Marie 6 (Quai des Charbonnages)
B-1080 Brussels
Belgium
Tel: 32-2-673-61-00
Fax: 32-2-660-10-72
http://www.uitp.org

TAXICAB, LIMOUSINE, AND PARATRANSIT
    ASSOCIATION
3200 Tower Oaks Blvd., Suite 220
Rockville, MD 20852
Tel: (301) 984-5700
Fax: (301) 984-5703
http://www.tlpa.org

TRANSPORTATION RESEARCH BOARD, THE
    NATIONAL ACADEMIES
500 5th St. NW
Washington, DC 20001
Tel: (202) 334-2934
Fax: (202) 334-2519
http://www.trb.org

ABOUT THE AUTHOR

April D. Ingram is a freelance writer and researcher in British Columbia, Canada. She is a graduate of the University of Calgary and has been associated with the passenger transportation industry since 2000, originally in a communications role and later as a research officer for transportation engineering research at the University of British Columbia.

FURTHER READING

Cudahy, Brian. *Cash, Tokens, and Transfers: A History of Urban Mass Transit in North America.* New York: Fordham University Press, 1990.

Guess, George. *Public Policy and Transit System Management.* New York: Greenwood Press, 1990.

Landefeld, Steven, Brent R. Moulton, and Cindy M. Vojtech. "Chained-Dollar Indexes: Issues, Tips on Their Use, and Upcoming Changes." *Survey of Current Business* (November, 2003): 8-16.

McDavid, Richard, and Susan Echaore-McDavid. *Career Opportunities in Transportation.* New York: Ferguson, 2009.

Transit Cooperative Research Program. *2008 Annual Report.* Washington, D.C.: Transportation Research Board, 2008.

U.S. Bureau of Labor Statistics. *Career Guide to Industries*, 2010-2011 ed. http://www.bls.gov/oco/cg.

U.S. Census Bureau. North American Industry Classification System (NAICS), 2007. http://www.census.gov/cgi-bin/sssd/naics/naicsrch?chart=2007.

U.S. Department of Commerce. International Trade Administration. Office of Trade and Industry Information. Industry Trade Data and Analysis. http://ita.doc.gov/td/industry/otea/OTII/OTII-index.html.

Personal Services

©Dreamstime.com

INDUSTRY SNAPSHOT

General Industry: Personal Services

Career Cluster: Human Services

Subcategory Industries: Astrology, Fortune-Telling, Psychic, and Phrenology Services; Barber Shops; Beauty Salons; Body Piercing Services and Tattoo Parlors; Concierge Services; Dating Services; Dry Cleaning and Laundry Services (Except Coin-Operated); Escort Services; Event Planning Services; Garment Alteration and Repair; Hair, Nail, and Skin Care Services; Hair Removal Services; Massage Parlors; Nail Salons; Parking Lots and Garages; Personal Care Services; Personal Shopping Services; Spas, Saunas, and Baths

Related Industries: Animal Care Services; Day-Care Services; Furniture and Home Furnishings Industry; Health and Fitness Industry; Home Maintenance Services; Landscaping Services; Rental and Leasing Services; Retail Trade and Service Industry

Annual Domestic Revenues: $588.8 billion USD (U.S. Bureau of Economic Analysis, 2008)

NAICS Numbers: 8121, 81232, 81293, 81299, 811490

INDUSTRY DEFINITION

Summary

The personal services industry provides a wide range of private services to individual consumers. The industry comprises dating services, massage parlors, hair and beauty salons, escort services, valet parking services, laundry services, event planning, and a host of other services. It consists largely of small businesses and individuals, making it one of the most fragmented industries in the U.S. economy.

History of the Industry

The personal services industry includes services that were once performed in the home or were not available to a family. Before the 1960's, most women worked in the home. They did the housecleaning, cooking, laundry, shopping, and errands. The majority of women now work outside the home, so they do not have time to perform all these household tasks. Their presence in the workforce is projected to keep growing. For this reason, many of these domestic tasks have been transferred to the marketplace. Another reason for the growth of personal services is the increase in unmarried people who hold jobs and most likely live alone. Personal services providers run errands and plan parties for working people who lack the time to perform such tasks themselves.

Other causes of the emergence of personal services in the public market include the rising wealth of families and the low cost of immigrant labor. In addition, successful personal service business models, such as franchising, have increased outsourcing of household tasks and growth of the personal services industry. In addition, technology has created a demand for services requiring specialized knowledge.

Despite the great diversity of personal services, they are all focused on helping individuals and families in their daily lives. The goal of all of them is to help people. Most service workers enjoy the feeling of satisfaction they get from helping others.

The personal service industry has four main functions: to help people feel better about themselves and look better, to provide care to people at different ages who need physical or emotional help, to help people when in crisis or when going

Hair and beauty are a large part of the personal services industry. (©Dreamstime.com)

through major changes in their lives, and to save clients time. The jobs available in this industry match a wide range of interests, skills, and education levels. Some are new jobs, whereas others have been around a long time. Some people want advice on what to buy. Others want help caring for their possessions. Others want their animals groomed, closets organized, pianos tuned, clothes washed or dry-cleaned, or items repaired. Personal service providers may save people time by running errands, standing in line for event tickets, or waiting at one's house for an appliance to be repaired. They might plan children's birthday parties or supervise the redecorating of one's home. They may clean out or organize one's closets and drawers, or every room in one's home, including the garage.

In the late 1990's, leading personal services in terms of capital included the Aramark Corporation in Philadelphia; Weight Watchers International, headquartered in New York; GE Capital Mortgage in Cherry Hill, New Jersey; and Unifirst Corporation in Wilmington, Massachusetts.

Companies are taking advantage of the personal services tag. A car dealer, for example, may advertise quality factory repairs that feature personal service. The personal feeling of the service, including staff attitude and amenities provided, can encourage repeat business. In other words, many providers of services in general seek to market them as personal services.

The Industry Today

The personal services industry is now well established and includes a number of niche industries. Major segments of the industry include laundry and cleaning services, garment repair, and hair and beauty services. More specialized niche services include baby shoe bronzing and phrenology. New segments have emerged, such as tanning salons and spray tanning. Among the largest business segments of this industry is dating services.

Miscellaneous personal services listed by the NEC Corporation include many but not all personal services available today. These services, some of which are classified in the personal services industry and some of which are classified within other industries, comprise 160,829 U.S. companies.

The "other" sector is the largest within personal services and includes a number of distinct indus-

The Contribution of Personal Services to the U.S. Economy

Value Added	Amount
Gross domestic product	$365.5 billion
Gross domestic product	2.5%
Persons employed	7.093 million
Total employee compensation	$239.5 billion

Note: Comprises miscellaneous services that are not primarily financial, professional, scientific, technical, educational, business-oriented, medical or health-related, food-related, entertainment-related, governmental, or geared toward social assistance.

Source: U.S. Bureau of Economic Analysis. Data are for 2008.

tries. Some, such as formal wear and costume rental, have operated for decades, while others are relatively new. Online dating and matchmaking is one of the newer categories. Its growth in revenue averaged 17.8 percent per year between 2002 and 2007.

Extermination, insect, and pest control services generate the second-highest profit margin among all personal services categories, at 12 percent. This is behind only hair-loss treatment and hair removal. The extermination sector is in a growth phase. This service, however, has moderate barriers to entry and heavy regulatory requirements that make it difficult for start-up operations to succeed.

Some personal services industries are good lending prospects, while others are not. Finding good investments among millions of personal services is not easy. Industry fundamentals have to be evaluated, including revenue growth, risk, historical performance, and profits.

According to IBISWorld, funeral homes and the "linen supply and diaper service" category exhibit the lowest risk ratings. These industries have been around a long time, but their growth predictions are low. Expected revenue growth through 2013 is below 2 percent per year. Nevertheless, these industries are considered to be low risk, even though returns will be low. The pluses, in addition to low risk, are low levels of volatility and moderate barriers to entry. Both lower the risk of default. Returns are not favorable, but investing in and lending to these businesses are considered relatively safe.

Businesses that are not safe for investment include shoe-repair shops and nanny, butler, and other such household services. These services are in decline. Their revenue is predicted to fall during the coming years. Shoe repair is in decline because consumers buy new shoes instead of having older shoes fixed. Nanny and butler services are being replaced by more specialized personal services that achieve better results and save time. Shoe repair, nanny, and butler services are threatened by default and bankruptcy. Cash and revenue is static and at a low level. All these factors make these services unsafe for lending and investment.

The best services for lenders and investors are child day care, pet grooming and boarding, and weight-loss centers. These industries are expected to experience strong revenue growth in the coming years. Profits are predicted to occur above the industry average, at 8 percent, 12 percent, and 9 percent, respectively. Profits will be higher as a result of franchising and low capital requirements.

Franchises can also fade away. To maintain

Inputs Consumed by Personal Services

Input	Value
Energy	$6.8 billion
Materials	$39.3 billion
Purchased services	$177.2 billion
Total	$223.3 billion

Note: Comprises miscellaneous services that are not primarily financial, professional, scientific, technical, educational, business-oriented, medical or health-related, food-related, entertainment-related, governmental, or geared toward social assistance.

Source: U.S. Bureau of Economic Analysis. Data are for 2008.

growth, they need to introduce new products and services. This often includes developing a technology component. Franchises may also explore new demographic niches and markets in order to expand operations and develop more profits.

Most personal services involve face-to-face communication between providers and clients and tend to serve the household market, although some serve businesses. Through the Internet, new virtual opportunities have also developed. New markets that used to be local may be made global by the Internet. For example, personal fitness training can take place online. Clients can ask questions about fitness goals online with a trainer, and they can watch exercise videos. Similar Web sites can offer many other services, such as those of wedding consultants and florists. One can become trained and certified online in some fields, such as the dry cleaning industry.

In addition, virtual personal assistants can be of help in business for minimal cost. A business does not have to hire a full-time office assistant, provide office space, or buy office equipment. A virtual assistant communicates with the employer through the Internet, e-mail, telephone calls, or fax. This person can do many things such as help out on a new project, compile data, manage workload, or find new marketing opportunities. Personal assistants can also hire grass cutters and snow removal services or order groceries to be delivered to one's home. They can hire babysitters or housekeepers, pay bills, make travel reservations, confirm reservations, and book rental cars or hotel rooms.

Numbering more than 4 million businesses and employing nearly 7 million people, the personal services sector is increasingly important to the U.S. economy, which overall is a service-based, rather than manufacturing-based, economy. The number of businesses in the industry is growing faster than the overal rate for all types of businesses in the

Dry cleaning businesses receive clothes and cleaning instructions from consumers, assign identifying tags to the clothes, and assign them priorities and complete-by dates. (©Lisa Mckown/Dreamstime.com)

United States. Personal services have expanded at an annualized rate of 2 percent, compared to an average of 1.4 percent for the overall economy. One of the reasons for this fast growth is that the personal services industry has low barriers to entry. It requires relatively small amounts of capital investment, for example. New business owners need to make relatively few purchases to support their businesses. As a result, thousands of people enter this industry every year.

For new services, a steady flow of income can be difficult to achieve, but one new category, online dating and matchmaking, has grown substantially in revenue. This trend of growth in personal services is sometimes difficult to track, because various personal services are categorized as parts of other industries. Little information on all personal services is consolidated within an individual category or set of categories, and isolating comprehensive data on personal services requires a great deal of effort.

INDUSTRY MARKET SEGMENTS

Because so much of the personal services industry comprises individuals and small businesses, it is not useful to segment the industry by size. Instead, each type of service may be treated as its own industry segment. The sections below list some of these segments and their function within the industry and the economy.

Laundry and Dry Cleaning

Laundry and dry cleaning businesses receive clothes and cleaning instructions from consumers, assign identifying tags to them, and assign them priorities and complete-by dates. Once a schedule and service is determined, these businesses place the clothes in the appropriate washing or dry cleaning machines; mix and add detergents, bleaches, starches, and other chemicals that clean, stiffen, color, and dry clothes; sort clothes removed from dryers; and fold, wrap, or hang them on racks. They then sort the finished clothes according to their expected pickup date.

In addition to knowledge of the principles and processes of laundry and dry cleaning, workers in this business have to be aware of and evaluate customer satisfaction and uphold the quality of their services. The laundry and dry cleaning industry has seen significant restructuring over the last two decades. Businesses in the industry used to be, and to some degree still are, family-owned neighborhood services, but a dramatic change has taken place, as much of this work is increasingly being done in industrial plants owned by corporations.

Garment Sewing and Alteration

Tailors work by sewing. They make dresses, do alterations, hem clothes, or mend clothes. They

OCCUPATION SPECIALTIES

Laundry/Dry Cleaning Machine Operators

Specialty	Responsibilities
Dry cleaners	Operate dry-cleaning machines, which clean clothing, drapes, and other materials that cannot be washed in water.
Fur cleaners	Restore fur garments by hand or machine, using brushes, pads, sawdust, corncob dust, and cleaning fluids.
Laundry operators	Perform various duties, such as receiving, marking, washing, finishing, checking, and wrapping laundry articles.
Machine washers	Tend one or more machines that wash commercial, industrial, or household articles, such as apparel, blankets, curtains, and rugs.

A seamstress fits a bridal gown. (©Ron Chapple Studios/Dreamstime.com)

work with many different kinds of fabrics. They may also make home accessories such as curtains, tablecloths, and pillows. They may work full or part time, for themselves, for businesses, or on a client-by-client basis. As long as there is clothing, there will always be a need for qualified people who can sew, but it is difficult to make a living solely by sewing.

Hair and Beauty Services

Generally, beauty and hair-care salons offer hair, nail, and skin care. They provide haircuts, hair styling, highlights, hair coloring, hair weaves, permanents, curling, scalp treatments, hair treatments, manicures, pedicures, nail sculptures, nail re-

OCCUPATION PROFILE

Barber

Considerations	Qualifications
Description	Cuts and trims hair, mostly of male customers.
Career cluster	Human Services
Interests	Data; people; things
Working conditions	Work inside
Minimum education level	On-the-job training; junior/technical/community college; apprenticeship
Physical exertion	Light work
Physical abilities	Unexceptional/basic fitness
Opportunities for experience	Apprenticeship; military service
Licensure and certification	Required
Employment outlook	Average growth expected
Holland interest score	ESR

Note: See volume 1, "Publisher's Note," for an explanation of the Holland interest score.

pair, facials, makeup application, and other services. Manicurists work on customers' hands. Most manicurists also are pedicurists and also work on feet. In many salons, manicurists also remove unwanted hair from clients' faces, legs, bikini areas, or arms. Manicuring is one of the fastest-growing specialties in the cosmetology business.

Child-Care Workers

Helping children learn and gain new skills can be rewarding. Child-care workers often

---

OCCUPATION SPECIALTIES

Cosmetologists

Specialty	Responsibilities
Electrologists	Remove hair from the skin by using a round-tipped needle.
Hair stylists	Dress hair according to the instructions of the customer or the makeup person.
Makeup artists	Apply makeup.
Manicurists	Clean, shape, and polish customers' fingernails and toenails; may also apply false nails, wrap nails, and provide other beauty services.

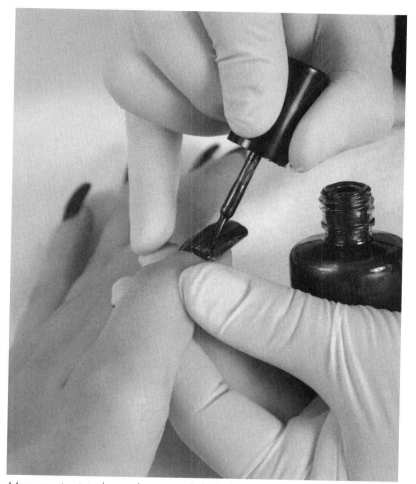

Many manicurists also work on toenails. (©Stefan Nedelchev/Dreamstime.com)

improve their own communication, learning, and other personal skills in their work. Jobs are available all year long for daytime or live-in child-care workers. Parents who travel with their children may hire child-care workers to travel with them.

Fashion Consultants

Some fashion consultants go into business for themselves or work in department stores. They can also become motivational speakers, become cosmeticians, or move into doing fashion design shows. Some travel to fashion hubs to learn about the latest trends in the fashion industry. Some specialize in bridal work or work with only one gender.

Housekeepers

Housekeepers work in private homes, cleaning them for the owners. Housekeeping is the systematic process of making a home neat and clean. Housekeepers can also become household managers. For example, they can be called on to manage

OCCUPATION SPECIALTIES

Housekeepers

Specialty	Responsibilities
Butlers	Coordinate the activities of the household workers, receive and announce guests, answer telephones, deliver messages, serve food and drinks, chauffeur clients, or act as personal attendants.
Caretakers	Perform heavy housework and general home maintenance. They wash windows, wax floors, and hang draperies. They maintain heating and other equipment and perform light carpentry and gardening if the household does not have a gardener.
Child monitors	Attend to children in private homes.
Companions	Care for the elderly, disabled persons, or persons recovering from illness or injury in home settings.
Cooks	Plan menus, cook meals, clean the kitchen, order groceries and supplies, and may also serve meals.
General house workers	Clean homes, care for children, plan and cook meals, do laundry, administer the household account books, and perform numerous other duties. Many household workers work for two or more employers.
Personal attendants	Perform personal services for their employers in home settings.

organizational, financial, and day-to-day operations of a house or estate.

Parking Valets

Parking valets park and retrieve vehicles at parking lots, restaurants, and hotels. American Valet, a company that hires parking lot valets, describes other requirements of this job:

- One must be hospitable, attentive, friendly, and efficient with all clients.
- One must park and retrieve vehicles in a prompt and safe way.
- One must assist with whatever the client wants such as baby strollers and suit jackets.
- If requested, provide driving directions and other information to clients.
- One is responsible for following American Valet's Safety and Loss Prevention Policies.
- One must receive claim checks before issuing keys.

- One must work independently with minimal or no direct supervision.
- One must be able to run fast and stand during the entire shift.
- One must have good vision.
- One must tolerate long hours.
- One must have at least a high school diploma.

Personal Assistants

A personal assistant helps in business and personal tasks, For example, a business person may have a personal assistant help with time and diary management, scheduling of meetings, correspondence, and note taking. Personal assistants also work with disabled people. Families in which both parents work may also employ personal assistants.

Personal Services

All these personal services vary widely in job description, earnings, and related features because they are so dependent upon the individual situations in which they are provided. Personal services providers may be employed primarily by a few individuals or may serve hundreds of customers. They may work for upper-class clients seeking luxuries, or they may serve clients on relatively tight budgets who are seeking to save money by "outsourcing" their household chores to free more time to work. Thus, the variation in experiences within the industry is even greater than the variation in most other industries.

Potential Annual Earnings Scale. According to the U.S. Bureau of Labor Statistics (BLS), the average annual income of all workers in the personal and laundry services industry in 2009 was $27,500. Hair dressers, hair stylists, and cosmetologists earned an average of $27,250, manicurists and pedicurists earned an average of $21,990, laundry and dry cleaning workers earned an average of $20,160, parking lot attendants earned an average of $20,080,

and tailors engaged in garment alteration and repair earned an average of $24,680. Depending on the circumstances, a personal services provider may earn significantly more or less than these mean salaries.

Clientele Interaction. All personal services providers must cultivate client relationships. They must be good communicators and able to relate to all types of clients. They should be approachable, cheerful, and tactful. Many providers develop close personal relationships with their clients—which may be gratifying but may also interfere with their business relationships.

Amenities, Atmosphere, and Physical Grounds. If a personal service provider works out of an office or other commercial space, location is crucial. Offices should be easily accessible for clients and enjoy significant foot traffic. The atmosphere should be physically appealing and look relaxing

Valet parking is offered by many hotels, restaurants, hospitals, and shopping malls. (©Les Palenik/Dreamstime.com)

and professional. Buildings should be landscaped so as to present an appealing entrance. Services should provide coffee and drink machines. Some of the services should have extended business hours to accommodate clients' schedules. Those working as a team should be top employees in ability and work attitudes. Reputation is crucial, as is providing superior personal services.

Typical Number of Employees. Personal services providers may be self-employed sole proprietors or may have several employees. Larger groups may work in corporate headquarters, such as laundries.

Traditional Geographic Locations. Service providers may be located almost anywhere, depending on the service being provided. More luxury-oriented providers are likely to be located in urban or suburban areas, while more universally necessary services, such as dry cleaning, may be located in rural areas as well.

Pros of Working as a Personal Services Provider. Americans value attractive appearances, so the demand for hair and beauty services will continue to thrive. Some hair and beauty salons are located in business buildings to be accessible to business people working there. Other providers travel to nursing and retirement homes. Some may specialize in makeup and hair styling for weddings or other special occasions.

Some salons provide other services, such as massages and facials. Manicurists and pedicurists often work in salons. Waxing can be done to remove hair. Manicurists also work in nail salons separate from hair salons. An increasing number of nail salons are in cities. Some of them have spas.

Fashion consultants have numerous opportunities. Some go into business for themselves or work for a business such as a department store and help customers choose clothes. They do not spend much time at a desk. Fashion designers develop skills in advertising, promoting, displaying, selling, and buying fashions. They may work in jobs such as fashion buying, public relations for fashion companies, sales in showrooms, and working on catalogs. Fashion journalism is also a possibility. In this field, consultants write and edit fashion magazines, trade journals, and Web sites.

Tailors make their living with needle and thread. This is a very popular occupation for a mother or father who needs money but does not want to be away from the children. The basic tailoring skill is sewing, but it is possible to put this skill to work in many contexts, such as dressmaking, gown design, handbag making, or costume design. Those who can work outside the home may be able to work in the fashion industry. This industry needs people who can sew and construct apparel. Certificate programs teach tailoring and the use of specialty fabrics.

Child-care work sometimes seems routine, but new activities and challenges come each day.

Housekeepers have income potential, are paid daily, have flexible hours, and do not work nights. There is great demand for this service. Workers can often choose where and when to work.

Personal assistants often interact with high-level executives and may have opportunities for permanent employment if they are good at their contract jobs. They may accompany executives to business dinners, private parties, or working vacations. They may work with hotels when executives travel to be sure they have the desired personal services at their hotels. Some hotel chains are developing guest histories to track and anticipate the preferred services of each guest. Personal assistants can consult with hotels to help them develop profiles of their clients and anticipate their needs, even on an initial visit when a history has not yet been constructed.

Usually, clients are happy to retrieve clean and well-pressed clothes. Compliments on their work can be satisfying to laundry workers.

Parking valets are in demand, and they may enjoy flexible hours or tips depending on the position.

Cons of Working as a Personal Services Provider. Classes required to work in hair and beauty can be expensive. Also, most states require providers to purchase and renew licenses to practice this occupation. New services in particular have to work hard to gain clients. It helps to be located where people notice the business. People in this business must stand a lot, wash towels, keep the floors clean of hair, and collect money from each client for their services.

Fashion consultants have to be available when clients are available. This could include nights and weekends. Buying trendy clothes can be expensive, but people in this business must keep up with fashion changes. It also takes time to shop. If the economy is good, some personal shoppers get a lot of business, but in a recession there is considerable competition for work.

Work in apparel production can be physically demanding. Some workers sit for long periods, and others spend many hours on their feet, leaning over tables and operating machinery. Operators must be attentive while running sewing machines, pressers, and automated cutters. They may need to wear protective clothing, such as gloves. Garment workers' wages are low, and they face a constant threat of unemployment because of unregulated overseas competition. This industry is expected to lose 245,000 jobs by 2012, probably more than any other industry.

Child care can be physically taxing, as workers are always standing or walking. They may have to stoop to the level of the child or lift the child. They constantly have to attend to each child's needs and problems. Child-care workers must be constantly alert to possible trouble and deal effectively with troublesome children. Child-care workers may become dissatisfied with their jobs' stressful conditions, low pay, and lack of benefits. They may eventually leave this work.

The caregiving sector was hurt by the recession of 2007-2009. Higher unemployment has caused more people to be at home with their children, reducing the demand for child-care services. Revenue will decline in this sector. Still, the caregiving industry remains robust. Profit margins are high, averaging 10 percent.

Laundries and dry cleaning establishments are often hot and noisy. Employees also may be exposed to harsh solvents, although there are now less toxic cleaning solvents. In addition to being exposed to contaminants, workers spend considerable time standing.

Outside unionized plants, working conditions and wages are poor in laundries and dry cleaning. Workers mostly earn minimum wage. Workdays and workweeks are long, and hardly any laundry or dry cleaning business pays overtime. Dry cleaning workers inhale a cleaning fluid that is a carcinogen, and this can cause health problems. Summertime heat exposure is also physically taxing. Pressers suffer year-round from burns.

Salaries are low for parking valets, and when cleaning cars, safety is a consideration because some cleaning products are toxic. Also, cleaning cars is physically demanding.

Housecleaning is hard physical work. One is exposed to germs on a daily basis. Cleaning toilets is not the most respectable job. One cannot depend on a certain salary every week.

To do their job well, personal assistants have to develop many skills across numerous areas. They have to be experts in these areas and produce error-free results. Their jobs are often high pressure and stressful.

Costs

Payroll and Benefits: Most personal service providers earn hourly wages, many of which are low. Benefits do not exist for self-employed persons, unless they are able to afford pension or other retirement plans. Benefits are offered to employees at the discretion of the employer and are relatively rare in the industry.

Supplies: For hair and beauty workers, supplies include a washbasin, faucets, a styling register, styling chairs, supply trolleys, hair dryers, mirrors, scissors, shampoo, hair steaming machines, towels, clothes covers, and salon loungers. Other supplies include combs, brushes, curling irons, gloves, hairspray, and mousse. Manicure supplies include manicure sets, cuticle remover, towels, massage tables, magazines, pedicure equipment, and razors. Later, one might get a computer and software that provides clients a virtual view of a hair cut before the actual haircut is done.

Fashion consultants require mirrors, makeup, color swatches, and fashion books and magazines. A video camera can help clients judge their body language and how well clothes look on them.

Parking valets who clean and finish car interiors and exteriors need cleaning products. They also clean wheels, tires, fabrics, and other parts of a car. For some cleaning, they need a pressure washer. Other needed supplies include a vacuum cleaner, broom, and mop. Supplies such as cleaning solutions, polish, and sponges are also required.

Laundry and dry cleaning businesses need washing and dry cleaning machines, clothes hangers and stands to hang clothes, tags for clothes identification, cash registers, and bags for clothes.

Housekeepers need supplies such as brooms,

brushes, buckets, cleaning and rinsing solutions, dusters, mops, squeegees, steam cleaners, vacuums, paper towels, polish, spray bottles, and steam cleaners. Some clients have these items on hand, but some do not and want the cleaner to bring supplies. Some have these supplies but still want the cleaner to bring them. This can be costly for the housekeeper.

External Services: Personal service providers require minimal external services, but they may contract cleaning and maintenance of office facilities, as well as accounting or tax preparation services.

Utilities: Depending on the service, utilities used may be supplied by clients. Businesses with storefronts or offices require water, sewage, electricity, gas, telephone, and perhaps Internet access.

Taxes: Personal services providers must pay local, state, and federal taxes on their business income, which they may claim on their personal returns if self-employed. In such cases, they must pay self-employment taxes. Business owners with employees must pay payroll taxes. Many providers must also collect and pay sales taxes on their services.

ORGANIZATIONAL STRUCTURE AND JOB ROLES

The personal services industry contains a mix of different structures and job roles. Some service providers are commonly self-employed or own very small, often home-based, businesses. In this case, the owner fulfills most or all job roles and is responsible for the success or failure of the business. Garment cleaners and beauty salons require storefronts and generally have some employees, but even then multiple job roles must often be assumed by each person. Some personal services providers, such as fashion consultants and personal assistants, may act as contractors and fill several roles within several different businesses simultaneously. All these jobs are specialized in the sense that workers have to have the skills and knowledge to apply to their jobs. They also must often provide their own supplies. Some have to be licensed to practice with clients.

The following umbrella categories apply to the organizational structure of businesses in the personal services industry:

- Business Management
- Customer Services
- Sales and Marketing
- Facilities, Security, and Technology

Business Management

Business managers oversee the operations of their companies. In small personal services companies, the business managers are usually the owners. They are often responsible not only for business decisions and staff management but also for staff training and dispatching. Sole proprietors must perform all necessary tasks themselves, including seeking work, performing work, and managing company finances. Some small businesses are partnerships. Often, co-owners of such businesses have complementary skill sets.

Business management occupations may include the following:

- Owner
- Partner
- Manager

Customer Services

Customer services are the products provided by personal service providers. They include everything from sewing a button on a shirt to coordinating a large wedding. Service providers strive to simultaneously deliver requested services and promote themselves by cultivating lasting business relationships.

Customer service occupations may include the following:

- Stylist
- Planner
- Consultant
- Housekeeper
- Dry Cleaner
- Caregiver
- Valet
- Personal Assistant

Sales and Marketing

While most personal services providers thrive on client recommendations and word of mouth, they cannot assume such recommendations will occur on their own. Providers must create the necessary infrastructure to generate referrals, by checking in with clients, requesting reviews to post on Web sites and elsewhere, attending trade events, and taking advantage of other business promotion opportunities. Some personal service providers, even small ones, have dedicated promotional staff. In such cases, there may be one partner who provides service and a second partner who both secures clients and maintains the work schedule.

Sales and marketing occupations may include the following:

- Owner/Partner
- Customer Relations Representative

Facilities, Security, and Technology

Most personal services providers do not have dedicated facility staffs: They must provide for their own cleaning, maintenance and security or contract such services. One exception, however, is in the parking segment. Many parking lots in urban areas require visible security staffs, not only to prevent damage to vehicles for which providers may be liable but also because potential clients may not be willing to park in lots that lack security guards.

The workers who can best use technology are fashion consultants and personal assistants. They can use video cameras, computers, and other technology to assist their clients. Fashion consultants use computer-aided design (CAD) software to create clothing on virtual models. Many businesses rely upon the World Wide Web to promote and even sell, schedule, or coordinate their services. Few small businesses have dedicated information technology staffs, but some employ office staff or other workers with technical knowledge who oversee their use of computers in addition to their other duties.

Facilities, security, and technology occupations may include the following:

- Security Guard
- Maintenance and Repair Worker
- Custodian/Janitor
- Web Designer
- Webmaster
- Computer Technician

INDUSTRY OUTLOOK

Overview

The outlook for this industry shows it for the most part to be on the rise. The number of businesses in the industry is growing faster than the average growth rate for all businesses combined. Personal services have expanded at an annualized rate of 2 percent, compared to an average of 1.4 percent for the overall economy. Service occupations will increase by 13.8 percent between 2008 and 2018, compared with an average increase of 11 percent across all occupations. There are so many different personal services that almost all people could find one they would enjoy providing.

Among the major occupational groups, only professional occupations outpace personal service occupations and only by 1 percent. The industry with the most change is laundry and dry cleaning. Small neighborhood businesses in some areas have been replaced by coin-operated laundry facilities. Institutions such as hospitals, hotels, restaurants, and other industries are subcontracting their cleaning to industrial laundries, plants that may have as many as several hundred workers. Dry cleaners also had small operations but are now increasingly using large dry cleaning plants. These plants are squeezing out the small, locally owned operations. They have found a labor supply in immigrant women, although jobs of drivers, pressers, and cleaners or spotters are still mostly filled by men.

There is not much change in hair and beauty salons, fashion consultants, child caregivers, valets, housekeeping, or personal assistants. Tailors have become more specialized, focusing their sewing skills on dressmaking, sail making, or wedding gown design.

Prospects in child care are good because the industry has a high rate of turnover, so many workers leaving the occupation need to be replaced. They leave because of responsibilities in their own families, to study further, or for other reasons. Others leave to pursue other occupations or because of the low wages in child-care work. Child-care workers often work as assistants to preschool teachers. This helps them gain experience in child care. More states instituting preschool education could increase employment growth for child-care workers. Qualified people who want to be child-care workers should have little trouble finding and keeping a job.

Earnings in fashion design can vary widely based on the employer and years of experience. Starting salaries in fashion design tend to be very low, until designers become established in this occupation. Salaried fashion designers usually earn higher and more stable incomes than self-employed or freelance designers. Self-employed fashion designers also must provide their own benefits and for their retirement. A few of the most successful self-employed fashion designers, however, may earn many times the salary of the highest paid salaried designers.

Jobs as parking valets will be plentiful and probably easy to get. Most do not clean cars. Instead they just park them and return them when the owner gets back.

Job prospects are expected to be good in housecleaning. Most job openings will result from turnover. Many new jobs are expected in private households as more people purchase residential cleaning services. There will also be more companies that supply cleaning services on a contract basis. Employment of supervisors and managers of these workers is projected to grow more slowly than the cross-occupation average, increasing by only 5 percent between 2008 and 2018. An increasing number of supervisors will be needed, however, to manage the growing number of housekeepers.

Much of the growth in personal assistants resulted from laid-off workers who attempted to start their own businesses. Starting a personal assistant business involves overcoming a relatively low barrier to entry, as well as low overhead costs. All one needs is a home office, phone, voicemail, and insurance.

Hair and beauty will always be a thriving business because both women and men want to look good.

Employment Advantages

Personal services constitute a feel-good industry. People who help others feel good about what they do. There are many career paths available, with a wide range of roles and salaries. They range from housecleaning to working as a personal assistant to becoming a business executive. Many kinds of other personal assistants operate within almost every occupation.

Annual Earnings

According to the U.S. Bureau of Economic Analysis, all personal services providers earned combined gross revenues of $588.8 billion in 2009 and had a combined gross operating surplus of $108.2 billion.

RELATED RESOURCES FOR FURTHER RESEARCH

American Association of Family and
  Consumer Sciences
400 N Columbus St., Suite 202
Alexandria, VA 22314
Tel: (800) 424-8080
http://www.aafcs.org

PROJECTED EMPLOYMENT FOR SELECTED OCCUPATIONS

Personal and Laundry Services

Employment		
2009	Projected 2018	Occupation
62,290	72,200	Counter and rental clerks
22,870	30,200	First-line supervisors/ managers of personal service workers
319,040	435,500	Hairdressers, hairstylists, and cosmetologists
108,420	119,000	Laundry and dry-cleaning workers
49,100	51,000	Pressers, textile, garment, and related materials

Source: U.S. Bureau of Labor Statistics, Industries at a Glance, Occupational Employment Statistics and Employment Projections Program.

NATIONAL ASSOCIATION FOR FAMILY CHILD CARE
5202 Pinemont Dr.
Salt Lake City, UT 84123
Tel: (800) 359-3817
http://www.nafcc.org

NATIONAL ASSOCIATION FOR THE EDUCATION OF
YOUNG CHILDREN
1313 L St. NW, Suite 500
Washington, DC 20005
Tel: (866) 623-9248
Fax: (202) 328-1846
http://www.naeyc.org

NATIONAL ASSOCIATION OF CHILD CARE
RESOURCE AND REFERRAL AGENCIES
3101 Wilson Blvd., Suite 350
Arlington, VA 22201
Tel: (703) 341-4410
http://www.naccrra.net

NATIONAL CHILD CARE ASSOCIATION
1325 G St. NW, Suite 500
Washington, DC 20005
http://www.nccanet.org

NATIONAL CHILD CARE INFORMATION CENTER
10530 Rosehaven St., Suite 400
Fairfax, VA 22030
http://www.nccic.org

NATIONAL EXTENSION ASSOCIATION OF FAMILY
AND CONSUMER SCIENCES
P.O. Box 849
Winchester, VA 22604
Tel: (800) 808-9133
http://www.neafcs.org

ABOUT THE AUTHOR

Ski Hunter, Ph.D., is a professor at the School of Social Work, University of Texas at Arlington. She teaches in the areas of human behavior, adult development, and personal relationships.

FURTHER READING

Brown, Bobbi, and Sally Wadyka. *Bobbi Brown Beauty Evolution: A Guide to a Lifetime of Beauty.* New York: HarperCollins, 2002.

Careers in Focus: Personal Services. 2d ed. New York: Ferguson, 2007.

Clarke-Stewart, A., and V. D. Allhusen. *What We Know About Childcare.* Cambridge, Mass.: Harvard University Press, 2005.

Ferri, E., and M. E. Siegel. *Finger Tips: A Professional Manicurist's Techniques for Beautiful Hands and Feet.* New York: C. N. Potter, 1988.

Mendelson, C. *Home Comforts: The Art and Science of Keeping House.* New York: Scribner, 1999.

Riordan, T. *Inventing Beauty: A History of the Innovations That Have Made Us Beautiful.* New York: Broadway Books, 2004.

Smith, G., and T. V. Beeck. "Personal Services: A Fast Growing Sector with Unique Risks." *RMA Journal,* July/August, 2009, 60-64.

U.S. Bureau of Labor Statistics. *Career Guide to Industries,* 2010-2011 ed. http://www.bls.gov/oco/cg.

U.S. Census Bureau. North American Industry Classification System (NAICS), 2007. http://www.census.gov/cgi-bin/sssd/naics/naicsrch?chart=2007.

U.S. Department of Commerce. International Trade Administration. Office of Trade and Industry Information. Industry Trade Data and Analysis. http://ita.doc.gov/td/industry/otea/OTII/OTII-index.html.

Wittenberg, R. *Opportunities in Child Care Careers.* New York: McGraw-Hill, 2007.

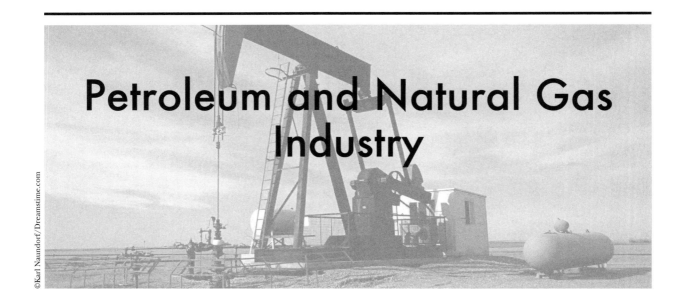

© Karl Naundorf/Dreamstime.com

Petroleum and Natural Gas Industry

INDUSTRY SNAPSHOT

General Industry: Natural Resources

Career Clusters: Agriculture, Food, and Natural Resources; Manufacturing

Subcategory Industries: Drilling Oil and Gas Wells; Oil and Gas Extraction; Petroleum Refineries; Petroleum and Petroleum Products Merchant Wholesalers; Pipeline Transportation of Crude Oil; Pipeline Transportation of Natural Gas; Pipeline Transportation of Refined Petroleum Products; Support Activities for Oil and Gas Operations

Related Industries: Biofuels Industry; Coal Mining Industry; Electrical Power Industry; Natural Resources Management

Annual Domestic Revenues: $1.9 trillion USD (Congressional Reference Service, 2007)

Annual Global Revenues: $4 trillion USD (estimate based on Forbes "Global 2000," 2007)

NAICS Numbers: 211, 486, 4247, 32411, 213111-213112

INDUSTRY DEFINITION

Summary

The petroleum and natural gas industry is concerned with all facets of gas and oil operations, from exploration and extraction to the fuels' delivery to sales outlets and end users. Some energy companies produce both oil and gas, while others produce only one or the other. Both oil and gas have upstream operations involving exploration, development, and production, as well as downstream operations encompassing refining, transporting, retailing, and accounting. Transportation includes loading and unloading terminals, as well as pipelines and transportation fleets. Collectively, these activities place the industry among the United States' and world's largest and offer a wide variety of career possibilities. By the industry's accounting, more than 2 million of the 138.5 million people in the U.S. workforce in 2010 were directly employed in the gas and oil industry, and approximately 9.2 million people were working either in the industry itself or in businesses dependent on it. In terms of gross domestic product (GDP), industry publicists calculate that the industry annually adds over $1 trillion to the U.S. economy (approximately 7.5 percent of the country's wealth).

History of the Industry

Although gas can occur in pockets apart from oil, oil and gas are normally both present at oil wellheads. Despite this geological copresence, however, the histories of these two industries in North America have differed considerably. The modern petroleum industry is older than the natural gas industry by a half century, and oil remains the more versatile and lucrative of the two commodities to this day. Initially focused on the production of kerosene, and with antecedents stretching back a thousand years to Baku, the American oil industry was born in the latter half of the nineteenth century when John D. Rockefeller established his Standard Oil monopoly by cornering the refining market and deploying a fleet of kerosene tankers to carry his product abroad.

The invention of the incandescent lightbulb soon cut into kerosene's appeal as a home lighting source, but the versatility of oil as a means of powering industry, heating homes, and moving naval and passenger ships quickly spurred the industry's growth, as did government policy. Great Britain and other European countries founded national companies to locate, gain access to, and develop the foreign oil fields that their navies needed to protect their empires, even as at home they continued to rely upon coal for the preponderance of their energy needs. In time, two giant international oil companies emerged from their actions: BP (British Petroleum) and Royal Dutch Shell. Meanwhile, in the United States, the era of laissez-faire capitalism that had characterized the country's economy gave way at the end of the nineteenth century to trust-busting. In 1911, the United States Supreme Court sanctioned the breakup of Rockefeller's oil industry giant into its regional components.

Even as separate entities, Standard Oil's California, New York, and New Jersey units (later known as Chevron, Mobil Oil, and Exxon, respectively) remained among the largest petroleum corporations in the world. Not all of them remained vertically integrated, however. Those chronically

An oil rig off the coast of California. (©David Stelmach/Dreamstime.com)

"crude short," such as Mobil, were forced to join the European companies and, eventually, a pair of U.S.-based corporations (Gulf Oil and Texaco) in seeking oil abroad. World War I temporarily interrupted that search, even as it underscored the strategic importance of oil, but with the spread of low-cost, assembly-line-produced automobiles in postwar America and the economic boom of the 1920's, the search for petroleum became more intense. The development of the Oklahoma and Texas fields and the discovery of oil in Saudi Arabia during the interwar period triggered momentary concerns of a glut on the oil market. Since World War II, however, the dominant fear has been one of oil shortages, either as the result of increased demand (especially from 1945 to 1950 and from 2003 to 2008) or as the result of producer states withholding oil shipments (as during the 1973 Arab oil embargo).

In the era stretching from the end of World War II until the 1973 energy crisis, Western nations came to depend on oil they did not possess for the energy upon which their lifestyles depended. Japan and western Europe, which relied on local coal for at least 70 percent of their total energy when World War II ended, recovered from the ravages of that war based primarily on Middle Eastern oil. Consequently, by the time of the 1973 crisis, it was imported oil that accounted for more than 70 percent of their energy. Meanwhile, 1957 was the last year that domestically produced oil met the United States' petroleum demands, and by the time of the oil embargo, the country was importing oil to satisfy approximately 14 percent of its total energy needs.

For years, the growing dependency on outside energy sources was masked by the fact that the global oil market was dominated by the Seven Sisters—Exxon, Mobil, Standard Oil of California, Gulf, Texaco, BP, and Royal Dutch Shell. As late as 1970, this Western oil consortium still accounted for approximately 80 percent of all oil produced outside North America and the communist world, as well as 70 percent of that area's refining capacity.

An oil pump jack in southern Alberta, Canada. (©Karl Naundorf/Dreamstime.com)

The consortium either leased or owned oil tankers carrying over 50 percent of the oil moving from producer to consumer countries.

Nevertheless, even in 1970, the movement into international operations of several formerly domestic oil companies was undercutting the Seven Sisters' ability to establish the market price of oil. In the aftermath of the 1973 energy crisis, that power passed to the major producer-exporting states that constituted the Seven Sisters' replacement cartel, the Organization of Petroleum Exporting Countries (OPEC). Likewise, as OPEC states bought out the private petroleum corporations' holdings inside their borders, control over reserves passed to a new set of "majors"—the state-owned oil companies, now capped by such giants as Saudi Aramco, the National Iranian Oil Company, Petroleos de Venezuela, and the Kuwait Petroleum Corporation.

By the time these events were occurring in the petroleum industry, the American natural gas industry had been established for nearly four decades. In the early 1930's, electronic welding techniques made it possible for gas producers to create a pipeline network capable of transporting natural gas to consumers throughout the country. This pipeline allowed producers to sell the gas that had previously been burnt off as a nuisance at oil well-heads in the gas fields of Oklahoma, Louisiana, Texas, and elsewhere.

The natural gas industry blossomed, finding a growing market for its product in the utility companies supplying power to home consumers. It did so

Inputs Consumed by the Oil and Natural Gas Extraction Industry

Input	Value
Energy	$9.7 billion
Materials	$47.8 billion
Purchased services	$62.1 billion
Total	$119.6 billion

Source: U.S. Bureau of Economic Analysis. Data are for 2008.

within the framework of the regulatory state that emerged during the Franklin D. Roosevelt administration. Because its primary purchasers were utility companies, which operated as government-regulated monopolies, natural gas producers were soon regulated by federal statutes seeking to control the price of natural gas. These statutes prohibited natural gas producers from owning both the pipelines transporting gas and the utility companies utilizing it. U.S. natural gas producers moved out of the utility industry at that time, and they continue to lack the end-use supply network that petroleum corporations have in their service station outlets, even though most of the other regulations affecting the price of natural gas, as well as those limiting pipeline ownership, have subsequently been eliminated or relaxed.

The Oil and Gas Extraction Industry's Contribution to the U.S. Economy

Value Added	Amount
Gross domestic product	$203.8 billion
Gross domestic product	1.4%
Persons employed	161,000
Total employee compensation	$26.9 billion

Source: U.S. Bureau of Economic Analysis. Data are for 2008.

The Industry Today

Despite their different histories, the petroleum industry and the natural gas industry continue to have much in common. Both are capital- and technology-intensive industries in ways that differentiate them from midsize and small-scale operations in other energy-producing sectors, such as strip or deep-shaft coal mining. Both—especially in their upstream research, extraction, and development activities—rely on employees with extensive training across a wide range of professions. Because oil and gas are the principal energy sources in the energy-intensive

The Pipeline Transportation Industry's Contribution to the U.S. Economy

Value Added	Amount
Gross domestic product	$13.7 billion
Gross domestic product	0.1%
Persons employed	41,000
Total employee compensation	$4.7 billion

Source: U.S. Bureau of Economic Analysis. Data are for 2008.

Western world and are increasingly sought by developing states, both the private corporations and the state companies involved in the industry are expected to continue hiring new employees for years to come.

The natural gas industry continues to be primarily involved in the upstream production of natural gas and in building and maintaining the pipelines that carry it to public utility companies. Indeed, whether carried out by the producers themselves or by the large pipeline industry that has grown up around the oil and gas industry, building pipelines has become a major industry in its own right. Technological changes have also made the production of liquified gas into a bona fide export business for countries with large holdings and low consumption capacities. Thus, BP is committed to developing a market for its liquefied petroleum gas (LPG) in Asian and European areas, where populations dwelling beyond the reach of city utility services may find LPG attractive for home heating, cooking, and hot water generation.

Technological advances likewise continue to shape the petroleum industry. Large-scale investments in upstream and downstream activities continue to be made by both private petroleum corporations—many of which merged during the 1980's and 1990's—and the state-owned companies of the OPEC producers. Coupled with the rising, OPEC-set price of oil on the world market, these developments have widened the extraction end of the industry into offshore operations conducted even in turbulent waters such as those of the North Sea.

Projects also extract oil from such exotic sources as tar sands and oil shale.

New extraction techniques have permitted the commercially viable development of relatively low yield offshore pools and mile-deep wells on land whose development was not previously cost-effective. Lateral drilling is now capable of reaching oil deposits that would otherwise be unattainable. Oil fields once thought to be commercially exhausted have been revisited with secondary and tertiary recovery techniques capable of producing more oil from them.

New technologies have also affected downstream operations. For example, in 2010 Standard Oil increased the efficiency of its delivery and billing operations by introducing a wireless system to electronically track its shipments from refineries to distributors. The system enabled the company to plan more efficient routing, curtailing the number of miles its tankers needed to travel in order to deliver fuel to its service stations.

The petroleum and natural gas industry's job market is complex, so career options within the industry may be difficult to assess. The variety of jobs at all levels of skill and in a variety of different settings defies easy description. Many recent changes, such as the ability to extract oil from tar sands, have widened the job market, even as the introduction of more efficient technologies and practices have contracted that market in other areas. Economic swings have also negatively affected the job market

Inputs Consumed by the Pipeline Transportation Industry

Input	Value
Energy	$2.0 billion
Materials	$2.3 billion
Purchased services	$10.1 billion
Total	$14.4 billion

Source: U.S. Bureau of Economic Analysis. Data are for 2008.

Building pipelines has become a major industry in its own right. (©Keng Po Leung/Dreamstime.com)

when plunging demand and oil prices have encouraged industry restructuring and mergers, with a resultant downsizing of operations.

INDUSTRY MARKET SEGMENTS

The profiles of the various sectors in the petroleum and natural gas industry do not correspond directly to the profiles of other industries, which generally include small, midsize, and large businesses. Even the businesses that are small relative to others in the industry are large by most standards. Independent firms, such as Ashland and Marathon Oil Corporation in the United States, are often involved in large-scale, expensive energy extraction and refining operations, and some produce both natural gas and oil. It may be more useful to segment the industry into downstream retailing and distribution activities, downstream transportation activities, and mid- and upstream development and production activities. Various firms specialize in these segments. However, large, vertically integrated corporations also exist that operate within all three segments at once.

Retailing and Distribution

The principal businesses operating at the end of the downstream activities of the oil and gas industry are the public utility companies that purchase natural gas and distribute it to home and business customers, as well as the service stations and home fuel companies that distribute transportation fuels and home heating oil to local customers.

Potential Annual Earnings Scale. Earning opportunities related to work within the public utility sector depends on the position, with jobs running from engineering and managerial positions at the top to repair and meter reading positions in the trenches. Overall, according to the U.S. Bureau of Labor Statistics (BLS), the average salary among all workers in the utilities industry in 2009 was $61,530 per year.

Oil retailing is a thriving business with a massive number of outlets. BP alone estimates that it serves 10 million motorists daily with its 44,000 service stations around the world. The United States has approximately 175,000 retail outlets dispensing gasoline and diesel fuel—a number smaller than before the oil industry restructured in the 1990's, but also one that remained relatively stable throughout the first decade of the twenty-first century.

The earnings of proprietor-operated fuel stations vary depending on their location and nature. The highest profits are normally garnered at stations lining major highways and offering twenty-four-hour convenience-store shopping. These hybrids continue to grow in number and were already grossing slightly under $800,000 per year in 2000 through their convenience-store sales alone. Also profitable are fast food-service station hybrids and the now proportionally few stations still offering full-service automotive maintenance, with mechanics on duty and selling tires, batteries, and other automotive supplies. Their gross receipts are apt to be less, but their needed staff is also smaller because their hours of operation tend to be less as well. Profits also depend on the locale of an operation. According to the BLS, in 2009 the average annual salary of automotive mechanics and technicians employed at gasoline stations was $33,850, while the average salary of service station attendants was $19,890.

Clientele Interaction. Except perhaps for highway service stations, where most customers are transient in nature, clientele interaction is important for both the gas and oil outlets at the local level. As regulated monopolies, public utility companies enjoy captive markets, and customers can grow restive when rates increase substantially. Public relations thus becomes a major part of their business. Meanwhile, the high level of competition most service stations face from other service stations, convenience stores, and automotive repair shops makes customer satisfaction crucial to repeat business, whether the face of the business is that of a friendly cashier or a proprietor who knows the names of regular customers.

Amenities, Atmosphere, and Physical Grounds. The twenty-first century has witnessed significant changes in the distribution networks for oil and gas at the local level. Natural gas continues to be distributed through a network of over one

An engineer stands on pipes to look at part of the oil and gas refinery. (©Dreamstime.com)

thousand government-regulated natural gas distribution companies that collectively control over 1 million miles of pipeline linking them to their local home and business customers. The majority of these firms still operate as government-granted monopolies in their areas. Because state governments regulate them, those governments can impose minimum standards for hiring upon these companies. These standards must be investigated by anyone seeking employment at a natural gas utility.

Public utility companies consciously maintain a clean ambiance, so office workers generally enjoy orderly and climate-controlled workplaces. Field workers, by contrast, spend most of their time outdoors, in all kinds of weather. Those laying and repairing pipelines work with heavy machinery underground and are subject to industrial hazards common to such occupations.

Older cities still retain companies committed to delivering fuel oil for home heating systems, and the existing networks for delivering aviation fuel to airports have changed little. However, the typical neighborhood service station has been radically transformed since 1990. Most typically, it has turned into either a miniconvenience store-gasoline station hybrid or it has paired with a fast-food franchise—or both. Marquees have also changed, as oil industry mergers have occurred and the outlets of acquired companies have closed or hoisted the logos of their new parent companies. Not infrequently, abandoned properties have been purchased by smaller, independent oil company operatives or convenience store chains contracting with oil suppliers, such as the QuikTrip convenience store stations in the Southwest.

Convenience and food store hybrids necessarily must project clean appearances. However, given the price of land, whether purchased or leased, metropolitan full-service gasoline stations are not usually located in prime, attractive settings. Mechanics working in service bays are generally surrounded by the noise and grime associated with automotive repair throughout their workdays.

Typical Number of Employees. The positions available at all levels in the public utility field are directly proportional to the size of the metropolitan or rural districts being served. As for service stations, the principal variables are whether they are twenty-four-hour operations and whether they include convenience stores with one or two cashiers or fast-food establishments with separate food staffs. Twenty-four-hour operations need staff around the clock; however, given the fact that most pumps are now self-service, these operations can often function with staffs of three or four persons per day, or a total of six to seven employees on rotating schedules. Full-service stations with mechanics on duty can also suffice with three or so people, including their proprietors. However, they are usually open only ten to twelve hours per day, and only five or six days per week.

Traditional Geographic Locations. Gas distributors, public utility outlets, service stations, home fuel oil services, and suppliers of aviation fuel are nationwide sources of employment, given

the dependency of Americans on natural gas and transportation fuel.

Pros of Working in Retailing or Distribution. The principal advantage of employment in this segment is the ability to work in one's home locale, normally on a set schedule. Retail and distribution workers often have opportunities to interact with customers. Positions in the public utility field carry a high level of job security, and supervisors and home office staff enjoy white-collar working conditions.

Cons of Working in Retailing or Distribution. Public utilities are generally bureaucratic organizations. Service station-convenience store hybrids demand low energy but pay low wages. Mechanic jobs, while potentially gratifying, require multitasking and working under time pressures to keep customers happy. Managing or owning a service station involves shouldering the responsibilities of any small enterprise owner (managing payroll, paying bills, maintaining inventory, and so forth), but it may not come with the freedom usually associated with self-employment, as large corporations often set the prices to be charged at each station.

Costs

Payroll and Benefits: Public utilities pay salaries or hourly wages, and they generally offer relatively generous benefits. Service stations pay hourly wages and rarely pay benefits.

Supplies: Various businesses in this segment may require retailing supplies, such as cash registers and credit card machines; tools for automotive repair, pipeline repair, and road excavation or construction; cleaning supplies; vehicle fleets; office supplies and equipment; and so on.

External Services: Retailing and distribution businesses may contract accounting and tax preparation, maintenance, landscaping, security, or advertising services as necessary. They often require insurance as well, and may need to contract hazardous waste disposal services if those are not provided by local government.

Utilities: Businesses typically pay for electricity, water, sewage, oil or gas, telephone, and Internet access.

Taxes: Private businesses must pay local, state, and federal corporate and property taxes. Business owners may report income on their personal returns, in which case they must also pay self-employment taxes. Public utilities are exempt from local taxes.

Transportation

Pipeline companies transport natural gas from processing plants to public utility companies. Pipeline companies and land and sea transportation fleets transport oil from extraction sites to refineries to distribution terminals to service stations. Oil tanker trucks and sea-going oil tankers may be owned and operated either by oil producers or by contracted agents of the industry. The principal independent businesses in this segment are regional pipeline companies.

Potential Annual Earnings Scale. According to the BLS, the average salary of all employees of pipeline companies in 2009 was $62,700. Engineering managers in the field earned an average of $132,040, while operations managers earned an average of $112,060. Petroleum engineers in the field earned an average of $103,070, control and valve installers and repairers earned an average of $50,160, and front-line production workers earned an average of $56,110. Among land and sea workers, heavy truck drivers in the oil and gas industry earned an average of $38,400 in 2009. Sailors and marine oilers earned an average of $50,860, while captains, mates, and pilots earned an average of $89,060.

Clientele Interaction. Aside from lobbying state and federal officials, the pipeline business operates largely outside the sight of the public. Natural gas pipeline companies, when not owned by suppliers, necessarily attempt to maintain good customer relations with their suppliers and those at the opposite end of the pipeline charged with marketing their wares to utility companies and local consumers. However, because of the heavily automated nature of the pipelines themselves, clientele interaction is low overall in the pipeline industry.

Amenities, Atmosphere, and Physical Grounds. Those working in the headquarters and field offices of pipeline companies enjoy comfortable work environments, often in prime locales in major cities. Those who drive trucks, repair pipelines, and work on sea-going oil tankers lack most of these amenities and work long hours at physically demanding jobs, often in uncomfortable circumstances. For the latter, the amenities—like the

advantages of their jobs—are highly personal. The sea can be alluring and a life on it, even with hard work, pleasurable to some. The same is true of the open road, and the task of muscling an eighteen-wheeler from refinery to neighborhood station can be satisfying. The physical landscape of the truck driver is unlikely to inspire, however, and the work can be grueling.

Typical Number of Employees. The number of employees at all levels in the pipeline industry depends on the geographical scale of operations and the pipeline mileage being managed by the individual company. The average number of employees per company is in the low hundreds, including accountants and clerical employees operating at corporate headquarters. Specific numbers are particularly hard to locate for the petroleum wing of the pipeline business because many of those professionals (engineers, for example) who become involved with oil pipelines are also involved in upstream activities in the industry.

Estimates of the number of petroleum tanker drivers serving petroleum producers and refineries are even more difficult to report. This segment of the industry is now carefully watched by the Department of Homeland Security because of the danger of terrorists using oil tankers as rolling bombs. Land transport also occurs largely within vertically integrated companies that do not always differentiate in their reports the specific numbers performing each task when those tasks are similar, as in the case of truck driving, which can include driving tankers, rig hauling, carrying explosives, driving vacuum trucks transporting wastes, and driving supply trucks.

Finally, the number of seamen needed on board an oil tanker depends on the size of the tanker itself. Supertankers are becoming increasingly automated, shrinking jobs in the field. However, slots are not hard to find for qualified seamen. ExxonMobil alone maintains a fleet of over fifty tankers. Land drivers are likewise in demand, the number depending on the size of the petroleum corporation's refinery output and the area being served.

Traditional Geographic Locations. The oil pipelines transporting petroleum from wellheads to refineries in the United States tend to cover the short distances typically separating extraction operations from refineries. Work in this sector is thus concentrated in the states where the most oil is produced. Refined oil and processed gas enter the national network of pipelines, and pipeline managing positions can exist anywhere along that network. Trucks carrying petroleum normally serve areas within defined radii of oil refineries, as well as pipeline terminal points across the country.

Gas pipeline companies are regionally organized. Each company tends to operate in a general region such as the Southwest, the Pacific Northwest, and so forth. Thus, a career with one of these companies would be largely spent within one such region.

Pros of Working in Transportation. Working midstream in the oil and gas industry is not like working for a midsize business in most sectors. The regionalized gas pipeline companies tend to be well established, have somewhat captive client bases, and enjoy low competition. They offer very secure employment.

The same can largely be said of careers involving the transport of petroleum and petroleum products. Employers are most likely to be vertically integrated economic giants, capable of offering competitive wages and above-average benefits packages. Workers also enjoy the job security of dealing with commodities that are likely to remain in high demand throughout their lifetimes. Finally, the industry offers positions for people who like to work alone (such as truck drivers and pipeline maintenance workers), as well as for those who like to work on teams (at company headquarters).

Cons of Working in Transportation. There are no "walk-in" positions in the oil and natural gas transportation industry segment. College degrees and sometimes advanced work are required for many positions involving natural gas pipelines. Various certificates and licenses are absolutely required to drive a big rig or to become a merchant marine. In addition, many positions require security checks and drug testing. Elsewhere, although job security is good, some positions are being shrunk by further automation (electronic rather than spot testing for pipeline breaches, for example), and other positions (such as driving a tanker loaded with highly inflammable liquids) are hazardous.

Costs

Payroll and Benefits: Oil and natural gas transportation workers receive salaries or hourly wages. Both the pay and the benefits provided by firms within the industry are usually superior to the average pay and benefits across all industries. This high compensation reflects the lucrative nature of the business, the size of most companies, and the expertise necessary to obtain a job in the industry.

Supplies: The essential supplies required for oil and natural gas transportation are very large ticket items. Depending on the size of the pipeline (41 inch or 45 inch diameters, for example) and the nature of the terrain, the cost of laying a pipeline can average $500,000 or more per mile. Likewise, the cost and maintenance of a fleet of trucks equipped to transport refined oil can range into the tens of millions of dollars, and the cost of a single sea-going oil tanker starts at $100 million. Depending on the price of oil and the calmness of the sea, the cost of operating such a vessel begins at more than $30,000 per day.

External Services: To assure the integrity of stockholder reports and the management of pension funds (or stock options), and to satisfy tax authorities, outside auditors are commonly contracted by petroleum and natural gas companies. Most other functions at these large corporations are handled in-house, although they may contract lobbying consultants or public relations firms to supplement existing staff for specific projects. Insurance of a natural gas or oil corporation's holdings also represents a significant expense.

Utilities: Petroleum and natural gas corporations are not only capital-intensive businesses but also energy-intensive ones. Pipeline pumping stations and the equipment necessary to keep the pipelines within prescribed temperature ranges require electricity. Gas, electrical power, water, and sanitation services are also required in all facets of their operations, from home offices to field stations. Measured against the costliness of the supplies necessary for those involved in gas and petroleum transportation activity, however, these are comparatively small operating expenses.

Taxes: Oil and natural gas companies must pay local, state, federal, and international corporate and property taxes, as well as industry-specific taxes, such as severance fees and other taxes on fossil fuels. They also, however, have access to tax benefits that can greatly reduce their overall tax burdens. In addition, the international nature of the business can help reduce taxes, as, for example, profits or losses sustained in transporting petroleum and refined fuels can be enfolded for maximum tax benefit into the tax filings for overall corporate operations, in which taxes paid to foreign governments can offset part of their domestic tax bills.

Other Expenses: Transport companies must maintain large contingency funds in the event of accidents and may face very significant expenses in the rare event of an environmental disaster.

Development and Production

The largest segment of the petroleum and natural gas industry is the upstream segment. These companies and corporate divisions locate fossil fuel deposits, determine how to extract them, engage in extraction, and refine the raw resources into usable fuel and other products.

Geologists begin the search for oil and gas, using the newest techniques, which today means seismic instruments that use sound-waves to locate oil and gas deposits—a practice that has transformed the search process. Petroleum engineers, environmental engineers, and construction engineers all contribute to the installation of largely automated drilling and extraction equipment. This equipment is maintained by drilling supervisors with the assistance of various skilled personnel and general hands, still known as roustabouts in the industry.

Engineers plan pipelines to transport oil and gas from the fields to nearby processing plants. Gas plants purify natural gas and then add odor to it for safety purposes because purified natural gas is odorless and potentially lethal. Oil refineries, while typically near the fields, can also be half a world away.

Potential Annual Earnings Scale. Because of the skill levels required, the often arduous nature of work, and the frequently harsh conditions in which they work, wage and salaried personnel in the oil and gas industry are normally paid at least 10 percent more at all levels than are employees performing similar tasks in other sectors of the mining category. Highly skilled workers and employees drawn from professionals are similarly well paid.

According to the BLS, the average salary of general and operations managers in the oil and gas ex-

traction industry in 2009 was \$139,630. Industrial production managers earned an average of \$119,590, while engineering managers earned an average of \$151,650, and petroleum engineers earned an average of \$126,090. Engineering technicians earned an average of \$68,720, geoscientists earned an average of \$136,270, and geological and petroleum technicians earned an average of \$63,600. Petroleum pump and refinery operators earned an average of \$57,780, and gas plant operators earned an average of \$54,050. Roustabouts earned an average of \$36,400.

Clientele Interaction. The large revenue and profits that the oil and gas industry regularly report have frequently provoked public criticism and legislative action. Especially in the wake of the 2010 *Deepwater Horizon* disaster in the Gulf of Mexico, the industry has found itself targeted by public interest groups. For this reason, the industry maintains a highly skilled public relations staff and employs experienced lobbyists to make its case in the media and before governing bodies. Otherwise, the dialogues of those involved in the business of finding, developing, producing, and processing oil and gas tend to be in-house, not between producers and clients.

Amenities, Atmosphere, and Physical Grounds. Executives, scientists, accountants, and legal staffs working in home offices enjoy the creature comforts of modern civilization and, often, state-of-the-art facilities and equipment. The same is true of the industry's engineers and geologists when they are not in the field. However, field assignments can take these scientists far away from their amenities. Field workers engaged in construction, extraction, and refining activities, such as pipeline pumping station managers, are in the field most of the time and for the life of a given field. Moreover, even with automation technologies, field work can be arduous. It is performed in areas where the outside temperature may be uncomfortably high or low, generally around the clock.

Typical Number of Employees. There are approximately 161,000 Americans domestically employed in the development and production of oil and natural gas. Most of these work in the extraction end of the business, either in drilling operations or in general (roustabout) labor. Small independent producers concentrating primarily on extraction activities often operate with fewer than twenty full-time employees. They contract additional drillers, accountants, and other staff when needed. By contrast, ExxonMobil, the largest employer in the industry, employs nearly eighty-five thousand people worldwide.

Traditional Geographic Locations. The major oil firms have headquarters in major cities, notably in Houston and New York in the United States and in world capitals abroad. They also have regional offices in urban and international regional centers. Field operations occur wherever oil or natural gas are located and extractable, anywhere in the world. Domestically, the greatest oil-producing states are Texas, California, Oklahoma, and Louisiana. Refineries are normally located either near oil fields, outside industrial centers where the demand for refined oil is high, or at seaports large enough to serve oil tankers.

Pros of Working in Development and Production. Oil and natural gas companies are most likely to be vertically integrated economic giants, capable of offering competitive wages and above-average benefits packages. Workers also enjoy the job security of dealing with commodities that are likely to remain in high demand throughout their lifetimes.

Cons of Working in Development and Production. Because oil corporations are so large, employees may feel lost in the crowd and may be frustrated by corporate bureaucracy. Corporate decisions are made based on the bottom line, and during economic difficulties retrenchment decisions are made. Thus, individual companies may cut jobs in some areas to refocus on others as their circumstances change. Also, even when the overall picture is positive, the introduction of new technologies or changing oil prices can significantly affect specific career paths. Finally, the geologists, engineers, and general managers involved in the industry spend considerable time on the road. The members of drilling crews must also be willing to move as old fields become automated and experienced personnel are needed in new locales.

Costs

Payroll and Benefits: Petroleum and natural gas companies are large employers of personnel at all levels, offering competitive wages and fringe benefit packages, stock options, and attractive pension plans. For a major multinational concern, payrolls and benefits may represent a cost of tens of billions of dollars.

Supplies: Fossil fuel development and production requires extremely complex and heavy machinery, including massive drilling equipment. Refineries require industrial-scale machinery as well. Even the seismological equipment now used to prospect for oil and gas can be extremely expensive. In addition to these supplies, corporations require all standard office business supplies.

External Services: Oil and gas corporations contract outside auditors and security consultants. Large corporations tend to handle all other tasks in-house, whereas smaller independent concerns often contract maintenance, legal, engineering, custodial, and other services. All oil and gas companies require insurance.

Utilities: Utility costs ranging from the lighting of corporate headquarters to the powering of drilling and refining operations are significant for even independent oil companies, and they are very sizeable for the majors, albeit dwarfed by the cost of constructing and maintaining production and refining facilities. In some instances, those costs have encouraged petroleum companies to seek alternative energy sources. For example, solar power units requiring little maintenance have been installed when feasible for some purposes on offshore drilling platforms.

Taxes: Oil and natural gas companies must pay local, state, federal, and international corporate and property taxes, as well as industry-specific taxes, such as severance fees and other taxes on fossil fuels. They also, however, have access to tax benefits that can greatly reduce their overall tax burdens. In addition, the international nature of the business can help reduce taxes, as, for example, profits or losses sustained in transporting petroleum and refined fuels can be enfolded for maximum tax benefit into the tax filings for overall corporate operations, in which taxes paid to foreign governments can offset part of their domestic tax bills.

Other Expenses: Oil and gas companies must maintain large contingency funds in the event of accidents and may face very significant expenses in the rare event of an environmental disaster.

ORGANIZATIONAL STRUCTURE AND JOB ROLES

The U.S. natural gas industry encompasses 6,500 producers, 530 processing plants, 160 pipeline companies operating 300,000 miles of pipeline (including 180,000 miles interstate), 123 natural gas storage operators with 400 underground facilities, and 260 companies marketing natural gas. The oil industry is similarly spread out, with numerous companies involved in both oil and gas. The petroleum industry encompasses the global search for oil, its extraction, its refining into transportation fuel and chemical products, its transportation, and its distribution through a network of company-owned or -licensed service station retailers, whose customers can often charge their purchases on oil-company credit cards. Consequently, careers in this broad industry reflect its scope and the intertwined nature of its operations across the multiple hiring sectors it encompasses.

The following umbrella categories apply to the organizational structure of businesses in the petroleum and natural gas industry:

- Business Management
- Customer Service
- Sales and Marketing
- Facilities and Security
- Technology, Research, Design, and Development
- Production and Operations
- Distribution
- Human Resources

Business Management

There is an overwhelming consensus among objective observers that the oil and gas industry is well managed. Indeed, the term understates the case. Even during the global financial crisis of 2007-2009, with the resultant drop in demand for their products, the larger private oil and gas corporations continued to record overall profits on their vertically integrated concerns. Many also managed to increase their overall revenue even as the industry contracted, and several of the majors continued to expand their acquisitions, as in December of 2009 when ExxonMobil acquired XTO Energy for $31 billion in order to increase its natural gas holdings in the United States.

Top management tends to be drawn from people who have spent careers in the industry and includes those with field experience in engineering positions, as well as those who have made careers in business management. They oversee the overall and sector operations of their companies, make decisions involving resource allocation to upstream and downstream activities, and engage in long-term planning. Operational managers are accountable to them; they are accountable to stockholders.

Also at each corporate headquarters are the corporation's own certified public accountants and its legal staff. Outside auditors may be employed to help produce annual shareholders' reports. However, the large corporations have their own staffs and their own legal departments, composed of both lawyers and paralegals.

Finally, at the lower echelons, corporate headquarters require large support staffs of administrative assistants, general technicians, and clerical personnel, all of whom are normally able to rise to supervisory positions over time and most of whom are eligible to participate in corporate stock-option pension plans. Given the industry's performance over the past four decades, these pension plans have produced very comfortable retirements.

Business management occupations may include the following:

- President/Chief Executive Officer (CEO)
- Chief Financial Officer (CFO)
- Chief Operating Officer (COO)
- General Counsel
- Engineering Manager
- Billing Manager
- Vice President of Exploration and Development
- Vice President of Public and Government Relations
- Accountant/Auditor
- Certified Public Accountant

Customer Service

Two areas are subsumed under customer service. First, there are the managers in charge of coordinating the relationships among the internal components of the vertically integrated corporation, who are inwardly their own customers, or of communicating with the consumers of their products, such as refineries, brokers, and so on. Second, there are those who are involved in field operations. For example, schedulers coordinate the delivery of refined fuels to service station outlets, home heating oil companies, and airports. Direct contact with individual end users is normally left in the hands of the retail outlets in the oil industry, the utility companies in the gas industry, and other third parties.

Customer service occupations may include the following:

- Public Relations Director
- Public Relations Representative
- Information Services Specialist
- Scheduler

Sales and Marketing

Because of the structure of the industry, the similarity of the product from producer to producer, and the essential nature of that product, there is less aggressive sales and marketing activity in the oil and gas industry than in most other industries. Salesmanship is more likely to occur before a state legislature concerned with high gas prices than to be involved in inducing customers to purchase a particular brand of gasoline, although such ad campaigns occasionally occur. Those campaigns normally originate within the public relations departments of corporate headquarters, where advertising specialists are on staff. Public relations campaigns normally originate in, or are coordinated by, the American Petroleum Institute, which has looked after the industry's interests almost since the day when the Standard Oil monopoly was broken.

Either as a separate department or an ancillary to sales and marketing, those corporations with their own credit cards, which include the majors that operate retail station outlets, maintain their own credit card operations and hire staffs composed of programmers, computer technicians, customer service representatives, and clerical personnel.

Sales and marketing occupations may include the following:

- Vice President of Sales and Marketing
- Sales Manager
- Marketing Manager
- Market Research Analyst
- Sales Representative
- Credit Operations Director
- Account Executive
- Account Associate

Facilities and Security

The security of oil and gas property and holdings has always been of concern, if only because the equipment employed is valuable and requires guarding against theft. Environmentalists have sometimes been angered by drilling sites, and protecting facilities against political vandalism has become a more recent concern. Since the terrorist attacks of September 11, 2001, however, the security of all facets of this industry has been given priority, with concerns ranging from guarding refineries and gas fields from terrorist attacks to preventing the hijacking of oil tankers that could easily be made to function as rolling bombs.

Employment opportunities in the security sector go beyond interior patrolling. Perimeter guarding of facilities against intrusion, or even photographers, is needed, as are computer and network security experts. Small staffs of people with military, civil-government, or private-firm experience in the security field are becoming as basic to the operations of large energy corporations as are geologists and petroleum engineers. Salaries at all levels are at least competitive with similar jobs in the private sector.

Facilities and security occupations may include the following:

- Emergency Services Crew
- Computer Network Security Specialist
- Installation and Perimeter Security Specialist
- Risk Analyst
- Security Manager
- Security Guard
- Maintenance Supervisor
- Maintenance and Repair Worker
- Custodian/Janitor

Technology, Research, Design, and Development

The oil and natural gas industry is forward-looking: Each corporation is more concerned about running out of resources to develop than about competition with other corporations. As a result, research scientists, laboratory technicians, engineers, draftsmen, and others work to develop new methods for extracting, transporting, and processing petroleum and gas. The hiring market is not wide, but for those penetrating it a secure career awaits in an industry that relies on continuous innovation to reach difficult areas on- and offshore and to build pipelines that can sustain high pressures in extreme weather and temperature conditions. Indeed, research and development is an almost recession-proof area to which the industry usually allocates steady funding, even in times of declining revenues.

Technology, research, design, and development occupations may include the following:

- Engineering Manager
- Natural Sciences Manager
- Industrial Engineer
- Industrial Engineering Technician
- Petroleum Engineer
- Petroleum Engineering Technician
- Geologist
- Geological/Petroleum Technician

Production and Operations

Project engineers, drilling personnel, mechanical engineers, pipeline managers, and general managers oversee production and operations activities. Managerial pay reflects the size of the crew, with pay slightly higher in the area of refining (where a total of sixty thousand are domestically employed, despite the growing automation of refineries), as well as the technical competence needed for the position. As in most sectors of the industry, the top positions in production and operations require either on-site experience or area-specific college and graduate degrees.

Production and operations occupations may include the following:

- Petroleum Engineer
- Industrial Engineer
- Industrial Production Manager
- Construction Manager
- Roustabout
- Service Unit/Rotary Drill/Derrick Operator

- Construction Supervisor
- Petroleum Pump System Operator/ Refinery Operator/Gauger
- Gas Plant Operator
- Production Supervisor
- Wellhead Pumper
- Environmental Scientist

Distribution

Distribution personnel transport oil and natural gas products to wholesalers, public utilities, and other sellers and consumers. The best-paying positions are the white-collar and highly skilled ones in the utility companies distributing natural gas to end users, as well as proprietor-ownership positions involving hybrid gasoline stations along well-traveled routes.

Distribution occupations may include the following:

- Distribution Manager
- Heavy Truck Driver
- Dispatcher
- Shipping and Receiving Clerk
- Control and Valve Installer/Repairer
- Petroleum Pump System Operator/ Refinery Operator/Gauger
- Gas Compressor/Gas Pumping Station Operator
- Sailor/Marine Oiler
- Water Vessel Captain/Mate

Human Resources

Big corporations, such as those in the oil and natural gas industry, have large human resources departments to manage hiring, termination, benefit packages, and sometimes in-house pension funds. Career opportunities in managing these departments, in accounting services related to them, and in overseeing employee relations exist in all of the majors, the state-petroleum corporations, and most of the smaller oil and gas companies.

Human resources occupations may include the following:

- Human Resources Manager
- Recruiter
- Human Resources Generalist
- Payroll Clerk
- Benefits Specialist

- Administrative Assistant
- Pension Plan Manager

INDUSTRY OUTLOOK

Overview

The outlook for this industry shows it to be in decline. The BLS projects that between 2008 and 2018, employment in natural gas and oil extraction will decrease by 16 percent, while employment by natural gas utilities will decrease by 11 percent. At the same time, employment across all sectors of the economy is projected to grow by 11 percent. Automation will continue to reduce the number of employees needed at the extraction end of the business; however, the 2010 BLS report on the industry noted that the overall employment picture will be improved by the fact that many current employees are nearing retirement age and will need to be replaced. Skilled workers in some positions, espe-

cially involving exploration, will always be in demand, as finding and developing new sources of fossil fuels become increasingly difficult. Moreover the sheer breadth of activities within the industry guards against any across-the-board drying up of career opportunities, although many such opportunities may exist in Asia, Australia, and Latin America.

The private petroleum corporations, which lack and no longer have guaranteed access to deep reserves, are moving more into upstream activities. These involve not just exploring for new pools of oil but also pursuing extraction processes once thought to be exotic, such as seeking oil from tar sands and oil shale, and producing liquefied petroleum gas. In 2007, almost 80 percent of the net income of the U.S. oil and gas industry came from these upstream operations. Meanwhile, state companies within and outside OPEC, with their access to often very deep oil and gas reserves, are more inclined to balance their upstream and downstream investments or to expand their downstream operations. Thus, during the first quarter of 2010, Saudi Arabia launched an ambitious five-year expansion plan capitalized at $170 billion, divided almost evenly between upstream investments ($90 billion, focused on increasing natural gas development in order to free for export the oil now being used for electrical generation) and downstream refining and petrochemical operations ($80 billion).

PROJECTED EMPLOYMENT FOR SELECTED OCCUPATIONS

Support Activities for Mining

Employment		
2009	Projected 2018	Occupation
18,920	18,300	Derrick operators, oil and gas
15,000	23,900	First-line supervisors/managers of construction trades and extraction workers
20,980	20,400	Rotary drill operators, oil and gas
43,970	50,400	Roustabouts, oil and gas
29,590	30,700	Service unit operators, oil, gas, and mining

Source: U.S. Bureau of Labor Statistics, Industries at a Glance, Occupational Employment Statistics and Employment Projections Program.

Employment Advantages

Industry employers and career counseling guides frequently stress industry working conditions. Most positions work regular hours, leaving employees' time free after those hours. Some jobs are arduous; for example, working on an offshore oil rig normally involves working fourteen straight days on the job, but the shift is then followed by twenty-one days off work and on shore.

Industry salaries can be high, and benefits are generous. A rapid rise in income is not a feature of industry jobs, however. Those who begin in low-skill jobs (for example, roughnecks on off-

About 175,000 retail outlets in the United States dispense gasoline and diesel fuel. (©Michael Adams/Dreamstime.com)

shore rigs) have the opportunity to rise to supervisory positions as they acquire additional skill and experience.

Job skills in the industry are normally portable, insofar as the tasks are similar regardless of the locale, and multinational corporations hire globally. Saudi Aramco, for example, boasts that it is the employer of a workforce numbering fifty-four thousand drawn from more than fifty different countries. It can also be satisfying to help the world's nations obtain the energy they need to function. More elusive but important, employees, from oil rig roughnecks to top industry executives, tend to share a camaraderie unmatched in most if not all other industries.

PROJECTED EMPLOYMENT FOR SELECTED OCCUPATIONS

Oil and Gas Extraction

Employment		
2009	Projected 2018	Occupation
6,500	5,700	Geoscientists, except hydrologists and geographers
10,580	9,800	Petroleum engineers
8,720	8,000	Petroleum pump system operators, refinery operators, and gaugers
11,160	10,700	Roustabouts, oil and gas
7,750	6,400	Wellhead pumpers

Source: U.S. Bureau of Labor Statistics, Industries at a Glance, Occupational Employment Statistics and Employment Projections Program.

Annual Earnings

The world consumes over 30 billion barrels of oil per year, and, except when price increases force developing states to scale back their development agendas, that amount is expected to rise in the years ahead. Kenneth Deffeyes and others argue that the world may have already reached its peak capacity to meet that demand; however, even pessimists acknowledge that petroleum will remain the world's principal energy source until mid-century. Thus, oil is expected to remain extremely valuable for the foreseeable future, and the industry continues to deploy geologists to find, and drillers to extract, oil that would be unprofitable at lower rates.

Oil and natural gas remain a multitrillion-dollar industry. Indeed, ExxonMobil alone experienced global revenues of $442.85 billion in 2009, as well as profits of more than $45 billion, despite a decline in oil prices. The company's net worth was valued at one-third of $1 trillion. Moreover, the largest private corporations are not necessarily the most profitable. Thus, although three of 2009's five most profitable U.S. companies were ExxonMobil (first), Chevron (third), and ConocoPhillips (fifth), smaller corporations (in particular Marathon Oil and Occidental) also made *Fortune*'s 2009 list of the fifty most profitable companies in the United States.

Overall, though, the majors dominate, with the five largest oil and gas corporations (ExxonMobil, Royal Dutch Shell, BP, Chevron, and ConocoPhillips) accounting for over 75 percent of both the $1.9 trillion in revenue and the $155 billion in profits garnered by the private petroleum industry in 2007. In a similar manner, the large state petroleum enterprises dominate the international export market, with OPEC producers estimating their 2007 revenue at $660 billion. It is in the operations of these private and public majors that both the future of the oil and natural gas industry and jobs within it principally lie.

PROJECTED EMPLOYMENT FOR SELECTED OCCUPATIONS

Petroleum and Coal Products Manufacturing

Employment		
2009	Projected 2018	Occupation
5,570	4,100	First-line supervisors/managers of production and operating workers
2,510	1,700	Maintenance and repair workers, general
3,730	3,600	Mixing and blending machine setters, operators, and tenders
21,530	18,900	Petroleum pump system operators, refinery operators, and gaugers
3,090	2,200	Truck drivers, heavy and tractor-trailer

Source: U.S. Bureau of Labor Statistics, Industries at a Glance, Occupational Employment Statistics and Employment Projections Program.

RELATED RESOURCES FOR FURTHER RESEARCH

AMERICAN PETROLEUM INSTITUTE
1220 L St.
Washington, DC 20005-4070
Tel: (202) 682-8000
http://www.api.org

EXXONMOBIL
5959 Las Colinas Blvd.
Irving, TX 75039-2298
Tel: (972) 444-1000
http://www.exxonmobil.com

SAUDI ARAMCO
P.O. Box 1977
Dhahran 31311
Saudi Arabia

Tel: 966-3-877-2626
http://www.saudiaramco.com

SHELL
910 Louisiana St.
Houston, TX 77210
Tel: (713) 241-6161
Fax: (713) 241-4044
http://www.shell.us

ABOUT THE AUTHOR

Joseph R. Rudolph, Jr., holds a Ph.D. from the University of Virginia and has served as a consultant for various petroleum-related companies while chairing the Department of Political Science at Tulsa University during the years of great upheaval in the petroleum industry. He is currently a professor of political science at Towson University, in Maryland. The author of more than two dozen essays and book chapters on various topics relating to energy, he also published a short guide to the literature pertaining to energy in the Magill Bibliographies series in 1995.

FURTHER READING

Anderson, Robert O. *Fundamentals of the Petroleum Industry*. Norman: University of Oklahoma Press, 1984.

Bader, Jeffrey, et al. *The Global Politics of Energy*. Washington, D.C.: Aspen Institute, 2008.

Boudreaux, Terry. *Ethanol and Biodiesel: What You Need to Know*. McLean, Va.: Hart Energy, 2007.

Deffeyes, Kenneth S. *Hubbert's Peak: The Impending World Oil Shortage*. Princeton, N.J.: Princeton University Press, 2001.

Drapes, Michaela. *Vault Guide to the Top Energy and Oil and Gas Employers, 2009*. New York: Vault Reports, 2008.

Engler, Robert. *The Brotherhood of Oil: Energy Policy and the Public Interest*. Chicago: University of Chicago Press, 1977.

Falola, Toyin, and Ann Genova. *The Politics of the Global Oil Industry: An Introduction*. Westport, Conn.: Praeger, 2005.

Grace, Robert. *Oil: An Overview of the Petroleum Industry*. Houston, Tex.: Gulf, 2007.

Johnson, Arthur M. *Pipelines: A Study in Private Enterprise and Public Policy*. Ithaca, N.Y.: Cornell University Press, 1956. Reprint. Westport, Conn.: Greenwood Press, 1982.

Miesner, Thomas O., and William L. Leffier. *Oil and Gas Pipelines in Nontechnical Language*. Tulsa, Okla.: Pennwell, 2006.

Odell, Peter R. *Global Issues*. Vol. 1 in *Oil and Gas: Crises and Controversies, 1961-2000*. Brentwood, Essex, England: Multi-Science, 2004.

Raymond, Martin S., and William L. Leffier. *Oil and Gas Production in Nontechnical Language*. Tulsa, Okla.: Pennwell, 2005.

Roberts, Paul. *The End of Oil: On the Edge of a Perilous New World*. New York: Mariner Books, 2005.

Sampson, Anthony. *The Seven Sisters: The Great Oil Companies and the World They Shaped*. New York: Viking Press, 1980.

Simmons, Matthew R. *Twilight in the Desert: The Coming Saudi Oil Shock and the World Economy*. New York: Wiley, 2006.

U.S. Bureau of Labor Statistics. *Career Guide to Industries*, 2010-2011 ed. http://www.bls.gov/oco/cg.

U.S. Census Bureau. North American Industry Classification System (NAICS), 2007. http://www.census.gov/cgi-bin/sssd/naics/naicsrch?chart=2007.

U.S. Department of Commerce. International Trade Administration. Office of Trade and Industry Information. Industry Trade Data and Analysis. http://ita.doc.gov/td/industry/otea/OTII/OTII-index.html.

Pharmaceuticals and Medications Industry

©Catalin Plesa/Dreamstime.com

INDUSTRY SNAPSHOT

General Industry: Manufacturing

Career Clusters: Manufacturing; Science, Technology, Engineering, and Math

Subcategory Industries: Biological Product Manufacturing; Botanical Manufacturing; Drug Wholesalers; In-Vitro Diagnostic Substance Manufacturing; Medicinal Manufacturing; Pharmaceutical Preparation Manufacturing; Research and Development in Biotechnology; Research and Development in the Life Sciences

Related Industries: Medicine and Health Care Industry; Scientific and Technical Services; Scientific, Medical, and Health Equipment and Supplies Industry

Annual Domestic Revenues: $286.5 billion USD (IMS Health, 2008)

Annual International Revenues: Outside North America: $352.9 billion USD (IMS Health, 2007)

Annual Global Revenues: $643 billion USD (IMS Health, 2007)

NAICS Numbers: 3254, 4242, 54171

INDUSTRY DEFINITION

Summary

The pharmaceuticals and medications industry researches, develops, produces, and distributes medicinal products that are used to diagnose, treat, and prevent disease. These products include medications available only by prescription, as well as over-the-counter products available without a prescription. Most leading pharmaceutical companies also work in other business segments, including consumer health, animal health, nutritional products, and medical devices. Considerable amounts of time, resources, and money are invested in research and development of new drugs, and the United States is a leader in pharmaceutical research and innovation. The pharmaceutical and medications industry is one of the fastest-growing industries in the United States.

History of the Industry

Drugs and medicinal products have been used throughout recorded history, with varying degrees of sophistication and understanding. However, the modern pharmaceuticals and medications industry (or simply pharmaceutical industry) was born from the nineteenth century chemical industry. Most of the largest pharmaceutical companies were already well-established organizations involved in chemical research and production when they en-

Pharmacists are responsible for filling prescriptions and instructing patients on drug usage. (©Mangostock/Dreamstime.com)

tered the pharmaceutical business in the 1920's and 1930's. Groundbreaking medical discoveries at that time, including the use of penicillin as an antibiotic and the function of insulin in the human body, served as catalysts for large-scale manufacturing and marketing of medicinal products. Countless drugs were discovered, manufactured, and marketed throughout the 1950's and 1960's, but the industry remained relatively small.

Since the 1960's, the organization of the pharmaceutical industry has changed dramatically. Between 1960 and 1980, total U.S. pharmaceutical company sales and annual revenues were fairly static as a percentage of gross domestic product (GDP). Until the mid-1970's, most pharmaceutical companies were large, vertically integrated enterprises that participated in every step of the pharmaceutical manufacturing process, from drug discovery to regulatory affairs, to manufacturing, to marketing. In the late 1970's, the industry started growing at an unprecedented rate, introducing new players in the market that challenged the tra-

ditional function of science and research enterprises.

Between 1980 and 2000, total pharmaceutical sales tripled, owing to changes in regulation and in the processes by which drugs were discovered and ultimately marketed. In the early 1980's, the U.S. Congress enacted laws that sped the transition of tax-supported basic science and research into useful products. Other new laws extended patent protections for brand-name drugs. These changes improved the United States' standing in the high-tech world markets and allowed drug companies to rely on academic and federal institutions, rather than in-house development teams, to conduct research. Since the early 1980's, the pharmaceutical industry has been one of the most profitable industries in the United States each year. The industry achieved record-high growth in 1999, with revenues expanding more than 14 percent from the previous year. From 1998 to 2006, the industry grew at a rate of 7 to 10 percent each year.

The economic downturn that began in 2000 affected the pharmaceutical industry, as the government and private employers looked for ways to cut health care spending and pushed back against high drug and medical costs. Total pharmaceutical sales continued to grow, but at a slower rate, in part because many brand-name drugs lost their exclusivity, fewer new products were approved, the growth of Medicare's Part D prescription drug benefit leveled off, and safety issues arose that affected sales.

The landscape of the pharmaceutical and medications industry has changed considerably since the 1970's. The number of institutions in the industry, and the relationships among them, have adjusted as waves of mergers have transformed the industry's structure. Companies merged in order to pool resources and mitigate revenue losses in the face of low expected growth in earnings or patent expirations. While smaller pharmaceutical firms have disappeared and larger firms have consolidated, biotechnology firms have entered the marketplace to form an intermediate sector between academia and large, global pharmaceutical companies. So-called biotech companies are research-oriented and specialize in new drug discovery. Most biotech companies are private, for-profit endeavors, but they are smaller than traditional pharmaceutical companies, with close geographical, cultural, and contractual relationships to nonprofit research institutions. Many biotech companies are founded by academic research scientists and serve as suppliers of specialized technology to larger firms. Large pharmaceutical firms rely heavily on developments in the biotech industry, and 25 to 40 percent of pharmaceutical sales come from drugs that originated in the biotech sector.

The Industry Today

The pharmaceutical industry is dominated by a small number of private, for-profit companies. "Big Pharma" is the collective name for the world's ten to fifteen largest pharmaceutical companies, which lead the industry. More than half of these companies are headquartered in the United States. The pharmaceutical industry operates globally—in terms of research and development, manufacturing, and sales—but the United States is the dominant market in all industry segments.

The pharmaceutical industry is one of the most research-intensive industries in existence, spend-

ing 10 to 20 percent of its revenues on research and development, a very large percentage compared to other industries. Investments in research and development have increased exponentially since the 1980's, and Big Pharma now spends an estimated $50 billion collectively in research and development each year. Global sales are the primary funding source for research and development in large, private companies, while smaller, newer firms rely on venture capital and equity financing to fund research and development.

The industry's attention has moved from basic science to more focused research and a deeper understanding of the human body. Still, only one out of every five thousand candidate drugs proves to be both safe and effective and becomes an approved drug that enters the market. Drug companies spend an average of nearly $2 billion to bring each

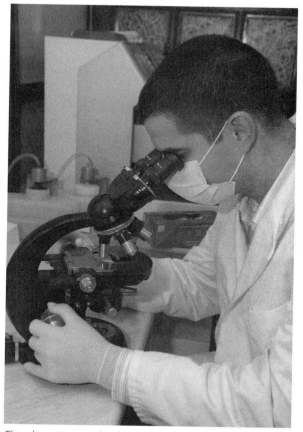

The pharmaceutical industry spends 10 to 20 percent of its revenues on research and development. (©Jovan Jaric/ Dreamstime.com)

new drug to market, through all the stages of drug discovery and development, testing, manufacturing, and distribution. As a result of rising costs and decreased research productivity, new drugs are not appearing as often as they once did. Most new approvals mark only small changes or improvements to existing drugs. The year 2007 witnessed the fewest new product launches in more than three decades.

The first stage in the industrial pharmaceutical process is drug discovery and the search for innovative products. This process involves identification of biological targets, validation of new chemical compounds, and screening and optimization of drug products. After a product has been optimized, the pharmaceutical company developing it files for a patent with the United States Patent and Trademark Office to safeguard its intellectual property rights. Most patents issued today provide twenty years of protection for a chemical or the processes involved in its production. Patent protection is one of the most significant issues facing the industry, as manufacturers attempt to recoup investments in research and development and to deter competitors from copying their original products.

Following discovery, pharmaceutical companies proceed with product design and development, which includes years of trials and submission for regulatory approval. This stage involves both preclinical testing involving animals and clinical testing involving human subjects to prove that a drug is safe and effective. Before it can begin trials, a company must file a new drug application with the United States Food and Drug Administration (FDA) detailing its research and plans for the trials. The clinical stage of drug testing is highly regulated by the government. While drug companies coordinate their trials and are responsible for their outcomes, most trials are actually conducted by separate, private clinical research organizations. Phase I trials include a small number of healthy volunteers to test the safety of a drug. Phase II trials test drug safety and efficacy and include patients who have

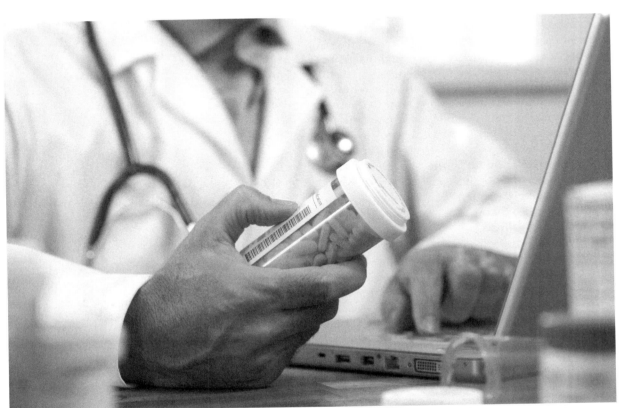

Generic drugs now represent more than half of all drugs sold in the United States. (©Dreamstime.com)

the disease or medical condition the drug is designed to treat. Phase III trials include large numbers of patients and establish safety, efficacy, and dosage regimens for the drug. After trials are complete, an FDA advisory panel reviews their findings and determines whether the drug is suitable to go to market, as well as the uses for which the drug can be prescribed and at what dosages.

Postmarketing, or Phase IV, trials and surveillance continue after a drug is on the market, since not all safety issues arise during the preapproval phase of testing. Manufacturers of generic drugs do not have to complete clinical trials, since the brand-name manufacturer of each drug has already completed them. Generic-drug manufacturers submit an abbreviated new drug application to the FDA and, upon approval, start producing drugs already developed by other companies once the original patent has expired.

Once a drug receives the necessary FDA approval, pharmaceutical companies proceed to manufacture the drug product. This stage is also heavily regulated by the government to ensure the quality of products and the safety of consumers. Manufacturing facilities are held to rigorous quality standards, and worker aptitude is routinely monitored.

Distribution, marketing, and sales represent the final stage in the life cycle of a pharmaceutical product or medication. This phase is directed at both physicians and consumers. Pharmaceutical companies have teams of sales representatives who report the findings of drug studies and detail drugs' benefits to physicians. Pharmaceutical companies are also involved in providing continuing education programs for physicians and other health care professionals. Direct-to-consumer advertising is a fast-growing expense in the marketing budgets of pharmaceutical companies. In 1997, rules regarding what information needed to be included in direct-to-consumer advertising were relaxed, resulting in an explosion of advertising.

Insurance companies are large players in the marketing and sales of pharmaceutical products, owing to strict formularies established by health maintenance organizations, hospitals, and other health care providers. Formularies limit the drugs that can be ordered or prescribed and can significantly affect the sales of certain products.

The pharmaceutical market is expected to continue to grow as the health care focus shifts away from primary-care, therapeutic classes of medication to specialty and biotech-driven therapies. Oncology and autoimmune products are currently the fastest-growing therapeutic classes. Specialty-driven products have nearly doubled their market share since 2000, accounting for more than 60 percent of the market's growth. Revenues from primary-care classes, in contrast, are shrinking, owing to the emergence of low-cost, high-quality generic drugs and switches from prescription-only to over-the-counter products. Generic drugs now represent more than half of all drugs sold in the seven key world markets: the United States, Canada, France, Germany, Italy, Spain, and the United Kingdom.

INDUSTRY MARKET SEGMENTS

Businesses within the pharmaceutical industry range from small start-up companies with only a few employees to large, multinational corporations that account for a considerable share of the market. The following divisions provide a comprehensive overview of businesses within the industry.

Small Businesses

Small pharmaceutical businesses are typically young start-up and biotech companies with no or few commercial products on the market. Most of these firms are exclusively research and development entities. Some small pharmaceutical businesses develop their own drugs, while others perform research and development functions for larger businesses. Revenues from small pharmaceutical businesses represent approximately 20 percent of global pharmaceutical revenues.

Potential Annual Earnings Scale. Low-level and unskilled workers may earn minimum wage or slightly more in a small pharmaceutical business. Throughout the industry, machine and equipment operators and manual laborers earn between $12 and $16 per hour. According to the U.S. Bureau of Labor Statistics (BLS), in 2009 the average annual salary of pharmaceutical biochemists and biophysicists was $91,070 and the average earnings of pharmaceutical epidemiologists were $92,920. Chemists in the industry earned $70,710, and microbiologists earned $69,830 on average. Biological technicians earned an average of $42,950, while chemical technicians earned an average of $46,740. Natural sciences managers earned $156,910. These wages do not tend to fluctuate significantly based on business size. Chief executive officers may earn between $100,000 in a small start-up company and $3 million in a strong biotech company.

Clientele Interaction. There is limited clientele interaction in small pharmaceutical businesses. Sales and marketing representatives may be employed to promote their companies' products to midsize or large pharmaceutical businesses or directly to health care providers or services.

Amenities, Atmosphere, and Physical Grounds. Small pharmaceutical businesses are primarily research-focused, and their facilities consist primarily of laboratory space. The available amenities and work atmosphere vary widely across the industry, depending on the location of the business, scope of the work, and number of employees.

Typical Number of Employees. In the pharmaceutical industry, business size is determined by revenue, rather than number of employees. However, smaller businesses in terms of revenue tend to have fewer employees than do larger businesses. Start-up companies may have only a few dozen employees, while other small manufacturers or distributors may have thousands. Small businesses employ a small fraction of workers in the pharmaceutical industry. According to the BLS, only 13 percent of workers in this industry are employed by businesses with fewer than one hundred employees.

Traditional Geographic Locations. Traditionally, small pharmaceutical companies and biotech firms have emerged from academic research institutions, and they tend to maintain close geographic proximity to large colleges and universities. Some small pharmaceutical businesses maintain close relationships with larger businesses, necessitating locations in the northeastern United States, where most large pharmaceutical companies are based. Many biotech companies are found near Boston, Massachusetts; San Francisco and San Diego, California; Princeton, New Jersey; Philadelphia, Pennsylvania; and Washington, D.C. Small pharmaceutical and biotech companies are emerging in developing countries, as demand for scientific and biotech innovation increases in these countries. The developing world imposes less regulation and provides greater financial incentives than the United States.

Pros of Working for a Small Pharmaceutical Business. Small start-up firms offer exciting opportunities to work with cutting-edge technology and develop groundbreaking products. Small businesses' employees often encounter less corporate bureaucracy and may be afforded greater flexibility than at large firms. This situation often leads to more efficient decision making and greater risk-taking. This, in turn, leads to increased discovery and innovation, and small companies sometimes make discoveries more quickly and cost-effectively than larger companies can.

With a small number of fellow employees, each worker may be able to gain valuable experience by taking on many different tasks. Such broad job descriptions allow workers to explore other related job opportunities and learn about every segment of their companies' operations. Also, workers usually enjoy more interaction with top management in small pharmaceutical businesses, providing them with opportunities for learning and career development. Each individual has the opportunity to stand out for his or her work in a small business; it is also easier for each worker to contribute actively to the success of the business and to feel a sense of personal accomplishment.

Citing employee satisfaction, *Fortune* magazine consistently lists several small pharmaceutical and biotech companies among its annual list of "One Hundred Best Companies to Work For." The magazine praises these companies for their compensation packages, family-friendly work environments, pride in products, workplace diversity, and community outreach programs. Growth is expected in the biotech sector of the pharmaceutical industry, positioning small businesses to expand their size, revenue, and market share. Opportunities for entrepreneurs and venture capitalists abound in the small business segment of the industry.

Cons of Working for a Small Pharmaceutical Business. Small pharmaceutical businesses are not always able to survive economic downturns or grow their staffs in climates of recession or decreased revenues, so they offer less job security than do large, established companies. Top management of small pharmaceutical or biotech companies often have more research- and academic-oriented experience than business management experience,

OCCUPATION SPECIALTIES

Pharmacists

Specialty	Responsibilities
Hospital pharmacists	Work in hospitals, clinics, or nursing homes. They may advise the medical staff on the selection and effects of drugs, perform administrative duties, and work in patient-care areas as members of medical teams. They may also monitor drug levels and fill medical orders.
Pharmacy services directors	Direct and coordinate the activities and functions of a hospital pharmacy and plan and implement procedures in the pharmacy according to hospital policy and legal requirements. They also direct pharmacy personnel programs, such as hiring, training, and intern programs.
Radiopharmacists	Prepare and dispense radioactive pharmaceuticals used for patient diagnosis and therapy, applying the principles and practices of pharmacology and radiochemistry. They verify that the specified radioactive substance prescribed by a physician will give the desired results in examination and treatment procedures.

and they may be unable to survive business challenges and industry fluctuations.

Small pharmaceutical businesses often focus the majority of their research and development attention on one or two therapeutic areas. They cannot sustain broader efforts or modify their areas of focus in response to changing client needs. With few staff, small businesses may require their employees to assume multiple job roles or perform several job functions, which may not appeal to all workers. Further, small businesses lack resources for training and education, which may limit employees' opportunities for career advancement.

Costs

Payroll and Benefits: Small pharmaceutical businesses employ workers at both hourly wages and annual salaries. Depending on employee job function, terms of employment, and size of the employer, benefits may or may not be included in a compensation package. However, most employees in the pharmaceutical industry receive paid sick leave and vacation time. Some small businesses offer pension plans or retirement benefits as well.

Supplies: Small pharmaceutical businesses require basic office supplies, as well as computers, telephones, and other communication supplies. Basic and sophisticated science tools and laboratory equipment are required for research and development teams. Production-specific equipment for manufacturing pharmaceutical products is required in manufacturing facilities. Raw materials and supplies are purchased for research, as well as for manufacturing operations.

External Services: Small pharmaceutical companies may own the buildings that house their corporate headquarters and manufacturing facilities, but they may pay mortgages or rent their properties. They may hire external vendors to manage janitorial or housekeeping services, as well as groundskeeping services, for their offices and manufacturing facilities. In order to maintain a small number of employees, small pharmaceutical businesses may hire contract workers for some job functions, such as human resources, legal counsel, or communications.

Utilities: Small pharmaceutical businesses pay utilities for all properties, including water and sew-

OCCUPATION PROFILE

Pharmacist

Considerations	Qualifications
Description	Dispenses medicines, looks at possible interactions with other medications, and advises customers on prescription and over-the-counter medications.
Career cluster	Health Science
Interests	Data; people; things
Working conditions	Work inside
Minimum education level	Doctor of pharmacy degree
Physical exertion	Light work
Physical abilities	Unexceptional/basic fitness
Opportunities for experience	Internship; military service
Licensure and certification	Required
Employment outlook	Faster-than-average growth expected
Holland interest score	IES

Note: See volume 1, "Publisher's Note," for an explanation of the Holland interest score.

age, gas service, electricity, telephone, and Internet access.

Taxes: Small pharmaceutical businesses pay federal, state, and local income, property, and sales taxes. Additional tariffs or duties are placed on all equipment, chemicals, and raw materials imported from foreign countries. Pharmaceutical companies collect applicable sales tax from product sales to distributors, wholesalers, or other entities. Small pharmaceutical businesses often obtain insurance to protect against loss, damage, theft, injury, and other liabilities.

Midsize Businesses

The global market share of midsize pharmaceutical companies has decreased considerably since the beginning of the twenty-first century, as the industry has been largely consolidated through a series of corporate mergers and acquisitions. Revenues from midsize pharmaceutical businesses represent less than 20 percent of global pharmaceutical revenues. Most manufacturers of generic drugs are midsize pharmaceutical businesses. They manufacture drugs that are no longer protected by patents and devote relatively small amounts of money to research and development, investing instead in manufacturing.

Potential Annual Earnings Scale. Low-level and unskilled workers may earn minimum wage or slightly more in a midsize pharmaceutical business. Throughout the industry, machine and equipment operators and manual laborers earn between $12 and $16 per hour. According to the BLS, in 2009 the average annual salary of pharmaceutical biochemists and biophysicists was $91,070 and the average earnings of pharmaceutical epidemiologists were $92,920. Chemists in the industry earned $70,710, and microbiologists earned $69,830 on average. Biological technicians earned an average of $42,950, while chemical technicians earned an average of $46,740. Natural sciences managers earned $156,910. Sales representatives earned an average of $80,700, sales supervisors earned an average of $97,010, and sales managers earned an average of $139,180. These wages do not tend to fluctuate significantly based on business size. Chief executive officers of midsize pharmaceutical companies generally earn between $1 million and $10 million in total compensation, including salary and stock options.

Clientele Interaction. The level of clientele interaction varies considerably in the midsize pharmaceutical business segment. Some midsize companies remain research-intensive, limiting interaction with clients. Sales and marketing representatives may be employed to promote companies' products to large pharmaceutical businesses or directly to health care providers or services. Midsize pharmaceutical businesses may also purchase technology or processes from smaller pharmaceutical or biotech companies.

Other pharmaceutical businesses manufacture and distribute drug products and compete with large pharmaceutical companies for commercial market share. These midsize companies employ sales and marketing staff to detail the benefits of their drug products to consumers, as well as to physicians, pharmacists, and other health care providers.

Amenities, Atmosphere, and Physical Grounds. As with all manufacturing sectors, midsize pharmaceutical manufacturers operate under strict regulatory and legal requirements. The pharmaceutical industry as a whole enjoys a low level of work-related accidents and injuries. Available amenities and work atmosphere vary widely across the industry, depending on the location of the business, scope of the work, and number of employees.

Typical Number of Employees. In the pharmaceutical industry, business size is determined by revenue rather than number of employees. Midsize pharmaceutical companies usually employ between one hundred and five hundred employees, but some have thousands of employees.

Traditional Geographic Locations. Midsize pharmaceutical companies are located throughout the United States. Some are located near smaller pharmaceutical or biotech firms with which they work. Midsize manufacturing and distribution companies often locate themselves in areas with strong transportation infrastructures, providing advantages for travel, transportation, or delivery. New Jersey and the surrounding areas in the northeastern United States have been home to the major pharmaceutical businesses since the modern industry's founding in the early twentieth century. Today, many midsize pharmaceutical businesses maintain locations along the East Coast, from Massachusetts to North Carolina.

Pros of Working for a Midsize Pharmaceutical Business. Midsize pharmaceutical companies work hard to expand market share and compete with large businesses. Many choose to focus on emerging technologies, challenging employees to innovate products on the cutting edge of the industry. Additionally, midsize pharmaceutical companies often choose to focus on less prevalent diseases, as opposed to common lifestyle conditions that produce blockbuster drugs for large pharmaceutical companies. This focus allows for personal and professional satisfaction when creating drugs to treat diseases that may have no widespread treatments yet available.

Midsize pharmaceutical businesses, while lacking the resources of large pharmaceutical companies, do possess sufficient capital to buy technology from small pharmaceutical and biotech companies. This process speeds innovation and allows for cost-effective research and development operations.

Citing employee satisfaction, *Fortune* magazine consistently lists several midsize pharmaceutical companies among its annual list of "One Hundred Best Companies to Work For." The magazine praises these companies for their compensation packages, family-friendly work environments, pride in products, workplace diversity, and community outreach programs. Many midsize pharmaceutical businesses also routinely appear on *Working Mother*'s similar annual "One Hundred Best Companies" list.

Manufacturers of generic drugs typically fall into the category of midsize pharmaceutical businesses. These manufacturers expect to grow in the near future, as many brand-name drug products will be losing their patent protection. At the same time, the U.S. government, health care providers, and patients seek cost-saving measures in the provision of health care services, making generic drugs an attractive treatment choice. The expected growth will result in more job growth and security in this segment of the industry.

Cons of Working for a Midsize Pharmaceutical Business. Midsize pharmaceutical businesses face challenges as the industry changes. Midsize companies are not large enough to compete with the world's largest pharmaceutical companies in terms of research and development resources or marketing budgets. Owing to financial, geographical, or discovery challenges, the proportion of midsize pharmaceutical businesses is shrinking. Multiple midsize companies have merged with one another, or they have been acquired by large firms. This trend leads to job insecurity, as newly merged companies may eliminate some resources and personnel to avoid redundancies and increase efficiency. Salaries tend to be slightly lower in midsize pharmaceutical companies than in large companies owing to smaller operating margins and lower total revenues and returns on investments.

Costs

Payroll and Benefits: Midsize pharmaceutical businesses employ workers at both hourly wages and annual salaries. Depending on employee job function and full- or part-time status, benefits may or may not be included in the compensation package. However, most employees in the industry receive paid sick leave and vacation time. Some midsize employers offer pension plans or retirement benefits as well. Some pharmaceutical businesses offer discounted medications to their employees.

Supplies: Midsize pharmaceutical businesses require basic office supplies, as well as computers, telephones, and other communication supplies. Basic and sophisticated science tools and laboratory equipment are required for research and development teams. Production-specific equipment is required in manufacturing facilities. Raw materials and supplies are purchased for research, as well as for manufacturing operations.

External Services: Midsize pharmaceutical companies may own the buildings that house their corporate headquarters and manufacturing facilities, or they may pay a mortgage or rent their properties. Midsize pharmaceutical companies may hire external vendors to manage janitorial or housekeeping services, as well as grounds-keeping services, for their offices and manufacturing facilities. In order to streamline business operations, midsize pharmaceutical businesses may hire contract workers for some job functions, such as human resources, legal counsel, or communications.

Other costs of midsize pharmaceutical businesses include premiums for insurance to protect against loss, damage, theft, injury, and other liabilities. Midsize pharmaceutical companies also pay smaller pharmaceutical and biotech companies fees to license promising research at various stages in the research and development process. These fees purchase the right to use the research or technology in the companies' own work.

Utilities: Midsize pharmaceutical companies pay utilities for all properties, including water and sewage, gas service, electricity, telephone, and Internet access.

Taxes: Midsize pharmaceutical companies pay federal, state, and local income, property, and sales taxes. Additional tariffs or duties are placed on all equipment, chemicals, and raw materials imported from foreign countries. Pharmaceutical companies collect applicable sales tax from product sales to distributors, wholesalers, or other entities. In some states, drug distributors are required to pay additional wholesale drug-distribution taxes.

Large Businesses

Large pharmaceutical companies are long-standing firms that have many approved drugs on the market. These companies share a majority of the total global pharmaceutical revenue; the 20 largest pharmaceutical companies represent 60 percent of the global pharmaceutical industry revenue.

Large pharmaceutical businesses invest a large percentage of financial and employee resources in research and development. Large pharmaceutical companies are not guaranteed success, but do enjoy advantages over small and midsize businesses.

Potential Annual Earnings Scale. Low-level and unskilled workers may earn minimum wage or slightly more in a large pharmaceutical business. Throughout the industry, machine and equipment operators and manual laborers earn between $12 and $16 per hour. According to the BLS, in 2009 the average annual salary of pharmaceutical biochemists and biophysicists was $91,070 and the average earnings of pharmaceutical epidemiologists were $92,920. Chemists in the industry earned $70,710, and microbiologists earned $69,830 on average. Biological technicians earned an average of $42,950, while chemical technicians earned an average of $46,740. Natural sciences managers earned $156,910. Sales representatives earned an average of $80,700, sales supervisors earned an average of $97,010, and sales managers earned an average of $139,180. These wages do not tend to fluctuate significantly based on business size. Chief executive officers of the largest pharmaceutical companies earn between $3 million and $35 million in total compensation, including salary and stock options.

Clientele Interaction. Large pharmaceutical businesses employ large sales and marketing teams to promote their products to physicians, pharmacists, and other health care providers. Alternatively, large pharmaceutical businesses may purchase technology or processes from small or midsize pharmaceutical or biotech companies.

Amenities, Atmosphere, and Physical Grounds. The largest pharmaceutical companies in the world maintain work sites on many acres of land that contain millions of square feet of office space, laboratories, and warehouses. The research facilities at these businesses are state-of-the-art and offer ideal scientific working conditions. As with all manufacturing sectors, large pharmaceutical manufacturers operate under strict regulatory and legal requirements. The industry as a whole enjoys a low level of work-related accidents and injuries.

Typical Number of Employees. In the pharmaceutical industry, business size is indicative of revenue, rather than number of employees. More than half of the employees in the industry are employed by pharmaceutical businesses that employ more than five hundred workers.

Traditional Geographic Locations. New Jersey and the surrounding areas in the northeastern United States have been home to the major pharmaceutical businesses since their founding in the early twentieth century. Most of the American pharmaceutical industry's employees work in New Jersey, New York, California, Puerto Rico, and Pennsylvania. The world's largest pharmaceutical companies have corporate offices and research facilities across the United States and Europe, primarily in or around major metropolitan areas to facilitate travel and distribution of goods. Manufacturing facilities are spread across the globe to facilitate distribution to crucial markets.

Large companies are increasingly moving their production facilities to developing nations. The economies of Asia, South America, and Central and Eastern Europe are growing quickly and offer attractive financial and regulatory benefits for large pharmaceutical companies. Skilled laborers in a variety of pharmaceutical business sectors are available in developing countries and require lower salaries than do workers in the United States. China and India are growing markets for pharmaceutical research and development processes, as they offer large populations of highly educated workers and industry-friendly regulations and tax incentives.

Pros of Working for a Large Pharmaceutical Corporation. Larger pharmaceutical companies are able to employ large numbers of workers and generally able to continue to grow their staffs during economic downturns. They have the managerial experience to succeed in the face of business challenges and industry fluctuations. Such businesses offer a multitude of resources to employees, including access to top-of-the-line equipment, funding for training and education, and opportunities to collaborate with world-renowned experts. These benefits can lead to career advancement and additional employment opportunities.

Large pharmaceutical businesses consistently appear on *Fortune* magazine's annual list of "One Hundred Best Companies to Work For." The magazine praises their compensation packages, family-friendly work environments, pride in products, workplace diversity, and community outreach programs. Many large pharmaceutical businesses also routinely appear on *Working Mother*'s similar annual "One Hundred Best Companies" list. Economies of scale in manufacturing, clinical trials, and marketing allow large companies to diversify their investments and expand their offerings. This diversification increases companies' job growth and employees' job security.

Cons of Working for a Large Pharmaceutical Corporation. Large companies operate with a high level of bureaucracy. Strict business structures and decision-making hierarchies lead to reduced research productivity, increased research and development costs, and longer discovery and manufacturing times. Such businesses are also fairly compartmentalized, with significant division of labor and job specialization. Thus, their employees may not be able to explore different job functions or business operations to the extent that they can at smaller companies. Indeed, each worker at a large business often has a specific, defined role, with little or no autonomy. Additionally, workers may not immediately see or feel the impact of their work on their companies or the larger world.

Costs

Payroll and Benefits: Large pharmaceutical businesses employ workers at both hourly wages and annual salaries. Depending on employee job function and full- or part-time status, benefits may or may not be included in a compensation package. However, most employees in the industry receive paid sick leave and vacation time. Many employers offer pension plans or retirement benefits as well, and some offer discounted medications to their employees.

Supplies: Large pharmaceutical businesses require basic office supplies, as well as computers, telephones, and other communication supplies. Basic and sophisticated science tools and laboratory equipment are required for research and development teams. Production-specific equipment is required in manufacturing facilities. Raw materials and supplies are purchased for research, as well as for manufacturing operations.

External Services: Large pharmaceutical companies often own the buildings that house their corporate headquarters and manufacturing facilities, but they may pay a mortgage or rent their properties. They may hire external vendors to manage janitorial or housekeeping services, as well as groundskeeping services, for their offices and manufacturing facilities. Large pharmaceutical businesses also pay tremendous insurance costs to protect against loss, damage, theft, injury, and other liabilities.

Large pharmaceutical companies pay small and midsize companies fees to license promising research at various stages in the research and development process. These fees purchase the rights to use the research or technology in the companies' own work.

Utilities: Large pharmaceutical companies pay utilities for all properties, including water and sewage, gas service, electricity, telephone, and Internet access.

Taxes: Large pharmaceutical companies pay federal, state, and local income, property, and sales taxes. Additional tariffs or duties are placed on all equipment, chemicals, and raw materials imported from foreign countries. Pharmaceutical companies collect applicable sales tax from product sales to distributors, wholesalers, and other entities. In some states, drug distributors are required to pay additional wholesale drug-distribution taxes.

ORGANIZATIONAL STRUCTURE AND JOB ROLES

The pharmaceuticals and medications industry employs nearly 300,000 workers in twenty-five hundred different places of employment throughout the United States. Some pharmaceutical companies locate all of their business functions in one geographic location, while others maintain distinct and separate research and development facilities, administrative headquarters, and manufacturing facilities. A large majority of pharmaceutical workers (87 percent) are employed by companies with more than one hundred employees. In the United States, more than half of industry employees work in California, New Jersey, Puerto Rico, Pennsylvania, and New York.

In general, industry workers are highly educated. More than 60 percent hold bachelor's, master's, professional, or doctoral degrees. Not all pharmaceutical jobs require advanced education, but entrance into the industry and career advancement may both depend on industry-specific training and expertise. The organizational structure and function of corporations within the pharmaceuticals and medications industry vary based on size, location, and business functions.

The following umbrella categories apply to the organizational structure of businesses within the pharmaceuticals and medications industry:

- Business Management
- Office and Administrative Support
- Sales and Marketing
- Facilities and Security
- Technology, Research, Design, and Development
- Manufacturing and Supply
- Production and Operations

- Distribution
- Infrastructure and Support Functions

Business Management

A small team of executives and managers makes policy and procedural decisions within a pharmaceutical company. Executive managers may decide matters of finance, marketing, or research for entire companies, while other managers direct specific departments. Overall, management and business occupations represent less than 20 percent of jobs within the industry.

Top managers include chief executive officers who oversee operational, financial, technological, and communications affairs. Depending on the size of each company, responsibilities within each job title may change, or one person may fulfill multiple roles. As a result of economic constraints, as well as anticipated corporate mergers and acquisitions, the number of top executive positions in the industry is not expected to increase in the short term. Other positions within the management structure are expected to increase, however, as demand for new pharmaceutical products and innovations continues to grow. Business operations specialists will be required to optimize companies' performance and business functions.

Salaries for top executives are typically much higher than salaries for similar positions in other industries. Compensation packages for many executives and managers combine salaries and stock options.

Business management occupations may include the following:

- President/Chief Executive Officer (CEO)
- Chief Financial Officer (CFO)
- Chief Medical Officer
- Chief Operating Officer (COO)
- Vice President
- Production Manager
- Natural Sciences Manager
- Business Operations Specialist
- Accountant
- Auditor
- General Counsel

Office and Administrative Support

Office and administrative support professionals maintain payroll, personnel, sales, and shipment records. They also perform tasks such as answering phones, scheduling and coordinating meetings, and maintaining office supplies. Excellent computer and organizational skills are essential for office and administrative support personnel.

Occupations in this area represent approximately 11 percent of jobs within the pharmaceutical industry. Job growth in the area has slowed relative to other areas, owing to corporate mergers and the consolidation of resources.

Office and administrative support occupations may include the following:

- Customer Service Representative
- Shipping and Receiving Clerk
- Administrative Assistant
- Executive Assistant
- Office Manager

Sales and Marketing

Sales and marketing personnel are the link between pharmaceutical companies and their clients. In large companies, they promote products to physicians, pharmacists, dentists, and retail and wholesale drug distributors, as well as other health services and health care providers. Sales and marketing jobs account for 3 percent of the jobs within the pharmaceutical industry.

Sales and marketing representatives working for small research-intensive pharmaceutical firms or biotech companies may focus on marketing their products or discoveries to larger pharmaceutical companies, rather than directly to health care providers or consumers. Sales and marketing representatives also work with production staff, engineers, and research and development teams to determine how existing products can be changed to meet new client needs.

Larger pharmaceutical companies have larger sales and marketing teams than do smaller companies. With more personnel, each representative covers a smaller geographical territory. Larger companies also provide sales representatives with more financial support for expense accounts, marketing outreach, and promotional support.

Sales representatives typically earn a combination of a salary and performance-based commissions. Most sales and marketing personnel have employment experience in a related industry, as well as scientific or technical expertise. Sales and marketing staffs typically grow when their parent companies grow, and the outlook for such growth is positive as the industry continues to grow.

A bachelor's degree is preferred for most sales and marketing positions, as are exceptional computer, technology, communication, and interpersonal skills. Course work or experience in economics, marketing, communication, and foreign languages is also desirable.

Sales and marketing occupations may include the following:

- Vice President of Sales and Marketing
- Regional Sales Supervisor
- Sales Manager
- Sales Representative
- Health Care Communications Professional
- Marketing Representative
- Market Research Analyst
- Marketing Manager

Facilities and Security

The pharmaceutical industry requires installation, maintenance, and repair specialists to maintain office space, research laboratories, and manufacturing facilities. Security is also important, as laboratories and manufacturing facilities develop and use proprietary chemicals and processes, as well as federally regulated controlled substances. Facilities and security workers account for approximately 4 percent of employees within the industry.

Facilities and security occupations may include the following:

- Industrial Machinery Mechanic
- Maintenance and Repair Worker
- Custodian/Janitor

OCCUPATION PROFILE

Pharmaceutical Sales Representative

Considerations	Qualifications
Description	Promotes the use of legal drugs and other pharmaceutical products to physicians, dentists, hospitals, and retail drug stores, informing potential customers of new drugs and explaining their characteristics and the results of relevant clinical studies.
Career clusters	Business, Management, and Administration; Human Services; Marketing, Sales, and Service
Interests	Data; people
Working conditions	Work inside
Minimum education level	Bachelor's degree
Physical exertion	Light work
Physical abilities	Unexceptional/basic fitness
Opportunities for experience	Part-time work
Licensure and certification	Usually not required
Employment outlook	Average growth expected
Holland interest score	ESA

Note: See volume 1, "Publisher's Note," for an explanation of the Holland interest score.

- Housekeeper
- Groundskeeper
- Security Guard
- Security Supervisor

Technology, Research, Design, and Development

Technology, research, design, and development staff perform every scientific step in the process from drug discovery through introduction to the market. Nearly one-third of all positions within the pharmaceutical industry are professional occupations, including scientists and science technicians.

Scientists collaborate with one another and with other industry professionals throughout the entire life cycle of a pharmaceutical product or medication. Life scientists may develop new drugs, study the effects of new chemical products on animals, investigate the action of drugs on the human body, or evaluate the safety or toxicity of drug products. Chemists may create models of chemical compounds, set standards for production or storage conditions, or test finished products for quality. Science technicians work under the supervision of scientists to operate and maintain laboratory equipment and conditions and to record results.

Engineers, who represent a small fraction of pharmaceutical professionals, improve equipment design, layout, and workflow and devise manufacturing processes. Specific disciplines include, but are not limited to, chemical, mechanical, biomedical, and industrial engineering. Statisticians help design clinical trials and validate study results. Medical writers communicate technical medical information throughout the drug development and distribution phases. They write policies and procedures for company operations, design research and clinical trial protocols, publish findings from research studies, and produce education and training materials for in-house staffs and health care personnel.

Salaries and wages within the technology and science professions vary widely based on education, work experience, and area of expertise, but overall earnings for most scientists and technicians are significantly higher than those for related professions in other industries. Significant growth is expected in research and development-related occupations through 2014.

Especially given that they pay higher average sal-aries than their competitors in other industries, pharmaceutical companies prefer to hire scientists with advanced degrees who have published scientific and academic papers. A bachelor's degree may or may not be required for a technician position; often, an associate's degree or specialized training is a minimum requirement. A bachelor's degree in computer science or information systems is a minimum requirement for most computer-systems analysts. Scientists and technology professionals with advanced degrees and several years of experience may have the opportunity for career advancement, becoming science or production managers or directors.

Technology, research, design, and development occupations may include the following:

- Computer Systems Analyst
- Engineer
- Chemist
- Biochemist
- Biophysicist
- Microbiologist
- Biological Technician
- Chemical Technician
- Pharmacist
- Physician
- Statistician
- Medical Writer

Manufacturing and Supply

The manufacturing sector of the pharmaceutical industry is focused on chemical manufacturing, raw material supply, and pharmaceutical production. Quality control and assurance are integral to pharmaceutical manufacturing, and most companies have full-time employees devoted to maintaining the quality and integrity of their products. Engineers working in pharmaceutical manufacturing are responsible for the quality and reliability of both equipment and work processes. Chemical, mechanical, electrical, and industrial engineers are needed to oversee the manufacturing processes, and they routinely collaborate with scientists and other professionals to optimize those processes.

All pharmaceutical manufacturing and supply personnel are tasked with producing drug products in large quantities while meeting regulatory demands and safety standards and preserving the

Pat the cat sits behind a vial of insulin. The diabetic cat has been receiving daily injections for four years. (AP/Wide World Photos)

health and safety of consumers and patients. Technology in the sector is quickly evolving, and workers remain continuously challenged to broaden their skills and knowledge base in order to improve their companies' products. Pharmaceutical manufacturing and supply personnel also face increasing pressure to design and implement environmentally conscious production facilities. Engineering positions require at least a bachelor's degree or significant work experience in a related discipline.

Manufacturing and supply occupations may include the following:

- Biomedical Engineer
- Chemical Engineer
- Industrial Engineer
- Industrial Engineering Technician
- Health and Safety Engineer
- Quality Assurance Analyst

Production and Operations

Most pharmaceutical manufacturing facilities are highly automated, but production-related occupations still account for more than one-quarter of all jobs within the pharmaceutical industry. Workers are needed to operate and control the machinery that produces bulk chemicals, mixes ingredients, and packages drug products. Workers

are also needed to inspect final drug products by sorting, sampling, testing, and weighing random product samples.

Pharmaceutical production and operations personnel work in scheduled shifts. Production and manufacturing facilities may operate twenty-four hours per day, allowing for flexible or nontraditional work schedules for employees. Working conditions in pharmaceutical manufacturing facilities are better than in most other types of manufacturing facilities, and work-related injuries are relatively rare. Most of the job functions in manufacturing and supply are not physically demanding. Career advancement to a supervisorial or managerial position is possible for production workers who excel at their jobs.

Wages in pharmaceutical production and operation occupations are higher than they are for similar occupations in other manufacturing industries. A bachelor's degree is not required for most production and operations positions. A high school diploma or the equivalent and specialized in-house training, along with computer skills, are often necessary.

Production and operations occupations may include the following:

- First-Line Production Supervisor
- Chemical Processing Machine Operator
- Mixing and Blending Machine Operator
- Packaging and Filling Machine Operator
- Inspector

Distribution

Pharmaceutical products and medications are distributed from manufacturing facilities first to drug wholesalers and then to physician offices, pharmacies, government agencies, and research labs, before they reach patient and consumers. The transfer of drug products from manufacturers to wholesalers and from wholesalers to dispensing entities is carefully regulated to avoid drug diversion.

The actual moving of drug products requires transportation and material-moving workers. Laborers and material movers move pharmaceutical freight or stock, as well as maintaining the equipment necessary to accomplish that task. Material movers include truck and tractor operators, loaders, and related personnel. Distribution work is unskilled, general labor and is often repetitive and physically demanding.

Workers in this area do not need formal or advanced education, but they should be attentive to detail and may be subject to security and background checks since they work with controlled substances. Wages are low compared to those of other pharmaceutical workers, but they are comparable to those of distribution workers in other manufacturing industries. Job growth is not expected in this area of the industry, owing to consolidation and streamlining of distribution and transportation processes.

Distribution occupations may include the following:

- Truck Driver
- Hand Freight Loader/Material Mover
- Machine Feeder and Offbearer
- Hand Packager
- Warehouse Supervisor

Infrastructure and Support Functions

All pharmaceutical companies, regardless of size or specific function, need a stable, knowledgeable infrastructure to support the work of their scientists and manufacturers. Management, regulation, and financing are important aspects of drug design, development, and distribution systems. Regulatory affairs professionals understand federal regulatory requirements and compile the information and applications necessary to secure drug approval. Similarly, lawyers and legal experts ensure that patents are obtained for new drug products and draft contractual agreements between their companies and others. The pharmaceutical industry also places heavy emphasis on training and continuing education for employees in topics including safety, quality control, and new technological and medical developments.

Pharmaceutical support workers assist and sustain company employees, as well as the communities in which companies are located. They also engage company stakeholders and improve corporate citizenship. Corporate outreach and community liaison roles help empower patients and improve access to medications.

Infrastructure and support occupations may include the following:

- Accountant
- Payroll Clerk
- Human Resources Manager
- Human Resources Generalist
- Benefits Specialist
- Information Technology Specialist
- Training Specialist
- Education and Training Director
- Legal Counsel
- Community Outreach Coordinator
- Administrative Assistant

INDUSTRY OUTLOOK

Overview

The outlook for the pharmaceutical industry shows it to be on the rise. The aging of the world's population will increase global demand for health care services and pharmaceutical products. The expansion of public and private health insurance companies will also contribute to increased growth of the pharmaceutical market.

The pharmaceutical industry has not been immune to the effects of the recession of 2007-2009. Most pharmaceutical companies imposed cost-cutting measures as a result of lower-than-expected growth and decreased profits during the global financial crisis. Similarly, a decrease in the amount of public and private funding available for pharmaceutical and biotech research and development has decreased the research productivity of the industry as a whole.

Today, the pharmaceutical industry faces challenges to its traditional mode of operation. Concerns about the transparency and integrity of the industry have compromised drug companies' images and resulted in increased government regulation and public scrutiny. Further, profitability and growth are at risk, as health care budgets are strained, patents expire, and generics take over a large percentage of the pharmaceutical and medications market. Comparative effectiveness research—analyses of the relative effectiveness of different treatments—will increase, resulting in amplified production and distribution of generic medications around the world. The U.S.

government may examine reimportation guidelines and adopt price controls on pharmaceutical and medical products, further reducing industry profits.

The success of pharmaceutical companies depends on their ability to improve their research and development productivity to mitigate the factors that limit their growth and profitability. The cost of drug discovery and development is the largest contributor to escalating costs and the declining number of new product launches. The costs of bringing a new drug to market will likely rise and will not vary between small biotech companies and large pharmaceutical companies.

Further, with a deepening understanding of the human body and its disease states, there is a continuing shift in the pharmaceutical industry away from producing primary-care, therapeutic classes of drugs and toward producing specialty and biotech-driven products. Oncology and autoimmune products represent the fastest-growing therapeutic classes. Also, generic medications continue to replace branded drugs in major therapeutic classes, challenging brand-name pharmaceutical compa-

nies to innovate new, profitable products. As a result, companies such as Johnson & Johnson and Abbott, two of the world's largest pharmaceutical companies, are growing their nonpharmaceutical business lines. Similarly, Roche, another large manufacturer of medicines and diagnostics, is expanding its oncology specialty franchise to generate increased revenue. Further large mergers, as well as small-scale acquisitions, by Big Pharma companies are expected, continuing industry trends.

Consumers are the ultimate payers in health care, and they are increasingly proactive in managing their own health at reasonable costs. As a result, patients and consumers influence regulatory approvals, market decisions, and physicians' prescribing practices. Owing to increased regulations, changes in pharmaceutical sales practices, and fear of lawsuits, physicians have become slower to adopt new products. Several notable black-box safety warnings have been issued in the twenty-first century, causing justifiable concern among consumers and prescribers. As public and private health care expands and the population ages, the demand for pharmaceuticals will continue around the world.

The pharmaceutical industry will continue to expand, but it faces a new era of modest growth, more narrowly focused medications, and increased scrutiny of safety issues.

Employment Advantages

Job prospects in the pharmaceutical industry are favorable. The industry is already one of the largest employers in the United States, employing 289,800 workers in 2008. The U.S. Department of Labor also reports that the industry will continue to grow by approximately 26 percent through at least 2014, exceeding the average growth rate of 14 percent for all industries combined during the same period. Workers in all stages of the pharmaceutical industry—from scientists involved in drug discovery to machine operators—will be in high demand.

A significant advantage to the pharmaceutical industry is that it needs workers with diverse education levels, backgrounds, and work experience.

PROJECTED EMPLOYMENT FOR SELECTED OCCUPATIONS

Pharmaceutical and Medicine Manufacturing

Employment		
2008	Projected 2018	Occupation
16,400	16,700	Chemists
1,200	1,200	Legal occupations
15,800	16,100	Life, physical, and social science technicians
1,700	1,900	Media and communication occupations
100	100	Pharmacists

Source: U.S. Bureau of Labor Statistics, Industries at a Glance, Occupational Employment Statistics and Employment Projections Program.

Production-related occupations account for slightly more than one-quarter of all jobs within the industry and include both low- and high-skilled tasks. Wages and salaries in the industry are higher than they are in other manufacturing industries. Professional occupations account for one-third of all jobs and include scientists, engineers, and science technicians. With industry growth expected and innovative drug products required, life scientists will be in particularly high demand in the future. The pharmaceutical industry offers exciting challenges and opportunities for growth, and job satisfaction within the industry is high.

Annual Earnings

Despite challenges to its traditional business model, the pharmaceutical industry enjoys continued growth and market expansion. In 2006, the global pharmaceutical market grew by 7 percent to earn $643 billion in revenue. This growth was due to an increase in prescribing volume in the United States owing to Medicare Part D, a government-paid prescription drug benefit for seniors. Strong innovations in oncology therapies also helped drive growth.

North America accounts for 45 percent of global pharmaceutical sales, with the United States claiming nearly all of the North American revenue. In 2007, the U.S. pharmaceutical industry's revenue was $286.5 billion, up nearly 4 percent from 2006. In total, North American revenues reached $290.1 billion in 2006. Outside the United States, the five major European markets (France, Germany, Italy, Spain, and the United Kingdom) have experienced slower growth than North America has, but they generated $123.1 billion in revenues in 2006. Latin American and African markets are experiencing higher growth than other countries because of increased life expectancies and improved standards of living and medical care. By 2013, the global pharmaceutical market is projected to exceed $975 billion. The rate of growth of the industry is likely to remain low, but strong demand for safe, effective, and innovative medications will continue.

BIOTECHNOLOGY INDUSTRY ORGANIZATION
1201 Maryland Ave. SW, Suite 900
Washington, DC 20024
Tel: (202) 962-9200
Fax: (202) 488-6301
http://www.bio.org

DRUG INFORMATION ASSOCIATION
800 Enterprise Rd., Suite 200
Horsham, PA 19044-3595
Tel: (215) 442-6100
Fax: (215) 442-6199
http://www.diahome.org

INTERNATIONAL FEDERATION OF PHARMACEUTICAL MANUFACTURERS AND ASSOCIATIONS
Chemin Louis-Dunant 15
P.O. Box 195
1211 Geneva 20
Switzerland
Tel: 41-22-338-3200
Fax: 41-22-338-3299
http://www.ifpma.org

INTERNATIONAL SOCIETY FOR PHARMACEUTICAL ENGINEERING
3109 W Dr. Martin Luther King, Jr., Blvd., Suite 250
Tampa, FL 33607-6240
Tel: (813) 960-2105
Fax: (813) 264-2816
http://www.ispe.org

PHARMACEUTICAL RESEARCH AND MANUFACTURERS ASSOCIATION OF AMERICA
950 F St. NW
Washington, DC 20004
Tel: (202) 835-3400
Fax: (202) 835-3414
http://www.phrma.org

ABOUT THE AUTHOR

Jennifer L. Gibson holds a bachelor of science degree in biochemistry from Clemson University, with a research emphasis in enzyme structure and function; she earned a doctorate in pharmacy from the Virginia Commonwealth University's School of Pharmacy. She has clinical practice expertise as a pharmacist in a hospital setting. She is also a medical communicator with experience in researching and preparing scientific publications for international journals and creating medical education resources and presentations for health care professionals.

FURTHER READING

Alliance for Retired Americans Educational Fund. *Outrageous Fortune: How the Drug Industry Profits from Pills.* Washington, D.C.: Author, 2007.

Angell, Marcia. *The Truth About Drug Companies: How They Deceive Us and What to Do About It.* New York: Random House, 2004.

Bastianelli, Enrico, Jurg Eckhardt, and Olivier Teirlynck. "Pharma: Can the Middle Hold?" *The McKinsey Quarterly*, May 29, 2001, 118.

Campbell, John J. *Understanding Pharma: The Professional's Guide to How Pharmaceutical and Biotech Companies Really Work.* 2d ed. Raleigh, N.C.: Pharmaceutical Institute, 2008.

Cockburn, Iain M. "The Changing Structure of the Pharmaceutical Industry." *Health Affairs* 23, no. 1 (January/February, 2004): 10-22.

Jacobsen, Thomas M., and Albert I. Wertheimer. *Modern Pharmaceutical Industry: A Primer.* Sudbury, Mass.: Jones and Bartlett, 2010.

McCarthy, Robert L., and Kenneth W. Schafermeyer. *Introduction to Health Care Delivery: A Primer for Pharmacists.* 2d ed. Gaithersburg, Md.: Aspen, 2001.

Niebyl, Jennifer R. "The Pharmaceutical Industry: Friend or Foe?" *American Journal of Obstetrics and Gynecology*, April, 2008, 435.

Organization for Economic Cooperation and Development. *Pharmaceutical Pricing Policies in a Global Market.* Paris: Author, 2008.

Paul, Steven M., et al. "How to Improve R&D Productivity: The Pharmaceutical Industry's Grand Challenge." *Nature Reviews: Drug Discovery* 9, no. 3 (March, 2010): 203-214.

U.S. Bureau of Labor Statistics. *Career Guide to Industries*, 2010-2011 ed. http://www.bls.gov/oco/cg.

U.S. Census Bureau. North American Industry Classification System (NAICS), 2007. http://www.census.gov/cgi-bin/sssd/naics/naicsrch?chart=2007.

U.S. Congressional Budget Office. *Research and Development in the Pharmaceutical Industry: A CBO Study.* Washington, D.C.: Author, 2006.

U.S. Department of Commerce. International Trade Administration. Office of Trade and Industry Information. Industry Trade Data and Analysis. http://ita.doc.gov/td/industry/otea/OTII/OTII-index.html.

U.S. Internal Revenue Service. "Pharmaceutical Industry Overview." http://www.irs.gov/businesses/article/0,,id=169579,00.html.

World Trade Organization. "TRIPS and Pharmaceutical Patents: Fact Sheet." Geneva, Switzerland: Author, 2006. http://www.wto.org/english/tratop_e/trips_e/factsheet_pharm00_e.htm.

Philanthropic, Charitable, Religious, Civic, and Grant-Making Industry

INDUSTRY SNAPSHOT

General Industry: Personal Services

Career Cluster: Human Services

Subcategory Industries: Business, Professional, Labor, Political, and Similar Organizations; Civic and Social Organizations; Grant-Making and Giving Services; Religious Organizations; Social Advocacy Organizations

Related Industries: Counseling Services; Higher Education Industry; Libraries and Archives Industry; Museums and Cultural Institutions Industry; Personal Services; Political Advocacy Industry; Public Elementary and Secondary Education Industry

Annual Domestic Revenues: $1.1 trillion (*The Nonprofit Almanac*, 2005)

NAICS Number: 813

INDUSTRY DEFINITION

Summary

The philanthropic, charitable, religious, civic, and grant-making industry is not, strictly speaking, an "industry," but a collection of organizations whose purpose is to provide services and that operate on a not-for-profit basis. This industry is diverse enough to include charities, religious institutions, service organizations, and foundations supporting scholarship, but these organizations have several features in common: Their purposes are to promote ideals and causes, not to make money; they are part of both the private sector and the government; and they are dependent on donations of money and goods and on volunteer labor.

History of the Industry

Philanthropic, charitable, religious, civic, and grant-making organizations have had a long, if not always cherished, place in American history and society. Their purposes have both overlapped and varied, but they have all sought a central place in the social and moral life of American society. Although Americans have always prided themselves on a society characterized by voluntarism, the diverse organizations that have both supported and been supported by this voluntarism were not always regarded with favor. Rather, changing political, social, and economic circumstances, along with competing ideas regarding charity and compassion, have had profound effects on their forms and practices. The overlapping role of the govern-

The Humane Society of the United States works to reduce suffering and improve the lives of animals, both directly through animal shelters and indirectly through advocacy. (©Michael Ledray/Dreamstime.com)

ment with private organizations has likewise changed throughout history.

The separation of church and state established in the U.S. Constitution firmly placed religious organizations outside the public sector and contributed to the creation of religious-based private social service organizations. It also influenced the establishment of a partial separation of charitable and philanthropic efforts from religion. Despite the resulting American voluntaristic tradition, responsibility for the social commonweal was considered a public effort, and private charitable and social service efforts did not enjoy widespread approval or support until the mid-nineteenth century. The period before the Civil War was one of massive social challenges resulting from urbanization, immigration, and industrialization, and these challenges only accelerated in the postwar decades. In particular, immigration created not only new challenges but also new promise, as newly arrived groups formed their own religious and ethnicity-based social services organizations.

The late nineteenth century, remembered as a period of unregulated industrial growth, was also the period when modern philanthropy was born, as industrialists sought to do good with their fortunes, resulting in the creation of many still existing foundations. Charity and social services, by then increasingly privatized efforts, were undergoing a shift to a "scientific" approach that emphasized determining "worthiness" and promoting "moral uplift." A burgeoning labor movement and its politically Progressive allies shifted the emphasis to a public and governmental responsibility for societal welfare, resulting in the strengthening and reforming of the public sector during the early twentieth century period known as the Progressive Era.

It was not until the Great Depression, however, that the primary role of the private sector for public welfare was seriously challenged. The New Deal, as well as the postwar efforts culminating in the 1960's Great Society, led to the creation of the modern welfare state, as well as of new roles for nonprofits of various descriptions. From the 1960's onward, these nonprofits created a kind of "shadow state" that had significant influence in shaping government policy. This increased public role for nonprofits, however, led to an increasingly close relationship with the government that included not only the support of public money but also greater regulation regarding permissible activities, financial practices, and even compensation for top executives.

The 1980's would bring further changes to the roles and relationship of public and private nonprofit organizations. Increasing political conservatism and conservative religious revivalism led to a denigration of the welfare state, eventual cutting of public welfare, and an increased emphasis on private charity and voluntarism. However, fiscal conservativism and, later, declining revenues led to decreasing financial support for the same private organizations that were expected to play an increased public role. Paradoxically, although religious organizations were traditionally excluded from government support, recent presidential administrations have sought to change that tradition, first through the 1996 Charitable Choice Act and then through the creation of the Office of Faith-Based and Community Initiatives.

The Industry Today

The public and private nonprofit industry today is the only sector of the American economy that is defined by what it is not—namely, that its primary purpose is not the creation of economic profits. It is also more varied in focus and purpose than ever before and covers numerous diverse categories, including government agencies and private organizations created to promote a sometimes intangible social, intellectual, or spiritual public welfare. In many of these areas, there are overlapping roles for public organizations and private agencies. The notable exception has traditionally involved interaction with religious organizations, where government support is more limited. Nonetheless, religious organizations enjoy tax exemption and other

privileges similar to those of secular organizations.

The degree and type of political activity and advocacy practiced by all nonprofit organizations can affect (though not necessarily eliminate) their tax-exempt classification. The public and private nonprofit sectors, therefore, closely interact in a variety of ways, to the point that private nonprofits have come to be regarded as the "third sector" of the American economy, alongside government and private, for-profit industry. For all the popular political emphasis on the importance of private charities, philanthropies, and social services, however, government support has remained an integral part of the functioning of this sector, with all but the smallest organizations required to register with the Internal Revenue Service (IRS) and to accept a certain degree of IRS monitoring. In some cases, this has led to increased conservatism in the purposes and services of many private organizations.

In recent years, there has been a noticeable blurring of lines between for-profit and not-for-

In 2007, about 13,000 cyclists participated in a two-day bike tour from Houston to Austin to benefit people with multiple sclerosis. The National Multiple Sclerosis Society holds similar events across the country. (AP/Wide World Photos)

profit activity, both in the sense that organizations devoted to the services traditionally provided by nonprofits have experienced unprecedented for-profit competition and in the sense that some for-profit enterprises make social action part of their business. These efforts have naturally been a source of controversy, as have the increasingly close partnerships between for-profit enterprise and not-for-profit organizations. Such partnerships lead to concerns regarding whether nonprofits can maintain a vital degree of independence from private industry and remain noncommercialized.

Corporate sponsorship and support has long been a hallmark of many officially not-for-profit institutions, as has corporate participation on governing boards. Along with the mixed blessings of for-profit collaboration with nonprofits, there has been recent controversy over the increased use of administrative and financial practices from the for-profit sector. In particular, there has been a slow eroding of the social stigma and even legal prohibi-

In 2010, a UPS employee, in partnership with United Way, rebuilds homes devastated by Hurricane Katrina in the New Orleans area. That same year, Forbes *magazine ranked United Way as the largest charity in the United States. (AP/Wide World Photos)*

tions against nonprofit executives accepting the payment and perks of their counterparts in the for-profit sector. In 1991, a scandal involving the United Way resulted in the disaffiliation of many local federations from the national organization and the downfall of the organization's president, William J. Aramony. This scandal is a key example of the real and imagined perils of the not-for-profit sector becoming too similar to the for-profit sector.

Some industry observers argue that the restrictions on nonprofit organizations' financial activities and structures are based on sometimes outmoded ideas regarding altruism and self-sacrifice and that they needlessly hamper the successful functioning of nonprofits. It is argued that restrictions on compensation in particular drive the most talented people to choose careers in the for-profit sector rather than in nonprofit or public service. At the lower level, these expectations can mean poor compensation for employees, especially in organizations that rely heavily on volunteer labor. They can sometimes put charitable organizations at odds with living wage campaigns. Among religious organizations, there are a variety of views and practices concerning compensation for institutional employees. Conversely, pay rates for public employment are usually set either directly or indirectly via legislation and may involve labor agreements with collective bargaining units.

As the roles of the public sector and private nonprofits have shifted, another important trend among private not-for-profit organizations has been a move away from federation-based disbursement of funds toward increased donor control over that disbursement, even by small donors. This has resulted in an unprecedented diversity among organizations, not only in clientele and purpose but also in leadership and donation, including an increasing presence of women among top executives and boards. This increased diversity comes along with a greater, if still controversial, demand for the equal inclusion of faith-based organizations in the public-private nonprofit partnership. This demand has provoked the most controversy when applied to religious organizations whose religious principles may sanction otherwise publicly unacceptable forms of discrimination, frequently regarding gender and leadership or the acceptability of homosexuality.

Another significant change in the nonprofit sector has been the increasingly universal use of the Internet, as well as the increasing use of social networking sites, such as Facebook. Indeed, not only is fund-raising increasingly conducted via the Internet, but there is also a small but growing number of legitimate organizations whose presence on the Web greatly outpaces their brick-and-mortar facilities. Finally, the recession of 2007-2009 has once again highlighted the depth of the partnership between public services and the private not-for-profit sector. As governments struggle to balance budgets and rein in debts, public welfare has been heavily affected. At the same time, public funding for private nonprofit organizations has dried up, even though the need for their services has not decreased and, in many cases, has increased. Although the future of many individual organizations remains uncertain, the not-for-profit industry remains a vital and important sector of the American economy and polity.

INDUSTRY MARKET SEGMENTS

Generally speaking, nonprofit organizations are those that qualify for tax-exempt status under the U.S. Tax Code. They may be almost any size, from an organization with one full- or even part-time employee that subsists on volunteer labor, to an international nongovernmental organization (NGO) with a worldwide employee base. Almost all have fewer paid staff than do organizations with equivalent budgets in the for-profit sector, and their unpaid volunteers and interns may therefore have significant operational responsibilities.

Small Organizations

Small organizations in the nonprofit world include local organizations and foundations, as well as local churches, synagogues, and other religious institutions. In the public sector, they may include local government agencies. Though they vary in size and purpose, most remain small-scale, and many private agencies are heavily dependent on volunteer labor.

Potential Annual Earnings Scale. According to the U.S. Bureau of Labor Statistics (BLS), the overall average annual salary of all employees in the nonprofit sector was $41,080 in 2009. On average, members of the clergy earned $46,480, community and social service specialists earned $39,750, social and human service assistants earned $31,690, and child, family, and school social workers in the industry earned $36,820. Lawyers in the nonprofit sector earned an average of $113,980. General and operations managers earned an average of $104,900, while social and community service managers earned an average of $60,320.

Clientele Interaction. In small organizations, clientele interaction is more likely to be individualized and one-on-one. Projects of these organizations tend to be comparatively few, local, and small-scale. Clientele may be further limited for organizations that are dedicated to serving distinct populations, including religious groups. In some cases, individual organizations may work on a federated basis through larger organizations in order to effectively serve their client pools. Nonetheless, for many of these organizations, client service is the point of being, and dedication to this purpose is the expectation.

Amenities, Atmosphere, and Physical Grounds. Although many small nonprofit organizations, especially most houses of worship, are likely to have their own buildings and grounds, many others may merely have offices or office suites, located in larger professional buildings. Amenities in these settings may be basic, and in some organizations equipment and supplies may be donated. Depending on the organization, the atmosphere may be more informal and less bureaucratic than in larger organizations.

Typical Number of Employees. Small nonprofit organizations, especially in the private sector, are almost invariably characterized by small staffs, which may include as few as one full-time paid employee. Depending on the type of organization, five may be a typical number, but many nonprofits may not have any full-time employees, and many are heavily dependent on volunteer labor.

Traditional Geographic Locations. Small nonprofit organizations may be located anywhere but are more likely than larger organizations to be found in smaller towns and communities. They are also less likely to have multiple locations or branch offices. As with larger organizations, however, a growing number in recent years have been developing a presence in cyberspace.

Pros of Working for a Small Organization. Working in a small nonprofit organization has many advantages, not the least of which is less bureaucratization and more opportunity to work one-to-one with people of different backgrounds and perspectives. There tends to be a closer relationship among the paid staff and boards, as well as with the community, and there may also be more opportunities to work in multiple areas and for direct involvement with clients and donors alike. Finally, for nonprofit entrepreneurs, small organizations may require only low overhead to start.

Cons of Working for a Small Organization. Although working for a small nonprofit organization can bring much personal and professional satisfaction, it may also involve numerous headaches and disadvantages peculiar to small organizations. First, in a smaller, less formal workplace, office politics have the potential to become personal, especially among the often dedicated and idealistic people who choose nonprofit work. Additionally, because idealism is emphasized and budgets may be limited, small organizations may suffer from a limited leadership pool. Although there are possibilities for advancement and specialization within the organization, they may be limited. Smaller organizations also are likely not only to be more dependent on volunteer labor but also to require greater staff deference to volunteer boards. With limited budgets and infrastructures, not only is pay likely to be poor, but the managerial leadership is also likely to be less professional, providing fewer opportunities for professional development and networking to employees. In short, small organizations have all the problems of nonprofit organizations, exacerbated by small size and budget.

Costs

Payroll and Benefits: This form of overhead is likely to be minimal in small nonprofit organizations, thanks in large part to reliance on volunteer labor and leadership. The relatively few full-time positions are likely to be salaried, but part-time employees may be paid on an hourly basis. Benefits likewise may be minimal, especially in entrepreneurial nonprofits whose staff may be essentially self-employed. Notably, this expense may be especially affected by available revenues.

Supplies: Supply requirements depend on the type of organization, although nearly all require general office, computer, and communication supplies and equipment. Some organizations may also require self-publishing supplies and library material, and the needs of religious organizations may include the appropriate religious sancta and books, as well as musical instruments and sheet music. Many organizations also require food for social and fund-raising events.

External Services: In small organizations, services such as computer and equipment maintenance and repairs, legal counsel, financial services, publicity and public relations, and consulting are likely to be contracted out, along with maintenance and security, although many religious organizations are likely to employ at least part-time staff for building cleaning, maintenance, and groundskeeping. Some maintenance and even clerical services may also be donated.

Utilities: Utilities for small organizations include the basics of electricity, water, sewage, garbage collection, telephone, and Internet access. Many organizations, notably churches and synagogues, have begun attempting to minimize their environmental and carbon footprints.

Taxes: Although small nonprofit organizations are by definition tax exempt, they must adhere to the appropriate IRS codes and accept monitoring as necessary. Most employee pay remains taxable.

Midsize Organizations

Midsize nonprofit organizations are a varied group that can sometimes be more diverse than either small or large organizations. These organizations may be local, regional, or national private entities or government agencies. In the case of religious institutions, they may include both individual congregations and larger religious organizations.

Potential Annual Earnings Scale. Midsize nonprofit organizations are likely to have a more stable and diverse donor population than their small counterparts, though even that may depend on the type and nature of the organization. Their donor pool is more likely to include corporate donors and sponsors from the for-profit sector, and partnerships with for-profit organizations are more common in this sector. Depending on the type of organization, there is more likely to be fee-based revenue, and as with small public agencies, midsize ones are supported by taxes and fees.

According to the BLS, the overall average annual salary of all employees in the nonprofit sector was $41,080 in 2009. On average, members of the clergy earned $46,480, community and social service specialists earned $39,750, social and human service assistants earned $31,690, and child, family, and school social workers in the industry earned $36,820. Lawyers in the nonprofit sector earned an average of $113,980. General and operations managers earned an average of $104,900, while social and community service managers earned an average of $60,320.

Clientele Interaction. The type of clientele interaction depends on the size, type, and purpose of the institution, but it is likely to be less individualized and more bureaucratic than in small organizations. There may be less direct employee-client interaction, but there may also be opportunities to work with a larger and more diverse clientele than is served by smaller organizations.

Amenities, Atmosphere, and Physical Grounds. Midsize organizations are more likely than their small counterparts to have their own buildings and grounds, or at least multiple offices or office suites, depending on the type of organization. There may be more personal and professional amenities available within midsize organizations than in small ones, and their availability may be less dependent on direct donations.

Typical Number of Employees. In the nonprofit world, the number of employees may be absolutely smaller at a midsize organization than it would be at its for-profit counterpart, especially since organizational size is determined by amount of revenue rather than number of employees. As a result, midsize organizations may be categorized as those that have between five and twenty-five full-time employees, supplemented by larger numbers of part-time employees and significant volunteer labor.

Traditional Geographic Locations. Like nonprofit organizations, midsize organizations may be

located anywhere, though they are less likely than their small counterparts to be located in small towns and communities. Many have multiple regional, if not always national, branches, and they are increasingly likely to have an additional presence in cyberspace.

Pros of Working for a Midsize Organization. Working for a midsize nonprofit organization may offer the best of both small and large organizations. Midsize organizations may be more financially and organizationally stable than small organizations and may have fewer problems with excess bureaucracy than large organizations. There may be better compensation, greater career mobility, and greater opportunities for specialization and professional growth than in small organizations. Plus, midsize organizations are more likely than small organizations to offer the satisfaction of name recognition, and, depending on the type of organization, they may offer better financial and professional resources.

Cons of Working for a Midsize Organization. Although midsize nonprofit organizations may on average have greater financial and organizational viability than their small counterparts, they may nonetheless have fewer resources, and therefore be less likely to survive economic downturns, than large organizations. As with midsize for-profit corporations, their ambitions may outpace their available resources, leading to more frustrated and unfulfilled organizational goals. In addition, they may have less professional management than large organizations, and paid staff may be more dependent on volunteer labor and beholden to volunteer boards.

Costs

Payroll and Benefits: There are more salaried full-time positions available in midsize organizations, though they may still be few compared to positions paid on an hourly basis. Top executives are unlikely to be compensated at rates comparable to those of the private sector, and the pay rate for hourly positions in some cases may not be much more than the minimum wage. In public agencies, pay rates are determined by legislation, union contracts, or some combination, and pay and benefits are likely to be more generous in the public sector. On the other hand, public agencies are increasingly contracting out certain job categories to private, for-profit vendors.

Supplies: Supply requirements vary according to the type of organization but are likely to include all of the necessary office, computer, and communications equipment and supplies. Library and self-publishing supplies may be included, along with the appropriate sancta, religious books, and musical supplies for religious organizations. Less commonly than in small organizations, some supplies may be donated, although in some cases, they may be purchased at a discount.

External Services: Although computer and equipment repair and maintenance may be performed by in-house staff, it may also be contracted out, and the same is true for maintenance and security, although midsize institutions are more likely to maintain most of these positions in-house. In addition, midsize institutions are more likely to engage outside consultants, legal counsel, accounting services, publicity and public relations services, catering, and entertainment services.

Utilities: Midsize nonprofit institutions require all the essential utilities to function, including electricity, water, sewage, garbage removal, telephone, and Internet access.

Taxes: Although nonprofit organizations are by definition tax exempt, their type and degree of tax exemption may depend on the nature and amount of political advocacy they engage in. All private nonprofit organizations are required to register with the IRS and accept a certain degree of public monitoring in order to maintain their tax-exempt status.

Large Organizations

Large not-for-profit organizations include the big-name national and international charities and foundations. Although they may be the projects of individuals or families, they are more likely to be broad-based organizations whose identities transcend those of individuals and families. They may also be public agencies or subsectors of government departments.

Potential Annual Earnings Scale. According to the BLS, the overall average annual salary of all employees in the nonprofit sector was $41,080 in 2009. On average, members of the clergy earned $46,480, community and social service specialists earned $39,750, social and human service assistants earned $31,690, and child, family, and school social workers in the industry earned $36,820. Lawyers in the nonprofit sector earned an average of $113,980. General and operations managers earned an average of $104,900, while social and community service managers earned an average of $60,320.

Clientele Interaction. Clientele interaction is on average far less personalized and more bureaucratic in large organizations and agencies than in smaller ones, except in the cases of some local branches. Depending on the type of organization, client interaction may involve less interaction with private individuals and more with other organizations and their representatives.

Amenities, Atmosphere, and Physical Grounds. Large nonprofit organizations are the most likely to have their own building and grounds and to have multiple offices and even campuses. Office amenities are more likely to go beyond the basic and may be similar to those found in the offices of for-profit businesses. The atmosphere at these organizations may be more formalized and bureaucratized than in smaller organizations but may still emphasize a sense of mission that differentiates them from for-profit corporations.

Typical Number of Employees. The number of full-time employees in a nonprofit organization, for which size is gauged by revenue rather than personnel, is likely to be smaller than for a comparably sized for-profit corporation, but one operative definition for a large organization is one that employers twenty-five or more full-time employees. These numbers may not account for larger numbers of part-time employees and certainly not for the numerous volunteers whose leadership and labor help many nonprofits carry out their missions. In any case, the size and prestige of private nonprofit organizations may not necessarily be correlated with the number of employees.

Traditional Geographic Locations. Large not-for-profit organizations are most likely to be found in major metropolitan centers, and private nonprofits are the most likely to have multiple locations in the form of headquarters and regional field offices, sometimes located nationwide. Most large nonprofit organizations also maintain a strong presence in cyberspace.

Pros of Working for a Large Organization. Working for a large nonprofit organization offers a variety of opportunities to associate with and enjoy the prestige of a widely recognized organization. For career changers moving from the for-profit to the not-for-profit sector, large organizations may offer the most opportunities for transference of professional skills and, for all professional employees in the nonprofit sector, may offer the best opportunities for specialization, career advancement, professional development, and networking. They may also offer some categories of nonprofit employees the most glamour in terms of opportunities for interaction with prominent individual and corporate donors. Finally, pay and benefits, especially at the top executive level, are more likely to be generous, though not necessarily approaching those offered by the for-profit sector.

Cons of Working for a Large Organization. As with large for-profit organizations, one chief disadvantage of working for large nonprofit organizations or public agencies is greater bureaucracy, with all of its attendant problems, including the sense of being merely a "cog in the machine." There may be less opportunity for direct client and donor interaction than in smaller organizations. Because large organizations are more likely to work closely with for-profit corporate partners, the effects of commercialization may diminish the sense of organizational idealism. Paradoxically, legal restrictions and social stigmas regarding compensation for nonprofit employees may make jobs at these organizations less attractive to those who have the potential to earn much more in the for-profit sector.

Costs

Payroll and Benefits: Large organizations and agencies maintain the most full-time, salaried employees, but salary costs may be kept down through formal and informal limits on nonprofit employee compensation. Likewise, full-time employees in nonprofit organizations are more likely to have benefits, though they may be less than those available in the for-profit sector. Even so, it is possible in some organizations for top executives to earn six-figure salaries. Beyond full-time employees, payroll expenses may include compensation for part-time and hourly employees.

Supplies: As with smaller organizations, supply needs for large nonprofit organizations may depend on the size of the organization but invari-

ably include office, computer, and communication supplies and equipment. They may also include necessary library, self-publishing, and mailing equipment

External Services: Although large not-for-profit organizations are the most likely to maintain in-house maintenance, repair, and security staff, they are increasingly likely to contract these services to for-profit vendors, an increasing trend among public organizations as well as private agencies. Large nonprofit organizations are also the most likely to engage outside consultants on a regular and sustained basis. They may also contract catering and entertainment for fund-raising events and benefits, legal counsel, financial services, lobbying, publicity, public relations, and software design and administration.

Utilities: Large nonprofit organizations require the most significant use of basic utilities, including electricity, water, sewage, garbage removal, telephone, and Internet access.

Taxes: Although nonprofit organizations may receive tax exemption regardless of size, the type and degree of tax exemption may be dependent upon how much and what type of political activity a given organization practices. For that reason, large organizations, as with their smaller counterparts, must register with the IRS and accept a certain degree of monitoring in order to maintain tax-exempt status. The close partnerships with for-profit enterprises that some large nonprofits maintain may create additional complications regarding tax exemptions. It is becoming increasingly common for umbrella organizations to operate simultaneously multiple nonprofit entities, such as a 501(c)3 and a 501(c)4, each of which has different limitations on permissible activities. Thus, for example, the organization may conduct its lobbying efforts through its 501(c)4 while conducting its nonpartisan activities through its 501(c)3.

ORGANIZATIONAL STRUCTURE AND JOB ROLES

Although the not-for-profit industry is regarded as almost synonymous with volunteer work and voluntarism, there are numerous professional roles and opportunities available within this sector. Although some opportunities may require skills and training similar to those required in the for-profit world, some may require more specialized preparation. Similarly, while many professional opportunities with not-for-profit organizations may involve more mundane and less glamorous duties than the voluntary opportunities, other nonprofit professional roles may offer unique opportunities to educate, influence, and even inspire. In the case of religious organizations, there may be significant religious requirements, chief among them faith membership, for entry into certain job categories, while for other job categories, religious requirements may be negligible or nonexistent. On the other hand, in some organizations even low-level support staff may be required to subscribe to the organization's culture and mission. In nearly all of these categories, working conditions and compensation may vary widely, sometimes even for the same type of position. Finally, although it is not true for all job categories, for some nonprofit jobs, it is possible to gain entry to paid positions via volunteer work, and in many cases previous relevant volunteer work may be considered advantageous.

The following umbrella categories apply to the organizational structure of organizations in the philanthropic, charitable, religious, civic, and grant-making industry:

- Management and Administration
- Client and Donor Services
- Public Relations
- Facilities and Security
- Technology, Research, and Development
- Financial and Legal Services
- Education and Spirituality
- Human Resources

Management and Administration

As in the for-profit economy, good administration and management are vital to the successful operation of philanthropic, charitable, civic, and grant-making organizations. There are notable differences, though, between working for these organizations, whether at the high or low levels of administration, and holding similar jobs in the for-profit sector. To begin with, administrators and their support staff at all levels are required to maintain at least a minimal adherence to the purpose and mission of the organizations they work for and to understand the differences between performance criteria for nonprofit organizations and those of for-profit enterprises. In high-level administrative positions, this may mean working closely with volunteer boards, organizational members and volunteers, spiritual or religious leaders, or some combination. Depending on the type of position and organization, administrative roles may merely involve responsibility for day-to-day management or may require long-term, visionary leadership.

In numerous instances, administrative occupations may require a careful balance of authority and deference to voluntary boards, as well as a focus on the less "glamorous," nuts-and-bolts aspects of nonprofit organizations. Also, depending on the size of the organization's paid staff, administrative occupations may involve multiple and sometimes diverse responsibilities. There are many entry points to administrative careers in this industry, and in many cases the required skills and background may be easily transferred from the for-profit world. However, compensation is likely to be significantly less than it is for similar positions in the for-profit sector.

Management and administrative occupations may include the following:

- Executive Director/Chief Executive Officer (CEO)
- Chief Operating Officer (COO)
- Program Officer
- Project Director
- Administrative Assistant
- Receptionist

Client and Donor Services

Among philanthropic, charitable, civic, and grant-making organizations, client services are what stand in for customer service in for-profit enterprises, and donor services constitute a relatively unique department. Combined, they form the lifeblood of nonprofit organizations, most of whose purposes are providing services and advancing social causes. For that reason, working in client relations, donor relations, or both requires a broad set of people skills for dealing with diverse populations that, depending on the organization, might even overlap. In both cases, working in either of these sectors may require specialized knowledge pertaining to the type of organization, and in some instances may require advanced degrees. Additionally, for some organizations, working in either of these sectors may require an awareness of broader class and economic issues and even political trends. For many organizations, it is also important for specialists in this sector to maintain awareness of changing donor and client pools. Occupations within this sector may also involve coordination and supervision of volunteer labor and, in the case of donor relations, may require knowledge of Internet and social networking technology. Notably, client and donor services are both areas where it may be possible to gain entry into professional positions via volunteer experience.

Client and donor relations occupations may include the following:

- Development Director
- Event Coordinator
- Program Director
- Project Director
- Fund-Raising Officer
- Case Worker
- Social Worker
- Psychologist

Public Relations

Public relations and publicity are vital to the workings of philanthropic, charitable, religious, civic, and grant-making organizations, as well as to public agencies. Specialists in this sector may engage not only in promoting the organization and its goals but also in creating the public face of the organization and, in some cases, frequently dealing with the press. In addition, for many private not-for-profit organizations, publicity and public relations are vital to successful fund-raising. Finally, the job of public relations specialists in the nonprofit sector is often to manage the brand of the organization they serve.

In some cases, public relations work may overlap with that of other departments, especially client and donor services. As partnerships between non-profit organizations and for-profit corporations become more common, especially among larger organizations, public relations specialists may find themselves working in ethically and legally dicey areas and may find that one of their most impor-

tant roles is to maintain a line between promotion and commercialization of their organization and its services. In addition to the appropriate professional education and background, working in public relations for nonprofit organizations is increasingly likely to require knowledge of Internet and even social networking technology. In some cases, skills may be transferable for those from for-profit public relations or journalistic backgrounds.

Public relations occupations may include the following:

- Marketing Director
- Assistant Marketing Director
- Publications Specialist
- Webmaster
- Public Relations Executive
- Press Agent
- Public Affairs Specialist
- Press Secretary
- Media Specialist

Facilities and Security

Although seemingly mundane, facilities management and security are often essential to the successful running of private, not-for-profit organizations, as well as public agencies. For nearly all organizations and agencies, maintaining clean, attractive, and inviting facilities is as important as it is for for-profit businesses. In addition, while security needs may vary (and may not always require specialized personnel), for many public agencies and for numerous private ones (sadly, Jewish agencies in particular), professional security service is a must for maintaining a safe environment and preventing disruption of operations.

Security needs may vary according to location, with institutions located in large metropolitan areas being more likely to require full-time security services. The number and type of facilities and security staff vary according to institutional needs and may be in-house, contracted out, or some combination. In addition, work in this area may be part or full time, and, while some institutions may mandate the payment of a living wage, many do not. Facilities service in particular may be strictly custodial or may involve a variety of duties. In the case of some religious institutions, some religion-specific duties may be involved, but denominational membership is not necessarily required as a result.

Training and skills for occupations within the facilities and security sector are usually easy to transfer to and from other industries.

Facilities and security occupations may include the following:

- Security Guard
- Custodian/Janitor
- Caretaker
- Sexton

Technology, Research, and Development

Beyond the grant-making organizations and agencies that specialize in the support of research and development, technology, research, and development is a broadly categorized department within the philanthropic, charitable, religious, civic, and grant-making industry and may include everything from program and project development to development of Internet capacity, as well as research in a variety of areas. Research and development is also important to retroactive assessment of the success of nonprofit programming. This department therefore, may require broad-based technological skills, business skills, specialized knowledge pertinent to the organization's mission, or a combination of these skills. Full-time opportunities in this department are most likely to be available in large organizations, whereas smaller organizations may be more likely to rely on part-time and volunteer labor for some functions and outside consultants for others.

Because of the broad-based nature of this department, there are numerous career entry points, and for potential entrants, technological skills may be most easily transferable from the for-profit sector. Research and development are broad categories but frequently involve financial research skills that may be transferable from the for-profit sector, albeit with necessary refocusing. Additionally, private and public nonprofit organizations that specialize in research grants or social services may require more social-science-based research skills, and offer opportunities for skill transference in this case from higher education.

Technology, research, and development occupations may include the following:

- Management Information Systems Director

- Chief Technology Officer (CTO)
- Special Projects Manager
- Development Director
- Webmaster
- Researcher
- Statistician

Financial and Legal Services

Financial and legal services are essential to the successful management of private philanthropic, charitable, religious, civic, and grant-making organizations, as well as to the functioning of public agencies. Legal services are often necessary for managing potentially difficult legal issues organizations may face and to assist in settling lawsuits and legal disputes. In addition, some nonprofit organizations or agencies may specialize in legal services or in legal advocacy and therefore retain lawyers and legal staff for that purpose.

The roles of financial service specialists in nonprofit organizations are more varied and complex. Competent financial management is vital to the solvency of nonprofit organizations and includes monitoring income, outflows, and disbursement of funds. Beyond day-to-day duties, specialists in financial services also play key roles in long-term financial planning, risk management, and fundraising, and they may work in tandem with legal specialists to deal with the requirements regarding tax exemptions. Specialized professional training is usually required for this group of occupations. In many cases, skills and qualifications are transferable from the for-profit sector, and financial services occupations in this industry may be especially attractive to those with business school backgrounds. Nonetheless, those who transfer to this sector from for-profit organizations must be prepared to adapt to a different kind of business culture and, in most cases, be willing to accept compensation that is notably below that of comparable occupations in for-profit industries.

Financial and legal occupations may include the following:

- Chief Financial Officer (CFO)
- Certified Public Accountant
- Development Officer
- Finance Officer
- Grants Manager
- Special Projects Manager

OCCUPATION PROFILE

Clergy

Considerations	Qualifications
Description	Provides religious services for believers.
Career cluster	Human Services
Interests	People
Working conditions	Work inside
Minimum education level	Bachelor's degree; master's degree
Physical exertion	Light work
Physical abilities	Unexceptional/basic fitness
Opportunities for experience	Military service; volunteer work
Licensure and certification	Usually not required
Employment outlook	Average growth expected
Holland interest score	SAI

Note: See volume 1, "Publisher's Note," for an explanation of the Holland interest score.

- Attorney
- Paralegal
- Legal Secretary

Education and Spirituality

Although this segment may be pertinent only to certain sectors of the not-for-profit industry, religious and spiritual leaders, along with religious education and sacred music specialists, play vital roles in religious institutions. In most houses of worship, ministers, priests, rabbis, imams, and other spiritual leaders are the recognized heads of the organizations they serve, yet in some cases they also may be regarded as employees, with little difference from other religious institution personnel. Spiritual leaders of all faiths are increasingly likely to be found working in nonprofit settings other than houses of worship, including charitable and educational institutions. They must meet the requirements of their respective faiths, which frequently include formal ordination by the appropriate religious organization. In addition, depending on the size and type of the institution, job description and

compensation may vary, notably in that spiritual leaders may also take on educational and even musical roles. In large institutions, they are more likely to be assisted, especially in musical duties, by specialists in the appropriate sacred music or religious education field. Occupations in these areas, therefore, require specialized education and training and frequently (though not universally) membership in the appropriate faith. Most of these occupations may involve some supervisory duties, and some may involve specialized work with children and youth. Nearly all require some weekend work, and in some cases those who practice these occupations may also be members of or participants in the institution they serve.

Education and spirituality occupations may include the following:

- Minister/Priest/Rabbi/Imam
- Chaplain
- Cantor/Cantorial Soloist/Church Soloist
- Organist/Musician
- Music/Choir Director

- Educational Director
- Religious School Teacher

Human Resources

The human resources department within the philanthropic, charitable, religious, civic, and grant-making industry deals with essentially the same issues as its counterparts in for-profit industries, including hiring and firing, organizational discipline, and dispute resolution, along with contract negotiations of various kinds. There are, however, some key differences that create complications for specialists in this department. Chief among them is the small size of most not-for-profit organizations, which frequently makes it impossible to have even one full-time specialist in human resources. The other, which is genuinely unique to the nonprofit industry, is the high reliance on volunteer labor. This reliance requires a different type of human resource management method, one that treats volunteer labor with the appropriate seriousness but also recognizes the different conditions involved in volunteer versus paid work. In any case, the role of employer-employee relations may vary according to the size and type of organization. Although larger organizations have specialized personnel officers, more often, human resources is fully integrated into general management, and there may be only one full-time personnel specialist, if any. The heavy reliance on volunteer labor may affect or limit the role of the human resources department as conventionally defined, and in the case of higher-level management and leadership roles, hiring decisions may require close cooperation with organizational boards and even, in some cases, membership.

Human resources occupations may include the following:

- Human Resources Manager
- Personnel Manager
- Ombudsman
- Volunteer Coordinator/Supervisor

INDUSTRY OUTLOOK

Overview

The outlook for the philanthropic, charitable, religious, civic, and grant-making industry appears to be stable, even in hard economic times, although the outlook varies among different subsets of the industry. This variation makes the outlook for the nonprofit industry difficult to compare to those of many for-profit industries, particularly given the different ways of measuring success in the two sectors. The recession of 2007-2009 in particular highlights the interdependence among many not-for-profit organizations, as well as between the public and private sectors of the industry. In practice, this set of interdependencies means that, while there will definitely be an increased need for the services of many kinds of nonprofit organizations, public, private, and corporate funding sources may be less available. The programming and even functioning of many organizations has been affected by the declining donor pools and availability of (tax-deductible) disposable income. Public agencies and private organizations alike have been and will be affected by state budget cuts, and while fee-based income may help make up the difference for some organizations, it is not likely to do so completely. Many organizations, moreover, will not have this option readily available to them.

The upshot is that the persistent need for nonprofit organizations may not translate into the steady availability of full-time paid employment within these organizations, especially in sectors that traditionally have relied on part-time and volunteer labor. While an increasingly business-oriented approach to nonprofit management may stabilize some organizations and make it possible to encourage greater experimentation and risk-taking, the business approach may also result in greater conservatism in mission and methods in order to limit the risk of offending potential donors, especially institutional donors from the for-profit corporate world. Additionally, an increased blurring of lines between not-for-profit and for-profit organizations may entail risks of increased commercialization and obscuring of mission, even as some nonprofit organizations might see this shift as necessary in order to remain competitive, especially as some services that traditionally have been the purview of nonprofits are being taken up by for-profit enterprises. Even with these issues, however, not-for-profit organizations should maintain a steady role as the "third sector" of the American economy and furthermore one that many regard as vital to the health and functioning of American democracy. The continued presence and perceived necessity of the nonprofit industry also highlights the enduring place of voluntarism and altruism in an otherwise increasingly commercialized American society.

The continued economic and social presence of nonprofit organizations also does not stop at the borders of the United States. A growing number of organizations, especially the larger ones, are or are becoming international in scope and operation, some with the sponsorship, assistance, and even active management of prominent individuals. Beyond these, however, there are numerous nonprofits and NGOs that play important charitable, cultural, economic, and even diplomatic roles on an international and global scale. Notably, in countries that feature more advanced welfare states than the United States, charitable organizations may not be perceived as playing the same essential role, but they nonetheless remain a significant part of national economies. In other parts of the world, there may be sometimes uncomfortable negotiations between international nonprofits and indigenous organizations, especially regarding control of the disbursement of funds and goods. Nonetheless, the success of internationally focused nonprofits and of NGOs both require and promote international cooperation, providing these organizations with an often unacknowledged role in the global economy.

Employment Advantages

Although full-time employment in many sectors of the philanthropic, charitable, religious, civic, and grant-making industry may sometimes be hard to secure and may never offer comparable pay and benefits to those of for-profit industries, jobs in this industry can offer intangible benefits that few for-profit enterprises can match—namely the opportunity to perform intellectually stimulating work and to work for the advancement of causes that one genuinely cares about. It is best, therefore, to pursue a career in the nonprofit industry with a healthy balance of idealism and realism, along with the willingness to put in the necessary hours and seek the appropriate training for the particular subset of the industry in which one is interested. That said, the nonprofit industry offers many points of entry and comparatively uniquely involves the possibility of securing paid employment via volunteer work. Additionally, in some departments, it is comparatively easy to transfer from for-profit employment, and in some cases there are even possibilities for entrepreneurship. In summation, while it is difficult at best to become rich working for nonprofit organizations, most people who go into this industry enjoy the satisfaction of working for an organization dedicated to advancing societal good.

Annual Earnings

In some ways, it is difficult to gauge the annual earnings of the philanthropic, charitable, religious, civic, and grant-making industry, precisely because it is broad-based enough to include a variety of organizations with widely differing structures, purposes, and budgets. Aside from the seeming philosophical contradiction of measuring the earnings of not-for-profit organizations, there are also practical obstacles. Chief among them is

PROJECTED EMPLOYMENT FOR SELECTED OCCUPATIONS

Religious, Grantmaking, Civic, Professional, and Similar Organizations

Employment		
2008	Projected 2018	Occupation
650,800	733,300	Clergy
8,800	10,000	Counselors
77,900	87,800	Directors, religious activities and education
24,800	27,800	Social workers

Source: U.S. Bureau of Labor Statistics, Industries at a Glance, Occupational Employment Statistics and Employment Projections Program.

that annual earnings are just one measure for rating nonprofit institutions and not even the chief one. Another difficulty is that annual income frequently includes donations of time and goods, rather than simply money. In addition, the differing structures and resources of nonprofits, as well as the understandable emphasis on disbursement over income, make acquiring aggregate data difficult. *The Nonprofit Almanac* reports the combined domestic assets for all nonprofit organizations as totaling $3.4 trillion in 2005. International figures can be even more difficult to come up with, especially when figuring in different factors that account for widely varying levels of giving. While reports are available for individual countries, most of which are major powers in the global economy, most of them focus on disbursement statistics and similar rankings, rather than absolute dollar numbers or equivalents.

RELATED RESOURCES FOR FURTHER RESEARCH

ALLIANCE FOR NONPROFIT MANAGEMENT
  1899 L St. NW, 7th Floor
  Washington, DC 20036
  Tel: (202) 955-8406
  Fax: (202) 822-0669
  http://www.allianceonline.org

ASSOCIATION FOR RESEARCH ON NONPROFIT ORGANIZATION AND VOLUNTARY ACTION
  550 W North St., Suite 301
  Indianapolis, IN 46202
  Tel: (317) 684-2120
  Fax: (317) 684-2128
  http://www.arnova.org

COUNCIL ON FOUNDATIONS
  2121 Crystal Dr., Suite 700
  Arlington, VA 22202
  Tel: (800) 673-9036
  http://www.cof.org

FOUNDATIONS CENTER
  79 5th Ave.
  New York, NY 10003-3076
  Tel: (212) 620-4230
  http://foundationcenter.org

NATIONAL COUNCIL OF CHURCHES
  475 Riverside Dr., Suite 800
  New York, NY 10115
  Tel: (212) 870-2228
  Fax: (212) 870-2030
  http://www.nccsusa.org

ABOUT THE AUTHOR

Susan Roth Breitzer holds a Ph.D. in U.S. history with specialties in social, cultural, immigration, urban, and labor history. She has taught U.S. and world history at Fayetteville State University and additionally worked with manuscript collections for several nonprofit institutions. She is the author of numerous encyclopedia articles for reference works that include *Issues: Understanding Controversies and Society, The Dictionary of American History, Encyclopedia of American Labor History*, and *Work in America: An Encyclopedia of History, Policy, and Society.*

FURTHER READING

Boris, Elizabeth T., et al. *What Drives Foundation Expenses and Compensation: Results of a Three-Year Study.* New York: Urban Institute, Foundation Center, and Philanthropic Research, 2008. Available at http://foundationcenter.org/gainknowledge/research/pdf/fec_report.pdf.

Charities Aid Foundation. *International Comparison of Charitable Giving, November, 2006.* Kings Hill, West Malling, Kent, England: Author, 2006. Available at http://www.cafonline.org/pdf/International Giving highlights.pdf.

Elazar, Daniel J. *Community and Polity: The Organizational Dynamics of American Jewry.* Philadelphia: Jewish Publication Society of America, 1976.

Gassler, Robert Scott. *The Economics of Nonprofit Enterprise: A Study in Applied Economic Theory.* Lanham, Md.: University Press of America, 1986.

Grobman, Gary M., and Gary B. Grant. *The Non-Profit Internet Handbook.* Harrisburg, Pa.: White Hat Communications, 1997.

Independent Sector. "The Sector's Economic

Impact." http://www.independentsector.org/economic_role.

Keating, Barry P., and Maryann O. Keating. *Not-for-Profit*. Glen Ridge, N.J.: Thomas Horton and Daughters, 1980.

Knauft, E. B., Renee A. Berger, and Sandra T. Gray. *Profiles of Excellence: Achieving Success in the Nonprofit Sector*. San Francisco: Josey-Bass, 1991.

Lowell, Stephanie. *Careers in the Nonprofit Sector*. Cambridge, Mass.: Harvard Business School, 2000.

Olasky, Marvin. *The Tragedy of American Compassion*. Preface by Charles Murray. Washington, D.C.: Regnery, 1992.

Organization for Economic Cooperation and Development. *The Non-profit Sector in a Changing Economy*. Paris: Author, 2003.

Pallotta, Dan. *Uncharitable: How Restraints on Nonprofits Undermine Their Potential*. Hanover, N.H.: University Press of New England, 2008.

Raymond, Susan U. *The Future of Philanthropy: Economics, Ethics, and Management*. Hoboken, N.J.: John Wiley & Sons, 2004.

Shaw, Sondra C., and Martha A. Taylor. *Reinventing Fundraising: Realizing the Potential of Women's Philanthropy*. San Francisco: Jossey-Bass, 1995.

U.S. Bureau of Labor Statistics. *Career Guide to Industries*, 2010-2011 ed. http://www.bls.gov/oco/cg.

_____. *Occupational Outlook Handbook*, 2010-2011 ed. http://www.bls.gov/oco.

U.S. Census Bureau. North American Industry Classification System (NAICS), 2007. http://www.census.gov/cgi-bin/sssd/naics/naicsrch?chart=2007.

U.S. Department of Commerce. International Trade Administration. Office of Trade and Industry Information. Industry Trade Data and Analysis. http://ita.doc.gov/td/industry/otea/OTII/OTII-index.html.

Von Drehle, David. "The Other Financial Crisis." *Time*, June 28, 2010, 22-28.

White, Michelle J., ed. *Nonprofit Firms in a Three-Sector Economy*. Washington, D.C.: Urban Institute, 1991.

Wing, Kennard T., Katie L. Roediger, and Thomas H. Pollak. *The Nonprofit Sector in Brief: Public Charities, Giving, and Volunteering, 2009*. Washington, D.C.: Urban Institute, 2010. http://www.urban.org/uploadedpdf/412085-nonprofit-sector-brief.pdf.

Wolch, Jennifer L. *The Shadow State: Government and Voluntary Sector in Transition*. New York: Foundation Center, 1990.

Plastics and Rubber Manufacturing Industry

INDUSTRY SNAPSHOT

General Industry: Manufacturing

Career Cluster: Manufacturing

Subcategory Industries: Birth Control Device Manufacturing; Laminated Plastics Plate, Sheet (Except Packaging), and Shape Manufacturing; Plastics Bottle Manufacturing; Plastics Packaging Materials and Unlaminated Film and Sheet Manufacturing; Plastics Pipe, Pipefitting, and Unlaminated Profile Shape Manufacturing; Plastics Plumbing Fixture Manufacturing; Plastics Product Manufacturing; Polystyrene Foam Product Manufacturing; Resilient Floor Covering Manufacturing; Rubber and Plastic Hoses and Belting Manufacturing; Rubber Product Manufacturing; Rubber Product Manufacturing for Mechanical Use; Tire Manufacturing; Urethane and Other Foam Product (except Polystyrene) Manufacturing

Related Industries: Automobiles and Personal Vehicles Industry; Chemicals Industry; Petroleum and Natural Gas Industry; Toys and Games Industry

Annual Domestic Revenues: $215 billion USD (*Business Wire*, 2009)

Annual International Revenues: $2.8 trillion USD (IBISWorld, "Plastics & Rubber Machinery Manufacturing," U.S. Industry Report, 2010)

Annual Global Revenues: $3.015 trillion USD (*Business Wire*, 2009, and IBISWorld, 2010)

NAICS Number: 326

INDUSTRY DEFINITION

Summary

The plastics and rubber manufacturing industry is part of the basic chemicals industry, sometimes called commodity chemicals. Plastics and rubber are polymers, very large natural or synthetic molecules consisting of numerous repeating and linked units or building blocks. Polymers such as synthetic plastics and rubber constitute a major portion of the basic chemicals market. The industry manufactures a variety of products, from plastic resins to natural, synthetic, and reclaimed rubber. The term "plastic" is derived from a Greek word meaning pliable, and in modern usage plastics are natural or synthetic materials that can be molded into products using heat, pressure, or a combination of both.

Traditionally, plastics have been divided into two types: thermoplastics, such as polyvinyl chloride, which soften and melt under high heat, and thermosetting plastic materials, such as vulcanized rubber, which retain their shape after solidification. Throughout the twentieth century, the manufacture of plastics and rubber products constituted an increasingly high percentage of developed and developing countries' output. In the United States, this industry has been variously estimated to comprise ten thousand to sixteen thousand companies that play a pivotal role in the nation's economy.

History of the Industry

Though often linked in contemporary practice, the histories of rubber and plastics were largely separate until the twentieth century. Modern scholars have shown that Native American Maya used rubber as far back as 1600 B.C.E. Ancient artisans used the sap of certain plants and trees (later called latex) to make balls, containers, human figures, and footwear. They also discovered that the juice from such plants as the morning glory, when mixed with latex sap, formed a durable, elastic material that proved advantageous for binding axe heads to handles, as well as for waterproofing clothing and headgear. The most notable use of what subsequently came to be called rubber, which caught the attention of colonizing Europeans in the fifteenth and sixteenth centuries, was to make a ball about the size of a modern basketball that was central to a dangerously violent game played by the Maya. Christopher Columbus, after his second voyage to the New World in 1496, took back some of these bounceable rubber balls to Europe. In 1615, the Spanish in Mexico learned how to use latex to waterproof leather, and they were also able to apply their technique to other fabrics, leading to a thriving waterproof fabric industry.

In the eighteenth century, following an expedition to South America, Charles de la Condamine and François Fresneau were the first to study rubber scientifically, reporting to the French Academy of Sciences about their discovery of substances that dissolved rubber. In 1770, Joseph Priestley, the accomplished English chemist, bestowed the name "rubber" on this material because of its ability to rub out pencil marks. The French built the world's first rubber factory near Paris in 1803, and the English rubber industry got its start from chemist Charles Macintosh's discovery that dissolving rubber in a certain way enabled him to waterproof cotton materials for raincoats (which were named "mackintosh" for him).

Thomas Hancock is called the founder of the British rubber industry because he invented the "masticator," which produced a rubber material that could be rolled into sheets. American inventor Charles Goodyear, after experimenting with numerous substances, accidentally discovered in 1839 that natural rubber, when heated with sulfur, generated a material that, unlike earlier products, remained flexible in hot and cold weather. Goodyear's "vulcanized" rubber proved to be water-resistant and electrically nonconductive, and it came to be used in a variety of commercial prod-

Latex is collected from a rubber tree. (©Chan Yew Leong/ Dreamstime.com)

ucts. In the second half of the nineteenth century, the rubber industry in several countries prospered because of such inventions as the pneumatic tire, golf and tennis balls, and rubber toys. During this time, Brazil dominated the natural rubber market, but in 1876 rubber-tree seeds were smuggled from Brazil to England, enabling the British to breed new, disease-resistant trees that were sent to their colonies in Asia, particularly Malaysia and Ceylon, where colonists established large rubber plantations.

Concomitant with these developments in the rubber industry were changes in the science of chemistry that would deepen understanding of natural rubber while enabling organic chemists to create synthetic rubber and originate the new field of plastics. Through the experiments and theories of organic chemists, rubber was revealed to consist of very long chains of carbon and hydrogen atoms. After plastics were discovered and developed in the second half of the nineteenth century, they, too, were eventually shown by organic chemists to consist of very long chains of carbon, hydrogen, oxygen, and a variety of other atoms. Though scholars have traced certain precursors of plastics from antiquity to the nineteenth century, most agree that English chemist Alexander Parkes discovered the first plastic in the 1850's when he evaporated a solution of camphor and partially nitrated cellulose in alcohol and ether. This process produced a ma-

terial called pyroxylin that could be shaped and molded. Parkes's attempts to market his material failed, but John Wesley Hyatt, an American inventor, improved his process. In 1869, Hyatt patented a method of making billiard balls out of celluloid, the name that he gave to his plastic. After a patent dispute was favorably settled, Hyatt's Celluloid Manufacturing Company flourished.

The Industry Today

The plastics and rubber industry of the twenty-first century evolved from a series of twentieth century developments and products, several of which remain an integral part of the industry today. The pattern was set when, in 1909, Belgian American chemist Leo Baekeland made public Bakelite, the first totally synthetic plastic and the first thermoset plastic, which kept its shape under a variety of stresses of heat, pressure, and shock. Bakelite's stress-resistant properties, as well as its resistance to electricity, led to several successful products, making it the first plastic to achieve worldwide acceptance. The American military used Bakelite in lightweight war machinery in World War II, and it is still part of many products today. Following Baekeland's example, other inventors came up with such plastics as cellophane, the first flexible moisture-proof wrapping; polyvinyl chloride (PVC), a thermoplastic resin used in such products as rainwear, phonograph records, and floor tiles; and nylon, a thermoplastic material discovered by Wallace Carothers that proved to be better and cheaper than natural substances in such products as toothbrushes and silk stockings.

Although nineteenth century chemists had made modest progress in converting certain substances into rubber-like materials, synthetic rubber's creation was a twentieth century development. A patent for the world's first synthetic rubber was granted in 1909. Before World War I, Russian, German, and English chemists created various elastic polymers that, unfortunately, were inferior to their natural counterpart. Deprived of natu-

Raw plastic granules, ready for processing. (©Ari Sanjaya/Dreamstime.com)

The Plastics and Rubber Products Industry's Contribution to the U.S. Economy

Value Added	Amount
Gross domestic product	$66.7 billion
Gross domestic product	0.5%
Persons employed	726,000
Total employee compensation	$40.5 billion

Source: U.S. Bureau of Economic Analysis. Data are for 2008.

were producing more than 700,000 tons of synthetic rubber annually. The exigencies of war also fostered progress in plastics, especially the creation of inexpensive and reliable substitutes for materials that could no longer be imported. Such plastics as polyethylene, polystyrene, polyester, polyethylene terephthalate (PET), and several others, including silicones, owe their maturation and, in some cases, their origin and development to wartime pressures (many of these plastics would achieve great commercial success in the postwar period).

After World War II, the plastics and rubber manufacturing industries expanded rapidly. In order to commercialize products researched and developed during the war, massive investments were needed to make the many kinds of plastics and synthetic rubbers into goods that would succeed in the marketplace. Consequently, such massive and long-established businesses as Goodyear Tire & Rubber Company, Firestone, Michelin, DuPont, Shell, BASF, Dow, and Exxon were able to make plastics and synthetic rubbers for companies making automobiles and tires, footwear, and construction materials. Small and midsize businesses were able to find market niches in making such things as specialized polymers. New synthetic rubbers introduced in the 1950's and 1960's included Hypalon and Viton by DuPont, Natsyn by Goodyear, and polyurethane by Bayer. Thermoplastic rubbers were introduced in

ral rubber during World War I, German chemists manufactured a synthetic rubber from dimethylbutadiene, but it had limited uses, especially since tires made from it were mediocre. However, high prices for natural rubber in the 1920's encouraged the experimental and theoretical blossoming of synthetic rubber.

Herman Staudinger, a German theoretical chemist, proved that plastics and rubber were polymers with long, orderly arrangements of basic units (and not disorderly agglomerations, as many believed). Experimental advances included the creation of a copolymer of butadiene and styrene that was a forerunner of styrene-butadiene rubber (SBR), whose properties of strength and processability made it a success in the rest of the twentieth and into the twenty-first century. Julius Nieuwland, a Belgian American chemist and Roman Catholic priest, discovered how acetylene could generate various polymers, and Carothers, working for DuPont, capitalized on Nieuwland's studies and created neoprene, a synthetic rubber that was better than natural rubber in its resistance to oxidizing chemicals and sunlight. During the 1930's, Germany and Russia built plants capable of producing over 100,000 tons of synthetic rubber annually, while the United States developed synthetic rubbers that were resistant to oil and oxidants.

During World War II, the Japanese captured Asian natural rubber plantations, stimulating the U.S. government to invest heavily in the production of styrene-butadiene and other synthetic rubbers. By the end of the war, North American plants

Inputs Consumed by the Plastics and Rubber Products Industry

Input	Value
Energy	$4.4 billion
Materials	$107.6 billion
Purchased services	$25.9 billion
Total	$137.9 billion

Source: U.S. Bureau of Economic Analysis. Data are for 2008.

the 1960's; they were more easily molded than vulcanized rubbers. Their elastomeric and plastic properties led to a variety of applications, especially in the footwear and adhesive industries.

By the mid-1960's, synthetic rubber constituted about 75 percent of the market, but since these polymers were made from oil, market share could change dramatically with political developments. For example, during the oil embargo of 1973, the price of synthetic rubber doubled and market share declined precipitously. During the remaining decades of the twentieth century, the environmental movement had an increasing influence on the way that the public viewed plastics and synthetic rubber. The multiplication of plastics in automobiles, aircraft, computers, and many other mass-produced products led to wastes that harmed the environment.

Some plastics played a role in consumer crazes, such as the flexible, shiny vinyl plastic that found favor with certain fashion designers in the late 1970's. Plastics played a major role in the expansion of global communications in the 1980's and 1990's, since such devices as computers, fiber optic cables, and telephones make extensive use of plastics. The ability of various plastics to mimic and even surpass natural products led to such goods as laminated and even completely plastic furniture, clothing made with polyvinyl chloride that was better than leather, and solid materials that were harder than wood, mimicked marble, and found wide use in kitchens.

By the twenty-first century, the plastics and synthetic rubber industries had grown into mammoth enterprises, and their products constituted a major part of all chemicals manufactured throughout the world. In the United States, for example, the plastics and rubber products manufacturing industry has thousands of companies that occupy hundreds of market niches, determined by the kinds of plastic and synthetic rubber manufactured and their commercial uses.

Although, overall, these industries have experienced phenomenal expansion throughout the twentieth and into the twenty-first century, they have also undergone declines, for example, during the recession of 2007-2009. These industries continued to be attacked by environmental groups because nondegradable plastic containers and other discarded plastic products remain in landfills and

A 400-meter athletic track made of polyurethane. (©Ioana Davies/Dreamstime.com)

the environment for dangerously extended periods of time. Researchers at plastics companies have sought to develop various biodegradable plastics. Because traditional and new plastics and synthetic rubbers comprise materials that are essential to modern industrialized societies and because the public has accepted many of these commodities as necessary to the quality of their lives, making plastics the most utilized materials in the world, most analysts believe that ways will be found to minimize the negative properties of these substances and to maximize their benefits to society.

INDUSTRY MARKET SEGMENTS

As the rubber and plastics manufacturing industries developed, they diversified (or fragmented) into hundreds of thousands of firms, ranging in size from specialty shops employing a handful of workers to such gigantic corporations as BASF, ExxonMobil, and DuPont, which employ many thousands of people. By using some examples from this large number of companies, the following sections provide an overview of small, midsize, and large rubber and plastics businesses.

Small Businesses

According to the *Profile of the Rubber and Plastics Industry* (2d ed., 2005), 84 percent of the facilities in the United States involved in making plastics and synthetic rubber have fewer than one hundred employees. Twenty-two percent have twenty to forty-nine employees, while 2,649 facilities (19 percent) have only one to four employees. Surprisingly, then, small firms dominate this industry, which, in the public mind, is often associated with such giants as Goodyear and DuPont.

Potential Annual Earnings Scale. According to a U.S. Bureau of Labor Statistics (BLS) report on plastics and rubber products manufacturing, hourly earnings for all American employees in this industry averaged $19.71 between March and June, 2010 (though earnings decreased slightly from month to month). When multiplied by the average weekly hours, 41.7, the result is a weekly pay of $821.91, and for those who work fifty weeks per year, this results in an annual salary of $41,095. The average hourly earnings for production employees was about $4 per hour less than the industry average, whereas the hourly wages for supervisors and managers was about $4 more. Annual wages for production personnel in 2009 ranged from about $30,000 for machine operators, setters, and tenders, to about $51,000 for supervisors. Mechanical engineers earned an average of $75,490, industrial engineers earned an average of $67,730, and industrial engineering technicians earned an average of $46,960.

Clientele Interaction. Although certain countries such as China and the United States tend to dominate the market (despite the troubling American trade deficit in plastic products with China), smaller countries, such as Mexico and Israel, have been able to satisfy clients in their maquiladoras (assembly plants along the U.S.-Mexican border) and kibbutz industries (based in collective Israeli settlements). Similarly, in North America, industry giants such as Goodyear and Michelin typically garner over half of all tire sales, but small businesses have been successful in providing parts for the automotive and electronics industries, in distributing and recycling tires, and in specializing in manufacturing rubber products for roofing, flooring, and weather-stripping. Small companies also tend to be more agile than giant ones in responding quickly to changes in their clients' needs and desires.

Amenities, Atmosphere, and Physical Grounds. Small businesses find it much easier to get to know the needs of their employees than do large businesses. For example, since the manufacture of certain rubber and plastic products often entails exposure to hazardous materials, workers have been able to influence managers to improve the work environment by introducing hoods for those handling toxic substances and ventilation systems to remove unsafe materials from the air.

Typical Number of Employees. For small businesses, as for large ones, the number of people employed by the plastics products industry is much larger than that employed by the rubber products industry. Employees involved in the manufacture of a great variety of plastics products tend to be concentrated in small businesses. For example, in the United States about half of all plastics products es-

In North America, industry giants such as Goodyear and Michelin typically garner more than half of all tire sales. (©Mark Winfrey/Dreamstime.com)

tablishments have fewer than twenty employees. Similarly, the rubber products industry manufactures many different products and, excluding tire manufacturers, well over half of the rubber products businesses have fewer than twenty employees.

Traditional Geographic Locations. Worldwide, the principal producers of rubber and plastics historically have been China, the United States, and the countries of the European Union. Within the United States, principal producers of rubber and plastics traditionally have included such states as Ohio, California, and Illinois. In terms of the geographic distribution of plastic products industries for 1997, the states with the largest number of facilities were California (1,708), Texas (842), and Illinois (836). For the rubber products industry in 1997, California led with 299 facilities, followed by Ohio with 279 and Texas with 190.

Pros of Working for a Small Business. The great variety of small synthetic rubber and plastics firms and their locations in greatly diverse settings allow potential employees wide selectivity in matching their talents, needs, and desires to a particular workplace. Unlike the mass-production products of large companies, small businesses often make customized goods that allow greater scope for creativity and individuality. With their small numbers of employees, these firms tend to have closer and more satisfying employer-employee personal relationships than do large firms.

Cons of Working for a Small Business. As statistics reveal, salaries for employees at all levels tend to be lower in small firms than they are in large corporations. In the highly competitive world of this industry, small businesses tend to fail at a much higher rate than large companies. Leaders of small businesses do not possess the capital to give their employees generous health and retirement plans, and they sometimes cannot even afford to make use of the new technologies that create a safe and healthy work environment.

Costs

Payroll and Benefits: How much workers in the rubber and plastics manufacturing industry are paid and what benefits they receive are dependent on their abilities, level of education, where they are employed (nation and region), the politics and economics of the time, the presence or absence of a union, and so on. Small businesses generally have lower pay and poorer benefits than midsize or large businesses.

Supplies: Both the rubber and plastics industries are highly dependent on the petroleum industry for their raw materials, and small businesses, because of this dependence, often disappear by failure or merger with larger companies when the oil business is under economic duress. These petroleum chemicals constitute a major manufacturing expense, often exceeding 50 percent of revenues. Certain companies need such devices as injection, transfer, and compression molding machines. Depending on their products, they also need supplies of other chemicals, for example, those used as catalysts. Small businesses additionally require office supplies and computers. Vehicles are needed to bring raw materials in and send finished products out.

External Services: Small synthetic rubber and plastics industries often have to purchase chemicals and machines that they are unable to make for themselves. Some firms frequently hire outside help for their accounting and payroll, machine maintenance, and food services.

Utilities: Small firms manufacturing synthetic rubbers and plastics need access to water supplies and electricity. They generally depend on local utilities for natural gas, telephone service, and Internet access.

Taxes: Some plastics and rubber manufacturing industries have located part or all of their businesses in such countries as Mexico, where the taxes and environmental regulations are not as burdensome as in the United States. Some state governments in the United States (and some federal laws) have provided tax breaks and incentives to small American synthetic rubber and plastics companies, but they, as well as firms that have not received these advantages, still have to pay their share of local, state, and federal taxes. Because these businesses often have significant trade with other countries, they may be subject to various foreign taxes.

Midsize Businesses

Variation exists among analysts, statisticians, and government agencies about precisely how to define midsize businesses. Some define them as facilities employing from one hundred to five hundred workers, while others extend the upper limit to one thousand. The Bureau of the Census counts numbers of employees per facility in increments of 5, 10, 30, 50, 150, 250, 500, and 1,500. For those defining midsize businesses as having between one hundred and five hundred employees per facility, the number of midsize U.S. plastic businesses in 2005 was 2,170, constituting 15 percent of all facilities. The number of midsize U.S. rubber products facilities was 349, constituting 13 percent of all businesses. In terms of numbers, then, midsize businesses are much fewer than small businesses but much greater than large ones.

Potential Annual Earnings Scale. According to the BLS, in 2009 annual wages for production personnel in this industry ranged from about $30,000 for machine operators, setters, and tenders, to about $51,000 for supervisors. Mechanical engineers earned an average of $75,490, industrial engineers earned an average of $67,730, and industrial engineering technicians earned an average of $46,960. Production managers earned an average of $86,750, and general and operations managers earned an average of $119,470. Sales representatives earned an average of $65,640; shipping, receiving, and traffic clerks earned an average of $30,970; and installation, maintenance, and repair workers earned an average of $42,940.

Clientele Interaction. Midsize plastics and rubber manufacturing industries, while often specializing in machinery that molds parts and generates plastic sheeting, have several advantages over small companies. Typical customers are large companies such as DuPont and Farrel that require devices for manipulating and manufacturing their raw plastic materials. Midsize companies can readily adapt to customer needs through their engineering flexibility. They are not wedded to traditional mechanical designs but are able to fashion mechanical systems to meet their customers' requirements.

Amenities, Atmosphere, and Physical Grounds. The facilities involved in the manufacture of plastics for midsize companies typically comprise equipment that can compress, extrude, and mold plastics. Rubber factories have machinery to make tires as well as recap them. In America, some states have developed support networks to aid companies in their competition with other states and countries, and they have tried to make the amenities at these polymer research centers as attractive to workers as possible. Some of these cen-

ters are associated with universities. While many of the facilities are owned and operated by U.S. companies, some states have succeeded in attracting foreign-owned plastics and synthetic rubber companies to establish their facilities at these centers by providing funding for construction materials, machines, and employee job training.

Typical Number of Employees. The number of employees in the plastics and rubber manufacturing industry varies according to occupations within the industry. In 2009, U.S. employment was largest (57,430) for molding and casting machine operators and tenders, but employment was also substantial for team assemblers (45,220) and for operators and tenders of extruding and drawing machines (34,370). While these data apply to the industry as a whole, similar job distributions apply for midsize companies. While employment in the rubber product manufacturing industry was high in 2009 (about 164,000), it is expected to decline to 133,000 by 2014.

Traditional Geographic Locations. In 2009, the U.S. plastics and rubber industry imported from 76 countries and exported to 139, which shows the extensive geographic locations of this industry. Traditionally, the United States and western Europe accounted for about two-thirds of the plastics market, but competition from Latin America and particularly China reduced this proportion to about one-half by the year 2000. In 1997, with the exception of Alaska, all American states had plastics industries, with states such as California, Ohio, Texas, Illinois, Indiana, and Pennsylvania having the greatest numbers of factories. Plastics and rubber manufacturing facilities are generally located in or near cities, but advocates for the plastics industry in Kentucky (which, in 2005, had nearly 200 facilities) point out that this state is equidistant from the Great Lakes, the Gulf of Mexico, and the Atlantic seaboard, making it a prime distribution center for plastics products.

Pros of Working for a Midsize Business. Since the demand for synthetic rubber and plastic products as replacement parts in automobiles and aircraft continued to increase in the second half of the twentieth century, the possibility for growth in the twenty-first century exists. Demand is also increasing in the packaging and container markets, as officials in these companies prefer plastic over glass and metal for containers. Synthetic chemists have the opportunity to research and develop new plastic and synthetic rubber materials, and chemical engineers are then able, for marketable new substances, to design and construct facilities to manufacture products made of these new plastics and synthetic rubbers.

Cons of Working for a Midsize Business. Midsize manufacturers of plastic and synthetic rubber products often do not have the capital to invest in new technologies and machinery. They also can be hampered by increasing health-care and pension costs. Because exports constitute a significant proportion of their business, midsize companies may find the high costs associated with exports prohibitive, such as compliance with burdensome regulations and testing. U.S. environmental regulations can also lower profits, as do increasingly high prices for energy and petroleum.

Costs

Payroll and Benefits: Compensation and entitlements tend to correlate with the educational level and experience of the employee. Midsize plastics and synthetic rubber companies hire managers, engineers, technicians, and machine operators on contract. These contracts often contain provisions for health benefits, vacation time, and incentives for ideas that improve the quantity and quality of the company's products.

Supplies: As with small and large companies, midsize plastics and synthetic rubber industries are heavily dependent on petroleum as a raw material for their products. They often depend on other companies for basic equipment and machinery. While some raw materials and machinery can be bought from concerns in the United States, midsize firms have become increasingly dependent on imports from foreign countries. Administrative staff, engineers, and technicians need computers and office supplies.

External Services: Midsize plastics and rubber industries typically purchase their bulk, basic, and specialty chemicals from other concerns. Machinery in their factories and equipment in their offices usually comes from external sources. Outside firms generally take care of accounting and payroll, on-site food, and on- and off-site medical services.

Utilities: Because of the great variety of products made by the plastics and synthetic rubber indus-

tries, their needs for public utilities vary, but midsize companies generally rely on local water, sewage, electricity, and gas or oil services. Their facilities also depend on telephone, cable television, and Internet services.

Taxes: Some midsize plastics and rubber manufacturing industries have been able to take advantage of tax breaks and incentives provided by state and federal programs meant to improve competitiveness in a global economy, but all companies have to pay certain local, state, and federal taxes, and their sizable imports and exports also necessitate duty payments.

Large Businesses

Despite their relatively small number of facilities when compared to small and midsize plastics and rubber industries, such large companies as BASF, Dow, Eastman Chemical, and DuPont dominate the market because of their advanced technologies and thousands of highly trained workers. According to 1997 Bureau of the Census data, only twenty-one facilities in the U.S. plastic products industry had more than a thousand employees per facility, and only thirty-three rubber products facilities had more than a thousand employees. These large companies are worth hundreds of millions, even billions, of dollars. They have many more divisions and produce greater assortments and quantities of products than do small or midsize firms. Although several of these gigantic corporations retain ties to particular countries (even regions within a country), their focus has become increasingly international, and they have branches all over the world.

Potential Annual Earnings Scale. According to the BLS, in 2009 annual wages for production personnel in this industry ranged from about $30,000 for machine operators, setters, and tenders, to about $51,000 for supervisors. Mechanical engineers earned an average of $75,490, industrial engineers earned an average of $67,730, and industrial engineering technicians earned an average of $46,960. Production managers earned an average of $86,750, and general and operations managers earned an average of $119,470. Sales representatives earned an average of $65,640; shipping, receiving, and traffic clerks earned an average of $30,970; and installation, maintenance, and repair workers earned an average of $42,940.

Because large corporations have facilities in

many countries, salary scales differ from nation to nation. For example, according to statistics from the Canadian census for 1996, about 35 percent of workers in the rubber industry earned less than $29,000 per year, 60 percent earned between $30,000 and $59,000, and 5 percent had annual salaries exceeding $60,000. The pay scale for workers in large U.S. rubber companies was substantially higher than these Canadian averages, whereas the pay scales for Mexican workers in maquiladoras were substantially lower. Gender is a factor in potential annual earnings. Women typically make up about one-fourth of the plastics and rubber industry labor force, but their pay, despite government efforts, continues to be less than that of males working at comparable jobs.

Clientele Interaction. Large businesses, which often generate substantial profits, can afford to set up specific divisions for dealing with clients, both domestically and internationally. Large companies have extensive budgets for advertising to attract new clients and customer-relations departments for retaining old clients while increasing sales to them. Since client-company interactions occur more and more frequently via computers or telephone, companies save money by outsourcing their relations with clients to concerns in such countries as India.

Amenities, Atmosphere, and Physical Grounds. Plastics and synthetic rubber companies are part of the chemical industry, and leaders in this industry have issued mission statements emphasizing that, besides making products efficiently and economically, they aspire to create working environments that are safe and healthy. They also realize that they have a duty to the communities in which their facilities are located and, more generally, to the environment. Despite the presence of hazardous chemicals, high temperatures, and noisy machinery, modern plastics and synthetic rubber plants are safer and more comfortable than the average chemical factory.

Because of the modern environmental movement, governments around the world have passed laws designed to improve the quality of air, water, soil, and the habitats for animals as well as the living and working conditions for humans. For example, in the United States, plastics and rubber products manufacturers have had to comply with the Clean Air Act, the Clean Water Act, the Resource Conser-

vation and Recovery Act, the Toxic Substances Control Act, and many other laws. Large companies have found that the best way to reduce pollution is to prevent it, which they have done by such changes as reengineering their processing technology to reuse by-products. Furthermore, they have discovered substitutes for toxic chemicals, while improving techniques for cleaning wastewater and recycling solid wastes.

Large companies generally have facilities with extensive grounds on which are located buildings housing machinery for making various products. Other buildings are used for administration and for storing and handling raw materials. These facilities have been located in suburbs as well as exurbs, with administrative facilities often within cities.

Typical Number of Employees. According to the BLS, the employment of all workers (seasonally adjusted) in the plastics and rubber industry in the months of March through June, 2010, was 631,800; the employment for production and nonsupervisory workers was 477,425. The unemployment rate for this period averaged 11.8 percent, which was higher than the national average. Companies were laying off workers at the rate of about 8,000 per month. The recession of 2007-2009 affected large companies as well as small ones.

Traditional Geographic Locations. Historically, the plastics and synthetic rubber industries were located in the United States and western Europe, but in the twenty-first century such countries as China have become major producers. In America, such states as Ohio, which in 2006 employed more people in the plastics and rubber products industry than any other state, also had an ample number of such large corporations as Goodyear, Eaton Corporation, and Hamilton Parker Company, whose revenues were from $10 billion to $20 billion in 2006. Other states with substantial numbers of large businesses were California, Illinois, Texas, and Indiana.

Pros of Working for a Large Company. Over the course of the twentieth and into the twenty-first century, large companies making plastic and rubber products have generally progressed in terms of their employee numbers, market share, economic success, and job security. This has led to better salaries and benefits for their employees when compared to small and midsize businesses. North America and western Europe continue to be excellent places to work in these industries, but as more plastics and synthetic rubber are made in Asia and Latin America, benefits of working for companies in these regions increase.

Cons of Working for a Large Company. Analysts have pointed out that, as globalization has made large companies richer than ever before, it has made small companies and ordinary workers poorer. Multinational corporations have been accused of social injustice, for example, by manufacturing plastics and synthetic rubber in regions of the world where workers can be hired at drastically substandard wages. Even in prosperous Western nations, poorly managed large companies have sometimes experienced dramatic failures. Other companies have been slow to comply with environmental and health legislation, thereby exposing their employees to unsafe conditions. These large companies are not recession-proof, as evidenced by large layoffs in the years after 2008.

Costs

Payroll and Benefits: The payroll structure and benefits of large companies depend not only on the country within which their facilities are located but also on the education, experience, and talent of their employees. Salaries range from many millions of dollars for chief executive officers, whose increasing compensation even for poorly managed businesses has generated passionate criticism, to the $25,000 annual salaries paid to unskilled workers. Highly skilled employees such as polymer chemists earn in excess of $100,000 a year.

Supplies: Large companies making synthetic rubber and plastic products depend heavily on raw materials supplied by the petroleum industry. They also need specialized chemicals, semifinished products, and modern machines that improve productivity. They require plastics with better heat resistance, more effective pigmentation processes, and increased biodegradability. They have to have access to fibers for use in reinforced plastics. The administrative and sales divisions of these large companies need office supplies, and the scientific and engineering personnel need chemicals, laboratory equipment, and computers.

External Services: When it is to their economic benefit, large companies contract with outside firms to take care of their payroll, accounting, computer-maintenance, and food-and-health services. Large companies also make extensive use of original equipment manufacturers (OEMs), when these can fulfill their requirements more economically and efficiently than their own engineers.

Utilities: Large manufacturers of plastics and synthetic rubber use great amounts of electrical power, generally supplied by local public utilities. Their water-and-sewage needs, as well as their use of gas and oil, are similarly taken care of. Administrative, sales, and research and development sections of large companies make use of locally supplied telephone, cable, and Internet services.

Taxes: State and federal laws require large companies to pay local property taxes, as well as state and federal taxes. Large companies have increasingly depended on imports and exports as significant parts of their business, and these transactions often involve tariffs and surcharges.

ORGANIZATIONAL STRUCTURE AND JOB ROLES

Because the plastics and rubber manufacturing industry involves the creation of thousands of different plastic and synthetic rubber products, and because the number of job roles increased dramatically in the final decades of the twentieth century (as evidenced by economic censuses during this period, whose coverage of the range of industries and job roles within them expanded and deepened), no single organizational structure or list of jobs will suit every company or cluster of companies. Nevertheless, some commonalities in company organizations and job roles do exist, though these, too, have evolved and changed over time. This volatility has forced many companies to be flexible in order to survive in a highly competitive marketplace.

Plastics and synthetic rubber products initially succeeded because of their low cost (compared to such traditional materials as glass and metals), ease of manufacture, and resistance to water and other chemicals. New plastics and synthetic rubber products have continued this trend, acting as substitutes for such materials as wood, stone, bone, leather, and even ceramics. During the last third of the twentieth and initial decade of the twenty-first century, environmental concerns have dampened the former optimism for plastic and synthetic rubber products because of the pollution associated with their creation and the environmental problems created when they are discarded after use. The increasing price of petroleum and questions as to its future availability are other concerns for leaders of these businesses, which they have attempted to meet with biodegradable plastics and petroleum substitutes.

Analysts who have studied the evolution of modern business organizations in the plastics and synthetic rubber industries have developed theories about their functioning, although some important questions remain unanswered, such as the role that market performance plays in determining the organizational structure of these industries. For example, the synthetic rubber industry's development was accelerated under government control during World War II, when the United States was unable to import sufficient quantities of natural rubber. After the war, in 1953, this industry, the first large one ever built by the federal government, was transferred into private hands under the Rubber Producing Facilities Disposal Act, with the goal of creating "a free, competitive, synthetic rubber industry." This law, for the first time in American history, gave Congress the power of setting up the organizational structure of a private business. Although the propelling idea was a competitive industry within which no single company could unduly influence the market price of various synthetic rubber products, the reality turned out to be many small and a few gigantic companies, and these large corporations have been able, to some extent, to manipulate the market, though attempts have been made by concerned citizens, groups, and government agencies to rein in their excesses.

The following umbrella categories apply to organizational structures of businesses within the plastics and rubber manufacturing industry:

- Executive Management
- Marketing and Sales
- Customer Service
- Research and Development
- Office and Administrative Support
- Production
- Distribution
- Information Technology

Executive Management

In their early evolution, the plastics and rubber industries developed separately, with executive managers generally chosen for their understanding of how to market the specialized products of each industry. Since World War II, government agencies and others have treated the plastics and rubber manufacturing industry as one, because of the many common characteristics between its subindustries, such as their foundation in polymer chemistry, highly specialized and fragmented subdivisions, dependence on rapid technological innovation, and so on. While some companies manufacture both plastic and synthetic rubber products, others maintain their historical allegiance to rubber or plastics. For example, Norman H. Cohan, with a background in chemical engineering, founded Security Plastics in 1955, and by inventing a revolutionary injection molding technology and by enlightened leadership, he created a highly successful company, for which he has been honored.

Executive management occupations may include the following:

- President/Chief Executive Officer (CEO)
- Administrative Support Manager
- Advertising and Marketing Manager
- Research and Development Director
- Domestic Sales Manager
- International Sales Manager
- Customer Service Manager

Marketing and Sales

Marketing deals with those processes concerned with getting goods from producers to consumers, whereas sales involves processes concerned with the actual selling of goods to consumers. When the plastics and rubber industry created highly desirable products, such as Bakelite and nylon, marketing could be kept to a minimum, but as domestic and global competition became intense, companies created sales and marketing divisions whose purpose was to alert the public to the benefits of their new plastics or synthetic rubber products or to remind consumers of what made their traditional products so successful. Persons marketing and selling plastics and synthetic rubber products should understand something of the science and technology that created them as well as their potential risks to consumers and the environment. Those marketing these products to foreign countries should have an understanding of the customers' cultures and languages.

Marketing and sales occupations may include the following:

- Marketing Director
- Sales Director
- Domestic Sales Manager
- International Sales Manager
- Sales and Marketing Expert in Plastics
- Sales and Marketing Expert in Synthetic Rubber

Customer Service

The plastics and synthetic rubber industry produces a great diversity of items sold to both individuals and companies, which means that customer service representatives have many responsibilities. For example, they typically deal with misunderstandings about the properties and functions of a particular product, complaints about defective products, and requests for information about new products. Since they often have to handle detailed technical questions about specific plastics, such as vinyl, acrylics, or PVC, they should either have the requisite scientific and technical background to deal knowledgeably with customers or be able to direct them to scientists, engineers, or technicians in the firm who can effectively deal with such questions, complaints, and misconceptions about their purchases.

Customer service occupations may include the following:

- Customer Service Representative for Plastics
- Customer Service Representative for Synthetic Rubber Products
- Customer Relations Manager

Research and Development

Most plastics and synthetic rubber industries originated through the research and development of particular inventions, such as Goodyear's invention of vulcanized rubber. This tradition has contin-

ued, and most large manufacturers of plastics and synthetic rubber products have research and development divisions whose purpose is to improve their well-known merchandise and to introduce innovative plastics and synthetic rubbers. Research and development divisions often maintain helpful relations with researchers in colleges, universities, and technical institutes, where discoveries of new manufacturing procedures and innovative products have contributed to the progress of the industry.

Polymer chemists specialize in creating new kinds of plastics and synthetic rubber materials. If these new substances have a good chance of being successful in the marketplace, then chemical engineers develop industrial processes for manufacturing them and machinery for molding them into products. Materials engineers are similarly concerned with techniques for the production of materials that meet the commercial requirements of the company.

Research and development occupations may include the following:

- Chemist
- Chemical Engineer
- Materials Scientist
- Materials Engineer
- Polymer Chemist
- Plastics Technology Expert
- Synthetic Rubber Technology Expert

Office and Administrative Support

The sizes of administrative staffs in the plastics and synthetic rubber industry depend on the sizes of companies, with large companies needing extensive staffs in multiple divisions to keep their thousands of employees working efficiently and to manage their national and international operations. Many workers are necessary to keep track of raw material inputs and finished product outputs. Because so much of information processing is now computerized, staff members need to have computer expertise, particularly in information management systems.

Office and administrative support occupations may include the following:

- Bookkeeper
- Accountant
- Auditor

- Shipping and Receiving Clerk
- Administrative Assistant
- Secretary
- Computer Specialist

Production

Many plastic products are made through injection and compression molding, in which heat is the chief agent, but some are made through reaction injection molding, which employs liquids, and blow molding, which uses compressed air. Most rubber manufactured in the United States is synthetic, and added chemicals change synthetic rubber's properties, making it soft, resilient, or hard, depending on the rubber product's ultimate use. Typical products include plastic pipes, rubber hoses, and rubber tires. To make these products requires the efforts of workers skilled in a variety of operations.

Production occupations may include the following:

- Production Manager
- Production Supervisor
- Inspector, Tester, Sorter, Sampler, and Weigher
- Molding and Casting Machine Setter and Operator
- Extruding Machine Setter and Operator
- Packager
- Specialist in the Manufacture of Rubber, Plastic Hoses, and Belting
- Specialist in the Manufacture of Machines for Manipulating Plastics and Synthetic Rubber

Distribution

Supplying products to wholesalers or retailers is often an important part of the synthetic rubber business. Some tire distributors, for example, specialize in tires from certain companies, such as Goodyear or Firestone. Because of environmental concerns, recycling old tires has become an increasingly necessary part of the tire business. Most tire distributors offer a selection of tires with different features such as longevity and all-weather use.

Distribution occupations may include the following:

- Warehouse Manager
- Distribution Manager

- Dispatcher
- Heavy Truck Driver
- Light Truck Driver
- Shipping and Receiving Clerk
- Freight Loader/Unloader

Information Technology

Computer specialists play important roles in such divisions as administration, marketing, and sales, but they have also become an increasingly important part of production, since processes for making certain plastics and synthetic rubber products have been automated through computers.

Information technology occupations may include the following:

- Information Technology Director
- Computer Scientist
- Computer Hardware Engineer
- Software Engineer
- Computer Technician
- Computer Programmer
- Computer Maintenance and Repair Technician

INDUSTRY OUTLOOK

Overview

Because of its many enterprises around the world and the large number of facilities within certain countries, determining the outlook for the plastics and rubber manufacturing industry is complex. Throughout the twentieth century, a trend of escalating growth, in general, characterized the production and consumption of plastic and synthetic rubber products, despite occasional dips during times of economic stress and despite changes in the nature of the market. For example, natural rubber was dominant before World War II, and synthetic rubber was dominant after it. Both global and U.S. production of plastics materials grew steadily in the postwar period. For example, in 1951 global production was 2 million tons and U.S. production was 810,000 tons; in 1967, global production was 18 million tons and U.S. production was 5.567 million tons; in 1980, global production reached 50 million tons, of which the U.S. share was 16.117 million tons. In 1998, global production exceeded 135 million tons and U.S. pro-

Plastic bottles account for 5 percent of the plastic industry's products. (©Ann Murie/Dreamstime.com)

duction was 33.5 million tons, or about 25 percent of the world's total.

Economic trends for the plastics and synthetic rubber industry in the twenty-first century have been variable, with a few good years and several bad ones. For example, shipments in the U.S. plastics industry decreased 6.6 percent from 2000 to 2002, and at the end of the decade the BLS reported that, for 2009, there was a decline in the number of plastics and rubber manufacturing establishments from 13,790 in the first quarter to 13,664 in the fourth quarter. On the other hand, during this decade, sales of industrial rubber products rose nearly 6 percent per year from 2001 to 2006.

Compared to the North American and European markets, which analysts describe as mature, China represents a young market, eager for Western technology, investment, and skilled workers. The United States has responded with roughly $30 billion of annual investment in China, though some analysts believe that the Chinese plastics and synthetic rubber industry confronts investors with considerable risks. Some optimistic companies have already shifted their manufacturing and production to China, taking advantage of much lower labor costs than in the West, as well as less stringent environmental regulations. One shortcoming is China's lack of significant oil and gas reserves, necessitating costly imports from the Middle East. Nevertheless, China has been increasing plastics production to meet surging domestic and global demands, and, if growth trends exhibited in the first decade of the twenty-first century continue, China is projected to be the world's biggest plastics market by around 2026.

Diversification and fragmentation characterized the U.S. plastics and synthetic rubber industries in the twentieth century, and many experts predict that they will continue to do so in the twenty-first. By the end of the twentieth century, general products constituted 55 percent of the plastics industry, with the following percentages for other products: plastic films and sheets (12 percent), plastic foam products (10 percent), custom resins (6 percent), plastic bottles (5 percent), unsupported plastics (4 percent), plastic pipes (3 percent), laminated plastic plates and sheets (3 percent), and plastic plumbing fixtures (3 percent). The rubber products industry was somewhat less diverse, with the following percentages for various products: tires (36 percent), fabricated rubber products (22 percent), mechanical rubber goods (16 percent), gaskets and sealing devices (13 percent), rubber hoses and belting (10 percent), and rubber footwear (3 percent). The plastics and rubber manufacturing industry has been and will continue to be very sensitive to the economic ups and downs of the petroleum industry, since petroleum is the source of over half of its raw materials. Other industries that have an economic effect on the plastics and rubber manufacturing industry are construction and health care.

Exports are important for the U.S. plastics industry, and the three largest export markets have been Canada, Mexico, and Japan. At the start of the twenty-first century the United States had a trade surplus in plastics products of $894 million, but this turned into increasing deficits beginning in 2001. The basic reason for this change was the inability of U.S. producers to compete with facilities in developing nations in the manufacture of inexpensive plastic goods. Besides labor costs, the divergence between the United States and less developed countries also involves different laws and product standards that make American goods more expensive. Despite cultural differences, most large-scale U.S. manufacturers of plastic and rubber products have overseas facilities. Industry analysts emphasize that many opportunities exist for American manufacturers to expand to such developing countries as China, Brazil, India, and Mexico.

Despite declines after the recession of 2007-2009, some analysts are predicting better than average growth in the second decade of the twenty-first century, although others predict that the economic recovery will be slow. A *Business Wire* report forecast that the demand for natural and synthetic rubber would rise. This prediction is based on the increasing expansion of the Chinese automobile industry. Other experts believe that economic turmoil in Europe and high unemployment in the United States and other countries will have a negative influence on the markets for plastic and rubber products. In this

PROJECTED EMPLOYMENT FOR SELECTED OCCUPATIONS

Plastics and Rubber Products Manufacturing

Employment		
2009	Projected 2018	Occupation
34,370	36,300	Extruding and drawing machine setters, operators, and tenders, metal and plastic
19,710	27,700	Extruding, forming, pressing, and compacting machine setters, operators, and tenders
30,420	30,800	First-line supervisors/ managers of production and operating workers
23,170	23,300	Inspectors, testers, sorters, samplers, and weighers
57,430	59,300	Molding, coremaking, and casting machine setters, operators, and tenders, metal and plastic
25,660	24,300	Packers and packagers, hand
46,220	47,600	Team assemblers

Source: U.S. Bureau of Labor Statistics, Industries at a Glance, Occupational Employment Statistics and Employment Projections Program.

uncertain economic situation, giant companies have been merging with small and midsize competitors, while also moving facilities to low-cost locations. What government officials do or do not do in terms of economic stimulus, regulation of large companies, and the encouragement of green technologies may also affect the plastics and synthetic rubber industry.

Employment Advantages

According to the BLS, the plastics and rubber products manufacturing industry will decline early in the second decade of the new millennium, though workers who can operate multiple machines will have an advantage in an increasingly competitive workforce. Highly skilled polymer chemists and chemical engineers will also fare better than less educated competitors. According to the *Occupational Outlook Handbook*, employment for all manufacturing jobs is expected to decline rapidly in the second decade of the twenty-first century, perhaps by as much as 13 percent. Nevertheless, because of an expected increase in the number of retirements by workers in the baby-boom generation, many jobs for workers with a thorough background in machine operations will open. For example, those with a good knowledge of plastics and synthetic rubber materials will have distinct advantages in what is expected to be a tortuously changing jobs environment.

Annual Earnings

Even though annual global revenues for the plastics and synthetic rubber industry are in excess of $3 trillion a year, with U.S. revenues as 14 percent of this value, uncertainties exist in calculating annual earnings in this industry, especially since it is difficult to count companies in certain foreign countries and even more difficult to get accurate figures on their earnings and employment. Data are much better for the American plastics and rubber products manufacturing industry. For example, employment was over 600,000 in the first half of 2010, with average weekly earnings of over $800. Work-related fatalities averaged 19.5 annually for the 2005-2008 period. For the same period, labor productivity (in terms of output per hour) declined from 108.721 to 102.71. This last statistic is surprising and somewhat troubling in the context of what had been overall increases in productivity

that had characterized the plastics and synthetic rubber industry in earlier decades, driven by dramatic advances in American technology.

RELATED RESOURCES FOR FURTHER RESEARCH

AMERICAN CHEMICAL SOCIETY
1155 16th St. NW
Washington, DC 20036
Tel: (800) 227-5558
Fax: (202) 872-6257
http://www.acs.org

AMERICAN INSTITUTE OF CHEMICAL ENGINEERS
3 Park Ave.
New York, NY 10016-5991
Tel: (800) 242-4363
Fax: (203) 775-5777
http://www.aice.org

INTERNATIONAL INSTITUTE OF SYNTHETIC RUBBER PRODUCERS
2077 S Gessner Rd., Suite 133
Houston, TX 77063
Tel: (713) 783-7511
Fax: (713) 783-7253
http://www.azom.com

PLASTICS INDUSTRY TRADE ASSOCIATION
1667 K St. NW, Suite 1000
Washington, DC 20006
Tel: (202) 974-5200
Fax: (202) 296-7005
http://www.plasticsindustry.org

SOCIETY OF PLASTICS ENGINEERS
23 Church Hill Rd.
Newtown, CT 06470
Tel: (203) 775-0471
Fax: (203) 775-8490
http://www.4spe.org

ABOUT THE AUTHOR

Robert J. Paradowski is a historian of science and technology who specializes in the history of chemistry, with a particular emphasis on the life and work of Linus Pauling. He is a summa cum laude graduate of Spring Hill College, with a master's degree in chemistry from Brandeis University and a Ph.D. in the history of science from the University of Wisconsin (1972). He has taught at Brooklyn College, Eisenhower College, and the Rochester Institute of Technology, where he is a professor in the Science, Technology, and Society/Public Policy Department.

FURTHER READING

Aftalion, Fred. *A History of the International Chemical Industry*. Philadelphia: University of Pennsylvania Press, 1991.

Chamis, Alice Yanosoko. "The Literature of Synthetic Rubber." In *Literature of Chemical Technology*, edited by Julian F. Smith. Washington, D.C.: American Chemical Society, 1968.

Chandler, Alfred D. *Shaping the Industrial Century: The Remarkable Story of the Evolution of the Modern Chemical and Pharmaceutical Industries*. Cambridge, Mass.: Harvard University Press, 2005.

Ciesielski, Andrew. *An Introduction to Rubber Technology*. Shawsbury, Shrewsbury, Shropshire, England: RAPRA Technology, 1999.

International Institute of Synthetic Rubber Producers. *Synthetic Rubber: The Story of an Industry*. New York: Author, 1973.

Kaufman, M. *The First Century of Plastics: Celluoid and Its Sequel*. London: Plastics Institute, 1963.

Mossman, Susan, ed. *Early Plastics: Perspectives, 1850-1950*. London: Leicester University Press, 1997.

Schidrowitz, P., and T. R. Dawson. *History of the Rubber Industry*. London: Institution of the Rubber Industry, 1952.

Stevens, Eugene S. *Green Plastics: An Introduction to the New Science of Biodegradable Plastics*. Princeton, N.J.: Princeton University Press, 2001.

U.S. Bureau of Labor Statistics. *Career Guide to Industries*, 2010-2011 ed. http://www.bls.gov/oco/cg.

U.S. Census Bureau. North American Industry Classification System (NAICS), 2007. http://www.census.gov/cgi-bin/sssd/naics/naicsrch?chart=2007.

U.S. Department of Commerce. International Trade Administration. Office of Trade and Industry Information. Industry Trade Data and Analysis. http://ita.doc.gov/td/industry/otea/OTII/OTII-index.html.

U.S. Environmental Protection Agency. Office of Compliance. *Profile of the Rubber and Plastics Industry*. 2d ed. Washington, D.C.: Author, 2005.

Political Advocacy Industry

©Dreamstime.com

INDUSTRY SNAPSHOT

General Industry: Communications

Career Cluster: Arts, A/V Technology, and Communication

Subcategory Industries: Business Associations; Environment, Conservation, and Wildlife Organizations; Human Rights Organizations; Labor Organizations; Lobbying Services; Political Consulting Services; Political Organizations; Professional Organizations; Social Advocacy Organizations

Related Industries: Advertising and Marketing Industry; Civil Services: Planning; Civil Services: Public Safety; Defense Industry; Federal Public Administration; Legal Services and Law Firms; Local Public Administration; Philanthropic, Charitable, Religious, Civic, and Grant-Making Industry

Annual Domestic Revenues: $3.2 billion USD (Center for Responsive Politics, 2008)

NAICS Numbers: 8133, 8139, 541820

INDUSTRY DEFINITION

Summary

The political advocacy industry focuses on creating connectivity and access between private businesses, organizations, and associations on one hand and government officials and legislators on the other. Central to the industry's activities is lobbying, or attempting to influence the creation, passage, or defeat of legislation. The political advocacy industry represents nearly every major industry that has an interest in the decisions made by legislators and other political leaders on the local, state, and national levels.

History of the Industry

It is believed that the first manifestations of the practice of political advocacy occurred during the Roman Empire (27 B.C.E to 476 C.E.). At the time, there was no government bureaucracy through which public policy was conducted. Instead, members of the Roman senate acted not just as legislators but also as government administrators, bureaucrats, and even diplomats. Senators therefore enjoyed a great deal of contact with a broad range of people, both within the empire and in other nations. Those individuals and groups, with whom the senators enjoyed strong relationships, consistently traveled to Rome to seek senatorial audiences to promote their public pol-

1458

icy agendas in the Senate. Senators, in turn, experienced a great deal of increased stature in the light of their large circle of friends and peers. In many cases, they saw a significant increase in their own personal wealth as a result of their public advocacy contacts.

In 1215, political advocacy was integrated into one of the most pivotal legal documents of Western civilization, the Magna Carta. The Magna Carta, as a foundational document, granted individuals the right to petition their government in the event that their interests were threatened, established legal systems, bound the king to the rule of law, and became the basis for many national constitutions and governments. More than five hundred years later, the failure of the British crown to heed the petitions of American colonies was a central theme in the Declaration of Independence of 1776.

Following the American Revolution, the U.S. Constitution was drafted in 1787. The First Amendment, added in 1789, contained a provision similar to that offered by the Magna Carta—the private cit-izen's right to petition the government for a redress of grievances. This constitutional clause not only allowed a person the right to protect his or her interests but also helped form public interest groups and organizations. As a result, the focus of political advocacy grew from a system to protect individual rights and needs to a much broader collection of industries and networks that sought representation and protection from negative public policy actions.

The ability of interest groups and individuals to solicit support from the U.S. government, granted by the Constitution, created a new industry that worked closely with the federal government and its officials. In fact, political advocacy, at least in terms of modern government, was founded only three years after the Constitution was signed. General William Hull, who was considered a hero of the American Revolution, was hired by veterans of the Continental Army who were seeking financial compensation from Congress for their wartime duty.

Political advocacy also became one of the cen-

Lobbyists gather outside the Michigan State Capitol House chambers in November, 2010. The state had 2,783 registered lobbyists in 2010, outnumbering state lawmakers nearly nine to one. (AP/Wide World Photos)

tral vehicles in the abolitionist movement that preceded the Civil War. In the 1830's, while Congress and the federal government avoided issuing any antislavery measure that superseded states' rights, the movement's supporters cleverly petitioned Congress to ban slavery within the nation's capital, the District of Columbia, which is governed by Congress itself. Though the effort ultimately failed, as Congress tabled any such legislation, it helped fuel the antislavery movement and contributed to the North-South schism.

The political advocacy industry continued to grow in strength during the post-Civil War era. President Ulysses S. Grant is credited with coining the term "lobbyist" during his presidency. As president, he often left the White House to relax in the public rooms of the nearby Willard Hotel. However, he complained that, during his visits to that establishment, people constantly approached him with questions, requests, and solicitations; he would eventually refer to these people as "those damn lobbyists."

By the late nineteenth and twentieth centuries, the political advocacy industry had become one of the more controversial and widespread industries in America. Popular opinion painted the industry as either one that encouraged political corruption (by granting access to political power to a relative few insiders) or one that ensured that those who previously lacked a voice in their local, state, or federal government would have an agent making that voice heard. A number of efforts on the federal and state levels throughout the late 1800's and 1900's sought more extensively to regulate lobbying. In some cases, outright bans of the practice were issued (although never fully enforced), while other laws were passed to identify and register lobbyists and the companies for which they worked. In the mid- to late twentieth century, a more comprehensive set of laws was passed to update antiquated post-World War II lobbying laws. These laws created strict guidelines on practices involving political contributions, gifts, meetings, and other aspects of political advocacy on all levels.

The Industry Today

The political advocacy industry is a multibillion-dollar sector spanning virtually every industry and connected to every level of government. Lobbying, which is the act of soliciting government officials to support or oppose public policy initiatives, composes only one part of the industry's endeavors. Lobbying activities also entail fund-raising efforts, such as sponsoring or holding events for political candidates to generate contributions. Additionally, political advocates help companies, associations, and organizations activate their grassroots members by assisting in grassroots campaigns. Lobbying firms also help develop their clients' legislative agendas by writing bills and monitoring the progress of those bills through the legislative process.

The lobbying industry has taken advantage of the increased prevalence of media technology as part of its resurgence over the last few decades. Lobbyists are often teamed with or employed by public relations firms to ensure that their clients' interests are heard not just in the capitol building but on the airwaves as well. The Internet also plays a criti-

Zine and Rose Hosein, right, are paid $15 an hour to hold places in line for lobbyists outside crowded congressional hearing rooms. (AP/Wide World Photos)

cal role in how lobbyists acquire and use information. Because such information is so readily available online, lobbyists are able to access and monitor a greater number of political developments on behalf of a greater number of clients without being stretched too thin.

Even in times of economic downturn, the political advocacy industry remains in high demand. Special interest groups spent nearly $2.6 billion on lobbying activities in 2007, a sharp increase of 10 percent from 2005. The industry saw a slight decline in the number of practicing federal lobbyists in 2009, a reflection of the 2007-2009 recession and the attitude of the new presidential administration toward officially registered lobbyists. Nonetheless, the decline in the lobbying field was slower than in other industries.

Lobbyists and political advocates operate in a number of different organizational arenas, and many companies are dedicated solely to the practice of lobbying. Some lobbying organizations, however, are part of larger law firms that conduct business that may or may not be relevant to the political advocacy they offer. In addition, many corporations, organizations, and trade associations have their own lobbyists on staff, overseeing their lobbying efforts in addition to all other aspects of government relations and affairs.

Lobbyists themselves come from a wide range of backgrounds. Many begin their careers in government, either as staff members or as legislators themselves. Others are attorneys who are intimately familiar with the laws and the legislative process. Still others are business professionals who act as their companies' lobbyists while also performing nonpolitical corporate duties. The political advocacy industry is a dynamic environment that often calls for long days and nights (especially during legislative sessions and budget hearings). Because of this profession's prevalence across a broad range of industries, those employed as lobbyists and advocates must generally have an understand-

New Jersey Education Association president Barbara A. Keshishian responds after hearing Governor Chris Christie's budget address in March, 2010. The association spent $6.9 million during the year, making it the biggest spender among lobbying groups. (AP/Wide World Photos)

ing of—or be able quickly to familiarize themselves with—a number of often divergent issue areas.

While the U.S. government, by virtue of its propensity to remain transparent and accessible to private citizens, is seemingly the target of the majority of the world's lobbyists, in truth most modern democracies are heavily solicited by such professionals. Today, lobbyists are found in democracies around the world. The access granted by the U.S. system of government, as well as its importance as a major market, has made the United States the apparent epicenter of the lobbying industry. Many foreign governments invest heavily in lobbying the U.S. government, as do foreign-based corporations.

The United States is the most transparent democracy in this arena. For example, many countries and regional governments do not require lobbyists to register in the same manner as the United

States. As a result, the U.S. industry is far more quantifiable (both in terms of number of political advocates and in terms of the revenues generated by the industry) than are foreign industries.

INDUSTRY MARKET SEGMENTS

Political advocacy is conducted by a variety of individuals, corporate entities, and organizations, both for-profit and nonprofit. In the United States, individuals who engage directly in lobbying activities must register with the entity that they lobby. In other words, they must register as federal lobbyists, as state lobbyists in specific states, and so on. Those who work for firms that engage in lobbying do not need to register if they work in a support or other indirect capacity. The industry may be divided into several segments by function rather than size: law firms, nonprofit organizations and trade associations, individual corporations, and consultants.

Law Firms

It has become increasingly common for lobbyists not merely to suggest legislative provisions but also to write the legislative language they wish to see in final bills. For this reason, legal expertise—rather than expertise only in the area to be covered by the law—is crucial to political advocacy. As a result, lobbying and political advocacy have become specialties of entire law firms. Generally speaking, such firms locate themselves in national or state capitals, where they can enjoy maximum access to legislators. Other laws firms may specialize in representing specific industries, such as the motion picture industry. They will engage in lobbying and political advocacy as part of their overall job of representing their industries' interests.

Potential Annual Earnings Scale. Lobbyists working as part of law firms earn varying wage levels, depending on the level of government with which they work, as well as the contract parameters established between the firm and the client. The geographic location of the position is also a factor. According to Salary.com, in 2009 the nationwide average annual salary for political advocates was $96,000. Additionally, according to a 2009 survey on associate salaries conducted by the National Association for Legal Professionals (NALP), the over-

all median starting salary for law firm associates was $130,000.

Clientele Interaction. In political advocacy, client interaction is a high priority. Advocates and lobbyists must be in constant communication with their clients in order to report on developments in the government and receive the clients' recommendations for action. Because many clients are unfamiliar with the legislative process and the inner workings of government, lobbyists need to hold many meetings with clients, sometimes on a weekly or monthly basis. They may also engage in e-mail and telephone correspondence. These interactions might take place on multiple occasions during a week in which relevant political activity is increased.

Amenities, Atmosphere, and Physical Grounds. Law firms maintain a professional office environment with varying degrees of employee and physical amenities. Such offices are usually part of larger buildings, although some firms are located in ground-level or two-level "storefront" settings. Depending on an employee's professional standing, individual offices may be available, although cubicles and shared offices are also common. The office atmosphere is usually high-paced, with many meetings and strategizing sessions. Hours are variable depending on the level of work performed, but for higher-level employees, the workday is often longer than average.

Typical Number of Employees. The number of political advocates and lobbyists at law firms varies based on the size of firm, the number of clients, and the size of the contracts on which they work. Some are national and even international corporations, employing hundreds of staff dedicated to political advocacy, while others are small and may operate on a local level, working for only a handful of clients at a time.

Traditional Geographic Locations. Law firms that conduct political advocacy tend to occupy office space in or near the capitals whose governments they solicit. Firms that have federal pursuits in the United States, for example, tend to be located in the greater Washington, D.C., area, while lobbyists who work with state governments tend to stay closer to state capital areas. Other firms that conduct both state and federal lobbying activities operate in major urban centers that provide them with access to transportation that can easily take them to their target government entity.

Pros of Working for a Law Firm. Law firms that offer political advocacy services present great opportunities for new and midlevel attorneys. Well-established and reputable law firms help such individuals enhance their own reputations and standing among clients and the government officials with whom they work. Lobbyists with legal qualifications are not only able to create connectivity between client and government entities, but also able to write public policy. Additionally, the salary and benefits of a political advocate working in a law firm, particularly a well-established firm, are typically above average.

Cons of Working for a Law Firm. The individual reputations of political advocates who work within law firms are closely tied to their firms' public reputations. Advocates may find themselves turned away by government officials based not on their own qualifications but on their firms' public standing and reputed political ideology. In addition, lobbyists may find themselves pulled in several directions at once—having less time to dedicate to one or two clients when the larger obligations of the firm require their attention.

Costs

Payroll and Benefits: Pay for lobbying and political advocacy activities vary based on the manner in which the activity is contracted. For example, some lobbyists operate on an hourly rate, while others are paid on a monthly, quarterly, or yearly basis. Benefits such as health and dental insurance are usually included.

Supplies: Law firms require computer hardware and software, basic office supplies, photocopiers, scanners, postage machines, and other office hardware. Because lobbyists are often mobile, wireless and mobile technology such as smart phones are often a necessity.

External Services: Political advocates operating out of law firms may call upon temporary employees to provide administrative support. Firms that own their own office space also often contract custodial services and, in many cases, security services. Because communications are so critical, they also utilize external telecommunications vendors to provide up-to-date cellular, voice-mail, and Web capabilities. As the nature of advocacy often requires travel, transportation can also be a significant cost, albeit often reim-

bursable, for lobbyists and their firms. Additionally, because they conduct a number of client luncheons and political fund-raisers, they often contract catering services.

Utilities: Law firms pay standard utilities, including telephone, Internet access, electricity, and heat. Larger firms that own their own property must also pay for trash removal, water, and sewage. Depending on the size of the firm and the number of contracts on which the company works, utilities may or may not comprise a significant portion of a law firm's monthly expenses.

Taxes: Law firms pay corporate taxes based on the income they generate. If they own their own property, they must also pay commercial real estate taxes and other local and state taxes. Lobbyist registration expenses, not technically considered taxes but rather fees, must also be paid in states that have such protocols (although some clients pay these fees as part of negotiated contracts).

Nonprofits and Trade Associations

Nonprofit organizations and trade associations advocate on behalf of often broad and diverse constituencies, such as retired persons, energy companies, medical professionals, or animal lovers. As a result, they are responsible to sometimes extremely large and diverse constituencies. It is sometimes difficult or impossible for such organizations to please their entire membership, so they must strive to influence legislation in a manner that matches their perceived mission and the interests expressed in that mission. Nonprofits and trade associations are more likely than other political advocates to spend a significant amount of time advocating directly to their own membership as well as to legislators.

Potential Annual Earnings Scale. Most nonprofits and trade associations pay in the lower end of the lobbyist income range. The higher education Web site eLearnPortal.com reports that U.S. Bureau of Labor Statistics (BLS) figures show that the median annual salary for a lobbyist with a nonprofit organization was $49,717 as of 2009. Salaries trend upward if the nonprofit or trade association employer has a large membership or a significant political agenda that may command a larger-than-average percentage of its budget expenditures.

Clientele Interaction. As is the case for all political advocates, client interaction is paramount for a lobbyist. In the case of nonprofits and trade associations, however, it is particularly important that the lobbyist work closely with the client, since in most cases, the clients are either individuals or members of the organization who are relatively inexperienced in political affairs. Lobbyists must conduct frequent meetings with clients and be in consistent contact (if not consistently available).

Amenities, Atmosphere, and Physical Grounds. Most nonprofit and trade associations maintain professional work atmospheres in their office space. Depending on the space available, offices may be shared or unavailable for lower-level employees. Because nonprofits and trade associations are typically smaller than corporations, their personnel are often required to perform multiple tasks in addition to their primary duties. With the exception of high-activity periods (such as legislative budget sessions, receptions, and other events at which pertinent bills are reviewed), the average workday is generally not as demanding as it is in other political advocacy environments.

Typical Number of Employees. Nonprofit and trade associations, in general, have relatively few employees on site. However, many such organizations also have broad memberships that are led by boards of directors. Additionally, many organizations may have a number of key leadership committees containing varying numbers of volunteer members who are tasked with driving the organizations' political activities.

Traditional Geographic Locations. Nonprofits and trade associations that conduct political advocacy and lobbying efforts are generally located in or near major urban centers (if not state or national capital cities) in order to facilitate government relations efforts. In many cases, however, they are positioned in a geographic location central to their membership, traveling to and from the capital from that base of operations.

Pros of Working for a Nonprofit or Trade Association. Political advocates and lobbyists who are part of nonprofits or trade associations have the benefit of focusing on one agenda and, thus, a relevant set of legislative pursuits. A single-minded approach such as this helps with organization and minimizes the amount of information that must be obtained from the thousands of legislative bills that are filed in each legislature every session. Additionally, by virtue of the relatively small size of most

nonprofits and trade associations, employees may have many tasks to manage in addition to their own, making work fast-paced and exciting.

Cons of Working for a Nonprofit or Trade Association. Nonprofit organizations and professional trade associations rely heavily on membership dues and external donations. Salaries for staff members are generally lower than in other business sectors. Additionally, although the association or organization is expected to have a single mind on political issues, its stances must be formulated through the often challenging process of reconciling the disparate opinions and attitudes of its members. Furthermore, the relatively small size of such organizations requires employees to handle many tasks. This situation can create confusion when dealing with the complex environment of legislative policy.

Costs

Payroll and Benefits: Nonprofits and trade associations usually pay staff members annual salaries. They are aware that the salaries they pay are lower than those paid for similar work and job descriptions in other arenas, so when budgetary constraints allow, they attempt to make up for lower pay with excellent benefits. Off-site meetings and other travel expenses are usually reimbursed if they are not included in a lobbyist's base salary.

Supplies: Nonprofit and trade associations need basic office supplies, as well as computers and smart phones (particularly for political advocates who will conduct business in the capital environment), fax machines, photocopiers, postage machines, and other such equipment.

External Services: Because of the relatively small size and budgets of trade associations and nonprofit organizations, much of their work may be distributed among external vendors. Computer and telecommunications consultants may help support operating systems, while accountants may handle member dues and contributions, as well as tax preparation. Additionally, such groups often use publishers or printing companies to produce pamphlets and promotional materials.

Utilities: Like most office environments, nonprofits and trade associations must pay for electricity and heat. In some cases, they must also pay for trash removal and recycling services. Additionally, such groups must pay for telephone and Internet service, which may include rental fees for equipment such as fax machines.

Taxes: Trade associations and nonprofit groups may pay a number of taxes, although a large volume of such organizations are tax-exempt. Some associations may be nonprofit in nature but, because they are driven by member dues revenues, must still pay commercial and corporate taxes. If they own their own real estate, such groups must also pay property taxes. Furthermore, while they may be exempt from sales taxes, they may still be subject to state and local taxes, such as hotel occupancy and meals taxes, provided that they are not on official government business.

Corporations

Many lobbyists work directly for large corporations that find their interests constantly engaged—whether positively or negatively—by legislation and public policy initiatives. These corporations find it more practical and cost-effective to engage lobbyists full time, rather than employing an outside law or consulting firm. Lobbyists of corporations in the same or related industries, such as banks or oil companies, may cooperate in their efforts on specific legislation. Sometimes, however, the interests of different companies in the same sector may diverge, particularly if they are of different sizes, are in different geographic regions, or have different attitudes toward expansion. In that case, the lobbyists working for one health insurer, for example, may pressure legislators to vote in precisely the opposite way as the lobbyists from a different health insurer.

Potential Annual Earnings Scale. A chief corporate lobbyist with ten to twenty years of experience may earn from just over $80,000 to well over $100,000 annually.

Clientele Interaction. A corporate lobbyist and political advocate's primary client is the corporation for which that individual works. However, the work performed is usually not just on behalf of one company, but rather on behalf of an entire industry or segment thereof. In both situations, the lobbyist will be expected to report to and communicate with executives as frequently as the situation merits, in order to ensure that the proper legislation is filed, meetings are conducted, and information is disseminated among the clients.

Amenities, Atmosphere, and Physical Grounds. Corporations that conduct political advocacy or lobbying activities maintain a professional office environment. Lobbyists may or may not be located in a corporate headquarters, however, as their work may require consistent placement in a capitol building or area that may be far from the main office. In other situations, lobbyists may be placed near public relations and external affairs offices. Corporate political advocates and lobbyists usually work in a fast-paced atmosphere, particularly when items on the company's agenda are under consideration.

Typical Number of Employees. Corporations vary in terms of personnel size. Political advocacy and lobbying activities within a corporate environment may be somewhat smaller and compartmentalized, with only a handful of lobbyists and administrative staff to support the political advocates while off site. The size of a political advocacy department depends on the amount of lobbying done, as well as the levels on which the lobbying takes place. For example, corporations that have local, state, and federal agendas employ a larger number of political advocates, lobbyists, and grassroots organizers than do companies that work solely on the state or local level.

Traditional Geographic Locations. Corporations that conduct lobbying and political advocacy may or may not be located near the target of that activity. Usually, larger corporations (which are more likely to have political interests) are located in or near major metropolitan areas in order to better conduct their main business. Lobbyists may be located on site as well, traveling to the capital in question from time to time. However, many larger corporations have satellite offices in Washington, D.C., London, and other capitals. Typically, these offices are dedicated fully to the pursuit of political advocacy and lobbying on the company's behalf. In still other cases, companies may have regional offices dedicated to regional lobbying or grassroots organizing.

Pros of Working for a Corporation. Corporations offer a degree of stability and financial security to lobbyists and political advocates, as well as above-average salaries. They may also provide better benefits, such as insurance, profit sharing, and retirement plans, than other potential employers. Corporate lobbyists and political advocates are also usually involved in the coordination of government affairs activities, such as grassroots mobilization, position-paper writing, and speaking at seminars and conferences. These activities, among others, help diversify a corporate political professional's daily activities. Additionally, with the clout of a major corporation behind them, those who work for such companies often enjoy a strong degree of backing among the legislators and officials with whom they meet and conduct business.

Cons of Working for a Corporation. Lobbyists and political advocates working directly for corporations may be limited in their level of access by virtue of the fact that they work for just one company. For example, they may not be seen as representative of an entire industry by legislators. Professionally, there is also a potential advancement issue for corporate political advocates, since such activities are but one part of the corporation's overall activities. Beyond certain upper-level positions, such as vice president of government affairs or a similar executive title, political advocates do not have much room for professional growth or upward mobility within a given corporation.

Costs

Payroll and Benefits: Corporate political advocates and lobbyists are usually paid on a salary basis. These salaries are dependent on the individual's experience and qualifications, as well as the financial strength of the corporation in question. Benefits are usually above average in quality, negotiated as part of an overall corporate package with insurance and financial consulting companies.

Supplies: Corporations require a general range of office supplies, as well as telecommunications and computer hardware such as printers, phones, and copiers. They also typically require audiovisual supplies such as screens, projectors, and related hardware. In many cases, rather than (or in addition to) personal computers, they may require laptop computers and smart phones (such as BlackBerries) for their mobile personnel.

External Services: Corporations, depending on their size, may use a number of external vendors for such tasks as printing and publications, off-site data storage and management, landscaping and custodial services, and caterers for profes-

sional luncheons and meetings. Larger companies may also employ security staff and even cafeteria staff that may be externally based. Additionally, they may use various modes of transportation, from taxis to corporate jets, to transport mobile staff to and from meeting sites.

Utilities: Corporations use a number of key utilities, such as telephone and Internet services, electricity, and heat. Larger corporations that own their own properties or lease large properties may also pay for water and sewage, as well as garbage-collection and recycling services.

Taxes: Corporations are required to pay corporate taxes, as well as commercial real estate taxes. They may also be expected to pay capital gains taxes on financial transactions. Additionally, they may pay taxes for state unemployment insurance programs.

Consultants

Political consultants advise clients on their political advocacy needs. Advocacy professionals who are based in consultancies rather than law firms may still have law degress, but they see themselves as offering a wider or differently focused range of services than do legal professionals. Because lobbyists must often have expertise in the industry or sphere within which they advocate, many consultants specialize in a particular type of lobbying, such as environmental lobbying. They may also specialize in advocacy techniques that are ancillary to a law firm's lobbying efforts, such as grassroots organizing or mounting public relations campaigns.

Potential Annual Earnings Scale. Political advocates and lobbyists who work as consultants receive salaries commensurate with their skills and reputations, as well as the scope of work performed. For example, some simply provide government affairs strategy information, while others act as their clients' official lobbyists. According to Simply Hired, the average salary for political advocacy consultants as of September, 2009, was approximately $66,000 per year.

Clientele Interaction. As is the case for most political advocates and lobbyists, client interaction and communication is imperative. Political consultants generally remain in consistent contact, whether via phone or e-mail, with the client. On many occasions, a consultant will meet with senior executives or board members to create and implement legislative strategies. During periods of particularly high legislative activity (such as hearings on relevant bills, budget sessions, and other key events), the frequency of such interactions will increase significantly.

Amenities, Atmosphere, and Physical Grounds. Political consultants, by virtue of being independent of corporate or legal oversight, vary in terms of their respective professional atmospheres. Still, they are expected to demonstrate professional characteristics and appearance, particularly when in contact with clients. The atmosphere of a consultant's workplace varies depending on the number of ongoing client projects, as well as the level of legislative or agency activity taking place. Consultants are located in a number of settings, such as urban office spaces. However, if the consultant is self-employed, he or she may work in a home office.

Typical Number of Employees. Political consultancies vary in staff size based on the number of clients and the types of activity they perform. In some cases, consultants have a number of staff, including lower-level lobbyists, researchers, interns, and administrative personnel. In others, the consultant is the sole staff representative, working out of a home office or similar venue.

Traditional Geographic Locations. Political advocacy consultants typically conduct their business close to or in capital cities, depending on the level of government with which they work. They may choose to locate in major noncapital urban areas in order to generate the largest volume of business, traveling to capitol buildings and legislative events as their work requires.

Pros of Working for a Consultancy. Political advocacy consultants generally act as independent agents outside a singular corporate or business framework. As a result, they are better able to organize their own schedules and pursuits. This arrangement may also allow them to work with a wide range of clients, industries, or issue areas. Additionally, they are generally able to avoid certain stigmas, such as political ideologies, that may attach to certain corporations or other lobbyists. Thus, they may be more able to stand on the merits of their own qualifications and professional reputations. Furthermore, for small advocacy consultant businesses, overhead expenses tend to be minimal. As a result, such businesses may present themselves as cost-effective alternatives to more expensive political advocacy firms and companies.

Cons of Working for a Consultancy. Political advocates and lobbyists who are independent of other companies, firms, and organizations must gain access to key government personnel by virtue of their own reputations. Consultants who are relatively new to the environment may have difficulty competing against more well-established lobbyists, particularly those with greater financial assets or backing. Consultants without the financial backing of major corporations or firms have expenses that must be deducted from their revenue streams. As a result, they must have enough clients and business to ensure that bills are paid and salaries are issued. In heavily saturated political advocacy markets or in economic downturns, such challenges can have a negative impact on a consultant's financial condition. Additionally, those consultants with limited staff must often assume the workloads of others within the firm, which may hinder their ability to complete their own work.

Costs

Payroll and Benefits: Political consultants are typically paid on an hourly, monthly, or quarterly basis, depending on their contracts. Smaller consultant businesses may not have as many competitive benefits, such as health care or financial planning services, as a result of their smaller staffs. However, those smaller staffs may also result in each employee garnering a higher percentage of major client agreements and contracts, translating into higher salaries.

Supplies: Political consultants require a general range of office supplies, including stationery, computers, and smart phones (such as BlackBerries). They also need fax machines, photocopiers, and related hardware. In some cases, they need overhead projectors and other audiovisual equipment. Advocates who conduct research may need computer software that enables them to conduct survey analyses and monitor targeted legislative and regulatory processes.

External Services: Consultants may contract caterers for client luncheons and fund-raisers, as well as custodial, accounting, and printing services. Many consultants subscribe to government news services, which provide real-time e-mailed reports of political events, sessions, and developments. Most require external companies to handle computer data storage and telecommunication services. They also incur the same necessary travel expenses incurred by other lobbyists.

Utilities: Political consultants must pay all relevant utilities, such as electricity, water, telecommunications, garbage pickup, recycling, and sewage.

Taxes: Consultants pay corporate taxes and property taxes. They must also account for taxation pertaining to any political donations to candidates or incumbent officials.

ORGANIZATIONAL STRUCTURE AND JOB ROLES

The organizational structure and distribution of tasks within a political advocacy business depends largely on the size of the company and the number of clients or projects being served. Independent consultants, for example, are likely to manage all of the major tasks of their businesses, while larger corporations and organizations have defined organizational structures and hierarchies. The tasks themselves, however, generally remain similar throughout the political advocacy and lobbying industry.

The following umbrella categories apply to the organizational structure of businesses in the political advocacy industry:

- Executive Management
- Business Development
- Communications and Public Relations
- Research
- Lobbying
- Legal Counsel
- Information Technology/Multimedia
- Human Resources
- Administrative Support

Executive Management

Executive management handles the general operations of a political advocacy company, corporation, organization, or consultancy. Managers oversee all aspects of their companies' endeavors, setting goals and strategies, assigning tasks to personnel, drafting and implementing budgets, and approving all new business. They are usually well educated, with graduate degrees such as a master of business administration (M.B.A.) or juris doctor (J.D.).

Executive managers generally earn the highest salaries in their companies. Their job is to manage the overall functions of the organization, address systemic issues, guide political activities, and ensure that all departments are functioning in such a way that clients' needs are fully satisfied. In most cases, they are the public face of their companies. Because of this visibility, executive managers of political advocacy organizations often come from high-profile positions themselves, thereby giving the organization a positive or immediate reputation.

Executive management occupations may include the following:

- President/Chief Executive Officer (CEO)
- Vice President
- Government Relations Director
- Operations Director
- Chief Financial Officer (CFO)
- New Business Director

Business Development

The business development department of a political advocacy firm, organization, or corporation is responsible for researching, contacting, securing, and maintaining the firm's client base. Business development personnel serve as the initial point of contact for new business, seeking out key groups whose interests may be well served by their companies. They must also monitor trends and issues in the political sphere in order to gauge the best areas for client contacts.

Business development specialists and personnel are well trained in business, although those who work in the field of political advocacy and lobbying must also have experience in government. A college and, in many cases, graduate degree such as an M.B.A. are usually preferred by the hiring company. Salaries vary based on the position, the organization's financial status, and the geographic location of the company. According to Simply Hired, the 2009 national average for a high-level business development staff member was about $70,000 per year.

Business development occupations may include the following:

- Vice President/Director of Business Development
- Business Development Manager/ Coordinator
- Administrative Assistant

Communications and Public Relations

Communications and public relations staff ensure that the political activities of their organization are shared with association members, clients, potential members, and the media. They serve as the primary point of contact for media representatives who have questions or need public statements concerning the organization's activities or clients. They also draft press releases and communications pieces (such as e-newsletters, mass e-mails, publications, and brochures) to ensure that the positive and negative developments on the organization's agenda are given light. They may also be tasked with Web site management.

Communications and public relations personnel are experienced in communications, having typically received undergraduate and sometimes graduate degrees in the field. They may also have backgrounds in government, often as spokespeople for legislators or executive agency officials. According to Salary.com, on average, a high-level communications and public relations manager in the United States earns about $129,000 per year.

Communications and public relations occupations may include the following:

- Vice President/Director of Public Relations
- Communications/Public Relations Manager
- Press Secretary
- Press Assistant
- Administrative Assistant
- Intern

OCCUPATION SPECIALTIES

Public Relations Specialists

Specialty	Responsibilities
Fund-raising directors	Direct and coordinate the solicitation and disbursement of funds for community social-welfare organizations. They establish fund-raising goals according to the financial needs of the agency and formulate policies for collecting and safeguarding the contributions.
Funds development directors	Plan, organize, and coordinate ongoing and special project funding programs for museums, zoos, public broadcasting stations, and similar institutions. They prepare a statement of planned activities and enlist support from members of the institution staff and volunteer organizations.
Lobbyists	Contact and confer with members of the legislature and other holders of public office to persuade them to support legislation favorable to their clients' interests.
Sales-service promoters	Generate sales and create goodwill for a firm's products by preparing displays and touring the country. They call on merchants to advise them of ways to increase sales and demonstrate products.

Research

Many political organizations have on-site individuals dedicated to researching and analyzing key issues and data in order to assist the company in developing key strategies. Researchers are required to analyze complex accounts, budgets, and statutes, as well as to write position papers and studies.

Researchers and analysts usually have college or graduate degrees in such fields as economics, political science, public policy, public administration, or sociology. They must be able to analyze and communicate complex and detailed material to those who will use it for the benefit of clients—and sometimes to the clients themselves. Additionally, qualified researchers and analysts must be experienced in the use of statistical-analysis and other types of specialized computer software, such as survey software. They must be experienced in the computer systems used to track legislation and legal precedents. This expertise is usually garnered in undergraduate and graduate programs before potential researchers emerge onto the job market. Salaries are dependent on the type of research performed and the individual's experience and issue familiarity. According to the Economic Research Institute, the average U.S. salary for political researchers and analysts is approximately $71,000 per year.

Research occupations may include the following:

- Research Director
- Research Coordinator/Project Manager
- Researcher
- Analyst
- Administrative Assistant
- Intern

Lobbying

Lobbyists form the field staff of a political advocacy firm or organization. They meet and com-

---

OCCUPATION PROFILE

Public Relations Specialist

Considerations	Qualifications
Description	Promotes or creates goodwill for individuals, companies, or organizations, often by creating promotional materials.
Career clusters	Business, Management, and Administration; Marketing, Sales, and Service
Interests	Data; people
Working conditions	Work inside
Minimum education level	Junior/technical/community college; apprenticeship; bachelor's degree
Physical exertion	Light work
Physical abilities	Unexceptional/basic fitness
Opportunities for experience	Internship; apprenticeship; military service; volunteer work; part-time work
Licensure and certification	Recommended
Employment outlook	Faster-than-average growth expected
Holland interest score	EAS

municate with clients on a consistent basis, helping clients develop strategies for achieving their objectives, writing legislation, and helping guide and monitor bills as they travel through the legislative process. In many cases, lobbyists also facilitate meetings between their clients and key agency personnel in order to achieve regulatory (rather than legislative) goals. Furthermore, lobbyists frequently host or attend political fund-raisers on behalf of their clients, guiding money to the campaign committees of legislators whom the clients support.

Lobbyists are usually college educated, with considerable experience in the political fields and geographical areas in which they work. They may have advanced degrees, such as a law degree or a master's degree in public policy, public administration, or political science. In addition to this academic experience, most lobbyists must register with state or federal government regulatory agencies in order to comply with state and federal lobbying laws. Often, legislators who have either lost or given up their elected seats choose to stay in Washington to act as lobbyists.

Lobbyists must be able to organize their schedules to account for a wide range of meetings and meeting topics. Therefore, they must have strong administrative and project management skills. The salary range for a lobbyist is diverse in nature. Salary.com lists the 2009 national average salary for a lobbyist at about $96,000, while The Learning House lists the median annual salary for a lobbyist as $45,000. The difference between mean and median salaries may be telling: Former legislators with significant experience can garner significantly more money for their services than can the average lobbyist.

Lobbying occupations may include the following:

- Government Relations Director
- Lobbyist
- Administrative Assistant
- Intern

Legal Counsel

Any organization that conducts political advocacy and lobbying activities must employ experts in the relevant state and federal laws. These staff members are tasked not only with analyzing relevant bills and existing statutes but also with assessing the liability of their companies and personnel as a result of their lobbying activities. Legal counsels have law degrees and must have passed the local bar examination, which determines whether candidates can practice law in a certain jurisdiction. In some cases, they have additional degrees, such as a master's degree in public administration. Furthermore, they must be familiar with the industry or industries in which they work.

Legal occupations may include the following:

- General/Chief Counsel
- Attorney
- Paralegal
- Administrative Assistant

Information Technology/Multimedia

Large political advocacy and lobbying organizations may have on-site personnel dedicated to ensuring the smooth operation of computers, telephones, and audiovisual systems. This department maintains the internal computer operations of the company and may be called upon to set up and operate presentations for meetings and receptions, as needed by clients.

Information technology (IT) personnel tend to have either college or vocational training in computer systems management. They must be familiar with the latest systems available and understand the most up-to-date antivirus and security software in order to maintain the integrity of the client-company relationship. According to the BLS, the national average salary for IT specialists is about $65,000 per year.

IT and multimedia occupations may include the following:

- Information Technology Specialist
- Systems Analyst
- Audiovisual Support Specialist
- Administrative Assistant

Human Resources

The human resources department is responsible for personnel management and the administration of employee benefits, such as insurance, retirement funds, and other employee incentives. It also assists employees with obtaining on-the-job training. Human resources managers are well trained in their field, both through experience and through college-level education. According to the BLS, human resource managers in the United States earn an average of about $104,000 per year.

Human resources occupations may include the following:

- Human Resources Director
- Human Resources Manager
- Administrative Assistant

Administrative Support

Administrative personnel are found throughout most political advocacy organizations, assisting each department in its overall operations. They assist at the front desk in answering phones during high-activity periods, run errands for executives, make photocopies and sending faxes for in-house personnel and clients, and perform a host of other associated office tasks. In many cases, they are the nucleus of a given department, providing support to managers through scheduling, data entry, filing, and other activities.

Administrative personnel have a wide range of backgrounds and professional training experience. Many are temporary employees, while others are brought in as entry-level staff for managers and other personnel. Many have college degrees and are hired with the potential for upward mobility. Their salaries are often hourly. According to PayScale.com, the national average salary for an administrative assistant is about $14 per hour.

Administrative occupations may include the following:

- Administrative Assistant
- Secretary
- Cooperative Employee
- Intern

INDUSTRY OUTLOOK

Overview

The political advocacy and lobbying industry has been both one of the most maligned and one of the steadiest industries in the modern economy. The industry is political in nature but, as is the case in government, has permutations in virtually every other industry in a given economy. Any company that has an interest in federal, state, or local legislation or regulations likely has direct access or, through trade associations, indirect access to a lobbyist.

The increased number of Western-style democracies (which promote the open solicitation of government officials by private citizens) in the twenty-first century indicates that the political advocacy industry will continue to play a major role in public policy making and public administration. Still, it is likely that the lobbying industry will need to undergo another evolution as government and industries alike experience fundamental changes.

In the United States, the 2008 election of Democratic presidential candidate Barack Obama, coupled with a strong showing by Democrats in both the House and Senate, led to a fundamental shift in leadership in the federal government. Campaigners—both Republican and Democrat—railed against "special interests" (another name for lobbyists), and the new administration instituted new rules making it more difficult for former lobbyists to work for the executive branch of government and for government employees to become lobbyists. Even so, the so-called revolving door between lobbying firms and government has continued. However, the rules have resulted in fewer people becoming officially registered lobbyists, as more seek to accomplish the same goals through less direct means. Moreover, despite the administration's avowed distrust of lobbyists, many lobbyists work to support the agendas promoted by President Obama, his administration, and the Democratic Party. Others represent right-leaning corporate interests, particularly in battles over the desirability or undesirability of new and increased regulation of the private sphere.

Thus, while the industry outlook is strong, political advocates and lobbyists are still faced with change. To address this change, lobbying and political advocacy firms are seeking seasoned veterans to head their efforts. In other words, lobbying firms may prefer to hire lobbyists with proven legislative experience, such as former state representatives and senators, as well as others who have strong relationships with the current legislature. They may prefer such candidates over those who are simply experienced lobbyists.

In addition to personnel adjustments, political

organizations must also change their tactics. The success of President Obama in the 2008 election is widely attributed to his grassroots organization, as well as his use of the Internet and emerging social media. Twenty-first century lobbyists must also be skilled at using the latest technologies to advance their causes. They must prove effective in organizing or helping organize grassroots campaigns that will send more than one message to targeted legislators.

The evolution of lobbying practices is not limited to the United States. The cohesion of the European Union means that lobbyists, while working with national governments on issues of local importance, must now also attempt to gain access to a much larger European political organization. Corporate political advocates must create new strategies in order to advance their clients' agendas among British, French, German, and other European leaders. Such an undertaking, challenging in and of itself, is complicated by the complexity of the EU structure, whose decision-making processes alternate between the national and supranational levels.

Political advocacy and lobbying will not continue unfettered, however. There are already strict rules in place that govern and regulate lobbying on the federal and state levels. Public outcry over the influence of special interests on the U.S. government led to a series of changes in lobbying and campaign finance rules in 2002. It is widely believed that such regulatory measures will continue to be pursued in Congress, in state governments, and in other governments. Even as the European Union continues to take shape, there is a growing call for lobbying regulations in Europe similar to those passed in the United States. While campaign finance itself is not an issue in Europe (EU policy makers are not elected), the issue of access has taken a larger portion of the spotlight in recent years, and it will most likely continue to influence the industry in that region.

Lobbyists and political advocates continue to be in high demand, particularly as leaders address complex issues such as health care, international terrorism, and the further development of the global economy. Although lobbyists will remain under scrutiny from the public, the industry will continue to play a major role in the establishment of public policy.

Employment Advantages

The political advocacy industry, while focused in terms of its own activities, has broad applications across a wide range of industries and levels of governments. Lobbyists and political advocates may enjoy working with a number of industries and issue areas—a lobbyist is hired largely because of the individual's expertise in government, knowledge of the political process, and relationships with key legislative leaders and officials. Additionally, the breadth of the industry's domain signifies industry stability. While the key leaders and issues may change, lobbyists and political advocates remain in high demand among companies and organizations seeking access to government.

Although the 2007-2009 global economic crisis tightened budgets around the world (and, as a result, placed limitations on lobbyist pay scales), the increased demand for qualified political advocates will likely translate into competitive salaries and benefits for such advocates. (According to a report in *The Wall Street Journal*, prior to the 2007-2009 recession, from 2000 until 2005, the number of registered lobbyists in Washington, D.C., more than doubled, and the amounts they charged clients increased by as much as 100 percent.)

Political advocacy is also a good occupation for activists who seek to be part of a dynamic vehicle for advancing their agendas. Individuals with a strong interest in the political process and a desire to work in a fast-paced environment often find satisfaction in the industry, as advocacy provides a voice in government for those who did not previously have or could not utilize one. Furthermore, lobbying presents employees with strong chances for advancement, either within the field itself or within another industry. This open-ended quality is due to the fact that a political advocate must become familiar with a number of industries and issue areas; the basic skills and personal characteristics political advocates must have and hone during their tenures may help significantly further their careers.

Annual Earnings

The political advocacy industry continues to generate significant earnings. In 2008, industry members were paid roughly $3.2 billion to lobby Congress. The largest political advocacy groups worked on behalf of the pharmaceutical industry—

in 2007, pharmaceutical companies paid $168 million to lobbyists to press their agenda on Capitol Hill. Lobbying on an international scale is also expected to see strong earnings. (According to Public Affairs Links, as of 2007, the lobbying industry was estimated to be worth over $3 billion in the United Kingdom.) Contributing to demand for international lobbyists are issues such as HIV/AIDS, climate change, and poverty. These issues increase the activity of nonprofit and nongovernmental organizations (NGOs) that, in turn, activate their grassroots bases to push local, national, and regional governments into addressing their concerns.

RELATED RESOURCES FOR FURTHER RESEARCH

AMERICAN LEAGUE OF LOBBYISTS
P.O. Box 30005
Alexandria, VA 22310
Tel: (703) 960-3011
http://www.alldc.org

ASSOCIATION OF ACCREDITED LOBBYISTS TO THE EUROPEAN PARLIAMENT
Rond Point Schuman 6
B-1040 Brussels
Belgium
Tel: 32-2-735-9339
http://www.eulobby.net

CASSIDY AND ASSOCIATES
700 13th St. NW, Suite 400
Washington, DC 20005
Tel: (202) 347-0773
Fax: (202) 347-0785
http://www.cassidy.com

CENTER FOR PUBLIC INTEGRITY
910 17th St. NW, Suite 700
Washington, DC 20006
Tel: (202) 466-1300
http://www.publicintegrity.org

LIBRARY OF CONGRESS
101 Independence Ave. SE
Washington, DC 20540
Tel: (202) 707-5000
http://thomas.loc.gov

PUBLIC AFFAIRS COUNCIL
2033 K St. NW, Suite 700
Washington, DC 20006
Tel: (202) 872-2790
Fax: (202) 835-8343
http://www.pac.org

ABOUT THE AUTHOR

Michael P. Auerbach has over sixteen years of professional experience in public policy and administration, economic development, and the hospitality industry. He is a 1993 graduate of Wittenberg University and a 1999 graduate of the Boston College Graduate School of Arts and Sciences. He is a veteran of state and federal government, having worked for seven years in the Massachusetts legislature and four years as a federal government contractor.

FURTHER READING

Birnbaum, Jeffrey H. "In a Harsh Climate for Lobbyists, the Forecast Calls for . . . More Lobbyists." *The Washington Post*, August 12, 2008.

"Biography of Ulysses S. Grant." Incredible People. http://profiles.incredible-people.com/ulysses-s-grant.

Center for Responsive Politics. Communications. "Washington Lobbying Grew to $3.2 Billion Last Year, Despite Economy." *Capitol Eye Blog*, January 29, 2009. http://www.opensecrets.org/news/2009/01/washington-lobbying-grew-to-32.html.

Clarke, Conor. "The Dire State of the Lobbying Industry." *The Atlantic*, March 12, 2009. http://politics.theatlantic.com/2009/03/the_dire_state_of_the_lobbying_industry.php.

Cummings, Jeanne. "Inside the Lobbying Industry's Evolution." *Politico*. August 14, 2007. http://www.politico.com/news/stories/0807/5368.html.

Danziger, Danny, and John Gillingham. *1215: The Year of Magna Carta*. New York: Simon and Schuster, 2004.

Hrebenar, Ronald J., and Bryson B. Morgan. *Lobbying in America: A Reference Handbook*. Santa Barbara, Calif.: ABC-CLIO, 2009.

Luneburg, William V., Thomas M. Susman, and Rebecca H. Gordon. *The Lobbying Manual: A Complete Guide to Federal Lobbying Law and Practice.* 4th ed. Chicago: American Bar Association, 2009.

McGrath, Conor. *Interest Groups and Lobbying in the United States and Comparative Perspectives: Essays in Ethics, Institutional Pluralism, Regulation, and Management.* Lewiston, N.Y.: Edwin Mellen Press, 2009.

Mahoney, Christine. *Brussels Versus the Beltway: Advocacy in the United States and the European Union.* Washington, D.C.: Georgetown University Press, 2008.

_____. "Why Lobbying in America Is Different." EuropeanVoice.com, April 6, 2009. http://www.europeanvoice.com/article/2009/06/why-lobbying-in-america-isdifferent/65078.aspx.

Newton, Adam, and Ronald K. L. Collins. "Petition." First Amendment Center. http://www.firstamendmentcenter.org/petition/overview.aspx.

Public Affairs Links. http://www.publicaffairs links.co.uk.

Public Citizen. "History of the Lobbying Disclosure Act." July 23, 2005. http://www.lobbyinginfo.org/laws/page.cfm?pageid=15.

Salary Expert. "Political Analyst Compensation Data." http://www.salaryexpert.com/index.cfm?fuseaction=Browse.Political-Analyst-salary-data-details&PositionId=17475.

Salent, Jonathan D., and Kristin Jensen. "Lobbyist-Bashing by Obama Doesn't Dim Industry's Boom Forecast." Bloomberg.com, November 20, 2008. http://www.bloomberg.com/apps/news?pid=20601070&refer=home&sid=aEZoCjCjrYDE.

SimplyHired. "Average Business Development Salaries." http://www.simplyhired.com/a/salary/search/q-business+development.

_____. "Average Political Consultant Salaries." http://www.simplyhired.com/a/salary/search/q-Political+Consultant.

Taminiau, Yvette, and Arnold Wilts. "Corporate Lobbying in Europe: Managing Knowledge and Information Strategies." *Journal of Public Affairs* 6, no. 2 (May, 2006): 122-130.

U.S. Bureau of Labor Statistics. *Career Guide to Industries,* 2010-2011 ed. http://www.bls.gov/oco/cg.

_____. *Occupational Outlook Handbook,* 2010-2011 ed. http://www.bls.gov/oco.

U.S. Census Bureau. North American Industry Classification System (NAICS), 2007. http://www.census.gov/cgi-bin/sssd/naics/naicsrch?chart=2007.

U.S. Department of Commerce. International Trade Administration. Office of Trade and Industry Information. Industry Trade Data and Analysis. http://ita.doc.gov/td/industry/otea/OTII/OTII-index.html.

Vance, Stephanie D. *The Advocacy Handbook: A Practitioner's Guide to Achieving Policy Goals Through Organization Networks.* Bethesda, Md.: Columbia Books, 2009.

Young, McGhee. *Developing Interests: Organizational Change and the Politics of Advocacy.* Lawrence: University Press of Kansas, 2010.

Postal and Package Delivery Services

INDUSTRY SNAPSHOT

General Industry: Transportation, Distribution, and Logistics

Career Clusters: Government and Public Administration Occupations; Transportation, Distribution, and Logistics

Subcategory Industries: Air Courier Services; Bicycle Courier Services; Courier Services; Direct Mail Advertising Services; Express Delivery Services; Local Letter and Parcel Delivery Services; Mailbox Rental Centers; Messenger Services; Parcel Mailing Services; Postal Station Operation; Private Mail Centers

Related Industries: Freight Transport Industry; Retail Trade and Service Industry

Annual Domestic Revenues: Postal services: $79.97 billion USD (U.S. Postal Service, 2008); courier services: $58.16 billion USD (U.S. Census Bureau, 2002)

Annual International Revenues: Postal services: $135.28 billion USD (Universal Postal Union, 2007); courier services: $71.84 billion USD (Oxford Economic Forecasting, 2003)

Annual Global Revenues: Postal services: $215.25 billion USD (Universal Postal Union, 2007); courier services: $130 billion USD (Oxford Economic Forecasting, 2003)

NAICS Number: 491-492

INDUSTRY DEFINITION

Summary

Postal and package delivery services encompass a highly strategic network of carefully coordinated tasks that moves mail and parcels efficiently. These services include government-regulated postal services with regular home delivery, such as the United States Postal Service, as well as local and ground messenger services and worldwide express carriers, such as FedEx Corporation, UPS, DHL, TNT, and Purolator. These corporations have grown with improvements in transportation and technology, and they have evolved to meet the demands of their customers. Globally, postal services employ more than 5.5 million people and move more than 440 billion letters and parcels annually. The United States Postal Service moves over half of the world's mail, making it the largest postal service in the world, with over 780,000 staff.

History of the Industry

References to delivery services date back to 2000 B.C.E. in Egypt and 1100 B.C.E. in China. In China, an organized system of relay messengers on horseback incorporated post houses, strategically placed throughout the kingdom, where messengers could pass along their packets to other messengers or collect fresh horses to continue the delivery themselves. Similar configurations existed in Egypt and the rest of the Persian Empire. Mounted messengers, using the relay stations, were able to travel approximately 170 miles in twenty-four hours. Early postal systems were reserved for royal, governmental, and military communications.

International business and commerce emerged during the Renaissance, creating a need for commercial communication. Related businesses and banking institutions established their own networks of postal systems. Late in the fifteenth century, after the invention of the printing press, mail volume vastly increased. Soon, private, for-profit postal services carried both commercial and personal mail. One of the largest services, Thurn and Taxis, received a patent to conduct business from

Roman emperor Maximillian I, employed over twenty thousand messengers, and carried mail throughout much of lower Europe between 1512 and 1867.

Successful public mail delivery in London, the Penny Post, was established in 1680 by William Dockwa, but within two years it was shut down because the duke of York deemed its profits and efficiency an infringement of the government monopoly on postal systems. Rowland Hill, an English tax reformer, is credited with the development of the modern postal system. In 1837, he wrote *Post Office Reform: Its Importance and Practicability*, which suggested a uniform rate of postage based on weight, regardless of distance, using prepaid stamps.

The vast geographic territory of the United States posed challenges for mail delivery. The famous Pony Express was established in 1860 but only lasted for a year. Soon thereafter, the transcontinental railroad connected the two sides of America. A railway post office was created in 1864,

The U.S. Postal Service sorts and delivers about 703 million pieces of mail to more than 146 million businesses and homes, six days per week. (AP/Wide World Photos)

but the railway did not run everywhere, so stage-coaches became the most reliable form of mail transport. Airmail began in 1911 in Britain and in 1918 in the United States. The first transcontinental airmail flight occurred in 1921.

For international mail to become feasible, various countries had to enter into agreements with one another promising to deliver foreign mail and establishing costs and protocols. In 1874, the Swiss government called for a meeting of twenty-two countries that led to the creation of the General Postal Union, which became the Universal Postal Union in 1878. The union regulates and communicates mail standards of rate and delivery between countries. It became a specialized agency of the United Nations in 1948.

The United States Postal Service is an independent agency of the federal executive branch. It began in the late eighteenth century under George Washington as part of the Treasury Department; during Washington's administration, only seventy-six post offices existed in the United States. The of-fice separated from the Treasury, becoming its own cabinet-level department, the Post Office Department, headed by the postmaster general. On July 1, 1971, the Post Office Department became the United States Postal Service (USPS), in accordance with the 1970 Postal Reorganization Act.

Home delivery of mail began in the United States in 1863, with 440 letter carriers serving forty-nine cities. Before that, street letter boxes were used, beginning in 1858, or a fee could be paid to have mail delivered to home and business addresses. Private parcel delivery from department stores began in 1913 with Merchants Parcel Delivery, which changed its name to United Parcel Service (UPS) in 1919 and slowly expanded service throughout the country. UPS provided air service as early as 1929, but the Depression halted that service in 1932; it resumed in 1953.

Express service began in 1973, when FedEx (Federal Express) began operations. Deregulation of the air cargo industry in 1977 allowed cargo carriers to purchase and operate their own aircraft:

As of 2011, FedEx had 684 aircraft and 43,000 motorized vehicles. (AP/Wide World Photos)

They no longer had to rely on the schedules of air forwarders, such as passenger jets. In the 1980's, many air couriers competed to provide overnight and express delivery, but by 2000 only a few companies remained, including FedEx, DHL (originally Dalsey, Hillblom, and Lynn), UPS, USPS, Purolator, TNT (originally Thomans Nationwide Transport), and Airborne Express.

The Industry Today

The Universal Postal Union, a special agency of the United Nations based in Bern, Switzerland, now has 191 member countries. Its purpose is to set the rules and standards for international mail exchange. It does not, however, interfere in nations' domestic postal operations. Individual postal services can set their own postage rates and determine how to manage their postal operations and staffs. There are more than 5.5 million postal employees worldwide. In many countries, the roles of postal clerks and delivery personnel are very different from what they are in North America. Some post offices require employees to collect specific taxes, sell pet or hunting licenses, distribute welfare benefits, and even distribute antimalarial medications.

USPS was put into operation on July 1, 1971, following implementation of the 1970 Postal Reorganization Act. At that time, taxpayers subsidized 23 percent of USPS; those subsidies were phased out completely by 1983. In order to compensate for unprofitable postal outlets, USPS is authorized to receive approximately $460 million annually; however, this funding has not been requested or received in over eighteen years, saving taxpayers more than $13 billion. Since 1971, USPS has been a self-supporting government agency that covers its operating costs with revenues generated through the sale of postage and related products and services.

USPS operates almost forty thousand post offices and sorts and delivers approximately 703 million of pieces of mail to over 146 million businesses and homes, six days per week. It is the largest postal

This UPS package sorter in Hodgkins, Illinois, reads codes and automatically sorts packages into bags ready for the delivery trucks. (AP/Wide World Photos)

system in the world, handling over half of the world's mail. Russia has more post offices, nearly ninety thousand, but the volume of mail handled by those offices is much less than the volume of American mail.

The modern process for moving mail is extremely streamlined and efficient and involves several different stages. Mail that is collected each day is brought to centrally located facilities to undergo a cancellation process. Mail handlers unload the mail and separate it based on size and priority. Letter mail is then fed onto conveyors, where automated machines check it for appropriate postage. Each item's postage (whether a stamp, meter mark, or prepaid insignia) is canceled, so it cannot be reused. A bar code is then printed on each envelope to assist in tracking and sorting. Each letter is scanned and visually analyzed by computer software, which produces Postnet bar codes through character recognition. This automated procedure can process 95 percent of all letters, almost forty thousand per hour. The remaining 5 percent have to be manually sorted. Once bar codes have been applied, the mail can be further sorted for local or other distribution.

Letter carriers arrive at depots early each morning to complete the final sorts for their mail routes. They typically stand at their sorting cases for approximately three hours a day, inserting the day's mail by street and address. The balance of the eight-hour workday is spent delivering the sorted mail, which is carried in satchels or pushed in carts. Letter carriers may also have smaller bundles left at secured relay boxes, strategically placed throughout their delivery zones, for them to pick up and deliver in addition to the mail they sort at their depots.

Large express package delivery services operate in a centralized hub-and-spoke system. Companies may have several hubs interconnected around the country and the world. Their drivers travel around each city, picking up and delivering packages. The collected packages are all placed in trucks or aircraft containers, depending on their destinations. Most truck- and aircraft-based package transport occurs at night, lessening the likelihood of interference from road- and air-traffic congestion. Moreover, many of the large companies have sufficient extra trucks and aircraft to continue operating at full capacity even when some of their vehicles must be removed from operation for maintenance and repair.

When packages arrive at a hub, they are unloaded and sorted by destination. Automation, bar coding, and other technologies increase the speed and accuracy of the sorting. After being sorted, packages are loaded back into containers and carried by truck and aircraft to their final destinations.

Express couriers and messengers deliver packages to residences and businesses within a certain route contracted in advance. At the start of a route, drivers go to local warehouse facilities, where all packages for their routes have been previously sorted for them by automated technology and parcel handlers. Their shifts are spent driving their routes and hand-delivering packages to recipients. Packages that cannot be delivered are returned to distribution centers for later delivery or pickup by customers. Some drivers service the same routes and become familiar with their regular customers.

Small and independent courier and messenger companies pick up packages and documents from individuals and businesses and take them directly to their intended recipients. These items do not get sorted. Some businesses keep couriers and delivery drivers on contract for regular transport of their important documents and packages. Some couriers transport sensitive or hazardous packages, such as laboratory specimens.

Electronic documents have affected the postal system by causing a consistent reduction in letter mail volume. However, some documents and materials cannot be sent electronically. Courier and messenger services are often hired to transport important documents and items, such as passports, legal documents, blueprints, laboratory specimens, or even organs for transplant.

INDUSTRY MARKET SEGMENTS

The postal and package delivery industry includes a wide variety of business structures. Industry players range from individual contractors running sole proprietorships, to multimillion-dollar international express delivery services, to government postal services. The following sections outline small, medium, and large businesses within the postal and package delivery industry.

Small Businesses

Small courier and messenger services may employ anywhere from one to one hundred people. They are local and regional businesses, operating within specific geographic areas. Because they are confined to small areas, many small businesses specialize in same-day or within-the-hour delivery. They are contracted to pick up, carry, and deliver messages, documents, packages, and other items between offices, businesses, and individuals. Items can include important and time-sensitive documents and medical specimens, depending on the needs of their customers. Their mode of transportation may be foot, bicycle, motorcycle, or automobile. These small businesses may be contracted by larger corporations on an on-call service basis.

Potential Annual Earnings Scale. According to the U.S. Bureau of Labor Statistics (BLS), the average annual earnings for local couriers and messengers in 2009 were $24,500. These earnings can vary widely by region and depending on the consistency of work availability. Approximately 19 percent of couriers and messengers are independent contractors.

Courier businesses that hold permanent or long-term contracts to provide services within branches of larger corporations, such as making steady trips between bank branches, law firms, medical offices, or laboratories, tend to have more reliable, steady sources of income. Many other small businesses are independent and can see variability in their work volume, as they respond to individual requests for service garnered through local advertising and marketing.

According to the BLS, dispatchers for local courier and messenger services earned an average of $35,000 in 2009, while sales representatives earned $55,200 and chief executives earned $137,580. These figures include salaries of large companies that operate multiple local-delivery offices in different cities. Earnings at small businesses may be significantly less than these averages.

Clientele Interaction. Small messenger and courier businesses most often pick up parcels directly from their customers and bring them directly to recipients. Couriers therefore have direct clientele interactions several times each day. Customers contact dispatchers by telephone to arrange service, and dispatchers assign messengers to respond to requests based on their locations, schedules, and workloads. In some very small businesses, the dispatcher and the messenger are the same person. Repeat business and recommendations from happy customers are keys to success, so all clientele interaction must be positive. Employees are often required to maintain standards of appearance, as they are the representatives of their companies.

Amenities, Atmosphere, and Physical Grounds. Small courier and messenger companies may have a small hub or office space, but delivery personnel most often consider their transport vehicles to be their offices. Dispatch centers may be located in home offices or in vehicles, and calls may be managed by cellular telephone. Most small businesses do not maintain retail or drop-off locations.

Typical Number of Employees. Small couriers, like other small businesses, attempt to keep expenses low and revenues high. A courier company can be managed by a single individual, depending on the workload and the geographic area it serves. Quite often, a central dispatch center receives requests for service and assigns them to independent couriers who work for the business as subcontrac-

tors. The typical number of employees for a small courier and messenger service ranges from one to one hundred.

Traditional Geographic Locations. Most small businesses serve specific geographic areas, such as a single city or district within a city. Many couriers offer service only to downtown office areas or have employees dedicated to specific city quarters or districts. Dispatch offices tend to be located in the center of their territories. Fuel and other transportation expenses make it difficult to keep costs low enough to attract customers while covering large areas.

Pros of Working for a Small Courier Business. Independent subcontractors can decide how much and when they want to work. Small companies or individuals that hold contracts for service with other companies have regular delivery points, allowing them to become familiar with their areas and customers. Employees usually do not experience a great deal of direct supervision, as they most often work alone.

Cons of Working for a Small Courier Business. Small courier companies offer very little room for advancement. Often, without set service contracts, fluctuations in business and income are common. Time and delivery commitments can cause a great deal of stress for delivery personnel, who may need to work long hours and may face penalties in pay if they fail to make their deliveries on time.

Costs

Payroll and Benefits: Typically, small courier and messenger companies pay their full-time delivery personnel an hourly wage or pay independent contractors per delivery. Full-time employees usually receive the same benefits as other workers, at the discretion of the owner or manager. However, many independent contractors do not receive benefits.

Supplies: Small courier and messenger services may need vehicles or may require their employees to provide their own transportation. In either case, the employer generally pays for fuel. They all require communication systems, such as mobile telephones or two-way radios, as well as some standard office supplies. They may provide some packaging services at an additional fee, in which case they require packaging supplies.

External Services: Small delivery services may contract vehicle maintenance and repair or may employ in-house specialists. They may also contract maintenance and repair of communication systems and computer systems as necessary, as well as advertising or accounting services.

Utilities: Many small courier businesses do not have central offices or service centers, so their utility costs may be minimal.

Taxes: Small businesses are required to pay local, state, and federal income taxes, as well as regional business and service taxes and permitting fees.

Midsize Businesses

Midsize package delivery companies usually operate within larger geographic areas and provide a greater range of services than do small companies. They typically provide only ground-based transportation services, operating within a specific area, often among several cities or states. Midsize businesses have centralized dispatch hubs and may offer online services, including order placement and package tracking, to compete with large express companies.

Potential Annual Earnings Scale. Midsize package delivery businesses have a broader range of positions. They may employ delivery drivers, dispatchers, sorting clerks, managers, supervisors, and technical support staff. Wages for these positions vary by region and job responsibilities. According to the BLS, the average annual salary of couriers and messengers employed by express delivery companies was $25,920 in 2009. Dispatchers earned an average of $42,360; shipping, receiving, and traffic clerks earned an average of $33,930; delivery-truck drivers earned an average of $45,780; and large commercial truck drivers in the industry earned an average of $51,640. Sales representatives averaged $56,620 in earnings. Transportation and distribution managers earned $95,660, on average, while general managers earned $102,200, sales managers earned $107,680, and chief executives earned $179,010. Employees of midsize businesses often receive salaries below these averages.

Clientele Interaction. As package and delivery businesses get larger, a greater proportion of their employees experience little direct clientele interaction. Midsize companies still take orders for service by telephone, and personnel still pick up packages in person, but many midsize businesses have started to offer online service orders and strategically placed drop boxes as well. As with any service industry, repeat business and recommendations from happy customers are keys to success, so all clientele interaction must be positive. Employees are often required to maintain standards of appearance and to wear uniforms, as they are the representatives of their companies and need to be recognizable as such.

Amenities, Atmosphere, and Physical Grounds. Midsize package delivery businesses often maintain central warehouses or package sorting hubs, dispatch offices, retail spaces, and lots for fleets of delivery vehicles. These businesses are committed to providing fast service, which can create a highly organized but frequently stressful atmosphere. Some employees, such as service clerks, may work in retail spaces, providing assistance to customers. Others spend most of their working hours in delivery vehicles or service warehouses.

Typical Number of Employees. The number of employees of a given midsize package and delivery business depends on its workload and the geographic area it serves. Midsize companies generally employ between one hundred and one thousand persons.

Traditional Geographic Locations. Midsize delivery companies usually cover larger territories and offer more services than do small companies. Sorting hubs are generally located in or outside urban or suburban areas near major highways to provide easy access to both transportation infrastructure and retail and dispatch centers. Retail centers are usually located conveniently for customers, in business centers and highly populated urban and suburban areas.

Pros of Working for a Midsize Courier or Express Delivery Company. Midsize companies tend to employ their workers directly, rather than engaging independent subcontractors. Employees are thus more likely to be guaranteed full-time work and may receive annual salaries rather than hourly wages, increasing their income stability and the likelihood of receiving benefits. Midsize companies often provide corporate uniforms and delivery vehicles, saving employees the expense of providing and maintaining their own.

Cons of Working for a Midsize Courier or Express Delivery Company. Midsize companies usually institute more structured work schedules than do small companies, reducing the flexibility of employees' work hours and increasing the amount of direct supervision they receive. Because couriers must cover larger areas, their routes may require greater time commitments than those at small companies, and drivers are more likely to be unfamiliar with some portion of their routes. Both of these factors may increase worker stress.

Costs

Payroll and Benefits: Midsize delivery companies pay hourly wages or annual salaries; delivery drivers may be paid per completed trip. Full-time employees usually receive vacation and benefits, at the discretion of the owner or manager.

Supplies: As the size of a parcel and package delivery service increases, so does the volume and range of supplies and items required to provide service to customers. Midsize companies must usually maintain fleets of delivery vehicles. In addition to the vehicles themselves, they need fuel, maintenance tools, and spare parts. They also require computerized inventory and parcel-tracking systems, including mobile scanning equipment, as well as radio or cellular communication systems. Midsize companies provide their employees with uniforms and other items to increase brand and logo recognition among their customers.

External Services: Midsize delivery companies may contract external vendors to maintain their vehicles, or they may employ maintenance crews directly. They must obtain vehicle and other liability insurance. Communication system and computer maintenance may also be contracted, and companies may engage advertising consultants, accountants, or legal counsel as necessary.

Utilities: Midsize companies must pay for electricity, heating, water, and sewage, as well as Internet and telephone service.

Taxes: Midsize businesses are required to pay local, state, and federal income taxes, as well as regional business and service taxes and permitting fees.

Large Businesses

Large postal and package delivery businesses are the best known companies in the industry, employing millions of people and serving the entire globe. The highly competitive worldwide delivery industry has annual revenues of over $75 billion. Globally, postal services employ over 5.5 million people to move more than 450 billion pieces of letter and parcel mail. Large courier express companies such as UPS, DHL, and FedEx have their own impressive statistics. They each employ over 275,000 people and use fleets of more than ninety thousand vehicles and hundreds of aircraft to move more than 1.5 billion packages annually.

Potential Annual Earnings Scale. The annual earnings for large postal and delivery service businesses have tremendous variability, depending on geographic area and job responsibilities. At the U.S. Postal Service, there are over four thousand distinct positions, most of which pay salaries of $32,000 to $55,000 annually. The express couriers have a similar number of unique positions, ranging from meteorologists and pilots to delivery drivers and sorting clerks.

According to the BLS, the average annual salary for a postal service mail carrier in 2009 was $48,940. Postal service clerks earned an average of $51,920, and first-line supervisors earned an average of $71,660. Postmasters and mail superintendents earned an average of $59,600. The postmaster general of the United States earned a base salary of more than $250,000 in 2008, as well as a six-figure bonus, and several other top managers in the USPS also received salaries of more than $200,000. The highest-paid postmaster, the head of Germany's Deutsche Post, receives $4 million per year.

According to the BLS, the average annual salary of couriers and messengers employed by express delivery companies was $25,920 in 2009. Dispatchers earned an average of $42,360; shipping, receiving, and traffic clerks earned an average of $33,930; delivery-truck drivers earned an average of $45,780; and large commerical truck drivers in the industry earned an average of $51,640. Sales representatives averaged $56,620 in earnings. Transportation and distribution managers earned $95,660, on average, while general managers earned $102,200, sales managers earned $107,680, and chief executives earned $179,010. The salaries at the major delivery corporations are significantly higher than these averages: The chief executive officer (CEO) of FedEx earned $8.67 million in 2007, and the CEO of UPS earned $3.1 million.

Clientele Interaction. Package and delivery services in general are becoming more high-tech and automated. Clients can easily request pickup and other services online. FedEx reports that more than 3 million people visit its Web site each day. Customer service at large delivery companies is most often provided online or by telephone. Delivery personnel, including counter workers, have the greatest amount of clientele interaction during package receipt, pickup, and delivery. The situation is similar for postal services: Most clientele interaction occurs with letter carriers, delivery staff, and post office counter workers. Such personnel, as the recognizable face of their companies, are required to wear uniforms, adhere to standards of appearance, have good communication skills, and be knowledgeable about the services and policies of their companies.

Amenities, Atmosphere, and Physical Grounds. The physical grounds of large postal and delivery companies are vast and vastly distributed. Postal services operate within specific countries but have agreements with other national postal services through the Universal Postal Union to provide continuity of service on an international scale. There are over 650,000 post offices worldwide providing public service, as well as an additional 650,000 administrative and corporate offices. Large express delivery companies have large hubs and offices. DHL, for example, has 450 hubs, where sorting and delivery is managed, in addition to 6,500 offices and a fleet of 76,000 vehicles and 420 aircraft. The other large express delivery companies have similar structures and facilities. Delivery personnel and loading-dock and other workers spend a great deal of time outside, which can be challenging. The atmosphere can be stressful, as billions of packages have to be accurately tracked and delivered in a timely manner.

Typical Number of Employees. Large postal and package delivery companies typically have thousands of employees, most of them full-time employees. Casual and part-time staff are sometimes engaged during high-volume periods, such as Christmas, or to cover entry-level positions. USPS employs over 685,000 career employees and over 100,000 noncareer staff, making it the second-largest employer in the United States after Walmart.

Traditional Geographic Locations. Postal services and large express delivery corporations have facilities throughout the world. Corporate and agency headquarters are generally located in ma-

jor cities and government centers, while sorting and distribution hubs are most often located on the outskirts of major urban areas, facilitating access both to population centers and to transportation infrastructure. Local front-line offices and drop points exist in all communities. Often, in more remote locations, express couriers collaborate with local postal services to provide delivery service. Letter carriers and some express delivery personnel have specific areas or districts that they deliver to on a daily basis, which allows them to become very familiar with their territories and customers.

Pros of Working for the Postal Service or Large Delivery Company. Postal workers in many countries, including the United States, are federal employees with the ability to unionize and collectively bargain for better wages and benefits. Benefits provided to almost all workers include cost-of-living adjustment payments, overtime payments, health insurance, and pensions. Wages and benefits for postal services are comparable to those of large express delivery couriers. Employees at larger companies are normally responsible for specific jobs, rather than covering multiple roles as they would at smaller companies. Some of the large express couriers have appeared many times on lists of best places to work; in 2009, FedEx was ranked on one such list at number ninety.

Cons of Working for the Postal Service or Large Delivery Company. Large delivery corporations and the Postal Service represent a very popular career choice for many people; therefore, hiring processes are highly competitive. USPS requires potential employees to take a qualification examination and then remain on a waiting list until positions open or their examination results expire. The agency services 146 million homes and businesses six days per week in the United States, and many express couriers make pickups and deliveries seven days per week. In order to provide such services, many large delivery companies operate twenty-four hours per day, requiring a significant amount of second- and third-shift work. This environment, as well as necessary time commitments and constant mail volumes, can be stressful for some people.

Costs

Payroll and Benefits: Large companies employ thousands of people with varying skills and job descriptions. Large teams of people are hired solely to manage employee payrolls and benefits. USPS pays out over $50 billion annually in salaries and benefits, and UPS and FedEx each pay between $12 billion and $18 billion annually.

Supplies: Large delivery corporations and the USPS each maintain massive fleets of ground vehicles and sizeable aircraft fleets as well. They require fuel for all these vehicles, as well as the tools and spare parts necessary to maintain and service them. The express delivery companies have each purchased over 90,000 vehicles, and FedEx and DHL own and operate over 400 aircraft. USPS operates a fleet of over 260,000 vehicles. It has been calculated that each time fuel prices increase by a single cent per gallon, USPS's total fuel costs increase by $5.5 million. Many of the large express couriers use a fuel-hedging program in an attempt to stabilize their fuel costs. Larger companies are currently testing the use of electric, hybrid, and hydrogen fuel cell vehicles.

External Services: Large postal and delivery companies tend to have internal staff to cover all requirements for operations, including maintenance of facilities and equipment. Communication (Internet, telephone, radio, and Global Positioning System) services are provided by national carriers and need to be of the highest quality and reliability. Companies that have large fleets of vehicles and aircraft are required to pay landing and service fees that can reach almost $2 billion annually. It is common for even the largest companies to consult with external public relations and advertising experts when launching new national ad campaigns.

Utilities: Large companies operate thousands of offices, retail spaces, warehouses, and hubs. Utilities include water, sewage, electricity, heat, and communication services. The U.S. Postal Service has implemented a utility management system (UMS) to facilitate central utility bill verification and payment and to capture energy-use and cost data for electricity, natural gas, and steam.

Taxes: Large express delivery corporations are required to pay local, state, and federal income taxes, as well as business and service taxes and permitting fees as required in each region. International carriers also pay customs and duty charges. The U.S. Postal Service is exempt from federal taxes.

ORGANIZATIONAL STRUCTURE AND JOB ROLES

The organizational structure of delivery companies is usually based on the size of each company and the service being provided. Some small independent couriers may have only a single or a few employees, who stay with each shipped item throughout its journey from pickup to delivery. By contrast, the U.S. Postal Service has over four thousand different job classifications, and FedEx has over 275,000 employees worldwide.

The following umbrella categories apply to the organizational structure of businesses in the postal and package delivery industry:

- Business Management
- Customer Service
- Sales and Marketing
- Facilities and Security
- Technology, Research, Design, and Development
- Operations
- Distribution
- Human Resources

Business Management

Management and executive positions are the highest-ranking positions within postal and package delivery corporations. The management staff is normally composed of a small group of individuals who are supported by a larger team of administrative and other professionals. The goal of this staff is to make decisions that ensure that their company generates maximum revenue, reduce costs, and improve service.

Most countries have appointed postmasters general who head their national postal services. The very first postmaster general of the United States was Benjamin Franklin, appointed in 1775. The annual salaries for national heads of postal services are quite considerable. Germany's postmaster earns $4 million annually, and the CEO of New Zealand's postal service earns over $730,000. In

2008, the total compensation package of the U.S. postmaster general—including base salary, bonus, perks, and significant increases in two pensions—totaled more than $800,000. In comparison, large nongovernmental express couriers compensate their high-ranking executives quite substantially. CEOs routinely earn salaries in the millions annually.

Business management occupations may include the following:

- Postmaster General
- President/Chief Executive Officer (CEO)
- Deputy Postmaster General/Chief Operating Officer (COO)
- Chief Financial Officer (CFO)
- Chief Technology Officer (CTO)
- Executive Vice President
- Vice President of Government Relations and Public Policy
- Vice President of Human Resources/ Chief Human Resources Officer
- Vice President of Sales and Marketing/ Chief Marketing Officer
- General Counsel

Customer Service

Customer service is critical to success. Positions in customer service often provide a company's customers with their very first and most lasting impressions of it. Personnel must provide accurate information and assistance to customers, respond to inquiries, resolve problems, and sell company services.

Customer service employees proactively provide answers and resolutions to customer inquiries. They assist customers to determine their pickup or delivery needs, trace shipments, quote rates, resolve tariff discrepancies, and answer billing and invoicing questions. Postal service clerks work at post offices and retail outlets, where they measure and weigh packages and sell postage, money orders, insurance, registration services, and mailing materials.

Positions in customer service do not often require previous training or specialized education. Employees often need to demonstrate excellent communication skills, professionalism, patience, and telephone etiquette, as well as problem-solving and multitasking skills.

Customer service occupations may include the following:

- Telephone/Online Customer Service Representative
- Retail Outlet Clerk
- Customer Relations Representative
- Customer Relations Manager
- Service Agent
- Postal Service Clerk

Sales and Marketing

Postal and package delivery is a competitive industry. Customers have many choices depending on their service requirements, so brand recognition and associated superior service reputation are critical to a company's success. Sales and marketing departments seek to ensure that advertising dollars are well spent, their brands remain at the forefront of customer choice, and exceptional relationships with customers are maintained. All businesses, large or small, have dedicated advertising budgets with which to develop and implement strategies to increase sales. A company's advertising may target the downtown blocks of a single city or the entire world, and its marketing team may be a single individual or a team of thousands.

Marketing and communications personnel seek to project their messages to potential customers; they also seek to protect their companies' reputations by identifying and managing emerging issues that may harm those reputations. Effective media relations and media monitoring are critical to handling crises and other issues that may arise. A key measurement of corporate success is revenue, so sales of products and services are imperative. A sales team needs to contact customers and prospective customers to be certain that they are aware of current and upcoming products and services and are satisfied with their current service. Sales and marketing analysts determine whether allocated advertising budgets have been used effectively. They report whether sales goals and targets have been achieved and develop analyses and recommendations for future sales opportunities and problems.

Sales positions are often compensated according to pay structures that incorporate base salaries and performance-based commissions, allocated either to individuals or to teams. Key skills include communication, persuasion, negotiation, problem solving, and organization. Sales positions often require travel, depending on the service being sold and the territory being covered.

Marketing and communications positions usually require degrees or training in the field, and salaries can start near $25,000 annually for entry-level or fellowship positions and in excess of $90,000 for marketing managers and directors. Key skills include communication, organization, knowledge of branding and promotions, trade-show and event planning, database marketing, telemarketing, advertising, and research.

Sales and marketing occupations may include the following:

- Sales Manager
- Sales Account Executive
- Sales Account Associate
- Sales Representative
- Sales Analyst
- Sales Clerk
- Corporate Communications Specialist
- Marketing Manager
- Media Relations Representative
- Business Solutions Specialist
- Business Liaison
- Market Research Manager
- Market Research Analyst
- Shipping/Mailing Solutions Specialist

Facilities and Security

The security and protection of shipped materials is extremely important, as is the protection and safety of postal and package delivery employees. The maintenance of facilities and equipment is also critical to the operation of any courier or delivery company.

During the early twenty-first century, security has increased and evolved to meet growing concerns over identity theft, privacy protection, drug transport, and terrorist threats. Mail and delivery personnel receive training and continuing education in identifying and dealing with suspicious packages and in general security awareness. Security is taken very seriously. For example, FedEx has more than five hundred security personnel around the world. Security personnel inspect aircraft, trucks, and facilities for a range of threats.

Security workers at large express delivery companies protect against both outside threats and those from within. They work with local and federal law enforcement to investigate thefts, pilferages, acts of vandalism, misconduct, and other activities detrimental to the company, its employees, or its customers. They may also protect management and executives in the corporation. Specialized security personnel normally require training and experience in law enforcement and transportation security, as well as familiarity with theft detection and applicable technical devices. Security analysts use statistical and scientific methods to detect trends or suspicious patterns in delivery data to identify thefts and other criminal acts. They design and implement preventive security methods and programs. The annual salary for a security analyst begins at about $55,000.

The United States Postal Inspection Service is one of the oldest federal law enforcement agencies, founded by Benjamin Franklin. Its agents carry firearms, make arrests, and serve federal search warrants and subpoenas. Postal inspectors perform protective functions at mail facilities and escort high-value mail shipments. They also staff and operate a forensic crime laboratory staffed with forensic scientists and technical specialists. Postal inspectors must have college degrees and complete a twelve-week training program. The annual salary for a postal inspector begins at about $54,000.

Facilities positions cover a wide range of job descriptions that ensure the smooth running and maintenance of equipment and grounds. Facilities personnel make minor repairs and provide routine maintenance for office, shop, dock, and yard facilities. Basic knowledge of electrical repair, plumbing, and carpentry are required. Specialized maintenance of equipment and vehicles is often contracted out to other companies, but some large companies keep individuals on staff to repair and maintain fleet vehicles.

Facilities and security occupations may include the following:

- Security Specialist
- Security Guard
- Loss Prevention Specialist
- Postal Inspector
- Security Analyst
- Maintenance and Repair Technician

- Mechanic
- Electrical Engineer
- Cleaner
- Custodian/Janitor

Technology, Research, Design, and Development

Technology is a critical and fast-paced area of postal and package delivery. Programming, analysis, and technical support jobs are experiencing the greatest growth. Customers want to be able to use their computers to purchase postage and services, request pickup service, track their packages, view recipients' signatures for registered items, and conduct numerous other technical operations, all securely and without delays. To meet this demand, package delivery companies use specialized equipment to scan and track parcels throughout the entire transportation and delivery process. In order to remain competitive in the industry, companies must quickly incorporate relevant advances in technology design. Technology design is constantly changing because systems need to be extremely efficient and effective while remaining easy for customers and employees to use.

Positions in the technology, research, design, and development area require specialized training for specific roles, such as degrees in computer science and information systems. Programmer analysts and systems programmers earn salaries beginning at about $35,000 and ranging up to $80,000 annually.

Postal and package delivery companies are beginning to employ scientists as well. Research and development teams look for more cost-effective transportation options, including cleaner-burning fuels, in order to combat rising fuel costs and minimize the environmental impact of their companies' operations. Consumers are increasingly demanding service that does less damage to the environment while maintaining standards of speed and efficiency. Large express companies must meet rigorous and complex air and ground transport schedules. Some employ dedicated meteorologists to track and predict weather patterns that may interfere with their service. UPS has had meteorologists on staff since 1994, and it employs five of them on rotating shifts to monitor weather patterns around the world that may affect delivery schedules.

Technology, research, design, and development occupations may include the following:

- Programmer Analyst
- Systems Analyst
- Technical Analyst
- Application Manager
- Application Analyst
- Technical Specialist
- Technology Consultant
- Technology and Application Support Staff
- Application Project Manager
- Technological Adviser
- Meteorologist
- Environmental Impact Analyst

Operations

Operations personnel conduct and oversee the inner workings of the postal and package delivery system, determining what happens to each item after it has left the sender's possession. At smaller courier companies, an article may not change hands between pickup and delivery, but at larger companies articles—especially those that have to travel great distances—may go through several points of processing on the way. As efficiency improves with the development of new technology, many operations tasks are automated or semiautomated.

Dispatchers are the liaisons between customers and couriers. A small delivery service may have a single dispatcher, while larger companies have single or multiple dispatch centers. Dispatchers collect pickup and delivery requests, whether directly from customers, through an automated online system, or in the form of lists assembled by support staff. They then assign jobs to field personnel as appropriate. Dispatchers communicate with customers in case of any delays and also serve as the primary contacts for couriers while they are on the road. Dispatchers normally do not require any specialized training or diplomas, but they need to be extremely organized, patient, and good multitaskers. The average annual salary for postal service dispatchers was $39,900 in 2009.

Postal and express couriers have specific drop-off and collection points, often within retail outlets or dedicated service centers. They pick up packages from these points and directly from customers and take them to central operations plants or hubs for sorting. Courier packages, parcels, and registered mail are scanned and tracked at each step of the process; pieces of regular mail are not.

Operations staff, such as handlers, sorters, and processing-machine operators, prepare incoming and outgoing articles by different methods of sorting and distribution. This type of work can be physically demanding, involving standing for long periods and handling heavy parcels or bags of mail (up to one hundred pounds), as well as pushing containers weighing up to fifteen hundred pounds. Individual units and larger shipments may need to be inspected for damage or customs processing. Equipment and strict protocols are in place to ensure that the process is efficient and safe for personnel. Handler salaries usually start at around $25,000 annually.

Operations engineers oversee and apply standardization processes and improvement policies to develop increased service and cost performance in mail and package processing operations. Annual salaries for operations engineers start at approximately $50,000. Operations supervisors coordinate the activities and movement of freight and articles at sorting plants and hubs. This job often involves coordinating employees inside, those at loading and unloading docks, and the vehicles dropping off and picking up parcels at their sites.

Operations occupations may include the following:

- Operations Supervisor
- Operations Engineer
- Sorting Clerk
- Handler
- Dispatcher
- Processor
- Processing Machine Operator

Distribution

Distribution of mail and parcels is the end result and goal of the postal and package delivery industry. Successful delivery within an agreed-upon time

---

OCCUPATION PROFILE

Dispatcher

Considerations	Qualifications
Description	Schedules and dispatches workers for delivery and pickup of packages and letters.
Career cluster	Transportation, Distribution, and Logistics
Interests	Data; people
Working conditions	Work inside
Minimum education level	On-the-job training; high school diploma or GED
Physical exertion	Light work
Physical abilities	Unexceptional/basic fitness
Opportunities for experience	Part-time work
Licensure and certification	Usually not required
Employment outlook	Average growth expected
Holland interest score	CES; CSR; ECS; ERS; ESC; ESI; ESR; SEC

Note: See volume 1, "Publisher's Note," for an explanation of the Holland interest score.

is the service customers are paying for. Careers in distribution involve almost all methods of transportation, including aircraft, automobiles, light and heavy trucks, bicycles, motorcycles, Segways, and walking. Many distribution occupations overlap with customer service, as delivery personnel are often viewed as the faces of their companies and many enjoy a great deal of direct interaction with their customers.

Pilots and large-truck drivers transport parcels over long distances between hubs and sorting plants. They do not generally work regular 9-to-5 schedules. Trucks and planes often travel overnight, and employees spend a lot of time away from home. The large express-air companies are considered to be two of the best-paying airlines in the world, and captains at FedEx and UPS in their fifteenth year of service can earn more than $240 per hour.

Delivery drivers do much more than drive. They are often expected to load and unload aircraft and vehicles, sort packages, and provide efficient delivery and pickup of packages and related customer service functions. The job can be physically demanding and is often considered stressful because it is so tightly scheduled and deadline-driven. A good driving record is required to obtain a driving position, as is proper licensing, such as possession of a commercial driver's license (CDL) and a hazardous materials endorsement. Annual salaries for courier drivers usually start at about $23,000, and many are paid hourly. The average annual salary of a heavy-truck driver in the courier and messenger industry was $50,660 in 2009; delivery-truck drivers earned an average of $44,440. The same positions in the U.S. Postal Service paid average salaries of $53,020 and $50,850, respectively. Some private companies may require that their drivers be responsible for their own vehicles and expenses.

Letter carriers deliver and collect mail on foot or by vehicle under varying road and weather conditions in specific urban or rural areas. They are the most recognizable face of a postal service and need to maintain a positive and professional relationship with customers. Many are required to carry mail weighing up to 35 pounds in shoulder

OCCUPATION PROFILE

Mail Carrier

Considerations	Qualifications
Description	Sorts mail for delivery and delivers it.
Career cluster	Transportation, Distribution, and Logistics
Interests	Data
Working conditions	Work outside; work both inside and outside
Minimum education level	On-the-job training; high school diploma or GED
Physical exertion	Medium work
Physical abilities	Unexceptional/basic fitness
Opportunities for experience	Military service; part-time work
Licensure and certification	Required
Employment outlook	Decline expected
Holland interest score	SRC

Note: See volume 1, "Publisher's Note," for an explanation of the Holland interest score.

OCCUPATION SPECIALTIES

Mail Clerks and Messengers

Specialty	Responsibilities
Express clerks	Receive express parcels from customers, compute charges, route parcels according to destination, and release incoming parcels to consignees.
Mail handlers	Sort and process mail in government or business post offices. They may sort mail into sacks or place it in pigeonholes according to destination.
Parcel post clerks	Wrap, inspect, weigh, and affix postage to outgoing mail parcels. They also record cash-on-delivery and insurance information.
Post office clerks	Work the front counter of a post office. They weigh envelopes, sell stamps, complete forms, issue money orders, compute mailing costs, and handle registered mail.

satchels or other equipment and to load or unload containers of mail weighing up to 70 pounds. Most letter carriers start in casual or temporary positions and then move into more permanent routes. Annual salaries of letter carriers averaged $48,940 in 2009.

Rural mail carriers sort their routes at urban mail facilities and then drive to established routes outside town or city corporate limits to deliver mail. Many rural mail carriers use their own vehicles and are reimbursed for mileage or have vehicle allowances built into their salaries. Rural carriers also pick up outgoing mail, sell stamps, and issue money orders.

Distribution occupations may include the following:

- City Driver
- Courier
- Road Driver
- Long-Haul Driver
- Pickup and Delivery Driver
- Pilot
- Letter Carrier
- Rural Mail Carrier

Human Resources

Human resources (HR) personnel hire and fire employees and ensure that all employees have the tools and training they need in order to be effective and productive in their positions. They manage a variety of tasks, beginning with recruiting new employees. In addition to hiring, training, and developing employees, human resources personnel administer payrolls and benefits, including retirement benefits for former employees. They also ensure that all employee relations and practices comply with legal requirements and corporate policies and respond to employee grievances.

Most human resources positions require college degrees or equivalent experience. Human resources managers in the postal service earned an average of $124,750 in 2009, while those at courier and messenger firms earned $110,520. Human resources is often a challenging area, and employee relations require patience, collaboration, negotiation, and conflict-resolution skills.

Human resources occupations may include the following:

- Human Resources Director
- Human Resources Manager
- Human Resources Coordinator
- Human Resources Analyst
- Human Resources Generalist
- Payroll Clerk
- Benefits Specialist
- Administrative Assistant

Overview

The outlook for the postal and package delivery industry appears to be on the rise or holding stable in most areas. Concerns have been raised regarding the impact of electronic commerce and digital communication on the industry, as well as that of increasing fuel and transportation costs. As has been true of many industries in the wake of the 2007-2009 recession, postal and delivery companies are exploring ways to increase revenues and decrease expenses through innovation and modernization.

Globally, letter mail and parcel volumes have increased by 1 to 2 percent each year since 2004. However, the United States has experienced a 1 to 2 percent decrease in letter mail. A small increase in package and parcel volumes has kept domestic revenues across all categories relatively stable. Following a three-week congress of the Universal Postal Union in 2008, over twenty-five hundred representatives from 179 of the 191 member countries determined that the global postal service is looking toward "development—rather than downsizing." Participants in the congress determined that the issues at the forefront of postal services globally are the needs to modernize services at all levels, to reform postal security, and to minimize and mitigate the impact of the industry on the environment. They agreed that postal services are managing the changing needs of globalization and keeping pace with technological advances. The next congress was scheduled for 2012.

Concerns have been raised that postal systems would be unable to compete with express carriers, but it appears that these competitors have become customers. In the United States, FedEx and UPS are two of the postal service's largest customers, paying the U.S. Postal Service to deliver over 400 million packages to residential customers. The U.S. Postal Service is also a customer of FedEx and UPS, utilizing their air networks for contract transportation arrangements.

Package delivery services are constantly evolving to meet the needs of potential customers. They have developed more elaborate time structures to accommodate specific needs, allowing for two-, three-, or five-day delivery at reduced costs. Traditionally, packages are limited to 100 pounds; however, some businesses are now allowing heavier items in order to capture some market share from freight and cargo carriers. Networks of carefully located drop boxes are being expanded to accommodate customers. Partnerships have been forged between package delivery companies and retailers to include drop boxes in their establishments.

Online shipping solutions and services have been expanded and become more streamlined as well. Most packages can now be tracked moment-by-moment throughout their journeys to their recipients. FedEx claims to have more than 3 million visitors to its Web site every day.

Couriers and Messengers Industry

Employment		
2009	Projected 2018	Occupation
9,860	13,800	Customer service representatives
6,190	6,800	Dispatchers, except police, fire, and ambulance
8,950	9,600	First-line supervisors/managers of transportation and material-moving machine and vehicle operators
152,580	159,500	Laborers and freight, stock, and material movers, hand
147,930	157,400	Truck drivers, light or delivery services

Source: U.S. Bureau of Labor Statistics, Industries at a Glance, Occupational Employment Statistics and Employment Projections Program.

Delivery drivers travel billions of miles each year, tremendously affecting the environment and businesses' expenses. In order to save money and address customers' concerns for environmental conservation, most courier and package delivery services are exploring alternative operating options and cleaner-burning fuels. Oxford Economic Forecasting projects the express delivery industry to grow at an average annual rate of 6.7 percent between 2005 and 2015.

Employment Advantages

The postal and package delivery industry continues to be one of the world's largest sources of employment. There are 5.5 million postal employees around the world. The U.S. Postal Service is second only to Walmart as the largest employer in the United States, with over 685,000 career employees and over 100,000 noncareer staff. Despite the large number of jobs, employment in the industry is highly competitive. Many positions do not require advanced education, but larger companies provide above-average wages and benefits. Smaller and independent courier services determine their own benefits and working conditions. Employment in the industry is considered desirable because most corporations provide automatic pay raises, cost-of-living adjustments, paid vacation time, life and health insurance, retirement pensions, and career development opportunities. FedEx sets an example in this regard, as it has remained, for over a decade, on numerous lists of the best companies to work for.

Annual Earnings

Postal and package delivery services constitute a multibillion-dollar industry. The impact of the global economic downturn of 2007-2009 has been widespread; however, the delivery industry appears be resilient. Over six thousand businesses operate within the industry. Mail volumes have remained stable in most areas of the world, and postal systems are looking at ways to improve and modernize their services. The forecast from the Universal Postal Union is positive and focused on development. As e-commerce grows, the items purchased need to be shipped and delivered. Express couriers continue to experience growth, as the demand for fast service continues to grow and market expansion into Asia develops.

RELATED RESOURCES FOR FURTHER RESEARCH

ASSOCIATION OF INTERNATIONAL COURIER AND
    EXPRESS SERVICES
1st Floor, Unit 6, Poyle 14, Newlands Dr.
Colnbrook S13 0DX
United Kingdom
Tel: 44-1753-680-550
Fax: 44-1753-687-033
http://www.aices.org

PROJECTED EMPLOYMENT FOR SELECTED OCCUPATIONS

Postal Service Industry

Employment		
2009	Projected 2018	Occupation
6,410	5,200	First-line supervisors/ managers of transportation and material-moving machine and vehicle operators
73,050	61,600	Postal service clerks
339,030	339,400	Postal service mail carriers
162,860	12,200	Postal service mail sorters, processors, and processing machine operators
24,890	21,700	Postmasters and mail superintendents

Source: U.S. Bureau of Labor Statistics, Industries at a Glance, Occupational Employment Statistics and Employment Projections Program.

EXPRESS DELIVERY AND LOGISTICS ASSOCIATION
400 Admiral Blvd.
Kansas City, MO 64106
Tel: (816) 221-0254
Fax: (816) 472-7765
http://www.expressassociation.org

GLOBAL POSTAL STRATEGY
1 Elmcroft Rd.
Stamford, CT 06926-0700
Tel: (203) 351-7588
Fax: (203) 351-6371
http://www.postinsight.com

UNIVERSAL POSTAL UNION
3000 Bern 15
Switzerland
Tel: 41-31-350-3111
Fax: 41-31-350-3110
http://www.upu.int

ABOUT THE AUTHOR

April D. Ingram is a writer and researcher in British Columbia. She is a graduate of the University of Calgary and has been associated with the postal and delivery services industry since 1999.

FURTHER READING

Frock, Roger. *Changing How the World Does Business: FedEx's Incredible Journey to Success—The Inside Story.* San Francisco: Berrett-Koehler, 2006.

Hill, Rowland. *Post Office Reform: Its Importance and Practicability.* London: Charles Knight, 1837.

Kosar, Kevin. *The U.S. Postal Service's Financial Condition: Overview and Issues for Congress.* Washington, D.C.: Congressional Research Service, 2010.

Niemann, Greg. *Big Brown: The Untold Story of UPS.* San Francisco: Jossey-Bass, 2007.

Oxford Economics. *The Impact of the Express Delivery Industry on the Global Economy.* Oxford, England: Author, 2009.

Potter, John. "Five Myths About the U.S. Postal Service." *Washington Post,* February 28, 2010. http://www.washingtonpost.com/wp-dyn/content/article/2010/02/25/AR2010022504888.html.

Rubio, Philip F. *There's Always Work at the Post Office: African American Postal Workers and the Fight for Jobs, Justice, and Equality.* Chapel Hill: University of North Carolina Press, 2010.

U.S. Bureau of Labor Statistics. *Career Guide to Industries,* 2010-2011 ed. http://www.bls.gov/oco/cg.

U.S. Census Bureau. North American Industry Classification System (NAICS), 2007. http://www.census.gov/cgi-bin/sssd/naics/naicsrch?chart=2007.

U.S. Congress. House. Committee on the Judiciary. *Competition in the Package Delivery Industry.* Washington, D.C.: Government Printing Office, 2009.

U.S. Department of Commerce. International Trade Administration. Office of Trade and Industry Information. Industry Trade Data and Analysis. http://ita.doc.gov/td/industry/otea/OTII/OTII-index.html.

U.S. Postal Service. *Annual Report, 2009.* Washington, D.C.: Author, 2009.

_____. *Envisioning a Viable Postal Service for America: An Action Plan for the Future.* Washington, D.C.: Author, 2010.

_____. *2008 Sustainability Report: Delivering a Greener Tomorrow.* Washington, D.C.: Author, 2009. http://www.usps.com/green/report/2008/welcome.htm.

Workplace Economics. *The Relative Size of Labor Costs at UPS, FedEx, and the U.S. Postal Service.* Washington, D.C.: American Postal Workers Union, 2002.